USING THE THEORY

Chapter 2   46
Using the Theory: Are We Saving
Lives Efficiently?

Chapter 3   82
Using the Theory: College
Administrators Make a Costly Mistake

Chapter 5   129
Using the Theory: GDP After
September 11

Chapter 6   154
Using the Theory: The Use and
Misuse of an Imperfect CPI

Chapter 7   185
Using the Theory: Fiscal Policy
in the Classical Model

Chapter 8   220
Using the Theory: Economic Growth
in the Less-Developed Countries

Chapter 10   271
Using the Theory:
The Recession of 2001

Chapter 11   306
Using the Theory: Bank Failures and
Banking Panics

Chapter 12   333
Using the Theory: The Fed and
the Recession of 2001

Chapter 13   366
Using the Theory: The Story
of Two Recessions and
"Jobless" Expansions

Chapter 14   394
Using the Theory: Challenges for
Monetary Policy

Chapter 15   428
Using the Theory: The Bush
Tax Cuts of 2001 and 2003

Chapter 16   461
Using the Theory: The Stubborn
U.S. Trade Deficit

Chapter 17   499
Using the Theory:
The U.S. Sugar Quota

Using All The Theory   505
The Stock Market and
the Macroeconomy

MACROECONOMICS

PRINCIPLES AND APPLICATIONS

THIRD EDITION

2006 UPDATE

Robert E. Hall
Department of Economics
Stanford University

Marc Lieberman
Department of Economics
New York University

THOMSON

SOUTH-WESTERN

Australia · Brazil · Canada · Mexico · Singapore · Spain · United Kingdom · United States

THOMSON
───◆───
SOUTH-WESTERN
™

Macroeconomics: Principles and Applications, Third Edition, 2006 Update

Robert E. Hall and Marc Lieberman

VP/Editorial Director:
Jack W. Calhoun

Editor-in-Chief:
Alex von Rosenberg

Publisher:
Steve Momper

Sr. Acquisitions Editor:
Michael W. Worls

Sr. Developmental Editor:
Susanna C. Smart

Sr. Marketing Manager:
John Carey

Sr. Production Project Manager:
Deanna Quinn

Manager of Technology, Editorial:
Vicky True

Technology Project Editor:
Dana Cowden

Web Coordinator:
Karen Schaffer

Sr. Manufacturing Coordinator:
Sandee Milewski

Production House:
Pre-Press Company, Inc.

Printer:
Quebecor World
Versailles, KY

Sr. Art Director:
Michelle Kunkler

Internal and Cover Designer:
Ramsdell Design, Cincinnati

Cover Image:
© Getty Images, Inc.

Photography Manager:
John Hill

Library of Congress Control Number:
2005932192

For more information about our products, contact us at:
Thomson Learning Academic Resource Center
1-800-423-0563

Thomson Higher Education
5191 Natorp Boulevard
Mason, OH 45040
USA

Preface

Macroeconomics: Principles and Applications is about economic principles and how economists use them to understand the world. It was conceived, written, and for the third edition, substantially revised to help your students focus on those basic principles and applications.

The Third Edition Update reflects many of the changes the economy has experienced since the third edition came out. Adjustments have been made to all of the tables and figures, and the narrative based on them. There are also hundreds of small changes throughout the text — updates to examples, and in some cases replacement with new examples. Finally, this update comes with an entirely new set of Aplia problem sets, involving unusually close cooperation between the Aplia team and ourselves as textbook authors. (More on Aplia later, in the Teaching and Learning Aids section of this preface.)

We originally decided to write this book because we thought that existing books often confused students about economics and what it is all about. In our view, the leading texts can be divided into three categories. In the first category are the encyclopedias—the heavy tomes with a section or a paragraph on every topic or subtopic you might possibly want to present to your students. These books are often useful as reference tools. But because they cover too many topics—many of them superficially—the central themes and ideas are lost in the shuffle.

The second type of text we call the "scrapbook." In an effort to elevate student interest, these books insert multicolored boxes, news clippings, interviews, cartoons, and whatever else they can find to jolt the reader on each page. While these special features are often entertaining, there is a trade-off: these books sacrifice a logical, focused presentation of the material. Once again, the central themes and ideas are lost.

Finally, the third type of text, perhaps in response to the first two, tries to do less in every area—a *lot* less. But instead of just omitting the extraneous or inessential details, these texts attempt to redefine introductory economics by throwing out key ideas, models, and concepts. Students who use these books may think that economics is overly simplified and unrealistic. After the course, they may be unprepared to go on in the field, or to think about the economy on their own.

A DISTINCTIVE APPROACH

Our approach is very different. We believe that the best way to teach principles is to present economics as a coherent, unified subject. This does not happen automatically. On the contrary, principles students often miss the unity of what we call "the economic way of thinking." For example, they are likely to see the analysis of goods markets, labor markets, and financial markets as entirely different phenomena, rather than as a repeated application of the same methodology with a new twist here and there. So the principles course appears to be just "one thing after another," rather than the coherent presentation we aim for.

CAREFUL FOCUS

Because we have avoided encyclopedic complexity, we have had to think hard about what topics are most important. As you will see:

We avoid nonessential material. When we believed a topic was not essential to a basic understanding of economics, we left it out. However, we have strived to include core material to *support* an instructor who wants to present special topics in class. So, for example, we do not have comprehensive treatments of environmental economics, agricultural economics, urban economics, health care economics, or comparative systems *as separate subject matter*. But instructors should find in the text a good foundation for building any of these areas—and many others—into their course. And we have included examples from each of these areas as *applications* of core theory where appropriate throughout the text.

We avoid distracting features. This text does not have interviews, news clippings, or boxed inserts with only distant connections to the core material. The features your students *will* find in our book are there to help them understand and apply economic theory itself, to help them avoid common mistakes in applying the theory (the Dangerous Curves feature), and to help them explore sources of information on their own using the Internet.

We explain difficult concepts patiently. By freeing ourselves from the obligation to introduce every possible topic in economics, we can explain the topics we *do* cover more thoroughly and patiently. We lead students, step-by-step, through each aspect of the theory, through each graph, and through each numerical example. In developing this book, we asked other experienced teachers to tell us which aspects of economic theory were hardest for their students to learn, and we have paid special attention to the trouble spots.

We use concrete examples. Students learn best when they see how economics can explain the world around them. Whenever possible, we develop the theory using real-world examples. You will find numerous references to real-world corporations and government policies throughout the text. When we employ hypothetical examples because they illustrate the theory more clearly, we try to make them realistic. In addition, each chapter ends with a thorough, extended application (the "Using the Theory" section) focusing on an important real-world issue.

FEATURES THAT REINFORCE

To help students see economics as a coherent whole, and to reinforce its usefulness, we have included some important features in this book.

The Three-Step Process

Most economists, when approaching a problem, begin by thinking about buyers and sellers, and the markets in which they come together to trade. They move on to characterize a market equilibrium, then give their model a workout in a comparative statics exercise. To understand what economics is about, students need to understand this process, and see it in action in different contexts. To help them do so, we have identified and stressed a "three-step process" that economists use in analyzing problems. The three key steps are:

1. **Characterize the Market.** Decide which market or markets best suit the problem being analyzed, and identify the decision makers (buyers and sellers) who interact there.
2. **Find the Equilibrium.** Describe the conditions necessary for equilibrium in the market, and a method for determining that equilibrium.
3. **Determine What Happens When Things Change.** Explore how events or government policies change the market equilibrium.

A full statement of each key step appears toward the end of Chapter 3. Thereafter, when one or more of the three steps plays an important part in a section of a future chapter, you'll often see a "steps symbol" as shown above. (It will be up to the student to determine which step or steps are applied in a particular section.) Through the use of the three-step process, students learn how to think like economists, and in a very natural way. And they come to see economics as a unified whole, rather than as a series of disconnected ideas.

Dangerous Curves

Anyone who teaches economics for a while learns that, semester after semester, students tend to make the same familiar errors. In class, in office hours, and on exams, students seem pulled, as if by gravity, toward certain logical pitfalls in thinking about, and using, economic theory. We've discovered in our own classrooms that merely explaining the theory properly isn't enough; the most common errors need to be *confronted*, and the student needs to be shown *specifically* why a particular logical path is incorrect. This was the genesis of our Dangerous Curves feature—boxes that anticipate the most common traps in economics, and warn students just when they are most likely to fall victim to them. We've been delighted to hear from instructors how effective this feature has been in overcoming the most common points of confusion for their students.

Using the Theory

 This text is full of applications that are woven throughout the narrative. In addition, virtually every chapter ends with an extended application ("Using the Theory") that pulls together several of the tools learned in that chapter. These are not news clippings or world events that relate only tangentially to the material. Rather, they are step-by-step presentations that help students see how the tools of economics can explain things about the world—things that would be difficult to explain without those tools.

Capstone Chapter

Another way we stress the unity of economics is through the capstone chapter. This chapter pulls together the tools learned in *several* of the macroeconomic chapters, and applies them to a single real-world issue.

In macroeconomics, the capstone chapter is **Using *All* the Theory: The Stock Market and the Macroeconomy.** In it we use a variety of macro tools learned in earlier chapters, and applies them to an issue that students find intriguing—the stock market. More specifically, the chapter pulls together material on GDP, unemployment, inflation, the aggregate expenditure model, the money market, and Federal Reserve policy while focusing on the two-way relationship between the stock market and the macroeconomy.

Internet References

HTTP:// Throughout the book, we've included very brief Internet references where students can look at data, or explore topics further.

CONTENT INNOVATIONS

In addition to the special features just described, you will find some important differences from other texts in topical approach and arrangement. These, too, are designed to make the theory stand out more clearly, and to make learning easier. These are not pedagogical experiments, nor are they innovation for the sake of innovation. The differences you will find in this text are the product of years of classroom experience.

Innovations in Macroeconomics

Scarcity, Choice, and Economic Systems (Chapter 2): This early chapter, while covering standard material such as opportunity cost, also introduces some central concepts much earlier than other texts. Most importantly, it introduces the concept of *comparative advantage*, and the basic principle of *specialization and exchange*. We have placed them at the front of our book because we believe they provide important building blocks for much that comes later.

Long-Run Macroeconomics (Chapters 7 and 8): Our text presents long-run growth before short-run fluctuations. Chapter 7 develops the long-run, classical model at a level appropriate for introductory students, mostly using supply and demand. Chapter 8 then *uses* the classical model to explain the causes—and costs—of economic growth in both rich and poor countries.

We believe it is better to treat the long run before the short run, for two reasons. First, the long-run model makes full use of the tools of supply and demand, and thus allows a natural transition from the preliminary chapters (1, 2, and 3) into macroeconomics. Second, we believe that students can best understand economic fluctuations by understanding *how* and *why* the long-run model breaks down over shorter time periods. This, of course, requires an introduction to the long-run model first.

Economic Fluctuations (Chapter 9): This unique chapter provides a bridge from the long-run to the short-run macro model, and paves the way for the short-run focus on *spending* as the driving force behind economic fluctuations.

Aggregate Demand and Aggregate Supply (Chapter 13): One of our pet peeves about other introductory texts is the too-early introduction of aggregate demand

and aggregate supply curves, *before* teaching where these curves come from. Students then confuse the *AD* and *AS* curves with their microeconomic counterparts, requiring corrective action later. In this text, the *AD* and *AS* curves do not appear until Chapter 13, where they are fully explained. Our treatment of aggregate supply is based on a very simple mark-up model that our students have found easy to understand.

Exchange Rates and Macroeconomic Policy (Chapter 16): Many students find international macroeconomics the most interesting topic in the course, especially the material on exchange rates and what causes them to change. Accordingly, you will find unusually full coverage of exchange rate determination in this chapter. This treatment is kept simple and straightforward, relying exclusively on supply and demand. And it forms the foundation for the discussion of open-economy macro policy that ends the chapter.

Comparative Advantage and the Gains from International Trade (Chapter 17): We've found that international trade is best understood through clear numerical examples, and we've developed them carefully in this chapter. We also try to bridge the gap between the economics and politics of international trade with a systematic discussion of winners and losers.

ORGANIZATIONAL FLEXIBILITY

We have arranged the contents of each chapter, and the table of contents as a whole, according to our recommended order of presentation. But we have also built in flexibility.

Once the core chapters (1–13) have been taught, the remaining chapters (14–17) can be presented in any order. Some instructors may want to assign selections from Chapter 15 (Fiscal Policy) along with Chapter 10 (The Short-Run Macro Model). Similarly, parts of the capstone chapter (Using *All* the Theory: The Stock Market and the Macroeconomy) can be assigned with chapters 10, 13, and 14.

Finally, we have included only those chapters that we thought were essential and teachable in a semester long course. But not everyone will agree about what is essential. While we—as authors—cringe at the thought of a chapter being omitted in the interest of time, we have allowed for that possibility. Nothing in Chapter 9 (economic fluctuations), Chapter 14 (monetary policy), Chapter 15 (fiscal policy and the budget), Chapter 16 (exchange rates and macroeconomic policy), or Chapter 17 (international trade) is required to understand any of the other numbered chapters in the book. Skipping any of these should not cause continuity problems.

In many cases, a chapter can be assigned selectively. For example, an instructor who is anxious to get to the short-run macro model could freely select among the sections in Chapter 8 (economic growth and rising living standards) and Chapter 9 (economic fluctuations).

NEW TO THE THIRD EDITION

For the third edition, we've incorporated many excellent suggestions from reviewers and adopters. We've also conducted lengthy interviews with several adopters to refine their suggestions further. While the overall approach and philosophy of the book remain unchanged, you'll find that every chapter has been affected by the revision.

For example, we've worked hard to clarify and simplify figures, and we've increased the use of caption boxes that enable students to work their way through diagrams more easily. We've replaced examples and made adjustments in the narrative on every page, recognizing that often a more apt example or a slight change in phrasing can vastly improve clarity. We've added a few dozen new Dangerous Curves boxes, in response to some great suggestions from instructors. About a third of the end-of-chapter "Using the Theory" sections are either entirely new or substantially expanded from previous editions. And, of course, we've updated all tables and figures with new data, and adjusted content to reflect the rapid economic changes that have taken place over the past few years.

In addition, we've made some major changes that all instructors should know about in preparing their course.

- *Chapter 2 (Scarcity, Choice, and Economic Systems):* We've revised the discussion of opportunity and incorporated "the opportunity cost of college" as a running example. We've also added a new section on technological change and the PPF.
- *Chapter 3 (Supply and Demand):* We've added an entirely new appendix covering supply and demand equations that teaches students how to solve for equilibrium algebraically. We've also replaced "productive capacity" (as a shift variable for supply curves) with the simpler "number of firms."
- *Chapter 8 (Economic Growth and Rising Living Standards):* The chapter is organized around an

entirely new framework for understanding growth, leading to a new emphasis on the role of productivity.

- *Chapter 9 (Economic Fluctuations):* This chapter has been vastly simplified by removing the more technically difficult material on disequilibrium and the adjustment to the long run, while retaining and improving the material on why the classical model cannot explain fluctuations.

- *Chapters 10, 12, and 13 (Short-Run Model, The Money Market,* and *Aggregate Demand and Aggregate Supply):* The "Using the Theory" sections at the ends of these chapters are now organized around the theme of the 2001 recession and its aftermath. With each presentation, the analysis is deepened and extended, taking advantage of the new tools presented in each chapter.

- *Chapter 14 (Monetary Policy):* This chapter includes a new, integrated discussion of the Taylor rule.

- *Chapter 15 (Fiscal Policy):* We've thoroughly rewritten the section on the long-run consequences of large budget deficits, and included a new "Using the Theory" on the Bush tax cuts.

- *Chapter 17 (International Trade and Comparative Advantage):* Based on instructor interest, we are now including this chapter in the macroeconomic split. And in this edition, we've incorporated the ideas of the Heckscher-Ohlin model (without using the term) in explaining the origins of comparative advantage, and paid more attention to the power politics of protectionism.

Finally, to make the switch from the previous edition to this one as easy as possible, we have posted a more extensive list of chapter-by-chapter changes on our Web site at http://hall-lieb.swlearning.com.

TEACHING AND LEARNING AIDS

To help you present the most interesting principles courses possible, we have created an extensive set of supplementary items. Many of them can be downloaded from the Hall/Lieberman Web site (http://hall-lieb.swlearning.com). The list includes:

For the Instructor

- *Aplia* is an online product developed by world-renowned economist Paul Romer and used by thousands of economics students at hundreds of colleges and universities. It includes online interactive problem sets that follow the order of topics within the text. To ensure the highest level of correlation with our textbook, we (the authors) reviewed every Aplia question for suitability, modified hundreds of them for a closer fit, and wrote hundreds of new questions from scratch. We believe our involvement has ensured consistency in pedagogical approach and technical language, and will allow students to move seamlessly from our text to Aplia and back again.

- An *Instructor's Manual,* by Jane Himarios of the University of Texas, Arlington. The manual provides chapter outlines, teaching ideas, Experiential Exercises for many chapters, suggested answers to the end-of-chapter questions, solutions to all problems, and answers to the e-con @pps (Economic Applications) exercises.

- *Instructor's Resource CD-ROM.* This easy-to-use CD allows quick access to instructor ancillaries from your desktop. It also allows you to review, edit, and copy exactly the material you need. Or, you may choose to go to *Instructor Resources* on the *Product Support Web Site.* This site at http://halllieb.swlearning.com features the essential resources for instructors, password-protected, in downloadable format: the *Instructors Manual* in Word, the Test Banks in Word, and PowerPoint Lecture and Exhibit Slides.

- *Macroeconomics Test Bank,* revised by Dennis Hanseman, University of Cincinnati. This contains over 2,000 multiple-choice questions. The test questions have been arranged according to chapter headings and subheadings, making it easy to find the material needed to construct examinations.

- *Supplemental Test Bank for Macroeconomics,* by Jeffrey Johnson, Sullivan University. This includes approximately 1,500 new Multiple-Choice and True/False questions, arranged by chapter headings.

- *ExamView® Computerized Testing Software.* ExamView is an easy-to-use test creation package compatible with both Microsoft Windows and Macintosh client software, and contains all of the questions in all of the printed test banks. You can select questions by previewing them on the screen, selecting them by number, or selecting them randomly. Questions, instructions, and answers can be edited, and new questions can easily be added. You can also administer quizzes online—over the Internet, through a local area network (LAN), or through a wide area network (WAN).

- *Full-Color Transparency Acetates.* Acetates are available in both a micro and a macro version and consist of many key graphs and illustrations from the text.
- *PowerPoint® Lecture and Exhibit Slides.* Available only on the Web site and the IRCD are two versions of the PowerPoint presentations. The first, prepared by John F. Hall, is a comprehensive and user-friendly *Lecture* outline presentation for use in the classroom, consisting of speaking points in chapter outline format, accompanied by numerous graphs and tables from the main text. The second version, *Exhibit Slides*, provides the instructor with key graphs from the text, many with animation, which may be printed for use as transparency masters.
- *Principles of Economics Videotape. Principles of Economics* is a 40-minute videotape that offers students an insightful overview of ten common economic principles: Trade-offs, Opportunity Cost, Marginal Thinking, Incentives, Trade, Markets, Government's Role, Productivity, Inflation, and the Phillips Curve. *Principles of Economics* shows viewers how to apply economic principles to their daily lives. This video is filled with interviews from some of the country's leading economists, includes profiles of real students facing economic choices, and shows the economy's impact on U.S. and foreign companies. The video can be used at the beginning of a term to give students a general overview of economics, or used one section at a time prior to teaching each of these principles.
- *CNN Video with Integration Guide.* Professors can bring the real world into the classroom by using the CNN Principles of Economics Video Updates. This video provides current stories of economic interest. The accompanying integration guide provides a summary and discussion questions for each clip. The video is produced in cooperation with Turner Learning, Inc.
- *Favorite Ways to Learn Economics: Instructor's Edition.* Authors David Anderson of Centre College and Jim Chasey of Homewood-Flossmoor High School use experiments to bring economic education to life. This is a lab manual for the classroom and for individual study that contains experiments and problem sets that reinforce key economic concepts. The Instructor's Edition provides you the guidance and tips to ensure that these experiments are facilitated successfully.
- *MarketSim.* MarketSim, by Tod Porter at Youngstown State University, is an online simulation designed to help students in microeconomics classes better understand how markets work, by taking on the roles of consumers and producers in a simulated economy. In the simulations, students "make" and "accept" offers to buy and sell labor and goods asynchronously via the Internet. The goal of MarketSim is to provide instructors with a flexible teaching tool that can be used to motivate students to better understand a wide variety of microeconomic concepts.
- *TextChoice.* TextChoice is a custom format of Thomson Learning's online digital content. TextChoice provides the fastest, easiest way for you to create your own learning materials. You may select content from hundreds of best-selling titles, choose material from one of numerous databases, and add your own material. Contact your South-Western/Thomson sales representative for more information at http://thomsoncustom.com.
- *eCoursepacks.* Create a customizable, easy-to-use, online companion for any course with eCoursepacks, from Thomson companies South-Western and Gale. eCoursepacks give educators access to current content from thousands of popular, professional, and academic periodicals, including NACRA and Darden cases, and business and industry information from Gale. You also have the ability to easily add your own material—even collecting a royalty if you choose. Permissions for all eCoursepack content are already secured, saving you the time and worry of securing rights. eCoursepacks online publishing tools also save you time and energy by allowing you to quickly search the databases and make selections, organize all your content, and publish the final outline product in a clean, uniform, and full-color format. eCoursepacks are the best way to provide your audience with current information easily, quickly, and inexpensively. http://ecoursepacks. swlearning.com.
- *WebTutor Advantage. WebTutor Advantage* is an interactive, Web-based, student supplement on WebCT and/or BlackBoard that harnesses the power of the Internet to deliver innovative learning aids that actively engage students. The instructor can incorporate WebTutor as an integral part of the course, or the students can use it on their own as a study guide. Benefits to students include automatic and immediate feedback from quizzes and exams; interactive, multimedia-rich explanation of con-

cepts; online exercises that reinforce what students have learned; flash cards that include audio support; and greater interaction and involvement through online discussion forums. Visit WebTutor to see a demo and for more information at http://webtutor.swlearning.com.

- *WebTutor Toolbox.* WebTutor ToolBox provides instructors with links to content from the book companion Web site. It also provides rich communication tools to instructors and students, including a course calendar, chat, and e-mail. For more information about the WebTutor products, please contact your local Thomson sales representative.

For the Student

- The *Active Learning Guide*, by Geoffrey A. Jehle of Vassar College. This guide provides numerous exercises and self-tests for problem solving practice. It is a valuable tool for helping students strengthen their knowledge of economics, and includes a sample multiple-choice final exam, with answers and explanations.
- Answers to even-numbered end-of-chapter Questions and Problems can be found on the text Web site at http://hall-lieb.swlearning.com.
- The *Hall/Lieberman Xtra!* at http://hallxtra.swlearning.com. Xtra! provides students with access to the robust set of additional online learning tools found at the site. Here is a tour through some of the study support features you will find there:
  - **Diagnostic Pretests.** These innovative quizzes offer students diagnostic self-assessment of their comprehension of each chapter and an individualized plan for directed study based on the areas in which they are found to have a weaker understanding.
  - **Master the Learning Objectives.** Each chapter's Master the Learning Objectives gives step-by-step instructions associated with each learning objective to guide students systematically through all the activities that will deepen their understanding of that particular concept.
  - **The Graphing Workshop.** The Graphing Workshop is a one-stop learning resource for help in mastering the language of graphs, which is one of the more difficult aspects of an economics course for many students. It enables students to explore important economic concepts through a unique learning system made up of tutorials, interactive drawing tools, and exercises that teach how to interpret, reproduce, and explain graphs.
  - **Using the Theory Applications.** Activities and exercises are available that ask students to use the three key steps to analyze unique and real-world questions.
  - **CNN Video Clips.** CNN video segments bring the "real world" right to students' desktops. The accompanying CNN video exercises help to illustrate how economics is an important part of their daily lives, and help them learn the material by applying it to current events.
  - **Ask the Instructor Video Clips.** Via streaming video, difficult concepts from each chapter are explained and illustrated by an economics instructor, Dr. Peter Olson from Indiana University. These video clips can be extremely helpful review and clarification tools if a student had trouble understanding an in-class lecture or is more of a visual learner.
  - **Economic Applications** (e-con @pps). EconNews Online, EconDebate Online, EconData Online, and EconLinks Online features help to deepen students' understanding of theoretical concepts through hands-on exploration and analysis of the latest economic news stories, policy debates, and data.
  - NEW to this edition and in conjunction with these Xtra! features are: **Economic Applications exercises** at the end of every chapter. Prepared by Brian J. Peterson (Manchester College) and Hamid Azari-Rad (SUNY–New Paltz), the exercises direct students to one or more of the applications to solve problems through brief research. These exercises help students to understand the relationship of current issues to the theories studied in the chapters. Xtra! is available as an optional package with the text.
- *InfoTrac College Edition.* Students can receive anytime, anywhere, online access to a database of full-text articles from hundreds of scholarly and popular periodicals, such as *Newsweek, Fortune, American Economist,* and the *Quarterly Journal of Economics.* The InfoTrac subscription card is good for four months, and is a great way to practice online research using academically-based and reliable sources.
- The *Hall/Lieberman Web site* (http://hall-lieb.swlearning.com). The site contains a wealth of use-

ful teaching and learning resources. Important features available at the Web site include:

- *Interactive Quizzes* with feedback on answers. Completed quizzes can be e-mailed directly to the instructor.
- Links to the Internet addresses referred to in the text.
- PowerPoint slides for review and note-taking.
- A sample chapter from the *Active Learning Guide.*

- ***Economics: Hits on the Web.*** This resource booklet supports your students' research efforts on the World Wide Web. The manual covers materials such as: introduction to the World Wide Web, browsing the Web, finding information on the World Wide Web, e-mail, e-mail discussion groups, newsgroups, and documenting Internet sources for research. It also provides a listing of the hottest economic sites on the Web.
- ***Favorite Ways to Learn Economics.*** In *Favorite Ways to Learn Economics,* authors David Anderson of Centre College and Jim Chasey of Homewood-Flossmoor High School use experiments to bring economic education to life. This is a lab manual for the classroom and for individual study that contains experiments and problem sets that reinforce key economic concepts.
- ***9/11: Economic Viewpoints.*** The shape, pace, and spirit of the global economy have been greatly impacted by the events that occurred on September 11, 2001. With *9/11: Economic Viewpoints,* South-Western offers a collection of essays that provides a variety of perspectives on the economic effects of this event. Each essay is written by one of South-Western's economics textbook authors, all of whom are highly regarded for both their academic and professional achievements. This unique collaboration results in one of the most cutting-edge resources available to help facilitate discussions of September 11th's impact within the context of economics courses.
- ***The Economist's Handbook: A Research and Writing Guide,*** **Second Edition.** This reference book, by Thomas Wyrick of Southwest Missouri State University, is designed to help students develop skills in conducting and interpreting economic research. *The Economist's Handbook* provides commonsense explanations, relevant examples, and focused assignments, as well as an extensive glossary of economic terms, information about economics careers, and other useful reference materials.

- ***Macroeconomics Alive! CD-ROMs.*** These interactive multimedia study aids provide a high-tech, fun way to study economics. Through a combination of animated presentations, interactive graphing exercises, and simulations, the core principles of economics come to life in an upbeat and entertaining way. Visit the Economics Alive! Web site at http://econalive. swlearning.com.
- ***The Wall Street Journal.*** The Hall and Lieberman texts are available with a special 15-week *Wall Street Journal* subscription offer. Have your instructor contact your South-Western/Thomson Learning sales representative for package pricing and ordering information.

ACKNOWLEDGMENTS

Our greatest debt is to the many reviewers who carefully read the book and provided numerous suggestions for improvements. While we could not incorporate all their ideas, we did carefully evaluate each one of them. To these reviewers we are most grateful:

Ljubisa Adamovich	Florida State University
Brian A'Hearn	Franklin and Marshall College
Rashid Al-Hmoud	Texas Tech University
David Aschauer	Bates College
Richard Ballman	Augustana College
Chris Barnett	Gannon University
Sylvain Boko	Wake Forest University
Mark Buenafe	Arizona State University
Steven Call	Metropolitan State College
Kevin Carey	American University
Steven Cobb	Xavier University
Dennis Debrecht	Carroll College
Selahattin Dibooglu	Southern Illinois University
John Duffy	University of Pittsburgh
Stephen Erfle	Dickinson College
James Falter	Mount Marty College
Sasan Fayazmanesh	California State University, Fresno
Sarmila Ghosh	University of Scranton
Satyajit Ghosh	University of Scranton
Scott Gilbert	Southern Illinois University–Carbondale
Michael Gootzeit	University of Memphis
John Gregor	Washington and Jefferson University
Rik Hafer	Southern Illinois University

Andrew Hildreth	University of California, Berkeley
Thomas Husted	American University
David Kaun	University of California, Santa Cruz
Philip King	San Francisco State University
Kate Krause	University of New Mexico
Viju Kulkarni	San Diego State University
Nazma Latif-Zaman	Providence College
Teresa Laughlin	Palomar College
Judith Mann	University of California, San Diego
Shahruz Mohtadi	Suffolk University
Chris Niggle	University of Redlands
Farrokh Nourzad	Marquette University
Jim Palmieri	Simpson College
Yvon Pho	American University
Teresa Riley	Youngstown State University
William Rosen	Cornell University
Thomas Sadler	Pace University
Jonathan Sandy	University of San Diego
Ramazan Sari	Texas Tech University
Ghosh Sarmila	University of Scranton
Edward Scahill	University of Scranton
Mary Schranz	University of Wisconsin, Madison
Alden Shiers	California Polytechnic State University
Kevin Siqueira	Clarkson University
Kevin Sontheimer	University of Pittsburgh
Richard Steinberg	Indiana University–Purdue University Indianapolis
Martha Stuffler	Irvine Valley College
Mohammad Syed	Miles College
Mikayel Vardanyan	Oregon State University
Thomas Watkins	Eastern Kentucky University
Glen Whitman	California State University, Northridge
Robert Whaples	Wake Forest University

To help us with improvements to this third edition, we went through a number of special reviews, surveys, and phone conversations. We would like to thank the following instructors for their thoughtful comments and insights:

Parantap Basu	Fordham University
Tibor Besedes	Rutgers University
Gautam Bhattacharya	University of Kansas
James E. Dietz	California State University, Fullerton
Khosrow Doroodian	Ohio University
Debra S. Dwyer	SUNY–Stony Brook
Sasan Fayazmanesh	California State University, Fresno
Lehman B. Fletcher	Iowa State University
James R. Gale	Michigan Technological University
Arunee C. Grow	Mesa Community College
Dennis Hanseman	
Roger Hewett	Drake University
Shahruz Hohtadi	Suffolk University
Jeffrey Johnson	Sullivan University
Jacqueline Khorassani	Marietta College
Frederic R. Kolb	University of Wisconsin–Eau Claire
Brent Kreider	Iowa State University
Bruce Madariaga	Montgomery College
Mark McCleod	Virginia Tech University
Steve McQueen	Barstow Community College
William R. Melick	Kenyon College
Paul G. Munyon	Grinnell College
Rebecca Neumann	University of Wisconsin–Milwaukee
Emmanuel Nnadozie	Truman State University
Alannah Orrison Rosenberg	Saddleback Community College
Zaohong Pan	Western Connecticut State University
Gregg Pratt	Mesa Community College
Robert F. Schlack	Carthage College
Pamela M. Schmitt	U.S. Naval Academy
John Vahaly	University of Louisville
Mikayel Vardanyan	Oregon State University
Michael F. Williams	University of St. Thomas
Dirk Yandell	University of San Diego
and Petr Zemcik	Southern Illinois University–Carbondale

We also wish to acknowledge the talented and dedicated group of instructors who helped put together a supplementary package that is second to none. Geoffrey A. Jehle of Vassar College wrote the *Active Learning Guide* and created numerous improvements to this edition, making it even more user-friendly and active. Jane Himarios of the University of Texas, Arlington, revised the *Instructor's Manual*, the Test Bank was carefully revised by Dennis Hanseman, and the new Supplemental Test Bank was created by Jeffrey Johnson of Sullivan University. We appreciate the contributions of Hamid Azari-Rad of SUNY–New Paltz and Brian J. Peterson of

Manchester College, both of whom created the new Economic Applications exercises for this edition. And we are grateful to Mark Karscig of Central Missouri State University for his contributions to the "Using the Theory" exercises for the Web site. In addition, we appreciate the work of the three people who contributed to the Web site's Online Quizzes: Brian J. Peterson, Jeffrey Johnson, and Douglas Kinnear. Our thanks go also to John and Pamela Hall (Western Washington University), who thoroughly revised and improved the PowerPoint slides for this edition. Finally, special thanks go to Dennis Hanseman, who was our development editor for the first edition; his insights and ideas are still present in this third edition, and his continued assistance has proved invaluable.

The beautiful book you are holding would not exist except for the hard work of a talented team of professionals. Book production was overseen by Deanna Quinn, Senior Production Project Manager at South-Western, and undertaken by Pre-Press Company. At Pre-Press, all things are possible because of the dedicated work of Nicole Lochead. Deanna and Nicole showed remarkable patience, as well as an unflagging concern for quality throughout the process. We couldn't have asked for better production partners. A team of NYU students helped to locate and fix the few remaining errors. They included Leslie Miller, Abigail Trainer, Martin Paredes, and Wen-Jyh Chao.

The overall look of the book and cover was planned by Michelle Kunkler and executed by Craig Ramsdell of Ramsdell Design. John Hill managed the photo program, and Sandee Milewski made all the pieces come together in her role as Senior Manufacturing Coordinator.

We are especially grateful for the hard work of the dedicated and professional South-Western editorial, marketing, and sales teams. Mike Worls, Senior Acquisitions Editor, has once again shepherded this text through publication with remarkable skill and devotion. John Carey, Senior Marketing Manager, has done a first-rate job getting the message out to instructors and sales reps. Susan Smart, Senior Development Editor, delved into every chapter and contributed to their improvement; her patience, flexibility, and skill went far beyond the call of duty. Vicky True, Manager of Technology, Editorial, and Dana Cowden, Technology Project Editor, have put together a wonderful package of media tools. And the South-Western sales representatives have been extremely persuasive advocates for the book. We sincerely appreciate all their efforts!

Finally, for the Third Edition Update, we want to acknowledge the amazing team at Aplia, who helped us as we modified existing Aplia problems, and wrote new ones, to create the closest possible fit with our textbook. In particular, Paul Romer (CEO and Founder), Kristen Ford (Managing Editor) and Perkin Chung (Senior Content Developer) showed remarkable skill, knowledge and patience in working with us on content, and in coming up with clever ways to make our job easier. It was a pleasure to work with them.

A REQUEST

Although we have worked hard on the first three editions of this book, we know there is always room for further improvement. For that, our fellow users are indispensable. We invite your comments and suggestions wholeheartedly. We especially welcome your suggestions for additional "Using the Theory" sections and Dangerous Curves. You may send your comments to either of us care of South-Western.

Bob Hall
Marc Lieberman

About the Authors

Robert E. Hall is a prominent applied economist. He is the Robert and Carole McNeil Professor of Economics at Stanford University and Senior Fellow at Stanford's Hoover Institution where he conducts research on inflation, unemployment, taxation, monetary policy, and the economics of high technology. He received his Ph.D. from MIT and has taught there as well as at the University of California, Berkeley. Hall is Director of the research program on Economic Fluctuations of the National Bureau of Economic Research, and Chairman of the Bureau's Committee on Business Cycle Dating, which maintains the semiofficial chronology of the U.S. business cycle. He has published numerous monographs and articles in scholarly journals, and coauthored a popular intermediate text. Hall has advised the Treasury Department and the Federal Reserve Board on national economic policy, and has testified on numerous occasions before congressional committees.

Marc Lieberman is Clinical Associate Professor of Economics at New York University. He received his Ph.D. from Princeton University. Lieberman has presented his extremely popular Principles of Economics course at Harvard, Vassar, the University of California, Santa Cruz, and the University of Hawaii, as well as at NYU, where he won the university's Golden Dozen teaching award and also the Economics Society Award for Excellence in Teaching. He is coeditor and contributor to *The Road to Capitalism: Economic Transformation in Eastern Europe and the Former Soviet Union.* Lieberman has consulted for the Bank of America and the Educational Testing Service. In his spare time, he is a professional screenwriter. He co-wrote the script for *Love Kills,* a thriller that aired on the USA Cable Network, and he teaches screenwriting at NYU's School of Continuing and Professional Studies.

Brief Contents

Part I: Preliminaries

1. What Is Economics? 1
2. Scarcity, Choice, and Economic Systems 21
3. Supply and Demand 52

Part II: Macroeconomics: Basic Concepts

4. What Macroeconomic Tries to Explain 89
5. Production, Income, and Employment 103
6. The Monetary System, Prices, and Inflation 137

Part III: Long-Run Macroeconomics

7. The Classical Long-Run Model 163
8. Economic Growth and Rising Living Standards 193

Part IV: Short-Run Macroeconomics

9. Economic Fluctuations 228
10. The Short-Run Macro Model 240

Part V: Money, Prices, and the Macroeconomy

11. The Banking System and the Money Supply 283
12. The Money Market and the Interest Rate 312
13. Aggregate Demand and Aggregate Supply 339

Part VI: Macroeconomic Policy

14. Inflation and Monetary Policy 375
15. Fiscal Policy: Taxes, Spending, and the Federal Budget 404
16. Exchange Rates and Macroeconomic Policy 437
17. Comparitive Advantage and the Gains from International Trade 473

Using *All* The Theory: The Stock Market and the Macroeconomy 505

Glossary G-1

Index I-1

Contents

PART I: PRELIMINARIES

Chapter 1: What Is Economics?   1

Economics, Scarcity, and Choice   1
Scarcity and Individual Choice, 2 • Scarcity and Social Choice, 3 • Scarcity and Economics, 4

The World of Economics   5
Microeconomics and Macroeconomics, 5 • Positive and Normative Economics, 5

Why Study Economics?   6
To Understand the World Better, 7 • To Gain Self-Confidence, 7 • To Achieve Social Change, 7 • To Help Prepare for Other Careers, 7 • To Become an Economist, 8

The Methods of Economics   8
The Art of Building Economic Models, 9 • Assumptions and Conclusions, 9 • The Three-Step Process, 10 • Math, Jargon, and Other Concerns . . . 10

How to Study Economics   11

Appendix: Graphs and Other Useful Tools   14
Tables and Graphs, 14 • Linear Equations, 16 • How Straight Lines and Curves Shift, 18 • Solving Equations, 20

Chapter 2: Scarcity, Choice, and Economic Systems   21

The Concept of Opportunity Cost   21
Opportunity Cost for Individuals, 22 • Opportunity Cost and Society, 26 • Production Possibilities Frontiers, 26 • The Search for a Free Lunch, 29

Economic Systems   34
Specialization and Exchange, 34 • Resource Allocation, 39 • Resource Ownership, 43 • Types of Economic Systems, 44

Using the Theory: Are We Saving Lives Efficiently?   46

Chapter 3: Supply and Demand   52

Markets   53
How Broadly Should We Define the Market? 53 • Buyers and Sellers, 54 • Competition in Markets, 55 • Using Supply and Demand, 56

Demand   57
The Law of Demand, 58 • The Demand Schedule and the Demand Curve, 59 • Shifts vs. Movements Along the Demand Curve, 59 • Factors That Shift the Demand Curve, 61

Supply   65
The Law of Supply, 66 • The Supply Schedule and the Supply Curve, 67 • Shifts vs. Movements Along the Supply Curve, 68 • Factors That Shift the Supply Curve, 69

Putting Supply and Demand Together   73

What Happens When Things Change?   76
Income Rises, Causing an Increase in Demand, 76 • An Ice Storm Causes a Decrease in Supply, 77 • Handheld PCs in 2003: Both Curves Shift, 78

The Three-Step Process   80

Using the Theory: College Administrators Make a Costly Mistake   82

Appendix: Solving for Equilibrium Algebraically   88

PART II: MACROECONOMICS: BASIC CONCEPTS

Chapter 4: What Macroeconomics Tries to Explain 89

Macroeconomic Goals 89
Economic Growth, 90 • High Employment (or Low Unemployment), 92 • Stable Prices, 95

The Macroeconomic Approach 96
Aggregation in Macroeconomics, 97

Macroeconomic Controversies 98

As You Study Macroeconomics . . . 99

Chapter 5: Production, Income, and Employment 103

Production and Gross Domestic Product 104
GDP: A Definition, 105 • The Expenditure Approach to GDP, 107 • Other Approaches to GDP, 113 • Measuring GDP: A Summary, 116 • Real Versus Nominal GDP, 116 • How GDP Is Used, 117 • Problems with GDP, 118

Employment and Unemployment 120
Types of Unemployment, 120 • The Costs of Unemployment, 123 • How Unemployment Is Measured, 126 • Problems in Measuring Unemployment, 127

Using the Theory: GDP After September 11 139
The Direct Impact on GDP, 130 • Indirect Impacts on GDP,   130

Chapter 6: The Monetary System, Prices, and Inflation 137

The Monetary System 138
History of the Dollar, 138 • Why Paper Currency Is Accepted as a Means of Payment, 139

Measuring the Price Level and Inflation 140
Index Numbers, 140 • The Consumer Price Index, 141 • How the CPI Has Behaved, 142 • From Price Index to Inflation Rate, 142 • How the CPI Is Used, 142 • Real Variables and Adjustment for Inflation, 143 • Inflation and the Measurement of Real GDP, 145

The Costs of Inflation 145
The Inflation Myth, 146 • The Redistributive Cost of Inflation, 147 • The Resource Cost of Inflation, 150 • A Preliminary Word About Deflation, 151

Is the CPI Accurate? 151
Sources of Bias in the CPI, 152

Using the Theory: The Use and Misuse of an Imperfect CPI 154
Indexing, 154 • Long-Run Comparisons, 155 • The Bigger, Conceptual Problem, 156 • What the CPI Does Well, 157

Appendix: Calculating the Consumer Price Index 161

PART III: LONG-RUN MACROECONOMICS

Chapter 7: The Classical Long-Run Model 163

Macroeconomic Models: Classical Versus Keynesian 164
Assumptions of the Classical Model, 166

How Much Output Will We Produce? 167
The Labor Market, 168 • Determining the Economy's Output, 169

The Role of Spending 171
Total Spending in a Very Simple Economy, 172 • Total Spending in a More Realistic Economy, 174

The Loanable Funds Market 178
The Supply of Funds Curve, 179 • The Demand for Funds Curve, 180 • Equilibrium in the Loanable Funds Market, 181 • The Loanable Funds Market and Say's Law, 182

The Classical Model: A Summary 184

Using the Theory: Fiscal Policy in the Classical Model 185
Fiscal Policy with a Budget Deficit, 186 • Fiscal Policy with a Budget Surplus, 188

Chapter 8: Economic Growth and Rising Living Standards 193

The Importance of Growth 194

What Makes Economies Grow? 196
Economic Growth and Living Standards, 198

Growth in the Labor Force Participation Rate (LFPR) 199
How to Increase Employment, 202

Growth in Productivity 204
Growth in the Capital Stock, 204• Investment and the Capital Stock, 206 • How to Increase Investment, 206 • Human Capital and Economic Growth, 212

Technological Change 213

Growth Policies: A Summary 215

The Cost of Economic Growth 215
Budgetary Costs, 217 • Consumption Costs, 218 • Opportunity Costs of Workers' Time, 219 • Sacrifice of Other Social Goals, 220

Using the Theory: Economic Growth in the Less-Developed Countries, 220

PART IV: SHORT-RUN MACROECONOMICS

Chapter 9: Economic Fluctuations 228

Can the Classical Model Explain Economic Fluctuations? 230
Shifts in Labor Demand, 231 • Shifts in Labor Supply, 232 • Verdict: The Classical Model Cannot Explain Economic Fluctuations, 233

What Triggers Economic Fluctuations? 234
A Very Simple Economy, 234 • The Real-World Economy, 235 • Shocks that Push the Economy Away from Equilibrium, 236

Where Do We Go from Here? 237

Chapter 10: The Short-Run Macro Model 240

Consumption Spending 242
Consumption and Disposable Income, 244 • Consumption and Income, 247 • Shifts in the Consumption-Income Line, 248

Getting to Total Spending 251
Investment Spending, 251 • Government Purchases, 252 •

Net Exports, 252 • Summing Up: Aggregate Expenditure, 253 • Income and Aggregate Expenditure, 254

Finding Equilibrium GDP 255
Inventories and Equilibrium GDP, 256 • Finding Equilibrium GDP with a Graph, 257 • Equilibrium GDP and Employment, 261

What Happens When Things Change? 263
A Change in Investment Spending, 263 • The Expenditure Multiplier, 265 • The Multiplier in Reverse, 267 • Other Spending Shocks, 267 • A Graphical View of the Multiplier, 268 • Automatic Stabilizers and the Multiplier, 269

Comparing Models: Long Run and Short Run 271
The Role of Saving, 272 • The Effect of Fiscal Policy, 272

Using the Theory: The Recession of 2001 273

Appendix 1: Finding Equilibrium GDP Algebraically 280

Appendix 2: The Special Case of the Tax Multiplier 281

PART V: MONEY, PRICES, AND THE MACROECONOMY

Chapter 11: The Banking System and the Money Supply 283

What Counts as Money 283

Measuring the Money Supply 284
Assets and Their Liquidity, 285 • M1 and M2, 286

The Banking System 288
Financial Intermediaries, 288 • Commercial Banks, 289 • A Bank's Balance Sheet, 290

The Federal Reserve System 291
The Structure of the Fed, 292 • The Federal Open Market Committee, 294 • The Functions of the Federal Reserve, 294

The Fed and the Money Supply 295
How the Fed Increases the Money Supply, 295 • The Demand Deposit Multiplier, 298 • The Fed's Influence on the Banking System as a Whole, 300 • How the Fed Decreases the Money Supply, 301 • Some Important Provisos About the Demand Deposit Multiplier, 303 • Other Tools for Controlling the Money Supply, 304

Using the Theory: Bank Failures and Banking Panics 306

Chapter 12: The Money Market and the Interest Rate 312

The Demand for Money 312
An Individual's Demand for Money, 313 • The Economy-Wide Demand for Money, 314

The Supply of Money 316

Equilibrium in the Money Market 317
How the Money Market Reaches Equilibrium, 319

What Happens When Things Change? 322
How the Fed Changes the Interest Rate, 322 • How Do Interest Rate Changes Affect the Economy? 323 • Monetary Policy and the Economy, 324 • Fiscal Policy (and Other Spending Changes) Revisited, 327

Are There Two Theories of the Interest Rate? 330

Expectations and the Money Market 331

Using the Theory: The Fed and the Recession of 2001 333

Chapter 13: Aggregate Demand and Aggregate Supply 339

The Aggregate Demand Curve 340
Deriving the Aggregate Demand Curve, 342 • Understanding the *AD* Curve, 342 • Movements Along the *AD* Curve, 343 • Shifts of the *AD* Curve, 343

The Aggregate Supply Curve 346
Costs and Prices, 347 • GDP, Costs, and the Price Level, 348 • Deriving the Aggregate Supply Curve, 350 • Movements Along the *AS* Curve, 351 • Shifts of the *AS* Curve, 351

AD and *AS* Together: Short-Run Equilibrium 353

What Happens When Things Change? 355
Demand Shocks in the Short Run, 355 • Demand Shocks: Adjusting to the Long Run, 359 • The Long-Run Aggregate Supply Curve, 362 • Supply Shocks, 363

Some Important Provisos About the *AS* Curve 365

Using the Theory: The Story of Two Recessions and "Jobless" Expansions 366
The Recession of 1990–91, 366 • The Recession of 2001, 367 • Jobless Expansions, 369

PART VI: MACROECONOMIC POLICY

Chapter 14: Inflation and Monetary Policy 375

The Objectives of Monetary Policy 376
Low, Stable Inflation, 376 • Full Employment, 376

The Fed's Performance 378

Federal Reserve Policy: Theory and Practice 379
Responding to Changes in Money Demand, 380 • Responding to Other Demand Shocks, 382 • Responding to Supply Shocks, 385

Expectations and Ongoing Inflation 387
How Ongoing Inflation Arises, 388 • Ongoing Inflation and the Phillips Curve, 391 • Why the Fed Allows Ongoing Inflation, 393

Using the Theory: Challenges for Monetary Policy 394
Information Problems, 395 • The Natural Rate of Unemployment, 396 • Rules Versus Discretion and the "Taylor Rule," 397 • Deflation, 398

Chapter 15: Fiscal Policy: Taxes, Spending, and the Federal Budget 404

Thinking About Spending, Taxes, and the Budget 405

Spending, Taxes, and the Budget: Some Background 406
Government Outlays, 406 • Federal Tax Revenues, 412 • The Federal Budget and the National Debt, 416

The Effects of Fiscal Changes in the Short Run 418
How Economic Fluctuations Affect the Federal Budget, 419 • How the Budget Affects Economic Fluctuations, 420 • Countercyclical Fiscal Policy, 421

The Effects of Fiscal Changes in the Long Run 423
The National Debt, 424

Using the Theory: The Bush Tax Cuts of 2001 and 2003 428
The Short Run: Countercyclical Fiscal Policy? 428 • The Long Run: The Tax Cuts and the National Debt, 429

Chapter 16: Exchange Rates and Macroeconomic Policy 437

Foreign Exchange Markets and Exchange Rates 438
Dollars per Pound or Pounds per Dollar? 438

The Demand for British Pounds 440
The Demand for Pounds Curve, 440 • Shifts in the Demand for Pounds Curve, 441

The Supply of British Pounds 442
The Supply of Pounds Curve, 443 • Shifts in the Supply of Pounds Curve, 444

The Equilibrium Exchange Rate 445

What Happens When Things Change? 446
How Exchange Rates Change Over Time, 447 • The Very Short Run: "Hot Money," 448 • The Short Run: Macroeconomic Fluctuations, 449 • The Long Run: Purchasing Power Parity, 450

Government Intervention and Foreign Exchange Markets 452
Managed Float, 452 • Fixed Exchange Rates, 453 • Foreign Currency Crises, the IMF, and Moral Hazard, 455 • The Euro, 457

Exchange Rates and the Macroeconomy 459
Exchange Rates and Demand Shocks, 459 • Exchange Rates and Monetary Policy, 459

Using the Theory: The Stubborn U.S. Trade Deficit 461
From a Financial Inflow to a Trade Deficit, 463 • The Growing Trade Deficit with China, 466

Chapter 17: Comparative Advantage and the Gains from International Trade 473

The Logic of Free Trade 474

The Theory of Comparative Advantage 475
Opportunity Cost and Comparative Advantage, 476 • Specialization and World Production, 477 • How Each

Nation Gains from International Trade, 478 • The Terms of Trade 479

How Potential Gains Turn into Actual Gains   480
Some Important Provisos, 483

The Sources of Comparative Advantage   485

Why Some People Object to Free Trade   487
The Impact of Trade in the Exporting Country, 488 • The Impact of Trade in the Importing Country, 489 • Attitudes and Influence on Trade Policy, 489

How Free Trade Is Restricted   492
Tariffs, 492 • Quotas,   493

Protectionism   494
Myths About International Trade, 494 • Sophisticated Arguments for Protection, 496 • Protectionism in the United States, 497

Using the Theory: The U.S. Sugar Quota   499

USING *ALL* THE THEORY: THE STOCK MARKET AND THE MACROECONOMY   505

Basic Background   506
Why Do People Hold Stock? 507 • Tracking the Stock Market, 507

Explaining Stock Prices   509
Step 1: Characterize the Market, 509 • Step 2: Find the Equilibrium, 509 • Step 3: What Happens When Things Change? 511

The Stock Market and the Macroeconomy   513
How the Stock Market Affects the Economy, 513 • How the Economy Affects the Stock Market, 516

What Happens When Things Change?   517
A Shock to the Economy, 518 • A Shock to the Economy and the Stock Market: The High-Tech Boom of the 1990s, 519 • A Shock to the Economy and the Market: The High-Tech Bust of 2000 and 2001, 520 • The Fed and the Stock Market, 521

Glossary   G-1

Index   I-1

What Is Economics?

Economics, Scarcity, and Choice
  Scarcity and Individual Choice
  Scarcity and Social Choice
  Scarcity and Economics
The World of Economics
  Microeconomics and Macroeconomics
  Positive and Normative Economics
Why Study Economics?
  To Understand the World Better
  To Gain Self-Confidence
  To Achieve Social Change
  To Help Prepare for Other Careers
  To Become an Economist

The Methods of Economics
  The Art of Building Economic Models
  Assumptions and Conclusions
  The Three-Step Process
  Math, Jargon, and Other Concerns . . .
How to Study Economics
Appendix: Graphs and Other Useful Tools
  Tables and Graphs
  Linear Equations
  How Straight Lines and Curves Shift
  Solving Equations

Economics. The word conjures up all sorts of images: manic stock traders on Wall Street, an economic summit meeting in a European capital, a somber television news anchor announcing good or bad news about the economy. . . . You probably hear about economics several times each day. What exactly *is* economics?

First, economics is a *social science,* so it seeks to explain something about *society.* In this sense, it has something in common with psychology, sociology, and political science. But economics is different from these other social sciences, because of *what* economists study and *how* they study it. Economists ask fundamentally different questions, and they answer them using tools that other social scientists find rather exotic.

ECONOMICS, SCARCITY, AND CHOICE

A good definition of economics, which stresses the difference between economics and other social sciences, is the following:

> *Economics is the study of choice under conditions of scarcity.*

Economics The study of choice under conditions of scarcity.

1

This definition may appear strange to you. Where are the familiar words we ordinarily associate with economics: "money," "stocks and bonds," "prices," "budgets," . . . ? As you will soon see, economics deals with all of these things and more. But first, let's take a closer look at two important ideas in this definition: scarcity and choice.

Scarcity and Individual Choice

Think for a moment about your own life—your daily activities, the possessions you enjoy, the surroundings in which you live. Is there anything you don't have that you'd *like* to have? Anything you'd like *more* of? If your answer is "no," congratulations! You are well advanced on the path of Zen self-denial. The rest of us, however, feel the pinch of limits to our material standard of living. This simple truth is at the very core of economics. It can be restated this way: We all face the problem of **scarcity**.

Scarcity A situation in which the amount of something available is insufficient to satisfy the desire for it.

At first glance, it may seem that you suffer from an infinite variety of scarcities. There are so many things you might like to have right now—a larger room or apartment, a new car, more clothes . . . the list is endless. But a little reflection suggests that your limited ability to satisfy these desires is based on two other, more basic limitations: scarce *time* and scarce *spending power*.

> *As individuals, we face a scarcity of time and spending power. Given more of either, we could each have more of the goods and services that we desire.*

The scarcity of spending power is no doubt familiar to you. We've all wished for higher incomes so that we could afford to buy more of the things we want. But the scarcity of time is equally important. So many of the activities we enjoy—seeing a movie, taking a vacation, making a phone call—require time as well as money. Just as we have limited spending power, we also have a limited number of hours in each day to satisfy our desires.

Because of the scarcities of time and spending power, each of us is forced to make *choices*. We must allocate our scarce *time* to different activities: work, play, education, sleep, shopping, and more. We must allocate our scarce *spending power* among different goods and services: housing, food, furniture, travel, and many others. And each time we choose to buy something or do something, we also choose *not* to buy or do something else.

Economists study the choices we make as individuals and also the *consequences* of those choices. For example, in 2002 and 2003, large numbers of consumers in the United States decided to spend less on air travel, due to concerns about safety and increased delays at airport security checkpoints. Many shifted their vacation spending toward home-improvement projects. Collectively, these decisions led to a contraction and layoffs in the airline industry, and in businesses associated with air travel (e.g., hotels and car rental firms). At the same time, businesses associated with home improvement (e.g., lumber mills, contractors, hardware stores) expanded, and hired additional workers.

Economists also study the more subtle and indirect effects of individual choice on our society. Will most Americans continue to live in houses or—like Europeans—will most of us end up in apartments? Will we have an educated and well-informed citizenry? Will traffic congestion in our cities continue to worsen or is there relief in sight? These questions hinge, in large part, on the separate decisions of millions of people. To answer them requires an understanding of how individuals make choices under conditions of scarcity.

Scarcity and Social Choice

Now let's think about scarcity and choice from *society*'s point of view. What are the goals of our society? We want a high standard of living for our citizens, clean air, safe streets, good schools, and more. What is holding us back from accomplishing all of these goals in a way that would satisfy everyone? You already know the answer: scarcity.

In society's case, the problem is a scarcity of **resources**—the things we use to make goods and services that help us achieve our goals. Economists classify resources into four categories:

1. **Labor** is the time human beings spend producing goods and services.
2. **Capital** is something produced that is long-lasting, and used to make *other* things that we value. Note the word *long-lasting*. If something is used up quickly in the production process—like the flour a baker uses to make bread—it is generally *not* considered capital. A good rule of thumb is that capital should last at least a year, although most types of capital last considerably longer.

    It's useful to distinguish two different types of capital. **Physical capital** consists of things like machinery and equipment, factory buildings, computers, and even hand tools like hammers and screwdrivers. These are all long-lasting *physical* goods that are used to make other things.

    Human capital consists of the skills and knowledge possessed by workers. These satisfy our definition of capital: They are *produced* (through education and training), they help us produce *other* things, and they last for many years, typically through an individual's working life.[1]

    The **capital stock** is the total amount of capital at a nation's disposal at any point in time. It consists of all the physical and human capital made in previous periods that is still productively useful.
3. **Land/Natural resources** are the preexisting "gifts of nature" in a country. This includes land—the physical space on which production takes place—as well as useful materials found under it or on it, such as crude oil, iron, coal, or fertile soil.
4. **Entrepreneurship** is an individual's ability (and the willingness to *use* this ability) to combine the *other* resources into a productive enterprise. An entrepreneur may be an *innovator* who comes up with an original idea for a business or a *risk taker* who provides her own funds or time to nurture a project with uncertain rewards.

Anything *produced* in the economy comes, ultimately, from some combination of these resources. Think about the last lecture you attended at your college. You were consuming a service—a college lecture. What went into producing that service? Your instructor was supplying labor. Many types of capital were used as well. The physical capital included desks, chairs, a chalkboard or transparency projector, the classroom building itself, and the computer your instructor may have used to

Resources The labor, capital, land and natural resources, and entrepreneurship that are used to produce goods and services.

Labor The time human beings spend producing goods and services.

Capital Something produced that is long-lasting and used to produce other goods.

Physical capital The part of the capital stock consisting of physical goods, such as machinery, equipment, and factories.

Human capital The skills and training of the labor force.

Capital stock The total amount of capital in a nation that is productively useful at a particular point in time.

Natural resources Land as well as the naturally occurring materials that come with it.

Entrepreneurship The ability and willingness to combine the *other* resources—labor, capital, and natural resources—into a productive enterprise.

---

[1] An individual's human capital is ordinarily supplied along with her labor time. (When your instructor lectures or holds office hours, she is providing both labor time and her skills as an economist and teacher.) Still, it's often useful to distinguish the *time* a worker provides (her labor) from any skills or *knowledge* possessed (human capital).

compose lecture notes. In addition, there was human capital—your instructor's specialized knowledge and lecturing skills. There was a natural resource—land—the property on which your classroom building sits. And some individual or group had to play the role of innovator and risk taker in order to combine the labor, capital, and natural resources needed to create and guide your institution in its formative years. (If you attend a public college or university, this entrepreneurial role was largely filled by the state government and the risk takers were the state's taxpayers.)

The scarcity of resources like these causes the scarcity of all goods and services produced from them.

> *As a society, our resources—land and natural resources, labor, capital, and entrepreneurship—are insufficient to produce all the goods and services we might desire. In other words, society faces a scarcity of resources.*

This stark fact about the world helps us understand the choices a society must make. Do we want a more educated citizenry? Of course. But that will require more labor—construction workers to build more classrooms and teachers to teach in them. It will require more natural resources—land for classrooms and lumber to build them. And it will require more capital—cement mixers, trucks, and more. These very same resources, however, could instead be used to produce *other* things that we find desirable, things such as new homes, hospitals, automobiles, or feature films. As a result, every society must have some method of *allocating* its scarce resources—choosing which of our many competing desires will be fulfilled and which will not be.

Input— Anything (including a resource) used to produce a good or service.

Many of the big questions of our time center on the different ways in which resources can be allocated. The cataclysmic changes that rocked Eastern Europe and the former Soviet Union during the early 1990s arose from a very simple fact: The method these countries used for decades to allocate resources was not working.

DANGEROUS CURVES

Resources vs. Inputs The term *resources* is often confused with another, more general term—**inputs.** An input is *anything* used to make a good or service—including (but not limited to) a resource. *Resources,* by contrast, are the *special* inputs that fall into one of four categories: labor, natural resources (including land), capital, and entrepreneurship. What's so special about resources? They are the ultimate source of everything that is produced. If you think about any good or service that you use—say, an automobile—it is made from the four resources and *other* inputs (such as steel). But any of these *other* inputs can be traced back to the resources used to produce it (steel is made from iron ore, labor, capital, etc.). Goods and services, and the inputs used to make them, are all made from resources. This is why a nation's capacity to produce goods and services is limited by the amounts of the four resources at its disposal.

Closer to home, the never-ending debates between Democrats and Republicans in the United States about tax rates, government services, and even foreign policy reflect subtle but important differences of opinion about how to allocate resources. Often, these are disputes about whether the private sector can handle a particular issue of resource allocation on its own or whether the government should be involved.

Scarcity and Economics

The scarcity of resources—and the choices it forces us to make—is the source of all of the problems you will study in economics. Households have limited incomes for satisfying their desires, so they must choose carefully how they allocate their spending among different goods and services. Business firms want to make the highest possible profit, but they must pay for their resources; so they carefully choose *what* to produce, *how much* to produce, and *how* to produce it. Federal, state, and local government agencies work with limited budgets, so they must carefully choose which goals to pursue. Economists study these decisions made by households, firms, and governments to explain how our economic system operates, to forecast the future of our economy, and to suggest ways to make that future even better.

THE WORLD OF ECONOMICS

The field of economics is surprisingly broad. It extends from the mundane—why does a pound of steak cost more than a pound of chicken?—to the personal and profound—how do couples decide how many children to have? With a field this broad, it is useful to have some way of classifying the different types of problems economists study and the different methods they use to analyze them.

Microeconomics and Macroeconomics

The field of economics is divided into two major parts: microeconomics and macroeconomics. **Microeconomics** comes from the Greek word *mikros,* meaning "small." It takes a close-up view of the economy, as if looking through a microscope. Microeconomics is concerned with the behavior of *individual* actors on the economic scene—households, business firms, and governments. It looks at the choices they make and how they interact with each other when they come together to trade *specific* goods and services. What will happen to the cost of movie tickets over the next five years? How many management-trainee jobs will open up for college graduates? How would U.S. phone companies be affected by a tax on imported cell phones? These are all microeconomic questions because they analyze individual *parts* of an economy rather than the *whole.*

Microeconomics The study of the behavior of individual households, firms, and governments; the choices they make; and their interaction in specific markets.

Macroeconomics—from the Greek word *makros,* meaning "large"—takes an *overall* view of the economy. Instead of focusing on the production of carrots or computers, macroeconomics lumps all goods and services together and looks at the economy's *total output.* Instead of focusing on employment of management trainees or manufacturing workers, it considers *total employment* in the economy. Instead of asking why credit card loans carry higher interest rates than home mortgage loans, it asks what makes interest rates *in general* rise or fall. In all of these cases, macroeconomics focuses on the big picture and ignores the fine details.

Macroeconomics The study of the behavior of the overall economy.

Positive and Normative Economics

The micro versus macro distinction is based on the level of detail we want to consider. Another useful distinction has to do with our *purpose* in analyzing a problem. **Positive economics** deals with *how* the economy works, plain and simple. If someone says, "Recent increases in spending for domestic security have slowed the growth rate of the U.S. economy," she is making a positive economic statement. A statement need not be accurate or even sensible to be classified as positive. For example, "Government policy has no effect on our standard of living" is a false, but positive, statement. Whether true or not, it's a statement about how the economy works and its accuracy can be tested by looking at the facts—and just the facts.

Positive economics The study of how the economy works.

Normative economics concerns itself with what *should be.* It is used to make judgments about the economy, identify problems, and prescribe solutions. Rather

Normative economics The study of what *should be;* it is used to make value judgments, identify problems, and prescribe solutions.

DANGEROUS CURVES

Seemingly Positive Statements Be alert to statements that may *seem* positive but are actually normative. Here's an example: "If we want to reduce pollution, our society will have to use less gasoline." This may *sound* positive, because it seems to refer only to facts about the world. But it's actually normative. Why? Cutting back on gasoline is just *one* policy among many that could reduce pollution. To say that we *must* choose this method makes a value judgment about its superiority to other methods. A purely positive statement on this topic would be, "Using less gasoline—with no other change in living habits—would reduce pollution."

Similarly, be alert to statements that use vague terms with hidden value judgments. An example: "All else equal, the less gasoline we use, the better our quality of life." Whether you agree or disagree, this is *not* a positive statement. Two people who agree about the facts—in this case, the consequences of using less gasoline—might disagree over the meaning of the phrase "quality of life," how to measure it, and what would make it better. This disagreement could not be resolved just by looking at the facts.

than limiting its concerns to just "the facts," it goes on to say what we should *do* about them and therefore depends on our values.

If an economist says, "We should cut total government spending," she is engaging in normative economic analysis. Cutting government spending would benefit some citizens and harm others, so the statement rests on a value judgment. A normative statement—like the one about government spending above—cannot be proved or disproved by the facts alone.

Positive and normative economics are intimately related in practice. For one thing, we cannot properly argue about what we should or should not do unless we know certain facts about the world. Every normative analysis is therefore based on an underlying positive analysis. But while a positive analysis can, at least in principle, be conducted without value judgments, a normative analysis is always based, at least in part, on the values of the person conducting it.

Why Economists Disagree. The distinction between positive and normative economics can help us understand why economists sometimes disagree. Suppose you are watching a television interview in which two economists are asked whether the United States should eliminate all government-imposed barriers to trading with the rest of the world. The first economist says, "Yes, absolutely," but the other says, "No, definitely not." Why the sharp disagreement?

The difference of opinion may be *positive* in nature: The two economists may have different views about what would actually happen if trade barriers were eliminated. Differences like this sometimes arise because our knowledge of the economy is imperfect or because certain facts are in dispute.

More likely, however, the disagreement will be *normative*. Economists, like everyone else, have different values. In this case, both economists might agree that opening up international trade would benefit *most* Americans, but harm *some* of them. Yet they may still disagree about the policy move because they have different values. The first economist might put more emphasis on benefits to the overall economy, while the second might put more emphasis on preventing harm to a particular group. Here, the two economists have come to the same *positive* conclusion, but their *different values* lead them to different *normative* conclusions.

In the media, economists are rarely given enough time to express the basis for their opinions, so the public hears only the disagreement. People may then conclude that economists cannot agree about how the economy works, even when the *real* disagreement is over goals and values.

WHY STUDY ECONOMICS?

Students take economics courses for all kinds of reasons.

To Understand the World Better

Applying the tools of economics can help you understand global and catastrophic events such as wars, famines, epidemics, and depressions. But it can also help you understand much of what happens to you locally and personally—the worsening traffic conditions in your city, the raise you can expect at your job this year, or the long line of people waiting to buy tickets for a popular concert. Economics has the power to help us understand these phenomena because they result, in large part, from the choices we make under conditions of scarcity.

Economics has its limitations, of course. But it is hard to find any aspect of life about which economics does not have *something* important to say. Economics cannot explain why so many Americans like to watch television, but it *can* explain how TV networks decide which programs to offer. Economics cannot protect you from a robbery, but it *can* explain why some people choose to become thieves and why no society has chosen to eradicate crime completely. Economics will not improve your love life, resolve unconscious conflicts from your childhood, or help you overcome a fear of flying, but it *can* tell us how many skilled therapists, ministers, and counselors are available to help us solve these problems.

HTTP://

The Federal Reserve Bank of Minneapolis asked some Nobel Prize winners how they became interested in economics. Their stories can be found at http://www.minneapolisfed.org/pubs/region/int.cfm.

To Gain Self-Confidence

Those who have never studied economics often feel that mysterious, inexplicable forces are shaping their lives, buffeting them like the bumpers in a pinball machine, determining whether or not they'll be able to find a job, what their salary will be, whether they'll be able to afford a home, and in what kind of neighborhood. If you've been one of those people, all that is about to change. After you learn economics, you may be surprised to find that you no longer toss out the business page of your local newspaper because it appears to be written in a foreign language. You may no longer lunge for the remote and change the channel the instant you hear "And now for news about the economy. . . . " You may find yourself listening to economic reports with a critical ear, catching mistakes in logic, misleading statements, or out-and-out lies. When you master economics, you gain a sense of mastery over the world, and thus over your own life as well.

To Achieve Social Change

If you are interested in making the world a better place, economics is indispensable. There is no shortage of serious social problems worthy of our attention—unemployment, hunger, poverty, disease, child abuse, drug addiction, violent crime. Economics can help us understand the origins of these problems, explain why previous efforts to solve them have failed, and help us to design new, more effective solutions.

To Help Prepare for Other Careers

Economics has long been a popular college major for individuals intending to work in business. But it has also been popular among those planning careers in politics, international relations, law, medicine, engineering, psychology, and other professions. This is for good reason: Practitioners in each of these fields often find themselves confronting economic issues. For example, lawyers increasingly face judicial rulings based on the principles of economic efficiency. Doctors will need to understand how new technologies or changes in the structure of health insurance will affect their practices. Industrial psychologists need to understand the economic implications of workplace changes they may advocate, such as flexible scheduling or on-site child care.

To Become an Economist

Only a tiny minority of this book's readers will decide to become economists. This is welcome news to the authors, and after you have studied labor markets in your *microeconomics* course you will understand why. But if you do decide to become an economist—obtaining a master's degree or even a Ph.D.—you will find many possibilities for employment. Of 10,280 employed members of the American Economic Association who responded to a recent survey,[2] 62 percent were employed at colleges or universities. Most of the rest were employed in a variety of areas, including the private sector (19 percent), government (8 percent), and international organizations (1.5 percent). Economists are hired by banks to assess the risk of investing abroad; by manufacturing companies, to help them determine new methods of producing, marketing, and pricing their products; by government agencies, to help design policies to fight crime, disease, poverty, and pollution; by international organizations, to help create aid programs for less developed countries; by the media, to help the public interpret global, national, and local events; and by nonprofit organizations, to provide advice on controlling costs and raising funds more effectively.

THE METHODS OF ECONOMICS

One of the first things you will notice as you begin to study economics is the heavy reliance on *models*. Indeed, the discipline goes beyond any other social science in its insistence that every theory be represented by an explicit, carefully constructed *model*.

You've no doubt encountered many models in your life. As a child, you played with model trains, model planes, or model people—dolls. In a high school science course, you probably saw a model of an atom—one of those plastic and wire contraptions with red, blue, and green balls representing protons, neutrons, and electrons. You may have also seen architects' cardboard models of buildings. These are physical models, three-dimensional replicas that you can pick up and hold. Economic models, on the other hand, are built not with cardboard, plastic, or metal but with words, diagrams, and mathematical statements.

What, exactly, is a model?

Model An abstract representation of reality.

*A **model** is an abstract representation of reality.*

The two key words in this definition are *abstract* and *representation*. A model is not supposed to be exactly like reality. Rather, it *represents* the real world by *abstracting* or *taking from* the real world that which will help us understand it. In any model, many real-world details are left out.

---

[2] *American Economic Review,* Table of Employment, 2003 (*http://www.vanderbilt.edu/AEA/TblEmploy. htm*).

The Art of Building Economic Models

When you build a model, how do you know which details to include and which to leave out? There is no simple answer to this question. The right amount of detail depends on your purpose in building the model in the first place. There is, however, one guiding principle:

> *A model should be as simple as possible to accomplish its purpose.*

This means that a model should contain only the *necessary* details.

To understand this a little better, think about a map. A map is a model—it represents a part of the earth's surface. But it leaves out many details of the real world. First, maps are two-dimensional, so they leave out the third dimension—height—of the real world. Second, maps always ignore small details, such as trees and houses and potholes. Third, a map is much smaller than the area it represents. But when you buy a map, how much detail do you want it to have?

These maps are models. But each would be used for a different purpose.

Let's say you are in Boston, and you need a map to find the best way to drive from Logan Airport to the downtown convention center (your *purpose*). In this case, you would want a very detailed city map, with every street, park, and plaza in Boston clearly illustrated and labeled. A highway map, which ignores these details, wouldn't do at all.

But now suppose your purpose is different: to select the best driving route from Boston to Cincinnati. Now you want a highway map. A map that shows every street between Boston and Cincinnati would have *too much* detail. All of that extraneous information would only obscure what you really need to see.

Although economic models are more abstract than road maps, the same principle applies in building them: The level of detail that would be just right for one purpose will usually be too much or too little for another. When you feel yourself objecting to a model in this text because something has been left out, keep in mind the purpose for which the model is built. In introductory economics, the purpose is entirely educational. The models are designed to help you understand some simple, but powerful, principles about how the economy operates. Keeping the models simple makes it easier to see these principles at work and remember them later.

Of course, economic models have other purposes besides education. They can help businesses make decisions about pricing and production, help households decide how and where to invest their savings, and help governments and international agencies formulate policies. Models built for these purposes will be much more detailed than the ones in this text, and you will learn about them if you take more advanced courses in economics. But even complex models are built around very simple frameworks—the same frameworks you will be learning here.

Assumptions and Conclusions

Every economic model begins with *assumptions* about the world. There are two types of assumptions in a model: simplifying assumptions and critical assumptions.

A **simplifying assumption** is just what it sounds like—a way of making a model simpler without affecting any of its important conclusions. The purpose of a simplifying assumption is to rid a model of extraneous detail so its essential features can stand out more clearly. A road map, for example, makes the simplifying assumption, "There are no trees," because trees on a map would only get in the way. Similarly, in

Simplifying assumption Any assumption that makes a model simpler without affecting any of its important conclusions.

an economic model, we might assume that there are only two goods that households can choose from or that there are only two nations in the world. We make such assumptions *not* because they are true, but because they make a model easier to follow and do not change any of the important insights we can get from it.

Critical assumption Any assumption that affects the conclusions of a model in an important way.

A **critical assumption**, by contrast, is an assumption that affects the conclusions of a model in important ways. When you use a road map, you make the critical assumption, "All of these roads are open." If that assumption is wrong, your conclusion—the best route to take—might be wrong as well.

In an economic model, there are always one or more critical assumptions. You don't have to look very hard to find them, because economists like to make these assumptions explicit right from the outset. For example, when we study the behavior of business firms, our model will assume that firms try to earn the highest possible profit for their owners. By stating this assumption up front, we can see immediately where the model's conclusions spring from.

The Three-Step Process

As you read this textbook, you will learn how economists use economic models to address a wide range of problems. In Chapter 2, for example, you will see how a simple economic model can give us important insights about society's production choices. And subsequent chapters will present still different models that help us understand the U.S. economy and the global economic environment in which it operates. As you read, it may seem to you that there are a lot of models to learn and remember . . . and, indeed, there are.

But there is an important insight about economics that—once mastered—will make your job easier than you might think. The insight is this: There is a remarkable similarity in the types of models that economists build, the assumptions that underlie those models, and what economists actually *do* with them. In fact, you will see that economists follow the same *three-step process* to analyze almost any economic problem. The first two steps explain how economists *build* an economic model, and the last explains how they *use* the model.

What are these three steps that underlie the economic approach to almost any problem? Sorry for the suspense, but you'll have to wait a bit—until the end of Chapter 3—for the answer. By that time, you'll have learned a little more about economics, and the three-step process will make more sense to you.

Math, Jargon, and Other Concerns . . .

HTTP://

An online inroduction to the use of graphs can be found at http://syllabus.syr.edu/cid/graph/book.html.

Economists often express their ideas using mathematical concepts and a special vocabulary. Why? Because these tools enable economists to express themselves more precisely than with ordinary language. For example, someone who has never studied economics might say, "When used textbooks are available, students won't buy new textbooks." That statement might not bother you right now. But once you've finished your first economics course, you'll be saying it something like this: "When the price of used textbooks falls, the demand curve for new textbooks shifts leftward."

Does the second statement sound strange to you? It should. First, it uses a special term—a *demand curve*—that you haven't yet learned. Second, it uses a mathematical concept—a *shifting curve*—with which you might not be familiar. But while the first statement might mean a number of different things, the second statement—

as you will see in Chapter 3—can mean only *one* thing. By being precise, we can steer clear of unnecessary confusion.

If you are worried about the special vocabulary of economics, you can relax. All of the new terms will be defined and carefully explained as you encounter them. Indeed, this textbook does not assume you have any special knowledge of economics. It is truly meant for a "first course" in the field.

But what about the math? Here, too, you can relax. While professional economists often use sophisticated mathematics to solve problems, only a little math is needed to understand basic economic *principles*. And virtually all of this math comes from high school algebra and geometry.

Still, you may have forgotten some of your high school math. If so, a little brushing up might be in order. This is why we have included an appendix at the end of this chapter. It covers some of the most basic concepts—such as interpreting graphs, the equation for a straight line, and the concept of a slope—that you will need in this course. You may want to glance at this appendix now, just so you'll know what's there. Then, from time to time, you'll be reminded about it when you're most likely to need it.

HOW TO STUDY ECONOMICS

As you read this book or listen to your instructor, you may find yourself following along and thinking that everything makes perfect sense. Economics may even seem easy. Indeed, it *is* rather easy to *follow* economics, since it's based so heavily on simple logic. But *following* and *learning* are two different things. You will eventually discover (preferably *before* your first exam) that economics must be studied actively, not passively.

If you are reading these words lying back on a comfortable couch, a phone in one hand and a remote control in the other, you are going about it in the wrong way. Active studying means reading with a pencil in your hand and a blank sheet of paper in front of you. It means closing the book periodically and *reproducing* what you have learned. It means listing the steps in each logical argument, retracing the cause-and-effect steps in each model, and drawing the graphs that represent the model. It means *thinking* about the basic principles of economics and how they relate to what you are learning. It does require some work, but the payoff is a good understanding of economics and a better understanding of your own life and the world around you.

Summary

Economics is the study of choice under conditions of scarcity. As individuals, and as a society, we have unlimited desires for goods and services. Unfortunately, the *resources*—land and natural resources, labor, capital, and entrepreneurship—needed to produce those goods and services are scarce. Therefore, we must choose which desires to satisfy and how to satisfy them. Economics provides the tools that explain those choices.

The field of economics is divided into two major areas. *Microeconomics* studies the behavior of individual households, firms, and governments as they interact in specific markets. *Macroeconomics,* by contrast, concerns itself with the behavior of the entire economy. It considers variables such as total output, total employment, and the overall price level.

Economics makes heavy use of *models*—abstract representations of reality. These models are built with words, diagrams, and mathematical statements that help us understand how the economy operates. All models are simplifications, but a good model will have *just enough detail for the purpose at hand.*

When analyzing almost any problem, economists follow a three-step process in building and using economic models. This three-step process will be introduced at the end of Chapter 3.

Key Terms

Capital
Capital stock
Critical assumption
Economics
Entrepreneurship
Human capital

Input
Labor
Macroeconomics
Microeconomics
Model
Normative economics

Natural resources
Physical capital
Positive economics
Resources
Scarcity
Simplifying assumption

Review Questions
Answers to even-numbered Questions and Problems can be found on the text Web site at http://hall-lieb.swlearning.com.

1. What is a *resource*? What are the four different types of resources?

2. What determines the level of detail that an economist builds into a model?

3. What is the difference between a simplifying assumption and a critical assumption?

4. Would each of the following be classified as microeconomics or macroeconomics? Why?
   a. Research into why the growth rate of total production increased during the 1990s.

   b. A theory of how consumers decide what to buy.
   c. An analysis of Dell Computer's share of the personal computer market.
   d. Research on why interest rates were unusually high in the late 1970s and early 1980s.

5. What is the difference between an input and a resource?

Problems

1. Come up with a list of critical assumptions that could lie behind each of the following statements. Discuss whether each assumption would be classified as normative or positive.
   a. The United States is a democratic society.
   b. European movies are better than American movies.
   c. The bigger the city, the higher the quality of the newspaper.

2. Discuss whether each statement is an example of positive economics or normative economics or if it contains elements of both:
   a. An increase in the personal income tax will slow the growth rate of the economy.
   b. The goal of any country's economic policy should be to increase the well-being of its poorest, most vulnerable citizens.
   c. Excess regulation of small business is stifling the economy. Small business has been responsible for most of the growth in employment over the last 10 years, but regulations are putting a severe damper on the ability of small businesses to survive and prosper.

   d. The 1990s were a disastrous decade for the U.S. economy. Income inequality increased to its highest level since before World War II.

3. For each of the following, state whether economists would consider it a *resource*, and if they would, identify which of the four types of resources the item is.
   a. A computer used by an FBI agent to track the whereabouts of suspected criminals.
   b. The office building in which the FBI agent works.
   c. The time that an FBI agent spends on a case.
   d. A farmer's tractor.
   e. The farmer's knowledge of how to operate the tractor.
   f. Crude oil.
   g. A package of frozen vegetables.
   h. A food scientist's knowledge of how to commercially freeze vegetables.
   i. The ability to bring together resources to start a frozen food company.
   j. Plastic bags used by a frozen food company to hold its product.

These exercises require access to Hall/Lieberman Xtra! If Xtra! did not come with your book, visit http://hallxtra.swlearning.com to purchase.

1. Use your Xtra! password at the Hall and Lieberman Web site (http://hallxtra.swlearning.com), select Chapter 1, and under Economic Applications, click on EconDebates. Choose Economic Fundamentals; Scarcity, Choice and Opportunity Cost; and scroll down to find the debate, "Are Americans Overworked?" Read the debate, and use the information to answer the following questions.

   a. Is the question in the title of this debate an example of positive or normative economics? Why?

   b. Why is leisure time becoming scarcer over time?

   c. Identify three statements of positive economics in this debate.

APPENDIX

GRAPHS AND OTHER USEFUL TOOLS

TABLES AND GRAPHS

A brief glance at this text will tell you that graphs are important in economics. Graphs provide a convenient way to display information and enable us to immediately *see* relationships between different variables.

Suppose that you've just been hired at the advertising department of Len & Harry's—an up-and-coming manufacturer of high-end ice cream products, located in Texas. You've been asked to compile a report on how advertising affects the company's sales. It turns out that the company's spending on advertising has changed repeatedly in the past, so you have lots of data on monthly advertising outlays and monthly sales revenue, both measured in thousands of dollars.

Table A.1 shows a useful way of arranging this data. The company's advertising outlays in different months are listed in the left-hand column, while the right-hand column lists total sales revenue ("sales" for short) during the same month. Notice that the data here is organized so that spending on advertising increases as we move down the first column. Often, just looking at a table like this can reveal useful patterns. Here, it's clear that higher spending on advertising is associated with higher monthly sales. These two variables—advertising and sales—have a **positive relationship**.[3] A rise in one is associated with a rise in the other. If higher advertising had been associated with *lower* sales, the two variables would have a **negative** or **inverse relationship**: A rise in one would be associated with a fall in the other.

We can be even more specific about the positive relationship between advertising and sales: Logic tells us that the association is very likely *causal*. We'd expect that sales revenue *depends on* advertising outlays, so we call sales our **dependent variable** and advertising our **independent variable**. Changes in an independent variable cause changes in a dependent variable, but not the other way around.

To explore the relationship further, let's graph it. As a rule, the *independent* variable is measured on the *horizontal* axis and the *dependent* variable on the *vertical* axis. In economics, unfortunately, we do not always stick to this rule, but for now we will. In Figure A.1, monthly advertising outlays—our independent variable—are measured on the horizontal axis. If we start at the *origin*—the corner where the two axes intersect—and move rightward along the horizontal axis, monthly advertising outlays increase from $0 to $1,000 to $2,000 and so on. The vertical axis measures monthly sales—the dependent variable. Along this axis, as we move upward from the origin, sales rise.

The graph in Figure A.1 shows six labeled points, each representing a different pair of numbers from our table. For example, point *A*—which represents the

TABLE A.1 **Advertising and Sales at Len & Harry's**	Advertising ($1,000 per Month)	Sales ($1,000 per Month)
	2	46
	3	49
	6	58
	7	61
	11	73
	12	76

[3] Key Terms found in this appendix are defined at the end of the appendix and in the glossary.

numbers in the first row of the table—shows us that when the firm spends $2,000 on advertising, sales are $46,000 per month. Point *B* represents the *second* row of the table, and so on. Notice that all of these points lie along a *straight line*.

Straight-Line Graphs

You'll encounter straight-line graphs often in economics, so it's important to understand one special property they possess: The "rate of change" of one variable compared with the other is always the same. For example, look at what happens as we move from point *A* to point *B*: Advertising rises by $1,000 (from $2,000 to $3,000), while sales rise by $3,000 (from $46,000 to $49,000). If you study the graph closely, you'll see that anywhere along this line, whenever advertising increases by $1,000, sales increase by the same $3,000. Or, if we define a "unit" as "one thousand dollars," we can say that every time advertising increases by one unit, sales rise by three units. So the "rate of change" is three units of sales for every one unit of advertising.

The rate of change of the *vertically* measured variable for a one-unit change in the *horizontally* measured variable is also called the **slope** of the line. The slope of the line in Figure A.1 is three, and it remains three no matter where along the line we measure it. For example, make sure you can see that from point *C* to point *D*, advertising rises by one unit and sales rise by three units.

What if we had wanted to determine the slope of this line by comparing points *D* and *E*, which has advertising rising by four units instead of just one? In that case, we'd have to calculate the rise in one variable *per unit* rise in the other. To do this, we divide the change in the vertically measured variable by the change in the horizontally measured variable.

$$\text{Slope of a straight line} = \frac{\text{change in vertical variable}}{\text{change in horizontal variable}}.$$

We can make this formula even simpler by using two shortcuts. First, we can call the variable on the vertical axis "*Y*" and the variable on the horizontal axis "*X*." In our case, *Y* is sales, while *X* is advertising outlays. Second, we use the Greek letter Δ ("delta") to denote the words "change in." Then, our formula becomes:

$$\text{Slope of straight line} = \frac{\Delta Y}{\Delta X}.$$

Let's apply this formula to get the slope as we move from point *D* to point *E*, which causes advertising (*X*) to rise from 7 units to 11 units. This is an increase of 4, so Δ*X* = 4. For this move, sales rise from 61 to 73, an increase of 12, so Δ*Y* = 12. Applying our formula,

$$\text{Slope} = \frac{\Delta Y}{\Delta X} = \frac{12}{4} = 3.$$

This is the same value for the slope that we found earlier. Not surprising, since it's a straight line and a straight line has the same slope everywhere. The particular pair of points we choose for our calculation doesn't matter.

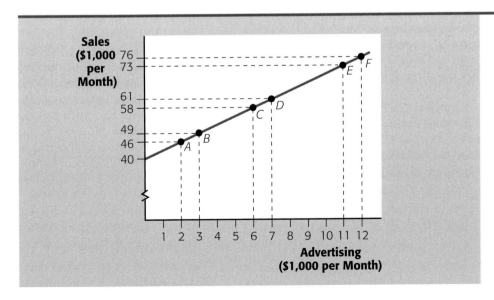

FIGURE A.1
A Graph of Advertising and Sales

FIGURE A.2
Measuring the Slope of a Curve

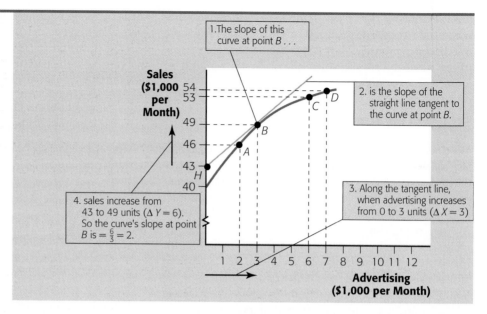

FIGURE A.2
Measuring the Slope of a Curve

Curved Lines

Although many of the relationships you'll encounter in economics have straight-line graphs, many others do not. Figure A.2 shows *another* possible relationship between advertising and sales that we might have found from a different set of data. As you can see, the line is curved. But as advertising rises, the curve gets flatter and flatter. Here, as before, each time we spend another $1,000 on advertising, sales rise. But now, the rise in sales seems to get smaller and smaller. This means that the *slope* of the curve is *itself changing* as we move along this curve. In fact, the slope is getting smaller.

How can we measure the slope of a curve? First, note that since the slope is different at every point along the curve, we aren't really measuring the slope of "the curve" but the slope of the curve *at a specific point along it*. How can we do this? By drawing a **tangent line**—a straight line that touches the curve at just one point and that has the same slope as the curve at that point. For example, in the figure, a tangent line has been drawn for point *B*. To measure the slope of this tangent line, we can compare any two points on it, say, *H* and *B*, and calculate the slope as we would for any straight line. Moving from point *H* to point *B*, we are moving from 0 to 3 on the horizontal axis ($\Delta X = 3$) and from 43 to 49 on the vertical axis ($\Delta Y = 6$). Thus, the slope of the tangent line—which is the same as the slope of the curved line at point *B*—is:

$$\frac{\Delta Y}{\Delta X} = \frac{6}{3} = 2.$$

This says that, at point *B*, the rate of change is two units of sales for every one unit of advertising. Or, going back to dollars, the rate of change is $2,000 in sales for every $1,000 spent on advertising.

The curve in Figure A.2 slopes everywhere upward, reflecting a positive relationship between the variables. But a curved line can also slope downward to illustrate a negative relationship between variables, or slope first one direction and then the other. You'll see plenty of examples of each type of curve in later chapters and you'll learn how to interpret each one as it's presented.

LINEAR EQUATIONS

Let's go back to the straight-line relationship between advertising and sales, as shown in Table A.1. What if you need to know how much in sales the firm could expect if it spent $5,000 on advertising next month? What if it spent $8,000, or $9,000? It would be nice to be able to answer questions like this without having to pull out tables and graphs to do it. As it turns out, anytime the relationship you are studying has a straight-line graph, it is easy to figure out an equation for the entire relationship—a *linear equation*. You then can use the equation to answer any such question that might be put to you.

All straight lines have the same general form. If *Y* stands for the variable on the vertical axis and *X* for the variable on the horizontal axis, every straight line has an equation of the form

$$Y = a + bX,$$

where *a* stands for some number and *b* for another number. The number *a* is called the vertical *intercept,* because it marks the point where the graph of this equation hits (intercepts) the vertical axis; this occurs when *X* takes the value zero. (If you plug *X* = 0 into the equation, you will see that, indeed, *Y* = *a*.) The number *b* is the slope of the line, telling us how much *Y* will change every time *X* changes by one unit. To confirm this, note that as *X* increases from 0 to 1, *Y* goes from *a* to *a* + *b*. The number *b* is therefore the change in *Y* corresponding to a one-unit change in *X*—exactly what the slope of the graph should tell us.

If *b* is a positive number, a one-unit increase in *X* causes *Y* to *increase* by *b* units, so the graph of our line would slope upward, as illustrated by the red line in panel (a) of Figure A.3. If *b* is a negative number, then a one-unit increase in *X* will cause *Y* to *decrease* by *b* units, so the graph would slope downward, as the blue line does in panel (a). Of course, *b* could equal zero. If it does, a one-unit increase in *X* causes no change in *Y*, so the graph of the line is flat, like the black line in panel (a).

The value of *a* has no effect on the slope of the graph. Instead, different values of *a* determine the graph's position. When *a* is a positive number, the graph will intercept the vertical *Y*-axis above the origin, as the red line does in panel (b) of Figure A.3. When *a* is negative, however, the graph will intercept the *Y*-axis *below* the origin, like the blue line in panel (b). When *a* is zero, the graph intercepts the *Y*-axis right at the origin, as the black line does in panel (b).

Let's see if we can figure out the equation for the relationship depicted in Figure A.1. There, *X* denotes advertising and *Y* denotes sales. Earlier, we calculated that

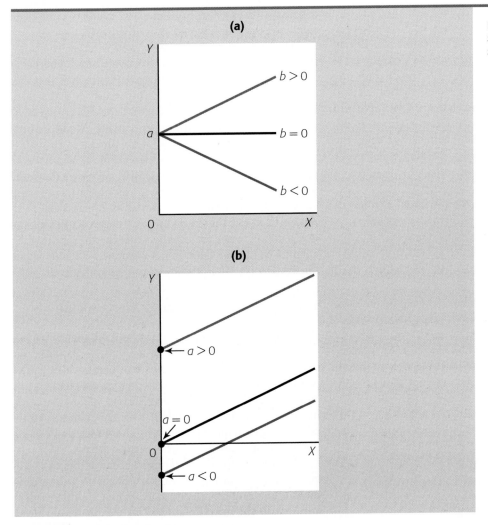

FIGURE A.3
Straight Lines with Different Slopes and Vertical Intercepts

the slope of this line, *b*, is 3. But what is *a*, the vertical intercept? On the graph, you can see that when advertising outlays are zero, sales are $40,000. That tells us that $a = 40$.[4] Putting these two observations together, we find that the equation for the line in Figure A.1 is

$$Y = 40 + 3X.$$

Now if you need to know how much in sales to expect from a particular expenditure on advertising, you'd be able to come up with an answer: You'd simply multiply the amount spent on advertising by 3, add $40,000, and that would be your sales. To confirm this, plug in for *X* in this equation any amount of advertising in dollars from the left-hand column of Table A.1. You'll see that you get the corresponding amount of sales in the right-hand column.

HOW STRAIGHT LINES AND CURVES SHIFT

So far, we've focused on relationships where some variable *Y* depends on a single other variable, *X*. But in many of our theories, we recognize that some variable of interest to us is actually affected by more than just one other variable. When *Y* is affected by both *X* and some third variable, changes in that third variable will usually cause a *shift* in the graph of the relationship between *X* and *Y*. This is because whenever we draw the graph between *X* and *Y*, we are holding fixed every other variable that might possibly affect *Y*.

> *A graph between two variables X and Y is only a picture of their relationship when all other variables affecting Y are held constant.*

But suppose one of these other variables *does* change? What happens then?

Think back to the relationship between advertising and sales. Earlier, we supposed sales depend only on advertising. But suppose we make an important discovery: Ice cream sales are *also* affected by how hot the weather is. What's more, all of the data in Table A.1 on which we previously based our analysis turns out to have been

from the month of June in different years, when the average temperature in Texas is 80 degrees. What's going to happen in July, when the average temperature rises to 100 degrees?

In Figure A.4 we've redrawn the graph from Figure A.1, this time labeling the line "June." Often, a good way to determine how a graph will shift is to perform a simple experiment like this: Put your pencil tip anywhere on the graph labeled June—let's say at point C. Now ask the following question: If I hold advertising constant at $6,000, do I expect to sell more or less ice cream as temperature rises in July? If you expect to sell more, then the amount of sales corresponding to $6,000 of advertising will be *above* point C, at a point such as C' (pronounced "C prime"), representing sales of $64,000. From this, we can tell that the graph will *shift upward* as temperature rises. In September, however, when temperatures fall, the amount of sales corresponding to $6,000 in advertising would be less than it is at point C. It would be shown by a point such as C'' (pronounced "C double-prime"). In that case, the graph would shift downward.

The same procedure works well whether the original graph slopes upward or downward and whether it is a straight line or a curved one. Figure A.5 sketches two examples. In panel (a), an increase in some third variable, *Z*, increases the value of *Y* for each value of *X*, so the graph of the relationship between *X* and *Y* shifts upward as *Z* increases. We often phrase it this way: "An increase in *Z* causes an increase in *Y*, *at any value of X*." In panel (b), an increase in *Z* *decreases* the value of *Y*, at any value of *X*, so the graph of the relationship between *X* and *Y* shifts *downward* as *Z* increases.

You'll notice that in Figures A.4 and A.5, the original line is darker, while the new line after the shift is drawn in a lighter shade. We'll use this convention—a lighter shade for the new line after a shift—throughout this book.

Shifts versus Movements Along a Line

If you look back at Figure A.1, you'll see that when advertising increases (say, from $2,000 to $3,000), we *move along* our line, from point A to point B. But you've just learned that when average temperature changes, the entire line *shifts*. This may seem strange to you. After all, in both cases, an independent variable changes (either advertising or temperature). Why should we move *along* the line in one case and *shift* it in the other?

The reason for the difference is that in one case (advertising), the independent variable is *in our graph*, measured along one of the axes. When an independent variable in the graph changes, we simply move along

---

[4] We could also use direct logic to find the vertical intercept. In the figure, locate any point—we'll use point A as our example, where $X = 2$ and $Y = 46$. From this point, to get to the vertical intercept, we'd have to decrease *X* by two units. But with a slope of 3, a two-unit decrease in *X* will cause a six-unit decrease in *Y*. Therefore, *Y* will decrease from 46 to 40. Summing up, we've found that when $X = 0$, $Y = 40$, so our vertical intercept is 40.

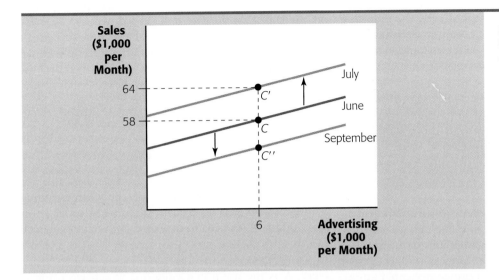

FIGURE A.4
Shifts in the Graph of Advertising and Sales

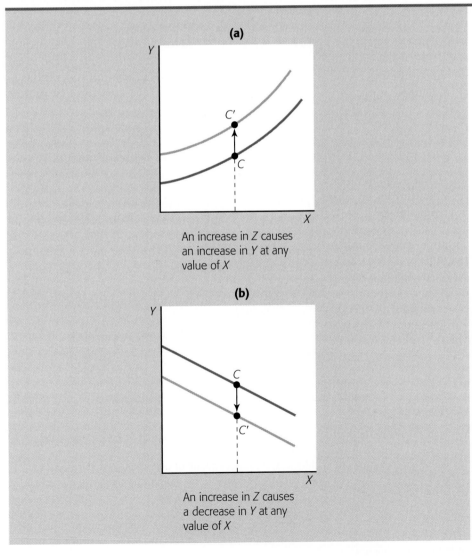

FIGURE A.5
Shifts of Curved Lines and Straight Lines

(a)

An increase in Z causes an increase in Y at any value of X

(b)

An increase in Z causes a decrease in Y at any value of X

the line. In the other case (temperature), the independent variable does *not* appear in our graph. Instead, it's been in the background, being held constant.

Here's a very simple—but crucial—rule:

> *Suppose Y is the dependent variable, which is measured on one of the axes in a graph. If the independent variable measured on the other axis changes, we move along the line. But if any other independent variable changes, the entire line shifts.*

Be sure you understand the phrase "any other independent variable." It refers to any variable that actually *affects* Y but is *not* measured on either axis in the graph.

This rule applies to straight lines as well as curved lines. And it applies even in more complicated situations, such as when *two different* lines are drawn in the same graph, and a shift of one causes a movement along the other. (You'll encounter this situation in Chapter 3.) But for now, make sure you can see how we've been applying this rule in our example, where the three variables are total sales, advertising, and temperature.

SOLVING EQUATIONS

When we first derived the equation for the relationship between advertising and sales, we wanted to know what level of sales to expect from different amounts of advertising. But what if we're asked a slightly different question? Suppose, this time, you are told that the sales committee has set an ambitious goal of $64,000 for next month's sales. The treasurer needs to know how much to budget for advertising, and you have to come up with the answer.

Since we know how advertising and sales are related, we ought to be able to answer this question. One way is just to look at the graph in Figure A.1. There, we could first locate sales of $64,000 on the vertical axis. Then, if

we read over to the line and then down, we find the amount of advertising that would be necessary to generate that level of sales. Yet even with that carefully drawn diagram, it is not always easy to see just exactly how much advertising would be required. If we need to be precise, we'd better use the equation for the graph instead.

According to the equation, sales (*Y*) and advertising (*X*) are related as follows:

$$Y = 40 + 3X.$$

In the problem before us, we know the value for sales, and we need to solve for the corresponding amount of advertising. Substituting the sales target of $64,000 for *Y*, we need to find that value of *X* for which

$$64 = 40 + 3X.$$

Here, *X* is the unknown value for which we want to solve.

Whenever we solve one equation for one unknown, say, *X*, we need to *isolate X* on one side of the equals sign and everything else on the other side of the equals sign. We do this by performing identical operations on both sides of the equals sign. Here, we can first subtract 40 from both sides, getting

$$24 = 3X.$$

We can then divide both sides by 3 and get

$$8 =$$

This is our answer. If we want to achieve sales of $64,000, we'll need to spend $8,000 on advertising.

Of course, not all relationships are linear, so this technique will not work in every situation. But no matter what the underlying relationship, the idea remains the same:

> *To solve for X in any equation, rearrange the equation, following the rules of algebra, so that X appears on one side of the equals sign and everything else in the equation appears on the other side.*

Key Terms

Dependent variable A variable whose value depends on the value of some other variable.

Independent variable A variable that causes changes in some other variable (the dependent variable).

Negative or inverse relationship A relationship between two variables that move in opposite directions to each other (when one increases the other decreases).

Positive relationship A relationship between two variables that move in the same direction (when one increases

so does the other; when one decreases so does the other).

Slope The rate of change of one variable with respect to another variable. In a graph, the change in the vertical-axis variable divided by the change in the horizontal-axis variable.

Tangent line A straight line that touches a curve at just one point, and has the same slope as the curve at that point.

Scarcity, Choice, and Economic Systems

CHAPTER OUTLINE

The Concept of Opportunity Cost
Opportunity Cost for Individuals
Opportunity Cost and Society
Production Possibilities Frontiers
The Search for a Free Lunch

Economic Systems
Specialization and Exchange
Resource Allocation

Resource Ownership
Types of Economic Systems

Using the Theory: Are We Saving Lives Efficiently?

What does it cost you to go to the movies? If you answered eight or nine dollars, because that is the price of a movie ticket, then you are leaving out a lot. Most of us are used to thinking of "cost" as the money we must pay for something. A Big Mac costs $2.90, a new Toyota Corolla costs $16,000, and the baby-sitter costs $8.00 an hour. Certainly, the money we pay for a good or service is a *part* of its cost. But economics takes a broader view of costs, recognizing monetary as well as nonmonetary components.

THE CONCEPT OF OPPORTUNITY COST

The total cost of any choice we make—buying a car, producing a computer, or even reading a book—is everything we must *give up* when we take that action. This cost is called the *opportunity cost* of the action, because we give up the opportunity to have other desirable things.

> The **opportunity cost** of any choice is what we must forego when we make that choice.

Opportunity cost What is given up when taking an action or making a choice.

Opportunity cost is the most accurate and complete concept of cost—the one we should use when making our own decisions or analyzing the decisions of others.

21

Opportunity Cost for Individuals

Virtually every action we take as individuals uses up scarce money, scarce time, or both. This money or time *could* have been used for other things that you value. Thus, the true cost of any choice you make—the *opportunity cost*—is everything you actually sacrifice in making the choice.

Suppose, for example, it's 8 P.M. on a weeknight and you're spending a couple of hours reading this chapter. As authors, that thought makes us very happy, especially because we know there are many other things you could be doing: going to a movie, having dinner with friends, playing ping pong, earning some extra money tutoring high school students, watching TV. . . . Some of these alternatives might be more fun than reading your economics text. But, assuming you're still reading—and you haven't just run out the door to do something else—let's relate this to opportunity cost.

What *is* the opportunity cost of reading this chapter? Is it *all* of those other possibilities we've listed? Not really, because if you weren't reading for these two hours, you'd probably have time to do only *one* of them. And you'd no doubt choose whichever one among these alternatives you regarded as best. So, by reading, you sacrifice the best choice among the alternatives that you could be doing instead.

The opportunity cost of a choice is the best among the available alternatives to that choice.

For many choices, a large part of the opportunity cost is the money sacrificed. If you spend $15 on a new DVD, you have to part with $15, which is money you could have spent on something else (whatever the best choice among the alternatives turned out to be). But for other choices, money may be only a small part, or no part, of what is sacrificed. If you walk your dog a few blocks, it will cost you time but not money. Still, economists often like to attach a monetary value even to costs that *don't* involve money. By translating such sacrifices into a dollar value, we can express opportunity cost as a single number, albeit a roughly estimated one. That, in turn, enables us to compare the cost of a choice with its benefits, which are also often expressed in dollars.

An Example: The Opportunity Cost of College. Let's consider an important choice you've made for this year: to attend college. What is the opportunity cost of this choice? A good starting point is to look at the actual monetary costs—the annual out-of-pocket expenses borne by you or your family for a year of college. Table 1 shows the College Board's estimates of these expenses for the average student. For example, the third column of the table shows that the average in-state resident at a four-year state college pays $5,132 in tuition and fees, $853 for books and supplies, $6,222 for room and board, and $2,433 for transportation and other expenses, for a total of $14,640 per year.

So, is that dollar figure the opportunity cost of a year of college for the average student at a public institution? Not really. Even if the entries are what you or your family actually pays out for college, there are two problems with using these figures to calculate the opportunity cost.

First, the table includes some expenses that are *not* part of the opportunity cost of college. For example, room and board is something you'd need no matter *what* you choose to do. That's obvious if, as part of your best choice among the

Type of Institution	Two-year Public	Four-year Public	Four-year Private
Tuition and fees	$ 2,076	$ 5,132	$20,082
Books and supplies	$ 773	$ 853	$ 870
Room and board	$ 5,747	$ 6,222	$ 7,434
Transportation and other expenses	$ 2,754	$ 2,433	$ 1,909
Total out-of-pocket costs	$11,350	$14,640	$30,295

TABLE 1

Average Cost of a Year of College, 2004–2005

Source: Trends in College Pricing, 2004. The College Board, New York, NY.

Notes: Averages are enrollment-weighted by institution, to reflect the average experience among students across the United States. Average tuition and fees at public institutions are for in-state residents only. Room and board charges are for students living on campus at four-year institutions, and off-campus (but not with parents) at two-year institutions.

alternatives, you'd have lived in an apartment and paid rent. But even living in your old room at home doesn't eliminate this cost: Your family *could* have rented out the room to someone else, or used it for some other valuable purpose. Either way, something is sacrificed. Let's suppose, for simplicity, that if you weren't in college, you or your family would be paying the same amount for room and board as your college charges. Then, that room and board expense should be excluded from opportunity cost. And the same applies to transportation and other expenses, at least the part that you would have spent anyway even if not in college.

Now we're left with payments for tuition and fees, and for books and other school supplies. For an in-state resident going to a state college, this averages $5,985 per year. Since these dollars are paid only when you attend college, they represent something sacrificed for that choice and are part of its opportunity cost. Costs like these—for which dollars are sacrificed through actual payments—are called **explicit costs,** and they are *part* of the opportunity cost.

Explicit cost The dollars sacrificed—and actually paid out—for a choice.

But college also has **implicit costs**—sacrifices for which no money changes hands. The biggest sacrifice in this category is *time.* But what is that time worth? That depends on what you *would* be doing if you weren't in school. For many students, the alternative would be working full-time at a job, something most students can't manage while attending college. If you are one of these students, attending college requires the sacrifice of the income you *could* have earned at a job—a sacrifice we call *foregone income.*

Implicit cost The value of something sacrificed when no direct payment is made.

How much income is foregone when you go to college for a year? In 2003, the average total income of an 18- to 24-year-old high school graduate who worked full-time was $21,521. If we assume that only nine months of work must be sacrificed to attend college, and that you could still work full-time in the summer, then foregone income is about 9/12 of $21,521, or $16,140.

Summing the explicit and implicit costs gives us a rough estimate of the opportunity cost of a year in college. For a public institution, we add $5,985 in explicit costs and $16,140 in implicit costs, giving us a total of $22,125 per year. Notice that this is significantly greater than the total charges estimated by the college board, which—in addition to including some expenses that are not part of opportunity cost—excludes the largest cost of all: foregone income. When you consider paying this opportunity cost for four years, its magnitude might surprise you. Without financial aid in the form of tuition grants or other fee reductions, the average in-state resident will sacrifice about $88,000 to get a bachelor's degree at a state college and about $148,000 at a private one.

Our analysis of the opportunity cost of college is an example of a general, and important, principle:

> *The opportunity cost of a choice includes both **explicit costs** and **implicit costs**.*

A Brief Digression: Is College the Right Choice? Before you start questioning your choice to be in college, there are a few things to remember. First, in addition to its high cost, college has substantial *benefits*, including financial ones. In fact, over a 40-year work life, the average college graduate will make about $2.5 million, which is about a million dollars *more* than the average high school graduate.[1] So, even when we properly add the foregone income into our measure of opportunity cost, attending college appears to be one of the best *financial* investments you can make.

Second, remember that we've left out of our discussion many important aspects of this choice that would be harder to estimate in dollar terms, but could be very important to you. Do you *enjoy* being at college? If so, it would be difficult (although not impossible) to value that enjoyment in dollars. But your enjoyment should still be considered—along with the more easily measured financial rewards—as part of your benefits. (Of course, if you *hate* college and are only doing it for the financial rewards or to satisfy your parents, that's an implicit cost—which is part of your opportunity cost—that we haven't included.)

Time Is Money. Our analysis of the opportunity cost of college points out a general principle, one understood by economists and noneconomists alike. It can be summed up in the expression, "Time is money." Those three words contain a profound truth: The sacrifice of time often means the sacrifice of money—in particular, the money that *could* have been earned during that time.

As a rule, economists have a simple technique to estimate the dollar value of time. First, we assume that working additional hours for pay is the best among the alternatives to the choice being considered. Then, each hour sacrificed for the choice is multiplied by the individual's hourly wage. (Even someone paid a monthly salary has an implied hourly wage: their total monthly income divided by the total monthly hours of work.)

For example, suppose Jessica is a freelance writer who decides to see a movie. The ticket price is $8, and the entire activity—including getting there and back—will take three hours out of her evening. What is the opportunity cost of seeing this

---

[1] Jennifer C. Day and Eric C. Newburger, "The Big Payoff: Educational Attainment and Synthetic Estimates of Work-Life Earnings," in *Current Population Reports* (U.S. Census Bureau), July 2002. There are two provisos. First, part of the additional earnings of college graduates may be due to the type of person that goes to college, rather than the degree itself. Second, remember that much of the additional income you'll earn with a college degree is postponed far into the future, which reduces its value to you right now. (If you are using the hardcover or the Microeconomics paperback version of this book, you'll learn—in a later chapter—some special techniques for estimating the value of postponed income.) These two provisos reduce the benefits of attending college. But even when economists account for these reductions in benefits, a college degree still appears to be one of the best financial investments you can make.

movie? Let's say Jessica earns an annual income of $40,000 by working 2,000 hours per year, giving her an implied hourly wage of $40,000 / 2,000 hrs = $20 per hour. Then for Jessica, the opportunity cost is the sum of the explicit costs ($8 for the ticket) and the implicit costs ($20 × 3 hrs = $60 in foregone income), giving her a total opportunity cost of $68.

The idea that a movie "costs" $68 might seem absurd to you. But if you think about it, $68 is a much better estimate than $8 of what the movie costs for Jessica. After all, Jessica gives up three hours that *could* have been spent working on an article that, on average, would provide her with another $60. Thus, in a very real sense, Jessica sacrifices $68 for the movie.[2]

Our examples about the cost of college and the cost of a movie point out an important lesson about opportunity cost:

> *The explicit (direct money) cost of a choice may only be a part—and sometimes a small part—of the opportunity cost of a choice.*

Indeed, the higher an individual's income, the less important is the direct money cost, and the more important the time cost of an activity. For example, suppose that Samantha is an attorney who bills out her time at $100 per hour. For her, the opportunity cost of the same movie—which entails three hours and the ticket—would be $308 dollars!

You might wonder if Samantha would ever see a movie at such a high cost. The answer for Samantha is the same as for Jessica or anyone else: yes, as long as the benefits of the movie are greater than the explicit and implicit costs. It's easy to see why Samantha might decide to see a movie. Imagine that she begins taking on more and more clients, working longer and longer hours, and earning more and more income. At some point, she will realize that leisure activities like movies are very important, while earning more income will seem less important. And at some point, the enjoyment of taking time off to see a movie might be well worth sacrificing the $308 that she could have had.

Once you understand the concept of opportunity cost and how it can differ among individuals, you can understand some behavior that might otherwise appear strange. For example, why do high-income people rarely shop at discount stores like Kmart or Target and instead shop at full-service stores where the same items sell for much higher prices? It's not that high-income people *like* to pay more for their purchases. But discount stores are generally understaffed and crowded with customers, so shopping there takes more time. While discount stores have lower *money* cost,

---

[2] In using the wage rate to measure the opportunity cost of time, we are assuming (1) that Jessica *could* work three additional hours and earn an additional $20 per hour; and (2) that among all the alternatives to the movie, working for pay is the best. Any violations of these assumptions would make our measure of opportunity cost less accurate. For example, suppose Jessica would *like* to work longer hours for additional pay, but her job doesn't permit this. Then she may already be diverting her nonwork time into an alternative she values at *less* than $20 per hour—say, $15 per hour. In this case, when Jessica considers a new choice, any time sacrificed would be worth only $15 an hour to her, so using her $20 hourly wage would *overestimate* the opportunity cost of the new choice.

On the other hand, if Jessica *could* work more hours but has chosen *not* to, she must already be doing other things that she values *more highly* than $20 per hour—say, at $25. In this case, a new choice would require giving up time worth $25 per hour, and using her $20 wage would *underestimate* the opportunity cost of the new choice.

they impose a higher *time cost*. For high-income people, discount stores are actually more costly than stores with higher price tags.

We can also understand why the most highly paid consultants, entrepreneurs, attorneys, and surgeons often lead such frenetic lives, doing several things at once and packing every spare minute with tasks. Since these people can earn several hundred dollars for an hour of work, every activity they undertake carries a correspondingly high opportunity cost. Brushing one's teeth can cost $10, and driving to work can cost hundreds! By combining activities—making phone calls while driving to work, thinking about and planning the day while in the shower, or reading the morning paper in the elevator—the opportunity cost of these routine activities is reduced.

And what about the rest of us? As our wages rise, we all try to cram more activities into little bits of free time. Millions of Americans now carry cell phones and use them while waiting for an elevator or walking their dogs. Books on tape are becoming more popular and are especially favored by runners. (Why just exercise when you can also "read" a book?) And for some, vacations have become more exhausting than work, as more and more activities are crammed into shorter and shorter vacation periods. These trends can be partly explained by the increasing opportunity cost of time.

Opportunity Cost and Society

For an individual, opportunity cost arises from the scarcity of time or money. But for society as a whole, opportunity cost arises from a different source: the scarcity of society's *resources*. Our desire for goods is limitless, but we have limited resources to produce them. Therefore,

> *virtually all production carries an opportunity cost: To produce more of one thing, society must shift resources away from producing something else.*

For example, we'd all agree that we'd like better health for our citizens. What would be needed to achieve this goal? Perhaps more frequent medical checkups for more people and greater access to top-flight medicine when necessary. These, in turn, would require more and better-trained doctors, more hospital buildings and laboratories, and more high-tech medical equipment such as positron emission tomography (PET) scanners and surgical lasers. In order for us to produce these goods and services, we would have to pull resources—land, labor, capital, and entrepreneurship—out of producing other things that we also enjoy. The opportunity cost of improved health care, then, consists of all the other goods and services we would have to do without.

Production Possibilities Frontiers

Let's build a simple model to help us understand the opportunity cost we must pay for improved health care. To be even more specific, we'll measure production of health care by the *number of lives saved*. This variable is plotted along the horizontal axis in Figure 1. To measure the opportunity cost of health care, we'll make a simplifying assumption: that all goods *other* than lifesaving health care can be lumped into a single category, and that we can measure how many units of these "other goods" we're producing. In Figure 1, the quantity of "other goods" is measured on the vertical axis.

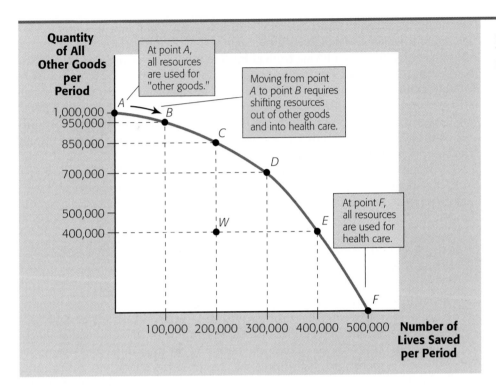

FIGURE 1
The Production Possibilities
Frontier

Now look at the curve drawn in Figure 1. It is society's **production possibilities frontier (PPF)**, *giving the different combinations of goods that can be produced with the resources and technology currently available.* More specifically, this PPF tells us the *maximum quantity* of all other goods we can produce for each number of lives saved and the maximum number of lives saved for each different quantity of other goods. Positions outside the frontier are unattainable with the technology and resources at the economy's disposal. Society's choices are limited to points *on* or *inside* the PPF.

Let's take a closer look at the PPF in Figure 1. Point *A* represents one possible choice for our society: to devote all resources to the production of "other goods" and none to health care. In this case, we would have 1,000,000 units of other goods, but we would have to forego every opportunity to save lives. Point *F* represents the opposite extreme: all available resources devoted to lifesaving health care. In that case, we'd save 500,000 lives, but we'd have no other goods.

If points *A* and *F* seem absurd to you, remember that they represent two *possible* choices for society but choices we would be unlikely to make. We want lifesaving health care to be available to those who need it, but we also want housing, clothing, entertainment, cars, and so on. So a realistic choice would include a *mix* of health care and other goods.

Suppose we desire such a mix, but the economy, for some reason, is currently operating at the undesirable point *A*—no health care but maximum production of everything else. Then we need to shift some resources from other goods to health care. For example, we could move from point *A* to point *B*, where we'd be saving 100,000 lives. But as a consequence, we'd have to cut back on other goods, producing 50,000 fewer units. The opportunity cost of saving 100,000 lives, then, would be 50,000 units of all other goods.

Production possibilities frontier (PPF) A curve showing all combinations of two goods that can be produced with the resources and technology currently available.

Increasing Opportunity Cost. Suppose we are at point *B* and now we want to save even more lives. Once again, we shift enough resources into health care to save an additional 100,000 lives, moving from point *B* to point *C*. This time, however, there is an even *greater* cost: Production of other goods falls from 950,000 units to 850,000 units, or a sacrifice of 100,000 units. The opportunity cost of saving lives has risen. You can see that as we continue to save more lives—by increments of 100,000, moving from point *C* to point *D* to point *E* to point *F*—the opportunity cost of producing other goods keeps right on rising, until saving the last 100,000 lives costs us 400,000 units of other goods.

The behavior of opportunity cost described here—the more health care we produce, the greater the opportunity cost of producing still more—applies to a wide range of choices facing society. It can be generalized as the *law of increasing opportunity cost*.

Law of increasing opportunity cost The more of something that is produced, the greater the opportunity cost of producing one more unit.

> *According to the **law of increasing opportunity cost**, the more of something we produce, the greater the opportunity cost of producing even more of it.*

The law of increasing opportunity cost causes the PPF to have a *concave* shape, becoming steeper as we move rightward and downward. To understand why, remember (from high school math) that the slope of a line or curve is just the change along the vertical axis divided by the change along the horizontal axis. Along the PPF, as we move rightward, the slope is the change in the quantity of other goods divided by the change in the number of lives saved. This is a negative number, because a positive change in lives saved means a negative change in other goods. The absolute value of this slope is the opportunity cost of saving another life. Now—as we've seen—this opportunity cost increases as we move rightward. Therefore, the absolute value of the PPF's slope must rise as well. The PPF gets steeper and steeper, giving us the concave shape we see in Figure 1.[3]

Why should there be a law of increasing opportunity cost? Why must it be that the more of something we produce, the greater the opportunity cost of producing still more?

Because most resources—*by their very nature*—are better suited to some purposes than to others. If the economy were operating at point *A*, for example, we'd be using all of our resources to produce other goods, including resources that are much better suited for health care. A hospital might be used as a food cannery, a surgical laser might be used for light shows, and a skilled surgeon might be driving a cab or trying desperately to make us laugh with his stand-up routine.

As we begin to move rightward along the PPF, say from *A* to *B*, we shift resources out of other goods and into health care. But we would *first* shift those resources *best suited to health care*—and *least* suited for the production of other things. For example, the first group of workers we'd use to save lives would be those who already have training as doctors and nurses. A surgeon—who would probably not make the best comedian—could now go back to surgery, which he does very well. Similarly, the first buildings we would put to use in the health care industry would be those that were originally built as hospitals and medical offices,

---

[3] You might be wondering if the law of increasing opportunity cost applies in both directions. That is, does the opportunity cost of producing "other goods" increase as we produce more of them? The answer is yes, as you'll see when you do Problem 1 at the end of this chapter.

and weren't really doing so well as manufacturing plants, retail stores, or movie studios. This is why, at first, the PPF is very flat: We get a *large* increase in lives saved for only a *small* decrease in other goods.

As we continue moving rightward, however, we shift away from other goods to those resources that are less and less suited to lifesaving. As a result, the PPF becomes steeper. Finally, we arrive at point F, where all resources—no matter how well suited for other goods and services—are used to save lives. A factory building is converted into a hospital, your family car is used as an ambulance, and comedic actor Jim Carrey is in medical school, training to become a surgeon.

The principle of increasing opportunity cost applies to all of society's production choices, not just that between health care and other goods. If we look at society's choice between food and oil, we would find that some land is better suited to growing food and some land to drilling for oil. As we continue to produce more oil, we would find ourselves drilling on land that is less and less suited to producing oil, but better and better for producing food. The opportunity cost of producing additional oil will therefore increase. The same principle applies in choosing between civilian goods and military goods, between food and clothing, or between automobiles and public transportation: The more of something we produce, the greater the opportunity cost of producing still more.

The Search for a Free Lunch

This chapter has argued that every decision to produce *more* of something requires us to pay an opportunity cost by producing less of something else. Nobel Prize–winning economist Milton Friedman summarized this idea in his famous remark, "There is no such thing as a free lunch." Friedman was saying that, even if a meal is provided free of charge to someone, society still uses up resources to provide it. Therefore, a "free lunch" is not *really* free: Society pays an opportunity cost by not producing other things with those resources. Therefore, some members of society will have to make do with less.

The same logic applies to other supposedly "free" goods and services. From society's point of view, there is no such thing as free Internet service, free broadcast television, or free medical care, even if those who enjoy these things don't pay for them as individuals. Providing any of these things requires us to sacrifice *other* things, as illustrated by a movement along society's PPF.

But there are some situations that seem, at first glance, to violate Freidman's dictum. Let's explore them.

Operating Inside the PPF. What if an economy is not living up to its productive potential, but is instead operating *inside* its PPF? For example, in Figure 1, suppose we are currently operating at point W, where the health care system is saving 200,000 lives and we are producing 400,000 units of other goods. Then we can move from point W to point E and save 200,000 more lives with no sacrifice of other goods. Or, starting at point W, we could move to point C (more of other goods with no sacrifice in lives saved) or to a point like D (more of *both* health care *and* other goods).

But why would an economy ever be operating inside its PPF? There are two possibilities.

Productive Inefficiency. One reason an economy might be operating inside its PPF is that resources are being wasted. Suppose, for example, that many people who could be outstanding health care workers are instead producing other goods, and many who would be great at producing other things are instead stuck in the health care industry. Then switching people from one job to the other could enable us to have more of *both* health care *and* other goods. That is, because of the mismatch of workers and jobs, we would be *inside* the PPF at a point like *W*. Creating better job matches would then move us to a point *on* the PPF (such as point *E*).

Economists use the phrase *productive inefficiency* to describe the type of waste that puts us inside our PPF.

Productive inefficiency A situation in which more of at least one good can be produced without sacrificing the production of any other good.

> *A firm, an industry, or an entire economy is **productively inefficient** if it could produce more of at least one good without pulling resources from the production of any other good.*

The phrase *productive efficiency* means the absence of any productive *inefficiency*. For example, if the computer industry is producing the maximum possible number of computers with the resources it is currently using, we would describe the computer industry as productively efficient. In that case, there would be no way to produce any more computers except to use more resources and shift them from the production of some other good. For an entire *economy* to be productively efficient, there must be no way to produce more of *any* good except by pulling resources from the production of some other good.

Although no firm, industry, or economy is ever 100 percent productively efficient, cases of gross inefficiency are not as common as you might think. When you study microeconomics, you'll learn that business firms have strong incentives to identify and eliminate productive inefficiency, since any waste of resources increases their costs and decreases their profit. When one firm discovers a way to eliminate waste, others quickly follow.

For example, empty seats on an airline flight represent productive inefficiency. Since the plane is making the trip anyway, filling the empty seat would enable the airline to serve more people with the flight (produce more transportation services) without using any additional resources (other than the trivial resources of the in-flight meal). Therefore, more people could fly without sacrificing any other good or service. When American Airlines developed a computer model in the late 1980s to fill its empty seats by altering schedules and fares, the other airlines followed its example very rapidly. And when—in the late 1990s— Priceline.com enabled airlines to auction off empty seats on the Internet, several airlines jumped at the chance and others quickly followed. As a result of this—and similar efforts to eliminate waste in personnel, aircraft, and office space—many cases of productive inefficiency in the airline industry were eliminated.

The same sorts of efforts have eliminated some easy-to-identify cases of productive inefficiency in all types of industries: banking, telephone service, Internet service, book publishing, and so on. There are certainly instances of inefficiency that remain (a possible example appears at the end of this chapter). But on the whole, if you search the economy for a free lunch due to productive inefficiency, you won't find as many hearty meals as you might think.

Recessions. Another reason an economy might operate inside its PPF is a *recession*— a slowdown in overall economic activity. During recessions, many resources are idle. For one thing, there is widespread *unemployment*—people *want* to work but are unable to find jobs. In addition, factories shut down, so we are not using all of our avail-

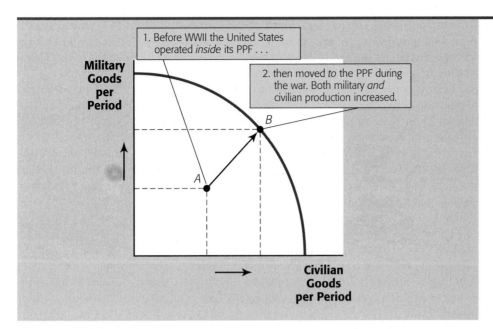

FIGURE 2
Production and Unemployment

able capital or natural resources either. An end to the recession would move the economy from a point *inside* its PPF to a point *on* its PPF—using idle resources to produce more goods and services without sacrificing anything.

This simple observation can help us understand an otherwise confusing episode in U.S. economic history. During the early 1940s, after the United States entered World War II and began using massive amounts of resources to produce military goods and services, the standard of living in the United States did *not* decline as we might have expected but actually improved slightly. Why?

Figure 2 helps to solve this puzzle. The PPF in Figure 2 is like the PPF in Figure 1. But this time, instead of pitting "health care" against "all other goods," we look at society's choice between *military* goods and *civilian* goods. When the United States entered the war in 1941, it was still suffering from the Great Depression—the most serious and long-lasting economic downturn in modern history, which began in 1929 and hit most of the developed world. For reasons you will learn when you study macroeconomics, joining the allied war effort helped end the Depression in the United States and moved our economy from a point like *A*, *inside* the PPF, to a point like *B*, *on* the frontier. Military production increased, but so did the production of civilian goods. Although there were shortages of some consumer goods, the overall result was a rise in the material well-being of the average U.S. citizen.

An economic downturn, such as the Great Depression of the 1930s, does seem to offer the possibility of a free lunch. And a war is only one factor that can reverse a downturn. In fact, no rational nation would ever *choose* war as an economic policy designed to cure a recession, since there are alternative policies that virtually everyone would find preferable. Still, eliminating a recession is not *entirely* cost-free. When you study macroeconomics, you will learn that policies to cure or avoid recessions can have risks and costs of their own. Of course, we may feel it is worth the possible costs, but they are costs nonetheless. Once again, a truly free lunch is hard to find.

Economic Growth. If the economy is already operating *on* its PPF, we cannot exploit the opportunity to have more of everything by moving *to* it. But what if the PPF itself were to change? Couldn't we then produce more of everything? This is exactly what happens when an economy's productive capacity grows.

Many factors contribute to economic growth, but they can be divided into two categories. First, the quantities of available *resources*—especially capital—can increase. An increase in physical capital—more factories, office buildings, tractors, or high-tech medical equipment—enables the economy to produce more of *everything* that uses these tools. The same is true for an increase in human capital—the skills of doctors, engineers, construction workers, software writers, and so on. In thinking about growth from greater resources, economists focus mostly on capital because, over time, increases in the capital stock have contributed more to higher living standards than other resources.

The second main factor behind economic growth is *technological change,* which enables us to produce more from a *given* quantity of resources. For example, the development of the Internet has enabled people to retrieve information in a few seconds that used to require hours of searching in a library. As a result, teachers, writers, government officials, attorneys, and physicians can produce more without working longer hours.

These two main causes of economic growth—increases in capital and technological change—often go hand in hand. In order for the Internet (a technological change) to be widely used, the economy had to produce and install servers, Internet-capable computers, and fiber-optic cable (increases in capital). In any case, both technological change and increases in the capital stock have the same type of effect on the PPF.

Let's explore a specific example that affects the PPF: body scanners that use PET. This technology enables doctors to quickly view every organ system in the body, and diagnose tumors, brain anomalies, cancers, and even potential heart problems more rapidly and accurately than previous scanning systems like magnetic resonance imaging (MRI). As this is being written (mid 2005), PET scanners are being installed in hospitals around the country. Once they're widely distributed, we'll be able to save thousands more lives every year even if we use unchanged quantities of *other* resources (doctors, nurses, hospitals, lab technicians, etc.).

What is the impact on the economy's PPF, like the one in Figure 3? First look at point *F*, where we assume *all* of our resources are devoted to lifesaving, with 500,000 lives saved per period. Under this assumption, having PET scanners would enable us to save even *more* lives—say, a total of 600,000 per period. Thus, the horizontal intercept of the PPF moves rightward, from *F* to *F'*.

Now consider point *A*, where we assume *none* of our resources would be devoted to lifesaving, and we'd produce 1,000,000 units of other goods. The new PET scanners have no productive use other than lifesaving, so having them would *not* change the vertical intercept, *A*.

As you can see, the impact of PET scanners is to stretch the PPF outward along the horizontal axis. Our society can then choose any point along the *new* PPF. For example, we could move from point *D* on the original PPF to point *H* on the new one. For this move, we'd be using all of the benefits of the new technology to save lives, with *unchanged* production of other goods. Or we could choose to move from point *D* to point *J* where, as you can verify, we produce more of *both* things that we value: more lives saved *and* more of other goods.

You may be wondering: How can a technological change in lifesaving enable us to produce more goods in *other* areas of the economy? The answer is: Society can

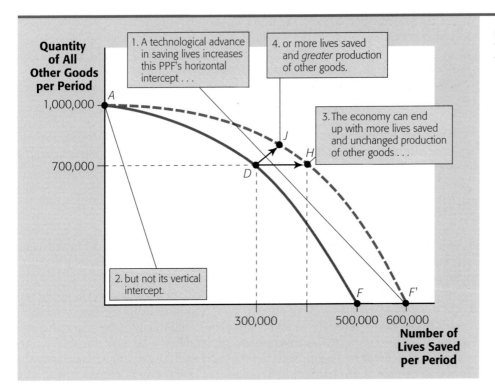

FIGURE 3
The Effect of a New Medical Technology

choose to use *some* of the increased lifesaving potential to shift other resources *out* of the medical care and into the production of other things. Because of the technological advance and the new capital, we can shift these resources without sacrificing lives.

We'd get a similar result from a technological change, or an increase in capital, that directly affected only *non*medical production. For example, the development and distribution of new assembly-line robots for the mass-production of automobiles, televisions, and home furniture would shift the *vertical* intercept of the PPF but leave its *horizontal* intercept unchanged. But once again, we could choose to save more lives *and* produce more of other goods. (You may want to draw the old and new PPFs for this case, and find a point that illustrates this choice.)

In general,

> *a technological change or an increase in the capital stock, even when the direct impact is to increase production of just one type of good, allows us to choose greater production of all types of goods.*

This conclusion certainly *seems* like a free lunch. After all, if we can produce more of the things that we value, without having to produce less of anything else, haven't we escaped from paying an opportunity cost?

Yes . . . and no. Figure 3 tells only *part* of the story, because it leaves out the steps needed to *create* this shift in the PPF in the first place. For example, technological innovation doesn't just "happen." Rather, resources must be used to create it—mostly by the research and development (R&D) departments of large corporations. In 2002, these corporations used $300 billion worth of resources on R&D, resources that *could* have been used to produce other things that we'd like right now—cars, apartments, entertainment, or even more *unimproved* medical services that can save lives in the present. The same is true when we produce and install new capital equipment; this, too, uses resources that could have been used for some other purpose.

> *In order to produce more goods and services **in the future**, we must shift resources toward R&D and capital production, and away from the production of things we'd enjoy right now.*

We must conclude that although economic growth—at first glance—*appears* to be a free lunch, someone ends up paying the check. In this case, the bill is paid by those members of society who will have to make do with less in the present.

ECONOMIC SYSTEMS

As you read these words—perhaps sitting at home or in the library—you are experiencing a very private moment. It is just you and this book; the rest of the world might as well not exist. Or so it seems. . . .

Actually, even in this supposedly private moment, you are connected to the rest of the world in ways you may not have thought about. In order for you to be reading this book, the authors had to write it. Someone had to edit it, to help make sure that all necessary material was covered and explained as clearly as possible. Someone else had to prepare the graphics. Others had to run the printing presses and the binding machines, and still others had to pack the book, ship it, unpack it, put it on a store shelf, and then sell it to you.

And there's more. People had to manufacture all kinds of goods: paper and ink, the boxes used for shipping, the computers used to keep track of inventory, and so on. It is no exaggeration to say that thousands of people were involved in putting this book in your hands.

And there is still more. The chair or couch on which you are sitting, the light shining on the page, the heat or the air conditioning in the room, the clothes you are wearing—all these things that you are using right now were *produced by somebody else*. So even now, as you sit alone reading this book, you are economically linked to others in hundreds—even thousands—of different ways.

Take a walk in your town or city, and you will see even more evidence of our economic interdependence: People are collecting garbage, helping schoolchildren cross the street, transporting furniture across town, constructing buildings, repairing roads, painting houses. Everyone is producing goods and services for *other people*.

Why is it that so much of what we consume is produced by other people? Why are we all so heavily dependent on each other for our material well-being? Why doesn't each of us—like Robinson Crusoe on his island—produce our own food, clothing, housing, and anything else we desire? And how did it come about that *you*—who did not produce any of these things yourself—are able to consume them?

These are all questions about our *economic system*—the way our economy is organized. Ordinarily, we take our economic system for granted, like the water that runs out of our faucets. But now it's time to begin looking at the plumbing—to learn how our economy serves so many millions of people, enabling them to survive and prosper.

Specialization and Exchange

If we were forced to, many of us could become economically *self-sufficient*. We could stake out a plot of land, grow our own food, make our own clothing, and build our own homes. But in no society is there such extreme self-sufficiency. On the contrary, every economic system over the past 10,000 years has been characterized by two features: (1) **specialization,** in which each of us concentrates on a limited number of productive activities, and (2) **exchange,** in which most of what we desire is obtained by trading with others rather than producing for ourselves.

> *Specialization and exchange enable us to enjoy greater production, and higher living standards, than would otherwise be possible. As a result, all economies exhibit high degrees of specialization and exchange.*

Specialization A method of production in which each person concentrates on a limited number of activities.

Exchange The act of trading with others to obtain what we desire.

There are three reasons why specialization and exchange enable us to enjoy greater production. The first has to do with human capabilities: Each of us can learn only so much in a lifetime. By limiting ourselves to a narrow set of tasks—fixing plumbing, managing workers, writing music, or designing Web pages—we are each able to hone our skills and become experts at one or two things instead of remaining amateurs at a lot of things. It is easy to see that an economy of experts will produce more than an economy of amateurs.

A second gain from specialization results from the time needed to switch from one activity to another. When people specialize, and thus spend more time doing one task, there is less unproductive "downtime" from switching activities.

Adam Smith first explained these gains from specialization in his book *An Inquiry into the Nature and Causes of the Wealth of Nations,* published in 1776. Smith explained how specialization within a pin factory dramatically increased the number of pins that could be produced there. In order to make a pin . . .

HTTP://

Economics is a subject that has benefited from specialization and the division of labor. To get a feel for the many different subjects that economists investigate, take a look at the *Journal of Economic Literature's* classification system at http:// www.econlit.org/ subject_descriptors.html.

> *One man draws out the wire, another straightens it, a third cuts it, a fourth points it, a fifth grinds it at the top for receiving the head; to make the head requires three distinct operations; to put it on is a [separate] business, to whiten the pins is another; it is even a trade by itself to put them into the paper; and the important business of making a pin is, in this manner, divided into about eighteen distinct operations, which, in some manufactories, are all performed by distinct hands.*

Smith went on to observe that 10 men, each working separately, might make 200 pins in a day, but through specialization they were able to make 48,000! What is true for a pin factory can be generalized to the entire economy: Total production will increase when workers specialize.

Notice that the production gains from specialization we've been discussing—and that Adam Smith described so well—do *not* depend on any differences in individuals' capabilities. Even in a society where initially everyone is *identical* to everyone else, specialization would still yield gains for the two reasons we've discussed: People would develop expertise over time and there would be less downtime from switching tasks.

Of course, in the real world, workers are *not* identically suited to different kinds of work. Nor are all plots of land, all natural resources, or all types of capital equipment identically suited for different tasks. This observation brings us to the *third* source of gains from specialization—one based on individual differences.

Further Gains to Specialization: Comparative Advantage. Imagine a shipwreck in which there are only two survivors—let's call them Maryanne and Gilligan—who wash up on opposite shores of a deserted island. Initially they are unaware of each other, so each is forced to become completely self-sufficient.

| **TABLE 2** | | **Labor Required for:** | |
Labor Requirements for Berries and Fish		1 Cup of Berries	1 Fish
	Maryanne	½ hour	1 hour
	Gilligan	2 hours	6 hours

On one side of the island, Maryanne finds that it takes her half an hour to pick one cup of berries and an hour to catch one fish, as shown in the first row of Table 2. On the other side of the island, Gilligan—who is less adept at both tasks—requires two hours to pick a cup of berries and six hours to catch one fish, as listed in the second row of the table. Since both castaways would want some variety in their diets, we can assume that each would spend part of the week catching fish and part picking berries.

Suppose that, one day, Maryanne and Gilligan discover each other. After rejoicing at the prospect of human companionship, they decide to develop a system of production that will work to their mutual benefit. Let's rule out any of the gains from specialization that we discussed earlier (minimizing downtime or developing expertise). Will it still pay for these two to specialize? The answer is yes, as you will see after a small detour.

Absolute Advantage: A Detour.   When Gilligan and Maryanne sit down to figure out who should do what, they might fall victim to a common mistake: basing their decision on *absolute advantage*. An individual has an **absolute advantage** in the production of some good when he or she can produce it using *fewer resources* than another individual can. On the island, the only resource being used is labor time, so the reasoning might go as follows: Maryanne can pick a cup of berries more quickly than Gilligan (see Table 2), so she has an *absolute advantage* in berry picking. It seems logical, then, that Maryanne should be the one to pick the berries.

But wait! Maryanne can also catch *fish* more quickly than Gilligan, so she has an absolute advantage in fishing as well. If absolute advantage is the criterion for assigning work, then Maryanne should do *both* tasks. This, however, would leave Gilligan doing nothing, which is certainly *not* in the pair's best interests. What can we conclude from this example? That absolute advantage is an unreliable guide for allocating tasks to different workers.

Comparative Advantage.   The correct principle to guide the division of labor on the island is comparative advantage:

> *A person has a **comparative advantage** in producing some good if he or she can produce it with a smaller opportunity cost than some other person can.*

Notice the important difference between absolute advantage and comparative advantage: You have an *absolute* advantage in producing a good if you can produce it using fewer *resources* than someone else can. But you have a *comparative* advantage if you can produce it with a smaller *opportunity cost*. As you'll see, these are not necessarily the same thing.

Absolute advantage The ability to produce a good or service, using fewer resources than other producers use.

Comparative advantage The ability to produce a good or service at a lower opportunity cost than other producers.

Let's see who has a *comparative* advantage in fishing, by calculating—for each of the castaways—the opportunity cost of catching one fish. For Maryanne, catching a fish takes an hour. This is time that could instead be used to pick *two* cups of berries. Thus, we can write

Maryanne: opportunity cost of 1 fish = 2 cups of berries

It takes Gilligan *six* hours to catch a fish, time with which he could pick *three* cups of berries. Thus,

Gilligan: opportunity cost of 1 fish = 3 cups of berries

Comparing the two results, we see that the opportunity cost of one fish is *lower* for Maryanne than it is for Gilligan. Therefore, *Maryanne has a comparative advantage in fishing*.

Even castaways do better when they specialize and exchange with each other, instead of trying to be self-sufficient.

Now let's determine who has a comparative advantage in berries by determining the opportunity cost of one cup of berries for both castaways. For Maryanne, one cup of berries takes half an hour, time that could be used to catch half a fish. Thus, we can write

Maryanne: opportunity cost of 1 cup berries = ½ fish

Of course, no one would ever catch *half* a fish, unless they were fishing with a machete. But it's still useful to know the *rate* of trade-off of one good for the other. It tells us, for example, that Maryann's opportunity cost for *two* cups of berries would be *one* fish—which is easier to imagine.

It takes Gilligan *two* hours to pick a cup of berries, time that could get him ⅓ fish instead. Thus,

Gilligan: opportunity cost of 1 cup berries = ⅓ fish

Comparing these results, we see that for berries, it's *Gilligan* who has the lower opportunity cost. Therefore, Gilligan—who has an absolute advantage in nothing—has a *comparative* advantage in berry picking.

Let's see what happens as the two decide to move toward *specializing* according to their comparative advantage. Let's have Gilligan catch *three fewer fish* each week, freeing up 18 hours that he can use to pick *nine* more cups of berries:

Gilligan: Fish ↓ 3 ⇒ Berries ↑ 9

Since Maryanne has the comparative advantage in fish, let's have her catch *four more fish* each week. This requires that she shift eight hours out of berry picking, sacrificing eight cups of berries:

$$\text{Maryanne: Fish} \uparrow 4 \Rightarrow \text{Berries} \downarrow 8$$

Now, what happens to *total* production as a result of these moves? As you can see, Maryanne *more* than makes up for the fish that Gilligan is no longer catching, and Gilligan *more* than makes up for the berries that Maryanne isn't picking. Taken together, the pair is producing one more fish *and* one more cup of berries, without requiring either to work more hours.

Since—by producing according to comparative advantage—total production on the island increases, total *consumption* can increase, too. Gilligan and Maryanne can figure out some way of trading fish for berries that makes each of them come out ahead. In the end, each of the castaways can enjoy a higher standard of living when they specialize and exchange with each other, compared to the level they'd enjoy under self-sufficiency.

What is true for our shipwrecked island dwellers is also true for the entire economy:

> *Total production of every good or service will be greatest when individuals specialize according to their comparative advantage. This is another reason why specialization and exchange lead to higher living standards than does self-sufficiency.*

When we turn from our fictional island to the real world, is production, in fact, consistent with the principle of comparative advantage? Indeed, it is. A journalist may be able to paint her house more quickly than a housepainter, giving her an *absolute* advantage in painting her home. Will she paint her own home? Except in unusual circumstances, no, because the journalist has a *comparative* advantage in writing news articles. Indeed, most journalists—like most college professors, attorneys, architects, and other professionals—hire house painters, leaving themselves more time to practice the professions in which they enjoy a comparative advantage.

Even comic book superheroes seem to behave consistently with comparative advantage. Superman can no doubt cook a meal, fix a car, chop wood, and do virtually *anything* faster than anyone else on the earth. Using our new vocabulary, we'd say that Superman has an absolute advantage in everything. But he has a clear comparative advantage in catching criminals and saving the known universe from destruction, which is exactly what he spends his time doing.

Specialization in Perspective. The gains from specialization, whether they arise from developing expertise, minimizing downtime, or exploiting comparative advantage, can explain many features of our economy. For example, college students need to select a major and then, upon graduating, to decide on a specific career. Those who follow this path are often rewarded with higher incomes than those who dally. This is an encouragement to specialize. Society is better off if you specialize, since you will help the economy produce more, and society rewards you for this contribution with a higher income.

The gains from specialization can also explain why most of us end up working for business firms that employ dozens, or even hundreds or thousands, of other employees. Why do these business firms exist? Why isn't each of us a *self-employed* expert, exchanging our production with other self-employed experts? Part of the answer is that organizing production into business firms pushes the gains from specialization still further. Within a firm, some people can specialize in working with their hands, others in managing people, others in marketing, and still others in keeping the books. Each firm is a kind of minisociety within which specialization occurs. The result is greater production and a higher standard of living than we would achieve if we were all self-employed.

Specialization has enabled societies everywhere to achieve standards of living unimaginable to our ancestors. But, it can have a downside as well. Adam Smith himself—while lauding specialization for raising living standards—worried that it could be taken too far, narrowing the range on an individual's interests and abilities, and damaging his character.

Of course, maximizing our material standard of living is not our only goal. In some instances, we might be better off *increasing* the variety of tasks we do each day, even if this means some sacrifice in production and income. For example, in many societies, one sex specializes in work outside the home and the other specializes in running the home and taking care of the children. Might families be better off if children had more access to *both* parents, even if this meant a somewhat lower family income? This is an important question. While specialization gives us material gains, there may be *opportunity costs* to be paid in the loss of other things we care about. The right amount of specialization can be found only by balancing the gains against these costs.

Resource Allocation

It was only 10,000 years ago—a mere blink of an eye in human history—that the Neolithic revolution began and human society switched from hunting and gathering to farming and simple manufacturing. At the same time, human wants grew beyond mere food and shelter to the infinite variety of things that can be *made*. Ever since, all societies have been confronted with three important questions:

1. *Which* goods and services should be produced with society's resources?
2. *How* should they be produced?
3. *Who* should get them?

Together, these three questions constitute the problem of **resource allocation**. The way a society chooses to answer these questions—that is, the method it chooses to allocate its resources—will in part determine the character of its economic system.

Resource allocation A method of determining which goods and services will be produced, how they will be produced, and who will get them.

Let's first consider the *which* question. Should we produce more health care or more movies, more goods for consumers or more capital goods for businesses? Where on its production possibilities frontier should the economy operate? As you will see, there are different methods societies can use to answer these questions.

The *how* question is more complicated. Most goods and services can be produced in a variety of different ways, each method using more of some resources and less of others. For example, there are many ways to dig a ditch. We could use *no capital at all* and have dozens of workers digging with their bare hands. We could use *a small amount of capital* by giving each worker a shovel and thereby use less labor, since each worker would now be more productive. Or we could use *even more capital*—a power trencher—and dig the ditch with just one or two workers. In every economic system, there must always be some mechanism that determines how goods and services will be produced from the infinite variety of ways available.

Finally, the *who* question. Here is where economics interacts most strongly with politics. There are so many ways to divide ourselves into groups: men and women, rich and poor, workers and owners, families and single people, young and old . . . the list is endless. How should the products of our economy be distributed among these different groups and among individuals within each group?

Determining *who* gets the economy's output is always the most controversial aspect of resource allocation. Over the last half-century, our society has become more sensitized to the way goods and services are distributed, and we increasingly ask whether that distribution is fair. For example, men get a disproportionately larger share of our national output than women do, whites get more than African-Americans and Hispanics, and middle-aged workers get more than the very old and the very young. As a society, we want to know *why* we observe these patterns (a positive economic question) and *what* we should do about them (a normative economic question). Our society is also increasingly focusing on the distribution of particular goods and services. Should scarce donor organs be rationed to those who have been waiting the longest so that everyone has the same chance of survival? Or should they be sold to the highest bidder so that those able to pay the most will get them? Should productions of Shakespeare's plays be subsidized by the government to permit more people—especially more poor people—to see them? Or should the people who enjoy these plays pay the full cost of their production?

The Three Methods of Resource Allocation. Throughout history, every society has relied primarily on one of three mechanisms for allocating resources. In a **traditional economy,** resources are allocated according to the long-lived practices of the past. Tradition was the dominant method of resource allocation for most of human history and remains strong in many tribal societies and small villages in parts of Africa, South America, Asia, and the Pacific. Typically, traditional methods of production are handed down by the village elders, and traditional principles of fairness govern the distribution of goods and services.

Traditional economy An economy in which resources are allocated according to long-lived practices from the past.

Economies in which resources are allocated mostly by tradition tend to be stable and predictable. But these economies have one serious drawback: They don't grow. With everyone locked into the traditional patterns of production, there is little room for innovation and technological change. Traditional economies are therefore likely to be stagnant economies.

In a **command economy,** resources are allocated mostly by explicit instructions from some higher authority. *Which* goods and services should we produce? The ones we're *ordered* to produce. *How* should we produce them? The way we're *told* to produce them. *Who* will get the goods and services? Whoever the authority *tells* us should get them.

Command or centrally planned economy An economic system in which resources are allocated according to explicit instructions from a central authority.

In a command economy, a government body *plans* how resources will be allocated. That is why command economies are also called **centrally planned economies.** But command economies are disappearing fast. Until about 15 years ago, examples would have included the former Soviet Union, Poland, Rumania, Bulgaria, Albania, China, and many others. Beginning in the late 1980s, all of these nations began abandoning central planning. The only examples left today are Cuba and North Korea, and even these economies—though still dominated by central planning—occasionally take steps away from it.

The third method of allocating resources—and the one with which you are no doubt most familiar—is "the market." In a **market economy,** neither long-held traditions nor commands from above guide most economic behavior. Instead, people are largely free to do what they want with the resources at their disposal. In the end, resources are allocated as a result of individual decision making. *Which* goods and services are produced? Whichever ones producers *choose* to produce. How are they produced? However producers *choose* to produce them. *Who* gets these goods and services? Anyone who *chooses* to buy them.

Market economy An economic system in which resources are allocated through individual decision making.

Of course, in a market system, freedom of choice is constrained by the resources one controls. And in this respect, we do not all start in the same place in the economic race. Some of us—like the Rockefellers and the Kennedys—have inherited great wealth; some—entrepreneur Bill Gates, the novelist Toni Morison, and the model Gisele Bündchen—have inherited great intelligence, talent, or beauty; and some, such as the children of successful professionals, are born into a world of helpful personal contacts. Others, unfortunately, will inherit none of these advantages. In a market system, those who control more resources will have more choices available to them than those who control fewer resources. Moreover, every market economy imposes limits on freeedom of choice. Some restrictions are imposed by government to ensure an orderly, just, and productive society. We cannot kill, steal, or break contracts—even if that is our desire—without suffering serious consequences. And we must pay taxes to fund government services. Still, in spite of the limitations imposed by government and the constraints imposed by limited resources, the market relies heavily on individual freedom of choice to allocate resources.

But wait . . . isn't there a problem here? People acting according to their own desires, without the firm hand of command or tradition to control them? This sounds like a recipe for chaos! How, in such a free-for-all, are resources actually *allocated*?

The answer is contained in two words: *markets* and *prices.*

The Nature of Markets. The market economy gets its name from something that nearly always happens when people are free to do what they want with the resources they possess. Inevitably, people decide to specialize in the production of one or a few things—often organizing themselves into business firms—and then sellers and buyers *come together to trade.* A **market** is a collection of buyers and sellers who have the potential to trade with one another.

Market A group of buyers and sellers with the potential to trade with each other.

In some cases, the market is *global*; that is, the market consists of buyers and sellers who are spread across the globe. The market for oil is an example of a global market, since buyers in any country can buy from sellers in any country. In other cases, the market is local. Markets for restaurant meals, haircuts, and taxi service are examples of local markets.

Markets play a major role in allocating resources by forcing individual decision makers to consider very carefully their decisions about buying and selling. They do so because of an important feature of every market: the *price* at which a good is bought and sold.

The Importance of Prices. A **price** is *the amount of money a buyer must pay to a seller for a good or service.* Price is not always the same as *cost.* In economics, as you've learned in this chapter, cost means *opportunity cost*—the *total* sacrifice needed to buy the good. While the price of a good is a *part* of its opportunity cost,

Price The amount of money that must be paid to a seller to obtain a good or service.

it is not the only cost. For example, the price does not include the value of the time sacrificed to buy something. Buying a new jacket will require you to spend time traveling to and from the store, trying on different styles and sizes, and waiting in line at the cash register.

Still, in most cases, the price of a good is a significant part of its opportunity cost. For large purchases such as a home or automobile, the price will be *most* of the opportunity cost. And this is why prices are so important to the overall working of the economy: They confront individual decision makers with the costs of their choices.

Consider the example of purchasing a car. Because you must pay the price, you know that buying a new car will require you to cut back on purchases of other things. In this way, the opportunity cost to *society* of making another car is converted to an opportunity cost *for you.* If you value a new car more highly than the other things you must sacrifice for it, you will buy it. If not, you won't buy it.

Why is it so important that people face the opportunity costs of their actions? The following thought experiment can answer this question. Imagine that the government passed a new law: When anyone buys a new car, the government will reimburse that person for it immediately. The consequences would be easy to predict. First, on the day the law was passed, everyone would rush out to buy new cars. Why not, if cars are free? The entire stock of existing automobiles would be gone within days—maybe even hours. Many people who didn't value cars much at all, and who hardly ever used them, would find themselves owning several—one for each day of the week or to match the different colors in their wardrobe. Others who weren't able to act in time—including some who desperately needed a new car for their work or to run their households—would be unable to find one at all.

Over time, automobile companies would drastically increase production to meet the surge in demand for cars. So much of our available labor, capital, natural resources, and entrepreneurial talent would be diverted to the automobile industry that we'd have to sacrifice huge quantities of all other goods and services. Thus, we'd end up *paying* for those additional cars in the end, by making do with less education, less medical care, perhaps even less food—all to support the widespread, frivolous use of cars. Almost everyone—even those who love cars—would conclude that society had been made worse-off with the new "free-car" policy. By eliminating a price for automobiles, and severing the connection between the opportunity cost of producing a car and the individual's decision to get one, we would have created quite a mess for ourselves.

> *When resources are allocated by the market, and people must* pay *for their purchases, they are forced to consider the opportunity cost to society of their individual actions. In this way, markets are able to create a sensible allocation of resources.*

Resource Allocation in the United States. The United States has always been considered the leading example of a market economy. Each day, millions of distinct items are produced and sold in markets. Our grocery stores are always stocked with broccoli and tomato soup, and the drugstore always has Kleenex and aspirin—all due to the choices of individual producers and consumers. The goods that are traded, the way they are traded, and the price at which they trade are determined by the traders themselves. No direction from above is needed to keep markets working.

But even in the United States, there are numerous cases of resource allocation *outside* the market. For example, families are important institutions in the United

States, and many economic decisions are made within them. Families tend to operate like traditional villages, not like market economies. After all, few families charge prices for goods and services provided inside the home.

Our economy also allocates some resources by command. Various levels of government collect, in total, about one-third of our incomes as taxes. We are *told* how much tax we must pay, and those who don't comply suffer serious penalties, including imprisonment. Government—rather than individual decision makers—spends the tax revenue. In this way, the government plays a major role in allocating resources—especially in determining which goods are produced and who gets them.

There are also other ways, aside from strict commands, that the government limits our market freedoms. Regulations designed to protect the environment, maintain safe workplaces, and ensure the safety of our food supply are just a few examples of government-imposed constraints on our individual choice.

What are we to make, then, of resource allocation in the United States? Markets are, indeed, constrained. But for each example we can find where resources are allocated by tradition or command, or where government restrictions seriously limit some market freedom, we can find hundreds of examples where individuals make choices according to their own desires. The things we buy, the jobs at which we work, the homes in which we live—in almost all cases, these result from market choices. The market, though not pure, is certainly the dominant method of resource allocation in the United States.

Resource Ownership

So far, we've been concerned with how resources are allocated. Another important feature of an economic system is how resources are *owned*. The owner of a resource—a parcel of land, a factory, or one's own labor time—determines how it can be used and receives income when others use it. And there have been three primary modes of resource ownership in human history.

Under *communal* ownership, resources are owned by everyone—or by no one, depending on your point of view. They are simply there for the taking; no person or organization imposes any restrictions on their use or charges any fees. It is hard to find economies with significant communal ownership of resources. Karl Marx believed that, in time, all economies would evolve toward communal ownership, and he named this predicted system **communism.** In fact, none of the economies that called themselves Marxist (such as the former Soviet Union) ever achieved Marx's vision of communism. This is not surprising: Communal ownership on a broad scale can work only when individuals have no conflicts over how resources are used. Therefore, communism requires the end of *scarcity*—an unlikely prospect in the foreseeable future.

Communism A type of economic system in which most resources are owned in common.

Nevertheless, there are examples of communal ownership on a smaller scale. Traditional villages maintain communal ownership of land and sometimes cattle. In some of the cooperative farms in Israel—called *kibbutzim*—land and capital are owned by all the members. Conflicts may result when individuals differ over how these resources should be used, but these conflicts are resolved by consensus rather than by decree or by charging fees for their use.

Closer to home, most families operate on the principle of communal ownership. The house, television, telephone, and food in the refrigerator are treated as if owned jointly. More broadly, who "owns" our sidewalks, streets, and public beaches? No one does, really. In practice, all citizens are free to use them as much and as often as they would like. This is essentially communal ownership.

Socialism A type of economic system in which most resources are owned by the state.

Under **socialism,** the *state* owns most of the resources. The prime example is the former Soviet Union, where the state owned all of the land and capital equipment in the country. In many ways, it also owned the labor of individual households, since it was virtually the only employer in the nation and unemployment was considered a crime.

State ownership also occurs in nonsocialist economies. In the United States, national parks, state highway systems, military bases, public colleges and universities, and government buildings are all state-owned resources. Over a third of the land in the country is owned by the federal government. The military, even under our current volunteer system, is an example in which the state owns the labor of soldiers—albeit for a limited period of time.

Capitalism A type of economic system in which most resources are owned privately.

Finally, the third system. When most resources are owned *privately*—as in the United States—we have **capitalism.** Take the book you are reading right now. If you turn to the title page, you will see the imprint of the company that published this book. This is a corporation owned by thousands of individual stockholders. These individuals own the buildings, the land under them, the office furniture and computer equipment, and even the reputation of the company. When these facilities are used to produce and sell a book, the company's profits belong to these stockholders. Similarly, the employees of the company are private individuals. They are selling a resource they own—their labor time—to the company, and they receive income—wages and salaries—in return.

The United States is one of the most capitalistic countries in the world. True, there are examples of state and communal ownership, as we've seen. But the dominant mode of resource ownership in the United States is *private* ownership. Resource owners keep *most* of the income they earn from supplying their resources, and they have broad freedom in deciding how their resources are used.

Types of Economic Systems

We've used the phrase *economic system* a few times already in this book. But now it's time for a formal definition.

Economic system A system of resource allocation and resource ownership.

> *An economic system is composed of two features: a mechanism for* allocating *resources and a mode of resource* ownership.

Let's leave aside the rare economies in which communal ownership is dominant and those in which resources are allocated primarily by tradition. That leaves us with four basic types of economic systems, indicated by the four quadrants in Figure 4. In the upper left quadrant, we have *market capitalism*. In this system, resources are *allocated* primarily by the market and *owned* primarily by private individuals. Today, most nations have market capitalist economies, including all of the countries of North America and Western Europe, and most of those in Asia, Latin America, and Africa.

HTTP://

The Center for International Comparisons at the University of Pennsylvania (**http://pwt.econ.upenn.edu/**) is a good source of information on the performance of economies around the world.

In the lower right quadrant is *centrally planned socialism,* under which resources are mostly allocated by command and mostly owned by the state. This *was* the system in the former Soviet Union and the nations of Eastern Europe until the late 1980s. But since then, these countries' economies have gone through cataclysmic change by moving from the lower right quadrant to the upper left. That is, these nations have simultaneously changed both their method of resource allocation and their systems of resource ownership.

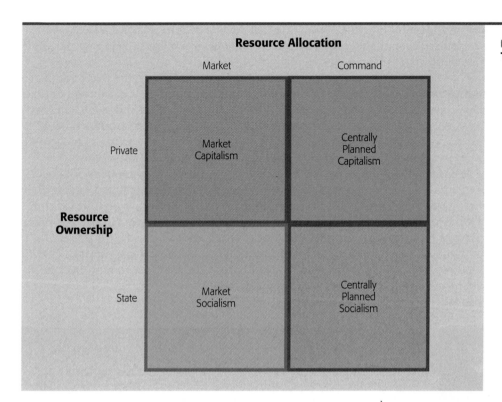

FIGURE 4
Types of Economic Systems

Although market capitalism and centrally planned socialism have been the two paramount economic systems in modern history, there have been others. The upper right quadrant represents a system of *centrally planned capitalism,* in which resources are owned by private individuals yet allocated by command. In the recent past, countries such as Sweden and Japan—where the government has been more heavily involved in allocating resources than in the United States—have flirted with this type of system. Nations at war—like the United States during World War II—also move in this direction, as governments find it necessary to direct resources by command in order to ensure sufficient military production.

Finally, in the lower left quadrant is *market socialism,* in which resources are owned by the state yet allocated by the market mechanism. The possibility of market socialism has fascinated many social scientists, who believed it promised the best of both worlds: the freedom and efficiency of the market mechanism and the fairness and equity of socialism. There are, however, serious problems—many would say "unresolvable contradictions"—in trying to mix the two. The chief examples of market socialism in modern history were short-lived experiments—in Hungary and the former Yugoslavia in the 1950s and 1960s—in which the results were mixed at best.

Economic Systems and This Book. In this book, you will learn how market capitalist economies operate. This means that the other three types of economic systems in Figure 4 will be, for the most part, ignored. Until 10 years ago, these statements would have been accompanied by an apology that would have gone something like this: "True, much of the world is characterized by alternative economic systems, but there is only so much time in one course . . ."

In the past 15 years, however, the world has changed dramatically: About 300 million people in Europe have come under the sway of the market as their nations abandoned centrally planned socialism; more than a billion have been added as China has changed course. The study of modern economies is now, more than ever, the study of market capitalism.

Understanding the Market. The market is simultaneously the most simple and the most complex way to allocate resources. For individual buyers and sellers, the market is simple. There are no traditions or commands to be memorized and obeyed. Instead, we enter the markets we *wish* to trade in and we respond to prices there as we *wish* to, unconcerned about the overall process of resource allocation.

But from the economist's point of view, the market is quite complex. Resources are allocated indirectly, as a *by-product* of individual decision making, rather than through easily identified traditions or commands. As a result, it often takes some skillful economic detective work to determine just how individuals are behaving and how resources are being allocated as a consequence.

How can we make sense of all of this apparent chaos and complexity? That is what economics is all about. And you will begin your detective work in Chapter 3, where you will learn about the most widely used model in the field of economics: the model of supply and demand.

USING THE THEORY
Are We Saving Lives Efficiently?

In this chapter, you learned that if resources are being wasted, we will operate *inside* our PPF rather than on the PPF. For example, suppose "all other goods" are being produced inefficiently. Then, by eliminating the productive inefficiency, we would free up resources. Some of the resources could be used to save more lives and some to produce more of other goods. In Figure 1, this would move us from a point like W to a point like D, where we end up saving more lives *and* having more of other goods.

But there could also be productive inefficiency in the saving of human lives. If that is the case—if it is possible to save more lives without devoting any additional resources to doing so—then we would, once again, be operating inside our PPF. And once again, we could have a free lunch—save more lives *and* have more of other goods—by eliminating the inefficiency.

Some economists have argued that we do, indeed, waste significant amounts of resources in our lifesaving efforts. How have they come to such a conclusion?

The first thing to remember is that saving a life—no matter how it is done—requires the use of resources. Any lifesaving action we might take—putting another hundred police on the streets, building another emergency surgery center, or running an advertising campaign to encourage healthy living—requires certain quantities of resources. In a market economy, resources sell at a price. This allows us to use the dollar cost of a lifesaving method to measure the value of the resources used up by that method.

Moreover, we can compare the "cost per year of life saved" of different methods. For example, in the United States we currently spend about $253 million on heart transplants each year and thereby add about 1,600 years to the lives of heart patients. Thus, the cost per year of life saved from heart transplants is $253,000,000/1,600 = $158,000 (rounded to the nearest thousand).

Method	Cost per Life-Year Saved
Brief physician antismoking intervention:	
Single personal warning from physician to stop smoking	$150
Sickle cell screening and treatment for African-American newborns	$236
Replacing ambulances with helicopters for medical emergencies	$2,454
Intensive physician antismoking intervention:	
Physician identification of smokers among their patients;	
three physician counseling sessions; two further sessions with	
smoking-cessation specialists; and materials—nicotine	
patch or nicotine gum	$2,587
Mammograms: Once every three years, for ages 50–64	$2,700
Chlorination of water supply	$4,000
Next step after suspicious lung X-ray:	
PET Scan	$3,742
Exploratory Surgery	$4,895
Needle Biopsy	$7,116
Vaccination of all infants against strep infections	$80,000
Mammograms: Annually, for ages 50–64	$108,401
Exercise electrocardiograms as screening test:	
For 40-year-old males	$124,374
Heart transplants	$157,821
Mammograms: Annually, for age 40–49	$186,635
Exercise electrocardiograms as screening test:	
For 40-year-old females	$335,217
Seat belts on school buses	$2,760,197
Asbestos ban in automatic transmissions	$66,402,402

TABLE 3
The Cost of Saving Lives

Sources: Electrocardiograms: Charles E. Phelps, *Health Economics,* 2nd ed. (Reading, MA: Addison-Wesley, 1997). Regular exercise: L. Goldman, A. M. Garber, S. A. Grover, & M. A. Hlatky (1996). Task Force 6. Cost-effectiveness of assessment and management of risk factors (Bethesda Conference). *JACC,* 27(5), 1020–1030. Anti-smoking intensive intervention: *Journal of the American Medical Association,* Dec. 3, 1997. Anti-smoking brief intervention: Malcolm Law and Jin Ling Tang, "An Analysis of the Effectiveness of Interventions Intended to Help People Stop Smoking," *Archives of Internal Medicine,* 1995; 155: pp. 1933–1941, and authors' calculations to convert "per life saved" to "per year of life saved." Annual mammograms: Kent Jeffreys, "Progressive Environmentalism: Principles for Regulatory Reform (Policy Report No. 194), National Center for Policy Analysis, June 1995. Benzene emission controls: Tammy O. Tengs et al., "Five Hundred Life-Saving Interventions and Their Cost-Effectiveness," *Risk Analysis,* 1994. All other figures: Tammy O. Tengs, "Dying Too Soon: How Cost-Effectiveness Analysis Can Save Lives," School of Social Ecology, University of California, Irvine, NCPA Policy Report No. 204, May 1997. Replacing ambulances with helicopters: Peter A. Gearhart, Richard Wuerz, A. Russell Localio, "Cost Effectiveness Analysis of Helicopter EMS for Trauma Patients," *Annals of Emergency Medicine,* Oct. 1997, 30:500–506. Chlorination of water supply: Kent Jeffreys, "Guide to Regulatory Reform: The Cost Benefit Rule," National Center for Policy Analysis, *Brief Analysis,* No. 150, January 31, 1995. Strep Vaccination: "A Pound of Prevention," in *News from Harvard Medical, Dental and Public Health Schools,* March 24, 2000 (based on price of $232 for a four-dose vaccination series with Prevnar). Lung cancer screening: M. Ditelin, D. Modka, K. Weber, P. Theiseen, H. Schicha, "Cost Effectiveness of PET in the Management Algorithms of Lung Tumors: Comparison of Health Economic Data," *Nuklearmedizin,* 40(4), August 2001, pp. 122–128, viewed at *http://www.acor.org/cnet/710582.html* (May 2003). Euros have been converted to dollars.

Table 3 lists several of the methods we currently use to save lives in the United States. Some of these methods reflect legal or regulatory decisions (such as the ban on asbestos) and others reflect standard medical practices (such as annual mammograms for women over 50). Other methods are used only sporadically (such as seat belts in school buses). You can see that the cost per life saved ranges widely—from $150 per year of life saved for a physician warning a patient to quit smoking, to over $66,000,000 per year of life saved from the ban on asbestos in automatic transmissions.

The table indicates that some lifesaving methods are highly cost effective. For example, our society probably exhausts the potential to save lives from brief physician antismoking intervention. Most doctors *do* warn their smoking patients to quit.

But the table also indicates some serious productive *in*efficiency in lifesaving. For example, screening and treating African-American newborns for sickle cell anemia is one of the least costly ways of saving a year of life in the United States—only $236 per year of life saved. Nevertheless, 20 percent of African-American newborns do *not* get this screening at all. Similarly, intensive intervention to discourage smoking is far from universal in the U.S. health care system, even though it has the relatively low cost of $2,587 per year of life saved.

Why is the less than universal use of these lower cost methods *productively inefficient?* To answer, let's do some thought experiments. First, let's imagine that we shift resources from heart transplants to *intensive* antismoking efforts. Then for each year of life we decided *not* to save with heart transplants, we would free up $157,821 in medical resources. If we applied those resources toward intensive antismoking efforts, at a cost of $2,587 per year of life saved, we could then save an additional $157,821/$2,587 = 61 life-years. In other words, we could increase the number of life-years saved without any increase in resources flowing to the health care sector, and therefore, without any sacrifice in other goods and services. If you look back at the definition of productive inefficiency given earlier in this chapter, you'll see why this is an example of it.

But why pick on heart transplants? Our ban on asbestos in automobile transmissions—which requires the purchase of more costly materials with greater quantities of scarce resources—costs us about $66 million for each life-year saved. Suppose these funds were spent instead to buy the resources needed to provide women aged 40 to 49 with annual mammograms (currently *not* part of most physicians' recommendations). Then for each life-year lost to asbestos, we'd save $66 million/186,635 = 354 life-years from earlier detection of breast cancer.

Of course, allocating lifesaving resources is much more complicated than our discussion so far has implied. For one thing, the benefits of lifesaving efforts are not fully captured by "life-years saved" (or even by an alternative measure, which accounts for improvement in *quality* of life). The cost per life-year saved from mandating seat belts on school buses is extremely high—almost $3 million. This is mostly because very few children die in school bus accidents—about 11 per year in the entire United States—and, according to the National Traffic Safety Board, few of these deaths would have been prevented with seat belts. But mandatory seat belts—rightly or wrongly—might decrease the anxiety of millions of parents as they send their children off to school. How should we value such a reduction in anxiety? Hard to say. But it's not unreasonable to include it as a benefit—at least in some way—when deciding about resources.

Another difficulty in allocating our lifesaving resources efficiently—which has become profoundly more serious in the last few years—is uncertainty. Consider, for example, our efforts to prevent a terrorist attack via hijacked airliners. What is the cost per life-year saved? We cannot know. An earlier study of antiterrorist efforts in the mid-1990s had estimated the cost at $8,000,000 per life-year saved, which seems productively inefficient.[4] But this study made two critical assumptions to

[4] "The Cost of Anti-terrorist Rhetoric," The Cato Review of Business and Government, Dec. 17, 1996, and authors' calculations to convert "per life saved" to "per year of life saved."

arrive at that number. First, that—without the new procedures—37 people would perish each year from airline-related terrorist incidents—equal to the rate we had had in the late 1980s and early 1990s. Second, the study assumed that the safety procedures being evaluated would be 100 percent effective in eliminating attacks.

Both of these assumptions were proven wrong by the events of September 11, 2001. On that day, we discovered that airline hijacking could take many more lives than we had imagined, dramatically reducing the cost per-life-year saved of antiterrorist measures. On the other hand, we also realized that our efforts to prevent such attacks could not be entirely successful—*increasing* the cost per life-year saved.

We confront similar uncertainties in allocating resources to protect against potential bioterrorism. Should our government be stockpiling smallpox vaccine? Should it go further, and press for vaccination of the entire population? The expected cost per life-year saved under each of these policies can range from minuscule to exorbitant, depending on the likelihood of a smallpox attack and how many lives the policy would save—things we can't realistically know. Clearly, trying to gauge and improve our productive efficiency in saving lives—which was never an exact science—has become even *less* exact in the post-9/11 era.

Summary

One of the most fundamental concepts in economics is *opportunity cost*. The opportunity cost of any choice is what we give up when we make that choice. At the individual level, opportunity cost arises from the scarcity of time or money; for society as a whole, it arises from the scarcity of resources—land and natural resources, labor, capital, and entrepreneurship. To produce and enjoy more of one thing, we must shift resources away from producing something else. The correct measure of cost is not just the money price we pay, but the opportunity cost: what we must give up when we make a choice. The *law of increasing opportunity cost* tells us that the more of something we produce, the greater the opportunity cost of producing still more.

In a world of scarce resources, each society must have an economic system—its way of organizing economic activity.

All *economic systems* feature *specialization*, where each person and firm concentrates on a limited number of productive activities—and *exchange*, through which we obtain most of what we desire by trading with others. Specialization and exchange enable us to enjoy higher living standards than would be possible under self-sufficiency.

Every economic system determines how resources are owned and how they are allocated. In a market capitalist economy, resources are owned primarily by private individuals and allocated primarily through markets. Prices play an important role in markets by forcing decision makers to take account of society's opportunity cost when they make choices.

Key Terms

Absolute advantage	Exchange	Price
Capitalism	Explicit cost	Production possibilities frontier (PPF)
Centrally planned economy	Implicit cost	Productive inefficiency
Command economy	Law of increasing opportunity cost	Resource allocation
Communism	Market	Socialism
Comparative advantage	Market economy	Specialization
Economic system	Opportunity cost	Traditional economy

Review Questions   *Answers to even-numbered Questions and Problems can be found on the text Web site at http://hall-lieb.swlearning.com.*

1. "Warren Buffett is one of the world's wealthiest men, worth billions of dollars. For someone like Buffet, the principle of opportunity cost simply doesn't apply." True or false? Explain.

2. What are some reasons why a country might be operating inside its production possibilities frontier (PPF)?

3. Why is a PPF concave—that is, bowed out from the origin? Be sure to give an *economic* explanation.

4. What are three distinct reasons why specialization leads to a higher standard of living?

5. What is the difference between comparative advantage and absolute advantage? Which is more important from an economic viewpoint?

6. List the three questions any resource allocation mechanism must answer. Briefly describe the three primary methods of resource allocation that have evolved to answer these questions.

7. What are the three primary ways in which resources are *owned*? Briefly describe each of them.

8. Why can't the United States economy be described as a *pure market capitalist economy*?

9. True or false?: "Resource allocation and resource ownership are essentially the same thing. Once you know who owns the resources in an economy, you also know by what mechanism those resources will be allocated." Explain your answer.

Problems and Exercises

1. Redraw Figure 1, but this time identify a different set of points along the frontier. Starting at point F (500,000 lives saved, zero production of other goods), have each point you select show equal increments in the quantity of other goods produced. For example, a new point H should correspond to 200,000 units of other goods, point J to 400,000 units, point K to 600,000 units, and so on. Now observe what happens to the opportunity cost of "200,000 more units of other goods" as you move leftward and upward along this PPF. Does the law of increasing opportunity cost apply to the production of "all other goods"? Explain briefly.

2. Suppose that you are considering what to do with an upcoming weekend. Here are your options, from least to most preferred: (1) Study for upcoming midterms; (2) fly to Colorado for a quick ski trip; (3) go into seclusion in your dorm room and try to improve your score on a computer game. What is the opportunity cost of a decision to play the computer game all weekend?

3. How would a technological innovation in lifesaving— say, the discovery of a cure for cancer—affect the PPF in Figure 1?

4. How would a technological innovation in the production of *other* goods—say, the invention of a new kind of robot that speeds up assembly-line manufacturing—affect the PPF in Figure 1?

5. Suppose that one day, Gilligan (the castaway) eats a magical island plant that turns him into an expert at everything. In particular, it now takes him just half an hour to pick a quart of berries, and 15 minutes to catch a fish.
   a. Redo Table 2 in the chapter.
   b. Who—Gilligan or Maryanne—has a comparative advantage in picking berries? In fishing? When the castaways discover each other, which of the two should specialize in which task?

   c. Can *both* castaways benefit from Gilligan's new abilities? How?

6. Suppose that two different castaways, Mr. and Mrs. Howell, end up on a different island. Mr. Howell can pick 1 pineapple per hour, or 1 coconut. Mrs. Howell can pick 2 pineapples per hour, but it takes her two hours to pick a coconut.
   a. Construct a table like Table 2 showing Mr. and Mrs. Howell's labor requirements.
   b. Who—Mr. or Mrs. Howell—has a comparative advantage in picking pineapples? In picking coconuts? Which of the two should specialize in which tasks?
   c. Assume that Mr. and Mrs. Howell had originally washed ashore on different parts of the island, and that they originally each spent 12 hours per day working, spending 6 hours picking pineapples and 6 hours picking coconuts. How will their total production change if they find each other and begin to specialize?

7. You and a friend have decided to work jointly on a course project. Frankly, your friend is a less than ideal partner. His skills as a researcher are such that he can review and outline only two articles a day. Moreover, his hunt-and-peck style limits him to only 10 pages of typing a day. On the other hand, in a day you can produce six outlines or type 20 pages.
   a. Who has an absolute advantage in outlining, you or your friend? What about typing?
   b. Who has a comparative advantage in outlining? In typing?
   c. According to the principle of comparative advantage, who should specialize in which task?

8. One might think that performing a mammogram once each year—as opposed to once every three years—would triple the cost per life saved. But according to Table 3, peforming the exam annually raises the cost per life-year saved by about 40 times. Does this make sense? Explain.

9. Use the information on 2003 college costs shown in the table below to calculate the average opportunity cost of a year in college for a student at a four-year public institution under the following assumptions:
   a. The student receives free room and board at home at no opportunity cost to the parents.
   b. The student receives an academic scholarship covering all tuition and fees (in the form of a grant, not a loan or a work study aid).
   c. The student works half time while at school at no additional emotional cost.

10. Work the following problems.
    a. Use the information on 2003 college costs shown in the table below to compare the opportunity cost of attending a year of college at a two-year public college, a four-year public college, and a four-year private college.

Type of Institution	Two-Year Public	Four-Year Public	Four-Year Private
Tuition and fees	$1,735	$4,081	$18,273
Books and supplies	$727	$786	$807
Room and Board	$5,430	$5,582	$6,779
Transportation and other expenses	$2,566	$2,394	$1,820
Total out-of-pocket costs	$10,458	$12,843	$27,679

Source: *Annual Survey of Colleges*, The College Board, New York, NY, 2003.

b. Consider Kylie, who has been awarded academic scholarships covering all tuition and fees at three different colleges. College #1 is a two-year public college. College #2 is a four-year public college, and College #3 is a four-year private college. Explain why, if the decision is based solely on opportunity cost, Kylie will turn down her largest scholarship offers.

c. Given your calculations in part b, what nonmonetary considerations might induce Kylie to go to the college with the highest opportunity cost? How large (in dollar terms) must these nonmonetary benefits be to persuade Kylie to choose the most expensive college?

11. Suppose the Internet enables more production of other goods *and* helps to save lives (for simplicity, assume proportional increases).
    a. Show how the PPF would be affected.
    b. Does this affect any of the general conclusions about economic growth?
    c. Graphically show the conclusion that more lives could be saved if technological change occurred that enabled greater production of other goods, but that did not directly affect the number of lives saved.

Challenge Question

1. Suppose that an economy's PPF is a straight line, rather than a bowed out, concave curve. What would this say about the nature of opportunity cost as production is shifted from one good to the other?

 These exercises require access to Hall/Lieberman Xtra! If Xtra! did not come with your book, visit http://hallxtra.swlearning.com to purchase.

1. Use your Xtra! password at the Hall and Lieberman Web site (http://hallxtra.swlearning.com), select Chapter 2, and under Economic Applications, click on EconDebates. Choose *Economic Fundamentals; Scarcity, Choice and Opportunity Cost* and scroll down to find the debate, "Should There Be a Market for Human Organs?" Read the debate, and answer the following questions.
   a. How (if at all) would compensation for organ donation offset the opportunity cost of donation?
   b. Now click on EconNews. Choose *Economic Fundamentals; Scarcity, Choice and Opportunity Cost* and scroll down to find the article, "What Price for a Life?" Does this form of compensation eliminate the same opportunity cost as organ donation? Why or why not?

2. Use your Xtra! password at the Hall and Lieberman Web site (http://hallxtra.swlearning.com), select Chapter 2, and under Economic Applications, click on EconNews. Choose *Economic Fundamentals; Production Possibility Frontier* and scroll down to find the article, "The Federal Budget: What a Difference a Day Makes." Read the summary, and answer the questions below.
   a. Does the article imply that the economy is producing efficiently? Why or why not?
   b. Draw a PPF between military spending on the horizontal axis, and all other government spending on the vertical axis. Where on the PPF does this article suggest the economy is moving?
   c. Is it possible for government to simultaneoiusly increase both military spending and domestic spending?

Supply and Demand

CHAPTER OUTLINE

Markets
  How Broadly Should We Define the Market?
  Buyers and Sellers
  Competition in Markets
  Using Supply and Demand

Demand
  The Law of Demand
  The Demand Schedule and the Demand Curve
  Shifts vs. Movements Along the Demand Curve
  Factors That Shift the Demand Curve

Supply
  The Law of Supply
  The Supply Schedule and the Supply Curve
  Shifts vs. Movements Along the Supply Curve
  Factors That Shift the Supply Curve

Putting Supply and Demand Together

What Happens When Things Change?
  Income Rises, Causing an Increase in Demand
  An Ice Storm Causes a Decrease in Supply
  Handheld PCs in 2003: Both Curves Shift

The Three-Step Process

**Using the Theory: College Administrators
  Make a Costly Mistake**

Appendix: Solving for Equilibrium Algebraically

Father Guido Sarducci, a character on the early *Saturday Night Live* shows, once observed that the average person remembers only about five minutes worth of material from college. He therefore proposed the "Five Minute University," where you'd learn only the five minutes of material you'd actually remember and dispense with the rest. The economics course would last only 10 seconds, just enough time for students to learn to recite three words: "supply and demand."

Of course, there is much more to economics than these three words. Still, Sarducci's observation had some truth. Many people *do* regard the phrase "supply and demand" as synonymous with economics. But surprisingly few people actually understand what the phrase means. In a debate about health care, poverty, recent events in the stock market, or the high price of housing, you might hear someone say, "Well, it's just a matter of supply and demand," as a way of dismissing the issue entirely. Others use the phrase with an exaggerated reverence, as if supply and demand were an inviolable physical law, like gravity, about which nothing can be done. So what does this oft-repeated phrase really mean?

First, supply and demand is just an economic model—nothing more and nothing less. It's a model designed to explain *how prices are determined in certain types of markets.*

Why has this model taken on such an exalted role in the field of economics? Because prices themselves play such an exalted role in the economy. In a market system, once the price of something has been determined, only those willing to pay that price will get it. Thus, prices determine which households will get which goods and services and which firms will get which resources. If you want to know why the cell phone industry is expanding while the video rental industry is shrinking, or why homelessness is a more pervasive problem in the United States than hunger, you need to understand how prices are determined. In this chapter, you will learn how the model of supply and demand works and how to use it. You will also learn about the strengths and limitations of the model. It will take more time than Guido Sarducci's 10-second economics course, but in the end you will know much more than just three little words.

MARKETS

Put any compound in front of a chemist, ask him what it is and what it can be used for, and he will immediately think of the basic elements—carbon, hydrogen, oxygen, and so on. Ask an economist almost any question about the economy, and he will immediately think about *markets.*

In ordinary language, a market is a specific location where buying and selling take place: a supermarket, a flea market, etc. In economics, a market is not a place, but rather a collection of *traders.* More specifically,

> *a market is a group of buyers and sellers with the potential to trade with each other.*

Economists think of the economy as a collection of individual markets. In each of these markets, the collection of buyers and sellers will be different, depending on what is being traded. There is a market for oranges, another for automobiles, another for real estate, and still others for corporate stocks, euros, and anything else that is bought and sold.

However, unlike chemistry—in which the set of basic elements is always the same—in economics, we can define a market in *different* ways, depending on our purpose. In fact, in almost any economic analysis, the first step is to define and characterize the market or collection of markets to analyze.

How Broadly Should We Define the Market?

Suppose we want to study the personal computer industry in the United States. Should we define the market very broadly ("the market for computers"), or very narrowly ("the market for ultra-light laptops"), or something in between ("the market for laptops")? The right choice depends on the problem we're trying to analyze.

For example, if we're interested in the price of equipment for connecting to the Internet, there would be no reason to divide computers into desktops and laptops, since the distinction would have nothing to do with e-mail access and would only get in the way. Thus, we'd treat all types of computers as if they were the same

Aggregation The process of combining distinct things into a single whole.

good. Economists call this process **aggregation**—combining a group of distinct things into a single whole.

But suppose we're asking a different question: Why do laptops always cost more than desktops with similar computing power? Then we'd aggregate all laptops together as one good, and all desktops as another, and look at each of these more narrowly defined markets.

The same general principle applies to the *geographic* breadth of the market. If we want to predict how instability in the Persian Gulf will affect gasoline prices around the world, we'd use the "global market for oil," in which the major oil producers in about 20 countries sell to buyers around the globe. But if we want to explain why gasoline is cheaper in the United States than in most of the rest of the world, we'd want to look at the "U.S. market for oil." In this market, global sellers choose how much oil to sell to U.S. buyers.

> *In economics, markets can be defined broadly or narrowly, depending on our purpose.*

How broadly or narrowly markets are defined is one of the most important differences between *macro*economics and *micro*economics. In macroeconomics, goods and services are aggregated to the highest levels. Macro models even lump all consumer goods—dishwashers, cell phones, blue jeans, and so forth—into the single category "consumption goods" and view them as if they are traded in a single, broadly defined market, "the market for consumption goods." Similarly, instead of recognizing different markets for shovels, bulldozers, computers, and factory buildings, macro models analyze the market for "capital goods." Defining markets this broadly allows macroeconomists to take an overall view of the economy without getting bogged down in the details.

In microeconomics, by contrast, markets are defined more narrowly. Instead of asking how much we'll spend on *consumer goods*, a microeconomist might ask how much we'll spend on *health care* or *video games*. Although microeconomics always involves some aggregation, the process stops before it reaches the highest level of generality.

Buyers and Sellers

A market is composed of the buyers and sellers that trade in it. But who, exactly, *are* these buyers and sellers?

When you think of a seller, your first image might be of a business. In many markets, you'd be right: The sellers *are* business firms. Examples are markets for restaurant meals, airline travel, clothing, and banking services. But businesses aren't the only sellers in the economy. For example, *households* are the primary sellers in labor markets, such as the markets for Web page designers, accountants, and factory workers. Households are also important sellers in markets for used cars, residential homes, and rare artworks. Governments, too, are sometimes important sellers. For example, state governments are major sellers in the market for education through state colleges and universities.

What about buyers? Your first thought may be "people" like yourself, or "households." Indeed, many goods and services are bought primarily by households: college education, movies, housing, clothing, and so on. But businesses and government agencies are the primary buyers in labor markets, and they are also important buyers of personal computers, automobiles, and airline transportation.

As you can see, the buyers in a market can be households, business firms, or government agencies. And the same is true of sellers. Sometimes, it's important to recognize that all three groups are on both sides of a market. But not always. Once again, it depends on our purpose.

Our purpose in this book—and your purpose in taking a college course in economics—is educational. We want to identify the major forces at work in the economy, the ones that cause prices to rise and fall, industries to expand and contract, and so on. Accordingly, we want to keep our models simple, so the important ideas stand out more clearly. This is why we'll usually (but not always) follow this guideline:

> *For the most part, in markets for consumer goods, we'll view business firms as the only sellers, and households as the only buyers.*

HTTP://

The Inomics search engine is devoted solely to economics (http://www.inomics.com/cgi/show). Use it to investigate topics related to supply and demand.

Similarly, when we analyze markets for labor or capital in later chapters, we'll generally view business firms as the only buyers, and households as the only sellers. Of course, we'll make exceptions whenever decisions by *other* groups of buyers or sellers matter to the problem at hand.

One last simplification should be mentioned. In many of our discussions, we'll be leaving out the "go-between." When analyzing, say, the market for books, we'll view book publishers as selling directly to households, rather than using retailers like Barnes and Noble or Amazon.com to do the selling for them. And in labor markets—such as say, the market for business managers—we'll view business firms as hiring workers directly, rather than using headhunting firms as intermediaries. Except for special issues in which retailers, headhunters or other intermediaries are important, including them would add complexity but not much else.

Competition in Markets

A final issue in defining a market is how individual buyers and sellers view the price of the product. In many cases, individual buyers or sellers have an important influence over the price they charge. For example, in the market for cornflakes, Kellogg's—an individual *seller*—simply sets its price every few months. It can raise the price and sell fewer boxes of cereal or lower the price and sell more. In the market for windshield wiper motors, Ford Motor Company—an individual *buyer*—can influence the price by negotiating special deals or by changing the number of motors it buys. The market for breakfast cereals and the market for windshield wiper motors are examples of *imperfectly competitive* markets.

> *In imperfectly competitive markets, individual buyers or sellers can influence the price of the product.*

Imperfectly competitive market
A market in which a single buyer or seller has the power to influence the price of the product.

But now think about the national market for wheat. Can an individual seller have any impact on the market price? Not really. On any given day there is a going price for wheat—say, $5.80 per bushel. If a farmer tries to charge more than that—say, $5.85 per bushel—he won't sell any wheat at all! His customers will instead go to one of his many competitors and buy the identical product from them for less. Each wheat farmer must take the price of wheat as a "given."

The same is true of a single wheat *buyer:* If he tries to negotiate a lower price from a seller, he'd be laughed off the farm. "Why should I sell my wheat to you for

$5.75 per bushel, when there are others who will pay me $5.80?" Accordingly, each buyer must take the market price as a given.

The market for wheat is an example of a *perfectly competitive market.*

Perfectly competitive market
A market in which no buyer or seller has the power to influence the price.

> *In perfectly competitive markets (or just competitive markets), each buyer and seller takes the market price as a given.*

What makes some markets imperfectly competitive and others perfectly competitive? You'll learn the complete answer when you are well into your study of *microeconomics,* along with more formal definitions. But here's a hint: In perfectly competitive markets, there are many small buyers and sellers, each is a small part of the market, and the product is standardized, like wheat. Imperfectly competitive markets, by contrast, have just a few large buyers or sellers, or else the product of each seller is unique in some way.

Using Supply and Demand

Supply and demand is a versatile model. It can be applied to broadly defined goods (the market for food) or narrowly defined goods (the market for Granny Smith apples). Households, business firms, or government agencies can appear in any combination on the buying side or the selling side. The buyers and sellers can reside within a small geographic area or be dispersed around the world.

But there is one important restriction in using supply and demand: We are implicitly assuming that the market is perfectly competitive.

> *The supply and demand model is designed to explain how prices are determined in perfectly competitive markets.*

This suggests that the model isn't very useful. After all, perfectly competitive markets—in which an individual buyer or seller has *no* influence on the market price—are not that common in the real world. However, many markets come reasonably close—close enough, in fact, that we can choose to view them as perfectly competitive.

Think of the market for fast-food hot dogs in a big city. On the one hand, every hot dog stand is somewhat different from every other one in terms of location, quality of service, and so on. This means an individual vendor has *some* influence over the price of his hot dogs. For example, if his competitors are all charging $1.50 for a hot dog, but he sells in a more convenient location, he might be able to charge $1.60 or $1.70 without losing too many customers. In this sense, the market for sidewalk hot dogs does not seem perfectly competitive.

On the other hand, there are rather narrow limits to an individual seller's freedom to change his price. With so many vendors in a big city, who are not *that* different from one another, one who charged $2.00 or $2.25 might soon find that he's lost all of his customers to the other vendors who are charging the market price of $1.50. Since no single seller can deviate *too* much from the market price, we could—if we wanted to—view the market as more or less perfectly competitive.

How, then, do we decide whether to consider a market, such as the market for big-city hot dogs, as perfectly or imperfectly competitive? You won't be surprised to hear that it depends on the question we want to answer. If we want to explain why there are occasional price wars among hot dog vendors, or why some of them routinely charge higher prices than others, viewing the market as perfectly competitive would be counterproductive—it would hide, rather than reveal, the answer. For these questions, the supply and demand model would not work, so we'd choose a *different* model—one designed for a type of *im*perfectly competitive market. (If your current course is *micro*economics, you will soon learn about these models and how to use them.)

But if we want to know why hot dogs are cheaper than most other types of fast foods, the simplest approach is to view the market for hot dogs as perfectly competitive. True, each hot dog vendor does have *some* influence over the price. But that influence is so small, and the prices of different sellers are so similar, that our assumption of perfect competition works pretty well.

Perfect competition then, is a matter of degree, rather than an all-or-nothing characteristic. While there are very few markets in which sellers and buyers take the price as completely given, there are many markets in which a *narrow range* of prices is treated as a given (as in the market for hot dogs). In these markets, supply and demand often provides a good approximation to what is going on. This is why it has proven to be the most versatile and widely used model in the economist's tool kit. Neither laptop computers nor orange juice is traded in a perfectly competitive market. But ask an economist to tell you why the cost of laptops decreases every year, or why the price of orange juice rises after a freeze in Florida, and he or she will invariably reach for supply and demand to find the answer.

Supply and demand are like two blades of a scissors: To analyze a market, we need both of them. In this and the next section, we will be sharpening those blades, learning separately about supply and demand. Then, we'll put them together and put them to use. Let's start with demand.

DEMAND

It's tempting to think of "demand" as just a psychological phenomenon, a pure "want" or "desire." But that notion can lead us astray. For example, you *want* all kinds of things: a bigger apartment, a better car, nicer clothes, more and better vacations. The list is endless. But you don't always *buy* them. Why not?

Because in addition to your wants—which you'd very much like to satisfy—you also face *constraints*. First, you have to *pay*. And in most cases, you don't have any influence over the price of what you buy—you just have to pay up or do without. You also have limited total funds with which to buy things, so every decision to buy one thing is also a decision *not* to buy something else. As a result, every purchase confronts you with an opportunity cost. (Even if you don't spend all of your income during the year, you still face an opportunity cost: Every purchase is money you are not saving for later, so you sacrifice future spending power.) Your "wants," together with the real-world constraints that you face, determine what you will choose to buy in any market. Hence, the following definition:

> A **household's quantity demanded** of a good is the specific amount the household would choose to buy over some time period, given (1) a particular price that must be paid for the good; (2) all other constraints on the household.

Household's quantity demanded The specific amount a household would choose to buy over some time period, given (1) a particular price, (2) all other constraints on the household.

When we add up the buying behavior of all households in a market, we get a similar definition:

Market quantity demanded The specific amount of a good that *all* buyers in the market would choose to buy over some time period, given (1) a particular price, (2) all other constraints they face.

*Market quantity demanded (often just **quantity demanded**) is the specific amount of a good that* all *buyers in the market would choose to buy over some time period, given (1) a particular price they must pay for the good; (2) all other constraints on households.*

Since this definition plays a key role in any supply and demand analysis, it's worth discussing briefly exactly what it means and doesn't mean.

Quantity Demanded Implies a *Choice*. Quantity demanded doesn't tell us the amount of a good that households feel they "need" or "desire" in order to be happy. Instead, it tells us how much households would like to buy *when they take into account the opportunity cost* of their decisions. The opportunity cost arises from the constraints households face, such as having to pay a given price for the good, limits on spendable funds, and so on.

Quantity Demanded Is *Hypothetical*. Will households actually be *able* to purchase the amount they want to purchase? Maybe yes, maybe no. There are special situations—analyzed in microeconomics—in which households are frustrated in buying all that they would choose to buy. But quantity demanded makes no assumptions about the availability of the good. Instead, it's the answer to a hypothetical question: How much would households *want* to buy, at a specific price, given real-world limits on their spending power?

Quantity Demanded Depends on *Price*. The price of the good is just one variable among many that influences quantity demanded. But because one of our main purposes in building a supply and demand model is to explain how prices are determined, we try to keep that variable front-and-center in our thinking. This is why for the next few pages we'll assume that all other influences on demand are held constant, so we can explore the relationship between price and quantity demanded.

The Law of Demand

How does a change in price affect quantity demanded? You probably know the answer to this already: When something is more expensive, people tend to buy less of it. This common observation applies to air travel, magazines, education, guitars, and virtually everything else that people buy. For all of these goods and services, price and quantity are *negatively related*: that is, when price rises, quantity demanded falls; when price falls, quantity demanded rises. This negative relationship is observed so regularly in markets that economists call it the *law of demand.*

Law of demand As the price of a good increases, the quantity demanded decreases.

*The **law of demand** states that when the price of a good rises and everything else remains the same, the quantity of the good demanded will fall.*

Read that definition again, and notice the very important words, "everything else remains the same." The law of demand tells us what would happen *if* all the other influences on buyers' choices remained unchanged, and only one influence—the price of the good—changed.

This is an example of a common practice in economics. In the real world, many variables change *simultaneously*. But to understand changes in the economy, we must first understand the effect of each variable *separately*. So we conduct a series of mental experiments in which we ask: "What would happen if this one variable—and only this variable—were to change?" The law of demand is the result of one such mental experiment, in which we imagine that the price of the good changes, but all other influences on quantity demanded remain constant.

The Demand Schedule and the Demand Curve

To make our discussion more concrete, let's look at a specific market: the market for real maple syrup in the United States. In this market, the buyers are all U.S. residents, whereas the sellers (to be considered later) are maple syrup producers in the United States or Canada.

Table 1 shows a hypothetical **demand schedule** for maple syrup in this market. This is *a list of different quantities demanded at different prices, with all other variables that affect the demand decision assumed constant.* For example, the demand schedule tells us that when the price of maple syrup is $2.00 per bottle, the quantity demanded will be 60,000 bottles per month. Notice that the demand schedule obeys the law of demand: As the price of maple syrup increases, the quantity demanded falls.

Now look at Figure 1. It shows a diagram that will appear again and again in your study of economics. In the figure, each price-and-quantity combination in Table 1 is represented by a point. For example, point *A* represents the price $4.00 and quantity 40,000, while point *B* represents the pair $2.00 and 60,000. When we connect all of these points with a line, we obtain the famous *demand curve*, labeled with a *D* in the figure.

> *The **market demand curve** (or just **demand curve**) shows the relationship between the price of a good and the quantity demanded, holding constant all other variables that influence demand. Each point on the curve shows the total quantity that buyers would choose to buy at a specific price.*

Notice that the demand curve in Figure 1—like virtually all demand curves—*slopes downward*. This is just a graphical representation of the law of demand.

> *The law of demand tells us that demand curves virtually always slope downward.*

Shifts vs. Movements Along the Demand Curve

Markets are affected by a variety of events. Some events will cause us to *move along* the demand curve; others will cause the entire demand curve to *shift*. It is crucial to distinguish between these two very different types of effects.

Let's go back to Figure 1. There, you can see that when

Demand schedule A list showing the quantities of a good that consumers would choose to purchase at different prices, with all other variables held constant.

Market demand curve The graphical depiction of a demand schedule; a curve showing the quantity of a good or service demanded at various prices, with all other variables held constant.

Price (per Bottle)	Quantity Demanded (Bottles per Month)
$1.00	75,000
2.00	60,000
3.00	50,000
4.00	40,000
5.00	35,000

TABLE 1
Demand Schedule for Maple Syrup in the United States

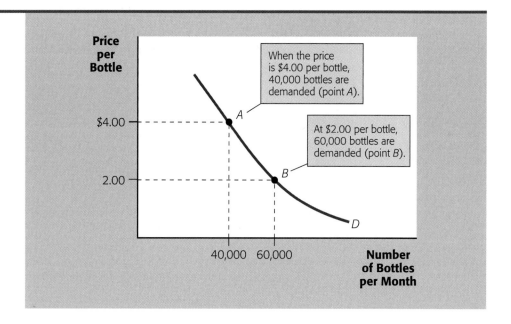

FIGURE 1
The Demand Curve

In Figure 1:

Price per Bottle

When the price is $4.00 per bottle, 40,000 bottles are demanded (point A).

At $2.00 per bottle, 60,000 bottles are demanded (point B).

$4.00

2.00

A

B

D

40,000   60,000

Number of Bottles per Month

the price of maple syrup rises from $2.00 to $4.00 per bottle, the number of bottles demanded falls from 60,000 to 40,000. This is a movement *along* the demand curve, from point *B* to point *A*. In general,

> *a change in the price of a good causes a movement* along *the demand curve.*

In Figure 1, a *fall* in price would cause us to move *rightward* along the demand curve (from point *A* to point *B*), and a *rise* in price would cause us to move *leftward* along the demand curve (from *B* to *A*).

Remember, though, that when we draw a demand curve, we assume all other variables that might influence demand are *held constant* at some particular value. For example, the demand curve in Figure 1 might have been drawn to give us quantity demanded at each price when average household income in the United States remains constant at, say, $40,000 per year.

But suppose average income increases to $50,000? With more income, we'd expect households to buy more of *most* things, including real maple syrup. This is illustrated in Table 2. At the original income level, households would choose to buy 60,000 bottles of maple syrup at $2.00 per bottle. But after income rises, they would choose to buy more at that price—80,000 bottles, according to Table 2. A similar change would occur at any other price for maple syrup: After income rises, households would choose to buy more than before. In other words, the rise in income *changes the entire relationship between price and quantity demanded*. We now have a *new* demand curve.

Figure 2 plots the new demand curve from the quantities in the third column of Table 2. The new demand curve lies to the *right* of the old curve. For example, at a price of $2.00, quantity demanded increases from 60,000 bottles on the old curve (point *B*) to 80,000 bottles on the *new* demand curve (point *C*). As you can see, the rise in household income has *shifted* the demand curve to the right.

Price (per Bottle)	Original Quantity Demanded (Bottles per Month)	New Quantity Demanded After Increase in Income (Bottles per Month)	
$1.00	75,000	95,000	**TABLE 2**
2.00	60,000	80,000	**Increase in Demand for Maple**
3.00	50,000	70,000	**Syrup in the United States**
4.00	40,000	60,000	
5.00	35,000	55,000	

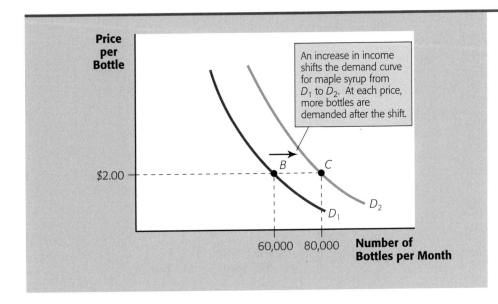

FIGURE 2
A Shift of the Demand Curve

More generally,

> *a change in any variable that affects demand—except for the good's price—causes the demand curve to shift.*

If buyers choose to buy a greater quantity at any price, the demand curve shifts *rightward*. If they decide to buy a smaller quantity at any price, the demand curve shifts *leftward*.

Factors That Shift the Demand Curve

Let's take a closer look at what might cause a change in demand (a shift of the demand curve). Keep in mind that for now, we're exploring *one factor at a time*, always keeping *all other determinants of demand constant*.

Income. In Figure 2, an increase in income shifted the demand for maple syrup to the right. In fact, a rise in income has the same effect on the demand for *most* goods. We call these **normal goods**. Housing, automobiles, health club memberships, and

Income The amount that a person or firm earns over a particular period.

Normal good A good that people demand more of as their income rises.

DANGEROUS CURVES

"Change in Quantity Demanded" vs. "Change in Demand." Language is important when discussing demand. The term *quantity demanded* means a *particular amount* that buyers would choose to buy at a specific price. It's a number represented by a single point on a demand curve. *Demand*, by contrast, means the *entire relationship* between price and quantity demanded, and is represented by the entire demand curve.

For this reason, when a change in the price of a good moves us *along* a demand curve, we call it a **change in quantity demanded**. For example, in Figure 1, the movement from point *A* to point *B* is an *increase* in quantity demanded. This is a change from one number (40,000 bottles) to another (60,000 bottles).

When something *other* than the price changes, causing the entire demand curve to shift, we call it a **change in demand**. In Figure 2, for example, the shift in the curve would be called an *increase in demand*.

Change in quantity demanded A movement along a demand curve in response to a change in price.

Change in demand A shift of a demand curve in response to a change in some variable other than price.

Inferior good A good that people demand less of as their income rises.

Wealth The total value of everything a person or firm owns, at a point in time, minus the total value of everything owed.

Substitute A good that can be used in place of some other good and that fulfills more or less the same purpose.

real maple syrup are all examples of normal goods.

But not all goods are normal. For some goods—called **inferior goods**—a rise in income would *decrease* demand—shifting the demand curve *leftward*. Regular-grade ground chuck is a good example. It's a cheap source of protein, but not as high in quality as sirloin. With higher income, households could more easily afford better types of meat—ground sirloin or steak, for example. As a result, higher incomes would cause the demand for ground chuck to decrease. For similar reasons, we might expect that Greyhound bus tickets (in contrast to airline tickets) and single-ply paper towels (in contrast to two-ply) are inferior goods.

A rise in income will increase *the demand for a* normal *good, and* decrease *the demand for an* inferior *good.*

Wealth. Your **wealth** at any point in time is the total value of everything you *own* (cash, bank accounts, stocks, bonds, real estate or any other valuable property) minus the total dollar amount you *owe* (home mortgage, credit card debt, auto loan, student loan, and so on). Although income and wealth are different (see the nearby Dangerous Curves box), they have similar effects on demand. Increases in wealth among buyers—because of an increase in the value of their stocks or bonds, for example—gives them more funds with which to purchase goods and services. As you might expect,

an increase in wealth will increase *demand (shift the curve rightward) for a normal good, and* decrease *demand (shift the curve leftward) for an inferior good.*

Prices of Related Goods. A **substitute** is a good that can be used in place of another good and that fulfills more or less the same purpose. For example, many people use real maple syrup to sweeten their pancakes, but they could use a number of other things instead: honey, sugar, jam, or *artificial* maple syrup. Each of these can be considered a substitute for real maple syrup.

When the price of a substitute rises, people will choose to buy *more* of the good itself. For example, when the price of jam rises, some jam users will switch to maple syrup, and the demand for maple syrup will increase. In general,

a rise in the price of a substitute increases the demand for a good, shifting the demand curve to the right.

Of course, if the price of a substitute falls, we have the opposite result: Demand for the original good decreases, shifting its demand curve to the left.

There are countless examples in which a change in a substitute's price affects demand for a good. A rise in the price of postage stamps would increase the demand for electronic mail. A drop in the rental price of videos would decrease the demand for movies at theaters. In each of these cases, we assume that the price of the substitute is the only price that is changing.

A **complement** is the opposite of a substitute: It's used *together with* the good we are interested in. Pancake mix is a complement to maple syrup, since these two goods are used frequently in combination. If the price of pancake mix rises, some consumers will switch to other breakfasts—bacon and eggs, for example—that *don't* include maple syrup. The demand for maple syrup will decrease.

Income vs. Wealth It's easy to confuse *income* with *wealth*, because both are measured in dollars and both are sources of funds that can be spent on goods and services. But they are not the same thing. Your income is how much you earn *over a period of time* (such as, $20 *per hour*, $3,500 *per month*, or $40,000 *per year*). Your wealth, by contrast, is the value of what you *own* minus the value of what you *owe* at a *moment in time*. (Such as, on December 31, 2005, the value of what you own is $12,000, but the value of what you owe is $9,000, so you have $3,000 in wealth.)

To help you see the difference: suppose you get a good job after you graduate, but you have very little in the bank, and you still have large, unpaid student loans. Then you'd have a moderate-to-high *income* (what you earn at your job each period), but your wealth would be negative (since what you would *owe* is greater than what you *own*).

DANGEROUS CURVES

Complement A good that is used *together with* some other good.

> *A rise in the price of a complement decreases the demand for a good, shifting the demand curve to the left.*

For this reason, we'd expect a higher price for automobiles to decrease the demand for gasoline. (To test yourself: How would a lower price for milk affect the demand for breakfast cereal?)

Population. As the population increases in an area, the number of buyers will ordinarily increase as well, and the demand for a good will increase. The growth of the U.S. population over the last 50 years has been an important reason (but not the only reason) for rightward shifts in the demand curves for food, rental apartments, telephones, and many other goods and services.

Expected Price. If buyers expect the price of maple syrup to rise next month, they may choose to purchase more *now* to stock up before the price hike, an increase in demand. If people expect the price to drop, they may postpone buying, hoping to take advantage of the lower price later.

> *In many markets, an expectation that price will rise in the future shifts the current demand curve rightward, while an expectation that price will fall shifts the current demand curve leftward.*

Expected price changes are especially important in the markets for financial assets such as stocks and bonds and in the market for real estate. People want to buy more stocks, bonds, and real estate when they think their prices will rise in the near future. This shifts the demand curves for these items to the right.

Tastes. Suppose we know the number of buyers in the United States, their expectations about the future price of maple syrup, the prices of all related goods, and the average levels of income and wealth. Do we have all the information we need to draw the demand curve for maple syrup? Not really. Because we do not yet know how consumers *feel* about maple syrup. How many of them eat breakfast? Of these, how many eat pancakes or waffles? How often? How many of them *like* maple syrup, and how much do they like it? And what about all of the other goods and services competing for consumers' dollars: How do buyers feel about *them*?

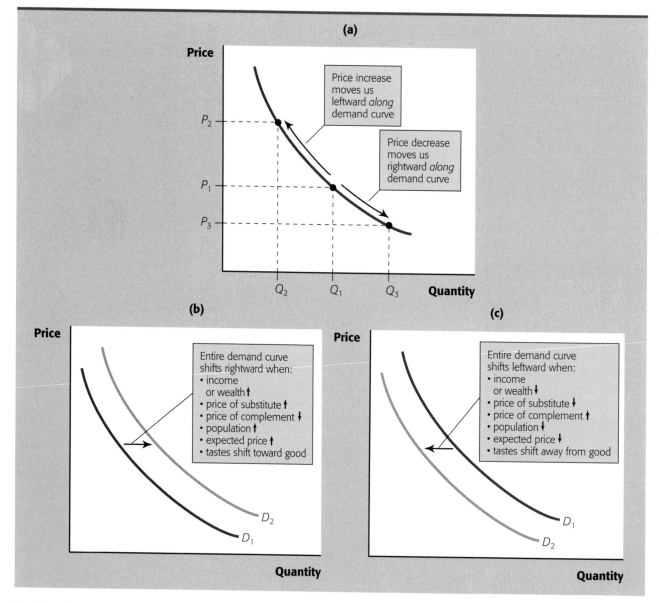

(a)

Price increase moves us leftward *along* demand curve

Price decrease moves us rightward *along* demand curve

(b)

Entire demand curve shifts rightward when:
• income or wealth↑
• price of substitute↑
• price of complement↓
• population↑
• expected price↑
• tastes shift toward good

(c)

Entire demand curve shifts leftward when:
• income or wealth↓
• price of substitute↓
• price of complement↑
• population↓
• expected price↓
• tastes shift away from good

FIGURE 3
Movements Along and
Shifts of the Demand Curve

The questions could go on and on, pinpointing various characteristics about buyers that influence their attitudes toward maple syrup. The approach of economics is to lump all of these characteristics of buyers together and call them, simply, *tastes*. Economists are sometimes interested in where these tastes come from or what makes them change. But for the most part, economics deals with the *consequences* of a change in tastes, whatever the reason for its occurrence.

When tastes change *toward* a good (people favor it more), demand increases, and the demand curve shifts to the right. When tastes change *away* from a good, demand decreases, and the demand curve shifts to the left. An example of this is the change in tastes away from cigarettes over the past several decades. The cause may have been an aging population, a greater concern about health among people of *all* ages, or successful antismoking advertising. But regardless of the cause, the effect has been to decrease the demand for cigarettes, shifting the demand curve to the left.

Figure 3 summarizes the variables we've discussed that affect the demand side of the market, and how their effects are represented with a demand curve. Notice the important distinction between movements *along* the demand curve and *shifts* of the entire curve.

Keep in mind that other variables, besides those listed in Figure 3, can influence demand. For example, weather can affect the demand for many goods: A rise in temperature can increase the demand for ice cream and decrease the demand for sweaters. Expectations other than the future price can matter too. If buyers expect a recession and fear their incomes may fall, demand may decrease for normal goods *now*, even though current income remains unchanged. Some of these other *shift-variables* for the demand curve will be discussed when they become relevant in a specific application. But we'll always use the same logic we used here: If an event makes buyers want to purchase more or less of a good *at any given price*, it causes the demand curve to shift.

Does Supply Affect Demand? A troubling thought may have occurred to you. Among the variables that shift the demand curve in Figure 3, shouldn't we include the amount of syrup available? Or to put the question another way, doesn't supply influence demand?

No—at least not directly. The demand curve answers a series of hypothetical questions about how much buyers *would like* to buy at each different price. A change in the amount available would not affect the answers, and so can't shift the demand curve. As you'll see later, a change in supply *will* change the *price* of the good, but this causes a movement along—not a shift of—the demand curve.

DANGEROUS CURVES

SUPPLY

When most people hear the word *supply*, their first thought is that it's the amount of something "available," as if this amount were fixed in stone. For example, someone might say, "We can only drill so much oil from the ground," or "There are only so many apartments for rent in this town." And yet, the world's known oil reserves—as well as yearly production of oil—have increased dramatically over the last quarter century, as oil companies have found it worth their while to look harder for oil. Similarly, in most towns and cities, short buildings have been replaced with tall ones, and the number of apartments has increased. Supply, like demand, can change, and the amount of a good supplied in a market depends on the *choices* made by those who produce it.

What governs these choices? We assume that business firms' managers have a goal: to earn the highest profit possible. But they also face constraints. First, in a competitive market, the price they can charge for their product is a *given*—the market price. Second, firms have to pay the *costs* of producing and selling their product. These costs will depend on the production process they use, the prices they must pay for their inputs, and more. A firm's desire for profit, together with the real-world constraints that it faces, determines how much it will choose to sell in any market. Hence, the following definition:

> A *firm's quantity supplied* of a good is the specific amount its managers would choose to sell over some time period, given (1) a particular price for the good; (2) all other constraints on the firm.

Firm's quantity supplied The specific amount a firm would choose to sell over some time period, given (1) a particular price for the good; (2) all other constraints on the firm.

When we add up the selling behavior of all firms in a market, we get a similar definition:

> *Market quantity supplied (often just **quantity supplied**) is the specific amount of a good that* all *sellers in the market would choose to sell over some time period, given (1) a particular price for the good; (2) all other constraints on firms.*

Let's briefly go over the notion of quantity supplied to clarify what it means and doesn't mean.

Quantity Supplied Implies a *Choice*. We assume that the managers of firms have a simple goal—to earn the highest possible profit. But they also face constraints: the specific price they can charge for the good, the cost of any inputs used, and so on. Quantity supplied doesn't tell us the amount of, say, maple syrup that sellers would like to sell *if* they could charge a thousand dollars for each bottle, and *if* they could produce it at zero cost.

Instead, it's the quantity that gives firms the highest possible profits *when* they take account of the constraints presented to them by the real world. Thus, each firm's quantity supplied reflects a *choice* made by its managers. Adding up those choices for all sellers in the market gives us the market quantity supplied.

Quantity Supplied Is *Hypothetical*. Will firms actually be *able* to sell the amount they want to sell at the going price? At this point, we don't know. But the definition makes no assumptions about firms' *ability* to sell the good. Quantity supplied answers the hypothetical question: How much would firms' managers *want* to sell, given the price of the good and all other constraints they must consider.

Quantity Supplied Depends on *Price*. The price of the good is just one variable among many that influences quantity supplied. But—as with demand—we want to keep that variable foremost in our thinking. This is why for the next few pages we'll assume that all other influences on supply are held constant, so we can explore the relationship between price and quantity supplied.

The Law of Supply

How does a change in price affect quantity supplied? When a seller can get a higher price for a good, producing and selling it become more profitable. Producers will devote more resources toward its production—perhaps even pulling resources out of other types of production—so they can sell more of the good in question. For example, a rise in the price of laptop computers will encourage computer makers to shift resources out of the production of other things (such as desktop computers) and toward the production of laptops.

In general, price and quantity supplied are *positively related:* When the price of a good rises, the quantity supplied will rise as well. This relationship between price and quantity supplied is called the law of supply, the counterpart to the law of demand we discussed earlier.

> *The **law of supply** states that when the price of a good rises, and everything else remains the same, the quantity of the good supplied will rise.*

Law of supply As the price of a good increases, the quantity supplied increases.

Once again, notice the very important words "everything else remains the same." Although many other variables influence the quantity of a good supplied, the law of supply tells us what would happen if all of them remained unchanged and only one—the price of the good—changed.

The Supply Schedule and the Supply Curve

Let's continue with our example of the market for maple syrup in the United States. Who are the suppliers in this market? Maple syrup producers are located mostly in the forests of Vermont, upstate New York, and Canada. The market quantity supplied is the amount of syrup all of these producers together would offer for sale at each price for maple syrup in the United States.

Table 3 shows the **supply schedule** for maple syrup—a *list of different quantities supplied at different prices, with all other variables held constant.* As you can see, the supply schedule obeys the law of supply: As the price of maple syrup rises, the quantity supplied rises along with it. But how can this be? After all, maple trees must be about 40 years old before they can be tapped for syrup, so any rise in quantity supplied now or in the near future cannot come from an increase in planting. What, then, causes quantity supplied to rise as price rises?

Price (per Bottle)	Quantity Supplied (Bottles per Month)
$1.00	25,000
2.00	40,000
3.00	50,000
4.00	60,000
5.00	65,000

TABLE 3
Supply Schedule for Maple Syrup in the United States

Supply schedule A list showing the quantities of a good or service that firms would choose to produce and sell at different prices, with all other variables held constant.

Many things. First, with higher prices, firms will find it profitable to tap existing trees more intensively. Second, evaporating and bottling can be done more carefully, so that less maple syrup is spilled and more is available for shipping. Finally, the product can be diverted from other areas and shipped to the United States instead. For example, if the price of maple syrup rises in the United States but not in Canada, producers would shift deliveries away from Canada so they could sell more in the United States.

Now look at Figure 4, which shows a very important curve—the counterpart to the demand curve we drew earlier. In Figure 4, each point represents a price-quantity pair taken from Table 3. For example, point *F* in the figure corresponds to a price of $2.00 per bottle and a quantity of 40,000 bottles per month, while point *G* represents the price-quantity pair $4.00 and 60,000 bottles. Connecting all of these points with a solid line gives us the *supply curve* for maple syrup, labeled with an *S* in the figure.

> *The **market supply curve** (or just **supply curve**) shows the relationship between the price of a good and the quantity supplied, holding constant the values of all other variables that affect supply. Each point on the curve shows the quantity that sellers would choose to sell at a specific price.*

Supply curve A graphical depiction of a supply schedule; a curve showing the quantity of a good or service supplied at various prices, with all other variables held constant.

FIGURE 4
The Supply Curve

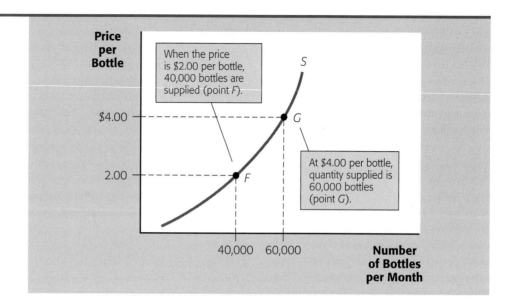

Notice that the supply curve in Figure 4—like all supply curves for goods and services—is *upward sloping*. This is the graphical representation of the law of supply.

> *The law of supply tells us that supply curves slope* upward.

Shifts vs. Movements Along the Supply Curve

As with the demand curve, it's important to distinguish those events that will cause us to *move along* a given supply curve for the good, and those that will cause the entire supply curve to *shift*.

If you look once again at Figure 4, you'll see that if the price of maple syrup rises from $2.00 to $4.00 per bottle, the number of bottles supplied rises from 40,000 to 60,000. This is a movement *along* the supply curve, from point *F* to point *G*. In general,

> *a change in the price of a good causes a movement* along *the supply curve.*

In the figure, a *rise* in price would cause us to move *rightward* along the supply curve (from point *F* to point *G*) and a *fall* in price would move us *leftward* along the curve (from point *G* to point *F*).

But remember that when we draw a supply curve, we assume that all other variables that might influence supply are *held constant* at some particular values. For example, the supply curve in Figure 4 might tell us the quantity supplied at each price when the cost of an important input—transportation from the farm to the point of sale—remains constant.

But suppose the cost of transportation drop. Then, at any given price for maple syrup, firms would find it more profitable to produce and sell it. This is illustrated in Table 4. With the original transportation cost, and a selling price of $4.00 per bottle, firms would choose to sell 60,000 bottles. But after transportation cost falls, they would choose to produce and sell more—80,000 bottles in our example—assuming they could still charge $4.00 per bottle. A similar change would occur for any other

Price (per Bottle)	Original Quantity Supplied (Bottles/Month)	Quantity Supplied After Decrease in Transportation Cost
$1.00	25,000	45,000
2.00	40,000	60,000
3.00	50,000	70,000
4.00	60,000	80,000
5.00	65,000	90,000

TABLE 4
Increase in Supply of Maple Syrup in the United States

price of maple syrup we might imagine: After transportation costs fall, firms would choose to sell more than before. In other words, *the entire relationship between price and quantity supplied has changed*, so we have a *new* supply curve.

Figure 5 plots the new supply curve from the quantities in the third column of Table 4. The new supply curve lies to the *right* of the old one. For example, at a price of $4.00, quantity supplied increases from 60,000 bottles on the old curve (point G) to 80,000 bottles on the *new* supply curve (point J). The drop in the transportation costs has *shifted* the supply curve to the right.

In general,

> *a change in any variable that affects supply—except for the good's price— causes the supply curve to shift.*

If sellers want to sell a greater quantity at any price, the supply curve shifts *rightward*. If sellers would prefer to sell a smaller quantity at any price, the supply curve shifts *leftward*.

"Change in Quantity Supplied" vs. "Change in Supply" As we stressed in our discussion of the demand side of the market, be careful about language when thinking about supply. The term *quantity supplied* means a *particular amount* that sellers would prefer to sell at a particular price. It's a number, represented by a single point on the supply curve. The term *supply*, however, means the *entire relationship* between price and quantity supplied, as represented by the entire supply curve.

For this reason, when the price of the good changes, and we move *along* the supply curve, we have a **change in quantity supplied.** For example, in Figure 4, the movement from point *F* to point *G* is an *increase* in quantity supplied.

When something *other* than the price changes, causing the entire supply curve to shift, we call it a **change in supply.** The shift in Figure 5, for example, would be called an *increase in supply.*

DANGEROUS CURVES

Change in quantity supplied A movement along a supply curve in response to a change in price.

Change in supply A shift of a supply curve in response to some variable other than price.

Factors That Shift the Supply Curve

Let's take a closer look at some of the *causes* of a change in supply (a shift of the supply curve). As always, we're considering *one* variable at a time, keeping all other determinants of supply constant.

Input Prices. In Figure 5, a drop in transportation costs shifted the supply curve for maple syrup to the right. But producers of maple syrup use a variety of other inputs, too: land, maple trees, evaporators, sap pans, labor, glass bottles, bottling machinery, and more. A lower price for any of these means a lower cost of producing and selling maple syrup, making it more profitable. As a result, we would expect producers to shift resources into maple syrup production, causing an increase in supply.

FIGURE 5
A Shift of the Supply Curve

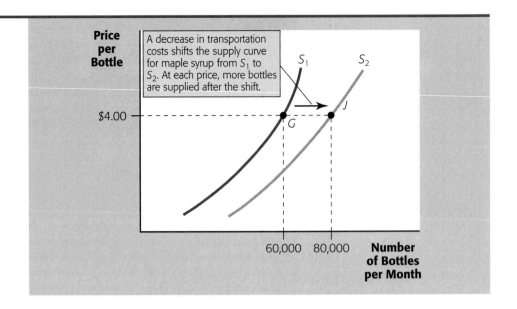

In general,

> *a fall in the price of an input causes an increase in supply, shifting the supply curve to the right. A rise in the price of an input causes a decrease in supply, shifting the supply curve to the left.*

If, for example, the wages of maple syrup workers rose, the supply curve in Figure 5 would shift to the left.

Price of Related Goods. Many firms can switch their production rather easily among several different goods or services, all of which require more or less the same inputs. For example, a dermatology practice can rather easily switch its specialty from acne treatments for the young to wrinkle treatments for the elderly. An automobile producer can—without too much adjustment—switch to producing light trucks. And a maple syrup producer could dry its maple syrup and produce maple *sugar* instead. Or it could even cut down its maple trees and sell maple wood as lumber. Other goods that firms *could* produce are called **alternate goods.**

Alternate goods Other goods that a firm could produce, using some of the same types of inputs as the good in question.

For example, if the price of maple *sugar* rose, then at any given price for maple *syrup*, producers would choose to shift some production from syrup to sugar. This would be a decrease in the supply of maple syrup. Alternatively, if firms already are producing maple sugar, and its price *falls*, the supply of syrup would increase. Remember that we are assuming—as always—that every *other* determinant that affects the supply of maple syrup remains unchanged.

> *When the price of an alternate good rises, the supply curve for the good in question shifts* leftward. *When the price of an alternate falls, the supply curve for the good in question shifts* rightward.

Technology. A *technological advance* in production occurs whenever a firm can produce a given level of output in a new and cheaper way than before. For exam-

ple, the discovery of a surgical procedure called Lasik—in which a laser is
used to reshape the interior of the
cornea rather than the outer surface—
has enabled eye surgeons to correct
their patients' vision with fewer fol-
low-up visits and smaller quantities of
medication than were used with previous procedures. This example is a
technological advance because it en-
ables firms to produce the same output (eye surgery) more cheaply than before.

Does Demand Affect Supply? In the list of variables that shift the supply curve in Figure 6 we've left out the amount that buyers would like to buy. Is this a mistake? Doesn't demand affect supply?

The answer is no—at least, not directly. The supply curve tells us how much sellers *would* choose to sell at alternative prices. Buyers' decisions don't affect this hypothetical quantity, so they cannot shift the supply curve. But—as you'll soon see—buyers *can* affect the price of the good, which in turn affects quantity supplied. But this is a movement *along* the supply curve—not a shift.

DANGEROUS CURVES

In maple syrup production, a technological advance might be a new, more efficient tap that draws more maple syrup from each tree, or a new bottling method
that reduces spillage. Advances like these would reduce the cost of producing maple
syrup, making it more profitable, and producers would want to make and sell more
of it at any price.

In general,

> *cost-saving technological advances increase the supply of a good, shifting
> the supply curve to the right.*

Number of Firms. A change in the number of firms in a market will change the quantity that all sellers together would want to sell at any given price. For example, if—
over time—more people decided to open up maple syrup farms because it was a profitable business, the supply of maple syrup would increase. And if maple syrup farms
began closing down, their number would be reduced and supply would decrease.

> *An increase in the number of sellers—with no other change—shifts the supply
> curve rightward, while a decrease in the number of sellers shifts it leftward.*

Expected Price. Imagine you're the president of Sticky's Maple Syrup, Inc., and
you've determined that the market price of maple syrup—over which you, as an individual seller, have no influence—will rise next month. What would you do? You'd
certainly want to postpone selling your maple syrup until the price is higher, and
profit greater. Therefore, at any given price *now*, you might slow down production,
or just slow down sales by warehousing more of what you produce. If other firms
have similar expectations of a price hike, they'll do the same. Thus, an expectation
of a *future* price hike will decrease supply *in the present.*

Suppose instead you expect the market price to *drop* next month. Then—at any
given price—you'd want to sell more *now*, by stepping up production and even selling out of your inventories. Now, an expected future drop in the price would cause
an increase in supply in the present. In terms of our supply curve:

> *In many markets, an expectation of a* future *price hike* shifts the current
> supply curve *leftward. Similarly, an expectation of a* future *price drop* shifts
> the current supply curve *rightward.*

Changes in Weather and Other Natural Events. Weather conditions are an especially important determinant of the supply of agricultural goods.

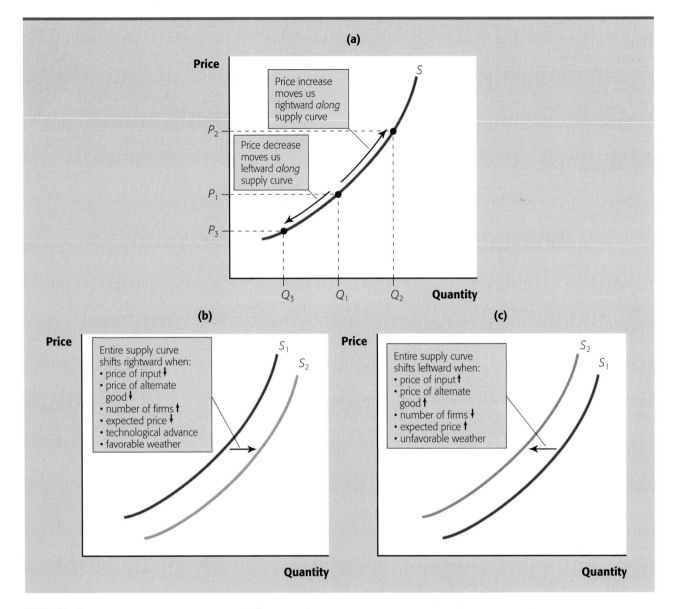

FIGURE 6
Changes in Supply and in Quantity Supplied

Favorable weather *increases crop yields, and causes a* rightward *shift of the supply curve for that crop.* Unfavorable weather *destroys crops and shrinks yields, and shifts the supply curve* leftward.

In addition to bad weather, natural disasters such as fires, hurricanes, and earthquakes can destroy or disrupt the productive capacity of *all* firms in a region. If many sellers of a particular good are located in the affected area, the supply curve for that good will shift leftward. For example, a sudden blight that destroyed many maple trees in Vermont would cause the supply curve to shift leftward in the market we've been analyzing.

Figure 6 summarizes the various factors we've discussed that affect the supply side of the market, and how we illustrate them using a supply curve. But the short list of *shift-variables* for supply is far from exhaustive. For example, a government tax on a good—or a government subsidy paid to producers—will shift the supply curve. So can other government policies, such as environmental and safety regulations. And man-made disasters, such as wars, riots, terrorist attacks, or epidemics, can have the same effects as natural disasters.

Even the *threat* of such events can seriously affect production. In mid-2003, in countries around the world, supply curves for children's toys shifted leftward. The reason? In China—where most of the world's toys are produced—tens of thousands of workers stayed away from their jobs for weeks, fearful of catching SARS (Severe Acute Respiratory Syndrome).

Some of the other shift-variables that shift supply curves will be discussed as they become relevant in future chapters. The basic principle, however, is always the same: Anything that makes sellers want to sell more or less *at any given price* will shift the supply curve.

PUTTING SUPPLY AND DEMAND TOGETHER

What happens when buyers and sellers, each having the desire and the ability to trade, come together in a market? The two sides of the market certainly have different agendas. Buyers would like to pay the lowest possible price, while sellers would like to charge the highest possible price. Is there chaos when they meet, with buyers and sellers endlessly chasing after each other or endlessly bargaining for advantage, so that trade never takes place? A casual look at the real world suggests not. In most markets, most of the time, there is order and stability in the encounters between buyers and sellers. In most cases, prices do not fluctuate wildly from moment to moment, but seem to hover around a stable value. Even when this stability is short-lived—lasting only a day, an hour, or even a minute in some markets—for this short-time the market seems to be at rest. Whenever we study a market, therefore, we look for this state of rest—a price and quantity at which the market will settle, at least for a while.

Economists use the word *equilibrium* when referring to a state of rest. When a market is in equilibrium, both the price of the good and the quantity bought and sold have settled into a state of rest. More formally,

> the **equilibrium price** and **equilibrium quantity** are values for price and quantity in the market that, once achieved, will remain constant—unless and until the supply curve or the demand curve shifts.

Equilibrium price The market price that, once achieved, remains constant until either the demand curve or supply curve shifts.

Equilibrium quantity The market quantity bought and sold per period that, once achieved, remains constant until either the demand curve or supply curve shifts.

What will be the price of maple syrup in the United States? And how much will people actually buy each month? We can rephrase these questions as follows: What is the *equilibrium* price of maple syrup, and what is the *equilibrium* quantity of maple syrup that will be bought and sold? These are precisely the questions that the supply and demand model is designed to answer.

Look at Figure 7, which combines the supply and demand curves for maple syrup. We'll use Figure 7 to find the equilibrium price in this market through the process of elimination.

Let's first ask what would happen if the price was $1.00 per bottle. At this price, buyers would want to buy 75,000 bottles each month, while sellers would offer to sell only 25,000. There would be an **excess demand** of 50,000 bottles. What would happen? Buyers would compete with each other to get more maple syrup than was

Excess demand At a given price, the excess of quantity demanded over quantity supplied.

FIGURE 7
Market Equilibrium

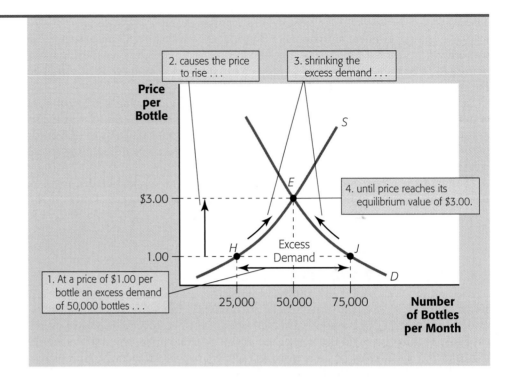

available, and would offer to pay a higher price rather than do without. The price would then rise.

We conclude that a price of $1.00—or *any* price we might imagine that is less than $3.00—cannot be an equilibrium price. Why not? As we've just seen, if the price starts below $3.00, it would start rising—*not* because the supply curve or the demand curve had shifted, but from natural forces within the market itself. This directly contradicts our definition of equilibrium price.

At this point, we should ask another question: If the price were initially $1.00, would it ever *stop* rising? Yes. Since excess demand is the reason for the price to rise, the process will stop when the excess demand is gone. And as you can see in Figure 8, the rise in price *shrinks* the excess demand in two ways. First, as price rises, buyers demand a smaller quantity—a leftward movement along the demand curve. Second, sellers increase supply to a larger quantity—a rightward movement along the supply curve. Finally, when the price reaches $3.00 per bottle, the excess demand is gone and the price stops rising.

This logic tells us that $3.00 is an *equilibrium* price in this market—a value that won't change as long as the supply and demand curves stay put. But is it the *only* equilibrium price? We've shown that any price *below* $3.00 is not an equilibrium, but what about a price *greater* than $3.00? Let's see.

Suppose the price of maple syrup was, say, $5.00 per bottle. Figure 8 shows us that, at this price, quantity supplied would be 65,000 bottles per month, while quantity demanded would be only 35,000 bottles—an **excess supply** of 30,000 bottles. Sellers would compete with each other to sell more maple syrup than buyers wanted to buy, and the price would fall. Thus, $5.00 cannot be the equilibrium price.

Moreover, the decrease in price would move us along both the supply curve (leftward) and the demand curve (rightward). As these movements continued, the

Excess supply At a given price, the excess of quantity supplied over quantity demanded.

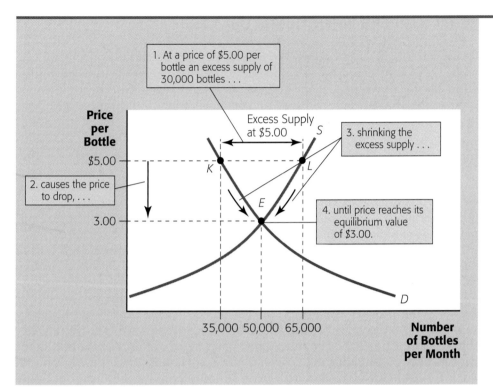

FIGURE 8
Excess Supply and Price Adjustment

excess supply of maple syrup would shrink until it disappeared, once again, at a price of $3.00 per bottle. Our conclusion: If the price happens to be above $3.00, it will fall to $3.00 and then stop changing.

You can see that is the equilibrium price—and the *only* equilibrium price—in this market. Moreover, at this price, sellers would want to sell 50,000 bottles—the same quantity that households would want to buy. So, when price comes to rest at $3.00, quantity comes to rest at 50,000 per month—the *equilibrium quantity*.

No doubt, you have noticed that $3.00 happens to be the price at which the supply and demand curves cross. This leads us to an easy, graphical technique for locating our equilibrium:

> To *find the equilibrium price and quantity in a competitive market, draw the supply and demand curves. The equilibrium price and equilibrium quantity can then be found on the vertical and horizontal axes, respectively, at the point where the supply and demand curves cross.*

This graphical insight helps make the logic of equilibrium even more apparent. In equilibrium, the market is operating on *both* the supply curve *and* the demand curve. Therefore, at the going price, quantity demanded and quantity supplied are equal. There are no dissatisfied buyers unable to find goods they want to purchase, nor are there any frustrated sellers unable to sell goods they want to sell. Indeed, this is why $3.00 is the equilibrium price. It's the only price that creates consistency between what buyers choose to buy and sellers choose to sell.

But we don't expect a market to stay at any particular equilibrium forever, as you're about to see.

WHAT HAPPENS WHEN THINGS CHANGE?

Remember that in order to draw the supply and demand curves in the first place, we had to assume particular values for all the other variables—besides price—that affect demand and supply. If one of these variables changes, then either the supply curve or the demand curve will shift, and our equilibrium will change as well. Let's look at some examples.

Income Rises, Causing an Increase in Demand

In Figure 9, point *E* shows an initial equilibrium in the U.S. market for maple syrup, with an equilibrium price of $3.00 per bottle, and equilibrium quantity of 50,000 bottles per month. Suppose that the incomes of buyers rise because the U.S. economy recovers rapidly from a recession. We know that income is one of the shift-variables in the demand curve (but not the supply curve). We also can reason that maple syrup is a *normal good,* so the rise in income will cause the demand curve to shift rightward. What happens then?

The old price—$3.00—is no longer the equilibrium price. How do we know? Because if the price *did* remain at $3.00, quantity demanded would exceed quantity supplied—an excess demand that would drive the price upward. The new equilibrium—at point *E'*—is the new intersection point of the curves *after* the shift in the demand curve. Comparing the original equilibrium at point *E* with the new one at point *E'*, we find that the shift in demand has caused the equilibrium price to rise (from $3.00 to $4.00) and the equilibrium quantity to rise as well (from 50,000 to 60,000 bottles per month).

Notice, too, that in moving from point *E* to point *E'*, we move *along* the supply curve. That is, a shift of the demand curve has caused a movement along he supply curve. Why is this? The demand shift causes the *price* to rise, and a rise in price always causes a movement *along* the supply curve. But the supply curve itself does not shift, because none of the variables that affect sellers—other than the price of the good—has changed.

In this example, the equilibrium price and quantity changed because income rose. But *any* event that shifted the demand curve rightward would cause both equilibrium price and quantity to rise. For example, if tastes changed in favor of maple syrup, or a substitute good like jam rose in price, or a complementary good like pancake mix became cheaper, the demand curve for

The Endless Loop of Erroneous Logic At some point, you might find yourself caught in an endless loop of erroneous logic about supply and demand. In our example in which income rises and demand increases, you might reason as follows: "The rise in income causes an increase in demand, which causes the price to rise. But a higher price increases supply. Higher supply, in turn, causes the price to fall. But then, when the price falls, demand will increase . . ." and so on. In this logic, the price bobs up and down and never stops moving.

What's the mistake here? The first sentence is indeed correct. But the second sentence—and all that follows from it—is wrong. The second sentence states that "a higher price increases supply," when it *should* say that a higher price increases *quantity supplied.*

This is more than just semantics. An "increase in supply" would be a rightward *shift* of the supply curve, which is what is implied in the incorrect statement. But look again at Figure 9. There is no supply shift, because none of the shift-variables for the supply curve have changed. Only *price* has changed, and that causes a movement *along* the supply curve. So a correct second sentence would be, "And the higher price increases quantity supplied until the new equilibrium is reached, at which point the price stops rising." End of story.

You can avoid this mistake by remembering that *a shift of one curve causes a movement along the other curve to the new equilibrium point.*

maple syrup would shift rightward, just as it did in Figure 9. So, we can summarize our findings as follows:

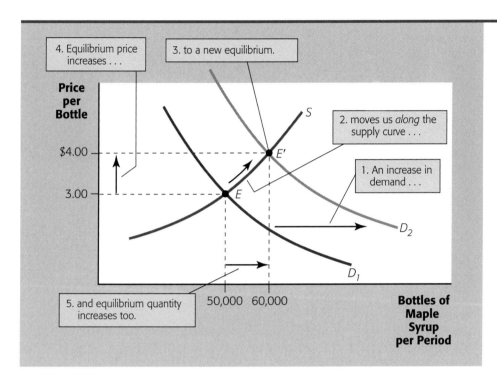

FIGURE 9
A Shift in Demand and a New Equilibrium

4. Equilibrium price increases . . .

3. to a new equilibrium.

Price per Bottle

2. moves us *along* the supply curve . . .

1. An increase in demand . . .

5. and equilibrium quantity increases too.

$4.00

3.00

50,000 60,000

E'

E

S

D_2

D_1

Bottles of Maple Syrup per Period

A rightward shift in the demand curve causes a rightward movement along the supply curve. Equilibrium price and equilibrium quantity both rise.

An Ice Storm Causes a Decrease in Supply

In January 1998, New England and Quebec were struck by a severe ice storm. Hundreds of thousands of maple trees were downed, and many more were damaged. In Vermont alone, 10 percent of the maple trees were destroyed. How did this affect the market for maple syrup?

As you've learned, weather is a shift-variable for the supply curve.

Figure 10 shows how the ice storm affected this market. Initially, the supply curve for maple syrup was S_1, with the market in equilibrium at Point *E*. After the ice storm, the supply curve shifted leftward—say, to S_2. The result: a rise in the equilibrium price of maple syrup (from $3.00 to $5.00 in the figure) and a fall in the equilibrium quantity (from 50,000 to 35,000 bottles).

Do Curves Shift Up and Down? Or Right and Left? When describing an increase in demand or supply, it's tempting to substitute "upward" for "rightward," and to substitute "downward" for "leftward" when describing a decrease in demand or supply. But be careful! While this interchangeable language works for the demand curve, it does *not* work for the supply curve. To prove this to yourself, look at Figure 6. There you can see that a rightward shift of the supply curve (an increase in supply) is also a *downward* shift of the curve. In later chapters, it will sometimes make sense to describe shifts as upward or downward. For now, it's best to avoid these terms and stick with *rightward* and *leftward*.

DANGEROUS CURVES

In this case, it was an ice storm that shifted the supply curve leftward. But suppose, instead, that the wages of maple syrup workers had increased or that evaporators became more expensive or that some maple syrup producers went out of business and sold their farms to housing developers. Any of these changes would have

FIGURE 10
**A Shift of Supply and
a New Equilibrium**

*An ice storm causes supply to
decrease from S₁ to S₂. At the
old equilibrium price of $3.00,
there is now an excess demand.
As a result, the price increases
until excess demand is eliminated at point E'. In the new
equilibrium, quantity demanded
again equals quantity supplied.
The price is higher, and fewer
bottles are produced and sold.*

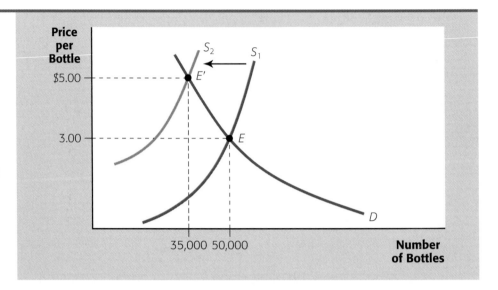

caused the supply curve for maple syrup to shift leftward, increased the equilibrium
price, and decreased the equilibrium quantity.

More generally,

> *any change that shifts the supply curve leftward in a market will increase the
> equilibrium price and decrease the equilibrium quantity in that market.*

Handheld PCs in 2003: Both Curves Shift

Since shifts in supply and demand work the same way in any market, let's leave maple
syrup for now and look at a different market: that for handheld computers like the
Palm, HP Ipaq, and Sony Clie. In early 2003, prices for these devices dropped. For
example, the price of both Palm's high-end Tungsten T model and Sony's new Clie
NX60V dropped from $500 to $400. At the same time, the number of handheld PCs
sold dropped—from 3.33 million (in the last quarter of 2002) to 2.45 million (first
quarter of 2003). What explains these movements in price and quantity?

*In 2003, a decrease in demand and an increase
in supply caused prices of handheld PCs to fall.*

To answer this question, we'll use the supply and demand
model. In doing so, we're assuming this is a perfectly competitive market, in which each producer sells a standardized product and treats the market price as a given. This is not too far
off: Product differences among manufacturers are rather modest, and to stay in business, each producer must charge a price
within a rather narrow *range*. Our assumption of perfect competition is, as in most cases, a useful approximation.

Figure 11 shows the market supply and demand curves for
handheld PCs in late 2002, labeled S_{2002} and D_{2002}, respectively.
Point *A* shows the equilibrium at that time, with an average
price of $500 and a quantity of 3.33 million PCs per quarter.

Now, what happened in this market between late 2002 and
mid-2003? Let's start with demand, where three factors combined to shift the demand curve leftward.

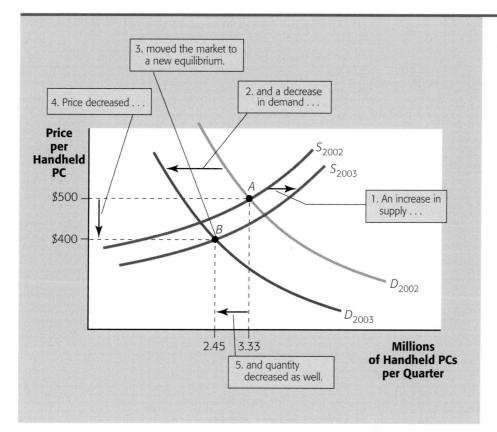

FIGURE 11
Changes in the Market for Handheld PCs

3. moved the market to a new equilibrium.

4. Price decreased . . .

2. and a decrease in demand . . .

Price per Handheld PC

S_{2002}

S_{2003}

$500

A

1. An increase in supply . . .

B

$400

D_{2002}

D_{2003}

2.45   3.33

Millions of Handheld PCs per Quarter

5. and quantity decreased as well.

First, by early 2003, handheld PCs had already been on the market for a few years. Most of those who regarded them as useful had already bought one. Since these first-time buyers had been behind the high demand in earlier periods, their withdrawal from the market amounted to a decrease in demand. (*The shift-variable: a change in market preferences for new handhelds*.)

Second, uncertainties caused by continued slow growth in the U.S. and European economies, and a looming U.S. war with Iraq, caused consumers to worry about their future income. These kinds of worries especially decrease the demand for goods that are relatively expensive and not considered necessities, such as handheld PCs. (*Shift-variable: a change in expectations*, in this case, about future income.)

Finally, in early 2003, cell phones that incorporated some of the key features of handheld PCs were becoming cheaper. Many of those who *would* have bought a handheld PC decided to purchase a cell phone with limited PC-capabilities instead. (*Shift-variable: a decrease in the price of a substitute good*.)

Any one of these three factors, by itself, would have caused a leftward shift in the demand curve for handhelds. When they all occurred together, the result was an even *larger* shift to the left. This is illustrated in Figure 11 by the shift from D_{2002} to D_{2003}.

What about supply? Throughout the early 2000s, new firms—at least, new to handheld PCs—entered the market. And entry continued through 2003, as Dell, Gateway, and Matsushita brought their first handhelds to the market. The entry of new firms increased the number of handhelds that would be offered for sale at any price, shifting the supply curve rightward (from S_{2002} to S_{2003} in the figure). (*Shift-variable: an increase in the number of firms.*)

As you can see in Figure 11, the result of all these events was a change in the market equilibrium—from point *A* to point *B*. In our diagram, the equilibrium price has fallen—from $500 to $400. This should not surprise you: *Either* a leftward shift in the demand curve *or* a rightward shift of the supply curve, by itself, would cause the price to drop. When these two shifts occur together, price drops even more.

But what about equilibrium quantity? Here, the two shifts work in *opposite* directions. The leftward shift in demand works to decrease equilibrium quantity, while the rightward shift in supply tends to increase equilibrium quantity. Figure 11 illustrates what *actually* happened: a decrease in quantity from 3.33 million to 2.45 million units sold. So we know that, over this period, the demand shift was *greater* than the supply shift.

To prove this to yourself, draw a graph that shows a leftward demand shift that is *smaller* than a rightward supply shift. What happens to equilibrium quantity in your diagram? Then draw a graph that shows equilibrium quantity remaining unchanged. If you draw these cases, you'll see that while the price *must* fall when the curves shift in the directions shown in Figure 11, the quantity could either rise, fall, or remain the same; it's *ambiguous*, unless we know the relative *sizes* of the shifts.

This example involves just *one* possible combination of directions that the two curves could shift. But remember that a leftward or rightward shift of one curve can occur together with either a leftward or rightward shift of the other curve. Table 5 lists all the possible combinations. It also shows what happens to equilibrium price and quantity in each case, and when the result is ambiguous (a question mark). For example, the top left entry tells us that when both the supply and demand curves shift rightward, the equilibrium *quantity* will always rise, but the equilibrium price could rise, fall or remain unchanged, depending on the relative *size* of the shifts.

The most general conclusion we can draw from this table is the following:

When just one *curve shifts, and we know the direction of the shift, we can determine the direction that* both *equilibrium price* and *quantity will move.*

When both *curves shift, and we know the* directions *of the shifts, we can determine the direction for* either *price or quantity—but not both. The direction of the other will depend on which curve shifts by more.*

Do *not* try to memorize the entries in Table 5. Instead, remember the advice in Chapter 1: to study economics actively, rather than passively. This would be a good time to put down the book, pick up a pencil and paper, and see whether you can draw a graph to illustrate each of the nine possible results in the table. When you see a question mark (?) for an ambiguous result, determine which shift would have to be greater for the variable to rise or to fall.

THE THREE-STEP PROCESS

In this chapter, we built a model—a supply and demand model—and then used it to analyze price changes in several markets. You may not have noticed it, but we took three distinct key steps as the chapter proceeded. Economists take these same three steps to answer almost *any* question about the economy. Why? Because they are so

	Increase in Demand (Rightward Shift)	No Change in Demand	Decrease in Demand (Leftward Shift)	
• **Increase in Supply** (Rightward Shift)	$P?\ Q\uparrow$	$P\downarrow\ Q\uparrow$	$P\downarrow\ Q?$	**TABLE 5**
• **No Change in Supply**	$P\uparrow\ Q\uparrow$	No change in P or Q	$P\downarrow\ Q\downarrow$	**Effect of Supply and Demand Shifts on Equilibrium Price (P) and Quantity (Q)**
• **Decrease in Supply** (Leftward Shift)	$P\uparrow\ Q?$	$P\uparrow\ Q\downarrow$	$P?\ Q\downarrow$	

effective in cutting through the chaos and confusion of the economy and helping us see how things really work.

In this book, we'll focus on this *three-step process,* which forms the core of economists' unique methodology. And we'll start right now by listing and discussing all three steps.

Key Step 1—Characterize the Market: *Decide which market or markets best suit the problem being analyzed, and identify the decision makers (buyers and sellers) who interact there.*

In economics, we make sense of the very complex, real-world economy by viewing it as a collection of *markets*. Each of these markets involves a group of *decision makers*—buyers and sellers—who have the potential to trade with each other. At the very beginning of any economic analysis, we must decide which market or markets to look at and how these markets should be *defined*.

To define a market, we decide how to view (a) the thing being traded (such as maple syrup); (b) the decision makers in the market (such as maple syrup producers in New England and Canada selling to U.S. households); and (c) the trading environment (such as our decision in this chapter to view the markets for maple syrup and handheld PCs as perfectly competitive).

Often, especially in microeconomics, we may want to define the specific *goals* and *constraints* of those who trade in the market. In the supply and demand model, for example, we assume that the goal of sellers is to earn the highest possible profit, but they are constrained by the market price they can charge, and the costs of production they must pay. Buyers are assumed to maximize their utility—their well-being or satisfaction. But they too are constrained by the market price they must pay, and by the limited funds at their disposal.

In addition to having goals, decision makers also face constraints. Firms are constrained by their production technology, the prices they must pay for their inputs, and the price they can get for their output. Households are constrained by the prices they must pay for their purchases and by their limited incomes. Government agencies are constrained by the prices of the things they buy and by limited budgets. And even entire nations, as a whole, are constrained in their choices by the resources at their disposal.

Key Step 2—Find the Equilibrium: *Describe the conditions necessary for equilibrium in the market, and a method for determining that equilibrium.*

Once we've defined a market, and put buyers and sellers together, we look for the point at which the market will come to rest—the equilibrium. In this chapter, we used supply and demand to find the equilibrium price and quantity in a perfectly competitive market, but this is just one example of how economists apply Step 2.

Key Step 3—What Happens When Things Change: Explore how events or government policies change the market equilibrium.

Once you've found the equilibrium, the next step is to ask how different events will *change* it. In this chapter, for example, we explored how an ice storm affected the equilibrium price and quantity for maple syrup, and how several events altered the equilibrium price and quantity for handheld PCs.

Do economists really follow this same procedure to analyze almost *any* economic problem? Indeed they do. They use it to answer important *microeconomic* questions. Why does government intervention to lower the price of a good (such as apartment rents) often backfire and sometimes harm the very people it was designed to help? Why do some people earn salaries that are hundreds of times higher than others? How will resources be reallocated to enable the United States to fight the war on terrorism that it declared in September 2001? If you're studying *micro*economics, you'll soon see how the three-step process helps us answer all of those questions.

Economists also use the procedure to address important *macroeconomic* questions. What caused the recession that began in early 2001, and what can we do to prevent recessions in the future? Why has the United States experienced such low inflation in recent years, and how long can we expect our recent good fortune to continue? How will concern about domestic security affect our standard of living over the next year? . . . over the next decade?

In *macro*economics, the three steps help us answer once again.

In this book, we'll be taking these three key steps again and again, every time we want to understand an aspect of the economy. From now on, you'll recognize these steps, because we'll be calling them to your attention as we use them.

To help you keep track you'll sometimes see an icon in the margins of this book when one or more of the steps is being used. If you pay attention to them, you will soon find yourself thinking like an economist.

USING THE THEORY
College Administrators Make a Costly Mistake

In the late 1980s, several East Coast colleges purchased expensive equipment that would enable them to switch rapidly from oil to natural gas as a source of heat. The idea was to protect the colleges from a sudden rise in oil prices, like the one they had suffered a decade earlier.

Finally, an event occurred that gave the colleges a chance to put their new equipment to use: In the fall of 1990, Iraq invaded Kuwait. As oil prices skyrocketed, the colleges switched from burning oil to burning natural gas. The college administrators expected big savings on their energy bills. But they were in for a shock. When they received the bills from their local utilities, they found that the price of natural gas—like the price of oil—had risen sharply. As a result, they did not save much in energy costs at all, certainly not enough to justify the costly switching equipment they had purchased. Many of these administrators were angry at the utility compa-

© BOB KRIST/CORBIS

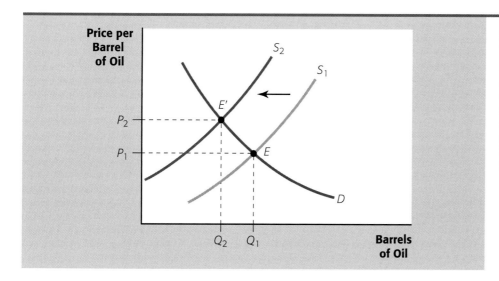

FIGURE 12
The Market for Oil

Before the Iraqi invasion of Kuwait, the oil market was in equilibrium at point E. The invasion and the resulting embargo on Iraqi oil decreased supply to S_2. Price increased to P_2, and the quantity exchanged fell to Q_2.

nies and accused them of price gouging. Iraq's invasion of Kuwait, they reasoned, had not affected natural gas supplies at all, so there was no reason for the price of natural gas to rise.

Were the college administrators right? Was this just an example of price gouging by the utility companies who were taking advantage of an international crisis to increase their profits? A simple supply and demand analysis will give us the answer. More specifically, it will enable us to answer two questions: (1) Why did Iraq's invasion of Kuwait cause the price of oil to rise, and (2) Why did the price of natural gas rise as well?

Figure 12 shows supply and demand curves in one of the markets relevant to our analysis: the market for crude oil. In this market, oil producers—including those in Iraq and Kuwait—sell to American buyers. Before the invasion, the market was in equilibrium at E with price P_1 and total output Q_1.

Then came the event that changed the equilibrium: Iraq's invasion and continued occupation of Kuwait—one of the largest oil producers in the world. Immediately after the invasion, the United States led a worldwide embargo on oil from both Iraq and Kuwait. As far as the oil market was concerned, it was as if these nations' oil fields no longer existed—a significant decrease in the oil industry's productive capacity. If you look back at Figure 6 you will see that a decrease in productive capacity shifts the supply curve to the left, and this is just what happened. The new equilibrium at E' occurred at a lower quantity and a higher price. This change in the oil market's equilibrium was well understood by most people—including the college administrators—and no one was surprised when oil prices rose.

But what has all this got to do with natural gas prices? Everything, as the next part of our analysis will show.

Figure 13 shows the next market relevant to our analysis: the market for natural gas. In this market, world producers (which did not include Iraq or Kuwait) sell natural gas to American buyers. In this market, the initial equilibrium—before the invasion and before the rise in oil prices—was at point F. How did the invasion affect the equilibrium?

Oil is a *substitute* for natural gas. A rise in the price of a substitute, we know, will increase the demand for a good. (Look back at Figure 3 if you need a reminder.) In this case, the increase in the price of oil caused the demand curve for natural gas to shift rightward. In Figure 13, the price of natural gas rose from P_3 to P_4.

FIGURE 13
The Market for Natural Gas

Oil is a substitute for natural gas. A rise in the price of oil increases the demand for natural gas. Here, demand for natural gas increases from D_1 to D_2 and the price rises from P_3 to P_4.

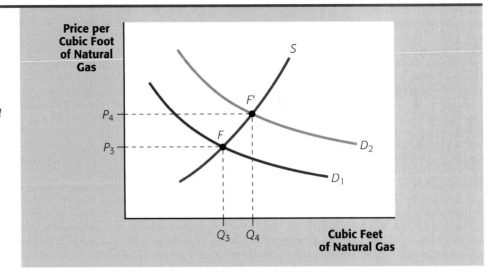

The administrators were right that the invasion of Kuwait did not affect the supply of natural gas. What they missed, however, was the invasion's effect on the *demand* for natural gas. With a fuller understanding of supply and demand, they could have predicted—*before* investing in their expensive switching equipment—that any rise in oil prices would cause a rise in natural gas prices. Armed with this knowledge, they would have anticipated a much smaller savings in energy costs from switching to natural gas and might have decided that there were better uses for their scarce funds.

Summary

In a market economy, prices are determined through the interaction of buyers and sellers in *markets. Perfectly competitive* markets have many buyers and sellers, and none of them individually can affect the market price. If an individual, buyer, or seller has the power to influence the price of a product, the market is *imperfectly competitive.*

The model of *supply and demand* explains how prices are determined in perfectly competitive markets. The *quantity demanded* of any good is the total amount buyers would choose to purchase at a given price. The *law of demand* states that quantity demanded is negatively related to price; it tells us that the *demand curve* slopes downward. The demand curve is drawn for given levels of income, wealth, tastes, prices of substitute and complementary goods, population, and expected future price. If any of those factors changes, the demand curve will shift.

The *quantity supplied* of a good is the total amount sellers would choose to produce and sell at a given price. According to the *law of supply*, supply curves slope upward. The supply curve will shift if there is a change in the price of an input, the price of an alternate good, the number of firms, or expectations of future prices.

Equilibrium price and quantity in a market are found where the supply and demand curves intersect. If either of these curves shifts, price and quantity will change as the market moves to a new equilibrium.

Economists use a three-step process to answer questions about the economy. The three steps—taken several times in this chapter—are to (1) characterize the market or markets involved in the question; (2) find the equilibrium in the market; and (3) ask what happens when something changes. This three-step process will be used throughout the textbook.

Key Terms

Aggregation	Change in quantity supplied	Equilibrium price
Alternate goods	Change in supply	Equilibrium quantity
Change in demand	Complement	Excess demand
Change in quantity demanded	Demand schedule	Excess supply

Firm's quantity supplied	Law of supply	Substitute
Household's quantity demanded	Market demand curve	Supply curve
Imperfectly competitive market	Market quantity demanded	Supply schedule
Income	Market quantity supplied	Wealth
Inferior good	Normal good	
Law of demand	Perfectly competitive market	

Review Questions
Answers to even-numbered Questions and Problems can be found on the text Web site at http://hall-lieb.swlearning.com.

1. How does the way each of the following terms is used in economics differ from the way it is used in everyday language?
   a. market
   b. demand
   c. normal good
   d. inferior good
   e. supply

2. What is the difference between *demand* and *quantity demanded*?

3. List and briefly explain the factors that can shift a demand curve and the factors that can shift a supply curve.

4. What is the difference between substitutes and complements? Which of the following pairs of goods are substitutes, which are complements, and which are neither?
   a. Coke and Pepsi
   b. Computer hardware and computer software
   c. Beef and chicken
   d. Salt and sugar
   e. Ice cream and frozen yogurt

5. Rank each of the following markets according to how close you think it comes to perfect competition:
   a. Wheat
   b. Personal computer hardware
   c. Gold
   d. Airline tickets from New York to Kalamazoo, Michigan

6. Is each of the following goods more likely to be *normal* or *inferior?*
   a. Lexus automobiles
   b. Secondhand clothes
   c. Imported beer
   d. Baby-sitting services
   e. Recapped tires
   f. Futons
   g. Home haircutting tools
   h. Restaurant meals

7. What does the term *equilibrium* mean in economics?

8. Explain why the price in a free market will not remain above or below equilibrium for long, unless there is outside interference.

9. Determine whether each of the following will cause a change in demand or a change in supply, and in which direction:
   a. Input prices increase.
   b. Income in an area declines.
   c. The price of an alternate good increases.
   d. Tastes shift away from a good.

10. In the Using the Theory section at the end of this chapter, the three-step process is used.
   a. Identify and briefly describe *where* each step is used.
   b. For each step, carefully explain how it is used.

Problems and Exercises

1. In the late 1990s, beef—which had fallen out of favor in the 1970s and 1980s—became popular again. On a supply and demand diagram, illustrate the effect of such a change on equilibrium price and quantity in the market for beef.

2. In the late 1990s and through 2000, the British public became increasingly concerned about "Mad Cow Disease," which could be deadly to humans if they ate beef from these cattle. Fearing the disease, many consumers switched to other meats, like chicken, pork, or lamb. At the same time, the British government ordered the destruction of thousands of head of cattle. Illustrate the effects of these events on the equilibrium price and quantity in the market for British beef. Can we determine with certainty the direction of change for the quantity? For the price? Explain briefly.

3. Discuss, and illustrate with a graph, how each of the following events will affect the market for coffee:
   a. A blight on coffee plants kills off much of the Brazilian crop.
   b. The price of tea declines.
   c. Coffee workers organize themselves into a union and gain higher wages.
   d. Coffee is shown to cause cancer in laboratory rats.
   e. Coffee prices are expected to rise rapidly in the near future.

4. The following table gives hypothetical data for the quantity of two-bedroom rental apartments demanded and supplied in Peoria, Illinois:

Monthly Rent	Quantity Demanded (Thousands)	Quantity Supplied (Thousands)
$ 800	30	10
$1,000	25	14
$1,200	22	17
$1,400	19	19
$1,600	17	21
$1,800	15	22

   a. Graph the demand and supply curves.
   b. Find the equilibrium price and quantity.
   c. Explain briefly why a rent of $1,000 cannot be the equilibrium in this market.
   d. Suppose a tornado destroys a significant number of apartment buildings in Peoria, but doesn't affect people's desire to live there. Illustrate on your graph the effects on equilibrium price and quantity.

5. The following table gives hypothetical data for the quantity of You-Snooze-You-Lose brand alarm clocks demanded and supplied per month.

Price per Alarm Clock	Quantity Demanded	Quantity Supplied
$ 5	3,500	700
$10	3,000	900
$15	2,500	1,100
$20	2,000	1,300
$25	1,500	1,500
$30	1,000	1,700
$35	500	1,900

   a. Graph the demand and supply curves.
   b. Find the equilibrium price and quantity.
   c. Illustrate on your graph how a decrease in the price of wake-up services would affect the market for You-Snooze-You-Lose alarm clocks.
   d. What would happen if there was a decrease in the price of wake-up services at the same time that the price of the plastic used to manufacture You-Snooze-You-Lose alarm clocks rose?

6. The following table gives hypothetical data for the quantity of electric scooters demanded and supplied per month.

Price per Electric Scooter	Quantity Demanded	Quantity Supplied
$150	500	250
$175	475	350
$200	450	450
$225	425	550
$250	400	650
$275	375	750

   a. Graph the demand and supply curves.
   b. Find the equilibrium price and quantity.
   c. Illustrate on your graph how an increase in the wage rate paid to scooter assemblers would affect the market for electric scooters.
   d. What would happen if there was an increase in the wage rate paid to scooter assemblers at the same time that tastes for electric scooters increased?

7. The following table gives hypothetical data for the quantity of gasoline demanded and supplied in Los Angeles per month.

Price per Gallon	Quantity Demanded (Millions of gallons)	Quantity Supplied (Millions of gallons)
$1.20	170	80
$1.30	156	105
$1.40	140	140
$1.50	123	175
$1.60	100	210
$1.70	95	238

   a. Graph the demand and supply curves.
   b. Find the equilibrium price and quantity.
   c. Illustrate on your graph how a rise in the price of automobiles would affect the gasoline market.

8. How would each of the following affect the market for blue jeans in the United States? Illustrate each answer with a supply and demand diagram.
   a. The price of denim cloth increases.
   b. An influx of immigrants arrives in the United States. (Explicitly state any assumptions you are making.)
   c. An economic slowdown in the United States causes household incomes to decrease.

9. Indicate which curve shifted—and in which direction—for each of the following. Assume that only one curve shifts.
   a. The price of furniture rises as the quantity bought and sold falls.
   b. Apartment vacancy rates increase while average monthly rent on apartments declines.
   c. The price of personal computers continues to decline as sales skyrocket.

10. Consider the following forecast: "In 2004, we predict that the demand curve for handheld PCs will continue its shift leftward, which will tend to lower price and quantity. However, with a lower price, supply will decrease as well, shifting the supply curve leftward. A leftward shift of the supply curve will tend to raise price and lower quantity. We conclude that as 2004 proceeds, quantity will decrease but the price of handheld PCs may either rise or fall." There is a serious mistake of logic in this forecast. Can you find it? Explain.

11. Draw supply and demand diagrams for market A for each of the following. Then use your diagrams to illustrate the impact of the following events. In each case, determine what happens to price and quantity in each market.

a. *A* and *B* are substitutes, and the price of good *B* rises.
b. *A* and *B* satisfy the same kinds of desires, and there is a shift in tastes away from *A* and toward *B*.
c. *A* is a normal good, and incomes in the community increase.

d. There is a technological advance in the production of good *A*.
e. *B* is an input used to produce good *A*, and the price of *B* rises.

Challenge Questions

1. Suppose that demand is given by the equation $Q^D = 500 - 50P$, where Q^D is quantity demanded, and *P* is the price of the good. Supply is described by the equation $Q^S = 50 + 25P$, where Q^S is quantity supplied. What is the equilibrium price and quantity? (See Appendix)

2. While crime rates have fallen across the country over the past few years, they have fallen especially rapidly in Manhattan. At the same time, there are some neighborhoods in the New York metropolitan area in which the crime rate has remained constant. Using supply and demand diagrams for rental housing, explain how a falling crime rate in Manhattan could make the residents in *other* neighborhoods *worse off*. (Hint: As people from around the country move to Manhattan, what happens to rents there? If someone cannot afford to pay higher rent in Manhattan, what might they do?)

3. A Wall Street analyst observes the following equilibrium price-quantity combinations in the market for restaurant meals in a city over a four-year period:

Year	P	Q (Thousands of Meals per Month)
1	$12	20
2	$15	30
3	$17	40
4	$20	50

She concludes that the market defies the law of demand. Is she correct? Why or why not?

 These exercises require access to Hall/Lieberman Xtra! If Xtra! did not come with your book, visit http://hallxtra.swlearning.com to purchase.

1. Use your Xtra! password at the Hall and Lieberman Web site (http://hallxtra.swlearning.com), select Chapter 3, and under Economic Applications, click on Econ-News. Choose *Economic Fundamentals: Equilibrium*, and scroll down to find the article "Sweet Home Improvement Market." Read the article summary, and answer the questions below.
   a. Show graphically, using supply and demand curves, the impact of the increase in new home sales on the home improvement market.
   b. Now click on EconData. Under Hot Data, scroll down to find *Housing Starts*. Click on it, and read the definition of Housing Starts. Then click on *Diagrams/Data*, and see how the level of housing starts relates to the 30-year mortgage rate. What relationship should this variable have with the mortgage rate? Do you see this in the graph? Why or why not?
   c. Next click on EconNews again. Choose *Economic Fundamental: Supply and Demand* and scroll down to find the article, "PC Price Cuts." Read the article summary, and describe, using supply and demand curves, how the effects of computer price cuts impacts the market for home improvement described in part a.

2. Use your Xtra! password at the Hall and Lieberman Web site (http://hallxtra.swlearning.com), select Chapter 3, and under Economic Applications click on EconDebate.

   Choose *Economic Fundamental: Supply and Demand*, and scroll down to find the debate, "Do slave redemption programs reduce the problem of slavery?" Read the debate and answer the questions below.
   a. What incentive problem is mentioned in the debate regarding slave redemption programs? Illustrate this using supply and demand curves.
   b. How could you modify the incentives of slave redemption programs to reduce the problem of increased slave raids?

3. Use your Xtra! password at the Hall and Lieberman Web site (http://hallxtra.swlearning.com), select Chapter 3, and under Economic Applications, click on Econ-News. Choose *Economic Fundamentals: Equilibrium*, and scroll down to find the article "Students Learn the Hard Way." Read the article summary, and answer the questions below.
   a. As the article points out, many schools are seeing an increase in costs as well as a reduction in state funds available. Illustrate, using a graph of supply and demand in the market for a college education, the effect of increasing costs of producing that education.
   b. Why would student government groups on college campuses with incentives like the ones described in the article be concerned about the quality of the education students were receiving?

APPENDIX

SOLVING FOR EQUILIBRIUM ALGEBRAICALLY

In the body of this chapter, notice that the supply and demand curves for maple syrup were *not* graphed as straight lines. This is because the data they were based on were not consistent with the straight-line graph. You can verify this if you look back at Table 2: When the price rises from $1.00 to $2.00, quantity demanded drops by 15,000 (from 75,000 to 60,000). But when the price rises from $2.00 to $3.00, quantity demanded drops by 10,000 (from 60,000 to 50,000). Since the change in the independent variable—price—is $1.00 in both cases, but the change in the dependent variable—quantity demanded—is different, we know that when the the relationship between quantity demanded and price is graphed, it will not be a straight line.

We have no reason to expect that demand or supply curves in the real world will be straight lines (to be *linear*). However, it's often useful to approximate a curve with a linear relationship that is reasonably close to the original curve. One advantage of doing this is that we can then express both supply and demand as simple equations, and solve for the equilibrium using basic algebra.

For example, suppose the demand for take-out pizzas in a modest-size city is represented by the following equation:

$$Q^D = 64,000 - 3,000\,P$$

where Q^D stands for the quantity of pizzas demanded per week. This equation tells us that every time the price of pizza rises by $1.00, the number of pizzas demanded each week *falls* by 3,000. As we'd expect, there is a negative relationship between price and quantity demanded. Moreover, since quantity demanded always falls at the same rate (3,000 fewer pizzas for every $1.00 rise in price), the equation is linear.[1]

Now we'll add an equation for the supply curve:

$$Q^S = -20,000 + 4,000\,P$$

where Q^S stands for the quantity of pizzas supplied per week. This equation tells us that when the price of pizza rises by $1.00, the number of pizzas supplied per week *rises* by 4,000—the positive relationship we expect of a supply curve.[2] And like the demand curve, it's linear: Quantity supplied continues to rise at the same rate (4,000 more pizzas for every $1.00 increase in price).

We know that if this market is in equilibrium, quantity demanded (Q^D) will equal quantity supplied (Q^S). So let's *impose* that condition on these curves. That is, let's require $Q^D = Q^S$. This allows us to use the definitions for Q^D and Q^S that have price as a variable, and set those equal to each other in equilibrium:

$$64,000 - 3,000\,P = -20,000 + 4,000\,P$$

This is one equation with a single unknown—P—so we can use the rules of algebra to isolate P on one side of the equation. We do this by adding 3,000 P to both sides, which isolates P on the right, and adding 20,000 to both sides, which moves everything that *doesn't* involve P to the left, giving us:

$$84,000 = 7,000\,P$$

Finally, dividing both sides by 7,000 gives us

$$84,000 / 7,000 = P$$

or

$$P = 12$$

We've found our equilibrium price: $12. What about equilibrium quantity? In equilibrium, we know quantity demanded and quantity supplied are equal, so we can *either* solve for Q^D using the demand equation, or solve for Q^S using the supply equation, and we should get the same answer. For example, using the demand equation, and using the equilibrium price of $12:

$$Q^D = 64,000 - 3,000\,(12)$$

or

$$Q^D = 28,000$$

To confirm that we didn't make any errors, we can also solve for quantity supplied at the same price:

$$Q^S = -20,000 + 4,000\,(12)$$

or

$$Q^S = 28,000$$

We've now confirmed that the equilibrium quantity is 28,000.

[1] If you try to graph the demand curve, don't forget that supply and demand graphs reverse the usual custom of graphing the independent variable on the horizontal axis and the dependent variable on the vertical axis. That is, quantity demanded is the dependent variable (it *depends* on price), and yet it's graphed on the *horizontal* axis.

[2] Don't be troubled by the negative sign (−20,000) in this equation. It helps determine a minimum price that suppliers must get in order to supply any pizza at all. Using the entire equation, we find that if price were $5.00, quantity supplied would be zero, and that price has to rise *above* $5.00 for any pizzas to be supplied in this market. But since a "negative supply" doesn't make sense, this equation is valid only for prices of $5.00 or greater.

What Macroeconomics Tries to Explain

CHAPTER OUTLINE

Macroeconomic Goals
Economic Growth
High Employment (or Low Unemployment)
Stable Prices

The Macroeconomic Approach
Aggregation in Macroeconomics

Macroeconomic Controversies

As You Study Macroeconomics . . .

You have no doubt seen photographs of the earth taken from satellites thousands of miles away. Viewed from that great distance, the world's vast oceans look like puddles, its continents like mounds of dirt, and its mountain ranges like wrinkles on a bedspread. In contrast to our customary view from the earth's surface—of a car, a tree, a building—this is a view of the big picture.

These two different ways of viewing the earth—from up close or from thousands of miles away—are analogous to two different ways of viewing the economy. When we look through the *microeconomic* lens—from up close—we see the behavior of *individual decision makers* and *individual markets*. When we look through the *macroeconomic* lens—from a distance—these smaller features fade away, and we see only the broad outlines of the economy.

Which view is better? That depends on what we're trying to do. If we want to know why computers are getting better and cheaper each year, or why the earnings of business professors are rising so rapidly, we need the close-up view of microeconomics. But to answer questions about the *overall* economy—about the overall level of economic activity, our standard of living, or the percentage of our potential workforce that is unemployed—we need the more comprehensive view of *macroeconomics*.

MACROECONOMIC GOALS

While there is some disagreement among economists about *how* to make the macroeconomy perform well, there is widespread agreement about the goals we are trying to achieve:

> *Economists—and society at large—agree on three important macroeconomic goals: economic growth, full employment, and stable prices.*

Why is there such universal agreement on these three goals? Because achieving them gives us the opportunity to make *all* of our citizens better off. Let's take a closer look at each of these goals and see why they are so important.

Economic Growth

Imagine that you were a typical American worker living at the beginning of the 20th century. You would work about 60 hours every week, and your yearly salary—about $450—would buy a bit less than $9,000 would buy today. You could expect to die at the age of 47. If you fell seriously ill before then, your doctor wouldn't be able to help much: There were no X-ray machines or blood tests, and little effective medicine for the few diseases that could be diagnosed. You would probably never hear the sounds produced by the best musicians of the day, or see the performances of the best actors, dancers, or singers. And the most exotic travel you'd enjoy would likely be a trip to a nearby state.

Today, the typical worker has it considerably better. He or she works about 35 hours per week and is paid about $37,000 per year, not to mention fringe benefits such as health insurance, retirement benefits, and paid vacation. Thanks to advances in medicine, nutrition, and hygiene, the average worker can expect to live into his or her late 70s. And more of a worker's free time today is really free: There are machines to do laundry and dishes, cars to get to and from work, telephones for quick communication, and personal computers to keep track of finances, appointments, and correspondence. Finally, during their lifetimes, most Americans will have traveled—for enjoyment—to many locations in the United States or abroad.

Economic growth The increase in our production of goods and services that occurs over long periods of time.

What is responsible for these dramatic changes in economic well-being? The answer is: **economic growth**—the increase in our production of goods and services that occurs over long periods of time. In the United States, as in most developed economies, the annual output of goods and services has risen over time, and risen faster than the population. As a result, the average person can consume much more today—more food, clothing, housing, medical care, entertainment, and travel—than in the year 1900.

Economists monitor economic growth by keeping track of *real gross domestic product (real GDP)*: the total quantity of goods and services produced in a country over a year. When real GDP rises faster than the population, output per person rises, and so does the average standard of living.

Figure 1 shows real GDP in the United States from 1929 to 2004, measured in dollars of output at 2000 prices. As you can see, real GDP has increased dramatically over the greater part of the century. Part of the reason for the rise is an increase in population: More workers can produce more goods and services. But real GDP has actually increased *faster* than the population: During this period, while the U.S. population did not quite triple, the quantity of goods and services produced per year has increased more than tenfold. Hence, the remarkable rise in the average American's living standard.

But when we look more closely at the data, we discover something important: Although output has grown, the *rate* of growth has varied over the decades. From

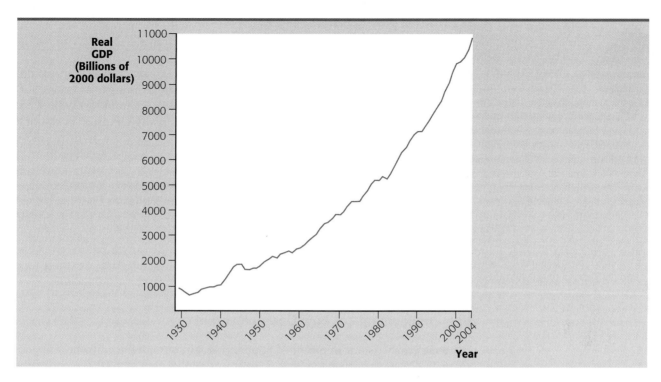

FIGURE 1

U.S. Real Gross Domestic Product, 1929–2004

Real GDP has increased dramatically over the past 75 years. In the figure, real GDP is measured in dollars of output valued at 2000 prices. (The measurement of real GDP will be discussed in more detail in the next two chapters.)

1959 to 1973, real GDP grew, on average, by 4.2 percent per year. But from 1973 to 1991, average annual growth slowed to 2.7 percent. Then, from 1991 to 2004, growth picked up again, averaging 3.1 percent per year. These may seem like slight differences. But over long periods of time, such small differences in growth rates can cause huge differences in living standards. For example, suppose that in each of the 20 years between 1984 and 2004, real GDP had grown by just one percentage point more than its actual rate. Then, over that entire period, the United States would have produced about $20 trillion *more* in goods and services than we *actually* produced over that period (valuing these goods and services at 2000 prices). That amounts to more than $65,000 for each person in the population.

Economists and government officials are very concerned when economic growth slows down. Growth increases the size of the economic pie, so it becomes possible—at least in principle—for every citizen to have a larger slice. This is why economists agree that growth is a good thing.

But in practice, growth does *not* benefit everyone. Living standards will always rise more rapidly for some groups than for others, and some may even find their slice of the pie shrinking. For example, since the late 1980s, economic growth has improved the living standards of the highly skilled, while less-skilled workers have benefited very little. Partly, this is due to improvements in technology that have lowered the earnings of workers whose roles can be taken by computers and machines. But very few economists would advocate a halt to growth as a solution to the problems of unskilled workers. Some believe that, in the long run, everyone will indeed benefit from growth. Others see a role for the government in taxing successful people and providing benefits to those left behind by growth. But in either case, economic

DANGEROUS CURVES

Growth Rates from Graphs In Figure 1, it looks like real GDP has not only been growing over time, but growing at a faster and faster rate, since the line becomes steeper over time. But the real GDP line would get steeper even if the growth rate were *constant* over the entire period. That's because as real GDP rises from an increasingly higher and higher level, the same *percentage* growth rate causes greater and greater *absolute* increases in GDP.

For example, when real GDP is $5 trillion, 3 percent growth would cause real GDP to rise by $5 trillion × 0.03 = $0.15 trillion. But when real GDP is $10 trillion, the same 3 percent growth would be $10 trillion × 0.03 = $0.30 trillion. Since the slope of the line depends on the *absolute* rise in real GDP each year rather than its *percentage* rise, the same percentage growth rate would create a steeper line when real GDP is higher.

In fact, the line can become steeper even if the percentage growth rate *decreases* over time. As you've read, real GDP actually grew faster from 1959 to 1973 (where the line is flatter) than during any subsequent period (where the line is steeper). In subsequent chapters, you'll see other graphs that make it easier to see changes in the growth rate of real GDP.

growth, by increasing the size of the overall pie, is seen as an important part of the solution.

Macroeconomics helps us understand a number of issues surrounding economic growth. What makes real GDP grow in the first place? Why does it grow more rapidly in some decades than in others? Why do some countries experience very rapid growth—some much faster than the United States—while others seem unable to grow at all? Can government policy do anything to alter the growth rate? And are there any downsides to such policies?

High Employment (or Low Unemployment)

Economic growth is one of our most important goals, but not the only one. Suppose our real GDP were growing at, say, a 3 percent annual rate, but 10 percent of the workforce was unable to find work. Would the economy be performing well? Not really, for two reasons. First, unemployment affects the distribution of economic well-being among our citizens. People who cannot find jobs suffer a loss of income. And even though many of the jobless receive some unemployment benefits and other assistance from the government, the unemployed typically have lower living standards than the employed. Concern for those without jobs is one reason that consistently high employment—or consistently low *unemployment*—is an important macroeconomic goal.

But in addition to the impact on the unemployed themselves, joblessness affects *all* of us—even those who *have* jobs. A high unemployment rate means that the economy is not achieving its full economic potential: Many people who *want* to work and produce additional goods and services are not able to do so. With the same number of people—but fewer goods and services to distribute among that population—the average standard of living will be lower. This general effect on living standards gives us another reason to strive for consistently high rates of employment and low rates of unemployment.

One measure economists use to keep track of employment is the *unemployment rate*—the percentage of the workforce that is searching for a job but hasn't found one. Figure 2 shows the average unemployment rate during each of the past 84 years. Notice that the unemployment rate is never zero; there are always *some* people looking for work, even when the economy is doing well. But in some years, unemployment is unusually high. The worst example occurred during the Great Depression of the 1930s, when millions of workers lost their jobs and the unemployment rate reached 25 percent. One in four potential workers could not find a job. More recently, in 1982 and 1983, the unemployment rate averaged almost 10 percent.

The nation's commitment to high employment has twice been written into law. With the memory of the Great Depression still fresh, Congress passed the *Employment Act of 1946*, which required the federal government to "promote maximum

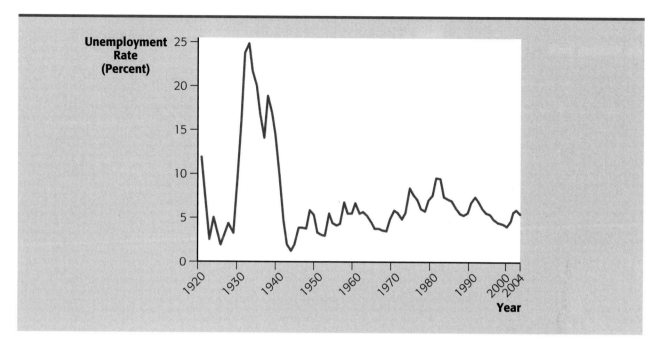

FIGURE 2
**U.S. Unemployment Rate,
1920–2004**

The unemployment rate fluctuates over time. During the Great Depression of the 1930s, unemployment was extremely high, reaching 25 percent in 1933. In the early 1980s, the rate averaged 10 percent. And during the 1990s, it fell rapidly, reaching 4 percent before turning up in the early 2000s.

employment, production, and purchasing power." It did not, however, dictate a target rate of unemployment the government should aim for. A numerical target was added in 1978, when Congress passed the *Full Employment and Balanced Growth Act,* which called for an unemployment rate of 4 percent.

A glance at Figure 2 shows how seldom we have hit this target over the last few decades. In fact, we did not hit it at all through the 1970s and 1980s. But in the 1990s, we came closer and closer and finally, in December 1999, we reached the 4 percent target for the first time since the 1960s. In 2001, the unemployment rate began to creep up again, and fluctuated between 5.2 and 6.3 percent through the first half of 2005.

Why has the unemployment rate been above its target so often? Why were we able to reach the target at the end of the 1990s, but not maintain it through the early 2000s? And what causes the average unemployment rate to fluctuate from year to year, as shown in Figure 2? These are all questions that your study of macroeconomics will help you answer.

Employment and the Business Cycle. When firms produce more output, they hire more workers; when they produce less output, they tend to lay off workers. We would thus expect real GDP and employment to be closely related, and indeed they are. In recent years, each 1 percent drop in output has been associated with the loss of more than half a million jobs. Consistently high employment, then, requires a high, stable level of output. Unfortunately, output has *not* been very stable. If you look back at Figure 1, you will see that while real GDP has climbed upward over time, it has been a bumpy ride. The periodic fluctuations in GDP—the bumps in the figure—are called **business cycles.**

Figure 3 shows a close-up view of a hypothetical business cycle. First, notice the thin upward-sloping line. This shows the long-run upward trend of real GDP, which

Business cycles Fluctuations in real GDP around its long-term growth trend.

FIGURE 3
The Business Cycle

Over time, real GDP fluctuates around an overall upward trend. Such fluctuations are called business cycles. *When output rises, we are in the expansion phase of the cycle; when output falls, we are in a* recession.

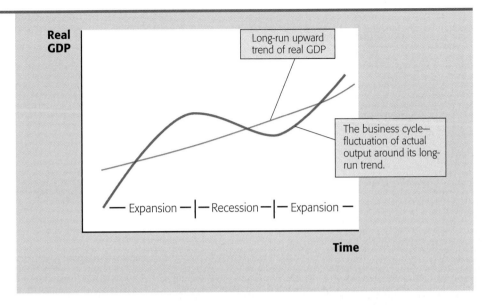

Expansion Versus Economic Growth Although the terms *expansion* and *economic growth* both refer to increases in real GDP, they are not the same. *Economic growth* refers to the long-run upward trend in output over a long period of time, usually more than a decade. It is measured as the *average* annual change in output over the entire period. An *expansion* refers to a usually shorter period of time during which output increases quarter by quarter or year by year.

Here's an example of the difference: From 1973 to 1991, output increased at an *average* rate of 2.7 percent per year over the entire period. This was the rate of economic growth during the period. But during a *part* of this long period—the early 1980s—output *fell* for several quarters. This was a contraction. During another part of this long period—the mid- and late 1980s—output *rose* every quarter. This was an expansion.

Expansion A period of increasing real GDP.

Recession A period of significant decline in real GDP.

Depression An unusually severe recession.

we refer to as *economic growth.* The thicker line shows the business cycle that occurs *around* the long-run trend. When output rises, we are in the **expansion** phase of the cycle; when output falls, we are in the *contraction* or **recession** phase. (Officially, a recession is a contraction considered significant —in terms of depth, breadth, and duration.)

Of course, real-world business cycles never look quite like the smooth, symmetrical cycle in Figure 3, but rather like the jagged, irregular cycles of Figure 1. Recessions can be severe or mild, and they can last several years or less than a single year. When a recession is particularly severe and long lasting, it is called a **depression.** In the 20th century, the United States experienced just one decline in output serious enough to be considered a depression—the worldwide *Great Depression* of the 1930s. From 1929 to 1933, the first four years of the Great Depression, U.S. output dropped by more than 25 percent.

But even during more normal times, the economy has gone through many recessions. Since 1959, we have suffered through two severe recessions (in 1974–75 and 1981–82) and several less severe ones, such as the recession from March to November of 2001.

Why are there business cycles? Is there anything we can do to prevent recessions from occurring, or at least make them milder and shorter? And why—even after a period of severe depression as in the 1930s—does the economy eventually move back toward its long-run growth trend? These are all questions that macroeconomics helps us answer.

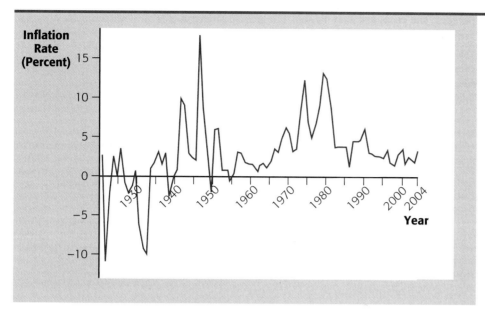

FIGURE 4

U.S. Annual Inflation Rate, 1922–2004

In most years, the inflation rate has been positive. The overall price level increased during those years.

Stable Prices

Figure 4 shows the annual inflation rate—the percentage increase in the average level of prices—from 1922 to 2004.[1] With very few exceptions, the inflation rate has been positive: On average, prices have risen in each of those years. But notice the wide variations in inflation. In 1979 and 1980, we had double-digit inflation: Prices rose by more than 12 percent in both years. During that time, polls showed that people were more concerned about inflation than any other national problem—more than unemployment, crime, poverty, pollution, or anything else. During the 1990s, the inflation rate averaged less than 3 percent per year, and it has averaged about 2½ percent during the 2000s (through June 2005). As a result, we hardly seem to notice it at all. Pollsters no longer include "rising prices" as a category when asking about the most important problems facing the country.

Other countries have not been so lucky. In the 1980s, several Latin American nations experienced inflation rates of thousands of percent per year. In the early 1990s, some of the newly emerging nations of Central Europe and the former Soviet Union suffered annual inflation rates in the triple digits. An extreme case was the new nation of Serbia, where prices rose by 1,880 percent in the single month of August 1993. If prices had continued to rise at that rate all year, the annual inflation rate would have been 363,000,000,000,000,000 percent.

Why are stable prices—a low inflation rate—an important macroeconomic goal? Because inflation is *costly* to society. With annual inflation rates in the thousands of

[1] Figure 4 is based on the Consumer Price Index, the most popular measure of the price level, as well as historical estimates of what this index *would* have been in the early part of the 20th century, before the index existed. We'll discuss the Consumer Price Index and other measures of inflation in more detail in later chapters.

percent, the costs are easy to see: The purchasing power of the currency declines so rapidly that people are no longer willing to hold it. This breakdown of the monetary system forces people to waste valuable time and resources bartering with each other—for example, trading plumbing services for dentistry services. With so much time spent trying to find trading partners, there is little time left for producing goods and services. As a result, the average standard of living falls.

With inflation rates of 12 or 13 percent—such as the United States experienced in the late 1970s—the costs to society are less obvious and less severe. But they are still significant. And when it comes time to bring down the inflation rate, painful corrective actions by government are sometimes required. These actions can cause output to decline and unemployment to rise. For example, in order to bring the inflation rate down from the high levels of the late 1970s (see Figure 4), government policy purposely caused a severe recession in 1981–82, reducing output and increasing unemployment.

Economists regard *some* inflation as good for the economy. In fact, in 2001 and 2002, policy makers worried that the inflation rate might fall *too low,* and that the economy might experience a harmful *deflation*—a period of *decreasing* prices. Price stabilization requires not only preventing the inflation rate from rising too high, but also preventing it from falling too *low,* where it would be dangerously close to turning negative.

The previous paragraphs may have raised a number of questions in your mind. What causes inflation or deflation? How would a *moderately* high inflation rate of 7 or 8 percent harm society? How does a recession bring down the inflation rate, and how does the government actually *create* a recession? And why might a period of decreasing prices—which sounds so wonderful—be a threat to the economy? Your study of macroeconomics will help you answer all of these questions.

THE MACROECONOMIC APPROACH

If you have already studied microeconomics, you will notice much that is familiar in macroeconomics. The *three-step process* plays an important role in both branches of the field. But the macroeconomic approach is different from the microeconomic approach in significant ways. Most importantly, in *microeconomics,* we typically apply our three steps to *one market at a time*—the market for soybeans, for neurosurgeons, or for car washes. In *macroeconomics,* by contrast, we want to understand how the entire economy behaves. Thus, we apply the steps to *all markets simultaneously.* This includes not only markets for goods and services, but also markets for labor and for financial assets like stocks and bonds.

How can we possibly hope to deal with all of these markets at the same time? One way would be to build a gigantic model that included every individual market in the economy. The model would have tens of thousands of supply and demand curves, which could be used to determine tens of thousands of prices and quantities. With today's fast, powerful computers, we could, in principle, build this kind of model.

But it would not be easy. We would need to gather data on every good and service in the economy, every type of labor, every type of financial asset, and so on. As you might guess, this would be a formidable task, requiring thousands of workers just to gather the data alone. And in the end, the model would not prove very useful. We would not learn much about the economy from it: With so many individual trees, we could not see the forest.

Moreover, the model's predictions would be highly suspect: With so much information and so many moving parts, high standards of accuracy would be difficult to maintain. Even the government of the former Soviet Union, which directed production throughout the economy until the 1990s, was unable to keep track of all the markets under its control. In a market economy, where production decisions are made by individual firms, the task would be even harder.

What, then, is a macroeconomist to do? The answer is a word that you will become very familiar with in the chapters to come: **aggregation,** the process of combining different things into a single category and treating them as a whole. Let's take a closer look at how aggregation is used in macroeconomics.

Aggregation The process of combining different things into a single category.

Aggregation in Macroeconomics

Aggregation is a basic tool of reasoning, one that you often use without being aware of it. If you say, "I applied for five jobs last month," you are aggregating five very different workplaces into the single category, *jobs*. Whenever you say, "I'm going out with my friends," you are combining several different people into a single category: people you consider *friends*.

Aggregation plays a key role in both micro- and macroeconomics. Microeconomists will speak of the market for automobiles, lumping Toyotas, Fords, BMWs, and other types of cars into a single category. But in macroeconomics, we take aggregation to the extreme. Because we want to consider the entire economy at once, and yet keep our model as simple as possible, we must aggregate all markets into the broadest possible categories. For example, we lump together all the goods and services that households buy—newspapers, pizza, couches, and personal computers—into the single category *consumption goods*. We combine all the different types of capital purchased by business firms—forklifts, factory buildings, office computers, and trucks—into the single category *investment goods*. Often we go even further, lumping consumption, investment, and all other types of goods into the single category *output* or *real GDP*. And in macroeconomics, we typically combine the thousands of different types of workers in the economy—doctors, construction workers, plumbers, college professors—into the category, *labor*. By aggregating in this way, we can create workable and reasonably accurate models that teach us a great deal about how the overall economy operates.

"Micro" Versus "Macro" In many English words, the prefix *macro* means "large" and *micro* means "small." As a result, you might think that in microeconomics, we study economic units in which small sums of money are involved, while in macroeconomics we study units involving greater sums. But this is not correct: The annual output of General Motors is considerably greater than the total annual output of many small countries, such as Estonia or Guatemala. Yet when we study the behavior of General Motors, we are practicing *microeconomics,* and when we study changes in the unemployment rate in Estonia, we are practicing *macroeconomics.* Why? Microeconomics is concerned with the behavior and interaction of *individual* firms and markets, even if they are very large; macroeconomics is concerned with the behavior of *entire economies,* even if they are very small.

DANGEROUS CURVES

MACROECONOMIC CONTROVERSIES

Macroeconomics is full of disputes and disagreements. Indeed, modern macroeconomics, which began with the publication of *The General Theory of Employment, Interest, and Money* by British economist John Maynard Keynes in 1936, originated in controversy. Keynes was taking on the conventional wisdom of his time, *classical economics,* which held that the macroeconomy worked very well on its own, and the best policy for the government to follow was *laissez faire*—"leave it alone." As he was working on *The General Theory,* Keynes wrote to his friend, the playwright George Bernard Shaw, "I believe myself to be writing a book on economic theory which will largely revolutionize—not, I suppose, at once but in the course of the next ten years—the way the world thinks about economic problems."

Keynes's prediction was on the money. After the publication of his book, economists argued about its merits, but 10 years later, the majority of the profession had been won over: they had become Keynesians. This new school of thought held that the economy does *not* do well on its own (one needed only to look at the Great Depression for evidence) and requires continual guidance from an activist and well-intentioned government.

From the late 1940s until the early 1960s, events seemed to prove the Keynesians correct. Then, beginning in the 1960s, several distinguished economists began to challenge Keynesian ideas. Their counterrevolutionary views, which in many ways mirrored those of the classical economists, were strengthened by events in the 1970s, when the economy's behavior began to contradict some Keynesian ideas. Today, much of this disagreement has been resolved and a modern consensus—incorporating both Keynsian and classical ideas—has emerged. But there are still controversies.

Consider, for example, the controversy over the Bush administration's $350 billion 10-year tax cut. In May 2003, the tax cut was approved by 231 to 200 in the House of Representatives, and passed the Senate only when Vice President Cheney cast his vote to break a 50–50 tie. Within hours of passage, the following appeared on CNN's Web site:

> *"This is a great victory for the American people," said Senate Majority Leader Bill Frist, R-Tennessee. "The wonderful thing is it really boils down to greater job security for people."*

> *"This is a policy of debt, deficits, and decline," said Sen. Kent Conrad, D-North Dakota, adding, "This is a scandal in the making. We're going to read there are perverse results as a result of this tax policy."*[2]

Similar opposing views were expressed by economists associated with the Bush administration on the one hand, and those associated with the Democratic Party on the other. What are we to make of macroeconomic policy controversies like these, which occur so often on the political scene?

Remember the distinction between *positive (what is)* and *normative (what should be)?* Some of these disagreements are *positive* in nature. While economists and policy makers often agree on the broad outlines of how the macroeconomy works, they may disagree on some of the details. For example, they may disagree about the economy's current direction or momentum, or the relative effectiveness of

---

[2] "Congress Approves Tax-Cut Package," CNN.com/Inside Politics, May, 23, 2002.

different policies in altering the economy's course. Indeed, the two opposing senators quoted above were expressing a positive disagreement: a disagreement about the *impact* that tax cuts would have on the economy.

But disagreements that *sound* postive often have *normative* origins. For example in 2003, Democrats in Congress criticized the Bush tax cut as unfair, because it gave the biggest tax reduction to those with the highest incomes. Republicans in Congress countered that the tax cut was fair, because taxpayers with the highest incomes paid higher taxes to begin with. In the competitive and confrontational arena of politics—with each side trying to muster all the arguments it can—positive economics is often enlisted. In 2003, Republicans who began with the view that the Bush tax cut was fair invariably *also* argued that it was the most effective policy to spur the economy into a healthy expansion phase (see Figure 3). And they found a number of economists—who may have had similar normative views—to support that argument. Democrats who began with the view that the tax cut was *un*fair invariably *also* argued that it would cause great harm to the economy. And they found a number of economists—who may have had similar normative views—to support *that* argument.

Because of such political battles, people who follow the news often think that there is little agreement among economists about how the macroeconomy works. In fact, the profession has come to a consensus on many basic principles, and we will stress these as we go. And even when there are disagreements, there is surprising consensus on the approach that should be taken to resolve them.

You won't find this consensus expressed in a hot political debate. But you *will* find it in academic journals and conferences, and in reports issued by certain nonpartisan research organizations or government agencies. And—we hope—you will find it in the chapters to come.

AS YOU STUDY MACROECONOMICS . . .

Macroeconomics is a fascinating and wide-ranging subject. You will find that each piece of the macroeconomic puzzle connects to all of the other pieces in many different ways. Each time one of your questions is answered, 10 more will spring up in your mind, each demanding immediate attention. This presents a problem for a textbook writer, and for your instructor as well: What is the best order to present the principles of macroeconomics? One way is to follow the order of questions as they would occur to a curious reader. For example, learning about unemployment raises questions about international trade, so we could then skip to that topic. But it also raises questions about government spending, economic growth, wages, banking, and much, much more. And each of these topics raises questions about still others. Organizing the material in this way would make you feel like a ball in a pinball machine, bouncing from bumper to bumper. This pinball approach—bouncing from topic to topic—is the one taken by the media when reporting on the economy. If you have ever tried to learn economics from a newspaper, you know how frustrating this approach can be.

In our study of macroeconomics, we will follow a different approach: presenting material as it is *needed* for what follows. In this way, what you learn in one chapter will form the foundation for the material in the next, and your understanding of macroeconomics will deepen as you go.

But be forewarned: This approach requires considerable patience on your part. Many of the questions that will pop into your head will have to be postponed until

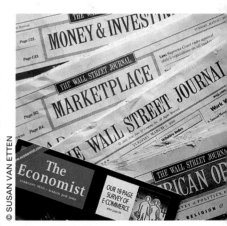

Two excellent print sources for news on the U.S. and world economies are The Wall Street Journal *and* The Economist, *a British magazine.*

the proper foundations for answering them have been established. It might help, though, to give you a *brief* indication of what is to come.

In the next two chapters, we will discuss three of the most important aggregates in macroeconomics: output, employment, and the price level. You will see why each of these is important to our economic well-being, how we keep track of them with government statistics, and how to interpret these statistics with a critical eye.

Then, in the remainder of the book, we study how the macroeconomy operates, starting with its behavior in the long run. Here, you will learn what makes an economy grow over long periods of time, and which government policies are likely to help or hinder that growth.

Next, we turn our attention to the short run for several chapters. You will learn why the economy behaves differently in the short run than in the long run, why we have business cycles, and how these cycles may be affected by government policies. We'll also expand our analysis to include the banking system and the money supply, and the special challenges they pose for government policy makers.

Finally, we'll turn our attention to the special problems of a global economy. You'll learn how trade with other nations constrains and expands our macro policy options at home and how economic events abroad influence our own economy. You will also learn why the United States has run persistent trade deficits with the rest of the world and what that means for our citizens.

This sounds like quite a lot of ground to cover, and indeed, it is. But it's not as daunting as it might sound. Remember that the study of macroeconomics—like the macroeconomy itself—is not a series of separate units, but an integrated whole. As you go from chapter to chapter, each principle you learn is a stepping-stone to the next one. Little by little, your knowledge and understanding will accumulate and deepen. Most students are genuinely surprised at how well they understand the macroeconomy after a single introductory course, and find the reward well worth the effort.

Summary

Macroeconomics is the study of the economy as a whole. It deals with issues such as economic growth, unemployment, inflation, and government policies that might influence the overall level of economic activity.

Economists generally agree about the importance of three main macroeconomic goals. The first of these is economic growth. If output, real gross domestic product, grows faster than population, the average person can enjoy an improved standard of living.

High employment is another important goal. In the United States and other market economies, the main source of household incomes is labor earnings. When unemployment is high, many people are without jobs and must cut back their purchases of goods and services.

The third macroeconomic goal is stable prices. This goal is important because inflation imposes costs on society. Keeping the rate of inflation low helps to reduce these costs.

Because an economy like that of the United States is so large and complex, the models we use to analyze the economy must be highly aggregated. For example, we will lump together millions of different goods to create an aggregate called "output" and combine all their prices into a single "price index."

Key Terms

Aggregation	Depression	Expansion
Business cycle	Economic growth	Recession

Review Questions *Answers to even-numbered Questions and Problems can be found on the text Web site at http://hall-lieb.swlearning.com.*

1. Discuss the similarities and differences between macro-economics and microeconomics.

2. What is the basic tool macroeconomists use to deal with the complexity and variety of economic markets and institutions? Give some examples of how they use this tool.

3. List the nation's macroeconomic goals and explain why each is important.

4. Consider an economy whose real GDP is growing at 4 percent per year. What else would you need to know in order to say whether the average standard of living is improving or deteriorating?

5. Explain the difference between a contraction, a recession, and a depression.

Problems and Exercises

1. In 1973, real GDP (at 1996 prices) was $4,123 billion. In 2000, it was $9,191 billion. During the same period, the U.S. population rose from 212 million to 281 million.
   a. What was the total percentage increase in real GDP from 1973 to 2000?
   b. What was the total percentage increase in the U.S. population during this period?
   c. Calculate real GDP per person in 1973 and in 2000. By what percentage did output per person grow over this period?

2. Suppose that real GDP had grown by 8 percent per year from 1973 to 2000. Using the data from Problem 1:
   a. What would real GDP have been in 2000?
   b. How much would output *per person* in 2000 have increased (compared to its actual value in 2000) if annual growth in real GDP over this period had been 8 percent?

3. a. The average growth rate for real GDP in the United States was 3.7 percent from 1991 to 2000. Use the information in the following table (which gives the actual GDP numbers measured in 1996 dollars) to calculate how much more we would have produced in 2000 if real GDP had grown by 4.7 percent over that period. [*Hint:* When real GDP grows at 4.7 percent annually, each year it will be 1.047 times its value of the year before.]

Year	Real GDP (Billions of 1996 dollars)
1991	$6,676.4
1992	$6,880.0
1993	$7,062.6
1994	$7,347.7
1995	$7,543.8
1996	$7,813.2
1997	$8,159.5
1998	$8,508.9
1999	$8,859.0
2000	$9,191.4

b. Calculate, for a 2000 population of 281 million people, how much higher the average output per person would have been in 2000 if the growth rate had been 4.7 percent over this period.

4. Assume that the country of Ziponia produced real GDP equal to $5000 (in billions) in the year 2000.
   a. Calculate Ziponia's output from 2000 to 2006, assuming that it experienced a constant growth rate of 6 percent per year over this period. Use your answers to construct a graph similar to the one in Figure 1. Is the slope of this graph constant? Explain.
   b. Calculate Ziponia's output from 2000 to 2006, assuming that its growth rate was 6 percent from 2000 to 2001, and then that it fell by 1 percent each year. Plot these points onto your graph from part (a). Is the slope of this graph constant? Explain.

5. Assume that the country of Zipinia produced real GDP equal to $5000 (in billions) in the year 2000.
   a. Calculate Zipinia's output from 2000 to 2006, assuming that it experienced a constant growth rate of 10 percent per year over this period. Use your answers to construct a graph similar to the one in Figure 1. Is the slope of this graph constant? Explain.
   b. Calculate Zipinia's output from 2000 to 2006, assuming that its growth rate was 10 percent from 2000 to 2001, and then that it fell by .5 percent each year (to 9.5, 9, 8.5, etc). Plot these points onto your graph from part (a). Is the slope of this graph constant? Explain.

Applications *These exercises require access to Hall/Lieberman Xtra! If Xtra! did not come with your book, visit http://www.thenation.com/ doc/20030630/greider to purchase.*

1. Use your Xtra! Password at the Hall and Lieberman Web site (http://hallxtra.swlearning.com), select this chapter, and under Economic Applications, click on EconDebate. Choose *Macroeconomics: Productivity and Growth*, and scroll down to find the debate, "Is More Spending on Infrastructure the Key to Economic Growth?" Read the debate and use the information to answer the following questions.

   a. In this chapter it is stated that economic growth, high employment, and stable prices are the main macroeconomic goals. Are these compatible or competing goals? Explain.

   b. What are the most common recommendations for increasing the rate of economic growth? Explain the debate on the appropriate role of government in economic growth.

2. Use your Xtra! Password at the Hall and Lieberman Web site (http://hallxtra.swlearning.com), select this chapter, and under Economic Applications, click on EconNews. Choose *Macroeconomics: Productivity and Growth*, and scroll down to find "Signs of Recovery." Read the full summary.

   a. Answer the three questions posed under the full summary.

   b. Read the article "Deflation" by William Greider http://www.thenation.com/doc/20030630/greider and explain why both Greenspan and Greider consider deflation to be an impediment to growth.

Production, Income, and Employment

CHAPTER OUTLINE

Production and Gross Domestic Product
GDP: A Definition
The Expenditure Approach to GDP
Other Approaches to GDP
Measuring GDP: A Summary
Real Versus Nominal GDP
How GDP Is Used
Problems with GDP

Employment and Unemployment
Types of Unemployment
The Costs of Unemployment
How Unemployment Is Measured
Problems in Measuring Unemployment

Using the Theory: GDP After September 11
The Direct Impact on GDP
Indirect Impacts on GDP

On the first Friday of every month, at 8:00 A.M., dozens of journalists mill about in a room in the Department of Labor. They are waiting for the arrival of the press officer from the government's Bureau of Labor Statistics. When she enters the room, carrying a stack of papers, the buzz of conversation stops. The papers—which she passes out to the waiting journalists—contain the monthly report on the experience of the American workforce. They summarize everything the government knows about hiring and firing at businesses across the country; about the number of people working, the hours they worked, and the incomes they earned; and about the number of people *not* working and what they did instead. But one number looms large in the journalists' minds as they scan the report and compose their stories: the percentage of the labor force that could not find jobs, or the nation's *unemployment rate*.

Every three months, a similar scene takes place at the Department of Commerce, as reporters wait for the release of the quarterly report on the nation's output of goods and services and the incomes we have earned from producing it. Once again, the report includes tremendous detail. Output is broken down by industry and by the sector that purchased it, and income is broken down into the different types of earners. And once again, the reporters' eyes will focus on a single number, a number that will dominate their stories and create headlines in newspapers across the country: the nation's *gross domestic product*.

The government knows that its reports on employment and production will have a major impact on the American political scene, and on financial markets in the United States and around the world. So it takes great pains to ensure fair and equal access to the information. For example, the Bureau of Labor Statistics allows

journalists to look at the employment report at 8:00 A.M. on the day of the release (the first Friday of every month). But they must stay inside a room—appropriately called the lockup room—and cannot contact the outside world until the official release time of 8:30 A.M. At precisely 8:29 A.M., the reporters are permitted to hook up their laptop modems, and then a countdown begins. At precisely 8:30 A.M., the reporters are permitted to transmit their stories. At the same instant, the Bureau posts its report on an Internet Web site (*http://www.bls.gov*).

And the world reacts. Within seconds, wire-service headlines appear on computer screens: "Unemployment Rate up Two-Tenths of a Percent" or "Nation's Production Steady." Within minutes, financial traders, for whom these news flashes provide clues about the economy's future, make snap decisions to buy or sell, moving stock and bond prices. And within the hour, politicians and pundits will respond with sound bites, attacking or defending the administration's economic policies.

In this chapter, we will take our first look at production and employment in the economy, focusing on two key variables: *gross domestic product* and the *unemployment rate*. The purpose here is not to explain what causes these variables to rise or fall. That will come a few chapters later, when we begin to study macroeconomic models. Here, we focus on the reality behind the numbers: what the statistics tell us about the economy, how the government obtains them, and how they are sometimes misused.

PRODUCTION AND GROSS DOMESTIC PRODUCT

You have probably heard the phrase *gross domestic product*—or its more familiar abbreviation, GDP—many times. It is one of those economic terms that is frequently used by the media and by politicians. In the first half of this chapter, we take a close look at GDP.

GDP: A Definition

The U.S. government has been measuring the nation's total production since the 1930s. You might think that this is an easy number to calculate, at least in theory: Simply add up the output of every firm in the country during the year. Unfortunately, measuring total production is not so straightforward, and there are many conceptual traps and pitfalls. This is why economists have come up with a very precise definition of GDP.

Gross domestic product (GDP)
The total value of all final goods and services produced for the marketplace during a given year, within the nation's borders.

> The nation's **gross domestic product** (GDP) *is the total value of all final goods and services produced for the marketplace during a given period, within the nation's borders.*

Quite a mouthful. But every part of this definition is absolutely necessary. To see why, let's break the definition down into pieces and look more closely at each one.

The total value . . .

An old expression tells us that "you can't add apples and oranges." But that is just what government statisticians must do when they measure our total output. In a typical day, American firms produce millions of *loaves* of bread, thousands of *pounds* of peanut butter, hundreds of *hours* of television programming, and so on.

These are *different* products, and each is measured in its own type of units. Yet, somehow, we must combine all of them into a single number. But how?

The approach of GDP is to add up the *dollar value* of every good or service—the number of dollars each product is *sold* for. As a result, GDP is measured in dollar units. For example, in 2004, the GDP of the United States was about $11,735,000,000,000—give or take a few billion dollars. (That's about $11.7 trillion.)

Using dollar values to calculate GDP has two important advantages. First, it gives us a common unit of measurement for very different things, thus allowing us to add up "apples and oranges." Second, it ensures that a good that uses more resources to produce (a computer chip) will count more in GDP than a good that uses fewer resources (a tortilla chip).

However, using the dollar prices at which goods and services actually sell also creates a problem: If prices rise, then GDP will rise, even if we are not actually *producing* more. For this reason, when tracking changes in production over time, GDP must be adjusted to take away the effects of inflation. We'll come back to this issue again a bit later in the chapter.

... of all final ...

When measuring production, we do not count *every* good or service produced in the economy, but only those that are sold to their *final users*. An example will illustrate why.

Figure 1 shows a simplified version of the stages of production for a ream (500 sheets) of notebook paper: A lumber company cuts down trees and produces $1.00 worth of wood chips, which it sells to a paper mill for $1.00. The mill cooks, bleaches, and refines the wood chips, turning them into $1.50 worth of paper rolls, which it sells to an office supplies manufacturer for that price. This manufacturer cuts the paper, prints lines and margins on it, and sells its to a wholesaler for $2.25. The wholesaler sells it to a retail store for $3.50, and then, finally, it is sold to a consumer—perhaps you—for $5.00.

Should we add the value of *all* this production, and include $1.00 + $1.50 + $2.25 + $3.50 + $5.00 = $13.25 in GDP each time a ream of notebook paper is produced? No, this would clearly be a mistake, since all of this production ends up creating a good worth only $5 in the end. In fact, the $5 you pay for this good already *includes* the value of all the other production in the process.

In our example, the goods sold by the lumber company, paper mill, office supplies manufacturer, and wholesaler are all **intermediate goods**—goods used up in the process of producing something else. But the retailer (say, your local stationery store) sells a **final good**—a product sold to its *final user* (you). If we separately added in the production of intermediate goods when calculating GDP, we would be counting them more than once, since they are already included in the value of the final good.

Intermediate goods Goods used up in producing final goods.

Final good A good sold to its final user.

> *To avoid overcounting intermediate products when measuring GDP, we add up the value of final goods and services only. The value of all intermediate products is automatically included in the value of the final products they are used to create.*

... goods and services ...

We all know a good when we see one: We can look at it, feel it, weigh it, and, in some cases, eat it, strum it, or swing a bat at it. Not so with a service: When you get a medical checkup, a haircut, or a car wash, the *effects* of the service may linger, but

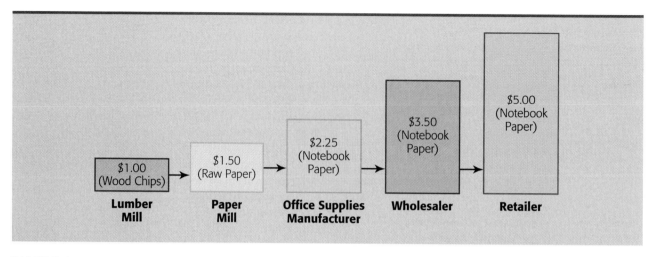

FIGURE 1
Stages of Production

the service itself is used up the moment it is produced. Nonetheless, final services count in GDP in the same way as final goods.

Services have become an increasingly important part of our total output in recent decades. The service sector has grown from about a third of U.S. output in 1950 to well over half of our output in 2002. These include the services produced by Internet providers, the health care industry, the banking industry, the educational system, and the entertainment industry.

. . . produced . . .

In order to contribute to GDP, something must be *produced*. This may sound obvious, but it is easy to forget. Every day, Americans buy billions of dollars worth of things that are *not* produced, or at least not produced during the period being considered, and so are not counted in that period's GDP. For example, people may buy land, or they may buy financial assets such as stocks or bonds. While these things cost money, they are not counted in GDP because they are not "goods and services *produced*." Land, for example, is not produced at all. Stocks and bonds represent a claim to ownership or to receive future payments, but they are not themselves goods or services.

. . . for the marketplace . . .

GDP does not include *all* final goods and services produced in the economy. Rather, it includes only the ones produced for the marketplace, that is, with the intention of being *sold*. Because of this restriction, we exclude many important goods and services from our measure. For example, when you clean your own home, you have produced a final service—housecleaning—but it is *not* counted in GDP because you are

DANGEROUS CURVES

The Services of Dealers, Brokers, and Other Sellers You've learned that GDP excludes the value of many things that are bought and sold—such as land, financial assets, and used goods—because they are not currently *produced goods and services*. But all of this buying and selling *can* contribute to GDP indirectly. How? If a dealer or broker is involved in the transaction, then that dealer or broker is producing a current service: bringing buyer and seller together. The value of this service is part of current GDP.

For example, suppose you bought a secondhand book at your college bookstore for $25. Suppose, too, that the store had bought the book from another student for $15. Then the purchase of the used book will contribute $10 to this year's GDP. Why? Because $10 is the value of the bookstore's services; it's the premium you pay to buy the book in the store, rather than going through the trouble to find the original seller yourself. The remainder of your purchase—$15—represents the value of the used book itself, and is *not* counted in GDP. The book was already counted when it was newly produced, in this or a previous year.

doing it for yourself, not for the marketplace. If you *hire* a housecleaner to clean your home, however, this final service *is* included in GDP; it has become a market transaction.

The same is true for many services produced in the economy. Taking care of your children, washing your car, mowing your lawn, walking your dog—none of these services are included in GDP if you do them for yourself, but all *are* included if you pay someone else to do them for you.

... *during a given period* ...

GDP measures production during some specific period of time. Only goods produced during that period are counted. But people and businesses spend billions of dollars each year on *used* goods, such as secondhand cars, previously occupied homes, used furniture, or an old photo of Elvis talking to an extraterrestrial. These goods were all *produced*, but not necessarily in the current period. And even if they *were* produced in the current period, they would only count when sold the *first* time, as new goods; to count them again each time they are resold would lead to an overestimate of total production for the period.

What duration of time should we use for GDP? In theory, we could use any duration. In 2004, for example, the United States produced an average of $32 billion worth of output each day, $978 billion each month, and $11,735 billion for the year as a whole. Thus, we could measure daily GDP, monthly GDP, and so on. In practice, however, GDP is measured for *each quarter* and then reported as an *annual rate* for that quarter.

To understand this, look at Table 1, which shows how GDP was actually reported by the government, for five recent quarters. During 2004–I (the first quarter, January through March of 2004), the U.S. economy actually produced about $2,868.15 billion in final goods and services. But you won't see that number in the table. What you *will* see is how much we *would* have produced during an entire year if we produced at that quarter's rate for *four* full quarters (4 × $2,868.15 billion = $11,472.6 billion).[1] Once the fourth-quarter figures are in, the government also reports the official GDP figure for the entire year—what we *actually* produced during the entire year.

... *within the nation's borders.*

U.S. GDP measures output produced *within U.S. borders*, regardless of whether it was produced by Americans. This means we *include* output produced by foreign-owned resources and foreign citizens located in the United States, and we *exclude* output produced by Americans located in other countries. For example, when the rock star Sting, a resident of Britain, gives a concert tour in the United States, the value of his services is counted in U.S. GDP but not in British GDP. Similarly, the services of an American nurse working in an Ethiopian hospital are part of Ethiopian GDP and not U.S. GDP.

The Expenditure Approach to GDP

The Commerce Department's Bureau of Economic Analysis (BEA), the agency responsible for gathering, reporting, and analyzing movements in the nation's output, calculates GDP in several different ways. The most important of these is the

---

[1] There is one other twist to the government's reporting: Before multiplying by 4, each quarter's production is *seasonally adjusted,* raised or lowered to eliminate any changes that usually occur during that time of year.

Quarter	2004–I	2004–II	2004–III	2004–IV	2005–I
GDP ($billions)	11,472.6	11,657.5	11,814.9	11,994.8	12,191.7

Source: Bureau of Economic Analysis, "National Income and Product Account Tables," accessed at *http://www.bea.gov.*

TABLE 1
GDP: Recent Quarters

expenditure approach. Because this method of measuring GDP tells us so much about the structure of our economy, we'll spend the next several pages on it.

In the expenditure approach, we divide output into four categories according to which group in the economy purchases it as the final user. The four categories are:

1. *Consumption goods and services (C),* purchased by households;
2. *Private investment goods and services (I),* purchased by businesses;
3. *Government goods and services (G),* purchased by government agencies;
4. *Net exports (NX),* purchased by foreigners.

This is an exhaustive list: Everyone who purchases a good or service included in U.S. GDP must be either a U.S. household, U.S. business, or U.S. government agency (including state and local government), or else is part of the foreign sector. Thus, when we add up the purchases of all four groups, we must get GDP:

Expenditure approach Measuring GDP by adding the value of goods and services purchased by each type of final user.

> *In the **expenditure approach** to measuring GDP, we add up the value of the goods and services purchased by each type of final user:*
>
> $$GDP = C + I + G + NX.$$

Table 2 shows the part of GDP purchased by each sector during the entire year 2004. Ignore the finer details for now and just concentrate on the last number in each column. Applying the expenditure approach to GDP in 2004 gives us GDP = $C + I + G + NX$ = $8,230 + $1,927 + $2,184 + (−$606) = $11,735 billion.

Now let's take a closer look at each of the four components of GDP.

Consumption Spending. Consumption (C) is the largest component of GDP— making up about three-quarters of total production in recent years—and the easiest to understand:

Consumption (C) The part of GDP purchased by households as final users.

> *Consumption is the part of GDP purchased by households as final users.*

Almost everything that households buy during the year—restaurant meals, gasoline, new clothes, doctors' visits, movies, electricity, and more—is included as part of consumption spending when we calculate GDP.

But notice the word *almost.*

Some of the things that households buy are *not* part of consumption in GDP. First, used goods or assets that households buy during the period are excluded. (Used goods were already counted when first produced, and assets are not goods or services, and therefore not part of GDP at all).

Second, *newly constructed homes*—even though part of GDP and usually purchased directly by households—are included as investment, rather than consumption. We'll discuss the reasons for this in the next section.

Finally, two things *are* included in consumption even though households don't actually buy them: (1) the total value of food products produced on farms that are

	Consumption Purchases		Private Investment Purchases		Government Purchases		Net Exports	
Services	$4,859	Plant, Equipment, and Sofware	$1,221	Government Consumption	$1,804	Exports	$1,176
Nondurable Goods	$2,377	New-Home Construction	$ 663	Government Investment	$ 380	Imports	$1,782
Durable Goods	$ 994	Changes in Business Inventories	$ 43				
Consumption =	**$8,230**	**Private Investment =**	**$1,927**	**Government Purchases =**	**$2,184**	**Net Exports =**	**−$ 606**

GDP = C + I + G + NX
= $8,230 + $1,927 + $2,184 + (−$606)
= $11,735

Source: Bureau of Economic Analysis, "National Income and Product Account Tables," accessed at *http://www.bea.gov.*

TABLE 2
GDP in 2004: The Expenditure Approach (Billions of Dollars)

consumed by the farmers and their families themselves; and (2) the total value of housing services provided by owner-occupied homes. The government estimates how much the food consumed on farms *could* have been sold for, and how much owner-occupied homes *could* have been rented for, and then includes these estimates as part of consumption.

Private Investment. What do oil-drilling rigs, cash registers, office telephones, and the house you grew up in all have in common? They are all examples of *capital goods*—goods that will provide useful services in future years. When we sum the value of all of the capital goods in the country, we get our **capital stock.**

Understanding the concept of capital stock helps us understand and define the concept of investment. A rough definition of **private investment** is *capital formation*—the *increase* in the nation's capital stock during the year.

More specifically,

> *private investment has three components: (1) business purchases of plant, equipment, and software; (2) new-home construction; and (3) changes in business firms' inventory stocks (changes in stocks of unsold goods).*

Each of these components requires some explanation.

Business Purchases of Plant, Equipment, and Software. This category might seem confusing at first glance. Why aren't plant, equipment, and software considered intermediate goods? After all, business firms buy these things in order to produce other things. Doesn't the value of their final goods include the value of their plant, equipment, and software as well?

Actually, no, and if you go back to the definition of intermediate goods, you will see why. Intermediate goods are *used up* in producing the current year's GDP. But a firm's plant, equipment, and software are intended to last for many years; only a

Capital stock The total value of all goods that will provide useful services in future years.

Private investment (*I*) The sum of business plant, equipment, and software purchases, new-home construction, and inventory changes; often referred to as just *investment*.

small part of them is used up to make the current year's output. Thus we regard new plant, equipment, and software as final goods, and we regard the firms that buy them as the final users of those goods.

For example, suppose our paper mill—the firm that turns wood chips into raw paper—buys a new factory building that is expected to last for 50 years. Then only a small fraction of that factory building—one-fiftieth—is used up in any one year's production of raw paper, and only a small part of the factory building's value will be reflected in the value of the firm's current output. But since the entire factory is produced during the year, we must include its full value *somewhere* in our measure of production. We therefore count the whole factory building as investment in GDP.

Plant, equipment, and software purchases are always the largest component of private investment. And 2004 was no exception, as you can see in the second column of Table 2. That year, businesses purchased and installed $1,221 billion worth of plant, equipment, and software, which was almost two-thirds of total private investment.

New-Home Construction. As you can see in Table 2, new-home construction made up a significant part of total private investment in 2004. But it may strike you as odd that this category is part of investment spending at all, since most new homes are purchased by households and could reasonably be considered consumption spending instead. Why is new-home construction counted as investment spending in GDP?

Largely because residential housing is an important part of the nation's *capital stock.* Just as an oil-drilling rig will continue to provide oil-drilling services for many years, so, too, a home will continue to provide housing services into the future. If we want our measure of private investment to roughly correspond to the increase in the nation's capital stock, we must include this important category of capital formation as part of private investment.

Changes in Inventories. Inventories are goods that have been produced but not yet sold. They include goods on store shelves, goods making their way through the production process in factories, and raw materials waiting to be used. We count the *change* in firms' inventories as part of investment in measuring GDP. Why? When goods are produced but not sold during the year, they end up in some firm's inventory stocks. If we did *not* count changes in inventories, we would be missing this important part of current production. Remember that GDP is designed to measure total *production,* not just the part of production that is sold during the year.

To understand this more clearly, suppose that in some year, the automobile industry produced $100 billion worth of automobiles, and that $80 billion worth was sold to consumers. Then the other $20 billion remained unsold and was added to the auto companies' inventories. If we counted consumption spending alone ($80 billion), we would underestimate automobile production in GDP. To ensure a proper measure, we must include not only the $80 billion in cars sold (consumption), but also the $20 billion *change* in inventories (private investment). In the end, the contribution to GDP is $80 billion (consumption) + $20 billion (private investment) = $100 billion, which is, indeed, the total value of automobile production during the year.

What if inventory stocks *decline* during the year, so that the change in inventories is negative? Our rule still holds: We include the change in inventories in our measure of GDP. But in this case, we add a *negative* number. For example, if the automobile industry produced $100 billion worth of cars this year, but consumers bought $120 billion, then $20 billion worth must have come from inventory stocks:

Unsold goods, like those pictured in this warehouse, are considered inventories. The change in these inventories is included as investment when calculating GDP.

© PHOTODISC/GETTY IMAGES

cars that were produced (and counted) in previous years, but that remained unsold until this year. In this case, the consumption spending of $120 billion *overestimates* automobile production during the year, so subtracting $20 billion corrects for this overcount. In the end, GDP would rise by $120 billion (consumption) − $20 billion (private investment) = $100 billion.

But why are inventory changes included in investment, rather than some other component of GDP? Because unsold goods are part of the nation's capital stock. They will provide services in the future, when they are finally sold and used. An increase in inventories represents capital formation: A decrease in inventories—negative investment—is a decrease in the nation's capital.

Inventory changes are generally the smallest component of private investment, but the most highly volatile in percentage terms. In 2004, for example, inventories rose by $43 billion; one year earlier, they fell by $1 billion, and the year before that they rose by $11 billion. Part of the reason for this volatility is that, while some inventory investment is intended, much of it is *unintended*. As the economy begins to slow, for example, businesses may be unable to sell all of the goods they have produced and had planned to sell. The unsold output is added to inventory stocks—an unintended increase in inventories. During rapid expansions, the opposite may happen: Businesses find themselves selling more than they produced—an unintended decrease in inventories.

Private Investment and the Capital Stock: Some Provisos. A few pages ago, it was pointed out that private investment corresponds only *roughly* to the increase in the nation's capital stock. Why this cautious language? Because changes in the nation's capital stock are somewhat more complicated than we are able to capture with private investment alone.

First, private investment *excludes* some production that adds to the nation's capital stock. Specifically, private investment does not include:

- *Government investment.* An important part of the nation's capital stock is owned and operated not by businesses, but by government—federal, state, and local. Courthouses, police cars, fire stations, schools, weather satellites, military aircraft, highways, and bridges are all examples of government capital. If you look at the third column of Table 2, for example, you'll see that the BEA estimated government investment to be $380 billion in 2004; that was the part of government spending that was devoted to capital formation in 2004.
- *Consumer durables.* Goods such as furniture, automobiles, washing machines, and personal computers for home use can be considered capital goods, since they will continue to provide services for many years. In 2004, households purchased $994 billion worth of consumer durables (see Table 2, first column).
- *Human capital.* Think about a surgeon's skills in performing a heart bypass operation, or a police detective's ability to find clues and solve a murder, or a Web-page designer's mastery of HTML and Java. These types of knowledge will continue to provide valuable services well into the future, just like plant and equipment or new housing. To measure the increase in the capital stock most broadly, then, we *should* include the additional skills and training acquired by the workforce during the year.

In addition to excluding some types of capital formation, private investment also errs in the other direction: It ignores depreciation—the capital that is used up during the year. Fortunately, the BEA estimates depreciation of the private and

Net investment Investment minus depreciation.

public capital stock, allowing us to calculate **net investment** (total investment minus depreciation) for these sectors. For example, for 2004, the BEA estimates that $1,178 billion of the private capital stock depreciated during the year (not shown in Table 2). So net private investment that year was only $1,927 billion − $1,178 billion = $749 billion. Similarly, the BEA estimates that $229 billion in government capital depreciated in 2004, so net government investment that year was $380 billion − $229 billion = $151 billion.

Government Purchases. In 2004, the government bought $2,184 billion worth of goods and services that were part of GDP—almost a fifth of the total. This component of GDP is called **government purchases,** although in recent years the Department of Commerce has begun to use the phrase *government consumption and investment purchases.* Government *investment,* as discussed earlier, refers to capital goods purchased by government agencies. The rest of government purchases is considered government *consumption:* spending on goods and services that are used up during the period. This includes the salaries of government workers and military personnel, and raw materials such as computer paper for government offices, gasoline for government vehicles, and the electricity used in government buildings.

Government purchases (G) Spending by federal, state, and local governments on goods and services.

Investment: Economics Versus Ordinary English Be *extremely* careful when using the term *investment* in your economics course. In economics, investment refers to capital formation, such as the building of a new factory, home, or hospital, or the production and installation of new capital equipment, or the accumulation of inventories by business firms. In everyday language, however, *investment* has a very different meaning: a place to put your wealth. Thus, in ordinary English, you invest whenever you buy stocks or bonds or certificates of deposit or when you lend money to a friend who is starting up a business. But in the language of economics, you have not invested but merely changed the form in which you are holding your wealth (say, from checking account balances to stocks or bonds). To avoid confusion, remember that investment takes place when there is new production of capital goods—that is, when there is *capital formation.*

DANGEROUS CURVES

There are a few things to keep in mind about government purchases in GDP. First, we include purchases by state and local governments as well as the federal government. In macroeconomics, it makes little difference whether the purchases are made by a local government agency like the parks department of Kalamazoo, Michigan, or a huge federal agency such as the U.S. Department of Defense.

Second, government purchases include *goods*—like fighter jets, police cars, school buildings, and spy satellites—and *services*—such as those performed by police, legislators, and military personnel. The government is considered to be the final purchaser of these things even if it uses them to make other goods or services. For example, if you are taking economics at a public college or university that produces educational services, then your professor is selling teaching services to a state or city government. His or her salary enters into GDP as part of government purchases.

Finally, it's important to distinguish between government *purchases*—which are counted in GDP—and government *outlays* as measured by local, state, and federal budgets and reported in the media. What's the difference? In addition to their purchases of goods and services, government agencies also disburse money for **transfer payments.** These funds are *given* to people or organizations—*not* to buy goods or services from them, but rather to fulfill some social obligation or goal. For example, Social Security payments by the federal government, unemployment insurance and welfare payments by state governments, and money disbursed to homeless shelters and soup kitchens by city governments are all examples of transfer payments. The important thing to remember about transfer payments is this:

Transfer payment Any payment that is not compensation for supplying goods or services.

Transfer payments represent money redistributed from one group of citizens (taxpayers) to another (the poor, the unemployed, the elderly). While transfers are included in government budgets as outlays, they are not purchases of currently produced goods and services, and so are not included in government purchases or in GDP.

Net Exports. There is one more category of buyers of output produced in the United States: *the foreign sector.* Looking back at Table 2, the fourth column tells us that in 2004, purchasers *outside* the nation bought approximately $1,176 billion of U.S. goods and services—about 10 percent of our GDP. These exports are part of U.S. production of goods and services and so are included in GDP.

However, once we recognize dealings with the rest of the world, we must correct an inaccuracy in our measure of GDP the way we've reported it so far. Americans buy many goods and services every year that were produced *outside* the United States (Chinese shoes, Japanese cars, Mexican beer, Costa Rican coffee). When we add up the final purchases of households, businesses, and government agencies, we *overcount* U.S. production because we include goods and services produced abroad. But these are *not* part of U.S. output. To correct for this overcount, we deduct all U.S. *imports* during the year, leaving us with just output produced in the United States. In 2004, these imports amounted to $1,782 billion, an amount equal to about 15 percent of our GDP.

Let's recap: To obtain an accurate measure of GDP, we must include U.S. production that is purchased by foreigners: total exports. But to correct for including goods produced abroad, we must subtract Americans' purchases of goods produced outside of the United States: total imports. In practice, we take both of these steps together by adding **net exports (NX)**, which are total exports minus total imports.

HTTP://
The main source of information on U.S. GDP is the Bureau of Economic Analysis. Its Web page can be found at http://www.bea.gov

Net exports (NX) Total exports minus total imports.

To properly account for output sold to, and bought from, foreigners, we must include net exports—the difference between exports and imports—as part of expenditure in GDP.

In 2004, when total exports were $1,176 billion and total imports were $1,782 billion, net exports (as you can see in Table 2) were $1,176 - $1,782 = -$606 billion. The negative number indicates that the imports we're subtracting from GDP are greater than the exports we're adding.

Other Approaches to GDP

In addition to the expenditure approach, in which we calculate GDP as $C + I + G + NX$, there are other ways of measuring GDP. You may be wondering: Why bother? Why not just use one method—whichever is best—and stick to it?

Actually, there are two good reasons for measuring GDP in different ways. The first is practical. Each method of measuring GDP is subject to measurement errors. By calculating total output in several different ways and then trying to resolve the differences, the BEA gets a more accurate measure than would be possible with one method alone. The second reason is that the different ways of measuring total output give us different insights into the structure of our economy. Let's take a look at two more ways of measuring—and thinking about—GDP.

The Value-Added Approach. In the expenditure approach, we record goods and services only when they are sold to their final users—at the end of the production process. But we can also measure GDP by adding up each *firm's* contribution to the product *as it is produced.*

A firm's contribution to a product is called its *value added.* More formally,

Value added The revenue a firm receives minus the cost of the intermediate goods it buys.

> *a firm's **value added** is the revenue it receives for its output, minus the cost of all the intermediate goods that it buys.*

Look back at Figure 1, which traces the production of a ream of notebook paper. The paper mill, for example, buys $1.00 worth of wood chips (an intermediate good) from the lumber company and turns it into raw paper, which it sells for $1.50. The value added by the paper mill is $1.50 − $1.00 = $0.50. Similarly, the office supplies maker buys $1.50 worth of paper (an intermediate good) from the paper mill and sells it for $2.25, so its value added is $2.25 − $1.50 = $0.75. If we total the value added by each firm, we should get the final value of the notebook paper, as shown in Table 3. (Notice that we assume the first producer in this process—the lumber company—uses no intermediate goods.)

The total value added is $1.00 + $0.50 + $0.75 + $1.25 + $1.50 = $5.00, which is equal to the final sales price of the ream of paper. For any good or service, it will always be the case that the sum of the values added by all firms equals the final sales price. This leads to our second method of measuring GDP:

Value-added approach Measuring GDP by summing the value added by all firms in the economy.

> *In the **value-added approach**, GDP is the sum of the values added by all firms in the economy.*

The Factor Payments Approach. If a bakery sells $200,000 worth of bread during the year and buys $25,000 in intermediate goods (flour, eggs, yeast), then its value added (its revenue minus the cost of its intermediate goods) is $200,000 − $25,000 = $175,000. This is also the sum that will be *left over* from its revenue after the bakery pays for its intermediate goods.

Where does this $175,000 go? In addition to its intermediate goods, the bakery must pay for the *resources* it used during the year: the land, labor, capital, and entrepreneurship that enabled it to add value to its intermediate goods.

Factor payments Payments to the owners of resources that are used in production

Payments to owners of resources are called **factor payments,** because resources are also called the factors of production. Owners of capital (the owners of the firm's buildings or machinery, or those who lend funds to the firm so that *it* can buy buildings and machinery) receive *interest payments.* Owners of land and natural resources receive *rent.* And those who provide labor to the firm receive *wages and salaries.*

Finally, there is one additional resource used by the firm: *entrepreneurship.* In every capitalist economy, the entrepreneurs are those who visualize society's needs, mobilize and coordinate the other resources so that production can take place, and gamble that the enterprise will succeed. The people who provide this entrepreneurship (often the owners of the firms) receive a fourth type of factor payment: *profit.*

Now let's go back to our bakery, which received $200,000 in revenue during the year. We've seen that $25,000 of this went to pay for intermediate goods, leaving $175,000 in value added earned by the factors of production. Let's suppose that

Firm	Cost of Intermediate Goods	Revenue	Value Added
Lumber Company	$ 0	$1.00	$1.00
Paper Mill	$1.00	$1.50	$0.50
Office Supplies Manufacturer	$1.50	$2.25	$0.75
Wholesaler	$2.25	$3.50	$1.25
Retailer	$3.50	$5.00	$1.50
			Total: $5.00

TABLE 3

Value Added at Different Stages of Production

$110,000 went to pay the wages of the bakery's employees, $10,000 was paid out as interest on loans, and $15,000 was paid in rent for the land under the bakery. That leaves $175,000 − $110,000 − $10,000 − $15,000 = $40,000. This last sum—since it doesn't go to anyone else—stays with the owner of the bakery. It, too, is a factor payment—profit—for the entrepreneurship she provides. Thus, when all of the factor payments, including profit, are added together, the total will be $110,000 + $10,000 + $15,000 + $40,000 = $175,000—precisely equal to the value added at the bakery. More generally,

In any year, the value added by a firm is equal to the total factor payments made by that firm.

Earlier, we learned that GDP equals the sum of all firms' value added; now we've learned that each firm's value added is equal to its factor payments. Thus, GDP must equal the total factor payments made by all firms in the economy. Since all of these factor payments are received by households in the form of wages and salaries, rent, interest, or profit, we have our *third* method of measuring GDP:

*In the **factor payments approach**, GDP is measured by adding up all of the income—wages and salaries, rent, interest, and profit—earned by all households in the economy.[2]*

Factor payments approach Measuring GDP by summing the factor payments earned by all households in the economy.

The factor payments approach to GDP gives us one of our most important insights into the marcoeconomy:

The total output of the economy (GDP) is equal to the total income earned in the economy.

This simple idea—output equals income—follows directly from the factor payments approach to GDP. It explains why macroeconomists use the terms "output"

---

[2] Actually, this is just an approximation. Before a firm pays its factors of production, it first deducts a small amount for depreciation of its plant and equipment, and another small amount for the sales taxes it must pay to the government. Thus, GDP and total factor payments are slightly different. We ignore this difference in the text.

and "income" interchangeably: They are one and the same. If output rises, income rises by the same amount; if output falls, income falls by an equal amount. We'll be using this very important insight in several chapters to come.

Measuring GDP: A Summary

You've now learned three different ways to calculate GDP:

Expenditure Approach: GDP = $C + I + G + NX$

Value-Added Approach: GDP = Sum of value added by all firms

Factor Payments Approach: GDP = Sum of factor payments earned by all households

= Wages and salaries + interest + rent + profit

= Total household income

We will use these three approaches to GDP again and again as we study what makes the economy tick. But for now, make sure you understand why each one of them should, in theory, give us the same number for GDP.

Real Versus Nominal GDP

Since GDP is measured in dollars, we have a serious problem when we want to track the change in output over time. The problem is that the value of the dollar—its purchasing power—is itself changing. As prices have risen over the years, the value of the dollar has steadily fallen. Trying to keep track of GDP using dollars in different years is like trying to keep track of a child's height using a ruler whose length changes each year. If we find that the child is three rulers tall in one year and four rulers tall in the next, we cannot know how much the child has grown, if at all, until we adjust for the effects of a changing ruler. The same is true for GDP and for any other economic variable measured in dollars: We usually need to adjust our measurements to reflect changes in the value of the dollar.

Nominal variable A variable measured without adjustment for the dollar's changing value.

Real variable A variable adjusted for changes in the dollar's value.

> *When a variable is measured over time with no adjustment for the dollar's changing value, it is called a **nominal variable**. When a variable is adjusted for the dollar's changing value, it is called a **real variable**.*

Most government statistics are reported in both nominal and real terms, but economists focus almost exclusively on real variables. This is because changes in nominal variables don't really tell us much. For example, from the second to the third quarter of 2001 (not shown in earlier tables), nominal GDP increased from $10,050 billion to $10,098 billion, an increase of one-half of one percent. But production as measured by *real GDP* actually *decreased* over that period. The increase in nominal GDP was due entirely to a rise in prices.

The distinction between nominal and real values is crucial in macroeconomics. The public, the media, and sometimes even government officials have been confused by a failure to make this distinction. Whenever we want to track significant changes in key macroeconomic variables—such as the average wage rate, wealth, income, and GDP or any of its components—we always use *real* variables.

Since our economic well-being depends, in part, on the goods and services we can buy, it is important to translate nominal values (which are measured in current dollars) to real values (which adjust for the dollar's changing value).

In the next chapter, you'll learn how economists translate some important nominal variables into real variables.

How GDP Is Used

We've come a long way since 1931. In that year—as the United States plummeted into the worst depression in its history—Congress summoned economists from government agencies, from academia, and from the private sector to testify about the state of the economy. They were asked the most basic questions: How much output was the nation producing, and how much had production fallen since 1929? How much income were Americans earning, how much were they spending? How much profit were businesses earning, and what were they doing with their profits? To the surprise of the members of Congress, no one could answer any of these questions, because *no one was keeping track of our national income and output!* The most recent measurement, which was rather incomplete, had been made in 1929.

Thus began the U.S. system of national income accounts, a system whose value was instantly recognized around the world and rapidly copied by other countries. Today, the government's reports on GDP are used to steer the economy over both the short run and the long run. In the short run, sudden changes in real GDP can alert us to the onset of a recession or a too-rapid expansion that can overheat the economy. Many (but not all) economists believe that, if alerted in time, policies can be designed to help keep the economy on a more balanced course.

GDP is also used to measure the long-run growth rate of the economy's output. Indeed, we typically define the average *standard of living* as *output per capita*: real GDP divided by the population. In order for output per capita to rise, real GDP must grow faster than the population. Since the U.S. population tends to grow by about 1 percent per year, a real GDP growth rate of 1 percent per year is needed just to *maintain* our output per capita; higher growth rates are needed to increase it.

Look at Figure 2, which shows the annual percentage change in real GDP from 1960 through 2004. The lower horizontal line indicates the 1 percent growth needed to just maintain output per capita. You can see that, on average, real GDP has grown by more than this, so that output per capita has steadily increased over time.

Growth in real GDP is also important for another reason: to ensure that the economy is generating sufficient new *jobs* for a workforce that is not only growing in number, but in productivity. Each year, the average worker is capable of producing more output, due to advances in technology, increases in the capital stock, and the greater skills of workers themselves. But if each worker produces more output, then output must increase even *faster* than the population to create enough jobs for everyone who wants to work. If not, the unemployment rate will rise.

In practice, an average annual growth rate of about 3.3 percent—the upper line in Figure 2—seems to prevent the unemployment rate from rising. And over the long run, growth in real GDP has been sufficiently high for this purpose. But you can also see that there are periods of time when GDP growth—even though positive—is too

Real GDP Growth Rate (Percent Change from Previous Period)

Actual GDP growth rate

GDP growth needed for constant unemployment rate

GDP growth needed for constant output per capita

Year

FIGURE 2

Real GDP Growth Rate, 1960–2004

Although the growth rate of real GDP has fluctuated over time, it has rarely dipped below the 1 percent rate needed to maintain output per capita. And although growth has frequently fallen below the 3.3 percent rate needed to prevent a rise in unemployment, it has met that threshold on average.

Source: Bureau of Economic Analysis, *National Economic Accounts,* Table 1.1.1.

low to prevent a rise in the unemployment rate. During the recession of 2001 and into the first half of 2003, for example, GDP growth lagged behind the 3.3 percent requirement, and the unemployment rate rose. However, most economists have confidence that over time, real GDP growth will exceed the 3.3 percent requirement by enough to make up for the periods it has fallen behind, and that the economy will continue to generate jobs for a growing and more productive workforce, just as it has in the past. Later, you'll learn the reasons for this confidence.

To sum up: We use GDP to guide the economy in two ways. In the short run, it alerts us to recessions and give us a chance to stabilize the economy. And over long periods it tells us whether our economy is growing fast enough to raise output per capita and our standard of living, and fast enough to generate sufficient jobs for a growing population.

Problems with GDP

You have seen that GDP is an extremely useful concept. But the measurement of GDP is plagued by some serious problems.

Quality Changes. Suppose a new ballpoint pen comes out that lasts four times as long as previous versions. What *should* happen to GDP? Ideally, each new pen should count the same as four old pens, since one new pen offers the same *writing services* as four old ones. But the analysts at the Bureau of Economic Analysis (BEA) would most likely treat this new pen the same as an old pen and record an increase in GDP only if the total number of pens increased. Why? Because the BEA has a limited budget. While it does include the impact of quality changes for many goods and services (such as automobiles and computers), the BEA simply does not have the resources to estimate quality changes for millions of different goods and services. These include many consumer goods (such as razor blades that shave closer and last longer), medical services (increased surgery success rates and shorter recovery periods), and retail services (faster checkout times due to optical scanners).

Ignoring these quality improvements causes GDP to understate the true growth in output from year to year.

The Underground Economy. Some production is hidden from government authorities, either because it is illegal (drugs, prostitution, most gambling) or because those engaged in it are avoiding taxes. Production in these hidden markets, which comprise the *underground economy,* cannot be measured accurately, so the BEA must estimate it. Many economists believe that the BEA's estimates are too low. As a result, GDP may understate total output. However, since the *relative* importance of the underground economy does not change rapidly, the BEA's estimates of *changes* in GDP from year to year should not be seriously affected.

Nonmarket Production. With a few exceptions, GDP does not include **nonmarket production:** goods and services that are produced but not sold in the marketplace. All of the housecleaning, typing, sewing, lawn mowing, and child rearing that people do themselves, rather than hiring someone else, are excluded from GDP. Whenever a nonmarket transaction (say, cleaning your apartment) becomes a market transaction (hiring a housecleaner to do it for you), GDP will rise, even though total production (cleaning one apartment) has remained the same.

Nonmarket production Goods and services that are produced but not sold in a market.

Over the last half-century, much production has shifted away from the home and to the market. Parenting, which was not counted in past years' GDP, has become day care, which *does* count—currently contributing several billion dollars annually to GDP. Similarly, home-cooked food has been replaced by takeout, talking to a friend has been replaced by therapy, and the neighbor who watches your house while you're away has been replaced by a store-bought alarm system or an increase in police protection. In all of these cases, real GDP increases, even though production has not. This can exaggerate the growth in GDP over long periods of time.

What do all these problems tell us about the value of GDP? That for certain purposes—especially interpreting *long-run* changes in GDP—we must exercise caution. For example, suppose that, over the next 20 years, the growth rate of GDP slows down. Would this mean that something is going wrong with the economy? Would it suggest a need to change course? Not necessarily. It *could* be that the underground economy or unrecorded quality changes are becoming more important. Similarly, if GDP growth accelerates, it could mean that our living standards are rising more rapidly. But it might instead mean that economic activity is shifting out of the home and into the market even more rapidly than in the past.

GDP works much better, however, as a guide to the short-run performance of the economy. Look back at the list of problems with GDP. The distortion in GDP measurement caused by each problem is likely to remain fairly constant from quarter to quarter. If GDP suddenly drops, it is extremely unlikely that the underground economy has suddenly become more important, or that there has been a sudden shift from market to nonmarket activities, or that we are suddenly missing more quality changes than usual. Rather, we can be reasonably certain that output and economic activity are slowing down.

Short-term changes in real GDP are fairly accurate reflections of the state of the economy. A significant quarter-to-quarter change in real GDP indicates a change in actual production, rather than a measurement problem.

This is why policy makers, businesspeople, and the media pay such close attention to GDP as a guide to the economy from quarter to quarter.

EMPLOYMENT AND UNEMPLOYMENT

When you think of unemployment, you may have an image in your mind that goes something like this: As the economy slides into recession, an anxious employee is called into an office and handed a pink slip by a grim-faced manager. "Sorry," the manager says, "I wish there were some other way. . . ." The worker spends the next few months checking the classified ads, pounding the pavement, and sending out résumés in a desperate search for work. And perhaps, after months of trying, the laid-off worker gives up, spending days at the neighborhood bar, drinking away the shame and frustration, and sinking lower and lower into despair and inertia.

For some people, joblessness begins and ends very much like this—a human tragedy, and a needless one. On one side, we have people who want to work and support themselves by producing something; on the other side is the rest of society, which could certainly use more goods and services. Yet somehow, the system isn't working, and the jobless cannot find work. The result is often hardship for the unemployed and their families, and a loss to society in general.

But this is just one face of unemployment, and there are others. Some instances of unemployment, for example, have little to do with macroeconomic conditions. And frequently, unemployment causes a lot less suffering than in our grim story.

Types of Unemployment

In the United States, people are considered unemployed if they are: (1) not working and (2) actively seeking a job. But unemployment can arise for a variety of reasons, each with its own policy implications. This is why economists have found it useful to classify unemployment into four different categories, each arising from a different cause and each having different consequences.

Frictional Unemployment. Short-term joblessness experienced by people who are between jobs or who are entering the labor market for the first time or after an absence is called **frictional unemployment**. In the real world, it takes time to find a job—time to prepare your résumé, to decide where to send it, to wait for responses, and then to investigate job offers so you can make a wise choice. It also takes time for employers to consider your skills and qualifications and to decide whether you are right for their firms. If you are not working during that time, you will be unemployed: searching for work but not working.

Because frictional unemployment is, by definition, short term, it causes little hardship to those affected by it. In most cases, people have enough savings to support themselves through a short spell of joblessness, or else they can borrow on their credit cards or from friends or family to tide them over. Moreover, this kind of unemployment has important benefits: By spending time searching rather than jumping at the first opening that comes their way, people find jobs for which they are better suited and in which they will ultimately be more productive. As a result, workers earn higher incomes, firms have more productive employees, and society has more goods and services.

HTTP://

Employment-related information for the United States can be found at the Bureau of Labor Statistics Web site: http://stats.bls.gov.

Frictional unemployment
Joblessness experienced by people who are between jobs or who are just entering or reentering the labor market.

Seasonal Unemployment. Joblessness related to changes in weather, tourist patterns, or other seasonal factors is called **seasonal unemployment**. For example, most ski instructors lose their jobs every April or May, and many construction workers are laid off each winter.

Seasonal unemployment, like frictional unemployment, is rather benign: It is short term and, because it is entirely predictable, workers are often compensated in advance for the unemployment they experience in the off-season. Construction workers, for example, are paid higher-than-average hourly wages, in part to compensate them for their high probability of joblessness in the winter.

However, seasonal unemployment complicates the interpretation of unemployment data. Seasonal factors push the unemployment rate up in certain months of the year and pull it down in others, even when overall conditions in the economy remain unchanged. For example, each June, unemployment rises as millions of high school and college students—who do not want to work during the school year—begin looking for summer jobs. If the government reported the actual rise in unemployment in June, it would *seem* as if labor market conditions were deteriorating, when in fact, the rise would be merely a predictable and temporary seasonal change. To prevent any misunderstandings, the government usually reports the *seasonally adjusted* rate of unemployment, a rate that reflects only those changes beyond normal for the month. For example, if the unemployment rate in June is typically one percentage point higher than during the rest of the year, then the seasonally adjusted rate for June will be the actual rate minus one percentage point.

Structural Unemployment. Sometimes, there are jobs available and workers who would be delighted to have them, but job seekers and employers are mismatched in some way. For example, in 2005, there were plenty of job openings for business professors; for nurses and nurse practitioners; for translators of strategic languages like Arabic, Persian, and Urdu; and in many other professions. Many of the unemployed, however, had been laid off from the airline, automobile and textile industries, and did not have the skills and training to work where the jobs were going begging. This is a *skill* mismatch. The mismatch can also be *geographic,* as when construction jobs go begging in Northern California, Oregon, and Washington, but unemployed construction workers live in other states.

Unemployment that results from these kinds of mismatches is called **structural unemployment,** because it arises from *structural change* in the economy: when old, dying industries are replaced with new ones that require different skills and are located in different areas of the country. Structural unemployment is generally a stubborn, *long-term* problem, often lasting several years or more. Why? Because it can take considerable time for the structurally unemployed to find jobs—time to relocate to another part of the country or time to acquire new skills. To make matters worse, the structurally unemployed—who could benefit from financial assistance for job training or relocation—usually cannot get loans because they don't have jobs.

In recent decades, structural unemployment has been a much bigger problem in other countries, especially in Europe, than it is in the United States. Table 4 shows average unemployment rates in the United States and several European countries from 1995 to 2004 as well as in early 2005. Unemployment rates were consistently higher in continental Europe than in the United States during this decade and, in most of these countries, were still high in early 2005. And the unemployed remain jobless longer in Europe (where more than a third of all the unemployed have been so for more than a year) than in the United States (where only 1 in 10 has been jobless for more than a year).

TABLE 4
Average Unemployment Rates in Several Countries, 1995–2004 and early 2005

Country	Average Unemployment Rate, 1995–2004	Unemployment Rate, early 2005
France	10.2 %	10.0 %
Italy	10.1 %	8.1 %
Canada	7.4 %	6.1 %
United Kingdom	6.2 %	4.7 %
Germany	8.9 %	11.2 %
Sweden	7.3 %	6.3 %
United States	5.2 %	5.2 %

Source: "Comparative Unemployment Rates in Nine Countries, 1995–2005," available online at Bureau of Labor Statistics, Foreign Labor Statistics page (www.bls.gov/fls/home.htm). European rates have been adjusted by the BLS for comparability to U.S. rates. Ten-year averages were calculated by authors from the BLS data. Early 2005 unemployment rates are for March, 2005 except for Italy (4th quarter, 2004) and the United Kingdom (February, 2005).

Within the United States, some areas have higher structural unemployment than others. For example, in March 2005 when the U.S. unemployment rate was 5.2 percent, the rate in Ohio was 6.3 percent; in South Carolina, 6.8 percent; and in Michigan, 6.9 percent.

The types of unemployment we've considered so far—frictional, structural, and seasonal—arise largely from *microeconomic* causes; that is, they are attributable to changes in specific industries and specific labor markets, rather than to the overall level of production in the country. This kind of unemployment cannot be entirely eliminated, as people will always spend some time searching for new jobs, there will always be seasonal industries in the economy, and structural changes will, from time to time, require workers to move to new locations or gain new job skills. Some amount of microeconomic unemployment is a sign of a dynamic economy. It allows workers to sort themselves into the best possible jobs, enables us to enjoy seasonal goods and services like winter skiing and summers at the beach, and permits the economy to go through structural changes when needed.

But frictional, structural, and seasonal unemployment rates are not fixed in stone, and government policy may be able to influence them. In the United States, many economists believe that we can continue to enjoy the benefits of a fast-changing and flexible economy with a lower unemployment rate. To achieve this goal, they advocate programs to help match the unemployed with employers and to help the jobless relocate and learn new skills. In Europe, by contrast, most economists believe that government labor and regulatory policies have been a *cause* of the structural unemployment problem. For example, government regulations make it costly or impossible for many European firms to lay off workers once they are hired. While that encourages firms to retain any *currently* employed workers, it also discourages new hiring, since firms regard any newly hired worker as a permanent obligation, even if future production turns down and the new worker is no longer needed. European unemployment benefits may also play a role. They are more generous than in the United States, and the benefits are given for longer durations with a greater fraction of the potential labor force eligible to receive them. While this certainly helps the unemployed deal with the hardship of job loss, it also means that European workers have less incentive to seek new work once they lose a job.

Note, however, that in both Europe and the United States, the proposed solutions for high seasonal, frictional, or structural unemployment are changes in labor or regulatory policies, rather than changes in macroeconomic policy designed to raise GDP.

Our fourth and last type of unemployment, however, has an entirely *macroeconomic* cause.

Cyclical Unemployment. When the economy goes into a recession and total output falls, the unemployment rate rises. Many previously employed workers lose their jobs and have difficulty finding new ones. At the same time, there are fewer openings, so new entrants to the labor force must spend more than the usual time searching before they are hired. This type of unemployment—because it is caused by the business cycle—is called **cyclical unemployment.**

Cyclical unemployment Joblessness arising from changes in production over the business cycle.

Look at Figure 3, which shows the unemployment rate in the United States for each quarter from 1960 to mid-2005, and notice the rises that occurred during periods of recession (shaded). For example, in the recessions of the early 1980s, the unemployment rate rose from about 6 percent to more than 10 percent. And in the more recent recession from March to November of 2001, the unemployment rate rose from 4.2 percent to 5.8 percent. These were rises in cyclical unemployment.

Since it arises from conditions in the overall economy, cyclical unemployment is a problem for *macroeconomic* policy. This is why macroeconomists focus almost exclusively on cyclical unemployment, rather than the other types of joblessness. Reflecting this emphasis, macroeconomists say we have reached **full employment** when *cyclical unemployment is reduced to zero,* even though substantial amounts of frictional, seasonal, and structural unemployment may remain:

Full employment A situation in which there is no cyclical unemployment.

> *In macroeconomics, full employment means zero cyclical unemployment. But the overall unemployment rate at full employment is greater than zero because there are still positive levels of frictional, seasonal, and structural unemployment.*

How do we tell how much of our unemployment is cyclical? Many economists believe that today, normal amounts of frictional, seasonal, and structural unemployment account for an unemployment rate of between 4.5 and 5.0 percent in the United States. Therefore, any unemployment beyond this is considered cyclical unemployment. For example, when the actual unemployment rate was 6.4 percent in June 2003, we would say that 1.4 to 1.9 percent of the labor force was cyclically unemployed.

The Costs of Unemployment

Why are we so concerned about achieving a low rate of unemployment? What are the *costs* of unemployment to our society? We can identify two different types of costs: economic costs, those that can be readily measured in dollar terms, and

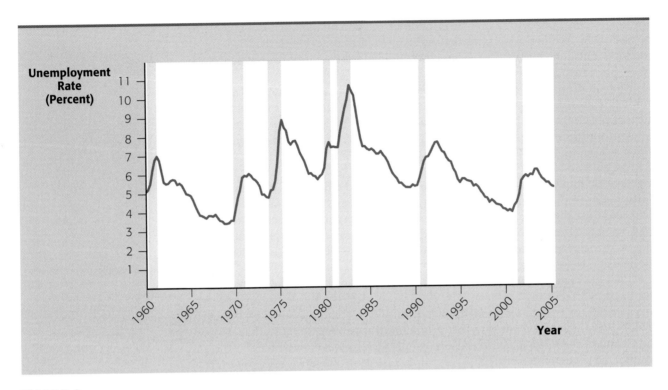

FIGURE 3
U.S. Quarterly Unemployment Rate, 1960–2005

The unemployment rate rises during recessions (shaded) and falls during expansions.

noneconomic costs, those that are difficult or impossible to measure in dollars, but that still affect us in important ways.

Economic Costs. The chief economic cost of unemployment is the *opportunity cost* of lost output: the goods and services the jobless *would* produce if they were working but do not produce because they cannot find work. This cost is borne by our society in general, although the burden may fall more on one group than another. If, for example, the unemployed were simply left to fend for themselves, then *they* would bear most of the cost. In fact, the unemployed are often given government assistance, so that the costs are spread somewhat among citizens in general. But there is no escaping this central fact:

> *When there is cyclical unemployment, the nation* produces *less output, and therefore some group or groups within society must* consume *less output.*

One way of viewing the economic cost of cyclical unemployment is illustrated in Figure 4. The green line shows real GDP over time, while the orange line shows the path of our **potential output**—the output we *could* have produced if the economy were operating at full employment.

Notice that actual output is sometimes *above* potential output. At these times, unemployment is *below* the full-employment rate. For example, during the expansion in the late 1960s, cyclical unemployment was eliminated and the sum of frictional, seasonal, and structural unemployment dropped below 4.5 percent, its normal level for those years. At other times, real GDP is *below* potential output,

Potential output The level of output the economy could produce if operating at full employment.

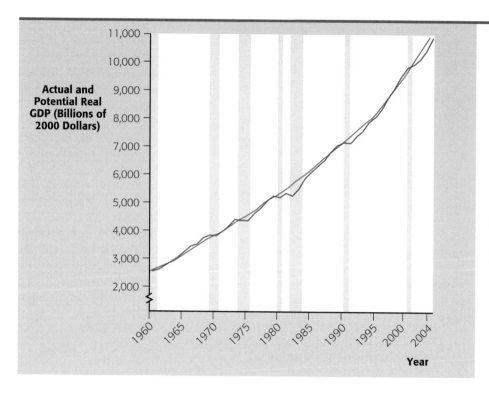

FIGURE 4
Actual And Potential Real GDP, 1960–2003

Measured in 2000 dollars. *Sources:* Real GDP from Bureau of Economic Analysis, "National Economic Accounts," Table 1.1.6 (www.bea.gov); Potential Real GDP from Congressional Budget Office, "Data Underlying Table 2-3: Key Assumptions in CBO's Projection of Potential Output" (By calendar year), The Budget and Economic Outlook: Fiscal Years 2004–2014, January 2004 (www.cbo.gov/Spreadsheet/4985_Table2-3.xls) and authors' conversion from 1996 to 2000 dollars.

most often during and following a recession. At these times, unemployment rises above the full-employment rate. During the 2001 recession, the unemployment rate rose from 4.2 percent to 5.6 percent, then hovered near or above 6 percent for the next two years.

In the figure, you can see that we have spent more of the last 40 years operating *below* our potential than above it. That is, the cyclical ups and downs of the economy have, on balance, led to lower living standards than we would have had if the economy had always operated just at potential output.

Broader Costs. There are also costs of unemployment that go beyond lost output. Unemployment—especially when it lasts for many months or years—can have serious psychological and physical effects. Some studies have found that increases in unemployment cause noticeable rises in the number of heart attack deaths, suicides, and admissions to state prisons and psychiatric hospitals. The jobless are more likely to suffer a variety of health problems, including high blood pressure, heart disorders, troubled sleep, and back pain. There may be other problems—such as domestic violence, depression, and alcoholism—that are more difficult to document. And, tragically, most of those who lose their job and remain unemployed for long periods also lose their health insurance, increasing the likelihood that these problems will have serious consequences.

Unemployment also causes setbacks in achieving important social goals. For example, most of us want a fair and just society where all people have an equal chance to better themselves. But our citizens do not bear the burden of unemployment equally. In a recession, we do not all suffer a reduction in our work hours;

TABLE 5
Unemployment Rates for Various Groups, May 2005

Group	Unemployment Rate
Whites	4.4%
Hispanics	6.0%
Blacks	10.1%
White Teenagers	15.4%
Black Teenagers	35.8%

Source: The Employment Situation: May 2005, Bureau of Labor Statistics News Release, June 3, 2005 (Tables A-2, A-3; seasonally adjusted data).

instead, some people are laid off entirely, while others continue to work roughly the same hours.

Moreover, the burden of unemployment is not shared equally among different groups in the population, but tends to fall most heavily on minorities, especially minority youth. As a rough rule of thumb, the unemployment rate for blacks is twice that for whites; and the rate for *teenage* blacks is triple the rate for blacks overall. Table 5 shows that the unemployment rates for May 2005 are roughly consistent with this general experience. Notice the extremely high unemployment rate for black teenagers: 35.8 percent. This contributes to a vicious cycle of poverty and discrimination: When minority youths are deprived of that all-important first job, they remain at a disadvantage in the labor market for years to come.

How Unemployment Is Measured

In May 2005, about 155 million Americans were not employed, according to official government statistics. Were all of these people unemployed? Absolutely not. In theory, the unemployed are those who are *willing and able* to work but do not have jobs. Most of the 155 million nonworking Americans were either *unable* or *unwilling* to work. For example, the very old, the very young, and the very ill were unable to work, as were those serving prison terms. Others were able to work, but preferred not to, including millions of college students, homemakers, and retired people. Still others were in the military and are counted in the population, but not counted when calculating civilian employment statistics.

But how, in practice, can we determine who is willing and able? This is a thorny problem, and there is no perfect solution to it. In the United States, we determine whether a person is willing and able to work by his or her *behavior*. More specifically, to be counted as unemployed, you must have recently *searched* for work. But how can we tell who has, and who has not, recently searched for work?

The Census Bureau's Household Survey. Every month, thousands of interviewers from the United States Census Bureau—acting on behalf of the U.S. Bureau of Labor Statistics (BLS)—conduct a survey of 60,000 households across America. This sample of households is carefully selected to give information about the entire population. Household members who are under 16, in the military, or currently residing in an institution like a prison or hospital are excluded from the survey. The interviewer will then ask questions about the remaining household members' activities during the *previous week*.

Figure 5 shows roughly how this works. First, the interviewer asks whether the household member has worked one or more hours for pay or profit. If the answer is yes, the person is considered employed; if no, another question is asked: Has she been *temporarily* laid off from a job from which she is waiting to be recalled? A yes means the person is unemployed whether or not the person searched for a new job; a no leads to one more question: Did the person actively *search* for work during the previous four weeks. If yes, the person is unemployed; if no, she is not in the labor force.

Figure 6 illustrates how the BLS, extrapolating from its 60,000-household sample, classified the U.S. population in May 2005. First, note that about 70 million people were ruled out from consideration because they were under 16 years of age, living in institutions, or in the military. The remaining 226 million people made up the civilian, noninstitutional population, and of these, 141.4 million were employed and 7.6 million were un-

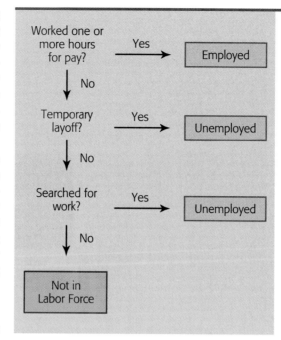

FIGURE 5
How the BLS Measures Employment Status

BLS interviewers ask a series of questions to determine whether an individual is employed, unemployed, or not in the labor force.

employed. Adding the employed and unemployed together gives us the **labor force,** equal to 141.4 million + 7.6 million = 149.0 million.

Finally, we come to the official **unemployment rate,** which is defined as the percentage of the labor force that is unemployed:

$$\text{Unemployment rate} = \frac{\text{Unemployed}}{\text{Labor Force}} = \frac{\text{Unemployed}}{(\text{Unemployed} + \text{Employed})}$$

Labor force Those people who have a job or who are looking for one.

Unemployment rate The fraction of the labor force that is without a job.

Using the numbers in Figure 6, the U.S. unemployment rate in May 2005 was calculated as 7.6/(7.6 + 141.4) = .051 or 5.1 percent. This was the number released to journalists at 8:00 A.M. on the first Friday of June 2005, and the number that made headlines in your local newspaper the next day.

Problems in Measuring Unemployment

The Census Bureau earns very high marks from economists for both its sample size—60,000 households—and the characteristics of its sample, which very closely match the characteristics of the U.S. population. Still, the official unemployment rate suffers from some important measurement problems.

Many economists believe that our official measure seriously underestimates the extent of unemployment in our society. There are two reasons for this belief: the treatment of *involuntary part-time workers* and the treatment of *discouraged workers.*

As you can see in Figure 5, anyone working one hour or more for pay during the survey week is treated as employed. This includes many people who would like a full-time job—and may even be searching for one—but who did some part-time work during the week. Some economists have suggested that these people, called

Employment Status of the U.S. Population—May 2005

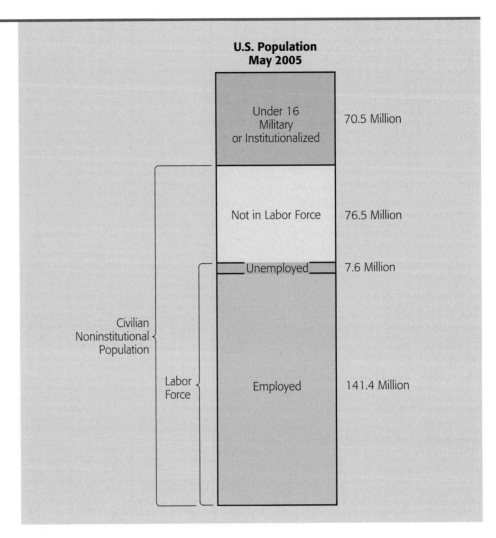

U.S. Population
May 2005

Under 16 Military or Institutionalized	70.5 Million
Not in Labor Force	76.5 Million
Unemployed	7.6 Million
Employed	141.4 Million

Civilian Noninstitutional Population

Labor Force

Involuntary part-time workers Individuals who would like a full-time job, but who are working only part time.

Discouraged workers Individuals who would like a job, but have given up searching for one.

involuntary part-time workers, should be regarded as partially employed and partially unemployed.

How many involuntary part-time workers are there? In May 2005, the BLS estimated that there were about 4.4 million.[3] If each of these workers were considered half-employed and half-unemployed, the unemployment rate in that month would have been 6.6 percent, instead of the officially reported 5.1 percent.

Another problem is the treatment of **discouraged workers,** individuals who would like to work but, because they feel little hope of finding a job, have given up searching. Because they are not taking active steps to find work, they are considered "not in the labor force" (see Figure 5). Some economists feel that discouraged workers should be counted as unemployed. After all, these people are telling us that they are willing and able to work, but they are not working. It seems wrong to exclude them just because they are not actively seeking work. Others argue that counting dis-

[3] This and other information about unemployment in May 2005 comes from *The Employment Situation: May 2005*, Bureau of Labor Statistics News Release, June 3, 2005. (All figures are seasonally adjusted except discouraged workers.)

couraged workers as unemployed would reduce the objectivity of our unemployment measure. Talk is cheap, they believe, and people may *say* anything when asked whether they would like a job; the real test is what people *do*. Yet even the staunchest defenders of the current method of measuring employment would agree that *some* discouraged workers are, in fact, willing and able to work and should be considered unemployed. The problem, in their view, is determining which ones.

How many discouraged workers are there? No one knows for sure. The BLS tries to count them, but defining who is genuinely discouraged is yet another thorny problem. Using the BLS's rather strict criteria, there were 392,000 discouraged workers in May 2005. But with a looser, unofficial definition of "discouraged worker"—people who are not working but say they want a job—the count rises to 5.4 million. Including some or all of these people among the unemployed could raise the unemployment rate significantly.

Still, the unemployment rate, as currently measured, tells us something important: the number of people who are *searching* for jobs, but have not yet found them. It is not exactly the same as the percentage of the labor force that is jobless even though willing and able to work. But if we could obtain a perfect measure of the latter, the unemployment rate, as currently measured, would be highly correlated with it.

Moreover, the unemployment rate tells us something unique about conditions in the macroeconomy. When the unemployment rate is relatively low—so that few people are actively seeking work—a firm that wants to hire more workers may be forced to lure them from other firms, by offering a higher wage rate. This puts upward pressure on wages and can lead to future inflation. A high unemployment rate, by contrast, tells us that firms can more easily expand by hiring those who are actively seeking work, without having to lure new workers from another firm and without having to offer higher wages. This suggests little inflationary danger. Later in the book, we will discuss the connection between unemployment and inflation more fully.

USING THE THEORY
GDP After September 11

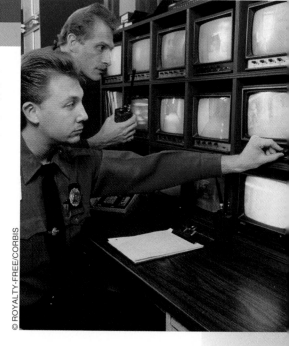

On September 11, 2001, the United States suffered an unprecedented terrorist attack when four airliners were hijacked and three of them were used to destroy the World Trade Center in New York and a section of the Pentagon in Washington D.C., killing more than 3,000 people. The most profound dimensions of this tragedy were the human lives lost and the continuing bereavement of those left behind—a loss that stunned and disoriented the nation.

But as the nation began to find its balance, it became clear that the events of September 11 would have a significant impact in another way: on the economy. Most economists suspected that the United States was already in recession (a suspicion that was confirmed later when the beginning of the recession was dated to March 2001). But what would happen after September 11? Would the recession deepen? How badly? Could the economy actually tilt into a depression? What was the appropriate economic policy, and how should it be orchestrated? As if the shock of the attacks weren't enough, millions of Americans now began to fear for their jobs.

© ROYALTY-FREE/CORBIS

How an event like September 11 affects the macroeconomy, and how the government responded, are issues you will learn about in later chapters of this book. Here, we look at just one aspect of the problem: the impact of the attacks on U.S. real GDP. By taking a brief look at this now—even before you've learned much about how the macroeconomy works—you'll be able to see how an understanding of GDP and its measurement can help us gauge the effects of September 11.

It will be helpful to distinguish between the *direct* impact on GDP (the direct result of the destruction itself) and the *indirect* impact (resulting from the choices of economic decision makers in the weeks, months, and even years following the attack).

The Direct Impact on GDP

At first, it seems that the direct impact of the attacks on GDP should be huge. For example, compared to the property loss from other recent man-made disasters, September 11 was orders of magnitude more destructive. The property loss from the Los Angeles riots of 1992 amounted to about $775 million; from the first World Trade Center bombing in 1993, $510 million; and from the 1995 bombing of the Federal Building in Oklahoma City, $125 million. By contrast, on September 11, the insured property damage in New York City alone was $16 billion.

But now consider the destruction caused by some recent *natural* disasters. The 1994 earthquake centered in Northridge, California, destroyed about $15 billion in property—almost as much as the direct damage to New York City. And Hurricane Andrew in 1992 caused even more damage—about $27 billion worth—significantly more than the damage to the World Trade Center and the Pentagon combined. The direct national economic impact of both of these natural disasters hardly appeared in the national statistics. And that is not surprising, since these magnitudes amount to only a fraction of a percentage point of our GDP, and an even smaller fraction of our total capital stock.

But as may have already occurred to you, measuring destruction of property—a loss of the capital stock—is beside the point of this section. GDP measures *production*, not the value of our capital stock. So the destruction caused by September 11—while it entered into another, related measure called *net domestic product* (GDP minus depreciation of the capital stock)—had *no direct impact at all* on GDP. Put another way, GDP is not designed to measure the resources at our disposal, but rather the production we get from those resources. While the loss of property did destroy resources capable of producing things, and thus caused production to drop in future quarters, the destroyed resources themselves did *not* count in GDP. Moreover, because our resources are so vast and our production so great, the actual drop in future production from having fewer resources was virtually unnoticeable.

> *The destruction caused by the terrorist attacks of September 11 had almost no direct impact on U.S. GDP.*

Indirect Impacts on GDP

By contrast, the *indirect* losses to GDP—those that resulted from our response to the attacks—were significant. Here, it will be useful to distinguish between the short-run impact (the weeks and months following the attacks) and the long-run impact (which we'll be experiencing for several years).

The Short Run. It did not take long for the aftermath of the attacks to affect economic decision making. First came a decision by the federal government, which immediately shut down airports nationwide for more than 48 hours. Thus, for two days, the number of flights in the United States declined from 30,000 per day to zero—an immediate decrease in airline production and therefore GDP. But the more important impact was the decision made by consumers *after* airports reopened: They no longer wanted to fly. Over the next four weeks, with dramatically reduced bookings, the airlines cut the number of flights offered by more than 20 percent and laid off 80,000 workers.

But that was only the beginning. With fewer people flying, hotel occupancy rates also decreased, by about 20 percent. The hotel industry responded with thousands of layoffs. And then—since there were fewer business travelers and tourists spending money on taxis, restaurants, and amusement parks—there were layoffs in those industries as well. The problem spread further: It wasn't long before the airlines canceled orders for new aircraft and hotels and other businesses halted construction projects, some of which had already started. Thus, the problem spread to the manufacturing and raw materials sectors of the economy.

Consumers made other decisions that affected production. Retail shopping declined dramatically, at first because millions of stunned viewers spent all their free time watching events unfold on television, and then because fears of deepening recession made them worry about their incomes.

There were also instances of *increased* production. On September 11, AT&T, which normally handles 300 million calls on a Tuesday, saw the number of calls spike to 431 million. For several weeks, state and local governments, seeking to beef up security, paid overtime to hundreds of thousands of police and firefighters. And millions of people—looking for emotional escape but not wanting to leave home—created a boom in video and DVD rentals. But these increases in production were swamped by the production cuts already rippling through the economy.

GDP did a good job of capturing all of these changes in spending and production, since that is just what it is designed to do. After taking account of changes in airline flights, hotel bookings, restaurant meals, video rentals, and hundreds of thousands of other changes in production, the Bureau of Economic Analysis reported that production turned southward in the third quarter of 2001, with much of the decline occurring during the three weeks of the quarter that remained after September 11.

The Long Run. What about the long run? Look again at Figure 4. It shows us that GDP can deviate from potential output for several quarters or even several years. But it also shows that, in the long run, GDP tends to rise at about the same rate as potential output. Thus, when we ask about the long-run impact of September 11 on GDP, we are really asking about its long-run impact on *potential* GDP.

What is this long-run impact? In the weeks following the attack, it became clear that the United States was about to start on a course it would follow for many years: a huge reallocation of national resources toward fighting terrorism abroad and achieving greater security at home. These are resources that would otherwise be used to produce other things.

Some of these resources are being purchased by the government. For example, in the first three months of U.S. attacks on terrorist camps and the associated Taliban regime in Afghanistan, the Department of Defense used more than $3.8 billion of additional resources (beyond its normal expenses) for jet fuel, munitions, and additional combat pay for 50,000 troops stationed in the region. Over the next four years, the United States spent billions of additional dollars pursuing a more aggressive foreign policy, including an invasion to overthrow the regime of Saddam Hussein in Iraq, and increased aid to allies—and potential allies—in the war against terrorism. At home, the federal government hired hundreds of air marshals to protect civilian aircraft, and thousands of new airport personnel to screen passengers and luggage.

But private businesses too, have been spending more for security each year than they did before September 11. More armed security guards are stationed at corporate headquarters and manufacturing plants; more sophisticated access-pass equipment and metal detectors have been installed in office buildings; new hires are more carefully screened and investigated; deliveries are more carefully monitored; and bomb-sniffing dogs and increased security have become a routine part of rock concerts and sporting events.

All of these security expenses are slowing the growth of our potential output, and are therefore slowing the growth of real GDP over the long run. Why? Because business security services are *intermediate goods*—things that firms use as inputs to produce final goods and services for sale to others. Just as Dell must use labor, computer chips, plastic, salespeople, and buildings as inputs when it makes computers, it must also hire people to guard its office buildings, to do background checks on employees, and to monitor deliveries to its national headquarters. These are all part of the cost of doing business.

Suppose, for example, that Dell now uses $25 more in security services for each computer it produces. The computer is not faster, lighter, or better in any way than before; it still contributes the same amount to real GDP as it did before. But the additional security uses up resources—land and natural resources, labor, capital, and entrepreneurship—that could otherwise have been used to produce *other* final goods, perhaps by Dell or by *other* firms in the economy. Since these other final goods are *not* being produced, our total output is lower than it would otherwise be.

To see this from another point of view, think about how technological advances normally work to increase our output of goods and services. Personal computers, the Internet, cell phones, assembly-line robots, and new medical devices have all enabled firms in various industries to produce whatever they produce using fewer resources. These freed-up resources are then used to produce other things, so potential output rises and—in the long run—so does our real GDP. But September 11 has had the *opposite* effect of a technological advance. It forces businesses to use *more* resources to produce output—resources that could have been used to make other things.

Of course, while increased security spending tends to reduce potential output, other forces are working to increase it, including technological advances, increases in the capital stock (both human and physical), increases in population. (You'll learn more about this in later chapters.) So increased security spending doesn't necessarily mean that potential output will fall, but it does create a force pulling the growth rate of potential output downward.

In the long run, as the nation shifts production away from other goods and services and toward security in the wake of September 11, the impact on our real GDP will be negative. Our potential output—and over the long run, our actual output—will grow more slowly than it otherwise would have.

Summary

This chapter discusses how some key macroeconomic aggregates are measured and reported. One important economic aggregate is *gross domestic product*—the total value of all final goods and services produced for the marketplace during a given year, within a nation's borders. GDP is a measure of an economy's total production.

In the *expenditure approach,* GDP is calculated as the sum of spending by households, businesses, government agencies, and foreigners on domestically produced goods and services. The *value-added approach* computes GDP by adding up each firm's contributions to the total product as it is being produced. Value added at each stage of production is the revenue a firm receives minus the cost of the intermediate inputs it uses. Finally, the *factor payments approach* sums the wages and salaries, rent, interest and profit earned by all resource owners. The three approaches reflect three different ways of viewing GDP.

Since nominal GDP is measured in current dollars, it changes when either production or prices change. *Real GDP* is nominal GDP adjusted for price changes; it rises only when production rises.

Real GDP is useful in the short run for giving warnings about impending recessions, and in the long run for indicating how fast the economy is growing. Unfortunately, it is plagued by important inaccuracies. It does not fully reflect quality changes or production in the underground economy, and it does not include many types of nonmarket production.

When real GDP grows, employment tends to rise and—if real GDP grows fast enough—the unemployment rate falls. In the United States, a person is considered unemployed if he or she does not have a job but is actively seeking one. Economists have found it useful to classify unemployment into four different categories. *Frictional unemployment* is short-term unemployment experienced by people between jobs or by those who are just entering the job market. *Seasonal unemployment* is related to changes in the weather, tourist patterns, or other predictable seasonal changes. *Structural unemployment* results from mismatches, in skills or location, between jobs and workers. Finally, *cyclical unemployment* occurs because of the business cycle. Unemployment, particularly the structural and cyclical forms, involves costs. From a social perspective, unemployment means lost production. From the individual viewpoint, unemployment often involves financial, psychological, and physical harm.

Key Terms

Capital stock	Government purchases	Private investment
Consumption	Gross domestic product (GDP)	Real variable
Cyclical unemployment	Intermediate goods	Seasonal unemployment
Discouraged workers	Involuntary part-time workers	Structural unemployment
Expenditure approach	Labor force	Transfer payment
Factor payments	Net exports	Unemployment rate
Factor payments approach	Net investment	Value added
Final good	Nominal variable	Value-added approach
Frictional unemployment	Nonmarket production	
Full employment	Potential output	

Review Questions *Answers to even-numbered Questions and Problems can be found on the text Web site at http://hall-lieb.swlearning.com.*

1. What is the difference between final goods and intermediate goods? Why is it that only the value of final goods and services is counted in GDP?

2. What is the relationship between private investment and the capital stock? What are the three components of private investment?

3. Describe the different kinds of factor payments.

4. What is the difference between nominal and real variables? What is the main problem with using nominal variables to track the economy?

5. Discuss the value and reliability of GDP statistics in both short-run and long-run analyses of the economy.

6. Real GDP (in 1996 dollars) was measured at around $8.8 trillion in 1999. Was the actual value of goods and services produced in the United States in 1999 likely to have been higher or lower than that? Why?

7. What, if anything, could the government do to reduce frictional and structural unemployment?

8. Categorize each of the following according to the type of unemployment it reflects. Justify your answers.

a. Workers are laid off when a GM factory closes due to a recession.

b. Workers selling software in a store are laid off when the store goes bankrupt due to competition from on-line software dealers.

c. Migrant farm workers' jobs end when the harvest is finished.

d. Lost jobs result from the movement of textile plants from Massachusetts to the South and overseas.

9. Can unemployment ever be good for the economy? Explain.

10. What are some of the different types of costs associated with unemployment?

11. Discuss some of the problems with the way the Bureau of Labor Statistics computes the unemployment rate. In what ways do official criteria lead to an overestimate or underestimate of the actual unemployment figure?

12. Explain this statement: "The Bureau of Economic Analysis reported a 2003 second quarter real GDP figure of $10,802.7 billion."

13. Summarize the three approaches to calculating GDP.

Problems and Exercises

1. Using the expenditure approach, which of the following would be directly counted as part of U.S. GDP in 2005? In each case, state whether the action causes an increase in C, I, G, or NX.

    a. A new personal computer produced by IBM, which remained unsold at the year's end

    b. A physician's services to a household

    c. Produce bought by a restaurant to serve to customers

    d. The purchase of 1,000 shares of Disney stock

    e. The sale of 50 acres of commercial property

    f. A real estate agent's commission from the sale of property

    g. A transaction in which you clean your roommate's apartment in exchange for his working on your car

    h. An Apple iMac computer produced in the United States, and purchased by a French citizen

    i. The government's Social Security payments to retired people

2. Calculate the total change in a year's GDP for each of the following scenarios:

    a. A family sells a home, without using a broker, for $150,000. They could have rented it on the open market for $700 per month. They buy a 10-year-old condominium for $200,000; the broker's fee on the transaction is 6 percent of the selling price. The condo's owner was formerly renting the unit at $500 per month.

    b. General Electric uses $10 million worth of steel, glass, and plastic to produce its dishwashers. Wages and salaries in the dishwasher division are $40 million; the division's only other expense is $15 million in interest that it pays on its bonds. The division's revenue for the year is $75 million.

    c. On March 31, you decide to stop throwing away $50 a month on convenience store nachos. You buy $200 worth of equipment, cornmeal, and cheese, and make your own nachos for the rest of the year.

    d. You win $25,000 in your state's lottery. Ever the entrepreneur, you decide to open a Ping-Pong ball washing service, buying $15,000 worth of equipment from SpiffyBall Ltd. of Hong Kong and $10,000 from Ball-B-Kleen of Toledo, Ohio.

    e. Tone-Deaf Artists, Inc. produces 100,000 new White Snake CDs that it prices at $15 apiece. Ten thousand CDs are sold abroad, but, alas, the rest remain unsold on warehouse shelves.

3. The country of Freedonia uses the same method to calculate the unemployment rate as the U.S. Bureau of Labor Statistics uses. From the data below, compute Freedonia's unemployment rate.

Population	10,000,000
Under 16	3,000,000
Over 16	
In military service	500,000
In hospitals	200,000
In prison	100,000
Worked one hour or more in previous week	4,000,000
Searched for work during previous four weeks	1,000,000

4. Toward the end of this chapter, it was stated that if half of the 4.4 million involuntary part-time workers in May 2005 were counted as unemployed, then the unemployment rate that month would have been 6.6 percent instead of 5.1 percent. Do the necessary calculations to confirm this statement, using the information in Figure 6. [*Hint:* The labor force will not be affected.]

5. In June 2003, the BLS estimated there were 9.4 million unemployed, 137.7 million employed, 478,000 discouraged workers, and 5.1 million people (including discouraged workers) who were not working but said they wanted a job. What would the unemployment rate have been in June 2003 if it had included among the unemployed:
   a. All officially discouraged workers?
   b. All those who were not working but said they wanted a job? [*Hint*: Don't forget about how these inclusions would affect the labor force.]

6. Ginny asks "If I buy a sweater that was produced in Malaysia, why is its purchase price subtracted from GDP?" How should you answer her question? (You may assume, for simplicity, that there was no value added to the sweater in the United States)

7. Ziponia, which uses the same method to calculate real GDP as the U.S. Bureau of Economic Analysis uses, has made the following calculations for 2004: $C = \$6{,}000$ million, $I = \$1{,}500$ million, $G = \$500$ million, and $NX = \$600$ million. Find Ziponia's real GDP for 2004 and explain how it changes for 2005 if the only difference between the two years is that Ziponia's citizens import an additional $5 million worth of DVD players in 2005. Does your answer depend on what Ziponia's firms produce? For instance, will your answer change if part of Ziponia's firms' production was $5 million worth of DVD players that they expected to sell to Ziponians, but were unable to because the Ziponians preferred imported DVD players?

8. a. The country of Ziponia uses the same method to calculate the unemployment rate as the U.S. Bureau of Labor Statistics uses. From the data below, compute Ziponia's unemployment rate.

Population	60,000
Under 16	9,000
Over 16	
In military service	600
In hospitals	60
In prison	200
Worked one hour or more in previous week	46,000
Searched for work during previous four weeks	2,140
Did not work in previous week but would have taken a job if one were offered	200

   b. How large is Ziponia's labor force?
   c. How many discouraged workers live in Ziponia?
   d. Not all of Ziponia's citizens are accounted for in part (a). How are the missing citizens classified? Give some examples of what they may be doing.
   e. How many of Ziponia's citizens are not in the labor force?

9. Refer to question 8. The 2,140 Ziponians who searched for work during the previous four weeks included: 54 ski resort employees who lost their winter jobs but expect to get them back in late fall; 200 recent high school graduates; 258 former textile workers who lost their jobs when their employers moved their operations overseas; 143 mothers and 19 fathers who had stayed at home to raise their children but who recently decided to reenter the work force; 394 high school and college students who want summer jobs; 115 people who live in West Ziponia and lost their jobs when their employers moved operations to East Ziponia, but who are not qualified for the remaining jobs in the west; 110 recent college graduates; 12 record-label designers who lost their jobs as consumers substituted CDs for records; and 32 retirees who decided to return to the workforce. The remaining job seekers lost their jobs due to a recession. Use this information to:
   a. Classify the job seekers by their type of unemployment, and calculate how many fell into each category.
   b. Find the frictional, seasonal, structural, and cyclical unemployment rates.
   c. Find how many Ziponians would be unemployed if Ziponia were to achieve full employment.

Challenge Questions

1. Suppose, in a given year, someone buys a General Motors automobile for $30,000. That same year, GM produced the car in Michigan, using $10,000 in parts imported from Japan. However, the parts imported from Japan themselves contained $3,000 in components produced in the United States.
   a. By how much does U.S. GDP rise?
   b. Using the expenditure approach, what is the change in each component (*C, I, G,* and *NX*) of U.S. GDP?
   c. What is the change in Japan's GDP and each of its components?

2. In the "Using the Theory" section of this chapter, you learned that business spending on security will work to reduce real GDP over the long run. Is the same true of government expenditures on security? Why or why not?

3. a. Federal Reserve Chairman Alan Greenspan came up with a novel (and facetious) way to measure the United States' output: by weight. Describe some of the problems inherent in measuring output by weight.
   b. What problems might arise if policy makers relied on a weight-based measure of output to determine the health of the U.S. economy?

ECONOMIC *Applications* | *These exercises require access to Hall/Lieberman Xtra! If Xtra! did not come with your book, visit http://hallxtra.swlearning.com to purchase.*

1. Use your Xtra! password at the Hall and Lieberman Web site (http://hallxtra.swlearning.com), select this chapter, and click on EconDebate. Choose *Macroeconomics: Employment, Unemployment, and Inflation* and scroll down to find the debate, "Do Technological Advances Result in Higher Unemployment?" Read the debate, and use the information to answer the following questions.
   a. How does technological change alter the composition of the demand for labor? Is the overall effect positive or negative? Why?
   b. What are the effects of technological change on productivity and growth? Explain.

2. Use your Xtra! password at the Hall and Lieberman Web site (http://hallxtra.swlearning.com), select this chapter, and under Economic Applications, click on EconDebate. Choose *Macroeconomics: Employment, Unemployment, and Inflation* and scroll down to find the *Real GDP.* Read the definition and click on Diagrams/Data and use the information to answer the following questions.
   a. Verify the inverse relationship between the economic growth rate and the unemployment rate. Explain this relationship.
   b. Why is there a direct relationship between real GDP and personal income?
   c. How well does the Index of Leading Economic Indicators perform in forecasting future economic conditions?

The Monetary System, Prices, and Inflation

CHAPTER OUTLINE

The Monetary System
History of the Dollar
Why Paper Currency Is Accepted as a Means of Payment

Measuring the Price Level and Inflation
Index Numbers
The Consumer Price Index
How the CPI Has Behaved
From Price Index to Inflation Rate
How the CPI Is Used
Real Variables and Adjustment for Inflation
Inflation and the Measurement of Real GDP

The Costs of Inflation
The Inflation Myth
The Redistributive Cost of Inflation
The Resource Cost of Inflation
A Preliminary Word About Deflation

Is the CPI Accurate?
Sources of Bias in the CPI

Using the Theory: The Use and Misuse of an Imperfect CPI
Indexing
Long-Run Comparisons
The Bigger, Conceptual Problem
What the CPI Does Well

Appendix: Calculating the Consumer Price Index

You pull into a gas station deep in the interior of the distant nation of Chaotica. The numbers on the gas pump don't make sense to you, and you can't figure out how much to pay. Luckily, the national language of Chaotica is English, so you can ask the cashier how much the gas costs. He replies, "Here in Chaotica, we don't have any standard system for measuring quantities of gas, and we don't have any standard way to quote prices. My pump here measures in my own unit, called the slurp, and I will sell you 6 slurps of gas for that watch you are wearing, or a dozen slurps of gas for your camera." You spend the next half hour trying to determine how many slurps of gas there are in a gallon and what form of payment you can use besides your watch and camera.

Life in the imaginary nation of Chaotica would be difficult. People would spend a lot of time figuring out how to trade with each other, time that could otherwise be spent producing things or enjoying leisure activities. Fortunately, in the real world, virtually every nation has a *monetary system* that helps to organize and simplify our economic transactions.

THE MONETARY SYSTEM

Unit of value A common unit for measuring how much something is worth.

A monetary system establishes two different types of standardization in the economy. First, it establishes a **unit of value**—a common unit for measuring how much something is worth. A standard unit of value permits us to compare the costs of different goods and services and to communicate these costs when we trade. The dollar is the unit of value in the United States. If a college textbook costs $100, while a round-trip airline ticket from Phoenix to Minneapolis costs $300, we know immediately that the ticket has the same value in the marketplace as three college textbooks.

Means of payment Anything acceptable as payment for goods and services.

The second type of standardization concerns the **means of payment,** the things we can use as payment when we buy goods and services. In the United States, the means of payment include dollar bills, personal checks, money orders, credit cards like Visa and American Express, and, in some experimental locations, prepaid cash cards with magnetic strips.

These two functions of a monetary system—establishing a unit of value and a standard means of payment—are closely related, but they are not the same thing. The unit-of-value function refers to the way we *think* about and record transactions; the means-of-payment function refers to how payment is actually made.

The unit of value works in the same way as units of weight, volume, distance, and time. In fact, the same sentence in Article I of the U.S. Constitution gives Congress the power to create a unit of value along with units of weights and measures. All of these units help us determine clearly and precisely what is being traded for what. Think about buying gas in the United States; you exchange dollars for gallons. The transaction will go smoothly and quickly only if there is clarity about both the unit of fluid volume (gallons) *and* the unit of purchasing power (dollars).

The means of payment can be different from the unit of value. For example, in some countries where local currency prices change very rapidly, it is common to use the U.S. dollar as the unit of value—to specify prices in dollars—while the local currency remains the means of payment. Even in the United States, when you use a check to buy something, the unit of value is the dollar but the means of payment is a piece of paper with your signature on it.

In the United States, the dollar is the centerpiece of our monetary system. It is the unit of value in virtually every economic transaction, and dollar bills are very often the means of payment as well. How did the dollar come to play such an important role in the economy?

History of the Dollar

Prior to 1790, each colony had its own currency. It was named the "pound" in every colony, but it had a different purchasing power in each of them. In 1790, soon after the Constitution went into effect, Congress created a new unit of value called the dollar. Historical documents show that merchants and businesses switched immediately to the new dollar, thereby ending the chaos of the colonial monetary systems. Prices began to be quoted in dollars, and accounts were kept in dollars. The dollar rapidly became the standard unit of value.

But the primary means of payment in the United States until the Civil War was paper currency issued by private banks. Just as the government defined the length of the yard but did not sell yardsticks, the government defined the unit of value but let private organizations provide the means of payment.

During the Civil War, however, the government issued the first federal paper currency, the greenback. It functioned as both the unit of value and the major means of payment until 1879. Then the government got out of the business of money creation for a few decades. During that time, currency was once again issued by private banks. But in 1913, a new institution called the **Federal Reserve System** was created to be the national monetary authority in the United States. The Federal Reserve was charged with creating and regulating the nation's supply of money, and it continues to do so today.

Federal Reserve System
The central bank and national monetary authority of the United States.

Why Paper Currency Is Accepted as a Means of Payment

You may be wondering why people are willing to accept paper dollars—or the promise of paper dollars—as a means of payment. Why should a farmer give up a chicken, or a manufacturer give up a new car, just to receive a bunch of green rectangles with words printed on them? In fact, paper currency is a relatively recent development in the history of the means of payment.

The earliest means of payment were precious metals and other valuable commodities such as furs or jewels. These were called *commodity money* because they had important uses other than as a means of payment. The non-money use is what gave commodity money its ultimate value. For example, people would accept furs as payment because furs could be used to keep warm. Similarly, gold and silver had a variety of uses in industry, as religious artifacts, and for ornamentation.

Precious metals were an especially popular form of commodity money. Eventually, to make it easier to identify the value of precious metals, they were minted into coins whose weight was declared on their faces. Because gold and silver coins could be melted down into pure metal and used in other ways, they were still commodity money.

Commodity money eventually gave way to paper currency. Initially, paper currency was just a certificate representing a certain amount of gold or silver held by a bank. At any time, the holder of a certificate could go to the bank that issued it and trade the certificate for the stated amount of gold or silver. People were willing to accept paper money as a means of payment for two reasons. First, the currency could be exchanged for a valuable commodity like gold or silver. Second, the issuer—either a government or a bank—could print new money only when it acquired additional gold or silver. This put strict limits on money printing, so people had faith that their paper money would retain its value in the marketplace.

But today, paper currency is no longer backed by gold or any other physical commodity. If you have a dollar handy, put this book down and take a close look at the bill. You will not find on it any promise that you can trade your dollar for gold, silver, furs, or anything else. Yet we all accept it as a means of payment. Why?

A clue is provided by the statement in the upper left-hand corner of every bill: *This note is legal tender for all debts, public and private.* The statement affirms that the piece of paper in your hands will be accepted as a means of payment (you can "tender" it to settle any "debt, public or private") by any American because the government says so. This type of currency is called **fiat money**. *Fiat*, in Latin, means "let there be," and fiat money serves as a means of payment by government declaration.

The government need not worry about enforcing this declaration. The real force behind the dollar—and the reason that we are all willing to accept these green pieces of paper as payment—is its long-standing acceptability by *others*. As long as you have confidence that you can use your dollars to buy goods and services, you won't mind giving up goods and services for dollars. And because everyone else feels the same way, the circle of acceptability is completed.

But while the government can declare that paper currency is to be accepted as a means of payment, it cannot declare the terms. Whether 10 gallons of gas will cost you 1 dollar, 10 dollars, or 20 dollars is up to the marketplace. The value of the

© PHOTODISC/GETTY IMAGES

Today, dollars are not backed by gold or silver, but we accept them as payment because we know that others will accept them from us.

Fiat money Anything that serves as a means of payment by government declaration.

dollar—its purchasing power—does change from year to year, as reflected in the changing prices of the things we buy. In the rest of this chapter, we will discuss some of the problems created by the dollar's changing value and the difficulty economists have measuring and monitoring the changes. We postpone until later chapters the question of *why* the value of the dollar changes from year to year.

MEASURING THE PRICE LEVEL AND INFLATION

Price level The average level of prices in the economy.

One hundred years ago, you could buy a pound of coffee for 15 cents, see a Broadway play for 40 cents, buy a new suit for $6, and attend a private college for $200 in yearly tuition.[1] Needless to say, the price of each of these items has gone up considerably since then. Microeconomic causes—changes in individual markets—can explain only a tiny fraction of these price changes. For the most part, these price rises came about because of a continually rising **price level**—the average level of dollar prices in the economy. In this section, we begin to explore how the price level is measured and how this measurement is used.

Index Numbers

Index A series of numbers used to track a variable's rise or fall over time.

Most measures of the price level are reported in the form of an **index**—a series of numbers, each one representing a different period. Index numbers are meaningful only in a *relative* sense: We compare one period's index number with that of another period and can quickly see which one is larger and by what percentage. But the actual value of an index number for a particular period has no meaning in and of itself.

In general, an index number for any measure is calculated as

$$\frac{\text{Value of measure in current period}}{\text{Value of measure in base period}} \times 100.$$

Let's see how index numbers work with a simple example. Suppose we want to measure how violence on TV has changed over time, and we have data on the number of violent acts shown in each of several years. We could then construct a TV-violence index. Our first step would be to choose a *base period*—a period to be used as a benchmark. Let's choose 1996 as our base period, and suppose that there were 10,433 violent acts on television in that year. Then our violence index in any current year would be calculated as

$$\frac{\text{Number of violent acts in current year}}{10,433} \times 100.$$

In 1996, the base year, the index will have the value $(10,433/10,433) \times 100 = 100$. Look again at the general formula for index numbers, and you will see that this is always true: *An index will always equal 100 in the base period.*

Now let's calculate the value of our index in another year. If there were 14,534 violent acts in 2000, then the index that year would have the value

$$\frac{14,534}{10,433} \times 100 = 139.3.$$

Index numbers compress and simplify information so that we can see how things are changing at a glance. Our media violence index, for example, tells us at a glance

[1] Scott Derks, ed., *The Value of the Dollar: Prices and Incomes in the United States: 1860–1989* (Detroit, MI: Gale Research Inc., 1994), various pages.

that the number of violent acts in 2000 was 139.3 percent of the number in 1996. Or, more simply, TV violence grew by 39.3 percent between 1996 and 2000.

The Consumer Price Index

The most widely used measure of the price level in the United States is the **Consumer Price Index (CPI)**. This index, which is designed to track the prices paid by the typical consumer, is compiled and reported by the Bureau of Labor Statistics (BLS).

Consumer Price Index An index of the cost, through time, of a fixed market basket of goods purchased by a typical household in some base period.

Measuring the prices paid by the typical consumer is not easy. Two problems must be solved before we even begin. The first problem is to decide which goods and services we should include in our average. The CPI tracks only *consumer* prices; it excludes goods and services that are not directly purchased by consumers. More specifically, the CPI excludes goods purchased by businesses (such as capital equipment, raw materials, or wholesale goods), goods and services purchased by government agencies (such as fighter-bombers and the services of police officers), and goods and services purchased by foreigners (U.S. exports). The CPI *does* include newly produced consumer goods and services that are part of consumption spending in our GDP—things such as new clothes, new furniture, new cars, haircuts, and restaurant meals. It also includes some things that are *not* part of our GDP but that are part of the typical family's budget. For example, the CPI includes prices for *used* goods such as used cars or used books, and imports from other countries—for example, French cheese, Japanese cars, and Mexican tomatoes.

The second problem is how to combine all the different prices into an average price level. In any given month, different prices will change by different amounts. The average price of doctors' visits might rise by 1 percent, the price of blue jeans might rise by a tenth of a percent, the price of milk might fall by half a percent, and so on. When prices change at different rates, and when some are rising while others are falling, how can we track the change in the *average* price level? It would be a mistake to use a simple average of all prices, adding them up and dividing by the number of goods. A proper measure must recognize that we spend very little of our incomes on some goods—such as Tabasco sauce—and much more on others—like car repairs or rent.

The CPI's approach is to track the cost of the *CPI market basket*—the collection of goods and services that the typical consumer bought in some base period. If the market basket's cost rises by 10 percent over some period, then the price level, as reported by the CPI, will rise by 10 percent. This way, goods and services that are relatively unimportant in the typical consumer's budget will have little weight in the CPI. Tabasco sauce could triple in price and have no noticeable impact on the cost of the complete market basket. Goods that are more important—such as auto repairs or rent—will have more weight.

In recent years, the base year[2] for the CPI has been 1983, so, following our general formula for price indexes, the CPI is calculated as

$$\frac{\text{Cost of market basket in current year}}{\text{Cost of market basket in 1983}} \times 100.$$

The appendix in this chapter discusses the calculation of the CPI in more detail.

---

[2] To be more specific: The typical consumer's market basket (used to determine the weights to apply to each good) is periodically updated. Currently, for example, the CPI uses information from its 2004 survey of consumer spending habits to determine the proper weights. But the BLS continues to use July 1983 as its official base period; that is, the value of the CPI is still set at 100 for July 1983.

TABLE 1
Consumer Price Index, December, Selected Years, 1970–2004

Year	Consumer Price Index (December)
1970	39.8
1975	55.6
1980	86.4
1985	109.5
1990	134.2
1995	153.9
2000	174.6
2001	177.3
2002	181.6
2003	185.0
2004	191.2

Source: Bureau of Labor Statistics, Consumer Price Index—All Urban Consumers, Seasonally adjusted. (www.bls.gov)

How the CPI Has Behaved

Table 1 shows the actual value of the CPI for December of selected years. Because it is reported in index number form, we can easily see how much the price level has changed over different time intervals. In December 2002, for example, the CPI had a value of 181.6, telling us that the typical market basket in that year cost 81.6 percent more than it would have cost in the July 1983 base period. In December 1970, the CPI was 39.8, so the cost of the market basket in that year was only 39.8 percent of its cost in July 1983. In July 1983 (not shown), the CPI's value was 100.

From Price Index to Inflation Rate

Inflation rate The percent change in the price level from one period to the next.

The Consumer Price Index is a measure of the price *level* in the economy. The **inflation rate** measures how fast the price level is changing, as a percentage rate. When the price level is rising, as it almost always is, the inflation rate is positive. When the price level is falling, as it did during the Great Depression, we have negative inflation, which is called **deflation.**

Deflation A *decrease* in the price level from one period to the next.

Figure 1 shows the U.S. rate of inflation, as measured by the CPI, since 1950. For each year, the inflation rate is calculated as the percentage change in the CPI from December of the previous year to December of that year. For example, the CPI in December 2003 was 185.0, and in December 2004 it was 191.2. The inflation rate for 2004 was $(191.2 - 185.0)/185.0 = 0.0335$ or 3.4 percent. Notice that inflation was low in the 1950s and 1960s, was high in the 1970s and early 1980s, and has been low since then. In later chapters, you will learn what causes the inflation rate to rise and fall.

How the CPI Is Used

The CPI is the most important and widely used measure of prices in United States. It is used in three ways:

More specifically, as a Policy Target. In the introductory macroeconomics chapter, we saw that price stability—or a low inflation rate—is one of the nation's important macroeconomic goals. The measure most often used to gauge our success in achieving low inflation is the CPI.

Indexation Adjusting the value of some nominal payment in proportion to a price index, in order to keep the real payment unchanged.

To Index Payments. A payment is **indexed** when it is set by a formula so that it rises and falls proportionately with a price index. An indexed payment makes up for the loss in purchasing power that occurs when the price level rises. It raises the nominal payment by just enough to keep its purchasing power unchanged. In the United States, 54 million Social Security recipients and government retirees have their benefit payments indexed to the CPI. About one-quarter of all union members—more than 2 million workers—have labor contracts that index their wages to the CPI. Since 1985, the U.S. income tax has been indexed as well: the threshold income levels at which tax rates change automatically rise at the same rate as the CPI. And the government now sells

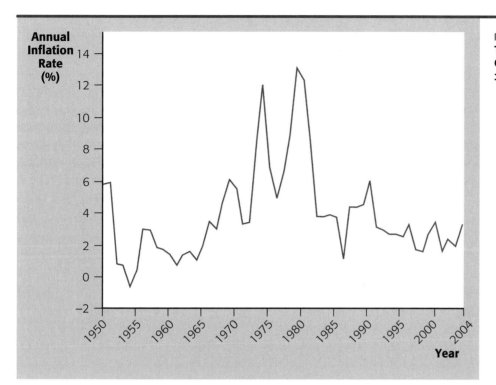

FIGURE 1
The Rate of Inflation Using the Consumer Price Index, 1950–2004

bonds that are indexed to the CPI. The owner of an indexed bond receives a payment each year to make up for the loss of purchasing power when the CPI rises.

To Translate from Nominal to Real Values. In order to compare economic values from different periods, we must translate *nominal variables,* measured in the number of dollars, into *real variables,* which are adjusted for the change in the dollar's purchasing power. The CPI is often used for this translation. Since calculating real variables is one of the most important uses of the CPI, we devote the next section to that topic.

HTTP://

You can find the latest information on the CPI at **http://www.bls.gov/bls/ newsrels.htm**—the Bureau of Labor Statistics Web site.

Real Variables and Adjustment for Inflation

Suppose that from December 2004 to December 2005, your nominal wage—what you are paid in dollars—rose from $15 to $30 per hour. Were you better off? That depends. You are earning twice as many dollars. But you should care not about how many green pieces of paper you earn, but how many goods and services you can buy with that paper. How, then, can we tell what happened to your purchasing power? By focusing not on the *nominal wage,* (the number of *dollars* you earn) but on the *real wage,* (the *purchasing power* of your wage). To track your real wage, we need to look at the number of dollars you earn *relative to the price level.*

Since the "typical worker" and the "typical consumer" are pretty

Rising Prices Versus Rising Inflation People often confuse the statement "prices are rising" with the statement "inflation is rising," but they do not mean the same thing. Remember that the inflation rate is the *rate of change* of the price level. To have rising inflation, the price level must be rising by a greater and greater percentage each period. But we can also have rising prices and *falling* inflation. For example, from 1996 to 1998, the CPI rose each year: "Prices were rising." But they rose by a smaller percentage each year than the year before, so "inflation was falling"—from 3.4 percent in 1996 to 1.7 percent in 1997 and to 1.6 percent in 1998.

DANGEROUS CURVES

much the same, the CPI is usually the price index used to calculate the real wage. The real-wage formula is as follows:

$$\text{Real wage in any year} = \frac{\text{Nominal wage in that year}}{\text{CPI in that year}} \times 100.$$

To see that this formula makes sense, let's go back to our fictional example: From 2004 to 2005, your nominal wage doubles from $15 to $30. Now, suppose the price of everything that you buy doubles at the same time. It is easy to see that in this case, your purchasing power would remain unchanged. And that is just what our formula tells us: If prices double, the CPI doubles as well. With 2004 as our base year, the CPI would increase from 100 in 2004 to 200 in the year 2005. The *real* wage would be ($15/100) ×100 = $15 in 2004 and ($30/200) × 100 = $15 in 2005. The real wage would remain unchanged.

Now suppose that prices doubled between 2004 and 2005, but your nominal wage remained unchanged at $15. In this case, your purchasing power would be cut in half. You'd have the same number of dollars, but each one would buy half as much as it did before. Our formula gives us a real wage of ($15/100) × 100 = $15 in 2004 and ($15/200) × 100 = $7.50 in 2005. The real wage falls by half.

Now look at Table 2, which shows the average hourly earnings of wage earners over the past four decades. In the first two columns, you can see that the average American wage earner was paid $4.87 per hour in December 1975, and more than triple that—$15.85—in December 2004. Does this mean the average hourly worker was paid more in 2004 than in 1975? In *dollars,* the answer is clearly yes. But what about in *purchasing power?* Or, using the new terminology you've learned: What happened to the *real wage* over this period?

Let's see. We know that the *nominal wage* rose from $4.87 in 1975 to $15.85 in 2004. But, according to the table, the CPI rose from 55.6 to 191.2 over the same period. Using our formula, we find that

$$\text{Real wage in 1975} = \frac{\$4.87}{55.6} \times 100 = \$8.76.$$

$$\text{Real wage in 2002} = \frac{\$15.85}{191.2} \times 100 = \$8.29.$$

Thus, although the average worker earned more *dollars* in 2004 than in 1975, when we use the CPI as our measure of prices, her purchasing power seems to have fallen over those years. *Why* this apparent decline in purchasing power? This is an interesting and important question, and one we'll begin to answer later in the chapter. The important point to remember here is that

when we measure changes in the macroeconomy, we usually care not about the number of dollars we are counting, but the purchasing power those dollars represent. Thus, we translate nominal values into real values using the formula

$$\text{real value} = \frac{\text{nominal value}}{\text{price index}} \times 100.$$

This formula, usually using the CPI as the price index, is how most real values in the economy are calculated. But there is one important exception: To calculate real GDP, the government uses a different procedure, to which we now turn.

Year	Nominal Wage, Dollars per Hour	CPI	Real Wage in 1983 Dollars per Hour
1970	3.50	39.8	8.79
1975	4.87	55.6	8.76
1980	7.12	86.4	8.24
1985	8.86	109.5	8.09
1990	10.33	134.2	7.70
1995	11.79	153.9	7.66
2000	14.26	174.6	8.17
2001	14.73	177.3	8.31
2002	15.19	181.6	8.36
2003	15.45	185.0	8.35
2004	15.85	191.2	8.29

TABLE 2
Nominal and Real Wages (in December of Each Year)

Source: Bureau of Labor Statistics, Statistical Tables, *http://www.bls.gov/data/*. Wage and CPI data for December of each year. Nominal wage: average hourly earnings of production or nonsupervisory workers in nonfarm private sector CPI: CPI-All Urban Consumers.

Inflation and the Measurement of Real GDP

In the previous chapter, we discussed the difference between nominal GDP and real GDP. After reading this chapter, you might think that real GDP is calculated just like the real wage: dividing nominal GDP by the Consumer Price Index. But the Consumer Price Index is *not* used to calculate real GDP. Instead, a special price index—which we can call the **GDP price index**—is used.

The most important differences between the CPI and the GDP price index are in the types of goods and services covered by each index. First, the GDP price index *includes* some prices that the CPI ignores. In particular, while the CPI tracks only the prices of goods bought by American *consumers,* the GDP price index must also include the prices of goods purchased by the government, investment goods purchased by businesses, and exports, which are purchased by foreigners.

Second, the GDP price index *excludes* some prices that are part of the CPI. In particular, the GDP price index leaves out used goods and imports, both of which are included in the CPI. This makes sense, because while used goods and imports are part of the typical consumer's market basket, they do not contribute to current U.S. GDP.

We can summarize the chief difference between the CPI and the GDP price index this way:

> *The GDP price index measures the prices of all goods and services that are included in U.S. GDP, while the CPI measures the prices of all goods and services bought by U.S. households.*[3]

GDP price index An index of the price level for all final goods and services included in GDP.

THE COSTS OF INFLATION

A high rate of inflation—whether it is measured by the CPI or the GDP price index—is never welcome news. What's so bad about inflation? As we've seen, it certainly

[3] The technical name for the GDP price index is the *chain-type annual weights GDP price index*. It differs from the CPI not only in goods covered, but also in its mathematical formula.

makes your task as an economics student more difficult: Rather than taking nominal variables at face value, you must do those troublesome calculations to convert them into real variables.

But inflation causes much more trouble than this. It can impose costs on society and on each of us individually. Yet when most people are asked *what* the cost of inflation is, they come up with an incorrect answer.

The Inflation Myth

Most people think that inflation, merely by making goods and services more expensive, erodes the average purchasing power of income in the economy. The reason for this belief is easy to see: The higher the price level, the fewer goods and services a given nominal income will buy. It stands to reason, then, that inflation—which raises prices—must be destroying the purchasing power of our incomes. Right?

Actually, this statement is mostly wrong.

To see why, remember that every market transaction involves *two* parties—a buyer and a seller. When a price rises, buyers of that good must pay more but sellers get more revenue when they sell it. The loss in buyers' real income is matched by the rise in sellers' real income. Inflation may *redistribute* purchasing power among the population, but it does not change the *average* purchasing power, when we include both buyers and sellers in the average.

In fact, most people in the economy participate on both sides of the market. On the one hand, they are consumers—as when they shop for food or clothing or furniture. On the other hand, they work in business firms that *sell* products, and may benefit (in the form of higher wages or higher profits) when their firms' revenues rise. Thus, when prices rise, a particular person may find that her purchasing power has either risen or fallen, depending on whether she is affected more as a seller or as a buyer. But regardless of the outcome for individuals, our conclusion remains the same:

> *Inflation can redistribute purchasing power from one group to another, but it does not directly decrease the average real income in the economy.*

Why, then, do people continue to believe that inflation robs the average citizen of real income? Largely because real incomes sometimes do decline—for *other* reasons. Inflation—while not the *cause* of the decline—will often be the *mechanism* that brings it about. Just as we often blame the messenger for bringing bad news, so too, we often blame inflation for lowering our purchasing power when the real cause lies elsewhere.

Let's consider an example. In Table 2, notice the decline in real wages during the late 1970s. The real wage fell from $8.76 in 1975 to $8.24 in 1980, a decline of about 6 percent. During this period, not only wage earners, but also salaried workers, small-business owners, and corporate shareholders all suffered a decline in their real incomes. What caused the decline?

There were several reasons, but one of the most important was the dramatic rise in the price of imported oil—from $3 per barrel in 1973 to $34 in 1981, an increase of more than 1,000 percent. The higher price for oil meant that oil-exporting countries, like Saudi Arabia, Kuwait, and Iraq, got more goods and services for each barrel of oil they supplied to the rest of the world, including the United States. But with these countries claiming more of America's output, less remained for the typical American. That is, the typical American family had to suffer a decline in real income. As always, a rise in price shifted income from buyers to sellers. But in this case, the sellers were *foreigners*, while the buyers were Americans. Thus, the rise in the price of foreign oil caused average purchasing power in the United States to decline.

But what was the mechanism that brought about the decline? Since real income is equal to (nominal income/price index) $\times$ 100, it can decrease in one of two ways: a fall in the numerator (nominal income) or a rise in the denominator (the price index). The decline in real income in the 1970s came entirely from an increase in the denominator. (Look back at Figure 1. You can see that this period of declining real wages in the United States was also a period of unusually high inflation; at its peak in 1979, the inflation rate exceeded 13 percent.) As a result, most workers blamed *inflation* for their loss of purchasing power. But inflation was not the cause; it was just the *mechanism*. The cause was a change in the terms of trade between the United States and the oil-exporting countries—a change that resulted in higher oil prices.

To summarize, the common idea that inflation imposes a cost on society by directly decreasing average real income in the economy is incorrect. But inflation *does* impose costs on society, as the next section shows.

The Redistributive Cost of Inflation

One cost of inflation is that it often redistributes purchasing power *within* society. But because the winners and losers are chosen haphazardly—rather than by conscious social policy—the redistribution of purchasing power is not generally desirable. In some cases, the shift in purchasing power is downright perverse—harming the needy and helping those who are already well off.

How does inflation sometimes redistribute real income? An increase in the price level reduces the purchasing power of any payment that is specified in nominal terms. For example, some workers have contracts that set their nominal wage for two or three years, regardless of any future inflation. The nationally set minimum wage, too, is set for several years and specified in nominal dollars. Under these circumstances, inflation can harm ordinary workers, since it erodes the purchasing power of their prespecified nominal wage. Real income is redistributed from these workers to their employers, who benefit by paying a lower real wage.

But the effect can also work the other way: benefiting ordinary households and harming businesses. For example, many homeowners sign fixed-dollar mortgage agreements with a bank. These are promises to pay the bank the same nominal sum each month. Inflation can reduce the *real* value of these payments, thus redistributing purchasing power away from the bank and toward the average homeowner.

In general,

> *inflation can shift purchasing power away from those who are awaiting future payments specified in dollars, and toward those who are obligated to make such payments.*

But does inflation *always* redistribute income from one party in a contract to another? Actually, no; if the inflation is *expected* by both parties, it should not redistribute income. The next section explains why.

Expected Inflation Need *Not* Shift Purchasing Power. Suppose a labor union is negotiating a three-year contract with an employer, and both sides agree that each year, workers should get a 3 percent increase in their *real wage*. Labor contracts, like most other contracts, are usually specified in nominal terms: The firm will agree to give workers so many additional *dollars per hour* each year. If neither side anticipates any inflation, they should simply negotiate a 3 percent *nominal* wage hike. With an unchanged price level, the *real* wage would then also rise by the desired 3 percent.

But suppose instead that both sides anticipate 10 percent inflation each year for the next three years. Then, they must agree to *more* than a 3 percent nominal wage increase in order to raise the real wage by 3 percent. How much more?

We can answer this question with a simple mathematical rule:

> *Over any period, the percentage change in a real value (%ΔReal) is approximately equal to the percentage change in the associated nominal value (%ΔNominal) minus the rate of inflation:*
>
> %ΔReal = %ΔNominal − Rate of inflation.

If the inflation rate is 10 percent and the real wage is to rise by 3 percent, then the change in the nominal wage must (approximately) satisfy the equation

3 percent = %ΔNominal − 10 percent ⇒ %ΔNominal = 13 percent.

The required nominal wage hike is 13 percent.

You can see that as long as both sides correctly anticipate the inflation, and no one stops them from negotiating a 13 percent nominal wage hike, inflation will *not* affect either party in real terms:

> *If inflation is fully anticipated, and if both parties take it into account, then inflation will not redistribute purchasing power.*

We come to a similar conclusion about contracts between lenders and borrowers. When you lend someone money, you receive a reward—an interest payment—for letting that person use your money instead of spending it yourself. The annual *interest rate* is the interest payment divided by the amount of money you have lent. For example, if you lend someone $1,000 and receive back $1,040 one year later, then your interest is $40, and the interest *rate* on the loan is $40/$1,000 = 0.04, or 4 percent.

But there are actually *two* interest rates associated with every loan. One is the **nominal interest rate**—the percentage increase in the lender's *dollars* from making the loan. The other is the **real interest rate**—the percentage increase in the lender's *purchasing power* from making the loan. It is the *real* rate—the change in purchasing power—that lenders and borrowers should care about.

Nominal interest rate The annual percent increase in a lender's dollars from making a loan.

Real interest rate The annual percent increase in a lender's purchasing power from making a loan.

In the absence of inflation, real and nominal interest rates would always be equal. A 4 percent increase in the lender's *dollars* would always imply a 4 percent increase in her purchasing power. But if there is inflation, it will reduce the purchasing power of the money paid back. Does this mean that inflation redistributes purchasing power? Not if the inflation is correctly anticipated, and if there are no restrictions on making loan contracts.

For example, suppose both parties anticipate inflation of 5 percent and want to arrange a contract whereby the lender will be paid a 4 percent *real* interest rate. What *nominal* interest rate should they choose? Since an interest rate is the *percentage change* in the lender's funds, we can use our approximation rule,

%ΔReal = %ΔNominal − Rate of inflation,

which here becomes

%Δ in Lender's purchasing power = %Δ in Lender's dollars − Rate of inflation or

$$\text{Real interest rate} = \text{Nominal interest rate} - \text{Rate of inflation.}$$

In our example, where we want the real interest rate to equal 4 percent when the inflation rate is 5 percent, we must have

$$4 \text{ percent} = \text{Nominal interest rate} - 5 \text{ percent}$$

or

$$\text{Nominal interest rate} = 9 \text{ percent.}$$

Once again, we see that as long as both parties correctly anticipate the inflation rate, and face no restrictions on contracts (that is, they are free to set the nominal interest rate at 9 percent), then no one gains or loses.

When inflation is *not* correctly anticipated, however, our conclusion is very different.

Unexpected Inflation *Does* Shift Purchasing Power. Suppose that, expecting no inflation, you agree to lend money at a 4 percent nominal interest rate for one year. You and the borrower think that this will translate into a 4 percent real rate. But it turns out you are both wrong: The price level actually rises by 3 percent, so the *real* interest rate ends up being 4 percent − 3 percent = 1 percent. As a lender, you have given up the use of your money for the year, expecting to be rewarded with a 4 percent increase in purchasing power. But you get only a 1 percent increase. Your borrower was willing to pay 4 percent in purchasing power, but ends up paying only 1 percent. *Unexpected* inflation has led to a better deal for your borrower and a worse deal for you, the lender.

That will not make you happy. But it could be even worse. Suppose the inflation rate is higher—say, 6 percent. Then your real interest rate ends up at 4 percent − 6 percent = −2 percent, a negative real interest rate. You get back *less* in purchasing power than you lend out—*paying* (in purchasing power) for the privilege of lending out your money. The borrower is *rewarded* (in purchasing power) for borrowing!

Negative real interest rates like this are not just a theoretical possibility. In the late 1970s, when inflation was higher than expected for several years in a row, many borrowers ending up paying negative real interest rates to lenders.

Now, let's consider one more possibility: Expected inflation is 6 percent, so you negotiate a 10 percent nominal rate, thinking this will translate to a 4 percent real rate. But the actual inflation rate turns out to be zero, so the real interest rate is 10 percent − 0 percent = 10 percent. In this case, inflation turns out to be *less* than expected, so the *real* interest rate is higher than either of you anticipated. The borrower is harmed and you (the lender) benefit.

These examples apply, more generally, to any agreement on future payments: to a worker waiting for a wage payment and the employer who has promised to pay it; to a doctor who has sent out a bill and the patient who has not yet paid it; or to a supplier who has delivered goods and his customer who hasn't yet paid for them.

When inflationary expectations are inaccurate, purchasing power is shifted between those obliged to make future payments and those waiting to be paid. An inflation rate higher than expected harms those awaiting payment and benefits the payers; an inflation rate lower than expected harms the payers and benefits those awaiting payment.

The Resource Cost of Inflation

In addition to its possible redistribution of income, inflation imposes another cost upon society. To cope with inflation, we are forced to use up time and other resources as we go about our daily economic activities (shopping, selling, saving) that we could otherwise have devoted to productive activities. Thus, inflation imposes an *opportunity cost* on society as a whole and on each of its members:

> *When people must spend time and other resources coping with inflation, they pay an opportunity cost—they sacrifice the goods and services those resources could have produced instead.*

Let's first consider the resources used up by *consumers* to cope with inflation. Suppose you shop for clothes twice a year. You've discovered that both The Gap and Banana Republic sell clothing of similar quality and have similar service, and you naturally want to shop at the one with the lower prices. If there is no inflation, your task is easy: You shop first at The Gap and then at Banana Republic; thereafter, you rely on your memory to determine which is less expensive.

With inflation, however, things are more difficult. Suppose you find that prices at Banana Republic are higher than you remember them to be at The Gap. It may be that Banana Republic is the more expensive store, or it may be that prices have risen at *both* stores. How can you tell? Only a trip back to The Gap will answer the question—a trip that will cost you extra time and trouble. If prices are rising very rapidly, you may have to visit both stores on the same day to be sure which one is cheaper. Now, multiply this time and trouble by all the different types of shopping you must do on a regular or occasional basis—for groceries, an apartment, a car, concert tickets, compact discs, restaurant meals, and more. Inflation can make you use up valuable time—time you could have spent earning income or enjoying leisure activities. True, if you shop for some of these items on the Internet, you can compare prices in less time, but not zero time. And most shopping is *not* done over the Internet.

Inflation also forces *sellers* to use up resources. First, remember that sellers of goods and services are also buyers of resources and intermediate goods. They, too, must do comparison shopping when there is inflation, which uses up hired labor time. Second, each time sellers raise prices, labor is needed to put new price tags on merchandise, to enter new prices into a computer scanning system, to update the HTML code on a Web page, or to change the prices on advertising brochures, menus, and so on.

Finally, inflation makes us all use up resources managing our financial affairs. When the inflation rate is high, we'll try to keep our funds in accounts that pay high nominal interest rates, in order to preserve our purchasing power. And we'll try to keep as little as possible in cash or in low-interest checking accounts. Of course, this means more frequent trips to the bank or the automatic teller machine, to transfer money into our checking accounts or get cash each time we need it.

All of these additional activities—inspecting prices at several stores or Web sites, changing price tags or price entries, going back and forth to the automatic teller machine—use up not only time, but other resources, too, such as the resources used to make gasoline or car repairs. From society's point of view, these resources could have been used to produce *other* goods and services that we'd enjoy.

You may not have thought much about the resource cost of inflation, because in recent years, U.S. inflation has been so low—averaging about 3 percent during the 1990s, and about $2\frac{1}{2}$ percent in the early 2000s. Such a low rate of inflation is often called *creeping inflation;* from week to week or month to month, the price level creeps up so slowly that we hardly notice the change. The cost of coping with creeping inflation is negligible. And (as you'll see in a later chapter) low, creeping inflation may actually be good for the economy.

But it has not always been this way. Three times during the last 50 years, we have had double-digit inflation: about 14 percent during 1947–48, 12 percent in 1974, and 13 percent during 1979 and 1980. Going back farther, the annual inflation rate reached almost 20 percent during World War I and rose above 25 percent during the Civil War.

And as serious as these episodes of American inflation have been, they pale in comparison to the experiences of other countries. In Germany in the early 1920s, the inflation rate hit thousands of percent *per month.* And more recently, in the late 1980s, several South American countries experienced inflation rates in excess of 1,000 percent annually. For a few weeks in 1990, Argentina's annual inflation rate even reached 400,000 percent! Under these conditions, the monetary system breaks down almost completely. Economic life is almost as difficult as in the mythical nation of Chaotica, discussed at the very beginning of this chapter.

A Preliminary Word About Deflation

In the early 2000s, as the annual inflation rate approached 2 percent, a new worry appeared on the American political and economic scene: *deflation* (a *negative* inflation rate). In some respects, deflation creates costs for society similar to those of inflation. For example, when the deflation rate is not correctly anticipated, purchasing power will be redistributed between borrowers and lenders. And if the deflation rate is high (prices are *falling* rapidly), resources are used up to cope with it: Prices must be updated more frequently, using up labor and raw materials, and more consumer time will be spent on comparison shopping.

However, deflation has some special costs and risks of its own, entirely different from those of inflation. To understand what's different about deflation, some understanding of macroeconomic models is required. For this reason, we'll postpone our comprehensive discussion of deflation until the chapter on Inflation and Monetary Policy.

IS THE CPI ACCURATE?

The Bureau of Labor Statistics spends millions of dollars gathering data to ensure that its measure of inflation is accurate. To determine the market basket of the typical consumer, the BLS randomly selects thousands of households and analyzes their spending habits. In the last such survey—completed in 2004—each of about 15,000 families kept diaries of their purchases for two weeks.

But that is just the beginning. Every month, the bureau's shoppers visit 23,000 retail stores and about 50,000 housing units (rental apartments and owner-occupied homes) to record 80,000 different prices. Finally, all of the prices are combined to determine the cost of the typical consumer's market basket for the current month.

The BLS is a highly professional agency, typically headed by an economist. Billions of dollars are at stake for each 1 percent change in the CPI, and the BLS deserves high praise for keeping its measurement honest and free of political manipulation. Nevertheless, conceptual problems and resource limitations make the CPI fall short of the ideal measure of inflation. Economists—even those who

HTTP://

To learn more about the strengths and weaknesses of the CPI, read Allison Wallace and Brian Motley, "A Better CPI" (**http://www.frbsf.org/econrsrch/wklyltr/wklyltr99/el99-05.html**).

work in the BLS—widely agree that the CPI overstates the U.S. inflation rate. By how much?

According to a report by an advisory committee of economists in 1996, the overall bias was at least 1.1 percent during the 1980s and early 1990s.[4] That is, in a typical year, the reported rise in the CPI was about 1 percentage point greater than the true rise in the price level. The BLS has been working hard to reduce this upward bias and—especially in the late 1990s—it made some progress. But significant bias remains.

Sources of Bias in the CPI

There are several reasons for the upward bias in the CPI.

Substitution Bias. Until recently, the CPI almost completely ignored a general principle of consumer behavior: People tend to *substitute* goods that have become relatively cheaper in place of goods that have become relatively more expensive. For example, in the seven years from 1973 to 1980, the retail price of oil-related products—like gasoline and home heating oil—increased by more than 300 percent, while the prices of most other goods and services rose by less than 100 percent. As a result, people found ways to conserve on oil products. They joined carpools, used public transportation, insulated their homes, and in many cases moved closer to their workplaces to shorten their commute. Yet throughout this period, the CPI basket—based on a survey of buying patterns in 1972–73—assumed that consumers were buying unchanged quantities of oil products.

The treatment of oil products is an example of a more general problem that has plagued the CPI for decades. Until recently, the CPI used fixed *quantities* to determine the relative importance of each item. That is, it assumed that households continued to buy each good or service in the same quantities in which they bought it during the most recent household survey—until the next household survey. Compounding the problem, the survey to determine spending patterns—and to update the market basket—was taken only about once every 10 years or so. So by the end of each 10-year period, the CPI's assumptions about spending habits could be far off the mark, as they were in the case of oil in the 1970s.

The BLS has *partially* fixed this problem, in two ways.[5] First, beginning in 2002, it began updating the market basket with a household survey every *two* years instead of every 10 years. This is widely considered an important improvement in CPI measurement.

Second, since January 1999, the CPI has no longer assumed that the typical consumer continues to buy the same *quantity* of each good that he bought in the last household "market basket" survey. Instead, the CPI now assumes that when a good's relative price rises by 10 percent, consumers buy 10 percent less of it, and switch their purchases to other goods whose prices are rising more slowly.

However, this is only a partial fix. The CPI still only recognizes the possibility of such substitution *within* categories of goods and *not among* them. For example, if the price of steak rises relative to the price of hamburger meat, the CPI now assumes that consumers will substitute away from steak and toward hamburger meat,

---

[4] See *Toward a More Accurate Measure of the Cost of Living,* Report to the Senate Finance Committee from the Advisory Commission to Study the Consumer Price Index, December 1996.

[5] For a discussion of these and other recent changes in the CPI, see "Planned Change in the Consumer Price Index Formula," Bureau of Labor Statistics, April 16, 1998 (*http://www.bls.gov/cpi/cpigm02.htm*), and "Future Schedule for Expenditure Weight Updates in the Consumer Price Index," Bureau of Labor Statistics, December 18, 1998 (*http://www.bls.gov/cpi/cpiupdt.htm*).

since both are in the same category: *beef.* However, if the price of all beef products rises relative to chicken and pork, the CPI assumes that there is *no* substitution at all from beef toward chicken and pork. As a result, beef products still would be overweighted in the CPI until the next survey.

Although the BLS has partially fixed the problem, the CPI still suffers from substitution bias. That is, categories of goods whose prices are rising most rapidly tend to be given exaggerated importance in the CPI, and categories of goods whose prices are rising most slowly tend to be given too little importance in the CPI.

New Technologies. New technologies are another source of upward bias in the CPI. One problem is that goods using new technologies are introduced into the BLS market basket only after a lag. These goods often drop rapidly in price after they are introduced, helping to balance out price rises in other goods. By excluding a category of goods whose prices are dropping, the CPI overstates the rate of inflation. For example, even though many consumers were buying and using cellular phones throughout the 1990s, they were not included in the BLS basket of goods until 1998. As a result, the CPI missed the rapid decline in the price of cell phones. Now that the market basket of the typical consumer is updated every two years instead of every 10, this source of bias has been reduced but not completely eliminated.

But there is another issue with new technologies: They often offer consumers a lower-cost alternative for obtaining the same service. For example, the introduction of cable television lowered the cost of entertainment significantly by offering a new, cheaper alternative to going out to see movies. This should have registered as a drop in the price of "seeing movies." But the CPI does not have any good way to measure this reduction in the cost of living. Instead, it treats cable television as an entirely separate service.

The CPI excludes new products that tend to drop in price when they first come on the market. When included, the CPI regards them as entirely separate from existing goods and services, instead of recognizing that they lower the cost of achieving a given standard of living. The result is an overestimate of the inflation rate.

Changes in Quality. Many products are improving over time. Cars are much more reliable than they used to be and require much less routine maintenance. They have features like air bags and antilock brakes that were unknown in the early 1980s. The BLS struggles to deal with these changes. As far back as 1967, it has recognized that when the price of a car rises, some of that price hike is not really inflation but instead the result of charging more because the consumer is *getting* more. In recent years, the BLS has adopted some routine statistical procedures to automatically adjust price changes for quality improvements for a variety of goods. Table 3 lists some important examples, along with the year that the CPI began measuring and adjusting for quality improvements.

Two things stand out in the table. First, for many of the goods, quality adjustment began very late, *after* huge advances in quality had already taken place. Up until that time, the CPI treated any price hike as pure inflation, thus contributing to an overestimate of the overall inflation rate. Second, while the list of goods in the table is impressive (and growing), most goods do *not* get this special treatment. For

TABLE 3
Goods Adjusted for Quality Changes in the CPI

Prices Adjusted for Quality Changes	Year Adjustment Began
Cars	1967
Used Cars	1987
Clothing	1991
Gasoline	1994
Personal Computers	1998
Televisions	1999
VCRs & DVD Players	2000
Refrigerators, Microwaves, Washing Machines	2000
College Textbooks	2000

Sources: "Program Report," *Monthly Labor Review,* May 2002, p. 47; and various BLS publications.

most goods, improvements in quality are effectively ignored.

Take the Internet. Every year, it offers more information and entertainment content, a greater number of retailers from which to buy things, and faster and more intelligent search engines to help you find it all. Yet, the Internet—which was introduced into the CPI in 1998—has been treated as a service whose quality has not changed. If the price of Internet service rises, the CPI considers it inflation rather than paying more to *get* more. And if the price stays the same, the CPI ignores the *decrease* in the cost per unit of available content and treats the price as unchanged.

> The CPI still counts as inflation many cases in which prices rise because of quality improvements. This causes the CPI to overstate the inflation rate.

Growth in Discounting. The CPI treats toothpaste bought at a high-priced drugstore and toothpaste bought at Wal-Mart or Drugstore. com as different products. And it assumes that we continue to buy from high- and low-priced stores in unchanged proportions. But that is not what has been happening. In fact, Americans are buying more and more of their toothpaste and other products from discounters, but the CPI does not consider this in measuring inflation. The purchasing power you have lost from inflation is not as great as the CPI says if you, like most Americans, are stretching your dollar by going more often to discount outlets, warehouse stores, and Web sites with low prices.

© SUSAN VAN ETTEN

USING THE THEORY
The Use and Misuse of an Imperfect CPI

The inaccuracies in measuring the Consumer Price Index discussed in the chapter, as well as an even more important conceptual issue to be discussed below, suggest that the CPI should be used and interpreted with great care. Unfortunately, the CPI is often used for purposes which it cannot handle accurately.

Indexing

Earlier in the chapter, we pointed out that more than 50 million Social Security recipients and other retirees, as well as 2 million workers, have their benefits *indexed* to the CPI: Their nominal (dollar) benefits automatically increase at the same rate as the CPI. The justification for indexing is to protect these people from any deterioration in living standards caused by inflation. But because changes in the CPI *overstate* inflation, these beneficiaries are *over*indexed. That is, their nominal benefit rises by a greater percentage than a more accurately measured price index would rise.

Let's take an example. Suppose that a Social Security recipient who retired in 1980 was promised $1,000 per month in Social Security benefits, indexed to the CPI each year. But suppose that each year from 1980 to 2002 (the period of retirement) the CPI *overstated* the annual rate of inflation by 1 percent. Then every year, the recipient receives 1 percent more in dollars than needed to maintain the *purchasing power* of the benefit, so the real benefit rises by 1 percent every year. At the end of the first year, the real payment is $1,000 \times 1.01 = \$1010$. For the second year, it's $[\$1,000 \times 1.01] \times 1.01 = \$1 \times (1.01)^2 = \$1,020.10$. And at the end of the 22nd year, it's $\$1,000 \times (1.01)^{22} = \$1,245$. Rather than just maintaining the real Social Security payment over time, indexing to the inaccurate CPI results in a continually rising *real* benefit, one that is 24 percent higher than in the initial period.

This will suit Social Security recipients just fine. And it may suit the rest of us too—when the economy is growing at a rapid pace. After all, why shouldn't retirees get a larger slice of the economic pie when the pie itself is growing rapidly and everyone else's slice is growing as well? But note that the increase in real benefits happens *automatically,* due to overindexing, *regardless* of the rate of economic growth. If the growth rate of real GDP slows down, the average Social Security recipient will *still* get a growing slice of the pie each year, even if everyone else's slice is shrinking. And because Social Security is financed by tax payments from the rest of society, any increase in real benefits shrinks the after-tax real income of nonretirees.

More generally,

> when a payment is indexed and the price index overstates inflation, the real payment increases over time. Purchasing power is automatically shifted toward those who are indexed and away from the rest of society.

This general principle applies whether the economy is growing rapidly or slowly, and it applies to anyone who is indexed: Social Security recipients, government pensioners, union workers with indexed wage contracts, or anyone else.

Long-Run Comparisons

If you look back at Table 2, you'll see a rather depressing story: The average hourly worker's real wage in 2004 was just a tiny bit higher than in 1980, and actually *lower* than in 1970. Has the purchasing power of the average wage really behaved this way? Not if the CPI—which was used in the table to calculate the real wage—overstates inflation.

We can get a *somewhat* more accurate view by asking the following question: What story would Table 2 tell if some of the recent improvements in the CPI measurement were applied retroactively? Fortunately, the BLS has attempted to answer this question by constructing an *unofficial* version of the CPI (called the CPI-U-RS, or the CPI for all Urban Consumers—Research Series) going back to 1978. This series is shown in Table 4. The first four columns of the data are selected rows from Table 2. They show the calculation of the wage using the *official* CPI. The fifth column shows the unofficial CPI—what the CPI *would* have been if some recent methodological improvements had been used in earlier years. Finally, the last column shows the recalculation of the real wage based on this somewhat more accurate CPI.

(1) Year	(2) Average Nominal Wage	(3) Official CPI	(4) Official Average Real Wage (1983 dollars) [(2)/(3)] × 100	(5) Partially Corrected CPI	(6) Partially Corrected Real Wage (1983 dollars) [(2)/(5)] × 100
1970	$3.50	39.8	$8.79	(no data available)	—
1980	$7.12	86.4	$8.24	86.0	$8.28
1990	$10.33	134.2	$7.70	130.8	$7.90
2000	$14.26	174.6	$8.17	165.2	$8.63
2002	$15.19	181.6	$8.36	171.7	$8.85
2004	$15.85	191.2	$8.29	180.6	$8.77

Source: "The Bureau of Labor Statistics' Statement on the Use of the CPI-U-RS," at *http://www.bls.gov/cpi/cpiurstx.htm* (modified April 27, 2005). Base year of CPI-U-RS was converted from 1977 to 1983 by authors.

TABLE 4
The Official and Partially Corrected Average Real Wage

As you can see in the last column, the story looks a bit different. From 1980 to 2004, instead of rising from $8.24 to $8.29 (in 1983 dollars), the partially corrected real wage rose from $8.28 to $8.77. Moreover, instead of falling from 1970 to 2004, the partially corrected real wage was essentially unchanged during this period. Keep in mind, too, that Columns 5 and 6 reflect only *some* of the BLS's improved measurement techniques, and these new techniques corrected only *some* of the acknowledged problems. A fuller correction would show a rise in the real wage over this period.

In any case, because the BLS never alters previously published data to reflect later improvements in methodology, the official history of the real wage remains that of Column 4, not Column 6. This is the story you will see on Web sites and press reports that discuss changes in real wages over time.

> *Because the BLS does not correct previously reported CPI numbers to reflect later methodological improvements, long-term comparisons of real variables based on the official CPI will remain inaccurate, even as CPI measurement improves.*

The Bigger, Conceptual Problem

An even more serious problem in using the CPI has to do with the way it is typically viewed: as a measure of the *cost of living*—the cost of maintaining a fixed living standard from purchased goods and services. Indexing, after all, is usually justified as a way to prevent any deterioration in living standards. And discussions about the real wage often end with conclusions about the average worker being better or worse off. These conclusions imply that the CPI—which is used to calculate the real wage—is tracking the cost of achieving a given living standard. However, viewed as a measure of the cost of living, the CPI is even more inaccurate than our discussion so far suggests. This is because of the way it treats new goods—a problem that will not be corrected by any of the BLS's planned improvements.

When a new good comes to market, it is dropped into the CPI market basket at some point, and the CPI tracks changes in its price from that time forward. But the increase in economic well-being made possible by *introducing* the good—and the good's continued availability—is never accounted for. Even if the BLS were able to in-corporate the good as soon as it came to market, and even if it accurately adjusted for subsequent quality improvements, it would still be missing the most important factor: the rise in living standards made possible by the new good's availability.

For example, we've already discussed the CPI's failure to account for quality *im-provements* in the Internet after it was dropped into the basket in 1998. But in ad-dition to this problem, the CPI has *never* recognized how the Internet has lowered the cost of achieving any given level of economic satisfaction (think of e-mail, on-line entertainment, online purchases, news, and more). The same is true for new medical procedures or prescription drugs that can treat or cure formerly untreat-able diseases. The CPI tracks increases in their prices *after* they appear in the bas-ket, but ignores the impact of these new treatments on our standard of living. In this way, the CPI misses a highly relevant fact: New goods raise the living standard we can achieve at any given dollar cost or, equivalently, they lower the dollar cost of achieving any given living standard.

How serious is this problem? No one knows for sure. But some authors have suggested that the error from ignoring the effect of new goods on living standards could be substantial. This error must be *added* to the combined effects of all the other errors discussed in this chapter.[6]

How might this change the story of the hourly real wage told in Table 2 (or Table 4)? Let's suppose that the ultimate, total overstatement in the cost of living has been 2 percent each year from 1970 to 2004. This would lead the CPI in 2004 to exaggerate the cost of living by about $(1.02)^{34} = 1.96$ or 96 percent. In Table 4, the official CPI over that period rose from 39.8 to 191.2, or a percentage increase of $(191.2 - 39.8)/39.8 = 3.80$ or 380 percent. Deducting the 96 percent error would leave a *true* cost of living increase of $380 - 96 = 284$ percent. Thus, to obtain an accurate CPI in 2004, we would increase 1970's CPI by 284 percent—instead of the official 380 per-cent. This would give us an accurate CPI in 2004 of $39.8 + (2.84 \times 39.8) = 152.8$. Finally, using this corrected CPI would give us a 2004 hourly real wage of $[\$15.85/152.8] \times 100 = \$10.37$. Comparing with 1970, we see that the real wage would have increased substantially—from \$8.79 to \$10.37—rather than falling, as the official story goes.

Of course, this example arbitrarily assumed a 2 percent overstatement of the annual rise in the cost of living. The actual overstatement could be less—or consid-erably more. But the general point is this:

> *Using the CPI as an index of the* cost of living *(the cost of achieving a given living standard) creates a further overstatement of inflation, because the CPI ignores the impact of new goods on living standards. Therefore, CPI-based indexing and CPI-based inferences about changes in well-being over time may be highly inaccurate.*

What the CPI Does Well

The CPI has another purpose besides indexing and making inferences about living standards: to measure inflationary tendencies in the economy. For this purpose, the CPI's interpretation as a cost-of-living index is irrelevant: The policy goal is to avoid

[6] See, for example, the suggestions of Jerry Hausman, "Sources of Bias and Solutions to Bias in the CPI," National Bureau of Economic Research, Working Paper 9298, October 2002 and also in Journal of Economic Perspectives, Vol.17, No.1 Winter 2003. Much of the discussion of this subsection is based on Hausman's work.

high costs to society when the price level—however it's interpreted—changes too rapidly. The CPI is one of several useful tools to help achieve this goal.

To see why, suppose the CPI-based inflation rate (or one of its useful variants, which leaves out volatile components like food or energy prices) suddenly jumps up. Because of its measurement errors, the official inflation rate will exaggerate the true rise in prices, but it's unlikely that measurement errors alone would cause the entire increase in reported inflation. (That would require a sudden change in the relative importance of the measurement errors themselves.) Instead, a sudden spike in the CPI would tell policy makers that prices in the economy are, indeed, rising at a faster rate, and that appropriate policy measures should be considered to prevent inflation from getting out of hand. The same might apply to a rapid *decrease* in officially measured inflation to very low levels, creating a danger of deflation.

Also, in times of high inflation—as in the late 1970s—using an imperfect CPI to estimate real wages or to index retirees may be preferable to not accounting for inflation at all. With official annual inflation of 13 percent, for example, indexing Social Security benefits to an exaggerated CPI might raise the living standards of retirees by a few percentage points at the expense of the rest of society. But *not* indexing Social Security benefits at all could cause retirees' living standards to fall by 10 percent or more.

This chapter has raised many questions and left some of them unanswered. What makes the inflation rate rise and fall? Who are these *policy makers* that monitor the inflation rate and often try to alter it? How do they actually change the inflation rate? And why would they worry about an inflation rate that is too *low*? These are all questions we'll address in future chapters, after you've learned about macroeconomic models—the subject we turn to now.

Summary

Money serves two important functions. First, it serves as a *unit of value* that helps us compare the costs of different goods and services. Second, it serves as a *means of payment* by being generally acceptable in exchange for goods and services. Without money, we would be reduced to barter, a very inefficient way of carrying out transactions.

The value of money is its purchasing power, and this changes as the prices of the things we buy change. The overall trend of prices is measured using a price index. Like any index number, a price index is calculated as: (value in current period/value in base period) × 100. The most widely used price index in the United States is the *Consumer Price Index (CPI)*, which tracks the prices paid for a typical consumer's "market basket." The percent change in the CPI is the inflation rate.

The most common uses of the CPI are for indexing payments, as a policy target, and to translate from nominal to real variables. Many nominal variables, such as the nominal wage, can be corrected for price changes by dividing by the CPI and then multiplying by 100. The result is a real variable, such as the real wage, that rises and falls only when its purchasing power rises and falls. Another price index in common use is the GDP price index. It tracks prices of all final goods and services included in GDP.

Inflation, a rise over time in a price index, is costly to our society. One of inflation's costs is an arbitrary redistribution of purchasing power. Unanticipated inflation shifts purchasing power away from those awaiting future dollar payments and toward those obligated to make such payments. Another cost of inflation is the resource cost: People use valuable time and other resources trying to cope with inflation.

It is widely agreed that the CPI has overstated inflation in recent decades, probably by more than one percentage point per year. As a result, the official statistics on real variables may contain errors, and people whose incomes are indexed to the CPI have actually been overindexed, enjoying an increase in real income that is paid for by the rest of society. The Bureau of Labor Statistics has been trying to eliminate the upward bias in the CPI. Much progress has been made, but some upward bias remains. The CPI is especially inaccurate as an index of the cost of achieving a given standard of living.

Key Terms

Consumer Price Index
Federal Reserve System
Fiat money
GDP price index

Index
Indexation
Inflation rate
Means of payment

Nominal interest rate
Price level
Real interest rate
Unit of value

Review Questions   *Answers to even-numbered Questions and Problems can be found on the text Web site at http://hall-lieb.swlearning.com.*

1. Distinguish between the *unit-of-value* function of money and the *means-of-payment* function. Give examples of how the U.S. dollar has played each of these two roles.

2. How does the price level differ from, say, the price of a haircut or a Big Mac?

3. Explain how you might construct an index of bank deposits over time. What steps would be involved?

4. What is the CPI? What does it measure? How can it be used to calculate the inflation rate?

5. Can the inflation rate be decreasing at the same time the price level is rising? Can the inflation rate be increasing at the same time the price level is falling? Explain.

6. What are the main uses of the CPI? Give an example of each use.

7. Explain the logic of the formula that relates real values to nominal values.

8. What are the similarities between the CPI and the GDP price index? What are the differences?

9. What are the costs of inflation?

10. Under what circumstances would inflation redistribute purchasing power? How? When would it *not* redistribute purchasing power?

11. How is a nominal interest rate different from a real interest rate? Which do you think is the better measure of the rate of return on a loan?

12. Explain the common misuses of the CPI.

Problems and Exercises

1. Calculate each of the following from the data in Table 1 in this chapter.
   a. The inflation rate for the year 2002.
   b. *Total* inflation (the total percentage change in the price level) from December 1970 to December 2002.

2. Using the data in Table 2, calculate the following for the period 1995–2000.
   a. The total percentage change in the nominal wage.
   b. The total percentage change in the price level.

3. Calculate the total percentage change in the real wage from 1995 to 2000 in two ways: (a) using your answers in problems 2a and b and the rule given earlier in this chapter; and (b) using the last column of Table 2. Which method is more accurate?

4. Suppose we want to change the base period of the CPI from July 1983 to December 1995. Recalculate December's CPI for each of the years in Table 1, so that the table gives the same information about inflation, but the CPI in December 1995 is now 100 instead of 153.9.

5. Which would be more costly: a steady inflation rate of 5 percent per year, or an inflation rate that was sometimes high and sometimes low, but that averaged 5 percent per year? Justify your answer.

6. Given the following *year-end* data, calculate the inflation rate for years 2, 3, and 4. Calculate the real wage in each year:

Year	CPI	Inflation Rate	Nominal Wage	Real Wage
1	100	____	$10.00	____
2	110	____	$12.00	____
3	120	____	$13.00	____
4	115	____	$12.75	____

7. Your friend asks for a loan of $100 for one year and offers to pay you 5 percent real interest. Your friend expects the inflation rate over that one-year period to be 6 percent; you expect it to be 4 percent. You agree to make the loan, and the actual inflation rate turns out to be 5 percent. Who benefits and who loses?

8. If there is 5 percent inflation each year for eight years, what is the *total* amount of inflation (i.e., the total percentage rise in the price level) over the entire eight-year period? (*Hint:* The answer is *not* 40 percent.)

9. Given the following data, calculate the real interest rate for years 2, 3, and 4. (Assume that each CPI number tells us the price level at the *end* of each year.)

Year	CPI	Nominal Interest Rate	Real Interest Rate
1	100		
2	110	15%	_____
3	120	13%	_____
4	115	8%	_____

If you lent $200 to a friend at the beginning of year 2 at the prevailing nominal interest rate of 15 percent, and your friend returned the money, with the interest, at the end of year 2, did you benefit from the deal?

10. (Requires appendix) An economy has only two goods, whose prices and typical consumption quantities are as follows:

	Dec. 2005		Dec. 2006	
	Price	Quantity	Price	Quantity
Fruit (lbs)	$1.00	100	$1.00	150
Nuts (lbs)	$3.00	50	$4.00	25

a. Using December 2005 as the base period for calculations and also as the year for measuring the typical consumer's market basket, calculate the CPI in December 2005 and December 2006.

b. What is the annual inflation rate for 2006?

c. Do you think your answer in b. would understate the actual inflation rate in 2006? Briefly, why or why not?

11. a. Use Table 4. For 1990 to 2002, calculate the following:
(i) the total percentage change in the official CPI;
(ii) the total percentage change in the partially corrected CPI;
(iii) the total percentage change in the official real wage; and
(iv) the total percentage change in the partially corrected real wage.

b. Suppose a fully corrected CPI would have increased only 25 percent over this entire period. What would be the percentage change in the fully corrected real wage?

c. Suppose the CPI overstates the cost of living by 2 percent, as discussed at the end of the "Using the Theory" section of this chapter. When this assumed overstatement is corrected, by what percentage would the real wage have increased from 1990 to 2002?

12. Complete the following table. (CPI numbers are for the end of each year).

Year	CPI	Inflation Rate	Nominal Wage	Real Wage
1	37		$ 5.60	
2	48		$ 7	
3		10%	$11.26	
4		19%		$25
5	60		$15	

13. a. Jodie earned $25,000 in year 1, when the CPI was 460. If the CPI in year 2 is 504, what would Jodie have to earn in year 2 to maintain a constant real wage?

b. What would she have to earn in year 2, to obtain a 5 percent increase in her real wage? What percentage increase in the nominal wage is this?

Challenge Questions

1. Inflation is sometimes said to be a tax on nominal money holdings. If you hold $100 and the price level increases by 10 percent, the purchasing power of that $100 falls by about 10 percent. Who benefits from this inflation tax?

2. During the late 19th and early 20th centuries, many U.S. farmers favored inflationary government policies. Why might this have been the case? (*Hint:* Do farmers typically pay for their land in full at the time of purchase?)

 These exercises require access to Hall/Lieberman Xtra! If Xtra! did not come with your book, visit http://hallxtra.swlearning.com to purchase.

1. Use your Xtra! password at the Hall and Lieberman Web site (http://hallxtra.swlearning.com), select this chapter, and click on EconDebate. Choose *Macroeconomics: Employment, Unemployment, and Inflation* and scroll down to find the debate, "Should the Federal Reserve Aim at a Zero Inflation Policy?" Read the debate and use the information to answer the following questions.

a. Explain the "Philips' Curve."

b. Argue from a new Classical perspective, whether an inflation rate of 0 percent is better or worse than an inflation rate of 3 percent.

2. Use your Xtra! password at the Hall and Lieberman Web site (http://hallxtra.swlearning.com), select this chapter, and under Economic Applications, click on EconData. Choose *Macroeconomics: Employment, Unemployment, and Inflation,* and scroll down to find *Consumer Price Index (CPI)*. Read the definition and click on Diagrams/Data and use the information to identify the periods when the relationship described by Philips' curve holds.

APPENDIX

CALCULATING THE CONSUMER PRICE INDEX

The Consumer Price Index (CPI) is the government's most popular measure of inflation. It tracks the cost of the collection of goods, called the *CPI market basket*, bought by a typical consumer in some *base period*. This appendix demonstrates how the Bureau of Labor Statistics (BLS) calculates the CPI. To help you follow the steps clearly, we'll do the calculations for a very simple economy with just two goods: hamburger meat and oranges (not a pleasant world, but a manageable one). Table A.1 shows prices for each good, and the quantities produced and consumed, in two different periods: December 2004 (the base period) and December 2005. The market basket (measured in the base period) is given in the third column of the table: In December 2004, the typical consumer buys 30 pounds of hamburger and 50 pounds of oranges. Our formula for the CPI in any period t is

CPI in period t

$$= \frac{\text{Cost of market basket at prices in period } t}{\text{Cost of market basket at 2004 prices}} \times 100,$$

where each year's prices are measured in December of that year.

TABLE A.1
Prices and Weekly Quantities in a Two-Good Economy

	December 2004		December 2005	
	Price (per lb.)	Quantity (lbs.)	Price (per lb.)	Quantity (lbs.)
Hamburger Meat	$5.00	30	$6.00	10
Oranges	$1.00	50	$1.10	100

Table A.2 shows the calculations we must do to determine the CPI in December 2004 and December 2005. In the table, you can see that the cost of the 2004 market basket at 2004 prices is $200. The cost of the *same* market basket at 2005's higher prices is $235.

TABLE A.2
Calculations for the CPI

	At December 2004 Prices	At December 2005 Prices
Cost of 30 lbs. of Hamburger	$5.00 × 30 = $150	$6.00 × 30 = $180
Cost of 50 lbs. of Oranges	$1.00 × 50 = $50	$1.10 × 50 = $55
Cost of Entire Market Basket	$150 + $50 = $200	$180 + $55 = $235

To determine the CPI in December 2004—the base period—we use the formula with period t equal to 2004, giving us

CPI in 2004

$$= \frac{\text{Cost of 2004 basket at 2004 prices}}{\text{Cost of 2004 basket at 2004 prices}} \times 100$$

$$= \frac{\$200}{\$200} \times 100 = 100.$$

That is, the CPI in December 2004—the base period—is equal to 100. (The formula, as you can see, is set up so that the CPI will always equal 100 in the base period, regardless of which base period we choose.)

Now let's apply the formula again, to get the value of the CPI in December 2005:

CPI in 2005

$$= \frac{\text{Cost of 2004 basket at 2005 prices}}{\text{Cost of 2004 basket at 2004 prices}} \times 100$$

$$= \frac{\$235}{\$200} \times 100 = 117.5.$$

From December 2004 to December 2005, the CPI rises from 100 to 117.5. The rate of inflation over the year 2005 is therefore 17.5 percent.

Notice that the CPI gives more weight to price changes of goods that are more important in the consumer's budget. In our example, the percentage rise in the CPI (17.5 percent) is closer to the percentage rise in the price of hamburger (20 percent) than it is to the percentage price rise of oranges (10 percent). This is because a greater percentage of the budget is *spent* on hamburger than on oranges, so hamburger carries more weight in the CPI.

But one of the CPI's problems, discussed in the body of the chapter, is *substitution bias*. The CPI recognizes that consumers substitute *within* categories of goods. For example, if we had a third good, steak, the CPI would recognize that consumers will buy more steak if the price of hamburger rises faster than the price of steak. But the CPI assumes there is no substitution *among* categories—between beef products and fruit, for example. No matter how much the relative price of beef products like hamburger rises, the CPI assumes that people will continue to buy the same quantity of it, rather than substitute goods in other categories like oranges. Therefore, as the price of hamburger rises, the CPI assumes that we spend a greater and greater percentage of our budgets on it; hamburger gets *increasing weight* in the CPI. In our example, spending on hamburger is assumed to rise from $150/$200 = 0.75, or 75 percent of the typical weekly budget, to $180/$235 = 0.766, or 76.6 percent. In fact, however, the rapid rise in price would cause people to substitute *away* from hamburger toward other goods whose prices are rising more slowly.

This is what occurs in our two-good example, as you can see in the last column of Table A.1. In 2005, the quantity of hamburger purchased drops to 10, and the quantity of oranges rises to 100. In an ideal measure, the decrease in the quantity of hamburger would reduce its weight in determining the overall rate of inflation. But the CPI ignores the information in the last column of Table A.1, which shows the new quantities purchased in 2005. This failure to correct for substitution bias across categories of goods is one of the reasons the CPI overstates inflation.

The Classical Long-Run Model

CHAPTER OUTLINE

Macroeconomic Models: Classical Versus Keynesian
  Assumptions of the Classical Model

How Much Output Will We Produce?
  The Labor Market
  Determining the Economy's Output

The Role of Spending
  Total Spending in a Very Simple Economy
  Total Spending in a More Realistic Economy

The Loanable Funds Market
  The Supply of Funds Curve
  The Demand for Funds Curve
  Equilibrium in the Loanable Funds Market
  The Loanable Funds Market and Say's Law

The Classical Model: A Summary

Using the Theory: Fiscal Policy in the Classical Model
  Fiscal Policy with a Budget Deficit
  Fiscal Policy with a Budget Surplus

Economists often disagree with each other. In news interviews, class lectures, and editorials, they give differing opinions about even the simplest matters. To the casual observer, it might seem that economics is little more than guesswork, where anyone's opinion is as good as anyone else's. But there is actually much more agreement among economists than there appears to be.

Take the following typical example: At a time when the economy is performing well, two distinguished economists appear on *CNN NewsNight*. In a somber tone, Aaron Brown—the anchor—asks each of them what should be done to maintain the health of the economy. "We need to reduce the government's budget deficit by cutting government spending or raising taxes," replies the first economist. "This will enable private businesses to borrow more, so they can purchase new capital and the economy can grow faster." (Don't worry if this chain of logic isn't clear to you yet; it will be by the end of the next chapter.)

"No, no, no," the second economist might interrupt. "Cutting the deficit is the *worst* thing we could do right now. The economy appears to be slowing, and if we raise taxes or cut government spending, we'd reduce the take-home pay of households, causing them to cut their own spending. We'd push the economy toward a recession—one that the U.S. Federal Reserve might not be able to prevent." (You'll begin learning what's behind this argument a few chapters later.)

Which of these economists would be right? Surprisingly, it's entirely possible for *both* of them to be correct. But how can this be? Aren't the two responses contradictory? Not necessarily, because each economist might be hearing—and answering—a different question. The first economist is addressing the likely *long-run* impact of a cut in the government's budget deficit: the impact we might expect after several years have elapsed. The second economist, by contrast, is focusing on a possible *short-run* impact: the effects we might see over the next year.

Once the distinction between the long run and the short run becomes clear, many apparent disagreements among macroeconomists dissolve. If Aaron Brown had asked our two economists about the *long-run* impact of cutting the deficit, both may well have agreed that it would lead to more investment by business firms and faster economic growth. If asked about the *short-run* impact, both may have agreed about the potential danger of recession. If no time horizon is specified, however, an economist is likely to focus on the horizon he or she feels is most important—something about which economists sometimes *do* disagree. The real dispute, though, is less over how the economy *works* and more about what our priorities should be in guiding it.

Ideally, we would like our economy to do well in both the long run and the short run. Unfortunately, there is often a trade-off between these two goals: Doing better in the short run can require some sacrifice of long-run goals, and vice versa. The problem for policy makers is much like that of the captain of a ship sailing through the North Atlantic. On the one hand, he wants to reach his destination (his long-run goal); on the other hand, he must avoid icebergs along the way (his short-run goal). As you might imagine, avoiding icebergs may require the captain to deviate from an ideal long-run course. At the same time, reaching port might require risking the occasional iceberg.

The same is true of the macroeconomy. If you flip back two chapters and look at Figure 4, you will see that there are two types of movements in total output: the long-run trajectory showing the growth of potential output and the short-run movements around that trajectory, which we call economic fluctuations or business cycles. Macroeconomists are concerned with both types of movements. But, as you will see, policies that can help us smooth out economic fluctuations may prove harmful to growth in the long run, while policies that promise a high rate of growth might require us to put up with more severe fluctuations in the short run.

MACROECONOMIC MODELS: CLASSICAL VERSUS KEYNESIAN

Classical model A macroeconomic model that explains the long-run behavior of the economy.

The **classical model**, developed by economists in the 19th and early 20th centuries, was an attempt to explain a key observation about the economy: Over periods of several years or longer, the economy performs rather well. That is, if we step back from current conditions and view the economy over a long stretch of time, we see that it operates reasonably close to its potential output. And even when it deviates, it does not do so for very long. Business cycles may come and go, but the economy eventually returns to full employment. Indeed, if we think in terms of decades rather than years or quarters, the business cycle fades in significance much like the waves in a choppy sea disappear when viewed from a jet plane.

In the classical view, this behavior is no accident: Powerful forces are at work that drive the economy toward full employment. Many of the classical economists went even further, arguing that these forces operated within a reasonably short period of time. And even today, an important group of macroeconomists continues to believe that the classical model is useful even in the shorter run.

Until the Great Depression of the 1930s, there was little reason to question these classical ideas. True, output fluctuated around its trend, and from time to time there were serious recessions, but output always returned to its potential, full-employment level within a few years or less, just as the classical economists predicted. But during the Great Depression, output was stuck far below its potential for many years. For some reason, the economy wasn't working the way the classical model said it should.

In 1936, in the midst of the Great Depression, the British economist John Maynard Keynes offered an explanation for the economy's poor performance. His new model of the economy—soon dubbed the *Keynesian model*—changed many economists' thinking.[1] Keynes and his followers argued that, while the classical model might explain the economy's operation in the long run, the long run could be a very long time in arriving. In the meantime, production could be stuck below its potential, as it seemed to be during the Great Depression.

Keynesian ideas became increasingly popular in universities and government agencies during the 1940s and 1950s. By the mid-1960s, the entire profession had been won over: Macroeconomics *was* Keynesian economics, and the classical model was removed from virtually all introductory economics textbooks. You might be wondering, then, why we are bothering with the classical model here. After all, it's an older model of the economy, one that was largely discredited and replaced, just as the Ptolemaic view that the sun circled the earth was supplanted by the more modern, Copernican view. Right?

Not really. The classical model is still important, for two reasons. First, in recent decades, there has been an active counterrevolution against Keynes's approach to understanding the macroeconomy. Many of the counterrevolutionary new theories are based largely on classical ideas. In some cases, the new theories are just classical economics in modern clothing, but in other cases significant new ideas have been added. By studying classical macroeconomics, you will be better prepared to understand the controversies centering on these newer schools of thought.

The second—and more important—reason for us to study the classical model is its usefulness in understanding the economy over the long run. Even the many economists who find the classical model inadequate for understanding the economy in the short run find it extremely useful in analyzing the economy in the long run.

> *Keynes's ideas and their further development help us understand economic fluctuations—movements in output around its long-run trend. But the classical model has proven more useful in explaining the long-run trend itself.*

This is why we will use the terms "classical view" and "long-run view" interchangeably in the rest of the book; in either case, we mean "the ideas of the classical model used to explain the economy's long-run behavior."

---

[1] Keynes's attack on the classical model was presented in his book *The General Theory of Employment, Interest and Money* (1936). Unfortunately, it's a very difficult book to read, though you may want to try. Keynes's assumptions were not always clear, and some of his text is open to multiple interpretations. As a result, economists have been arguing for decades about what Keynes really meant.

Assumptions of the Classical Model

Remember from Chapter 1 that all models begin with *assumptions* about the world. The classical model is no exception. Many of its assumptions are *simplifying;* they make the model more manageable, enabling us to see the broad outlines of economic behavior without getting lost in the details. Typically, these assumptions involve aggregation, such as ignoring the many different interest rates in the economy and instead referring to a single interest rate, or ignoring the many different types of labor in the economy and analyzing instead a single aggregate labor market. These simplifications are usually harmless: Adding more detail would make our work more difficult, but would not add much insight; nor would it change any of the central conclusions of the classical view.

There is, however, one assumption in the classical model that goes beyond mere simplification. This is an assumption about how the world works, and it is critical to the conclusions we will reach in this and the next chapter. We can state it in two words: *Markets clear.*

Market clearing Adjustment of prices until quantities supplied and demanded are equal.

> *A critical assumption in the classical model is that **markets clear**: The price in every market will adjust until quantity supplied and quantity demanded are equal.*

Does the market-clearing assumption sound familiar? It should: It was the basic idea behind our study of supply and demand. When we look at the economy through the classical lens, we assume that the forces of supply and demand work fairly well throughout the economy and that markets do reach equilibrium. An excess supply of anything traded will lead to a fall in its price; an excess demand will drive the price up.

The market-clearing assumption, which permeates classical thinking about the economy, provides an early hint about why the classical model does a better job over longer time periods (several years or more) than shorter ones. In many markets, prices might not fully adjust to their equilibrium values for many months or even years after some change in the economy. An excess supply or excess demand might persist for some time. Still, if we wait long enough, an excess supply in a market will eventually force the price down, and an excess demand will eventually drive the price up. That is, *eventually,* the market will clear. Therefore, when we are trying to explain the economy's behavior over the long run, market clearing seems to be a reasonable assumption.

In the remainder of the chapter, we'll use the classical model to answer a variety of important questions about the economy in the long run, such as:

- How is total employment determined?
- How much output will we produce?
- What role does total spending play in the economy?
- What happens when things change?

Keep in mind that, in our discussion of the classical model, we will focus on *real* variables: real GDP, the real wage, real saving, and so on. These variables are typically measured in the dollars of some base year, and their numerical values change only when their *purchasing power* changes. While our *actual* measures of the price level are imperfect, you can think of a real variable as one that reflects *true* purchasing power—the value we'd obtain if we used a perfectly accurate price index.

HOW MUCH OUTPUT WILL WE PRODUCE?

Over the last decade, on average, the U.S. economy produced about $8.2 trillion worth of goods and services per year (valued in 1996 dollars). How was this average level of output determined? Why didn't we produce $14 trillion per year? Or just $2 trillion? There are so many things to consider when answering this question, variables you constantly hear about in the news: wages, interest rates, investment spending, government spending, taxes, and more. Each of these concepts plays an important role in determining total output, and our task in this chapter is to show how they all fit together.

But what a task! How can we disentangle the web of economic interactions we see around us? Our starting point will be the first step of our *three-step process,* introduced toward the end of Chapter 3. To review, that first step was to *characterize the market*—to decide which market or markets best suit the problem being analyzed, which means indentifying the buyers and sellers and the type of environment in which they trade.

But which market should we start with?

The classical approach is to start at the beginning, with the *reason* for all this production in the first place: our desire for goods and services, and our need for income in order to buy them. In a market economy, people get their income from supplying labor and other resources to firms. Firms, in turn, use these resources to make the goods and services that people demand. Thus, a logical place to start our analysis is markets for resources: labor, land and natural resources, capital, and entrepreneurship.

For now we'll concentrate our attention on just one type of resource: labor. We'll assume that firms are already using the available quantities of the other resources. Moreover, since we are building a *macroeconomic* model, we'll aggregate all the different types of labor—office workers, construction workers, teachers, taxi drivers, waiters, writers and more—into a single variable, simply called *labor.*

Our question is: How many workers will be employed in the economy?

The Labor Market

The classical labor market is illustrated in Figure 1. The number of workers is measured on the horizontal axis, and the real hourly wage rate is measured on the vertical axis. Remember that the *real wage*—which is measured in the dollars of some base year—tells us the amount of goods that workers can buy with an hour's earnings.

Now look at the two curves in the figure. These are supply and demand curves, similar to the supply and demand curves for maple syrup, but there is one key difference: For a *good* such as maple syrup, households are the demanders and firms the suppliers. But for labor, the roles are reversed: Households supply labor and firms demand it.

The curve labeled L^S is the **labor supply curve** in this market; it tells us how many people will want to work at each wage. The upward slope tells us that the greater the real wage, the greater the number of people who will want to work. Why does the labor supply curve slope upward?

Labor supply curve Indicates how many people will want to work at various real wage rates.

To earn income, you must go to work and give up other activities such as school, parenting, or leisure. Thus, each of us will want to work only if the income we will earn *at least* compensates us for the other activities that we will give up.

The Labor Market

The equilibrium wage rate of $15 per hour is determined at point E, where the upward-sloping labor supply curve crosses the downward-sloping labor demand curve. At any other wage, an excess demand or excess supply of labor will cause an adjustment back to equilibrium.

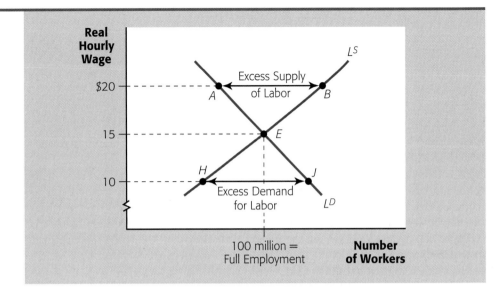

Of course, people value their time differently. Thus, for each of us, there is some critical wage rate above which we would decide that we're better off working. Below that wage, we would be better off not working. Thus, in Figure 1,

> *the labor supply curve slopes upward because, as the wage rate increases, more and more individuals are better off working than not working. Thus, a rise in the wage rate increases the number of people in the economy who want to work—to supply their labor.*

Labor demand curve Indicates how many workers firms will want to hire at various real wage rates.

The curve labeled L^D is the **labor demand curve,** which shows the number of workers firms will want to hire at any real wage. Why does this curve slope downward?

In deciding how much labor to hire, a firm's goal is to earn the greatest possible profit: the difference between sales revenue and costs. A firm will want to keep hiring additional workers as long as the output produced by those workers adds more to the firm's revenue than it adds to costs.

Now think about what happens as the wage rate rises. Some workers that added more to revenue than to cost at the lower wage will now cost more than they add in revenue. Accordingly, the firm will not want to employ these workers at the higher wage.

> *As the wage rate increases, each firm in the economy will find that, to maximize profit, it should employ fewer workers than before. When all firms behave this way together, a rise in the wage rate will decrease the quantity of labor demanded in the economy. This is why the economy's labor demand curve slopes downward.*

Remember that in the classical view, *all markets clear,* and that includes the market for labor. Specifically, the real wage adjusts until the quantities of labor supplied and demanded are equal. In the labor market in Figure 1, the market-clearing wage is $15 per hour, since that is where the labor supply and labor demand curves intersect. While every worker would prefer to earn $20 rather than $15, at $20 there would be an excess supply of labor equal to the distance *AB*. With not enough jobs to go around, competition among workers would drive the wage downward. Similarly, firms might prefer to pay their workers $10 rather than $15, but at $10, the excess demand for labor (equal to the distance *HJ*) would drive the wage upward. When the wage is $15, however, there is neither an excess demand nor an excess supply of labor, so the wage will neither increase nor decrease. Thus, $15 is the equilibrium wage in the economy. Reading along the horizontal axis, we see that at this wage, 100 million people will be working.

Notice that, in the figure, labor is fully employed; that is, the number of workers that firms want to hire is equal to the number of people who want jobs. Therefore, everyone who wants a job at the market wage of $15 should be able to find one. Small amounts of frictional unemployment might exist, since it takes some time for new workers or job switchers to find jobs. And there might be structural unemployment, due to some mismatch between those who want jobs in the market and the types of jobs available. But there is no *cyclical* unemployment of the type we discussed two chapters ago.

Full employment of the labor force is an important feature of the classical model. As long as we can count on markets (including the labor market) to clear, government action is not needed to ensure full employment; it happens automatically:

> *In the classical view, the economy achieves full employment on its own.*

Automatic full employment may strike you as odd, since it contradicts the cyclical unemployment we sometimes see around us. For example, in the recession of 2001, millions of workers around the country, in all kinds of professions and labor markets, were unable to find jobs for many months. Remember, though, that the classical model takes the long-run view, and over long periods of time, full employment is a fairly accurate description of the U.S. labor market. Cyclical unemployment, by definition, lasts only as long as the current business cycle itself; it is not a permanent, long-run problem.

Determining the Economy's Output

So far, we've focused on the labor market to determine the economy's level of employment. In our example, 100 million people will have jobs. Now we ask: How much output (real GDP) will these 100 million workers produce? The answer depends on two things: (1) the amount of other resources available for labor to use; and (2) the state of *technology*, which determines how much output we can produce with those resources.

In this chapter, remember that we're focusing on only one resource—labor—and we're treating the quantities of all other resources firms use as fixed during the period we're analyzing. Now we'll go even further: We'll assume that technology does not change.

Why do we make these assumptions? After all, in the real world technology *does* change, the capital stock *does* grow, new natural resources *can* be discovered, and the number and quality of entrepreneurs *can* change. Isn't it unrealistic to hold all of these things constant?

HTTP://
For the latest on economic output, visit the Economic Statistics Briefing Room at http://www.whitehouse.gov/fsbr/output.html.

Yes, but our assumption is only temporary. The most effective way to master a macroeconomic model is "divide and conquer": Start with a part of the model, understand it well, and then add in other parts. Accordingly, our classical analysis of the economy is divided into two separate questions: (1) What would be the long-run equilibrium of the economy *if* there were a constant state of technology and *if* quantities of all resources besides labor were fixed? And (2) What happens to this long-run equilibrium when technology and the quantities of other resources change? In this chapter, we focus on the first question. In the next chapter on economic growth, we'll address the second question.

The Production Function. With a constant technology, and given quantities of all resources other than labor, there is only one variable left that can affect total output: labor. So it's time to explore the relationship between total employment and total production in the economy. This relationship is given by the economy's *aggregate production function*.

Aggregate production function
The relationship showing how much total output can be produced with different quantities of labor, with quantities of all other resources held constant.

> *The **aggregate production function** (or just **production function**) shows the total output the economy can produce with different quantities of labor, given constant amounts of other resources and the current state of technology.*

The bottom panel of Figure 2 shows what a nation's aggregate production function might look like. The upward slope tells us that an increase in the number of people working will increase the quantity of output produced. But notice the shape of the production function: It flattens out as we move rightward along it.

The declining slope of the aggregate production function is the result of *diminishing returns to labor*: Output rises when another worker is added, but the rise is smaller and smaller with each successive worker. Why does this happen? For one thing, as we keep adding workers, gains from specialization are harder and harder to come by. Moreover, as we continue to add workers, each one will have less and less of the other resources to work with. For example, each time more agricultural workers are added to a fixed amount of farmland, output might rise. But as we continue to add workers and the ratio of workers to acres rises, output will rise by less and less with each new worker. The same is true when more factory workers are added to a fixed amount of factory floor space and machinery, or more professors are added to a fixed number of classrooms: Output continues to rise, but by less and less with each added worker.

Figure 2 also illustrates how the aggregate production function, together with the labor market, determines the economy's total output or real GDP. In our example, the labor market (upper panel) automatically generates full employment of 100 million workers, and the production function (lower panel) tells us that 100 million workers—together with the available amounts of other resources and the current state of technology—can produce $7 trillion worth of output. Since $7 trillion is the output produced by a fully employed labor force, it is also the economy's potential output level.

> *In the classical, long-run view, the economy reaches its potential output automatically.*

This last statement is an important conclusion of the classical model and an important characteristic of the economy in the long run: Output tends toward its potential,

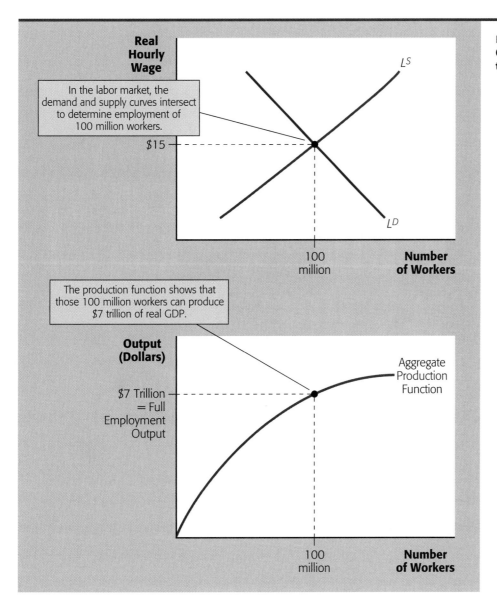

FIGURE 2
**Output Determination In
the Classical Model**

full-employment level *on its own*, with no need for government to steer the economy toward it. And we have arrived at this conclusion merely by assuming that the labor market clears and observing the relationship between employment and output.

THE ROLE OF SPENDING

Something may be bothering you about the classical view of output determination, a potential problem we have so far carefully avoided: What if business firms are unable to sell all the output produced by a fully employed labor force? Then the economy would not be able to sustain full employment for very long. Business firms will not continue to employ workers who produce output that is not being sold. Thus, if

FIGURE 3
The Circular Flow

The outer loop of the diagram shows the flows of goods and resources. Households supply resources to firms, which use them to produce goods. The inner loop shows money flows. Firms' factor payments become income to households. Households use the income to purchase goods from firms.

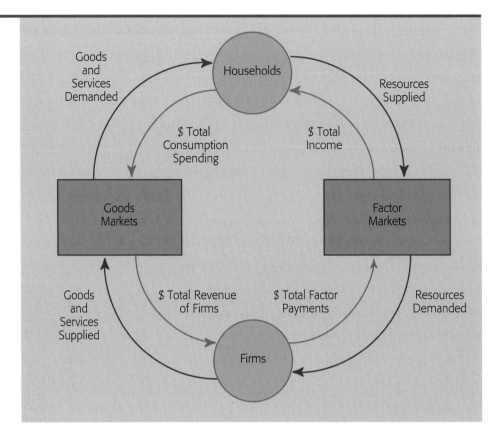

we are asserting that potential output is an equilibrium for the economy, we had better be sure that *total spending* on output is equal to *total production* during the year. But can we be sure of this?

In the classical view, the answer is, absolutely yes! We'll demonstrate this in two stages: first, in a very simple (but very unrealistic) economy, and then, under more realistic conditions.

Total Spending in a Very Simple Economy

Imagine a world much simpler than our own, a world with just two types of economic units: households and business firms. In this world, households spend all of their income on goods and services. They do not save any of their income, nor do they pay taxes. Such an economy is illustrated in the **circular flow** diagram of Figure 3.

Circular flow A diagram that shows how goods, resources, and dollar payments flow between households and firms.

The arrows on the right-hand side show that resources—labor, capital, land and natural resources, and entrepreneurship—are supplied by households, and demanded by firms, in *factor markets*. In return, households receive payments: wages, rent, interest, and profit. For example, if you were working part-time in a restaurant while attending college, you would be supplying a resource (labor) in a factor market (the market for waiters). In exchange, you would earn a wage. Similarly, the owner of the land on which the restaurant sits is a supplier in a factor market (the market for land) and would receive a payment (rent) in return. The payments received by resource owners are called *factor payments*.

On the left side of the diagram, the outer arrows show the flow of goods and services—food, new clothes, books, movies, and more—that firms supply, and households buy, in various *goods* markets. Of course, households must pay for these goods and services, and their payments provide revenue to firms, as shown by the inner arrows.

Now comes an important insight. As you learned two chapters ago, the total output of firms is equal to the total income of households. For example, if the economy is producing $7 trillion worth of output, then it also creates $7 trillion in household income. And in this simple economy—in which households spend all of their income—spending would equal $7 trillion as well.

In general,

> *in a simple economy with just households and firms, in which households spend all of their income, total spending must be equal to total output.*

This simple proposition is called **Say's law,** after the classical economist Jean Baptiste Say (1767–1832), who popularized the idea. Say noted that each time a good or service is produced, an equal amount of income is created. This income is spent, so it comes back to the business sector to purchase its goods and services. In Say's own words:

> A product *is no sooner created than it, from that instant, affords a market for other products to the full extent of its own value. . . . Thus, the mere circumstance of the creation of one product immediately opens a vent for other products.*[2]

Say's law The idea that total spending will be sufficient to purchase the total output produced.

For example, each time a shirt manufacturer produces a $25 shirt, it creates $25 in factor payments to households. (Forgot why? Go back two chapters and refresh your memory about the factor payments approach to GDP.) But in the simple economy we're analyzing, that $25 in factor payments will lead to $25 in total spending—just enough to buy the very shirt produced. Of course, the households who receive the $25 in factor payments won't necessarily buy a shirt with it; the shirt manufacturer must still worry about selling its own output. But in the *aggregate*, we needn't worry about there being sufficient demand for the total output produced. Business firms—by producing output—also create a demand for goods and services equal to the value of that output.

> *Say's law states that by producing goods and services, firms create a total demand for goods and services equal to what they have produced. Or, more simply, supply creates its own demand.*

Say's law is crucial to the classical view of the economy. Why? Remember that because the labor market is assumed to clear, firms will hire all the workers who want jobs and produce our *potential* or *full-employment* output level. But firms will only *continue* to produce this level of output if they can *sell* it all. In the simple economy of Figure 3, Say's law assures us that, in the aggregate, spending will be just high enough for firms to sell all the output that a fully employed labor force can produce. As a result, full employment can be maintained.

---

[2] J. B. Say, *A Treatise on Political Economy*, 4th ed. (London: Longman, 1821), Vol. I, p. 167.

But the economy in Figure 3 leaves out some important details of economies in the real world. Does Say's law also apply in a more realistic economy? Let's see.

Total Spending in a More Realistic Economy

The real-world economy is more complicated than the imaginary one we've just considered. In the real world,

1. Households don't spend *all* their income. Rather, some of their income is saved or goes to pay taxes.
2. Households are not the only spenders in the economy. Rather, businesses and the government also buy final goods and services.
3. In addition to markets for goods and markets for resources, there is also a *loanable funds* market where household saving is made available to business firms and the government.

All of these details complicate our picture of the economy. Will Say's law still apply?

Let's consider the economy of Classica, a fictional economy that behaves according to the classical model, but one that is more realistic than the economy of Figure 3. Data on Classica's economy in 2004 are given in Table 1. Notice that total output and total income are both equal to $7 trillion in 2004, which is assumed to be Classica's full-employment or potential output level.

Next come three entries that refer to spending by the final users who purchase Classica's GDP. Note that unlike the households in Figure 3, Classica's households spend only *part* of their income: $4 trillion on consumption goods (*C*). Skipping down to government purchases (*G*), we find that Classica's government sector—combining its national, regional, and local government agencies—purchases $2 trillion in goods and services.

Some New Macroeconomic Variables. In addition to consumption and government purchases—with which you are already familiar—Table 1 includes some new variables. Since these will be used throughout the rest of this book, it's worth defining and discussing them here.

Planned Investment Spending (I^P). Two chapters ago, you learned that total investment spending—the component labeled *I* in the expenditure approach to GDP—includes not only business spending on new capital but also *changes in firms' inventories* over a period of time. Inventory changes occur when firms produce more than they sell (an increase in inventories) or sell more than they produce (a decrease in inventories).

Our ultimate goal is to find out if Say's law works in Classica—if total spending exactly matches Classica's total output. Therefore, it would be a mistake to include inventory changes—which represent the mismatch between sales and production—as part of investment spending. When we exclude inventory changes from investment spending, we're left with *planned investment spending*.

Planned investment spending
Business purchases of plant and equipment.

> *Planned investment spending* (I^P) *over a period of time is total investment spending* (I) *minus the change in inventories over the period:*
>
> $$I^P = I - \Delta \ inventories.$$

Here, we're using the Greek letter Δ ("delta") to indicate a change in a variable.

Total Output (GDP)	$7 trillion	**TABLE 1**
Total Income	$7 trillion	**Flows in the Economy**
Consumption Spending (C)	$4 trillion	**of Classica, 2004**
Planned Investment Spending (I^P)	$1 trillion	
Government Purchases (G)	$2 trillion	
Net Taxes (T)	$1.25 trillion	
Household Saving (S)	$1.75 trillion	

Why do we call this new variable *planned* investment? In the real world, some inventory changes are, in fact, planned by firms. But they can also come as a surprise. For example, suppose Calvin Klein produces $40 million in clothing during a quarter, planning to sell all of it. But during the quarter, it actually ships and sells only $35 million. Then $5 million in unsold output would be an *unplanned increase in inventories*—a surprise, rather than a planned result. On the other hand, if Calvin Klein sold $43 million, then $3 million in sales would come out of inventories. This would be an *unplanned decrease in inventories*—a surprise in the other direction.

Changes in inventories are generally the only component of spending in GDP that is not planned. A firm does not "discover" at the end of a quarter that it has purchased a new factory. This type of investment is intended and planned in advance. And—other than Homer in *The Simpsons*—a consumer doesn't "discover" that he has purchased a new car or a lifetime supply of slurpies; consumption spending is intentional.

In this and future chapters, to keep our discussions simple we'll regard *all* inventory changes as unplanned surprises. This is why, after deducting inventory changes from total investment, we call what is left *planned investment*. In Table 1, you can see that Classica's planned investment spending—which excludes any changes in inventories—is $1 trillion.

Net Tax Revenue (T). Recall (from two chapters ago) that *transfer payments* are government outlays that are *not* spent on goods and services. These transfers—which include unemployment insurance, welfare payments, and Social Security benefits—are just *given* to people, either out of social concern (welfare payments), to keep a promise (Social Security payments), or elements of both (unemployment insurance).

In the macroeconomy, government transfer payments are like negative taxes: They represent the part of tax revenue that the government takes from one set of households (taxpayers) but gives right back to another set of households (such as Social Security recipients), and are not available for government purchases. Since we're interested in the funds that flow from the household sector *as a whole* to the government in any given year, and since transfer payments stay *within* the household sector, we can treat them as if they were never paid to the government at all. We do this by focusing on *net taxes*:

Net taxes (T) *are total government tax revenue minus government transfer payments:*

$$T = total \ tax \ revenue - transfers.$$

Net taxes Government tax revenues minus transfer payments.

For example, in 2005 net taxes in Classica are $1.25 trillion. This number might result from total tax revenue of $2 trillion and $0.75 trillion in government transfer payments. It could also result from $3 trillion in tax revenue and $1.75 trillion in transfers. From the macroeconomic perspective, net taxes—what the government has available for purchases—are $1.25 trillion in either case.

Household Saving (S). It's often useful to arrive at household saving in two steps. First, we determine how much income the household sector has left after payment of net taxes. This is the household sector's **disposable income:**

Disposable income Household income minus net taxes, which is either spent or saved.

$$\text{Disposable Income} = \text{Total Income} - \text{Net Taxes.}$$

The household sector can *dispose* of this disposable (after-tax) income in only two ways: either by spending it (*C*) or by *not* spending it. The part that is *not* spent is defined as (**household**) **saving** (*S*):

(Household) saving The portion of after-tax income that households do not spend on consumption.

$$S = \text{Disposable Income} - C.$$

The last entry in Table 1 tells us that in Classica, household saving is $1.75 trillion. Let's check this using disposable income. From the table, total income is $7 trillion and net taxes are $1.25 trillion, so disposable income (not shown in the table) is $7 trillion − $1.25 trillion = $5.75 trillion. Consumption spending is $4 trillion, so:

$$S = \text{Disposable Income} - C = \$5.75 \text{ trillion} - \$4 \text{ trillion} = \$1.75 \text{ trillion}$$

Total Spending in Classica. In Classica, total spending is the sum of the purchases made by the household sector (*C*), the business sector (I^P), and the government sector (*G*):[3]

$$\text{Total spending} = C + I^P + G.$$

Or, using the numbers in Table 1:

$$\text{Total spending} = \$4 \text{ trillion} + \$1 \text{ trillion} + \$2 \text{ trillion} = \$7 \text{ trillion.}$$

This may strike you as suspiciously convenient: Total spending is exactly equal to total output, just as we'd like to be if we want Classica to continue producing its potential output of $7 trillion. And just what we needed to illustrate Say's law in this more realistic economy.

But we haven't yet proven anything; we've just cooked up an example that made the numbers come out this way. The question is, do we have any reason to *expect* the economy to give us numbers like these automatically, with total spending precisely equal to total output?

The rectangles in Figure 4 provide some perspective on this question and suggest the way to an answer. Total output (represented by the first rectangle) is, by definition, always equal in value to total income (the second rectangle). As we've seen in Figure 3, if households *spent* all of this income, then consumption spending would equal total output.

But in Classica, households do *not* spend all of their income. Some income goes to pay net taxes ($1.25 trillion), and some is saved ($1.75 trillion). Saving and net

---

[3] Notice that to keep things simple, we've assumed that Classica does not trade with the rest of the world (no exports, no imports). Introducing exports and imports would not change any of our conclusions in important ways, but it would make it harder to see them.

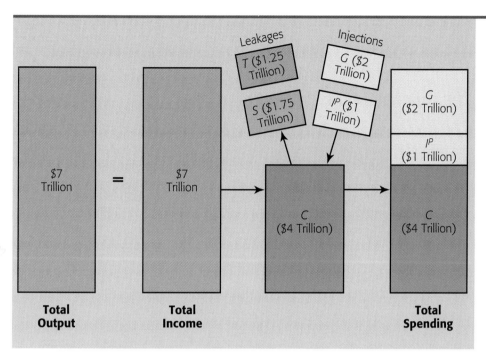

FIGURE 4
Leakages and Injections

By definition, total output equals total income. Leakages—net taxes (T) and saving (S)—reduce consumption spending below total income. Injections—government purchases (G) plus planned investment spending (I^P)—contribute to total spending. When leakages equal injections, total spending equals total output.

taxes are called **leakages** out of spending: the amount of income that households receive, but do not spend. Leakages reduce consumption spending below total income, as you can see in the third, lower rectangle. In Classica, total leakages = $1.75 trillion + $1.25 trillion = $3 trillion, and this must be subtracted from income of $7 trillion to get consumption spending of $4 trillion. Thus, if consumption spending were the only spending in the economy, business firms would be unable to sell their entire potential output of $7 trillion.

Fortunately, in addition to leakages, there are **injections**—spending from sources *other* than households. Injections boost total spending and enable firms to produce and sell a level of output greater than just consumption spending.

There are two types of injections in the economy. First is the government's purchases of goods and services. When government agencies—federal, state, or local—buy aircraft, cleaning supplies, cellular phones, or computers, they are buying a part of the economy's output.

The other injection is planned investment spending *(I^P)*. When business firms purchase new computers, trucks, or machinery, or they build new factories or office buildings, they are buying a part of the GDP along with consumers and the government.

Take another look at the rectangles in Figure 4. Notice that in going from total output to total spending, leakages are subtracted and injections are added. Clearly, total output and total spending will be equal only if leakages and injections are equal as well.

> *Total spending will equal total output if and only if total leakages in the economy are equal to total injections—that is, only if the sum of saving and net taxes is equal to the sum of planned investment spending and government purchases.*

Leakages Income earned, but not spent, by households during a given year.

Injections Spending from sources other than households.

And here is a surprising result: In the classical model, this condition will automatically be satisfied. To see why, we must first take a detour through another important market. Then we'll come back to the equality of leakages and injections.

THE LOANABLE FUNDS MARKET

Loanable funds market The market in which households make their saving available to borrowers.

The **loanable funds market** is where households make their saving available to those who need additional funds. When you save—that is, when you have income left over after paying taxes and buying consumption goods—you can put your surplus funds in a bank, buy a bond or a share of stock, or use the funds to buy a variety of other assets. In each of these cases, you would be a supplier in the loanable funds market

Households supply funds because they receive a reward for doing so. But the reward comes in different forms. When the suppliers *lend* out funds, the reward is *interest payments*. When the funds are provided through the stock market, the suppliers become part owners of the firm and their payment is called *dividends*. To keep our discussion simple, we'll assume that all funds made available by households are *loaned* and that the payment is simply *interest*.

> *The total supply of loanable funds is equal to household saving. The funds supplied are loaned out, and households* receive interest *payments on these funds.*

On the other side of the market are those who want to obtain funds—demanders in this market. Business firms are important demanders of funds. When Avis wants to add cars to its automobile rental fleet, when McDonald's wants to build a new beef-processing plant, or when the local dry cleaner wants to buy new dry cleaning machines, it will likely raise the funds in the loanable funds market. It may take out a bank loan, sell bonds, or sell new shares of stock. In each of these cases, a firm's planned investment spending would be equal to the funds it obtains from the loanable funds market. To keep the discussion simple, we'll assume that business firms *borrow* the funds they obtain in the loanable funds market.

> *Businesses' demand for loanable funds is equal to their planned investment spending. The funds obtained are borrowed, and firms pay interest on their loans.*

Aside from households and business firms, the other major player in the loanable funds market is the government sector. Government participates in the market whenever it runs a budget deficit or a budget surplus.

Budget deficit The excess of government purchases over net taxes.

Budget surplus The excess of net taxes over government purchases.

> *When government purchases of goods and services (G) are greater than net taxes (T), the government runs a **budget deficit** equal to G − T. When government purchases of goods and services (G) are less than net taxes (T), the government runs a **budget surplus** equal to T − G.*

In our example in Table 1, Classica's government is running a budget deficit: Government purchases are $2 trillion, while net taxes are $1.25 trillion, giving us a deficit of $2 trillion − $1.25 trillion = $0.75 trillion. This deficit is financed by borrowing in the loanable funds market. In any year, the government's demand for funds is equal to its deficit.

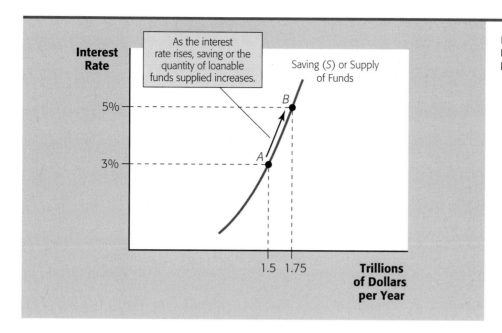

FIGURE 5
Household Supply of Loanable Funds

When the government runs a budget deficit, its demand for loanable funds is equal to its deficit. The funds are borrowed, and the government pays interest on its loans.

(What if Classica's government were running a surplus? We'll consider that toward the end of this chapter.)

We can summarize our view of the loanable funds market so far with these two points:

- The supply of funds is household saving.
- The demand for funds is the sum of the business sector's planned investment spending and the government sector's budget deficit, if any.

Now let's take a closer look at the behavior of each of the key players—households, business firms, and the government—in the market for loanable funds.

The Supply of Funds Curve

Since interest is the reward for saving and supplying funds to the financial market, a rise in the interest rate *increases* the quantity of funds supplied (household saving), while a drop in the interest rate decreases it. This relationship is illustrated by Classica's upward-sloping **supply of funds curve** in Figure 5. If the interest rate is 3 percent, households save $1.5 trillion, and if the interest rate rises to 5 percent, people save more and the quantity of funds supplied rises to $1.75 trillion.

Supply of funds curve Indicates the level of household saving at various interest rates.

The quantity of funds supplied to the financial market depends positively on the interest rate. This is why the saving or supply of funds curve slopes upward.

FIGURE 6
Business Demand for
Loanable Funds

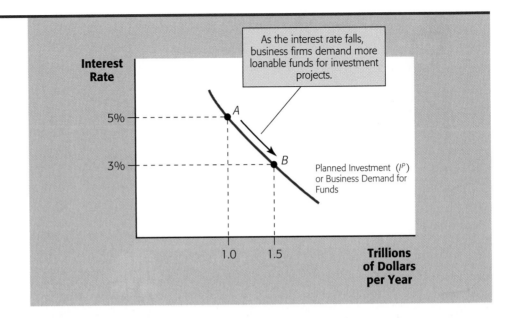

Of course, other things can affect saving besides the interest rate: tax rates, expectations about the future, and the general willingness of households to postpone consumption, to name a few. In drawing the supply of funds curve, we assume each of these variables is constant. In the next chapter, we'll explore what happens when some of these variables change.

The Demand for Funds Curve

Businesses buy plant and equipment when the expected benefits exceed the costs. Since businesses obtain the funds for their investment spending from the loanable funds market, a key cost of any investment project is the interest rate that must be paid on borrowed funds. As the interest rate rises and investment costs increase, fewer projects will look attractive, and planned investment spending will decline. This is the logic of the downward-sloping **business demand for funds curve** in Figure 6. At a 5 percent interest rate, firms would borrow $1 trillion and spend it on capital equipment; at an interest rate of 3 percent, business borrowing and investment spending would rise to $1.5 trillion.

Business demand for funds curve Indicates the level of investment spending firms plan at various interest rates.

> *When the interest rate falls, investment spending and the business borrowing needed to finance it rise. The business demand for funds curve slopes downward.*

What about the government's demand for funds? Will it, too, be influenced by the interest rate? Probably not very much. Government seems to be cushioned from the cost–benefit considerations that haunt business decisions. Any company president who ignored interest rates in deciding how much to borrow would be quickly out of a job. U.S. presidents and legislators have often done so with little political cost.

For this reason, when government is running a budget deficit, our classical model treats government borrowing as independent of the interest rate: No matter

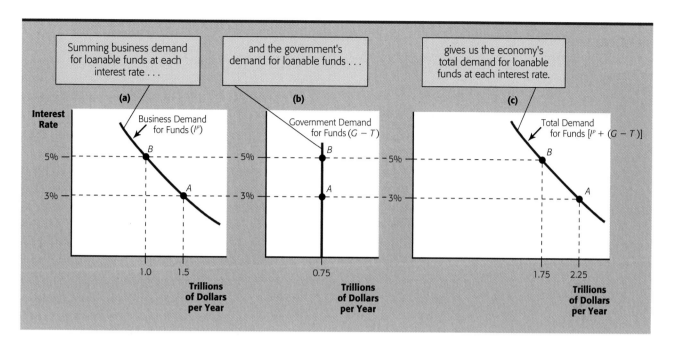

FIGURE 7
The Demand for Funds

what the interest rate, the government sector's deficit—and its borrowing—remain constant. This is why we have graphed the **government's demand for funds curve** as a vertical line in panel (b) of Figure 7.

The government sector's deficit and, therefore, its demand for funds are independent of the interest rate.

Government demand for funds curve Indicates the amount of government borrowing at various interest rates.

In the figure, the government deficit—and hence the government's demand for funds—is equal to $0.75 trillion at any interest rate.

Figure 7 also shows that the **total demand for funds curve** is found by horizontally summing the business demand curve [panel (a)] and the government demand curve [panel (b)]. For example, if the interest rate is 5 percent, firms demand $1 trillion in funds and the government demands $0.75 trillion, so that the total quantity of loanable funds demanded is $1.75 trillion. A drop in the interest rate—to 3 percent—increases business borrowing to $1.5 trillion while the government's borrowing remains at $0.75 trillion, so the total quantity of funds demanded rises to $2.25 trillion.

Total demand for funds curve Indicates the total amount of borrowing at various interest rates.

As the interest rate decreases, the quantity of funds demanded by business firms increases, while the quantity demanded by the government remains unchanged. Therefore, the total *quantity of funds demanded rises.*

Equilibrium in the Loanable Funds Market

In the classical view, the loanable funds market—like all other markets—is assumed to clear: The interest rate will rise or fall until the quantities of funds supplied and demanded are equal. Figure 8 illustrates the loanable funds market of Classica, our fictional economy. Equilibrium occurs at point *E*, with an interest rate of 5 percent and total saving equal to $1.75 trillion. (To convince yourself that 5 percent is the

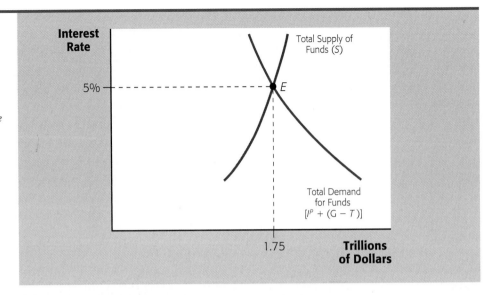

FIGURE 8
Loanable Funds Market Equilibrium

Suppliers and demanders of funds interact to determine the interest rate in the loanable funds market. At an interest rate of 5%, quantity supplied and quantity demanded are both equal to $1.75 trillion.

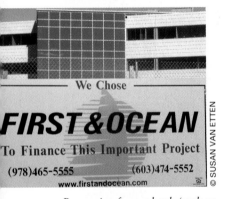

Borrowing from a bank (such as First and Ocean) is one way firms obtain loanable funds for investment projects.

equilibrium interest rate, mark an interest rate of 4 percent on the graph. Would there be an excess demand or an excess supply of loanable funds at this rate? How would the interest rate change? Then do the same for an interest rate of 6 percent.)

Once we know the equilibrium interest rate (5 percent), we can use the first two panels of Figure 7 to tell us exactly where the total household saving of $1.75 billion ends up. Panel (a) tells us that at 5 percent interest, business firms are borrowing $1 trillion of the total, and panel (b) tells us that the government is borrowing the remaining $0.75 trillion to cover its deficit.

So far, our exploration of the loanable funds market has shown us how three important variables in the economy are determined: the interest rate, the level of saving, and the level of investment. But it really tells us more. Remember the question that sent us on this detour into the loanable funds market in the first place: Can we be sure that all of the output produced at full employment will be purchased? We now have the tools to answer this question.

The Loanable Funds Market and Say's Law

In Figure 4 of this chapter, you saw that total spending will equal total output if and only if *total leakages* in the economy (saving plus net taxes) are equal to *total injections* (planned investment plus government purchases). Now we can see why this requirement will be satisfied automatically in the classical model. Look at Figure 9, which duplicates the rectangles from Figure 4. But there is something added: arrows to indicate the flows between leakages and injections.

Let's follow the arrows to see what happens to all the leakages out of spending. One arrow shows that the entire leakage of net taxes ($1.25 trillion) flows to the government, which spends it. Another arrow shows that $1.75 trillion of saving flows into the loanable funds market. And the last two arrows show that $0.75 trillion of this saving is borrowed by the government, while the rest—$1 trillion—is borrowed by business firms.

Now let's step back from the numbers, and think about the logic in the diagram. Remember our question: Will total spending be sufficient to purchase the economy's

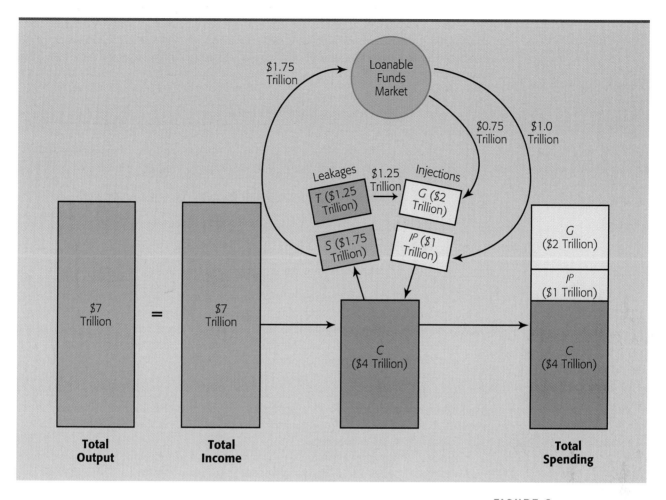

Total Output

Total Income

Total Spending

FIGURE 9

How the Loanable Funds Market Ensures that Total Spending = Total Output

Because the loanable funds market clears, we know that total leakages will automatically equal total injections. The leakage of net taxes goes to the government and is spent on government purchases. If the government is running a budget deficit, it will also borrow part of the leakage of household saving and spend that too. Any household saving left over will be borrowed by business firms and spent on capital. Thus, every dollar of leakages turns into spending by either government or private business firms.

total output? And remember what created some doubt about the answer: The household sector spends only *part* of its income, because of the leakages of net taxes and saving.

Now we can see that net taxes and savings don't just disappear from the economy. Net taxes go to the government, which *spends them*. And any funds saved go either to the government—which spends them—or to business firms—which spend them. But wait . . . how do we know that *all* funds that are saved will end up going to either the government or businesses? Because the loanable funds market clears: The interest rate adjusts until the quantity of loanable funds supplied (saving) is equal to the quantity of loanable funds demanded (government and business borrowing).

We can put all this together as follows: Every dollar of output creates a dollar of household income, by definition. And—as long as the loanable funds market clears—every dollar of income will either be spent by households themselves or passed along to some *other* sector of the economy that will spend it in their place.

Or, to put it even more simply,

as long as the loanable funds market clears, Say's law holds: Total spending equals total output. This is true even in a more realistic economy with saving, taxes, investment and a government deficit.

Here's another way to see the same result, in terms of a simple equation. Because the loanable funds market clears, we know that the interest rate—the price in this market—will rise or fall until the quantity of funds supplied (savings, S) is equal to the quantity of funds demanded (planned investment plus the deficit, or $I^P + (G - T)$):

$$\text{Loanable funds market clears} \quad \Rightarrow \quad \underbrace{S}_{\substack{\text{Quantity of} \\ \text{funds supplied}}} = \underbrace{I^P + (G - T)}_{\substack{\text{Quantity of} \\ \text{funds demanded}}}$$

Rearranging this equation by moving T to the left side, we have:

$$\text{Loanable funds market clears} \quad \Rightarrow \quad \underbrace{S + T}_{\text{Leakages}} = \underbrace{I^P + G}_{\text{Injections}}$$

Finally, remember that

$$\text{Leakages} = \text{Injections} \quad \Rightarrow \quad \text{Total spending} = \text{Total output}$$

In other words, market clearing in the loanable funds market *assures us* that total leakages in the economy will equal total injections, which in turn *assures us* that total spending will be just sufficient to purchase total output.

Say's law is a powerful concept. But be careful not to overinterpret it. Say's law shows that the *total* value of spending in the economy will equal the *total* value of output, which rules out a *general* overproduction or underproduction of goods in the economy. It does not promise us that each firm in the economy will be able to sell all of the particular good it produces. It is perfectly consistent with Say's law that there be excess supplies in some markets, as long as they are balanced by excess demands in other markets.

But lest you begin to think that the classical economy might be a chaotic mess, with excess supplies and demands in lots of markets, don't forget about the *market-clearing* assumption. In each market, prices adjust until quantities supplied and demanded are equal. For this reason, the classical, long-run view rules out over- or underproduction in individual markets, as well as the generalized overproduction ruled out by Say's law.

THE CLASSICAL MODEL: A SUMMARY

You've just completed a first tour of the classical model, our framework for understanding the economy in the long run. Before we begin to *use* this model, this is a good time to go back and review what we've done.

We began with a critical assumption: All markets clear. We then used the first two steps of our three-step process to organize our thinking about the economy. First, we focused on an important market—the labor market. We identified the buyers and sellers in that market, and then found the equilibrium by assuming that the market cleared.

We went through a similar process with the loanable funds market, identifying the suppliers and demanders, examining how each would be affected by changes in the interest rate, and finding the equilibrium in that market as well. Finally, we saw how market clearing in the loanable funds market assures us that total spending will be just sufficient to purchase our potential output level.

Our analysis leads us to two important policy conclusions:

> *In the classical model, the government needn't worry about employment: The economy will achieve full employment on its own;*

and

> *in the classical model, the government needn't worry about total spending: The economy will generate just enough spending on its own to buy the output that a fully employed labor force produces.*

But suppose the government wanted to make the economy do even better—to employ even *more* people and produce even *more* output than the classical model suggests. Could the government accomplish this by engineering an *increase* in total spending? We'll answer this question in the "Using the Theory" section.

 U S I N G   T H E   T H E O R Y
Fiscal Policy in the Classical Model

Could the government increase the economy's total employment and total output by raising total spending? It *seems* like an idea that should work. After all, with higher total spending, business firms would sell more output, so they might want to hire more workers and produce more. And two ideas for increasing spending come to mind. First, the government could simply purchase more output: more goods, like tanks and police cars, or more services, like those provided by high school teachers and judges. Second, the government could cut net taxes, letting households keep more of their income, so they would spend more on food, clothing, furniture, new cars, and so on. (Since net taxes are tax revenues minus government transfers, there are two ways to cut net taxes: decrease tax revenues, or increase transfers.)

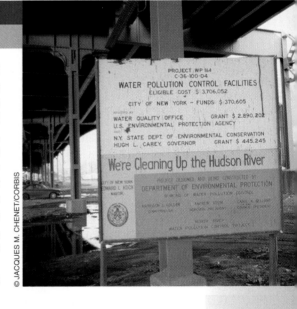

© JACQUES M. CHENET/CORBIS

If the government uses either of these steps, it would be engaging in *fiscal policy:*

> **Fiscal policy** *is a change in government purchases or in net taxes designed to change total spending in the economy and thereby influence the levels of employment and output.*

Fiscal policy A change in government purchases or net taxes designed to change total spending and thereby change total output.

The idea behind fiscal policy sounds sensible enough. But does it work?

Not if the economy behaves according to the classical model. As you are about to see, in the classical model, fiscal policy is completely ineffective. It cannot change total output or employment in the economy, period. It cannot even change total spending. Moreover, fiscal policy is *unnecessary,* since the economy achieves and sustains full employment on its own. Here, we'll demonstrate this conclusion for the case of an increase in government spending. In a challenge question at the end of this chapter, you are invited to demonstrate the same conclusion for the case of a cut in net taxes.

Fiscal Policy with a Budget Deficit

Let's first see what would happen if the government of Classica attempted to increase employment and output by increasing government purchases. More specifically, suppose the government raised its spending by $0.5 trillion, hiring people to fix roads and bridges, or hiring more teachers, or increasing its spending on goods and services for homeland security. What would happen?

To answer this, we must first answer another question: Where will Classica's government get the additional $0.5 trillion it spends? If net taxes are unchanged (as we are assuming), then the government deficit will rise, so the government must dip into the loanable funds market to *borrow* the additional funds.

Figure 10 illustrates the effects. Initially, with government purchases equal to $2 trillion, the demand for funds curve is D_1, and equilibrium occurs at point A with the interest rate equal to 5 percent. If government purchases increase by $0.5 trillion, with no change in taxes, the budget deficit increases by $0.5 trillion and so does the government's demand for funds. The demand for funds curve shifts rightward by $0.5 trillion to D_2, since total borrowing will now be $0.5 trillion greater at *any* interest rate. After the shift, there would be an excess demand for funds at the original interest rate of 5 percent. The total quantity of funds demanded would be $2.25 trillion (point H), while the quantity supplied would continue to be $1.75 trillion (point A). Thus, the excess demand for funds would be equal to the distance AH in the figure, or $0.5 trillion. This excess demand drives up the interest rate to 7 percent. As the interest rate rises, two things happen.

First, a higher interest rate chokes off some investment spending, as business firms decide that certain investment projects no longer make sense. For example, the local dry cleaner might wish to borrow funds for a new machine at an interest rate of 5 percent, but not at 7 percent. In the figure, as we move along the new demand for funds curve D_2, from point H to point B, planned investment declines by $0.2 trillion (from $2.25 trillion to $2.05 trillion). (Question: How do we know that only business borrowing, and not also government borrowing, adjusts as we move from point H to point B?) Thus, one consequence of the rise in government purchases is a *decrease in planned investment spending.*

But that's not all: The rise in the interest rate also causes saving to increase. Of course, when people save more of their incomes, they spend less, so another consequence of the rise in government purchases is a *decrease in consumption spending.* In the figure, as we move from point A to point B along the saving curve, saving increases (and consumption decreases) by $0.3 trillion—rising from $1.75 trillion to $2.05 trillion.

Let's recap: As a result of the increase in government purchases, both planned investment spending and consumption spending decline. The government's purchases have *crowded out* the spending of households (C) and businesses (I^P).

Crowding out A decline in one sector's spending caused by an increase in some other sector's spending.

> *Crowding out is a decline in one sector's spending caused by an increase in some other sector's spending.*

Complete crowding out A dollar-for-dollar decline in one sector's spending caused by an increase in some other sector's spending.

But we are not quite finished. If we sum the drop in C and the drop in I^P, we find that total private sector spending has fallen by $0.3 trillion + $0.2 trillion = $0.5 trillion. That is, the drop in private sector spending is *precisely equal* to the rise in government purchases, G. Not only is there crowding out, there is **complete crowding out:** Each dollar of government purchases causes private sector spending

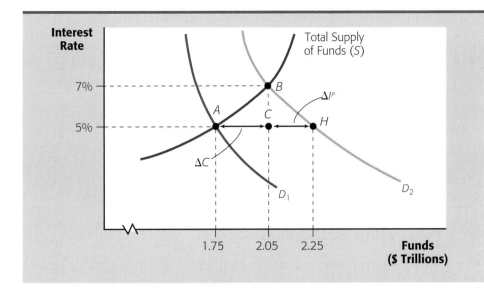

FIGURE 10

Crowding Out with an Initial Budget Deficit

Beginning from equilibrium at point A, an increase in the budget deficit created to finance additional government purchases shifts the demand for funds curve from D_1 to D_2. At point H, the quantity of funds demanded exceeds the quantity supplied, so the interest rate begins to rise. As it rises, households are led to save more, and business firms invest less. In the new equilibrium at point B, both consumption and investment spending have been completely crowded out by the increased government spending.

to decline by a full dollar. The net effect is that total spending ($C + I^P + G$) does not change at all!

> *In the classical model, a rise in government purchases completely crowds out private sector spending, so total spending remains unchanged.*

A closer look at Figure 10 shows that this conclusion always holds, regardless of the particular numbers used or the shapes of the curves. When G increases, the demand for funds curve shifts rightward by the same amount that G rises, or the distance from point A to point H. Then the interest rate rises, moving us along the supply of funds curve from point A to point B. As a result, saving rises (and consumption falls) by the distance AC. But the rise in the interest rate *also* causes a movement along the demand for funds curve, from point H to point B. As a result, investment spending falls by the amount CH.

The final impact can be summarized as follows:

- $G\uparrow = AH$
- $C\downarrow = AC$
- $I^P\downarrow = CH$

And since $AC + CH = AH$, we know that the combined decrease in C and I^P is precisely equal to the increase in G.

Because there is complete crowding out in the classical model, a rise in government purchases cannot change total spending. And the logic behind this result is straightforward. Each additional dollar the government spends is obtained from the loanable funds market, where *it would have been spent by someone else* if the government hadn't borrowed it. How do we know this? Because the loanable funds market funnels every dollar of household saving—no more and no less—to either the government or business firms. If the government borrows more, it just removes funds that would have been spent by businesses (the drop in I^P) or by consumers (the drop in C).

Remember that the goal of this increase in government purchases was to increase output and employment *by increasing total spending*. But now we see that the policy fails to increase spending at all. Therefore,

> *in the classical model, an increase in government purchases has no impact on total spending and no impact on total output or total employment.*

Of course, the opposite sequence of events would happen if government purchases *decreased*: The drop in G would *shrink* the deficit. The interest rate would decline, and private sector spending (C and I^P) would rise by the same amount that government purchases had fallen. (See if you can draw the graphs to prove this to yourself.) Once again, total spending and total output would remain unchanged.

Fiscal Policy with a Budget Surplus

What if the government were running a budget *surplus* instead of a budget deficit? The classical model works very much the same way and gives us the same conclusions. However, some of the details change.

The government sector runs a budget surplus when its net tax revenue (T) is greater than its purchases (G):

$$\text{Budget Surplus} = T - G$$

When the government runs a surplus, it pays back debts that it incurred while running deficits in previous years. At the federal level, for example, the federal government's unpaid debt is called the *national debt*. When the federal government runs a surplus (as it did for a few years in the late 1990s), it uses the net tax revenues that it doesn't spend to pay back part of the national debt, buying back government bonds that it issued in previous years when it ran deficits. In this sense, the government becomes a *supplier* of loanable funds, because it is putting funds back into the market, where they can be borrowed by others.

Figure 11 shows the equilibrium in the loanable funds market with a budget surplus. Now, the government *supplies* loanable funds rather than *demands* them. Therefore, the total demand for loanable funds in Figure 11 is equal to business investment spending alone. The supply of loanable funds, however, now consists of household saving *plus* the budget surplus. So, because of the surplus, the total supply of funds curve S_1 lies farther to the right than it otherwise would, by the amount of the initial surplus.

In the initial equilibrium at point *A*, the interest rate is 5 percent, and the total quantity of funds supplied and demanded are equal, at $1.75 trillion. If government spending rises by $0.5 trillion, with no change in taxes, the budget surplus will shrink by $0.5 trillion, shifting the supply of funds curve leftward by that amount to S_2. In new equilibrium at point *B*, the interest rate is higher (7 percent) and the quantity of funds supplied and demanded is lower ($1.55 trillion).

But that's not all: The rise in the interest rate also causes saving to increase, and consumption spending to decrease. This is represented by the movement from point *H* to point *B* along the new supply of funds curve, which causes saving to rise (consumption to decrease) by $0.3 trillion, or the distance *HC*. The rise in the interest rate also causes investment spending to decrease along the total demand for funds curve, from point *A* to point *B*. Investment spending falls by $0.2 trillion, or the

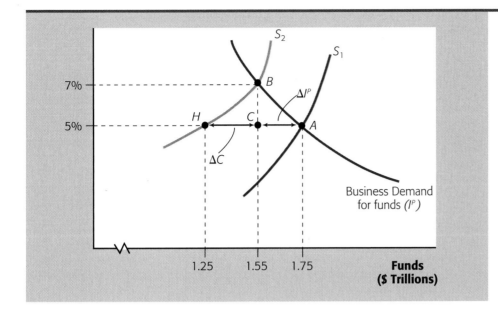

FIGURE 11
Crowding Out with an Initial Budget Surplus

Beginning from equilibrium at point A, *an increase in government purchases causes a decrease in the budget surplus, shifting the supply of funds curve from* S₁ *to* S₂. *At point* H, *the quantity of funds demanded exceeds the quantity supplied, so the interest rate begins to rise. As it rises, households are led to save more, and business firms invest less. In the new equilibrium at point* B, *both consumption and investment spending have been completely crowded out by the increased government spending.*

distance *AC*. Once again, we see that the rise in government spending has completely crowded out consumption and investment spending: A $0.5 trillion rise in government spending has caused consumption and investment spending to decrease by a total of $0.5 trillion. Total spending remains unchanged, and the fiscal policy is completely ineffective. This is the same conclusion we reached about fiscal policy in the previous section, with a government budget deficit.

If you look back over the conclusions we've reached in this chapter, you'll see that virtually all of them were preceded by the words, "In the classical model . . ." (Look back, for example, at the last highlighted statement about the effect of an increase in government purchases.) These words have been added for good reason: All of our conclusions followed from a critical assumption of the classical model: *markets clear.*

This assumption is most realistic when we take a very long-run view of the economy. In the labor market, for example, a persistent significant excess supply of labor—in which millions of qualified people are looking for work for long periods of time and not finding jobs—would *eventually* lead to falling wages, more hiring by firms, and the achievement of full employment.

Since the classical model's assumptions are most accurate over the long run, its conclusions, too, will be most accurate when we take the long-run view—when we look at the average performance of the economy over a period of many years.

Our exploration of fiscal policy shows us that, in the long run, government efforts to change total output by changing government spending or taxes are not only unnecessary, but also ineffective. What, then, *should* a government do to help manage the macroeconomy in the long run? And what *can* it do? These are questions we explore in the next chapter, where we use the classical model to analyze how potential output grows over the long run, and how government policy can help or hinder that growth.

Summary

The classical model is an attempt to explain the behavior of the economy over long time periods. Its most critical assumption is that markets clear—that prices adjust in every market to equate quantities demanded and supplied. The labor market is perhaps the most important part of the classical model. When the labor market clears, we have full employment and the economy produces the potential level of output.

Another important concept is the production function. It shows the total output the economy can produce with different quantities of labor and for given amounts of other resources and a given state of technology. When the labor market is at full employment, the production function can be used to determine the economy's potential level of output.

According to Say's law, total spending in the economy will always be just sufficient to purchase the amount of total output produced. By producing and selling goods and services, firms create a total demand equal to what they have produced. If households do not spend their entire incomes, the excess is channeled, as saving, into the loanable funds market, where it is borrowed and spent by businesses and government.

In the loanable funds market, the quantity of funds supplied equals household saving, which depends positively on the interest rate, and the budget surplus (if there is one). The quantity of funds demanded equals business investment, which depends negatively on the interest rate, and any government budget deficit, if there is one. The interest rate adjusts so that the quantity of funds supplied always equals the quantity demanded. Equivalently (with a budget deficit), it adjusts so that saving (S) equals the sum of planned investment spending (^{P}) and the government budget deficit ($G - T$).

Fiscal policy cannot affect total output in the classical model. An increase in government purchases results in complete crowding out of planned investment and consumption spending, leaving total spending and total output unchanged.

Key Terms

Aggregate production function	Disposable income	Loanable funds market
Budget deficit	Fiscal policy	Market clearing
Budget surplus	Government demand for funds curve	Net taxes
Business demand for funds curve	(Household) saving	Planned investment spending
Circular flow	Injections	Say's law
Classical model	Labor demand curve	Supply of funds curve
Complete crowding out	Labor supply curve	Total demand for funds curve
Crowding out	Leakages	

Review Questions

Answers to even-numbered Questions and Problems can be found on the text Web site at http://hall-lieb.swlearning.com.

1. Discuss the critical assumption on which the classical model is based. How does it relate to the length of time over which we are analyzing the economy?

2. Describe how, in the classical model, the economy reaches full employment automatically. Is this a "realistic" depiction of how the economy behaves?

3. Why does the classical model treat technology and the capital stock as constant?

4. Explain why the slope of the aggregate production function diminishes as more labor is employed.

5. "According to Say's law, all markets always clear." True or false? Explain.

6. What is the difference between net taxes and total tax revenue? Why is the distinction important?

7. Who are the two major groups on the demand side of the loanable funds market? Why does each seek funds there? What is the "price" of these funds?

8. What is the source of funds supplied to the loanable funds market?

9. Explain why the supply of funds curve slopes upward, and why the curve depicting business demand for funds slopes downward.

10. How will the *slope* of the demand for funds curve be affected if the government runs a budget deficit? Why?

11. Why does Say's law hold even after household saving and taxes are taken into account?

12. Explain the implications of the classical model for government economic policy. What are the two consequences

of an increase in government spending that the model predicts?

13. A senator asserts that deficit spending reduces business investment dollar for dollar—every dollar the government borrows means that business investment must fall by a dollar. Is he correct? Why or why not?

14. What is the only type of spending in GDP that is not planned? How does this type of spending occur?

Problems and Exercises

1. Use a diagram similar to Figure 2 to illustrate the effect, on aggregate output and the real hourly wage, of (a) an increase in labor demand, and (b) an increase in labor supply.

2. The following data give a complete picture of the household, business, and government sectors for 2005 in the small nation of Sylvania. (All dollar figures are in billions.)

Consumption spending	$50
Capital stock (end of 2004)	$100
Capital stock (end of 2005)	$103
Change in inventories	$0
Government welfare payments	$5
Government unemployment insurance payments	$2
Government payroll	$3
Government outlays for materials	$2
Depreciation rate	7%
Interest rate	6%

Assuming the government budget for 2005 was in balance, calculate each of the following (in order):
a. government purchases
b. net taxes
c. total investment
d. real GDP
e. total saving
f. total leakages
g. total injections

3. For the economy in Problem 2, suppose that the government had purchased $2 billion more in goods and services than you found in that problem, with no change in taxes.
a. Explain how each of the variables you calculated in Problem 2 would be affected (i.e., state whether it would increase or decrease).
b. Draw a graph illustrating the impact of the $2 billion increase in government purchases on the loanable funds market. Clearly label the equilibrium interest rate, saving, and total quantity of funds demanded at both the original and the new level of government purchases. (Note: You won't be able to find specific numbers.)

4. Once again, as in Problem 3, suppose that Sylvania's government increases its purchases by $2 billion. But this time, suppose Sylvania has a law that prohibits the interest rate from rising above 6 percent. Explain what will happen now in the loanable funds market, and in the economy as a whole. (*Hint:* Will leakages and injections be equal after the increase in government purchases?)

5. Draw a diagram (similar to Figure 10 in this chapter) illustrating the impact of a *decrease* in government purchases. Assume the government is running a budget deficit both before and after the change in government purchases. On your diagram, identify distances that represent:
a. the decrease in government purchases;
b. the increase in consumption spending; and
c. the increase in planned investment spending.

6. Consider the following statement: "In the classical model, just as an *increase* in government purchases causes complete crowding *out*, so a *decrease* in government purchases causes complete crowding *in*."
a. In this statement, explain what is meant by "crowding in" and "complete crowding in."
b. Is the statement true? (*Hint:* Look at the diagram you drew in Problem 5.)

7. Using a three-panel graph similar in style to Figure 7, illustrate how the *supply* of funds curve is obtained when the government is running a budget surplus.

8. Show that Say's law still holds when the government is running a surplus rather than a deficit. (*Hint:* Use a diagram similar to Figure 9.)

9. Use graphs to depict the effect on saving, investment, and the interest rate of a *decrease* in government spending when the government is running a budget *surplus*.

10. Redraw Figure 10 from the chapter, and label
a. the amount of government borrowing that occurs at point *B*; and
b. the amount of private borrowing that occurs at point *B*.

How do these amounts compare with the amounts at the original equilibrium at point *A*?

11. The following data ($ millions) are for the island nation of
     Pacifica.

Total output	$10
Total income	$10
Consumption	$ 6
Government Spending	$ 3
Total Tax Revenue	$ 2.5
Transfer Payments	$ 0.5

     a. Use this information to find Pacifica's net taxes, dis-
         posable income, and savings.
     b. Determine whether the government is running a sur-
         plus, deficit, or balanced budget.

     c. Find planned investment by calculating how much is
         available in the loanable funds market after the govern-
         ment has borrowed what it might need.
     d. Does total output equal total spending?
     e. Show your answers on a diagram similar to the one in
         Figure 9 in the chapter.

12. Return to Question 11. What will happen if consumption
     spending starts to rise? Assume no change in net taxes.
     Show the effect on the loanable funds market, and tell
     what will happen to C, I^P, and G. (*Note:* You won't be
     able to find specific numbers.)

Challenge Questions

1. Using an analysis similar to the one in the "Using the
    Theory" section, show that a tax cut (which decreases net
    taxes) cannot increase total spending in the economy, un-
    der each of the following two assumptions:
    a. Initially (before any change in the interest rate), *none*
        of the tax cut is saved, so that the supply of funds
        curve does not shift at all.
    b. Initially (before any change in the interest rate), the *en-
        tire* tax cut is saved, causing the supply of funds curve
        to shift rightward by an amount equal to the tax cut.

2. Assume the loanable funds market is in equilibrium. Influ-
    ential media pundits begin to warn about impending eco-
    nomic doom: recession, layoffs, and so forth. Using
    graphs, discuss what might happen to the equilibrium in-
    terest rate and the equilibrium quantity of loanable funds
    supplied and demanded. Assume that the government bud-
    get is in balance—neither a deficit nor a surplus. (*Hint:*
    How would these warnings separately affect household
    and business behavior in the loanable funds market?)

ECONOMIC *Applications*   *These exercises require access to Hall/Lieberman Xtra! If Xtra! did not come with your book, visit* http://hallxtra.swlearning.com
                           to purchase.

1. Use your Xtra! password at the Hall and Lieberman Web
    site (http://hallxtra.swlearning.com), select this chapter,
    and under Economic Applications, click on EconDebate.
    Choose *Macroeconomics: Employment, Unemployment,
    and Inflation* and scroll down to find the debate, "Does
    an Increase in the Minimum Wage Result in a Higher Un-
    employment Rate?" Read the debate and use the infor-
    mation to answer the following questions.
    a. The labor market is one of the most important parts
        of the classical model. What are the ramifications of
        the minimum wage laws on employment and output
        according to the classical model?
    b. Considering the effects of inflation on the minimum
        wage would you expect the labor markets to clear or

    unemployment to persist in the presence of the mini-
    mum wage laws? Explain.

2. Use your Xtra! password at the Hall and Lieberman
    Web site (http://hallxtra.swlearning.com), select this
    chapter, and under Economic Applications, click on
    EconDebate. Choose *Macroeconomics: Employment,
    Unemployment, and Inflation* and scroll down to find
    the *Real GDP*, Read the definition and click on Dia-
    grams/Data and use the information to answer the fol-
    lowing question. Does the empirical data on employ-
    ment support the classical assumption that labor
    markets clear? Explain why or why not.

Economic Growth and Rising Living Standards

CHAPTER OUTLINE

The Importance of Growth

What Makes Economies Grow?
  Economic Growth and Living Standards

Growth in the Labor Force Participation Rate (LFPR)
  How to Increase Employment and the LFPR

Growth in Productivity
  Growth in the Capital Stock
  Investment and the Capital Stock
  How to Increase Investment
  Human Capital and Economic Growth

Technological Change

Growth Policies: A Summary

The Costs of Economic Growth
  Budgetary Costs
  Consumption Costs
  Opportunity Costs of Workers' Time
  Sacrifice of Other Social Goals

Using the Theory: Economic Growth in the Less-Developed Countries

Economist Thomas Malthus, writing in 1798, came to a striking conclusion: "Population, when unchecked, goes on doubling itself every twenty-five years, or increases in a geometrical ratio. . . . The means of subsistence . . . could not possibly be made to increase faster than in an arithmetic ratio."[1] From this simple logic, Malthus forecast a horrible fate for the human race. There would be repeated famines and wars to keep the rapidly growing population in balance with the more slowly growing supply of food and other necessities. The prognosis was so pessimistic that it led Thomas Carlyle, one of Malthus's contemporaries, to label economics "the dismal science."

But history has proven Malthus wrong . . . at least in part. In the industrialized nations, living standards have increased beyond the wildest dreams of anyone alive in Malthus's time. Economists today are optimistic about these nations' long-run material prospects. At the same time, living standards in many of the less-developed countries have remained stubbornly close to survival level and, in some cases, have fallen below it.

What are we to make of this? Why have living standards steadily increased in some nations but not in others? And what, if anything, can governments do to speed the rise in living standards? These are questions about economic growth—the long-run increase in an economy's output of goods and services.

---

[1] Thomas Robert Malthus, *An Essay on the Principle of Population*, 1798.

In this chapter, you will learn what makes economies grow. Our approach will make use of the classical model, focusing on Step 3 of the three-step process: What Happens When Things Change? As you'll see, growth arises from *shifts* of the curves of the classical model. And by the end of this chapter, you will know why increasing the rate of economic growth is not easy. While nations can take measures to speed growth, each measure carries an opportunity cost. More specifically,

> *achieving a higher rate of growth in the long run generally requires some sacrifice in the short run.*

THE IMPORTANCE OF GROWTH

Why should we be concerned about economic growth? For one simple reason:

> *When output grows faster than the population, GDP per capita, which we call the **average standard of living**, will rise. When output grows more slowly than the population, the average standard of living will fall.*

Average standard of living Total output (real GDP) per person.

Measuring the standard of living by GDP per capita may seem limiting. After all, as we saw three chapters ago, many important aspects of our quality of life are not captured in GDP. Leisure time, workplace safety, good health, a clean environment—we care about all of these. Yet they are not considered in GDP.

Still, many aspects of our quality of life *are* counted in GDP: food, housing, medical care, education, transportation services, and movies and video games, to name a few. It is not surprising, then, that economic growth—measured by increases in GDP—remains a vital concern in every nation.

Economic growth is especially important in countries with income levels far below those of Europe, Japan, and the United States. The average standard of living in some third-world nations is so low that many families can barely acquire the basic necessities of life, and many others perish from disease or starvation. Table 1 lists GDP per capita, infant mortality rates, life expectancies, and adult literacy rates for some of the richest and poorest countries. The statistics for the poor countries are grim enough, but even they capture only part of the story. Unsafe and unclean workplaces, inadequate housing, and other sources of misery are part of daily life for most people in these countries. Other than emigration, economic growth is their only hope.

Growth is a high priority in prosperous nations, too. As we know, resources are scarce, and we cannot produce enough of everything to satisfy all of our desires simultaneously. We want more and better medical care, education, vacations, entertainment . . . the list is endless. When output per capita is growing, it's at least *possible* for everyone to enjoy an increase in material well-being without anyone having to cut back. We can also accomplish important social goals—helping the poor, improving education, cleaning up the environment—by asking those who are doing well to sacrifice part of the rise in their material well-being, rather than suffer a drop.

But when output per capita stagnates, material gains become a fight over a fixed pie: The more purchasing power my neighbor has, the less is left for me. With everyone struggling for a larger piece of this fixed pie, conflict replaces cooperation. Efforts to help the less fortunate, wipe out illiteracy, reduce air pollution—all are seen as threats, rather than opportunities.

Country	Real GDP per Capita	Infant Mortality Rate (per 1,000 Live Births)	Life Expectancy at Birth	Adult Literacy Rate
Rich Countries				
United States	$35,750	7	77.0	Greater than 99%
Japan	$26,940	3	81.5	Greater than 99%
France	$26,920	4	78.9	Greater than 99%
United Kingdom	$26,150	5	78.1	Greater than 99%
Italy	$26,430	4	78.7	98.5%
Poor Countries				
Azerbaijan	$ 3,210	74	72.1	97.0%
Ghana	$ 2,130	57	57.8	73.8%
Pakistan	$ 1,940	83	60.8	41.5%
Cambodia	$ 2,060	96	57.4	69.4%
Sierra Leone	$ 520	165	34.3	36.0%

TABLE 1

Some Indicators of Economic Well-Being in Rich and Poor Countries, 2002

Sources: United Nations Development Programme, *Human Development Report 2004*, pp. 139–142 and 176–179.

In the 1950s and 1960s, economic growth in the wealthier nations seemed to be taking care of itself. Economists and policy makers focused their attention on short-run movements around full-employment output, rather than on the growth of full-employment output itself. The real payoff for government seemed to be in preventing recessions and depressions—in keeping the economy operating as close to its potential as possible.

All of that changed starting in the 1970s, and economic growth became a national and international preoccupation. Like most changes in perception and thought, this one was driven by experience. Table 2 tells the story. It gives the average yearly growth rates of real GDP per capita for the United States and some of our key trading partners.

Over most of the postwar period, output in the more prosperous industrialized countries (such as the United States, the United Kingdom, and Canada) grew by 2 or 3 percent per year, while output in the less wealthy ones—those with some catching up to do—grew even faster. But beginning in the mid-1970s, all of these nations saw their growth rates slip.

In the late 1990s and early 2000s, only the United States and the United Kingdom returned to their previous high rates of growth, while the other industrialized countries continued to grow more slowly than their historical averages.

Looking at the table, you might think that this slowing in growth was rather insignificant. Do the tiny differences between the pre-1972 and the post-1972 growth rates really matter? Indeed, they do. Recall our example a few chapters ago in which an increase in the U.S. growth rate of around 1 percentage point over the past 20 years would mean $20 trillion in additional output over the entire period. Seemingly small differences in growth rates matter a great deal.

TABLE 2
Average Annual Growth Rate of Real GDP per Capita

Country	1948–1972	1972–1988	1988–1995	1995–2004
United States	2.2%	1.7%	1.0%	2.3%
United Kingdom	2.4	2.1	0.9	2.5
Canada	2.9	2.6	0.6	2.4
France	4.3	2.1	1.2	1.8
Italy	4.9	2.8	1.6	1.3
West Germany	5.7	2.2	1.3	1.2
Japan	8.2	3.3	2.1	1.3

Sources: Angus Maddison, *Phases of Capitalist Development* (Oxford: Oxford University Press, 1982); U.S. Census Bureau IDB Summary Demographic Data (*http://www.census.gov/ipc/www/idbsum.html*); and *Economic Report of the President*, 2002, 2005, Table B-112; and various OECD publications. *Note:* Data for Germany includes West Germany only through 1995, and all of Germany after 1995.

WHAT MAKES ECONOMIES GROW?

A useful way to start thinking about long-run growth is to look at what determines our potential GDP in any given period. Starting this process is very simple: We can say that real GDP depends on

- The amount of output the average worker can produce in an hour
- The number of hours the average worker spends at the job
- The fraction of the population that wants to work
- The size of the population

If you spend a moment considering each of these variables, you'll see that—all else equal—if any one of them increases, real GDP rises.

Before we start working with these determinants of growth, let's briefly discuss how the first three are measured. The amount of output the average worker produces in an hour is called **labor productivity**, or just **productivity**. It is measured by taking the total output (real GDP) of the economy over a period of time and dividing by the total number of hours that *everyone* worked during that period.

Labor productivity The output produced by the average worker in an hour.

$$\text{Productivity} = \text{Output per hour} = \frac{\text{Total output}}{\text{Total hours worked}}.$$

For example, if during a given month all workers in the United States spent a total of 25 billion hours at their jobs and produced $1 trillion worth of output, then on average, labor productivity would be $1 trillion / 25 billion hours = $40 per hour. Or in words, the average worker would produce $40 worth of output in an hour. As you'll see later in this chapter, increases in productivity are one of the most important contributors to economic growth.

Next, the hours of the average worker can be found by dividing the total hours worked over a period by total employment, the *number* of people who worked during the period. However—since we're ultimately interested in *potential* output rather than actual output in any particular period—we'll assume that, on average, the economy behaves according to the classical model: All those who *want* to work will find a job. Therefore, over the long run, total employment is equal to the number of people who want to work—the *labor force*.

$$\text{Average Hours} = \frac{\text{Total hours}}{\text{Labor Force}}.$$

For example, if the labor force is 200 million people and they would work a total of 25 billion hours per month if all were employed, then average hours per month would be 25 billion hours / 200 million workers = 125 hours per month.

Now let's turn to the fraction of the population working. Once again we'll take a long-run perspective—assuming that all those who want to work will find employment. Then the fraction of the population working is the **labor force participation rate (LFPR)**, and is found by dividing the labor force (all those who want to be working) by the population:[2]

$$\text{LFPR} = \frac{\text{Labor Force}}{\text{Population}}$$

Now that we understand how these variables are measured, let's multiply them together and cancel out the like terms:

$$\frac{\text{Total output}}{\text{Total hours}} \times \frac{\text{Total hours}}{\text{Labor Force}} \times \frac{\text{Labor Force}}{\text{Population}} \times \text{Population}$$

$$= \text{Total output}.$$

Thus, we can write our equation for total output as:

$$\text{Total output} = \text{Productivity} \times \text{Average Hours} \times \text{LFPR} \times \text{Population}.$$

Finally, there is one more step before turning our attention to *explaining* growth. We'll borrow a rule from mathematics that states that if two variables A and B are multiplied together, then the percentage change in their product is approximately equal to the sum of their percentage changes. In symbols:

$$\%\Delta\, (A \times B) \approx \%\Delta A + \%\Delta B.$$

Applying this rule to all four variables in the right side of our equation, as well as to total output on the left, we find that the growth rate of total output over any period of time is

$$\%\Delta\ \text{Total Output} \approx \%\Delta\ \text{productivity} + \%\Delta\ \text{average hours} +$$
$$\%\Delta\ \text{LFPR} + \%\Delta\ \text{Population}.$$

Table 3 shows estimates of how each of these variables have contributed to output growth during different periods of recent U.S. history, as well as a six-year future projection. For example, the first column tells us that from 1953 to 1973, real GDP grew, on average, by 3.6 percent per year. Of that growth, 1.6 percentage points were due to a growing population, and 0.2 percentage points were due to a rise in the labor force participation rate. Average hours—which decreased during the period—contributed negatively to growth, reducing it by a third of a percentage point. Finally, growth in labor productivity contributed 2.3 percent during this period.

Going across the rows and moving from period to period, you can see that almost all of the growth in real GDP over the last 50 years (and projected for the near

[2] In actual practice in the United States and many other countries, the LFPR is the fraction of the *civilian, noninstitutional population over the age of 16* that is either employed or seeking work. We'll ignore this technical definition in our analysis, and consider LFPR to be the fraction of the entire population that wants to be working.

TABLE 3	Annual Percentage Growth in Real GDP Due to:	1953 to 1973	1973 to 1995	1995 to 2004	2004 to 2010 (projected)
Factors Contributing to Growth in Real GDP	Population	1.6	1.4	1.2	1.1
	LFPR	0.2	0.4	−0.1	−0.1
	Average Hours	−0.3	−0.3	−0.3	0.1
	Productivity	2.3	1.3	2.7	2.2
	Total	3.6	2.8	3.5	3.3

Source: Economic Report of the President, 2005, Table 1–2, p. 45, and author calculations. (The *Economic Report* lists nonfarm business productivity only. In this table, annual productivity growth has been reduced by 0.1 to 0.2 percentage points in each period to account for slightly slower output growth in the government and farm sectors.)

future) has come from two factors: population growth and productivity growth. Increases in labor force participation have contributed somewhat in the past, and average hours have decreased slightly, slowing growth in real GDP.

Economic Growth and Living Standards

Ultimately, growth in real GDP—by itself—does not guarantee a rising standard of living. Imagine, for example, that real GDP grew by 10 percent over some period while the population doubled. With 10 percent more output divided among twice as many people, the average standard of living would clearly decrease even though real output was growing. What matters for the standard of living is *real GDP per capita*—our total output of goods and services *per person*. Over the long run, since real GDP tends to track along with *potential* output, living standards will depend on *potential* output per person.

To see more clearly what causes potential output per person to rise, let's go back to our basic growth equation:

$$\text{Total Output} = \text{Productivity} \times \text{Average Hours} \times \text{LFPR} \times \text{Population}$$

If we divide both sides of this equation by the population, we get:

$$\frac{\text{Total Output}}{\text{Population}} = \text{Productivity} \times \text{Average Hours} \times \text{LFPR}$$

And, in terms of percentage growth rates:

$$\%\Delta \text{ Total Output per person} \approx \%\Delta \text{ productivity} + \%\Delta \text{ average hours} + \%\Delta \text{ LFPR}.$$

Notice that population drops out of the equation. This tells us that the only way to raise the average standard of living is to increase productivity, increase average hours, or increase the labor force participation rate.

But as we saw in Table 3, average hours in the United States have decreased over the past several decades, and are projected to remain constant for several years. In continental Europe, the decrease in average hours has been even greater. This is why we'll focus our discussion on the remaining two factors in our equation: the LFPR and productivity.

> *To explain growth in output per person and living standards in the United States and other developed nations, economists look at two factors: increases in the labor force participation rate and growth in productivity.*

Now it's time to look more closely at *how* these two factors raise the average standard of living. And the classical model that you learned in the last chapter is very well suited to helping us understand this. We'll start by considering increases in the labor force participation rate.

GROWTH IN THE LABOR FORCE PARTICIPATION RATE (LFPR)

If the labor force were to grow at the same rate as the population, the labor force participation rate would remain unchanged. For example, if the labor force is 50 million out of a total population of 100 million, then the LFPR = 50 million / 100 million = 0.50. If the labor force and the population each grew by 10 percent, the LFPR would be 55 million / 110 million = 0.50—the same as before the change. In order for the LFPR to grow, the labor force must grow *faster* than the population. In our example, you can verify that if the labor force rose by *more* than 10 percent (say, from 50 million to 57 million) while the population still grew at 10 percent, the LFPR would *rise*.

Over the long run, when the economy operates at full employment, growth in the labor force is the same as growth in total employment. This leads us to the following observation:

> *Over the long run, the labor force participation rate rises when* employment *grows at a faster rate than the* population.

The classical model—which explains how equilibrium employment is determined over the long run—can help us understand long-run changes in the LFPR.

What causes employment to grow?

One possibility is an increase in labor *supply:* a rise in the number of people who would like to work at any given wage. This is illustrated in Figure 1 by a rightward shift in the labor supply curve. We'll discuss *why* the labor supply curve might shift later; here, we'll concentrate on the consequences of the shift.

Before the shift, the labor supply curve is L_1^S, the market clears at a wage of $15 per hour, and the fully employed labor force is 100 million workers. The aggregate production function tells us that, with the given amounts of other resources in the economy, and the given state of technology, 100 million workers can produce $7 trillion in goods and services—the initial value of full-employment output. When the labor supply curve shifts to L_2^S, the market-clearing wage drops to $12. Business firms, finding labor cheaper to hire, increase the number of workers employed along the labor demand curve, from point *A* to point *B*. The labor force increases to 120 million workers, and full-employment output rises to $8 trillion.

But growth in employment can also arise from an increase in labor demand: a rise in the number of workers that firms would like to hire at any given wage. Once again, we'll consider the *causes* of labor demand changes momentarily; here, we focus on the *consequences*.

FIGURE 1
An Increase in Labor Supply

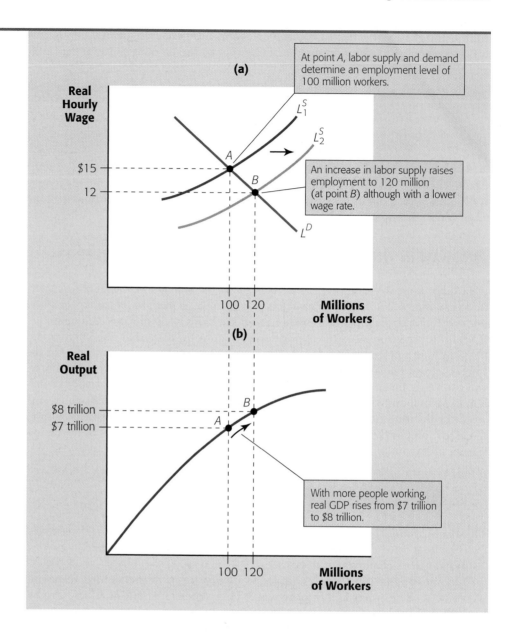

Graphically, an increase in labor demand is represented by a rightward shift in the labor demand curve, as in Figure 2. As the wage rate rises from $15 to its new equilibrium of $17, we move along the labor supply curve from point *A* to point *B*. More people decide they want to work as the wage rises. Equilibrium employment once again rises from 100 million to 120 million workers, so full-employment output will rise. Thus,

growth in employment can arise from an increase in labor supply (a rightward shift in the labor supply curve) or an increase in labor demand (a rightward shift of the labor demand curve).

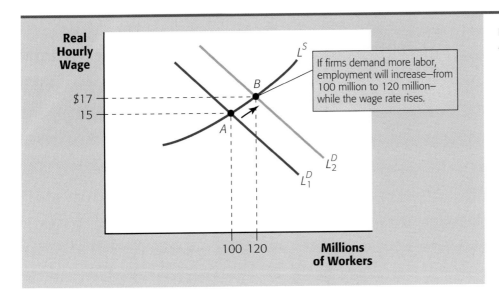

FIGURE 2
An Increase in Labor Demand

Real Hourly Wage

L^S

B

If firms demand more labor, employment will increase—from 100 million to 120 million—while the wage rate rises.

$17

15

A

L_2^D

L_1^D

100 120

Millions of Workers

You may have noticed one very important difference between the labor market outcomes in Figures 1 and 2: When labor *supply* increases, the wage rate falls (from $15 to $12 in Figure 1); when labor *demand* increases, the wage rate rises (from $15 to $17 in Figure 2). Which of the figures describes the actual experience of the U.S. labor market?

Actually, a combination of both: Over the past 50 years, the U.S. labor supply curve has shifted steadily rightward, sometimes slowly, sometimes more rapidly. Why the shift in labor supply? In part, the reason has been steady population growth: The more people there are, the more will want to work at any wage. But another reason has been an important change in tastes: an increase in the desire of women (especially married women) to work.

Over the past 50 years, as the labor supply curve has shifted rightward, the labor demand curve has shifted rightward as well. Why? Throughout this period, firms have been acquiring more and better capital equipment for their employees to use. Managers and accountants now keep track of inventories and other important accounts with lightning-fast computer software instead of account ledgers. Supermarket clerks use electronic scanners instead of hand-entry cash registers. And college professors or their research assistants now gather data by searching for a few hours on the Web instead of a few weeks in the library. At the same time, workers have become better educated and better trained. These changes have increased the amount of output a worker can produce in any given period, so firms have wanted to hire more of them at any wage.[3]

In fact, over the past century, increases in labor demand have outpaced increases in labor supply, so that, on balance, the average wage rate has risen and employment has increased. This is illustrated in Figure 3, which shows a shift in the labor supply curve from L_1^S to L_2^S, and an even greater shift in the labor demand curve from L_1^D to L_2^D.

---

[3] These changes in physical and human capital have also shifted the economy's production function, but we'll consider that in the next section.

FIGURE 3
The U.S. Labor Market Over a Century

Over the past century, increases in labor demand have outpaced increases in supply. As a result, both the level of employment and the average wage have risen.

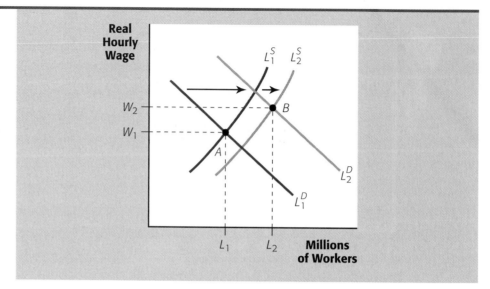

The impact of these changes on total employment has been dramatic. Between 1948 and 2004, the labor force rose from 59 million to 149 million—an increase of about 150 percent. And as the classical model predicts, employment rose by about the same percentage, from 56 million to 142 million.

But what about the labor force participation rate—the fraction of Americans who want to work? It did, in fact, rise—from 57 percent to 66 percent of the adult population. This tells us that employment grew *faster* than the population during this period. And as you've learned, such an increase in the LFPR causes not just real GDP, but real GDP *per capita*, to grow. However, most of the rise in the LFPR was due to a special factor that is unlikely to be repeated: the greater labor force participation rate of women—especially married women—during the 1960s, 1970s, and 1980s. But in the 1990s—as the female LFPR stabilized—this source of growth disappeared.

Currently, the U.S. Bureau of Labor Statistics predicts employment growth of 1 percent per year until the year 2010—about the same as the growth rate of the population. Thus, the labor force participation rate is not expected to grow at all. Employment growth—while it will raise real GDP—will not increase real GDP per capita, and so will not contribute to a rise in living standards.

Can we do anything about this? Can we speed up the rightward shifts in the labor demand and labor supply curves over the next few years, so that employment grows faster than the 1 percent annual growth rate of the population? Yes, we can. But as you read on, keep in mind that these measures to increase employment are not necessarily socially desirable. They would, most likely, accomplish the goal, but they would also have costs—costs that Americans may or may not be willing to pay. Later, we'll discuss these costs.

How to Increase Employment and the LFPR

One set of policies to speed the rise in employment focuses on changing labor supply. And an often-proposed example of this type of policy is a decrease in income tax rates. Imagine that you have a professional degree in accounting, physical therapy, or some other field, and you are considering whether to take a job. Suppose the going rate for your professional services is $30 per hour. If your average tax rate is 33 percent, then one-third of your income will be taxed away, so your take-home pay would be only $20 per hour. But if your tax rate were cut to 20 percent, you would take home $24 per hour. Since you care about your take-home pay, you will respond to a tax cut in the same way you would respond to a wage increase—even if the wage your potential employer pays does not change at all. If you would be willing to take a job that offers a take-home pay of $24, but not one that offers $20, then the tax cut would be just what was needed to get you to seek work.

When we extend your reaction to the population as a whole, we can see that a cut in the income tax rate can convince more people to seek jobs at any given wage, shifting the labor supply curve rightward. This is why economists and politicians who focus on the economy's long-run growth often recommend lower taxes on labor income to encourage more rapid growth in employment. They point out that many American workers must pay combined federal, state, and local taxes of more than 40 cents out of each additional dollar they earn, and that this may be discouraging work effort in the United States.

Indeed, this was an important part of the logic behind the two tax cuts engineered by President Bush early in his administration. For example, the first tax cut, which Congress passed after much debate in June 2001, called for gradually reduced tax rates over 10 years. It reduced the cumulative tax burden on households by about $1.35 trillion over that period.

In addition to tax rate changes, some economists have advocated changes in government transfer programs to speed the growth in employment. They argue that the current structure of many government programs creates disincentives to work. For example, families receiving welfare payments, food stamps, unemployment benefits, and Social Security retirement payments all face steep losses in their benefits if they go to work or increase their work effort. Redesigning these programs might therefore stimulate growth in labor supply.

This reasoning was an important motive behind the sweeping reforms in the U.S. welfare system passed by Congress, and signed by President Clinton, in August 1996. Among other things, the reforms reduced the number of people who were eligible for benefits, cut the benefit amount for many of those still eligible, and set a maximum coverage period of five years for most welfare recipients. Later in this chapter, we'll discuss some of the *costs* of potentially growth-enhancing measures like this. Here, we only point out that changes in benefit programs have the potential to change labor supply.

A cut in tax rates increases the reward for working, while a cut in benefits to the needy increases the hardship of not working. Either policy can cause a greater rightward shift in the economy's labor supply curve than would otherwise occur and speed the growth in employment, creating growth in labor force participation and output per person.

Government policies can also affect the labor *demand* curve. In recent decades, subsidies for education and training, such as government-guaranteed loans for college students or special training programs for the unemployed, have helped to increase the skills of the labor force and made workers more valuable to potential employers. Government also subsidizes employment more directly—by contributing part of the wage when certain categories of workers are hired—the disabled, college work-study participants, and, in some experimental programs, inner-city youth. By enlarging these programs, government could increase the number of workers hired at any given wage and thus shift the labor demand curve to the right:

> Government policies that help increase the skills of the workforce or that subsidize employment more directly shift the economy's labor demand curve to the right, increasing labor force participation and output per person.

Efforts to create growth in labor force participation are controversial. In recent decades, those who prefer an activist government have favored policies to increase labor *demand* through government-sponsored training programs, more aid to college students, employment subsidies to firms, and similar programs. Those who prefer a more *laissez-faire* approach have generally favored policies to increase the labor *supply* by *decreasing* government involvement—lower taxes or a less generous social safety net.

GROWTH IN PRODUCTIVITY

Our analysis of growth began with an equation explaining how total output is determined. Then—one by one—we eliminated variables that could not explain growth in total output—and living standards—over the long run. First, we ruled out population growth, based on the logic of the equation for total output per person. Second, we ruled out growth in average hours, based on the past and projected future behavior of this variable. And in the previous section, we ruled out increases in the labor force participation rate—at least as a source of continual, rapid economic growth in the near future. So only one variable remains: productivity.

HTTP://

For a more in-depth explanation of recent productivity behavior in the U.S., see the January 2005 speech by Federal Reserve Board Governor Ben Bernanke at http://www.federalreserve.gov/boarddocs/speeches/2005/20050119/default.htm.

If you look back at Table 3, you'll see that growth in productivity has been responsible for most of the growth in real GDP over the last 50 years. (The period from 1973 to 1995, when population growth led slightly, is the exception.) And as you've learned, population growth—while it can raise real GDP—cannot raise real GDP *per capita*. If we restrict ourselves to the three factors in Table 3 that *can* raise real GDP per capita, we see that

> over the past several decades, and into the near future, virtually all growth in the average standard of living can be attributed to growth in productivity.

Not surprisingly, when economists analyze rising living standards, they think first and foremost about growth in productivity.

Table 3 shows that productivity is expected to grow a bit more than 2 percent during the reminder of the 2000s. Can we make it grow even faster?

Growth in the Capital Stock

One key to productivity growth is the nation's capital stock or, more precisely, the amount of capital available for the average worker in the economy. You can dig more ditches with a shovel than with your hands, and even more with a backhoe. And the economy can produce more automobiles, medical services, and education

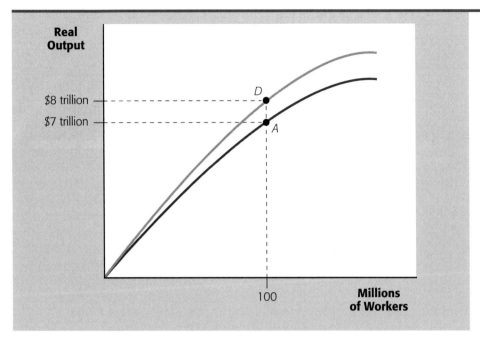

FIGURE 4
Capital Accumulation and the Production Function

An increase in the capital stock shifts the production function upward. At point A, 100 million workers could produce $7 trillion of real GDP. With more capital, those same workers could produce $8 trillion of real GDP.

when the average employee in these industries has more machinery, technical equipment, and computers to work with.

A rise in **capital per worker**—the total capital stock divided by the labor force—results in greater productivity. Figure 4 shows this from the perspective of the classical model. Initially, the economy operates at point *A* on the lower aggregate production function, where 100 million workers produce $7 trillion in output. An increase in the capital stock shifts the production function upward, since any given number of workers can produce more output if there is more capital to work with. Assuming that the labor force remains at 100 million, there will be more capital per worker, greater productivity, and the economy will move to point *D*. At this point, 100 million workers produce $8 trillion in output.

Capital per worker The total capital stock divided by total employment.

However, in the real world, as the capital stock grows, so does the labor force. While any increase in capital will shift up the production function as in the figure, productivity will rise only if capital *per worker* increases—that is, only if the nation's total capital stock grows *faster* than the labor force.

> *All else equal, if the capital stock grows faster than the labor force, then capital per worker will rise, and labor productivity will increase along with it. But if the capital stock grows more slowly than the labor force, then capital per worker will fall, and labor productivity will fall as well.*

In the United States and most other developed countries, the capital stock has grown more rapidly than the labor force. As a result, labor productivity has risen over time. But in some developing countries, the capital stock has grown at about the same rate as, or even more slowly than the labor force, and labor productivity has remained stagnant or fallen. We will return to this problem in the "Using the Theory" section of this chapter.

Investment and the Capital Stock

What determines how fast the capital stock rises, and whether it will rise faster than the labor force? The answer is: the rate of *planned investment spending* in the economy. Investment spending and the capital stock are related to each other, but they are different *kinds* of variables. Specifically, capital is a *stock* variable while investment spending is a *flow* variable.

Stock variable a variable measuring a quantity at a moment in time.

> A **stock variable** *measures a quantity at a moment in time.* A **flow variable** *measures a process over a period of time.*

Flow variable a variable measuring a *process* over some period of time.

To use an analogy, think of a bathtub being filled with water. The water *in* the tub is a stock variable—so many gallons at any given moment. The water *flowing into* the tub is a flow variable—so many gallons *per minute* or *per hour.* You can always identify a flow variable by the addition of "per period" in its definition. Even when not explicitly stated, some period of time is always implied in a flow variable.

Now let's think about capital again. The capital stock—the total amount of plant and equipment that exists in the economy—is like the quantity of water *in* the tub. It can be measured at any given moment. Investment spending—the amount of *new* capital being installed over some time interval—is like the water flowing *into* the tub. Investment spending is defined *per period*—such as *per quarter* or *per year.* In the simplest terms, investment spending *adds* to the capital stock over time.

But there is one more flow involved in the capital-investment relationship: *depreciation.* Each period, some of the capital stock is used up. If a computer is expected to last only three years, for example, then each year the computer depreciates by about a third of its initial value. Depreciation tends to *reduce* the capital stock over time. (In our tub analogy, depreciation is like the flow of water draining *out* each period.) *As long as investment is greater than depreciation* (more water flows into the tub than drains out), *the capital stock will rise.* Moreover, for any rate of depreciation, the greater the flow of investment spending, the faster the rise in the capital stock.

Pulling all of this together leads us to an important conclusion about investment spending and the capital stock:

> *For a given rate of depreciation and a given growth rate of the labor force, a higher rate of investment spending causes faster growth in capital per worker and productivity, and faster growth in the average standard of living.*

This is why when economists think about raising productivity via the capital stock, they focus on raising the rate of investment spending.

How to Increase Investment

A government seeking to spur investment has more than one weapon in its arsenal. It can direct its efforts toward businesses themselves, toward the household sector, or toward its own budget.

Targeting Businesses: Increasing the Incentive to Invest. One kind of policy to increase investment targets the business sector itself, with the goal of increasing planned investment spending. Figure 5 shows how this works. The figure shows a

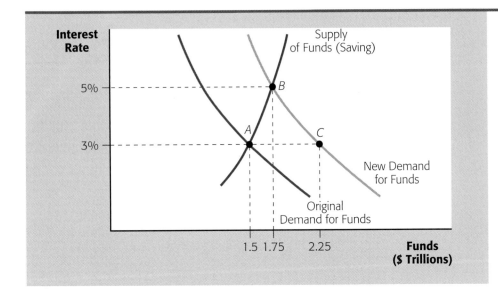

FIGURE 5
An Increase in Investment Spending

Government policies that make investment more profitable will increase investment spending at each interest rate. The resulting rightward shift of the investment demand curve leads to a higher level of investment spending, at point B.

simplified view of the loanable funds market where—to focus on investment—we assume that there is no budget deficit, so there is no government demand for funds. The initial equilibrium in the market is at point *A*, where household saving (the supply of funds) and investment (the demand for funds) are both equal to $1.5 trillion and the interest rate is 3 percent. Now suppose that the government takes steps to make investment more profitable, so that—at any interest rate—firms will want to purchase $0.75 trillion more in capital equipment than before. Then the investment curve would shift rightward by $0.75 trillion and the interest rate would rise from 3 percent to 5 percent. Note that, as the interest rate rises, some—but not all—of the original increase in planned investment is choked off. In the end, investment rises from $1.5 trillion to $1.75 trillion, and so each year $0.25 trillion more is added to the capital stock than would otherwise be added.

These are the mechanics of a rightward shift in the investment curve. But what government measures would *cause* such a shift in the first place? That is, how could the government help to make investment spending more profitable for firms?

One such measure would be a reduction in the **corporate profits tax**, which would allow firms to keep more of the profits they earn from investment projects. Another, even more direct, policy is an **investment tax credit**, which subsidizes corporate investment in new capital equipment.

Corporate profits tax A tax on the profits earned by corporations.

Investment tax credit A reduction in taxes for firms that invest in new capital.

> *Reducing business taxes or providing specific investment incentives can shift the investment curve rightward, thereby speeding growth in physical capital, and increasing the growth rate of living standards.*

Of course, the same reasoning applies in reverse: An *increase* in the corporate profits tax or the *elimination* of an investment tax credit would shift the investment curve to the left, slowing the rate of investment, the growth of the capital stock, and the rise in living standards.

Targeting Households: Increasing the Incentive to Save. While firms make decisions to purchase new capital, it is largely households that supply the funds, via

FIGURE 6

An Increase in Saving

If households decide to save more of their incomes, the supply of funds will increase. With more funds available, the interest rate will fall. Businesses will respond by increasing their borrowing, and investment will increase from $1.75 trillion to $2.25 trillion.

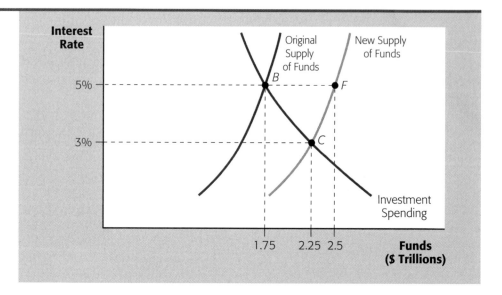

personal saving. Thus, an increase in investment spending can originate in the household sector, through an increase in the desire to save. This is illustrated in Figure 6. If households decide to save more of their incomes at any given interest rate, the supply of funds curve will shift rightward. The increase in saving drives down the interest rate, from 5 percent to 3 percent, which, in turn, causes investment to increase. With a lower interest rate, NBC might decide to borrow funds to build another production studio, or the corner grocery store may finally decide to borrow the funds it needs for a new electronic scanner at the checkout stand. In this way, an increase in the desire to save is translated, via the loanable funds market, into an increase in investment and faster growth in the capital stock.

What might cause households to increase their saving? The answer is found in the reasons people save in the first place. And to understand these reasons, you needn't look farther than yourself or your own family. You might currently be saving for a large purchase (a car, a house, a vacation, college tuition) or to build a financial cushion in case of hard times ahead. You might even be saving to support yourself during retirement, though this is a distant thought for most college students.

Given these motives, what would make you save *more*? Several things: greater uncertainty about your economic future, an increase in your life expectancy, anticipation of an earlier retirement, a change in tastes toward big-ticket items, or even just a change in your attitude about saving. Any of these changes—if they occurred in many households simultaneously—would shift the saving curve (the supply of funds curve) to the right, as in Figure 6.

But government policy can increase household saving as well. One way is to decrease the **capital gains tax.** A capital gain is the profit you earn when you sell an asset, such as a share of stock or a bond, at a higher price than you paid for it. By lowering the special tax rate for capital gains, households would be able to keep more of the capital gains they earn. As a result, stocks and bonds would become more rewarding to own, and you might decide to reduce your current spending in order to buy them. If other households react in the same way, total saving would rise, and the supply of funds to the loanable funds market would increase.

Capital gains tax A tax on profits earned when a financial asset is sold at more than its acquisition price.

This was the logic behind a key component of the Bush administration's second tax cut, signed into law in May 2003. The tax cut included a reduction in the capital gains tax, from 20 percent to 15 percent for higher income households, and from 10 percent to 5 percent (and down to 0% in 2008) for lower income households. The lower tax rates applied only to *long-term* capital gains—gains on assets held for a year or longer—to encourage people to put their funds into stocks and other assets and keep them there, rather than engage in short-term speculation.

The 2003 tax cut on capital gains was controversial for two reasons. First, there was an equity issue: since most of the capital gains in the economy are earned by higher income households, this part of the tax cut benefited high-income households more than low-income households. Second, the government was already running a substantial budget deficit in 2003, and the tax cuts threatened to raise it further. As you'll see in the next section, higher budget deficits can work *against* economic growth.

Another frequently proposed measure is to switch from the current U.S. income tax—which taxes all income whether it is spent or saved—to a **consumption tax,** which would tax only the income that households spend. A consumption tax could work just like the current income tax, except that you would deduct your saving from your income and pay taxes on the remainder. This would increase the reward for saving. By saving, you would earn additional interest on the part of your income that would have been taxed away under an income tax. Currently, individual retirement accounts, or IRAs, allow households to deduct limited amounts of saving from their incomes before paying taxes. A general consumption tax would go much further and allow *all* saving to be deducted.

Consumption tax A tax on the part of their income that households spend.

Another change that would increase household saving—if we were to choose this route—would be to modify the government programs that form our social safety net. Social security payments to the elderly, unemployment insurance payments for those who lose their jobs, and Medicaid for those too poor to afford health care—all help to guarantee a basic floor for living standards. But by reducing the fear and anxiety of possible adverse economic outcomes, these government transfer programs also reduce households' incentive to save as a precaution.

Government can alter the tax and transfer system to increase incentives for saving. If successful, these policies would make more funds available for investment, speed growth in the capital stock, and speed the rise in living standards.

(Do any of these methods of increasing saving disturb you? Remember, we are not advocating any measures here; rather, we are merely noting that such measures would increase saving and promote economic growth. We'll discuss the *costs* of growth-promoting measures later.)

Shrinking the Budget Deficit. A final pro-investment measure is directed at the government sector itself. The previous chapter showed that an increase in government purchases, financed by borrowing in the financial market, completely crowds out consumption and investment. A *decrease* in government purchases has the opposite effect: raising consumption and investment.

Figure 7 reintroduces the government to the loanale funds to show how this works. Initially, the budget deficit is $0.75 trillion, equal to the distance *EA*. The

FIGURE 7
**Deficit Reduction and
Investment Spending**

*Eliminating the government's
budget deficit will reduce government borrowing in the loanable funds market. As a result,
the total demand for funds will
fall, as will the interest rate. At
a lower interest rate, businesses
will increase their investment
spending from $1 trillion (point
E) to $1.5 trillion (point B).*

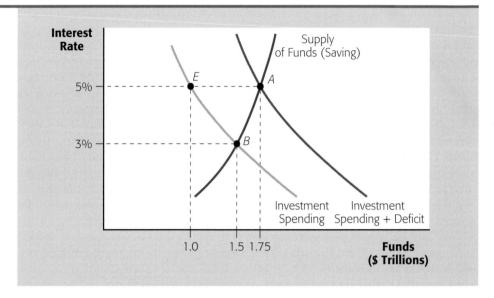

total demand for funds is now the sum of investment and the government's budget
deficit, given by the curve labeled "Investment Spending + Deficit." The demand for
funds curve intersects the supply of funds curve at point *A*, creating an equilibrium
interest rate of 5 percent and equilibrium saving of $1.75 trillion. At this interest
rate, investment spending is only $1 trillion. The part of saving not going to finance
investment spending ($1.75 trillion − $1 trillion = $0.75 trillion) is being used to fi-
nance the budget deficit.

Now consider what happens if the government eliminates the deficit—say, by
reducing its purchases by $0.75 trillion. The demand for funds would consist of
investment spending only. Since there would be no other borrowing, the new equilibrium would be point *B*, with an interest rate of 3 percent and investment equal
to $1.5 trillion—greater than before. By balancing its budget, the government no
longer needs to borrow in the loanable funds market, which frees up funds to
flow to the business sector instead. Initially, this creates an excess supply of funds.
But, as the loanable funds market clears, the interest rate drops and the excess
supply of funds disappears. (Why does a drop in the interest rate make the excess
supply disappear? *Hint:* What happens to saving and to investment as the interest
rate declines?)

The link between the government budget, the interest rate, and investment
spending is the major reason why the U.S. government, and governments around
the world, try to reduce and, if possible, eliminate budget deficits. They have
learned that

*a shrinking deficit or a rising surplus tends to reduce interest rates and in-
crease investment, thus speeding the growth in the capital stock.*

In the 1990s, Congress set strict limits on the growth of government spending,
and the budget deficit began shrinking. The restraints on spending, and rapid economic growth during the 1990s, finally turned the federal budget from deficit to
surplus in 1998, and continued surpluses were projected for more than a decade.

These surpluses were viewed as positive for economic growth: They would help keep the interest rate low, which in turn would lead to greater business investment spending.

When President George W. Bush took office in 2001, the direction of growth policy shifted away from preserving budget surpluses and toward lower tax rates. The first Bush tax cut in 2001(a total of $1.35 trillion over 10 years) purposely cut into potential future surpluses in order to reduce the tax burden on American households. Shortly afterward, a series of events pushed the budget into deficit. These included a continuing recession that had begun in March 2001 and the attacks of September 11, which resulted in large increases in military and homeland security spending. And a second tax cut in 2003—amounting to $350 billion over 10 years—increased current and projected deficits further.

The tax cuts included some elements (discussed earlier) to increase investment spending, such as a lower tax rate for capital gains and tax incentives for investment by small businesses. Also, you've learned that cutting income tax rates can have some effect on the labor force participation rate by shifting the labor supply curve rightward. But the tax cuts—by raising current and future budget deficits—would ultimately drive the interest rate higher than it would otherwise be, which works in opposition to the growth benefits of the tax cut. We'll discuss budget deficits and their effects on the economy more thoroughly toward the end of this book, in the chapter on fiscal policy.

An Important Proviso About the Budget Deficit. A reduction in the deficit or an increase in the surplus—even if they stimulate private investment—are not *necessarily* pro-growth measures. It depends on *how* the budget changes. By an increase in taxes? A cut in government spending? And if the latter, which government programs will be cut? Welfare? National defense? Highway repair? The answers can make a big difference to the impact on growth.

For example, in our discussions of the capital stock so far, we've ignored government capital—roads, communication lines, bridges, and dams. To understand the importance of government capital, just imagine what life would be like without it. How would factories obtain their raw materials or distribute their goods if no one repaired the roads? How would contracts between buyers and sellers be enforced if there were no public buildings to house courts and police departments? Government capital supports private economic activity in more ways than we can list here.

> *Government investment in new capital and the maintenance of existing capital makes an important contribution to economic growth.*

This important observation complicates our view of deficit reduction. It is still true that a decrease in government spending will lower the interest rate and increase private investment. But if the budget cutting falls largely on government investment, the negative effect of smaller public investment will offset some of the positive impact of greater private investment. Shrinking the deficit will then alter the *mix* of capital—more private and less public—and the effect on growth could go either way. A society rife with lawlessness, deteriorating roads and bridges, or an unreliable communications network might benefit from a shift toward public capital. For example, a study of public budgets in African nations—which have poor road conditions—found that each one-dollar-per-year cut in the road-maintenance budget increased vehicle operating costs by between $2 and $3 per year, and in one case, by as much as $22 per year.[4] This is an example of a cut in government spending that, even if it reduces the deficit, probably hinders growth. By contrast, in Sweden—a country with a fully developed and well-maintained public infrastructure—recent governments have decided to shift the mix away from public and toward private capital, in part because they believed this would speed growth.

> *The impact of deficit reduction on economic growth depends on which government programs are cut. Shrinking the deficit by cutting government investment will not stimulate growth as much as would cutting other types of government spending.*

Human Capital and Economic Growth

So far, the only type of capital we've discussed is physical capital—the plant and equipment workers use to produce output. But when we think of the capital stock most broadly, we include *human capital* as well. **Human capital**—the skills and knowledge possessed by workers—is as central to economic growth as is physical capital. After all, most types of physical capital—computers, CAT scanners, and even shovels—will contribute little to output unless workers know how to use them. And when more workers gain skills or improve their existing skills, output rises just as it does when workers have more physical capital:

Human capital Skills and knowledge possessed by workers.

> *An increase in human capital works like an increase in physical capital to increase output: It causes the production function to shift upward, raises productivity, and increases the average standard of living.*

There is another similarity between human and physical capital: Both are *stocks* that are increased by *flows* of investment. The stock of human capital increases whenever investment in new skills during some period, through education and training, exceeds the depreciation of existing skills over the same period, through retirement, death, or disuse. Therefore, greater investment in human capital will speed the growth of the human capital stock, increasing the growth rate of productivity and living standards.

Human capital investments are made by business firms (when they help to train their employees), by government (through public education and subsidized training), and by households (when they pay for general education or professional training). Human capital investments have played an important role in recent U.S. economic growth. Can we do anything to increase our rate of investment in human capital?

In part, we've already answered this question: Some of the same policies that increase investment in *physical* capital also work to raise investment in human capital. For example, a decrease in the budget deficit would lower the interest rate and make it cheaper for households to borrow for college loans and training programs. A change in the tax system that increases the incentive to save would have the same impact, since this, too, would lower interest rates. And an easing of the tax burden on business firms could increase the profitability of *their* human capital investments, leading to more and better worker training programs.

College-level courses are one important way that countries increase the stock of human capital and shift up their production function.

---

[4] This World Bank study was cited in *The Economist,* June 10, 1995, p. 72.

But there is more: Human capital, unlike physical capital, cannot be separated from the person who provides it. If you own a building, you can rent it out to one firm and sell your labor to another. But if you have training as a doctor, your labor and your human capital must be sold together, as a package. Moreover, your wage or salary will be payment for both your labor and your human capital. This means that income tax reductions—which we discussed earlier as a means of increasing labor supply—can also increase the profitability of human capital to households, and increase their rate of investment in their own skills and training. For example, suppose an accountant is considering whether to attend a course in corporate financial reporting, which would increase her professional skills. The course costs \$4,000, and will increase the accountant's income by \$1,000 per year for the rest of her career. With a tax rate of 40 percent, her take-home pay would increase by \$600 per year, so her annual rate of return on her investment would be \$600/\$4,000 = 15 percent. But with a lower tax rate—say, 20 percent—her take-home pay would rise by \$800 per year, so her rate of return would be \$800/\$4,000 = 20 percent. The lower the tax rate, the greater is the rate of return on our accountant's human capital investment, and the more likely she will be to acquire new skills. Thus,

many of the pro-growth policies discussed earlier—policies that increase employment or increase investment in physical capital—are also effective in promoting investment in human capital.

TECHNOLOGICAL CHANGE

So far, we've discussed how economic growth arises from greater quantities of resources—more labor, more physical capital, or more human capital. But another important source of growth is **technological change**—the invention or discovery of new inputs, new outputs, or new methods of production. Indeed, it is largely because of technological change that Malthus's horrible prediction (cited at the beginning of this chapter) has not come true. In the last 60 years, for example, the inventions of synthetic fertilizers, hybrid corn, and chemical pesticides have enabled world food production to increase faster than population.

Technological change The invention or discovery of new inputs, new outputs, or new production methods.

New technology affects the economy in much the same way as do increases in the capital stock. Flip back to Figure 4 of this chapter. There, you saw that an increase in the capital stock would shift the production function upward and increase output. New technology, too, shifts the production function upward, since it enables any given number of workers to produce more output.

In many cases, the new technology requires the acquisition of physical and human capital before it can be used. For example, a new technique for destroying kidney stones with ultrasound, rather than time-consuming surgery, can make doctors more productive—but not until they spend several thousand dollars to buy the ultrasound machine and take a course on how to use it. Similarly, the recent development of the Internet has enabled many businesses—both big and small—to order supplies and market their products using less labor time and other resources than ever before. But they can't take advantage of this technology until they purchase computer equipment and their employees learn how to master the operation of both hardware and software.

In some instances, however, a new technology can be used without any additional equipment or training, as when a factory manager discovers a more efficient way to organize workers on the factory floor. In either case, technological change will shift the production function upward and increase productivity. It follows that

> *the faster the rate of technological change, the greater the growth rate of productivity, and the faster the rise in living standards.*

It might seem that technological change is one of those things that just happens. Thomas Edison invents electricity, or Steve Jobs and Steve Wozniak develop the first practical personal computer in their garage. But the pace of technological change is not as haphazard as it seems. The transistor was invented as part of a massive research and development effort by AT&T to improve the performance of communications electronics. Similarly, the next developments in computer technology, transportation, and more will depend on how much money is spent on research and development (R&D) by the leading technology firms:

> *The rate of technological change in the economy depends largely on firms' total spending on R&D. Policies that increase R&D spending will increase the pace of technological change.*

What can the government do to increase spending on R&D? First, it can increase its own direct support for R&D by carrying out more research in its own laboratories or increasing funding for universities and tax incentives to private research labs.

Patent protection A government grant of exclusive rights to use or sell a new technology.

Second, the government can enhance **patent protection,** which increases rewards for those who create new technology by giving them exclusive rights to use it or sell it. For example, when the DuPont Corporation discovered a unique way to manufacture Spandex, it obtained a patent to prevent other firms from copying its technique. This patent has enabled DuPont to earn millions of dollars from its invention. Without the patent, other firms would have copied the technique, competed with DuPont, and taken much of its profit away. Hundreds of thousands of new patents are issued every year in the United States: to pharmaceutical companies for new prescription drugs, to telecommunications companies for new cellular technologies, and to the producers of a variety of household goods ranging from can openers to microwave ovens.

Since patent protection increases the rewards that developers can expect from new inventions, it encourages them to spend more on R&D. By broadening patent protection—issuing patents on a wider variety of discoveries—or by lengthening patent protection—increasing the number of years during which the developer has exclusive rights to market the invention—the government could increase the expected profits from new technologies. That would increase total spending on R&D and increase the pace of technological change. Currently in the United States, patents give inventors and developers exclusive marketing rights over their products for a period of about 20 years. Increasing patent protection to 30 years would certainly increase R&D spending at many firms.

Finally, R&D spending is in many ways just like other types of investment spending: The funds are drawn from the loanable funds market, and R&D programs require firms to buy something now (laboratories, the services of research scientists, materials for prototypes) for the uncertain prospect of profits in the future. Therefore, almost any policy that stimulates investment spending in general will also increase spending on R&D. Cutting the tax rate on capital gains or on corporate profits, or lowering interest rates by encouraging greater saving or by reducing the budget deficit, can each help to increase spending on R&D and increase the rate of technological change.

GROWTH POLICIES: A SUMMARY

In this chapter, you've learned about the forces that affect the economy's economic growth, as well as a host of government policies that can speed the economy's growth rate. If you are having trouble keeping it all straight, Table 4—which summarizes all of this information—might help.

As you look at the table, you may notice something interesting: Some of the policies that work to *increase* economic growth through one channel can simultaneously work *against* growth through another channel. For example, in the first row of the table, you can see that a *decrease* in income tax rates contributes to growth by increasing employment. But farther down, you'll see that an *increase* in taxes can aid growth by shrinking a budget deficit (implying that a *decrease* in taxes would have the opposite effect and harm growth). Thus, a decrease in tax rates simultaneously helps growth through one channel and harms growth through another.

The fact that a single policy can have two competing effects on the economy helps us understand one reason for controversy in macroeconomic policy. When we cut income taxes, for example, the ultimate effect on economic growth will depend on which of the two effects is stronger, something over which economists can and do disagree. This is why the Bush tax cut in 2001 was seen by some observers as a growth-enhancing measure (those who stressed the impact on employment) and by others as harmful to economic growth (those who stressed the reduction in the budget surplus and the effects on interest rates and investment).

THE COSTS OF ECONOMIC GROWTH

So far in this chapter, we've discussed a variety of policies that could increase the rate of economic growth and speed the rise in living standards. Why don't all nations pursue these policies and push their rates of economic growth to the maximum? For example, why did the U.S. standard of living (output per capita) grow by 2.3 percent per year between 1995 and 2004? Why not 4 percent per year? Or 6 percent? Or even more?

In this section, you will see that policies to increase a nation's rate of economic growth involve trade-offs.

Promoting economic growth involves unavoidable trade-offs: It requires some groups, or the nation as a whole, to give up something else that is valued. In order to decide how fast we want our economy to grow, we must consider growth's costs as well as its benefits.

Economics is famous for making the public aware of policy trade-offs. One of the most important things you will learn in your introductory economics course is that

TABLE 4
Factors That Influence Growth in Output per Capita

Source of Growth	Method		Examples of Pro-Growth Government Policies
Increase in Labor Force Participation Rate	Rightward shift in labor supply curve		• Lower income tax rates • Less generous transfer payments
	Rightward shift in labor demand curve		• Subsidized college loans • Subsidized training for the unemployed • Programs that target specific types of workers (e.g., disabled, inner-city youth)
Growth in Physical Capital Stock (Productivity Growth)	Rightward shift in investment demand curve		• Investment tax credit • Lower corporate profits tax
	Lower interest rate . . .	via rightward shift in saving curve	• Tax incentives for saving • Changes in government transfer programs • Lower capital gains tax
		via decrease in budget deficit (or increase in budget surplus)	• Cuts in government purchases • Cuts in transfer payments • Tax increase
Growth in Human Capital Stock (Productivity Growth)	Lower interest rate . . .	(see above)	• Any policy (above) that lowers the interest rate
	Other methods to make human capital investment more attractive		• Lower income tax rates • Subsidized student loans • Tax incentives for investment in human capital
Technological Progress (Productivity Growth)	Lower interest rate . . .	(see above)	• Any policy (above) that lowers the interest rate
	Other methods to make investment in R & D more profitable		• Investment tax credit for R&D • Lower corporate profits tax • Expansion of patent protection

there are no costless solutions to society's problems. Just as individuals face an opportunity cost when they take an action (they must give up something else that they value), so, too, policy makers face an opportunity cost whenever they pursue a policy: They must compromise on achieving some other social goal.

What are the costs of growth?

Budgetary Costs

If you look again at Table 4, you'll see that many of the pro-growth policies we've analyzed involve some kind of tax cut. Cutting the income tax rate may increase the labor force participation rate. Cutting taxes on capital gains or corporate profits will increase investment directly. And cutting taxes on saving will increase household saving, lower interest rates, and thus increase investment spending indirectly. Unfortunately, implementing any of these tax cuts would force the government to choose among three unpleasant alternatives: increase some other tax to regain the lost revenue, cut government spending, or permit the budget deficit to rise.

Who will bear the burden of this budgetary cost? That depends on which alternative is chosen. Under the first option—increasing some other tax—the burden falls on those who pay the other tax. For example, if income taxes are cut, real estate taxes might be increased. A family might pay lower income taxes, but higher property taxes. Whether it comes out ahead or behind will depend on how much income the family earns relative to how much property it owns.

The second option, cutting government spending, imposes the burden on those who currently benefit from government programs. These include not only those who directly benefit from a program—like welfare recipients or farmers—but also those who benefit from government spending more indirectly. Even though you may earn your income in the private sector, if government spending is cut, you may suffer from a deterioration of public roads, decreased police protection, or poorer schools for your children.

The third option—a larger budget deficit or a smaller budget surplus—is more complicated. Suppose a tax cut causes the government to end up with a larger deficit. Then greater government borrowing will increase the total amount of government debt outstanding—called the national debt—and lead to greater interest payments to be made by future generations, in the form of higher taxes. The same is true even if the government is running a budget surplus. In that case, a tax cut will *reduce* the size of the surplus and reduce the amount of the national debt the government pays back each year. Once again, the tax cut raises the interest payments that future generations must bear.

But that is not all. From the previous chapter, we know that a rise in the budget deficit (by increasing the demand for funds) or a drop in the budget surplus (by decreasing the supply of funds) drives up the interest rate. The higher interest rate will reduce investment in physical capital by businesses, as well as investment in human capital by households, and both effects will work to decrease economic growth. It is even possible that so much private investment will be crowded out that the tax cut, originally designed to boost economic growth, ends up slowing growth instead. At best, the growth-enhancing effects of the tax cut will be weakened. This is why advocates of high growth rates usually propose one of the other options—a rise in some other tax or a cut in government spending—as part of a pro-growth tax cut.

In sum,

> *while properly targeted tax cuts can increase the rate of economic growth, they will force us to either redistribute the tax burden or cut government programs.*

Consumption Costs

Any pro-growth policy that works by increasing investment—in physical capital, human capital, or R&D—requires a sacrifice of current consumption spending. The land, labor, capital and entrepreneurship we use to produce new cloth-cutting machines, oil rigs, assembly lines, training facilities, college classrooms, or research laboratories could have been used instead to produce clothing, automobiles, video games, and other consumer goods. In other words, we face a trade-off: The more capital goods we produce in any given year, the fewer consumption goods we can enjoy in that year.

The role of this trade-off in economic growth can be clearly seen with a familiar tool from Chapter 2: the production possibilities frontier (PPF). Figure 8 shows the PPF for a nation with some given amount of land, labor, capital and entrepreneurship that must be allocated to the production of two types of output: capital goods and consumption goods. At point *K*, the nation is using all of its resources to produce capital goods and none to produce consumption goods. Point *C* represents the opposite extreme: all resources used to produce consumption goods and none for capital goods. Ordinarily, a nation will operate at an intermediate point such as *A*, where it is producing both capital and consumption goods.

Now, as long as capital production at point *A* is greater than the depreciation of existing capital, the capital stock will grow. In future periods, the economy—with more capital—can produce more output, as shown by the outward shift of the PPF in the figure. If a nation can produce more output, then it can produce more consumption goods for the same quantity of capital goods (moving from point *A* to point *B*) or more capital goods for the same quantity of consumption goods (from point *A* to point *D*) or more of both (from point *A* to point *E*).

Let's take a closer look at how this sacrifice of current consumption goods might come about. Suppose that some change in government policy—an investment tax credit or a lengthening of the patent period for new inventions—successfully shifts the investment curve to the right. (Go back to Figure 5.) What will happen? Businesses—desiring more funds for investment—will drive up the interest rate, and households all over the country will find that saving has become more attractive. As families increase their saving, we move rightward along the economy's supply of funds curve. In this way, firms get the funds they need to purchase new capital. But a decision to *save more* is also a decision to *spend less*. As current saving rises, current consumption spending necessarily falls. By driving up the interest rate, *the increase in investment spending causes a voluntary decrease in consumption spending by households.* Resources are freed from producing consumption goods and diverted to producing capital goods instead.

Although this decrease in consumption spending is voluntary, it is still a cost that we pay. And in some cases, a painful cost: Some of the increase in the household sector's net saving results from a decrease in borrowing by households that—at higher interest rates—can no longer afford to finance purchases of homes, cars, or furniture. In sum,

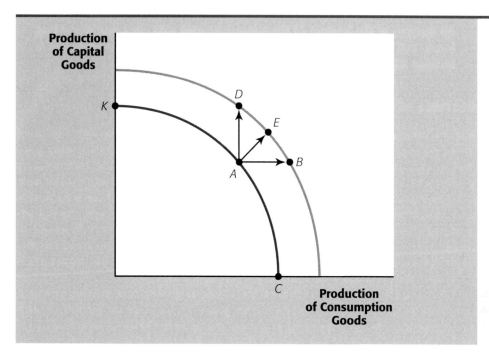

FIGURE 8

Consumption, Investment, and Economic Growth

In the current period, a nation can choose to produce only consumer goods (point C), or it can produce some capital goods by sacrificing some current consumption, as at point A. If investment at point A exceeds capital depreciation, the capital stock will grow, and the production possibilities frontier will shift outward. After it does, the nation can produce more consumption goods (point B), more capital goods (point D), or more of both (point E).

greater investment in physical capital, human capital, or R&D will lead to faster economic growth and higher living standards in the future, but we will have fewer consumer goods to enjoy in the present.

Opportunity Costs of Workers' Time

Living standards will also rise if a greater fraction of the population works or if those who already have jobs begin working longer hours. In either case, there will be more output to divide among the same population. But this increase in living standards comes at a cost: a decrease in time spent in nonmarket activities. For example, with a greater fraction of the population working, a smaller fraction is spending time at home. This might mean that more students have summer jobs, more elderly workers are postponing their retirement, or more previously nonworking spouses are entering the labor force. Similarly, an increase in average working hours would mean that the average worker will have less time for other activities— less time to watch television, read novels, garden, fix up the house, teach his or her children, or do volunteer work.

Thus, when economic growth comes about from increases in the labor force participation rate (or in average hours), we face a trade-off: On the one hand, we can enjoy higher incomes and more goods and services; on the other hand, we will have less time to do things other than work in the market. In a market economy, where choices are voluntary, the value of the income gained must be greater than the value of the time given up. No one forces a worker to reenter the labor force or to increase her working hours. Any worker who takes either of these actions must be better off for doing so. Still, we must recognize that *something* of value is always given up when employment increases:

An increase in the fraction of the population with jobs (or a rise in working hours) will increase output and raise living standards, but also requires us to sacrifice time previously spent in nonmarket activities.

Sacrifice of Other Social Goals

Rapid economic growth is an important social goal, but it's not the only one. Some of the policies that quicken the pace of growth require us to sacrifice other goals that we care about. For example, you've seen that restructuring and even reducing government transfer payments could increase saving, leading to more investment and faster growth. But such a move would cut the incomes of those who benefit from the current system and force some citizens into levels of poverty that society may find unacceptable. You've learned that extending patent protection would increase incentives for research and development. But it would also extend the monopoly power exercised by patent holders and force consumers to pay higher prices for drugs, electronic equipment, and even packaged foods.

Of course, the argument cuts both ways: Just as government policies to stimulate investment require us to sacrifice other goals, so, too, can the pursuit of other goals impede investment spending and economic growth. Most of us would like to see a cleaner environment and safer workplaces. But safety and environmental regulations have increased in severity, complexity, and cost over time, reducing the rate of profit on new capital and shrinking investment spending.

Does this mean that business taxes and government regulations should be reduced to the absolute minimum? Not at all. As in most matters of economic policy, we face a trade-off:

We can achieve greater worker safety, a cleaner environment, and other social goals, but we may have to sacrifice some economic growth along the way. Alternatively, we can achieve greater economic growth, but we will have to compromise on other things we care about.

When values differ, people will disagree on just how much we should sacrifice for economic growth or how much growth we should sacrifice for other goals.

© SUSAN VAN ETTEN

USING THE THEORY
Economic Growth in the Less-Developed Countries

In most countries, Malthus's dire predictions have not come true. One reason is that increases in the capital stock have raised productivity and increased the average standard of living. Increases in the capital stock are even more important in the less-developed countries (LDCs), which have relatively little capital to begin with. In these countries, even small increases in capital formation can have dramatic effects on living standards.

But how does a nation go about increasing its capital stock? As you've learned, there are a variety of measures, all designed to accomplish the same goal: shifting resources away from consumer-goods production toward capital-goods production. A very simple formula.

Country	Average Annual Growth Rate of Output per Capita	
	1975–2002	1990–2002
Bangladesh	1.9	3.1
Pakistan	2.6	1.1
Ghana	0.3	1.8
Benin	0.6	2.1
Kenya	0.3	−0.6
Haiti	−2.3	−3.0
Sierra Leone	−3.3	−5.9

TABLE 5
Economic Growth in Selected Poor Countries

Source: United Nations Development Programme, *Human Development Report 2004*, pp. 186–187.

Some countries that were once LDCs—like the four Asian tigers (Hong Kong, Singapore, South Korea, and Taiwan)—have applied the formula very effectively. Output per capita in these counties has grown by 5 or 6 percent per year over the past few decades. They were able to shift resources from consumption goods into capital goods in part by pursuing many of the growth-enhancing measures discussed in this chapter: large subsidies for human and physical capital investments, pro-growth tax cuts to encourage saving and investment, and the willingness to sacrifice other social goals—especially a clean environment—for growth.[5] These economies gave up large amounts of potential consumption during a period of intensive capital formation.

But other LDCs have had great difficulty raising living standards. Table 5 shows growth rates for several of them. In some cases—such as Pakistan, Bangladesh, and more recently, Ghana and Benin—slow but consistent growth has given cause for optimism. In other cases—such as Kenya—living standards have barely budged over the past few decades. In still other cases—for example, Haiti and Sierra Leone—output per capita has been falling ever more rapidly. Why do some LDCs have such difficulty achieving economic growth?

Much of the explanation for the low growth rates of many LDCs lies with three characteristics that they share:

1. *Very low current output per capita.* Living standards are so low in some LDCs that they cannot take advantage of the trade-off between producing consumption goods and producing capital goods. In these countries, pulling resources out of consumption would threaten the survival of many households. In the individual household, the problem is an inability to save: Incomes are so low that households must spend all they earn on consumption.

2. *High population growth rates.* Low living standards and high population growth rates are linked together in a cruel circle of logic. On the one hand, rapid population growth by itself tends to reduce living standards; on the other hand, a low standard of living tends to increase population growth. Why? First, the poor are often uneducated in matters of family planning. Second, high

[5] The Asian tigers also had some special advantages—such as a high level of human capital to start with.

mortality rates among infants and children encourage families to have many off-spring, to ensure the survival of at least a few to care for parents in their old age. As a result, while the average woman in the United States will have fewer than two children in her lifetime, the average woman in Haiti will have about five children, and the average woman in Rwanda will have more than six.

3. *Poor infrastructure.* Political instability, poor law enforcement, corruption, and adverse government regulations make many LDCs unprofitable places to invest. Low rates of investment mean a smaller capital stock and lower productivity. Infrastructure problems also harm worker productivity in another way: Citizens must spend time guarding against thievery and trying to induce the government to let them operate businesses—time they could otherwise spend producing output.

These three characteristics—low current production, high population growth, and poor infrastructure—interact to create a vicious circle of continuing poverty, which we can understand with the help of the familiar PPF between capital goods and consumption goods. Look back at Figure 8, and now imagine that it applies to a poor, developing country. In this case, an outward shift of the PPF does not, in itself, guarantee an increase in the standard of living. In the LDCs, the population growth rate is often very high, and employment grows at the same rate as the population. If employment grows more rapidly than the capital stock, then even though the PPF is shifting outward, capital per worker will decline. Unless some other factor—such as technological change—is raising productivity, then living standards will fall.

> *In order to have rising capital per worker—an important source of growth in productivity and living standards—a nation's stock of capital must not only grow, but grow faster than its population.*

Point N in Figure 9 shows the minimum amount of investment needed to increase capital per worker, labor productivity, and living standards for a given rate of population growth. For example, if the population is growing at 4 percent per year, then point N indicates the investment needed to increase the total capital stock by 4 percent per year. If investment is just equal to N, then capital per worker—and living standards—remains constant. If investment exceeds N, then capital per worker—and living standards—will rise. Of course, the greater the growth in population, the higher point N will be on the vertical axis, since greater investment will be needed just to keep up with population growth. (We assume throughout this discussion that the labor force and employment are both rising at the same rate as the population.)

The PPF in Figure 9 has an added feature: Point S shows the minimum acceptable level of consumption, the amount of consumer goods the economy *must* produce in a year. For example, S might represent the consumption goods needed to prevent starvation among the least well off, or to prevent unacceptable social consequences, such as violent revolution.

Now we can see the problem faced by the most desperate of the less-developed economies. Output is currently at a point like H in Figure 9, with investment just equal to N. The capital stock is not growing fast enough to increase capital per worker, and so labor productivity and living standards are stagnant. In this situation, the PPF shifts outward each year, but not quickly enough to improve people's lives. It could be even worse: Convince yourself that, at a point like R, the average standard of living declines even though the capital stock is growing—that is, even though the PPF will shift outward in future periods.

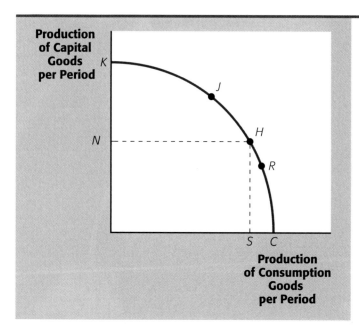

Production of Capital Goods per Period

Production of Consumption Goods per Period

FIGURE 9
LDC Growth and Living Standards

In order to increase capital per worker when population is growing, yearly investment spending must exceed some minimum level N. In any year, there is a minimum level of consumption, S, needed to support the population. If output is currently at point H, capital per worker and living standards are stagnant. But movement to a point like J would require an unacceptably low level of consumption.

The solution to this problem appears to be an increase in capital production beyond point *N*—a movement *along* the PPF from point *H* to a point such as *J*. As investment rises above *N*, capital per worker rises, and the PPF shifts outward rapidly enough over time to raise living standards. In a wealthy country, like the United States, such a move could be engineered by changes in taxes or other government policies. But in the LDCs depicted here, such a move would be intolerable: At point *H*, consumption is already equal to *S*, the lowest acceptable level. Moving to point *J* would require reducing consumption *below S*.

> *The poorest LDCs are too poor to take advantage of the trade-off between consumption and capital production in order to increase their living standards. Since they cannot reduce consumption below current levels, they cannot produce enough capital to keep up with their rising populations*

In recent history, countries have attempted several methods to break out of this vicious circle of poverty. During the 1930s, the dictator Joseph Stalin simply *forced* the Soviet economy from a point like *H* to one like *J*. His goal was to shift the Soviet Union's PPF outward as rapidly as possible. But, as you can see, this reduced consumption below the minimum level *S*, and Stalin resorted to brutal measures to enforce his will. Many farmers were ordered into the city to produce capital equipment. With fewer people working on farms, agricultural production declined and there was not enough food to go around. Stalin's solution was to confiscate food from the remaining farmers and give it to the urban workforce. Of course, this meant starvation for millions of farmers. Millions more who complained too loudly, or who otherwise represented a political threat, were rounded up and executed.

A less-brutal solution to the problem of the LDCs is to make the wealthy bear more of the burden of increasing growth. If the decrease in consumption can be limited to the rich, then *total* consumption can be significantly reduced—freeing up resources for investment—without threatening the survival of the poor. This, however, is not often practical, since the wealthy have the most influence with government in

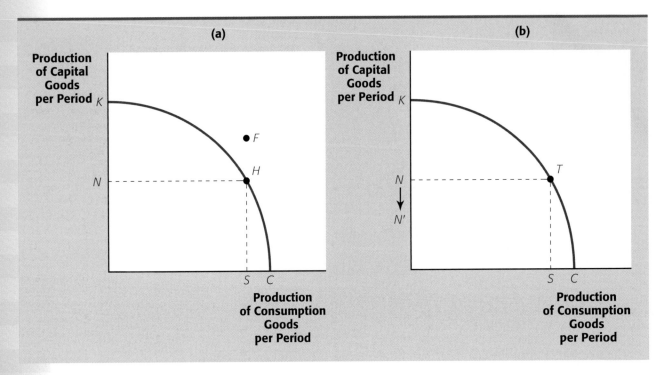

FIGURE 10
Growth Options for LDCs

Panel (a) shows an LDC producing at point H, where the available consumption goods are just sufficient to meet minimum standards (point S). If the nation can obtain goods externally, through foreign investment or foreign assistance, it can make use of capital and consumption goods at a point like F—outside of its PPF.

Panel (b) shows a case where capital production at point T is just sufficient to keep up with a rising population, but not great enough to raise capital per worker and living standards. If this nation can reduce its population growth rate, then the same rate of capital production will increase capital per worker and raise the standard of living.

LDCs. Being more mobile, they can easily relocate to other countries, taking their savings with them. This is why efforts to shift the sacrifice to the wealthy are often combined with restrictions on personal liberties, such as the freedom to travel or to invest abroad. These moves often backfire in the long run, since restrictions on personal and economic freedom are remembered long after they are removed and make the public—especially foreigners—hesitant to invest in that country.

A third alternative—and the one used increasingly since the 1940s—is *foreign investment* or *foreign assistance*. If the wealthier nations—individually or through international organizations such as the World Bank or the International Monetary Fund—provide the LDCs with capital, then the capital *available* to them can increase, with *no* cutbacks in consumption. This permits an LDC to *acquire* capital goods at a point like F in Figure 10(a), even though its *production* remains—for the moment—at point *H.*

A variation on this strategy is for foreign nations to provide consumer goods so that the poorer nation can shift its *own* resources out of producing them (and into capital production) without causing consumption levels to fall. Once again, if capital production exceeds point N during the year, capital per worker will grow, setting the stage for continual growth to higher standards of living.

Finally, there is a fourth alternative. Consider a nation producing at point *T* in Figure 10(b). Capital production is just sufficient to keep up with a rising population, so the PPF shifts outward each year, but not rapidly enough to raise living standards. If this nation can reduce its population growth rate, however, then less capital production will be needed just to keep up with population growth. In the figure, point N will move downward to N'. If production remains at point *T,* the PPF will continue to shift outward as before, but now—with slower population growth—productivity and living standards will rise. Slowing the growth in population has been an important (and successful) part of China's growth strategy, although it has required severe restrictions on the rights of individual families to have children. Policy trade-offs, once again.

Summary

The growth rate of real GDP is a key determinant of economic well-being. If output grows faster than the population, then output per person—and the average standard of living—will rise. But in order for output per person to rise, either average working hours, the labor force participation rate (LFPR), or productivity must increase. In developed countries, average hours have been decreasing and are unlikely to rise in the near future. Therefore, higher living standards can be attributed entirely to the last two factors—higher LFPR and higher productivity.

In order for the LFPR to rise, the labor force (and therefore, employment) must grow faster than the population. Employment growth arises from an increase in either labor supply or labor demand. Government tax and transfer policies can influence labor supply, and government subsidy and training programs can influence labor demand.

Productivity increases when capital per worker rises or there are advances in technology. When the flow of investment spending is greater than the flow of depreciation over some period of time, the capital stock will rise. An increase in the capital stock shifts the production upward, enabling any given number of workers to produce more output. If the capital stock rises at a faster rate than the labor force, then capital per worker rises, and so does productivity.

Investment can be encouraged by government policies. If the government reduces its budget deficit, the demand for loanable funds will fall, the interest rate will decline, and investment will increase. Investment can also be stimulated directly through reductions in the corporate profits tax or through subsidies to new capital. Finally, policies that encourage household saving can also lower the interest rate and contribute to capital formation.

Technological change—the application of new inputs or new methods of production—also raises productivity. The rate of technological change depends on spending on research and development, either by government or private firms. Almost any government policy that increases investment spending in general will also increase spending on research and development, and therefore increase the pace of technological change. In addition, patent protection can specifically influence research and development on new, patentable products and technologies.

Economic growth is not costless. Tax cuts that stimulate employment, capital formation, or technological progress require increases in other taxes, cuts in spending programs, or an increase in the national debt. Any increase in employment from a given population requires a sacrifice of leisure time and other nonmarket activities. More broadly, any increase in investment requires the sacrifice of consumption today.

Key Terms

Average standard of living
Capital gains tax
Capital per worker
Consumption tax
Corporate profits tax

Flow variable
Human capital
Investment tax credit
Labor force participation rate (LFPR)
Labor productivity

Patent protection
Stock variable
Technological change

Review Questions

Answers to even-numbered Questions and Problems can be found on the text Web site at http://hall-lieb.swlearning.com.

1. How do we calculate the average standard of living? Why should economic policy makers be concerned about economic growth?

2. Discuss the three major ways a country can increase its equilibrium level of output.

3. Why can population growth be a mixed blessing in terms of economic growth?

4. Explain how a tax cut could lead to *slower* economic growth.

5. If a country's PPF is shifting outward, is it necessarily the case that the country's standard of living is rising? Why or why not?

6. Why did Malthus's dire prediction fail to materialize? Do you think it could still come true? Explain your reasoning.

7. "Faster economic growth can benefit everyone and need not harm anyone. That is, there is no policy trade-off when it comes to economic growth." True or false? Explain.

8. Explain the following statement: "In some LDCs, it can be said that a significant cause of continued poverty is poverty itself."

9. Compare the effects on the real wage rate and output from an increase in labor demand and an increase in labor supply.

10. Describe four ways in which LDCs might improve their growth performance. Discuss the opportunity cost that must be borne in each case and identify the group that is most likely to bear it.

Problems and Exercises

1. Discuss the effect (holding everything else constant) each of the following would have on full-employment output, productivity, and the average standard of living. Use the appropriate graphs (e.g., labor market, loanable funds market, production function), and state your assumptions when necessary.
   a. Increased immigration
   b. An aging of the population with an increasing proportion of retirees
   c. A baby boom
   d. A decline in the tax rate on corporate profits
   e. Reduction of unemployment compensation benefits
   f. Expanding the scope of the federal student loan program
   g. Easier access to technical information on the Internet

2. Below are GDP and growth data for the United States and four other countries:

	1950 per Capita GDP (in Constant Dollars)	1990 per Capita GDP (in Constant Dollars)	Average Yearly Growth Rate
United States	$9,573	$21,558	2.0%
France	$5,221	$17,959	3.0%
Japan	$1,873	$19,425	5.7%
Kenya	$ 609	$ 1,055	1.3%
India	$ 597	$ 1,348	2.0%

Source: Angus Maddison, *Monitoring the World Economy, 1820–1992.* Paris, OECD, 1995.

   a. For both years, calculate each country's per capita GDP as a percentage of U.S. per capita GDP. Which countries appeared to be catching up to the United States, and which were lagging behind?
   b. If all these countries had continued to grow (from 1990 onward) at the average growth rates given, in what year would France have caught up to the United States? In what years (respectively) would India and Kenya have caught up to the United States?

3. Below are hypothetical data for the country of Barrovia:

	Population (Millions)	Employment (Millions)	Labor Productivity (Output per-Worker per-Year)	Total Yearly Output
1997	100	50	$ 9,500	____
1998	104	51	$ 9,500	____
1999	107	53	$ 9,750	____
2000	108	57	$ 9,750	____
2001	110	57	$10,000	____

   a. Fill in the entries for total output in each of the five years.

   b. Calculate the following for each year (except 1997):
      (1) Population growth rate (from previous year)
      (2) Growth rate of output (from previous year)
      (3) Growth rate of per capita output (from previous year)

4. In addition to shifting the production function upward, an increase in the capital stock will ordinarily make workers more productive and shift the labor demand curve rightward. Graphically illustrate the full impact of an increase in the nation's capital stock under this assumption.

5. Show what would happen to the production function if the capital stock decreased. Suppose, too, that the decrease in the capital stock—because it made workers less productive to firms—shifted the labor demand curve leftward. Graphically illustrate the full impact of a decrease in the nation's capital stock under this assumption. What government policies could cause a decrease in the capital stock?

6. State whether each of the following statements is true or false, and explain your reasoning briefly.
   a. "A permanent increase in employment from a lower to a higher level will cause an increase in real GDP, but not continued growth in real GDP."
   b. "A permanent increase in the nation's capital stock to a new, higher level will cause an increase in real GDP, but not continued growth in real GDP."
   c. "With constant population, work hours, and technology, as long as planned investment spending continues to be greater than depreciation, real GDP will continue to grow year after year."
   d. "All else equal, a permanent increase in an economy's rate of planned investment spending will cause real GDP to grow faster each year than it would at the old, lower level of investment spending."

7. On a diagram, draw an economy's production function. On the same diagram, add curves to illustrate where the production function would be in five years under each of the following assumptions. (Label your additional curves a, b, and c, and assume nothing else affecting economic growth changes.)
   a. Planned investment remains constant at its current level, which exceeds depreciation.
   b. Planned investment remains constant at its current level, which is less than depreciation.
   c. Planned investment rises above its current level, which exceeds depreciation.

8. Complete the following table, then find the growth rate of output from Year 1 to Year 2, from Year 2 to Year 3, and from Year 3 to Year 4, in terms of the percentage change in each of its components.

	Year 1	Year 2	Year 3	Year 4
Total hours worked	192 million	200 million	285 million	368 million
Labor force	1,200,000	1,400,000	1,900,000	2,100,000
Population	2,000,000	2,500,000	2,900,000	3,200,000
Productivity	$50 per hour	$52.50 per hour	$58 per hour	$60 per hour
Average hours per worker				
LFPR				
Total output				

9. Figure 1 in the chapter shows the effects of an increase in labor supply. Redraw both panels and show the effects of (a) an increase in labor demand, (b) a decrease in labor supply and (c) a decrease in labor demand.

10. Redraw Figure 10 from the chapter, and add the new PPF that the country would face in year 2 for each of the following scenarios: (i) the economy produces at point *J* in year 1, (ii) the economy produces at point *H* in year 1.

Challenge Questions

1. Economist Amartya Sen has argued that famines in underdeveloped countries are not simply the result of crop failures or natural disasters. Instead, he suggests that wars, especially civil wars, are linked to most famine episodes in recent history. Using a framework similar to Figure 10, discuss the probable effect of war on a country's PPF. Explain what would happen if the country were initially operating at or near a point like *S*, the minimum acceptable level of consumption.

2. All else equal, why might someone prefer to invest in physical capital in a less-developed country with a small capital stock than in a more-developed country that already has much capital? When wealth holders look for a place to invest and compare prospects in these two types of countries, is all else (other than existing capital stock) really equal? Explain.

 These exercises require access to Hall/Lieberman Xtra! If Xtra! did not come with your book, visit *http://hallxtra.swlearning.com* to purchase.

1. Use your Xtra! password at the Hall and Lieberman Web site (http://hallxtra.swlearning.com), select this chapter, and under Economic Applications, click on EconDebate. Choose *Productivity Growth* and scroll down to find the debate, "Is There a New Economy?" Read the debate, and use the information to answer the following questions.
   a. List and explain the contributing factors to the GDP growth, outlined in this chapter, during the 1980s and 1990s according to the economists who argue in favor of the existence of a "new economy" and those who question it.
   b. Which of the contributing factors, listed in this chapter, are responsible for GDP growth in the manufacturing and agricultural industries? Explain.

2. Use your Xtra! password at the Hall and Lieberman Web site (http://hallxtra.swlearning.com), select this chapter, and under Economic Applications, click on EconData. Choose *Macroeconomics: Employment, Unemployment, and Inflation* and scroll down to find *Labor Productivity*. Read the definition and click on Diagrams/Data for information to answer the following questions.
   a. Do the diagrams confirm the existence of a "new economy"?
   b. Does the relationship between the labor productivity and real compensation per hour indicate a rising living standard for workers? Explain.

Economic Fluctuations

CHAPTER OUTLINE

Can the Classical Model Explain Economic Fluctuations?
Shifts in Labor Demand
Shifts in Labor Supply
Verdict: The Classical Model Cannot Explain Economic
Fluctuations

What Triggers Economic Fluctuations?
A Very Simple Economy
The Real-World Economy
Shocks That Push the Economy Away from Equilibrium

Where Do We Go from Here?

If you are like most college students, you will be looking for a job when you graduate, or you will already have one and want to keep it for a while. In either case, your fate is not entirely in your own hands. Your job prospects will depend, at least in part, on the overall level of economic activity in the country.

If the classical model of the previous two chapters described the economy at every point in time, you'd have nothing to worry about. Full employment would be achieved automatically, so you could be confident of getting a job at the going wage for someone with your skills and characteristics. Unfortunately, this is not always how the world works: Neither output nor employment grows as smoothly and steadily as the classical model predicts. Instead, as far back as we have data, the United States and similar countries have experienced *economic fluctuations*.

Look at panel (a) of Figure 1, which you've seen before in this book. The orange line shows estimated full-employment or potential output since 1960—the level of real GDP predicted by the classical model. As a result of economic growth, full-employment output rises steadily.

But now look at the green line, which shows *actual* output. You can see that actual GDP fluctuates above and below the classical model's predictions. During *recessions*, which are shaded in the figure, output declines, occasionally sharply. During *expansions* (the unshaded periods) output rises quickly, usually faster than potential output is rising. Indeed, in the later stages of an expansion, output often *exceeds* potential output—a situation that economists call a **boom**.

Boom A period of time during which real GDP is above potential GDP.

Panel (b) shows another characteristic of expansions and recessions: fluctuations in employment. During expansions, such as the period from 1983 to 1990, employment grows rapidly. During recessions (shaded), such as 1990–91, employment declines.

Figure 1 shows us that employment and output move very closely together. But the figure doesn't tell us anything about the *causal* relationship between them.

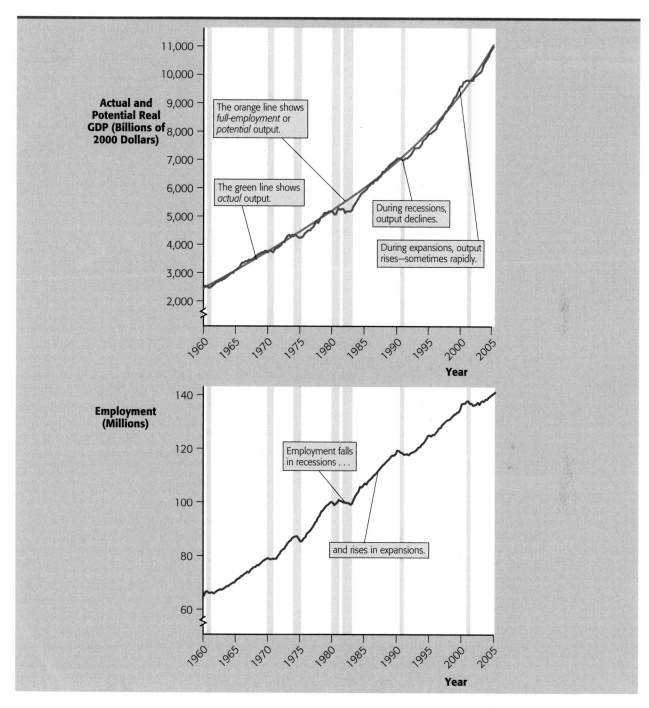

Actual and Potential Real GDP (Billions of 2000 Dollars)

The orange line shows *full-employment* or *potential* output.

The green line shows *actual* output.

During recessions, output declines.

During expansions, output rises—sometimes rapidly.

Year

Employment (Millions)

Employment falls in recessions . . .

and rises in expansions.

Year

FIGURE 1

Potential and Actual Real GDP and Employment, quarterly, 1960–2005

However, as you'll see in this chapter, we have good reason to conclude that over the business cycle, it is changes in output that cause firms to change their employment levels. For example, in a recession, many business firms lay off workers. If asked why, they would answer that they are reducing employment *because* they are producing less output.

FIGURE 2
U.S. Unemployment Rate,
quarterly, 1960–2005

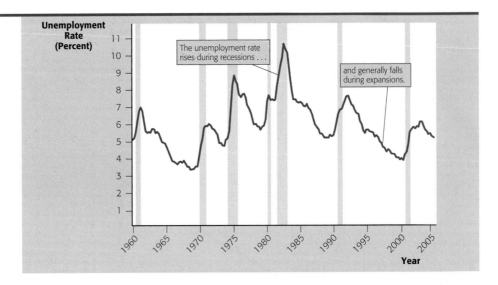

Finally, look at Figure 2, which presents the unemployment rate over the same period as in Figure 1. Figure 2 shows a critical aspect of fluctuations—the bulge of unemployment that occurs during each recession. When GDP falls, the unemployment rate increases. In the last few decades, the worst bulge in unemployment occured in 1982, when more than 10 percent of the labor force was looking for work. In expansions, on the other hand, the unemployment rate falls. In our most recent expansion, which began in March 1991 and ended in March 2001, unemployment dropped to 4 percent. In some expansions, the unemployment rate can drop even lower than the full-employment level. In the sustained expansion of the late 1960s, for example, it reached a low of just over 3 percent. At the same time, output exceeded its potential, as you can verify in Figure 1.

Figure 1 also shows something else: Expansions and recessions don't last forever. Indeed, sometimes they are rather brief. The recession of 1990–91, for example, ended within a year. And the recession that began in March 2001 officially ended in November of that year.

But if you look carefully at the figure, you'll see that the back-to-back recessions of the early 1980s extended over three full years. And during the Great Depression of the 1930s (not shown), it took more than a decade for the economy to return to full employment. Expansions too can last for extended periods. The expansion of the 1980s lasted about seven years, from 1983 to 1990. And the expansion that began in March 1991 turned out to be the longest expansion in U.S. economic history—a duration of 10 years.

The next several chapters deal with economic fluctuations. We have three things to explain: (1) *why* they occur in the first place, (2) why they sometimes last so long, and (3) why they do not last forever. But our first step is to see whether the macroeconomic model you've already studied—the classical, long-run model—can explain why economic fluctuations occur.

CAN THE CLASSICAL MODEL EXPLAIN ECONOMIC FLUCTUATIONS?

The classical model does a good job of explaining why the economy tends to operate near its potential output level, on average, over long periods of time. But can it help

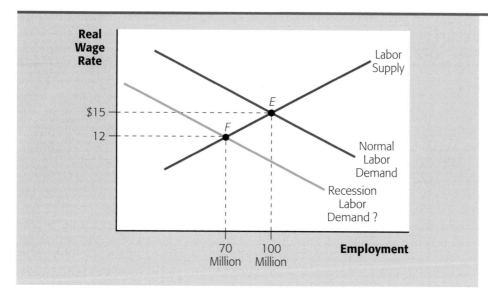

FIGURE 3

A Recession Caused by Declining Labor Demand?

In theory, a recession could be caused by a sudden leftward shift in the labor demand curve, causing employment to fall. In fact, large, sudden shifts in labor demand are an unlikely explanation for real-world fluctuations.

us understand the facts of economic fluctuations, as shown in Figures 1 and 2? More specifically, can the classical model explain why GDP and employment typically fall *below* potential during a recession and often rise above it in an expansion? Let's see.

Shifts in Labor Demand

One idea, studied by a number of economists, is that a recession might be caused by a leftward shift of the labor demand curve. This possibility is illustrated in Figure 3, in which a leftward shift in the labor demand curve would move us down and to the left along the labor supply curve. In the diagram, the labor market equilibrium would move from point *E* to point *F*, employment would fall and so would the real wage rate. Is this a reasonable explanation for recessions? Most economists feel that the answer is no, and for a very good reason.

The labor demand curve tells us the number of workers the nation's firms want to employ at each real wage rate. A leftward shift of this curve would mean that firms want to hire *fewer* workers at any given wage than they wanted to hire before. What could make them come to such a decision? One possibility is that firms are suddenly unable to sell all the output they produce. Therefore, the story would go, they must cut back production and hire fewer workers at any wage.

But as you've learned, in the classical model, total spending is *never* deficient. On the contrary, from the classical viewpoint, total spending is automatically equal to whatever level of output firms decide to produce. As you learned two chapters ago when we analyzed fiscal policy, a decrease in spending by one sector of the economy (such as the government) would cause an equal *increase* in spending by other sectors, with no change in total spending. While it is true that a decrease in output would cause total spending to decrease along with it (because Say's law tells us total spending is always equal to total output), the causation cannot go the other way in the classical model. In that model, changes in total spending cannot arise on their own. Therefore, if we want to explain a leftward shift in the labor demand curve using the classical model, we must look for some explanation other than a sudden change in spending.

Another possibility is that the labor demand curve shifts leftward because workers have become less *productive* and therefore less valuable to firms. This might happen if there were a sudden decrease in the capital stock, so that each worker had less equipment to work with. Or it might happen if workers suddenly forgot how to do things—how to operate a computer or use a screwdriver or fix an oil rig. Short of a major war that destroys plant and equipment, or an epidemic of amnesia, it is highly unlikely that workers would become less productive so suddenly. Thus, a leftward shift of the labor demand curve is an unlikely explanation for recessions.

What about booms? Could a *rightward* shift of the labor demand curve (not shown in Figure 3) explain them? Once again, a change in total spending cannot be the answer. In the classical model, as discussed a few paragraphs ago, changes in spending are caused by changes in employment and output, not the other way around. Nor can we explain a boom by arguing that workers have suddenly become more productive. While it is true that the capital stock grows over time and workers continually gain new skills—and that both of these movements shift the labor demand curve to the right—such shifts take place at a glacial pace. Compared to the amount of machinery already in place, and to the knowledge and skills that the labor force already has, annual increments in physical capital or knowledge are simply too small to have much of an impact on labor demand. Thus, a sudden rightward shift of the labor demand curve is an unlikely explanation for an expansion that pushes us beyond potential output.

> *Because shifts in the labor demand curve are not very large from year to year, the classical model cannot explain real-world economic fluctuations through shifts in labor demand.*

Shifts in Labor Supply

A second way the classical model might explain a recession is through a shift in the labor supply curve. Figure 4 shows how this would work. If the labor supply curve shifted to the left, the equilibrium would move up and to the left along the labor demand curve, from point E to point G. The level of employment would fall, and output would fall with it.

This explanation of recessions has almost no support among economists. First, remember that the labor supply schedule tells us, at each real wage rate, the number of people who *would like to* work. This number reflects millions of families' preferences about working in the market rather than pursuing other activities, such as taking care of children, going to school, or enjoying leisure time. A leftward shift in labor supply would mean that fewer people want to work at any given wage—that preferences have changed toward these other, nonwork activities. But in reality, preferences tend to change very slowly, and certainly not rapidly enough to explain recessions.

Second, even if such a shift in preferences did occur, it could not explain the facts of real-world downturns. Recessions are times when unusually large numbers of people are looking for work (see Figure 2). It would be hard to square that fact with a shift in preferences away from working.

The same arguments could be made about expansions: To explain them with labor supply shifts, we would have to believe that preferences suddenly change *toward* market work and away from other activities—an unlikely occurrence. And, in

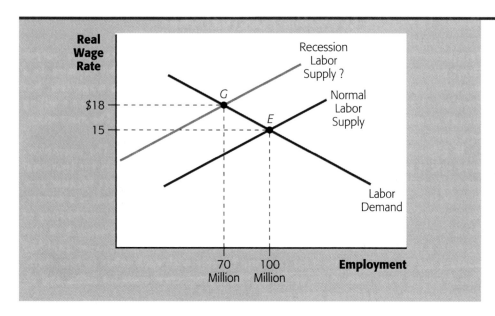

FIGURE 4
**A Recession Caused by
Declining Labor Supply?**

*In theory, a recession could be
caused by a sudden leftward
shift in the labor supply curve,
causing employment to fall. In
fact, shifts in labor supply occur
very slowly, so they cannot explain economic fluctuations.*

any case, expansions are periods when the unemployment rate typically falls to unusually low levels; *fewer*—not more—people are seeking work.

*Because sudden shifts of the labor supply curve are unlikely to occur, and
because they could not accurately describe the facts of the economic cycle,
the classical model cannot explain fluctuations through shifts in the supply
of labor.*

Verdict: The Classical Model Cannot Explain Economic Fluctuations

In earlier chapters, we stressed that the classical model works well in explaining the
movements of the economy in the longer run. Now we see that it does a rather poor
job of explaining the economy in the short run. Why is this? Largely because
the classical model involves assumptions about the economy that make sense in the
longer run, but not in the short run. Chief among these is the assumption that
the labor market clears—that is, that the labor market operates at the point of intersection of the labor supply and labor demand curves. As long as this assumption
holds, a boom or recession would have to arise from a sudden, significant *movement* in that intersection point, caused by a sudden and significant *shift* in either the
labor demand curve or the labor supply curve.

But now, we've seen that such sudden shifts are very unlikely. Moreover, even if
they did occur, they could not explain the changes in job-seeking activity that we
observe in real-world recessions. And this, in a nutshell, is why we must reject the
classical model when we turn our attention to the short run.

*We cannot explain the facts of short-run economic fluctuations with a
model in which the labor market always clears. This is why the classical
model, which assumes that the market always clears, does a poor job of explaining the economy in the short run.*

WHAT TRIGGERS ECONOMIC FLUCTUATIONS?

Recessions that bring output below potential and expansions that drive output above potential are periods during which the economy is going a bit haywire. In a recession, millions of qualified people *want* to work at the going wage rate, but firms won't hire them. Managers would *like* to hire them, but they aren't selling enough output—in part because so many people are unemployed. The macroeconomy seems to be preventing an opportunity for mutual gain.

In a boom, the economy is going haywire in a different way. The unemployment rate is so low the normal job-search activity—which accounts for frictional unemployment—is short-circuited. Firms, desperate to hire workers because production is so high, are less careful about whom they hire. The result is a poorer-than-normal match between workers and their jobs. Moreover, the overheating of the economy that occurs in a boom can lead to inflation. We'll discuss how this happens a few chapters from now. But the basic outline is this: Because qualified workers are so scarce, firms must compete fiercely with each other to hire them. This drives up wage rates in the economy, raises production costs for firms, and ultimately causes firms to raise their prices.

Booms and recessions are periods during which the economy deviates from the normal, full-employment equilibrium of the classical model. The question is, why do such deviations occur? Let's start to answer this question by looking at a world that is much simpler than our own.

A Very Simple Economy

Imagine an economy with just two people: Yasmin and Pepe. Yasmin is especially good at making popcorn, but she eats only yogurt. Pepe, by contrast, is very good at making yogurt, but eats only popcorn. If things are going well, Yasmin and Pepe will make suitable amounts of popcorn and yogurt and trade with each other. Because of the gains from specialization, their trade will make them both better off than if they tried to function without trading. And under ordinary circumstances, Yasmin and Pepe will take advantage of all mutually beneficial opportunities for trading. Our two-person economy will thus operate at full employment, since both individuals will be fully engaged in making products for the other. You can think of their trading equilibrium as being like the labor market equilibrium in the classical model.

Now, suppose there is a breakdown in communication. For example, Yasmin may get the impression that Pepe is not going to want as much popcorn as before. She would then decide to *make* less popcorn for Pepe. At their next trading session, Pepe will be offered less popcorn, so he will decide to produce less yogurt. The result: Total production in the economy declines, and our two traders will lose some of the benefits of trading. This corresponds to a recession.

Alternatively, suppose Yasmin thinks that Pepe will want *more* popcorn than before. This might lead her to *increase* her production, working more than she normally prefers to work so she can get more yogurt from Pepe before his demand for popcorn returns to normal. Yasmin's production of popcorn—and therefore, total output in the economy—rises even if Yasmin's expectations turn out to be wrong and Pepe does *not* want more popcorn. Temporarily, we are in a boom.

In reading the previous paragraph, you might be thinking, "Wait a minute. If either Yasmin or Pepe got the impression that the other might want less or more of the other's product, wouldn't a simple conversation between them straighten things out?" If these are your thoughts, you are absolutely right. A breakdown in communication and a sudden change in production would be extremely unlikely . . . *in a simple economy with just two people*. And therein lies the problem: The real-world economy is much more complex than the world of Yasmin and Pepe.

The Real-World Economy

Think about the U.S. economy, with its millions of businesses producing goods and services for hundreds of millions of people. In many cases, production must be planned long before goods are actually sold. For example, from inception to final production, it takes nearly a year to build a house and two years to develop a new automobile model or produce a Hollywood film. If one firm—say, General Motors—believes that consumers will buy fewer of its cars next year, it cannot simply call a meeting of all potential customers and find out whether its fears are justified. Nor can it convince people, as Yasmin can convince Pepe, that their own jobs depend on their buying a GM car. Most potential car buyers do *not* work for General Motors and don't perceive any connection between buying a car and keeping their own jobs. Under the circumstances, it may be entirely logical for General Motors to plan for a lower production level and lay off some of its workers.

Of course, this would not be the end of the story. By decreasing its workforce, GM would create further problems for the economy. The workers it has laid off, who will earn less income or none at all, will cut back on *their* spending for a variety of consumer goods—restaurant meals, movies, vacation travel—and they will certainly postpone any large purchases they'd been planning, such as a new large-screen television or that family trip to Disney World. This will cause other firms—the firms producing these consumer goods and services—to cut back on *their* production, laying off *their* workers, and so on. In other words, what began as a perceived decrease in spending in one sector of the economy can work its way through other sectors, causing a full-blown recession.

This example illustrates a theme that we will revisit in the next chapter: the interdependence between production and income. When people spend their incomes, they give firms the revenue they need to hire workers and pay them income! If any link in this chain is broken, output and income may both decline. In our example, the link was broken because of incorrect expectations by firms in one sector of the economy. But there are other causes of recessions as well, also centering on the interdependence between production and income, and a failure to coordinate the decisions of millions of firms and households.

The classical model, however, waves these potential problems aside. It assumes that workers and firms, with the aid of markets, can work things out—like Yasmin and Pepe—and enjoy the benefits of producing and trading. And the classical model is right: People *will* work things out . . . eventually. But in the short run, we need to look carefully at the problems of coordinating production, trade, and consumption in an economy with millions of people and businesses.

A boom can arise in much the same way as a recession. It might start because of an increase in production in one sector of the economy, say, the housing sector. With more production and more workers earning higher incomes, spending increases in other sectors as well, until output rises above the classical, full-employment level.

Shocks That Push the Economy Away from Equilibrium

Spending shock A change in spending that ultimately affects the entire economy.

In our discussion above, General Motors decided to cut back on its production of cars because its managers believed, rightly or wrongly, that the demand for GM cars had decreased. Often, many firms will face a real or predicted drop in spending at the same time. We call this a **spending shock** to the economy—a change in spending that initially affects one or more sectors and ultimately works its way through the entire economy.

In the real world, the economy is constantly buffeted by shocks, and they often cause full-fledged macroeconomic fluctuations. Table 1 lists some of the recessions and notable expansions of the last 50 years, along with the events and spending shocks that are thought to have caused them or at least contributed heavily. You can see that each of these shocks first affected spending and output in one or more sectors of the economy. For example, several recessions have been set off by increases in oil prices, which caused a decrease in spending on products that depend on oil and energy, such as automobiles, trucks, and new factory buildings. Other recessions were precipitated by military cutbacks. Still others came about when the Federal Reserve caused sudden increases in interest rates that led to decreased spending on new homes and other goods. (You'll learn about the Federal Reserve and its policies a few chapters from now.)

Strong expansions, on the other hand, have been caused by military buildups, and by falling oil prices that stimulated spending on energy-related products, or by bursts of planned investment spending. The long expansion of the mid- and late-1990s, for example, began when the development of the Internet, and improvements in computers more generally, led to an increase in investment spending. Once the economy began expanding, it was further spurred by other factors, such as a rise in stock prices and consumer optimism, both of which led to an increase in consumption spending.

In addition to these identifiable spending shocks, the economy is buffeted by other shocks whose origins are harder to spot. For example, consumption was higher than expected in the late 1980s, contributing to the rapid expansion that occurred in those years. In the early 1990s, consumption fell back to normal, helping to cause the recession of that period. There was no obvious event that caused these changes in consumption.

And each shock has momentum. When a decrease in spending causes production cutbacks, firms will lay off workers. The laid-off workers, suffering decreases in their incomes, cut back their own spending on other products, causing further layoffs in other sectors. The economy can continue sliding downward, and remain below potential output, for a year or longer. The same process works in reverse during an expansion: Higher spending leads to greater production, higher employment, and still greater spending, possibly leading to a boom in which the economy remains overheated for some time.

Booms and recessions do not last forever, however. The economy eventually adjusts back to full-employment output. Often, a change in government macroeconomic policy helps the adjustment process along, speeding the return to full employment. Other times, a policy mistake thwarts the adjustment process, prolonging or deepening a costly recession, or exacerbating a boom and overheating the economy even more.

How does this adjustment process work? This is a question we'll be coming back to a few chapters from now, after you've learned some new tools for analyzing the economy's behavior over the short run.

© PHOTODISC/GETTY IMAGES

Half of our recessions since the early 1950s have been caused, at least in part, by rapid rises in oil prices.

HTTP://

Katherine Bradbury's "Job Creation and Destruction in Massachusetts" http://www.bos.frb.org/economic/neer/neer1999/neer599c.pdf provides a case study of how the labor market adjusts.

Period		Event	Spending Shock
Early 1950s	Expansion	Korean War	Defense Spending ↑
1953	Recession	End of Korean War	Defense Spending ↓
Late 1960s	Expansion	Vietnam War	Defense Spending ↑
1970	Recession	Change in Federal Reserve Policy	Spending on New Homes ↓
1974	Recession	Dramatic Increase in Oil Prices	Spending on Cars and Other Energy-using Products ↓
1980	Recession	Dramatic Increase in Oil Prices	Spending on Cars and Other Energy-using Products ↓
1981–82	Recession	Change in Federal Reserve Policy	Spending on New Homes, Cars, and Business Investment ↓
Early 1980s	Expansion	Military Buildup	Defense Spending ↑
Late 1980s	Expansion	Huge Decline in Oil Prices	Spending on Energy-using Products ↑
1990	Recession	Large Increase in Oil Prices; Collapse of Soviet Union	Spending on Cars and Other Energy-using Products ↓; Defense Spending ↓
1991–2000	Expansion	Technological Advances in Computers; Development of the Internet; High Wealth Creation	Spending on Capital Equipment ↑; Consumption Spending ↑
2001	Recession	Investment in New Technology Slows; Technology-fueled Bubble of Optimism Bursts; Wealth Destruction	Spending on Capital Equipment ↓
2002–?	Expansion	Changes in Fiscal and Federal Reserve Policies; Rapid Rise in Housing Wealth	Consumption Spending ↑

TABLE 1
Expansions, Recessions, and Shocks That Caused Them

WHERE DO WE GO FROM HERE?

The classical model that you've learned in previous chapters is certainly useful: It helps us understand economic growth over time, and how economic events and economic policies affect the economy over the long run. But in trying to understand expansions and recessions—where they come from, and why they can last for one or more years—we've had to depart from the strict framework of the classical model.

One theme of our discussion has been the central role of spending in understanding economic fluctuations. In the classical model, spending could be safely ignored. First, Say's law assured us that total spending would always be sufficient to buy the output produced at full employment. Second, a change in spending—for example, a decrease in military spending by the government—would cause other categories of spending to rise by just the right amount to make up for the lower spending of the government. In the long run, we can have faith in the classical perspective on spending.

But in the short run, we've seen that spending shocks to the economy affect production, usually in one specific sector. When employment changes in that sector, the spending of workers *there* will change as well, affecting demand in still other sectors. Clearly, if we want to understand fluctuations, we need to take a close look at spending. This is what we will do in the next chapter, when we study the *short-run macro model*.

Summary

The classical model does not always do a good job of describing the economy over short time periods. Over periods of a few years, national economies experience economic fluctuations in which output rises above or falls below its long-term growth path. Significant periods of falling output are called recessions, while periods of rapidly rising output are expansions. If an expansion causes output to rise above potential (or full-employment) output, it is called a boom. When real GDP fluctuates, it causes the level of employment and the unemployment rate to fluctuate as well.

The classical model cannot explain economic fluctuations because it assumes that the labor market always clears; that is, it always operates at the point where the labor supply and demand curves intersect. Evidence suggests that this market-clearing assumption is not always valid over short time periods. And when we try to explain economic fluctuations using the classical model, we come up short. Neither shifts in the labor demand curve, nor shifts in the labor supply curve, offer a realistic explanation for what happens during a recession or a boom.

In a simple, two-person economy, decisions about spending and production could be easily coordinated, so economic fluctuations would be easy to avoid. But in a market economy with millions of people and firms, decisions about spending and production cannot be coordinated, making the economy vulnerable to changes in production that are harmful to everyone involved.

Deviations from the full-employment level of output are often caused by *spending shocks*—changes in spending that initially affect one sector and then work their way through the entire economy. Negative shocks can cause recessions, while positive shocks can cause expansions that lead to booms. Eventually, output will return to its long-run equilibrium level, but it does not do so immediately. The origins of economic fluctuations can be understood more fully with the short-run macro model, which we will study in the next chapter.

Key Terms

Boom   Spending shock

Review Questions   *Answers to even-numbered Questions and Problems can be found on the text Web site at* http://hall-lieb.swlearning.com.

1. How does a *recession* differ from an *expansion*? Describe the typical behavior of GDP and the unemployment rate during each of these periods.

2. Why can't a recession be explained in terms of a reduction in labor demand? In terms of a reduction in labor supply?

3. In an economy with just two people, economic fluctuations would be unlikely to occur. Why? What is the key difference in the real-world economy that makes economic fluctuations more likely?

4. "During the last half-century economic fluctuations in the United States have been caused entirely by changes in military spending." True or false? Explain.

5. Suppose the economy is disturbed by a decrease in spending. Describe how this leads to a recession. How would an increase in spending lead to a boom?

Problems and Exercises

1. Using the upper panel of Figure 1, identify two time spans during which the U.S. economy was enjoying an expansion but *not* a boom. [*Hint:* Reread the first page of this chapter.]

2. This chapter explains how a spending shock—such as a decrease in investment spending—could cause a recession. But in the classical model, a decrease in investment spending could *not* causes a recession. Why not? [*Hint:* Use the loanable funds market diagram.]

3. Imagine that you are an unemployed worker. Are you more likely to find a job quickly during a recession or a boom? Once you find a job, explain how your behavior will contribute to the recession or boom that is taking place.

 These exercises require access to Hall/Lieberman Xtra! If Xtra! did not come with your book, visit http://hallxtra.swlearning.com to purchase.

---

1. Use your Xtra! password at the Hall and Lieberman Web site (http://hallxtra.swlearning.com), select this chapter, and under Economic Applications, click on EconDebate. Choose *Macroeconomics: Employment, Unemployment, and Inflation,* and scroll down to find the debate, "Does an Increase in the Minimum Wage Result in a Higher Unemployment Rate?" Read the debate, and use the information to answer the following questions.

    a. The labor market is one of the most important parts of the classical model. What are the ramifications of the minimum wage laws on employment and output according to the classical model?

    b. Considering the effects of inflation on the minimum wage would you expect the labor markets to clear or unemployment to persist in the presence of the minimum wage laws? Explain.

2. Use your Xtra! password at the Hall and Lieberman Web site (http://hallxtra.swlearning.com), select this chapter, and under Economic Applications, click on EconData. Choose *Macroeconomics: Employment, Unemployment, and Inflation,* and scroll down to find *Real GDP.* Read the definition and click on Diagrams/Data and use the information to answer the following question.

    a. Does the real GDP and Personal Income diagram support the interplay of income and spending and their role in explaining short-term fluctuations, as indicated in this chapter? Explain.

The Short-Run Macro Model

CHAPTER OUTLINE

Consumption Spending
Consumption and Disposable Income
Consumption and Income
Shifts in the Consumption–Income Line

Getting to Total Spending
Investment Spending
Government Purchases
Net Exports
Summing Up: Aggregate Expenditure
Income and Aggregate Expenditure

Finding Equilibrium GDP
Inventories and Equilibrium GDP
Finding Equilibrium GDP with a Graph
Equilibrium GDP and Employment

What Happens When Things Change?
A Change in Investment Spending
The Expenditure Multiplier
The Multiplier in Reverse
Other Spending Shocks
A Graphical View of the Multiplier
Automatic Stabilizers and the Multiplier

Comparing Models: Long Run and Short Run
The Role of Saving
The Effect of Fiscal Policy

Using the Theory: The Recession of 2001

Appendix 1: Finding Equilibrium GDP Algebraically

Appendix 2: The Special Case of the Tax Multiplier

Every December, newspapers and television news broadcasts focus their attention on spending. You might see a reporter standing in front of a Circuit City outlet, warning that unless holiday shoppers loosen their wallets and spend big on computers, DVD players, vacation trips, toys, and new cars, the economy is in for trouble.

Of course, spending matters during the rest of the year, too. But holiday spending attracts our attention because the normal forces at work during the rest of the year become more concentrated in late November and December. Factories churn out merchandise and stores stock up at higher than normal rates. If consumers are in Scrooge-like moods, unsold goods will pile up in stores. In the months that follow, these stores will cut back on their orders for new goods. As a result, factories will decrease production and lay off workers.

And the story will not end there. The laid-off workers—even those who collect some unemployment benefits—will see their incomes decline. As a consequence, they will spend less on a variety of consumer goods. This will cause other firms—the ones that produce those consumer goods—to cut back on *their* production.

This hypothetical example reinforces a conclusion we reached in the last chapter: Spending is very important in the short run. And it points out an interesting circularity: The more income households have, the more they will spend. That is, *spending depends on income*. But the more households spend, the more output firms will produce—and the more income they will pay to their workers. Thus, *income depends on spending*.

> *In the short run, spending depends on income, and income depends on spending.*

In this chapter, we will explore this circular connection between spending and income. We will do so with a very simple macroeconomic model, which we'll call the *short-run macro model*. Many of the ideas behind the model were originally developed by the British economist John Maynard Keynes in the 1930s. The **short-run macro model** focuses on the role of spending in explaining economic fluctuations. It explains how shocks that initially affect one sector of the economy quickly influence other sectors, causing changes in total output and employment.

Short-run macro model A macroeconomic model that explains how changes in spending can affect real GDP in the short run.

To keep the model as simple as possible, we will—for the time being—ignore all influences on production *besides* spending. As a result, the short-run model may appear strange to you at first, like a drive along an unfamiliar highway. You may wonder: Where is all the scenery you are used to seeing along the classical road? Where are the labor market, the production function, the loanable funds market, and the market-clearing assumption? Rest assured that many of these concepts are still with us, lurking in the background and waiting to be exposed, and we will come back to them in later chapters. But in this chapter, we assume that spending—and *only* spending—determines how much output the economy will produce.

Thinking About Spending. Before we begin our analysis of spending, we have some choices to make.

First, spending on *what*? People spend on food, clothing, furniture, and vacations. They also spend to buy stocks and bonds, to buy homes, to buy used goods, and to buy things produced in foreign countries.

Remember that our main purpose in building the short-run macro model is to explain fluctuations in real GDP that the long-run, classical model cannot explain. Accordingly, we will ignore spending on things that are *not* part of our GDP, like stocks and bonds and real estate and goods produced abroad. Instead,

> *in the short-run macro model, we focus on spending in markets for currently produced U.S. goods and services—that is, spending on things that are included in U.S. GDP.*

Next, we need to organize our thinking about markets that contribute to GDP. We know who the sellers are: U.S. firms. But there are so many different types of buyers of U.S. goods and services: city dwellers and suburbanites; government agencies like the Department of Defense and the local school board; businesses of all types, ranging from the corner convenience store to a huge corporation such as AT&T; and foreigners from nearby Canada and distant Fiji. What's the best way to categorize all these buyers into larger groups so we can analyze their behavior?

Macroeconomists have found that the most useful approach is to divide those who purchase the GDP into four broad categories:

- Households, whose spending is called consumption spending (C)
- Business firms, whose spending is called planned investment spending (I^P)
- Government agencies, whose spending on goods and services is called government purchases (G)
- Foreigners, whose spending we measure as net exports (NX)

These categories should seem familiar to you. They were the same groups of buyers we used to break down GDP in the expenditure approach. In the first part of this chapter, we'll take another look at each of these types of buyers. Then, we'll add their purchases together to explore the behavior of *total* spending in the economy.

Finally, one more choice: Should we look at *nominal* or *real* spending? (Recall that a nominal variable is measured in current dollars, while a real variable is measured in the constant dollars of some base year.) Ultimately, we care more about real variables, such as real output and real income, because they are the more closely related to our economic well-being. For example, a rise in *nominal* output might mean that we are producing more goods and services, or it might just mean that prices have risen and production has remained the same or fallen. But a rise in *real* output always means that production has increased. For this reason, we will think about real variables right from the beginning. When we discuss "consumption spending," we mean "real consumption spending," "government purchases" means "real government purchases," and so on.

CONSUMPTION SPENDING

A natural place for us to begin our look at spending is with its largest component: *consumption spending*. In all, household spending on consumer goods—groceries, restaurant meals, rent, car repairs, movies, telephone calls, and furniture—averages about two-thirds of total spending in the economy. Total consumption spending in the economy is the sum of spending by over a hundred million U.S. households. What determines the *total* amount of consumption spending?

One way to answer is to start by thinking about yourself or your family. What determines your spending in any given month, quarter, or year?

Disposable Income. The first thing that comes to mind is your income: The more you earn, the more you spend. But in macroeconomics, small differences in language can be crucial. It's not exactly your *income* per period—what you are paid by your employer—that determines your spending, but rather what you get to *keep* from that income after deducting any taxes you have to pay. Moreover, some people receive a flow of transfer payments from the government—such as unemployment insurance benefits or Social Security payments—which they can spend in addition to any income received from an employer. If we start with the income you earn, deduct all tax payments, and then add in any transfer received, we would get your *disposable income*—a term introduced with the classical model. This is the income you are free to spend or save as you wish.

$$\text{Disposable Income} = \text{Income} - \text{Tax Payments} + \text{Transfers Received}.$$

This can be rewritten as:

$$\text{Disposable Income} = \text{Income} - (\text{Taxes} - \text{Transfers}).$$

Finally, remember that that the term in parentheses, Taxes − Transfers, is defined as *net taxes*. So the easiest way to think of your disposable income is:

Disposable Income = Income − Net Taxes.

All else equal, you'd certainly spend more on consumer goods with a disposable income of $50,000 per year than with $20,000 per year. For almost any household, *a rise in disposable income—with no other change—causes a rise in consumption spending.*

Wealth. Given your disposable income, how much of it will you spend and how much will you save? That will depend, in part, on your *wealth*—the total value of your assets (home, stocks, bonds, bank accounts and the like) minus your outstanding liabilities (student loans, mortgage loans, credit card debt, and so on). Even if your disposable income stayed the same, an increase in your wealth—say, because you own stocks or bonds that have risen in value—would probably induce you to spend more. In general, *a rise in wealth, with no other change, causes a rise in consumption spending.*

The Interest Rate. The interest rate is the reward people get for saving, or what they have to pay when they borrow. You would probably save more each year if the interest rate was 10 percent than if it was 2 percent. But when you save more of your disposable income, you spend less. *All else equal, a rise in the interest rate causes a decrease in consumption spending.*

It's worth noting that this relationship between the interest rate and consumption spending applies even for people who aren't "savers" in the common sense of the term. For example, suppose you've been living beyond your means and now you have thousands of dollars in credit card debt. Each month, you have to decide how much of your disposable income to spend and how much to use to pay down your credit card balance. If the interest rate on your unpaid balance is low, you might not worry too much, paying back very little each month. You might even go deeper into debt, continuing to spend *more* than your disposable income.

But at higher interest rates, you'd probably want to pay down more of the balance. To do so, you'd be spending *less* of your disposable income each period. So, whether you are earning interest on funds you've saved, or paying interest on funds you've borrowed, the higher the interest rate, the lower your consumption spending.

Expectations. Expectations about the future can affect your spending as well. If you become more optimistic about your job security or expect a big raise, you might spend more of your income *now*. Similarly, if you become more pessimistic—worried about losing your job or a pay cut—you'd probably spend less now. *All else equal, optimism about future income causes an increase in consumption spending.*

Other variables, too, can influence your consumption spending, including inheritances you expect to receive over your lifetime, and even how long you expect to live. But disposable income, wealth, the interest rate, and expectations are the key variables we'll be coming back to again and again in the short-run macroeconomic model. And just as these variables influence the consumption spending of each individual household, they also influence the consumption spending of the household sector as a whole.

FIGURE 1
U.S. Consumption and Disposable Income, 1985–2004

When real consumption expenditure is plotted against real disposable income, the resulting relationship is almost perfectly linear: As real disposable income rises, so does real consumption spending.

Source: Bureau of Economic Analysis, National Income and Product Accounts Tables, Tables 2.1 and 1.1.6.

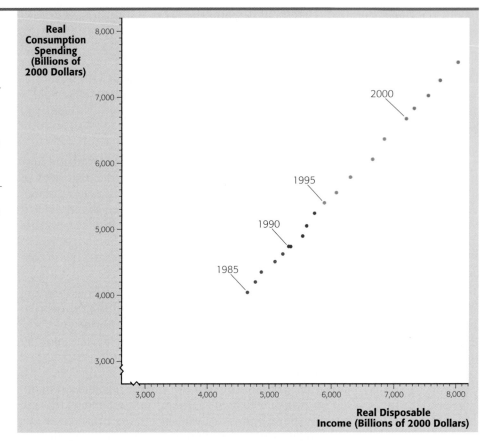

Unless we're focusing on an individual household to make a point (as in the preceding paragraphs), in macroeconomics, we use phrases like "disposable income," "wealth," or "consumption spending" to mean the *total* disposable income, *total* wealth, and *total* consumption spending of all households in the economy combined. So we can state our conclusions this way:

All else equal, consumption spending increases when:
- *disposable income rises*
- *wealth rises*
- *the interest rate falls*
- *households become more optimistic about the future*

Consumption and Disposable Income

Of all the factors that influence consumption spending, the most important and stable determinant is disposable income. Figure 1 shows the relationship between (real) consumption spending and (real) disposable income in the United States from 1985 to 2004. Each point in the diagram represents a different year. For example, the point labeled "2000" represents a disposable income in that year of $7,194 billion and consumption spending of $6,739 billion. Notice that as disposable income rises, consumption spending rises as well. Indeed, almost all of the variation

Real Disposable Income (Billions of Dollars per Year)	Real Consumption Spending (Billions of Dollars per Year)
0	2,000
1,000	2,600
2,000	3,200
3,000	3,800
4,000	4,400
5,000	5,000
6,000	5,600
7,000	6,200
8,000	6,800

TABLE 1

Hypothetical Data on Disposable Income and Consumption

in consumption spending from year to year can be explained by variations in disposable income. Although the other factors we've discussed do affect consumption spending, their impact appears to be relatively minor.

There is something even more interesting about Figure 1: The relationship between consumption and disposable income is almost perfectly *linear;* the points lie remarkably close to a straight line. This almost-linear relationship between consumption and disposable income has been observed in a wide variety of historical periods and a wide variety of nations. This is why, when we represent the relationship between disposable income and consumption with a diagram or an equation, we use a straight line.

Our discussion will be clearer if we move from the actual data in Figure 1 to the hypothetical example in Table 1. Each row in the table represents a combination of (real) disposable income and (real) consumption we might observe in an economy. For example, the table shows us that if disposable income were equal to $7,000 billion in some year, consumption spending would equal $6,200 billion in that year. When we plot this data on a graph, we obtain the straight line in Figure 2. This line is called the **consumption function,** because it illustrates the functional relationship between consumption and disposable income.

Like every straight line, the consumption function in Figure 2 has two main features: a vertical intercept and a slope. Mathematically, the intercept—in this case, $2,000 billion—tells us how much consumption spending there would be in the economy if disposable income were zero. However, the real purpose of the vertical intercept is not to identify what would actually happen at zero disposable income, but rather to help us identify the particular line that represents consumption spending in the diagram. After all, there are many lines we could draw that have the same slope as the one in the figure. But only one of them has a vertical intercept of $2,000.

The vertical intercept in the figure also has a name: **autonomous consumption spending.** It represents the influence on consumption spending of everything *other than* disposable income. For example, if household wealth were to increase, consumption would be greater at any level of disposable income. In that case, the entire consumption function in the figure would shift upward, so its vertical intercept would increase. We would call this *an increase in autonomous consumption spending.* Similarly, a decrease in wealth would cause a *decrease in autonomous consumption spending,* and shift the consumption function downward.

Consumption function A positively sloped relationship between real consumption spending and real disposable income.

Autonomous consumption spending The part of consumption spending that is independent of income; also the vertical intercept of the consumption function.

FIGURE 2
The Consumption Function

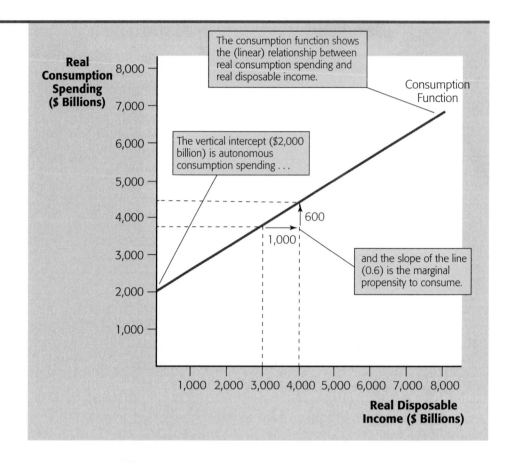

The second important feature of Figure 2 is the slope, which shows the change along the vertical axis divided by the change along the horizontal axis as we go from one point to another on the line:

$$\text{slope} = \frac{\Delta \text{Consumption}}{\Delta \text{Disposable Income}}.$$

As you can see in the table, each time disposable income rises by $1,000 billion, consumption spending rises by $600 billion, so that the slope is

$$\frac{\$600 \text{ billion}}{\$1,000 \text{ billion}} = 0.6$$

The slope in Figure 2 is an important feature not just of the consumption function itself, but also of the macroeconomic analysis we will build from it. This is why economists have given this slope a special name, the *marginal propensity to consume,* abbreviated *MPC.* In our example, the *MPC* is 0.6.

We can think of the *MPC* in three different ways, but each of them has the same meaning:

Marginal propensity to consume
The amount by which consumption spending rises when disposable income rises by one dollar.

The **marginal propensity to consume** (**MPC**) is *(1) the slope of the consumption function; (2) the change in consumption divided by the change in disposable income; or (3) the amount by which consumption spending rises when disposable income rises by one dollar.*

Logic suggests that the *MPC* should be larger than zero (when income rises, consumption spending will *rise*), but less than 1 (the rise in consumption will be *smaller* than the rise in disposable income). This is certainly true in our example where *MPC* is 0.6 and each one-dollar rise in disposable income causes spending to rise by 60 cents. This range of values for the MPC is also observed to be true in economies throughout the world. Accordingly,

we will always assume that $0 < \text{MPC} < 1$.

Representing Consumption with an Equation. Sometimes, we'll want to use an equation to represent the straight-line consumption function. The most general form of the equation is

$$C = a + b \times (\text{Disposable Income})$$

where *C* is consumption spending. The term *a* is the vertical intercept of the consumption function. It represents the theoretical level of consumption spending at disposable income = 0, which you've learned is called *autonomous consumption spending*. In the equation, you can see clearly that autonomous consumption (*a*) is the part of consumption that does *not* depend on disposable income. In our example in Figure 2, *a* is equal to $2,000 billion.

The other term, *b,* is the slope of the consumption function. This is our familiar marginal propensity to consume (*MPC*), telling us how much consumption *increases* each time disposable income rises by a dollar. In our example in Figure 2, *b* is equal to 0.6.

Consumption and Income

The consumption function is an important building block of our analysis. Consumption is the largest component of spending, and disposable income is the most important determinant of consumption. But there is one limitation of the line as we've drawn it in Figure 2: It shows us the value of consumption at each level of *disposable* income, whereas we will need to know the value of consumption spending at each level of *income*. Disposable income, you remember, is the income that the household sector has left after deducting net taxes. How can we convert the line in Figure 2 into a relationship between consumption and income?

Table 2 illustrates the consumption–income relationship when the household sector pays net taxes. In the table, we treat net taxes as a fixed amount—in this case, $2,000 billion. Some taxes are, indeed, fixed in this way, such as the taxes assessed on real estate by local governments. Other taxes, like the personal income tax and the sales tax, rise and fall with income in the economy. Still, treating net taxes as if they are independent of income, as in Table 2, will simplify our discussion without changing our results in any important way.

Notice that the last two columns of the table are identical to the columns in Table 1: In both tables, we assume that the relationship between consumption spending and *disposable* income is the same. For example, both tables show us that, when disposable income is $7,000 billion, consumption spending is $6,200 billion. But in Table 2, we see that disposable income of $7,000 is associated with *income* of $9,000. Thus, when income is $9,000, consumption spending is $6,200. By comparing the first and last columns of Table 2, we can trace out the

TABLE 2
The Relationship Between Consumption and Income

Income or GDP (Billions of Dollars per Year)	Tax Collections (Billions of Dollars per Year)	Disposable Income (Billions of Dollars per Year)	Consumption Spending (Billions of Dollars per Year)
2,000	2,000	0	2,000
3,000	2,000	1,000	2,600
4,000	2,000	2,000	3,200
5,000	2,000	3,000	3,800
6,000	2,000	4,000	4,400
7,000	2,000	5,000	5,000
8,000	2,000	6,000	5,600
9,000	2,000	7,000	6,200
10,000	2,000	8,000	6,800

Consumption–income line A line showing aggregate consumption spending at each level of income or GDP.

relationship between consumption and income. This relationship—which we call the **consumption–income line**—is graphed in Figure 3.

If you compare the consumption–income line in Figure 3 with the line in Figure 2, you will notice that both have the same slope of 0.6, but the consumption–income line is lower by $1,200 billion. Net taxes have lowered the consumption–income line. Why? Because at any level of income, taxes reduce disposable income and therefore reduce consumption spending.

But why is the consumption–income line lower by precisely $1,200 billion? We can reason it out as follows: Any increase in net taxes (T) will cause consumption spending to fall by $MPC \times \Delta T$. In our example, when we impose taxes of $2,000 billion on the population, disposable income will drop by $2,000 billion at any level of income. With an MPC of 0.6, consumption at any level of income falls by 0.6 × $2,000 billion = $1,200 billion.

Finally, we noted earlier that the *slope* of the consumption–income line is unaffected by net taxes. This is because with net taxes held at a fixed amount, disposable income rises dollar-for-dollar with income. With an MPC of 0.6, consumption spending will rise by 60 cents each time income rises by a dollar, just as it rises by 60 cents each time *disposable* income rises by a dollar. You can see this in Table 2: Each time income rises by $1,000 billion, consumption spending rises by $600 billion, giving the consumption–income line a slope of $600 billion / $1,000 billion = 0.6, just as in the case with no taxes. More generally,

when the government collects a fixed amount of taxes from households, the line representing the relationship between consumption and income is shifted downward by the amount of the tax times the marginal propensity to consume (MPC). The slope of this line is unaffected by taxes, and is equal to the MPC.

Shifts in the Consumption–Income Line

As you've learned, consumption spending depends positively on income: If income increases and net taxes remain unchanged, disposable income will rise, and consumption spending will rise along with it. The chain of causation can be represented this way:

In Figure 3, this change in consumption spending would be represented by a *movement along* the consumption–income line. For example, a rise in income from $7,000 billion to $8,000 billion would cause consumption spending to increase from $5,000 billion to $5,600 billion, moving us from point *A* to point *B* along the consumption–income line.

But consumption spending can also change for reasons other than a change in income, causing the consumption–income line itself to shift. For example, a decrease in net taxes will increase *disposable* income at each level of income. Consumption spending will then increase at any income level, shifting the entire line upward. The mechanism works like this:

| Taxes ↓ | ⇒ | Disposable income at each income level ↑ | ⇒ | Consumption at each income level ↑ | Shift Upward of the Consumption– Income Line |

In Figure 4, a decrease in taxes from $2,000 billion to $500 billion increases disposable income at each income level by $1,500 billion, and causes consumption at each income level to increase by 0.6 × $1,500 billion = $900 billion. This means that the consumption line shifts upward, to the upper line in the figure.

In addition to net taxes, all the other influences on consumption, other than disposable income, shift the consumption–income line as well. But these other shift-variables work by changing the value of *autonomous consumption*, the vertical intercept of the consumption function in Figure 2. By shifting the relationship between

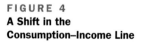

FIGURE 4
A Shift in the
Consumption–Income Line

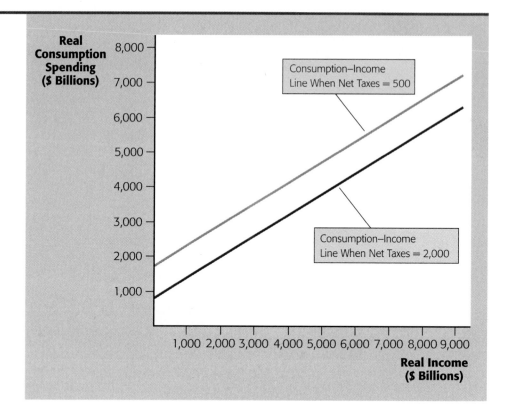

consumption and disposable income, we shift the relationship between consumption and income as well. For example, an increase in household wealth would increase autonomous consumption, and shift the consumption–income line upward, as in Figure 4. Increases in autonomous consumption could also occur if the interest rate decreased, or if households became more optimistic about the future. In general, increases in autonomous consumption work this way:

| Autonomous consumption (a) ↑ | ⇒ | Consumption at each level of *disposable* income ↑ | ⇒ | Consumption spending at at each level of *income* ↑ | } Shift Upward of the Consumption–Income Line |

We can summarize our discussion of changes in consumption spending as follows:

When a change in income causes consumption spending to change, we move along *the consumption–income line. When a change in anything else besides income causes consumption spending to change, the line will shift.*

Table 3 provides a more specific summary of how different types of changes in consumption spending are represented with the consumption–income line. Remember that all of the changes that *shift* the line—other than a change in taxes—work by increasing or decreasing autonomous consumption (a).

Rightward Movement Along the Line	Leftward Movement Along the Line	Entire Line Shifts Upward		Entire Line Shifts Downward		
When	When	When		When		
Income ↑	Income ↓	autonomous consumption (a) ↑	Taxes ↓ Household wealth ↑ Interest rate ↓ Greater optimism	Taxes ↑ Household wealth ↓ Interest rate ↑ Greater pessimism		autonomous consumption (a) ↓

TABLE 3

Changes in Consumption Spending and the Consumption–Income Line

GETTING TO TOTAL SPENDING

In addition to household consumption spending, there are three other types of spending on goods and services produced by American firms: investment, government purchases, and purchases by foreigners. Let's consider each of these types of spending in turn.

Investment Spending

Remember that in the definition of GDP, the word *investment* by itself (represented by the letter *I* by itself) consists of three components: (1) business spending on plant and equipment; (2) purchases of new homes; and (3) accumulation of unsold inventories. In this chapter, as we did when we studied the classical model, we focus not on investment, but on *planned investment* or *investment spending* (we'll use these two terms interchangeably).

Planned investment (I^p) is business purchases of plant and equipment, and construction of new homes.

Why do we focus on planned investment and leave out inventory accumulation? When we look at how spending influences the economy, we are interested in the purchases households, firms, and the government *want* to make. But some inventory changes, as you learned a few chapters ago, are an *unplanned* and *undesired* occurrence that firms try to avoid. While firms want to have *some* inventories on hand, sudden *changes* in inventories are typically not desirable. To keep the model simple, we treat *all* inventory changes as temporary, unplanned occurrences for the firm, and we exclude them when we measure spending in the economy. But even though they are excluded from spending, inventory changes will play an important part in our analysis, as you will see in a few pages.

In the short-run macro model, (planned) investment spending (I^P) is plant and equipment purchases by business firms, and new home construction. Inventory investment is treated as unintentional and undesired, and is therefore excluded from our definition of investment spending.

What determines the level of investment spending in a given year? In this chapter, we will regard investment spending as a *fixed value*, determined by forces outside of our analysis. This may seem surprising. After all, aren't there variables that affect investment spending in predictable ways? Indeed, there are.

For example, in the classical model, you learned that planned investment is likely to be affected by the interest rate. Indeed, in the real world, the investment–interest rate relationship is quite strong. Investment is also influenced by the general level of optimism or pessimism about the economy and by new technological developments. But if we introduced all of these other variables into our analysis, we would find ourselves working with a very complex framework, and much too soon. In future chapters, we'll explore some of the determinants of investment spending, but in this chapter, to keep things simple, we assume that investment spending is some given amount. We'll explore what happens when that amount changes, but we will not, in this chapter, try to explain what *causes* investment spending to change.

> For now, we regard investment spending (I^P) as a given value, determined by forces outside of our model.

Government Purchases

Government purchases include all of the goods and services that government agencies—federal, state, and local—buy during the year. We treat government purchases in the same way as investment spending: as a given value, determined by forces outside of our analysis. Why?

The relationship between government purchases and other macroeconomic variables—particularly income—is rather weak. In recent decades, the biggest changes in government purchases have involved military spending. These changes have been based on world politics rather than macroeconomic conditions. So assuming that government spending is a given value, independent of the other variables in our model, is realistic.

> In the short-run macro model, government purchases are treated as a given value, determined by forces outside of the model.

As with investment spending, we'll be exploring what happens when the "given value" of government purchases changes. But we will not try to explain what causes it to change.

Net Exports

If we want to measure total spending on U.S. output, we must also consider the international sector. About 11 percent of U.S.-produced goods are sold to *foreign* consumers, *foreign* businesses, and *foreign* governments. These U.S. *exports* are as much a part of total spending on U.S. output as the other types of spending we've discussed so far. Thus, exports must be included in our measure of total spending.

International trade in goods and services also requires us to make an adjustment to the other components of spending. A portion (about 16 percent) of the output bought by *American* consumers, firms, and government agencies was produced abroad. From the U.S. point of view, these are *imports:* spending on foreign, rather than U.S., output. These imports are included in our measures of consumption, investment, and government spending, giving us an exaggerated measure of spending on *American* output. But we can easily correct for this overcount by simply deducting imported consumption goods from our measure of consumption, deducting imported investment goods from our measure of investment spending, and deducting imported government purchases from our measure of government purchases. Combining all these deductions together, we are actually deducting *total* imports to correct our exaggerated measure of *total* spending.

In sum, to incorporate the international sector into our measure of total spending, we must add U.S. exports and subtract U.S. imports. These two adjustments can be made together by simply including *net exports (NX)* as the foreign sector's contribution to total spending.

$$\text{Net Exports} = \text{Total Exports} - \text{Total Imports}.$$

By including net exports, we simultaneously ensure that we have included U.S. output that is sold to foreigners, and excluded consumption, investment, and government spending on output produced abroad.

Net exports can change for a variety of reasons: changes in tastes toward or away from a particular country's goods, changes in the price of foreign currency on world foreign exchange markets, and more. In a later chapter of this book, we'll discuss in more detail how and why net exports change. But in this chapter, to keep things simple, we assume that net exports—like investment spending and government purchases—are some given amount. We'll explore what happens when that amount changes, but we will not, in this chapter, try to explain what causes net exports to change.

> *For now, we regard net exports as a given value, determined by forces outside of our analysis.*

It is important to remember that net exports can be *negative;* and in the United States, they have been negative since 1982. Negative net exports means that our imports are greater than our exports. Or, equivalently, Americans are buying more foreign goods and services than foreigners are buying of ours. In that case, net exports contribute *negatively* to total spending on U.S. output.

Summing Up: Aggregate Expenditure

Now that we've discussed all of the components of spending in the economy, we can be more precise about measuring total spending. First, we'll use the phrase *aggregate expenditure* to mean total spending on U.S. output over some period of time. More formally,

> *aggregate expenditure is the sum of spending by households, businesses, the government, and the foreign sector on final goods and services produced in the United States.*

Aggregate expenditure (AE) The sum of spending by households, business firms, the government, and foreigners on final goods and services produced in the United States.

Remembering that C stands for household consumption spending, I^p for investment spending, G for government purchases, and NX for net exports, we have

$$\text{Aggregate expenditure} = C + I^p + G + NX.$$

Aggregate expenditure plays a key role in explaining economic fluctuations. Why? Because over several quarters or even a few years, business firms tend to respond to

(1) Income or GDP (Billions of Dollars per Year)	(2) Consumption Spending (Billions of Dollars per Year)	(3) Investment Spending (Billions of Dollars per Year)	(4) Government Purchases (Billions of Dollars per Year)	(5) Net Exports (Billions of Dollars per Year)	(6) Aggregate Expenditure (AE) (Billions of Dollars per Year)	(7) Change in Inventories (Billions of Dollars per Year)
2,000	2,000	700	500	400	3,600	−1,600
3,000	2,600	700	500	400	4,200	−1,200
4,000	3,200	700	500	400	4,800	−800
5,000	3,800	700	500	400	5,400	−400
6,000	**4,400**	**700**	**500**	**400**	**6,000**	**0**
7,000	5,000	700	500	400	6,600	400
8,000	5,600	700	500	400	7,200	800
9,000	6,200	700	500	400	7,800	1,200
10,000	6,800	700	500	400	8,400	1,600

TABLE 4
The Relationship Between Income and Aggregate Expenditure

changes in aggregate expenditure by changing their level of output. That is, a rise in aggregate expenditure leads firms throughout the economy to raise their output level, while a drop in aggregate expenditure causes a decrease in output throughout the economy. While these changes are temporary, they persist long enough to create the kinds of economic fluctuations that you saw in the previous chapter's Figures 1 and 2. In the next section, we'll explore just how changes in spending create these economic fluctuations.

Income and Aggregate Expenditure

As we discussed earlier, the relationship between income and spending is circular: Spending depends on income, and income depends on spending. In Table 4, we take up the first part of that circle: how total spending depends on income. In the table, column 1 lists some possible income levels, and column 2 shows the level of consumption spending we can expect at each income level. These two columns are just the consumption–income relationship we introduced earlier, in Table 2.

Column 3 shows that business firms in this economy buy $700 billion per year in plant and equipment, regardless of the level of income. Government purchases are also fixed in value, as shown by column 4: At every level of income, the government buys $500 billion in goods and services. And net exports, in column 5, are assumed to be $400 billion at each level of income. Finally, if we add together the entries in columns 2, 3, 4, and 5, we get $C + I^p + G + NX$, or aggregate expenditure, shown in column 6. (For now, ignore column 7.)

DANGEROUS CURVES

GDP Versus Aggregate Expenditure The definition of aggregate expenditure looks very similar to the definition of GDP presented in the chapter entitled "Production, Income, and Employment." Does this mean that aggregate expenditure and total output are always the same number? Not at all. There is a slight—but important—difference in the definitions. GDP is defined as $C + I + G + NX$. Aggregate expenditure, by contrast, is defined as $C + I^p + G + NX$. The difference is that GDP adds actual investment (I), which includes business firms' inventory investment. Aggregate expenditure adds just planned investment (I^p), which *excludes* inventory investment. The two numbers will not be equal unless inventory investment is zero. (We'll use this fact to help us find the equilibrium GDP in the next section.)

Notice that aggregate expenditure increases as income rises. But notice also that the rise in aggregate expenditure is *smaller* than the rise in income. For example, you can see that when income rises from $5,000 billion to $6,000 billion (column 1), aggregate expenditure rises from $5,400 billion to $6,000 billion (column 6). Thus, a $1,000 billion increase in income is associated with a $600 billion increase in aggregate expenditure. This is because, in our analysis, consumption is the only component of spending that depends on income, and consumption spending always increases according to the marginal propensity to consume, here equal to 0.6.

> *When income increases, aggregate expenditure* (AE) *will rise by the* MPC *times the change in income:* $\Delta AE = MPC \times \Delta GDP$.

Notice that we've used ΔGDP to indicate the change in total income, because GDP and total income are always the same number.

FINDING EQUILIBRIUM GDP

Table 4 shows how aggregate expenditure depends on income. In this section, you will see how income depends on aggregate expenditure—that is, how spending determines the economy's *equilibrium income* or *equilibrium GDP*. That is, we are about to use Step 2 of our three-step process. As always, the equilibrium will be a point of rest of the economy: a value for GDP that remains the same until something we've been assuming constant begins to change. That part of Step 2 will be familiar to you.

However, be forewarned: Our method of *finding* equilibrium in the short run is very different from anything you've seen before in this text.

Our starting point in finding the economy's short-run equilibrium is to ask ourselves what would happen, hypothetically, if the economy were operating at different levels of output. Let's start with a GDP of $9,000 billion. Could this be the equilibrium GDP we seek? That is, if firms were producing this level of output, would they keep doing so? Let's see.

Table 4 tells us that when GDP, and therefore income, is equal to $9,000 billion, aggregate expenditure is equal to $7,800 billion. Business firms are *producing* $1,200 billion more than they are *selling*. Since firms will certainly not be willing to continue producing output they cannot sell, we can infer that, in future periods, they will slow their production. Thus, if the economy finds itself at a GDP of $9,000 billion, it will not stay there. In other words, $9,000 billion is *not* where the economy will settle in the short run, so it is *not* our equilibrium GDP. More generally,

What About Prices? You may be wondering why, in the short-run macro model, a firm that produces more output than it sells wouldn't just lower the price of its goods. That way, it could sell more of them and not have to lower its output as much. Similarly, a firm whose sales exceeded its production could take advantage of the opportunity to raise its prices rather than increase production.

To some extent, firms *do* change prices—even in the short run. But they change their output levels, too. To keep things as simple as possible, this first version of the short-run macro model assumes that firms adjust *only* their output to match aggregate expenditure. That is, we assume that *prices don't change at all*. In a later chapter, we'll make the model more realistic by assuming that firms adjust both prices and output.

DANGEROUS CURVES

> *when aggregate expenditure is less than GDP, output will decline in the future. Thus, any level of output at which aggregate expenditure is less than GDP cannot be the equilibrium GDP.*

Now let's consider the opposite case: a level of GDP of $3,000 billion. At this level of output. Table 4 shows aggregate expenditure of $4,200 billion; spending is actually *greater* than output by $1,200 billion. What will business firms do in response? Since they are selling more output than they are currently producing, we can expect them to *increase* their production in future months. Thus, if GDP is $3,000 billion, it will tend to rise in the future. So $3,000 billion is *not* our equilibrium GDP.

> *When aggregate expenditure is greater than GDP, output will rise in the future. Thus, any level of output at which aggregate expenditure exceeds GDP cannot be the equilibrium GDP.*

Now consider a GDP of $6,000 billion. At this level of output, our table shows that aggregate expenditure is precisely equal to $6,000 billion: Output and aggregate expenditure are equal. Since firms, on the whole, are selling just what they produce—no more and no less—they should be content to produce that same amount in the future. We have found our equilibrium GDP:

> *In the short run, equilibrium GDP is the level of output at which output and aggregate expenditure are equal.*

Equilibrium GDP In the short run, the level of output at which output and aggregate expenditure are equal.

Inventories and Equilibrium GDP

When firms *produce* more goods than they sell, what happens to the unsold output? It is added to their inventory stocks. When firms *sell* more goods than they produce, where do the additional goods come from? They come from firms' inventory stocks. You can see that the gap between output and spending determines what will happen to inventories during the year.

More specifically,

> *the change in inventories during any period will always equal output minus aggregate expenditure.*

For example, Table 4 tells us that if GDP is equal to $9,000 billion, aggregate expenditure is equal to $7,800 billion. In this case, we can find that the change in inventories is

$$\Delta \text{Inventories} = GDP - AE$$
$$= \$9,000 \text{ billion} - \$7,800 \text{ billion}$$
$$= \$1,200 \text{ billion.}$$

When GDP is equal to $3,000 billion, aggregate expenditure is equal to $4,200 billion, so that the change in inventories is

$$\Delta \text{Inventories} = GDP - AE$$
$$= \$3,000 \text{ billion} - \$4,200 \text{ billion}$$
$$= -\$1,200 \text{ billion.}$$

Notice the negative sign in front of the $1,200 billion; if output is $3,000 billion, then inventory stocks will *shrink* by $1,200 billion.

Only when output and total sales are equal—that is, when GDP is at its equilibrium value—will the change in inventories be zero. In our example, when GDP is at its equilibrium value of $6,000 billion, so that aggregate expenditure is also $6,000 billion, the change in inventories is equal to zero. At this output level, we have

$$\Delta \text{Inventories} = GDP - AE$$

$$= \$6,000 \text{ billion} - \$6,000 \text{ billion}$$

$$= \$0.$$

What you have just learned about inventories suggests another way to find the equilibrium GDP in the economy: Find the output level at which the change in inventories is equal to zero. Firms cannot allow their inventories of unsold goods to keep growing for very long (they would go out of business), nor can they continue to sell goods out of inventory for very long (they would run out of goods). Instead, they will desire to keep their production in line with their sales, so that their inventories do not change.

To recap,

$$AE < GDP \Rightarrow \Delta \text{Inventories} > 0 \Rightarrow GDP \downarrow \text{ in future periods.}$$

$$AE > GDP \Rightarrow \Delta \text{Inventories} < 0 \Rightarrow GDP \uparrow \text{ in future periods.}$$

$$AE = GDP \Rightarrow \Delta \text{Inventories} = 0 \Rightarrow \text{No change in } GDP.$$

Now look at the last column in Table 4, which lists the change in inventories at different levels of output. This column is obtained by subtracting column 6 from column 1. The equilibrium output level is the one at which the change in inventories equals zero, which, as we've already found, is $6,000 billion.

Finding Equilibrium GDP with a Graph

To get an even clearer picture of how equilibrium GDP is determined, we'll illustrate it with a graph, although it will take us a few steps to get there. Figure 5 begins the process by showing how we can construct a graph of aggregate expenditure. The lowest line in the figure, labeled C, is our familiar consumption–income line, obtained from the data in the first two columns of Table 4.

The next line, labeled $C + I^P$, shows the *sum* of consumption and investment spending at each income level. Notice that this line is parallel to the C line, which means that the vertical distance between them—$700 billion—is the same at any income level. This vertical difference is investment spending, which remains the same at all income levels.

The next line adds government purchases to consumption and investment spending, giving us $C + I^P + G$. The $C + I^P + G$ line is parallel to the $C + I^P$ line. The vertical distance between them—$500 billion—is government purchases. Like investment spending, government purchases are the same at all income levels.

Finally, the top line adds net exports, giving us $C + I^P + G + NX$, or aggregate expenditure. The distance between the $C + I^P + G + NX$ line and the $C + I^P + G$ line—$400 billion—represents net exports, which are assumed to be the same at any level of income.

Now look just at the aggregate expenditure line—the top line—in Figure 5. Notice that it slopes upward, telling us that as income increases, so does aggregate

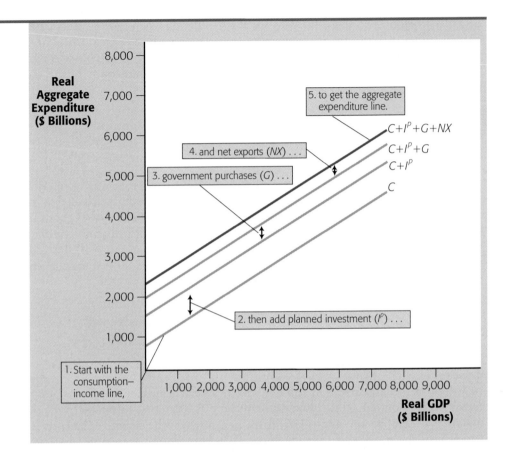

FIGURE 5
Deriving the Aggregate Expenditure Line

expenditure. And the slope of the aggregate expenditure line is less than 1: When income increases, the rise in aggregate expenditure is *smaller* than the rise in income. In fact, the slope of the aggregate expenditure line is equal to the *MPC*, or 0.6 in this example. This tells us that a one-dollar rise in income causes a 60-cent increase in aggregate expenditure. (Question: In the graph, which of the four components of aggregate expenditure rises when income rises? Which remain the same?)

Now we're almost ready to use a graph like the one in Figure 5 to locate equilibrium GDP, but first we must develop a little geometric trick.

Figure 6 shows a graph in which the horizontal and vertical axes are both measured in the same units, such as dollars. It also shows a line drawn at a 45° angle that begins at the origin. This 45° line has a useful property: Any point along it represents the same value along the vertical axis as it does along the horizontal axis. For example, look at point *A* on the line. Point *A* corresponds to the horizontal distance 0*B*, and it also corresponds to the vertical distance *BA*. But because the line is a 45° line, we know that these two distances are equal: 0*B* = *BA*. Now we have two choices for measuring the distance 0*B*: We can measure it horizontally, or we can measure it as the vertical distance *BA*. In fact, *any* horizontal distance can also be read vertically, merely by going from the horizontal value (point *B* in our example) up to the 45° line.

A 45° line is a translator line: It allows us to measure any horizontal distance as a vertical distance instead.

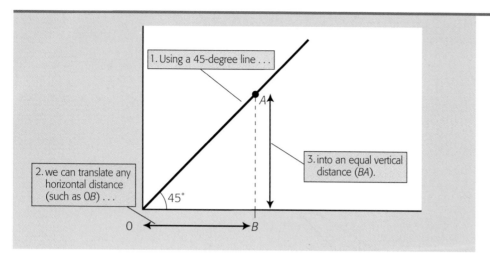

FIGURE 6
**Using a 45° to
Translate Distances**

Now we can apply this geometric trick to help us find the equilibrium GDP. In our aggregate expenditure diagram, we want to compare output with aggregate expenditure. But output is measured horizontally, while aggregate expenditure is measured vertically. Our 45° line, however, enables us to translate output into a vertical distance, and thus permits us to compare output and aggregate expenditure as two vertical distances.

Figure 7 shows how this is done. The blue line is the aggregate expenditure line ($C + I^P + G + NX$) from Figure 5. (We've dispensed with the other three lines that were drawn in Figure 6 because we no longer need them.) The black line is our 45° translator line. Now, let's search for the equilibrium GDP by considering a number of possibilities.

For example, could the output level $9,000 billion be our sought-after equilibrium? Let's see. We can measure the output level $9,000 billion as the vertical distance from the horizontal axis up to point A on the 45° line. But when output is $9,000 billion, aggregate expenditure is the vertical distance from the horizontal axis to point H on the aggregate expenditure line. Notice that, since point H lies below point A, aggregate expenditure is less than output. If firms *did* produce $9,000 billion worth of output, they would accumulate inventories equal to the vertical distance HA (the excess of output over spending). We conclude graphically (as we did earlier, using our table) that if output is $9,000 billion, firms will accumulate inventories of unsold goods and reduce output in the future. Thus, $9,000 billion is not our equilibrium. In general,

at any output level at which the aggregate expenditure line lies below the 45° line, aggregate expenditure is less than GDP. If firms produce any of these output levels, their inventories will grow, and they will reduce output in the future.

Now let's see if an output of $3,000 billion could be our equilibrium. First, we read this output level as the vertical distance up to point J on the 45° line. Next, we note that when output is $3,000 billion, aggregate expenditure is the vertical distance up to point K on the aggregate expenditure line. Point K lies *above* point J,

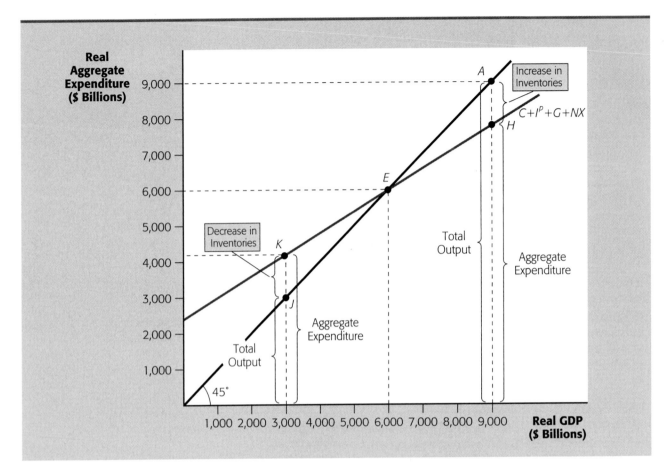

FIGURE 7
Determining Equilibrium
Real GDP

At point E, *where the aggregate expenditure line crosses the 45° line, the economy is in short-run equilibrium. With real GDP equal to $6,000 billion, aggregate expenditure equals real GDP. At higher levels of real GDP—such as $9,000 billion— total production exceeds aggregate expenditures, and firms will be unable to sell all they produce. Unplanned inventory increases equal to* HA *will lead them to reduce production. At lower levels of real GDP—such as $3,000 billion—aggregate expenditure exceeds total production. Firms find their inventories falling, and they will respond by increasing production.*

so aggregate expenditure is greater than output. If firms *did* produce $3,000 billion in output, inventories would *decrease* by the vertical distance *JK*. With declining inventories, firms would want to increase their output in the future, so $3,000 billion is not our equilibrium. More generally,

at any output level at which the aggregate expenditure line lies above *the 45° line, aggregate expenditure exceeds GDP. If firms produce any of these output levels, their inventories will decline, and they will increase their output in the future.*

Finally, consider an output of $6,000 billion. At this output level, the aggregate expenditure line and the 45° line cross. As a result, the vertical distance up to point *E* on the 45° line (representing output) is the same as the vertical distance up to point *E* on the aggregate expenditure line. If firms produce an output level of $6,000 billion, aggregate expenditure and output will be precisely equal, inventories will remain unchanged, and firms will have no incentive to increase or decrease output in the future. We have thus found our equilibrium on the graph: $6,000 billion.

> *Equilibrium GDP is the output level at which the aggregate expenditure line intersects the 45° line. If firms produce this output level, their inventories will not change, and they will be content to continue producing the same level of output in the future.*

Equilibrium GDP and Employment

Now that you've learned how to find the economy's equilibrium GDP in the short run, a question may have occurred to you: When the economy operates at equilibrium, will it also be operating at full employment? The answer is: *not necessarily.* Let's see why.

If you look back over the two methods we've employed to find equilibrium GDP—using columns of numbers as in Table 4 and using a graph as in Figure 7, you will see that in both cases we've asked only one question: How much will households, businesses, the government, and foreigners *spend* on goods produced in the United States? We did not ask any questions about the number of people who want to work. Therefore, it would be quite a coincidence if our equilibrium GDP happened to be the output level at which the entire labor force were employed.

Figure 8 illustrates the connection between employment and output in the economy. We'll be going back and forth between the panels, so it's good to make sure you understand each step before going on to the next. Let's start with the right-hand panel, which shows the economy's *aggregate production function*, introduced earlier as part of the classical model. This curve tells us the relationship between any given number of workers and the level of output, with the current state of technology and given quantities of other resources. In this economy, full employment is assumed to be 100 million workers, measured along the horizontal axis. Potential output—$7,000 billion on the vertical axis—is the amount of output a fully-employed labor force of 100 million workers could produce. This is the also the long-run equilibrium output level that the classical model would predict for the economy.

But will $7,000 billion be the economy's equilibrium in the *short run*? Not necessarily. One possible outcome is shown in the left panel. The short-run equilibrium occurs at point *E,* where the aggregate expenditure line crosses the 45° line. At this point, output (on the horizontal axis) is $6,000 billion.

How many people will have jobs? We can answer by using the 45° line to convert the $6,000 billion from a horizontal distance to a vertical distance, then (following the dashed line) carrying that vertical distance across to the right panel. The right panel's production function tells us that to produce $6,000 billion in output, only 75 million workers are needed. In short-run equilibrium, then, only 75 million workers will have jobs. The difference between *full* employment and *actual* employment is 100 million − 75 million = 25 million, which is the amount of cyclical unemployment in the economy.

But why? What prevents firms from hiring the extra people who want jobs? After all, with more people working, producing more output, wouldn't there be more income in the economy and therefore more spending? Indeed, there would be. But not *enough* additional spending to justify the additional employment. To prove this, just look at what would happen if firms *did* hire 100 million workers. Output would rise to $7,000 billion, but at this output level, the aggregate

During the Great Depression of the 1930s, the economy's short-run equilibrium output fell far below potential, and at least a quarter of the labor force became unemployed.

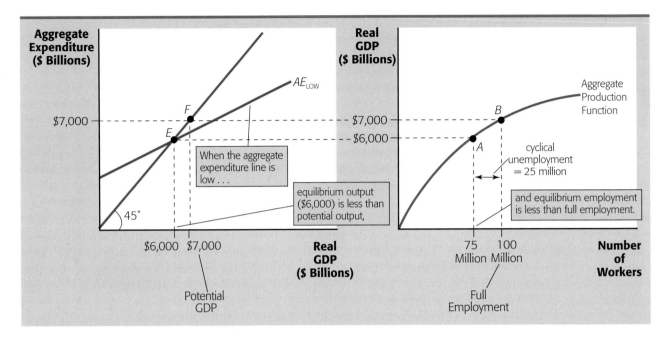

FIGURE 8

**Equilibrium GDP Can Be Less
than Full-Employment GDP**

expenditure line would lie below the 45° line so *firms would be unable to sell all their output.* Unsold goods would pile up in inventories, and firms would cut back on production until output reached $6,000 billion again, with employment back at 75 million.

In sum: Figure 8 shows that we can be in short-run equilibrium and yet have abnormally high unemployment. The reason: The aggregate expenditure line is *too low* to create an intersection at full-employment output.

> *In the short-run macro model, cyclical unemployment is caused by insufficient spending. As long as spending remains low, production will remain low and unemployment will remain high.*

What about the opposite possibility? In the short run, is it possible for spending to be *too high,* causing unemployment to be *too low?* Absolutely. Figure 9 illustrates such a case. Here, the aggregate expenditure line and the 45° line intersect at point *E′,* giving us a short-run equilibrium GDP at $8,000 billion. According to the production function, producing an output of $8,000 billion requires employment of 135 million workers. Since this is greater than the economy's full employment of 100 million, we will have abnormally high employment and abnormally low *un*employment.

> *In the short-run macro model, the economy can overheat because spending is too high. As long as spending remains high, production will exceed potential output, and unemployment will be unusually low.*

In the previous chapter, we concluded that the classical model could not explain economic fluctuations. The short-run macro model, on the other hand, does provide an explanation: The aggregate expenditure line may be low, meaning that in

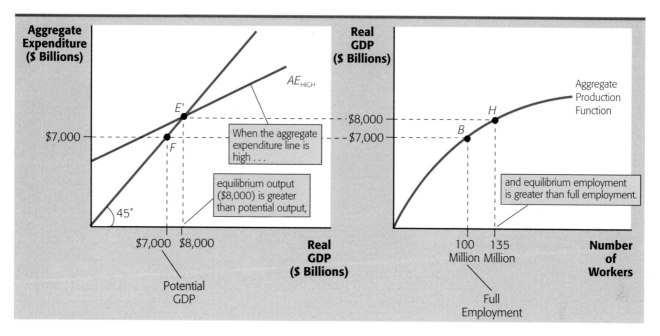

FIGURE 9
Equilibrium GDP Can Be Greater
than Full-Employment GDP

the short run, equilibrium GDP is below full employment. Or aggregate expenditure may be high, meaning that in the short run, equilibrium GDP is above the full-employment level. (Of course, this is just a first step in explaining economic fluctuations. In later chapters, we'll add more realism to the model.)

WHAT HAPPENS WHEN THINGS CHANGE?

So far, you've seen how the economy's equilibrium level of output is determined in the short run, and the important role played by spending in determining that equilibrium. But now it's time to use Step 3 and explore how a spending shock—a sudden change in spending—affects equilibrium output.

A Change in Investment Spending

Suppose the equilibrium GDP in an economy is $6,000 billion and then business firms increase their investment spending on plant and equipment. This might happen because business managers feel more optimistic about the economy's future, or because there is a new "must-have" technology (such as the Internet in the late 1990s), or because some new government policy increases the incentive for firms to buy new plant and equipment. Whatever the cause, firms decide to increase yearly planned investment purchases by $1,000 billion above the original level. What will happen?

First, sales revenue at firms that manufacture investment goods—firms like Dell Computer, Caterpillar, and Westinghouse—will increase by $1,000 billion. But remember, each time a dollar in output is produced, a dollar of income (factor payments) is created. Thus, the $1,000 billion in additional sales revenue will become $1,000 billion in additional income. This income will be paid out as wages,

TABLE 5
Cumulative Increases in Spending When Investment Spending Increases by $1,000 Billion

Round	Additional Spending in Each Round (Billions of Dollars per Year)	Total Additional Spending (Billions of Dollars per Year)
Initial Increase in Investment	1,000	1,000
Round 2	600	1,600
Round 3	360	1,960
Round 4	216	2,176
Round 5	130	2,306
Round 6	78	2,384
Round 7	47	2,431
Round 8	28	2,459
Round 9	17	2,476
Round 10	10	2,486
Round 20	0.06	Very close to 2,500

rent, interest, and profit to the households who own the resources these firms have purchased.[1]

What will households do with their $1,000 billion in additional income? Remember that with net taxes fixed at some value, a $1,000 rise in income is also a $1,000 rise in *disposable* income. Households are free to spend or save this additional income as they desire. What they will do depends crucially on the *marginal propensity to consume* (MPC) *in the economy*. If the MPC is 0.6, then consumption spending will rise by 0.6 × $1,000 billion = $600 billion. Households will save the remaining $400 billion.

But that is not the end of the story. When households spend an additional $600 billion, firms that produce consumption goods and services—firms such as McDonald's, Coca-Cola, American Airlines, and Disney—will receive an additional $600 billion in sales revenue, which, in turn, will become income for the households that supply resources to these firms. And when *these* households see *their* annual incomes rise by $600 billion, they will spend part of it as well. With an MPC of 0.6, consumption spending will rise by 0.6 × $600 billion = $360 billion, creating still more sales revenue for firms, and so on and so on. . . .

As you can see, an increase in investment spending will set off a chain reaction, leading to successive rounds of increased spending and income.

The process is illustrated in Table 5. The second column gives us the additional spending in each round of this chain reaction. The first entry shows the additional spending of $1,000 billion per year from the initial increase in investment. The next entry shows the $600 billion increase in consumption spending, then another $360 billion increase in consumption, and so on. Each successive round of additional spending is 60 percent of the round before. The third column adds up the additional spending created by all preceding rounds, to give the *total* additional spending as this chain reaction continues. For example, total additional spending after the first

---

[1] Some of the sales revenue will also go to pay for intermediate goods, such as raw materials, electricity, and supplies. But the intermediate-goods suppliers will also pay wages, rent, interest, and profit for the resurces *they* use, so that household income will still rise by the full $1,000 billion.

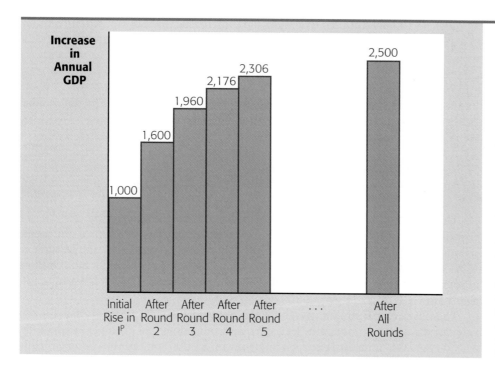

FIGURE 10

The Effect of a Change in Investment Spending

An increase in investment spending sets off a chain reaction, leading to successive rounds of increased spending and income. As shown here, a $1,000 billion increase in investment first causes real GDP to increase by $1,000 billion. Then, with higher incomes, households increase consumption spending by the MPC times the change in disposable income. In round 2, spending and GDP increase by another $600 billion. In succeeding rounds, increases in income lead to further changes in spending, but in each round the increases in income and spending are smaller than in the preceding round.

round is just $1,000 billion, the initial increase in annual investment spending. But after the second round, we add the $600 billion in additional consumption spending, to get $1,600 billion in additional spending per year. After the third round, additional spending rises to $1,960 billion per year.

Remember that each time spending rises, output rises to match it. Figure 10 illustrates what happens to GDP (at an annual rate) after each round of this chain reaction. When we analyze events like this in the U.S. economy, we find that the successive increases in spending and output occur quickly; the process is largely completed within a year. And at the end of the process, when the economy has reached its new equilibrium, total spending and total output are considerably higher.

But how much higher?

If you look at the second column of Table 5, you can see that each successive round adds less to total spending than the round before. And in Figure 10, you see that GDP rises by less and less with each round. Eventually, GDP rises by such a small amount that we can safely ignore it, and the GDP will be so close to its new equilibrium value that we can ignore any difference. In our example, when the chain reaction is virtually completed—equilibrium GDP will be $2,500 billion more than it was initially.

The Expenditure Multiplier

Let's go back and summarize what happened in our example: Business firms increased their investment spending by $1,000 billion, and as a result, spending and output rose by $2,500 billion. Equilibrium GDP increased by *more than* the initial increase in investment spending. In our example, the increase in equilibrium GDP ($2,500 billion) was two-and-a-half times the initial increase in investment spending ($1,000 billion). As you can verify, if investment spending had increased by half as much ($500 billion), GDP would have increased by 2.5 times *that* amount ($1,250 billion). In fact, *whatever* the rise in investment spending, equilibrium GDP would increase by a factor of 2.5, so we can write

$$\Delta GDP = 2.5 \times \Delta I^p.$$

In our example, the change in investment spending was *multiplied by* the number 2.5 in order to get the change in GDP that it causes. For this reason, 2.5 is called the *expenditure multiplier* in this example.

Expenditure multiplier The amount by which equilibrium real GDP changes as a result of a one-dollar change in autonomous consumption, investment spending, government purchases, or net exports.

> *The expenditure multiplier is the number by which the change in investment spending must be multiplied to get the change in equilibrium GDP.*

The value of the expenditure multiplier depends on the value of the *MPC* in the economy. If you look back at Table 5, you will see that each round of additional spending would have been larger if the *MPC* had been larger. For example, with an *MPC* of 0.9 instead of 0.6, spending in round 2 would have risen by $900 billion, in round 3 by $810 billion, and so on. The result would have been a larger ultimate change in GDP, and a larger multiplier.

There is a very simple formula we can use to determine the multiplier for *any* value of the *MPC*. To obtain it, let's start with our numerical example in which the *MPC* is 0.6. When investment spending rises by $1,000 billion, the change in equilibrium GDP can be written as follows:

$$\Delta GDP = \$1,000 \text{ billion} + \$600 \text{ billion} + \$360 \text{ billion} + \$216 \text{ billion} + \ldots$$

Factoring out the $1,000 billion change in planned investment, this becomes

$$\Delta GDP = \$1,000 \text{ billion } [1 + 0.6 + 0.36 + 0.216 + \ldots]$$
$$= \$1,000 \text{ billion } [1 + 0.6 + 0.6^2 + 0.6^3 + \ldots]$$

In this equation, $1,000 billion is the change in investment (ΔI^p), and 0.6 is the *MPC*. To find the change in GDP that applies to *any* ΔI^p and *any MPC*, we can write

$$\Delta GDP = \Delta I^p \times [1 + (MPC) + (MPC)^2 + (MPC)^3 + \ldots]$$

Now we can see that the term in brackets, the infinite sum $1 + MPC + (MPC)^2 + (MPC)^3 + \ldots$, is our multiplier. But what is its value?

We can borrow a rule from the mathematics of sums just like this one. The rule tells us that for any variable H that has a value between zero and 1, the infinite sum

$$1 + H + H^2 + H^3 + \ldots$$

always has the value $1/(1 - H)$. So we can replace H with the *MPC*, since the *MPC* is always between zero and 1. This gives us a value for the multiplier of $1/(1 - MPC)$.

> *For any value of the* MPC, *the formula for the expenditure multiplier is* $1/(1 - MPC)$.

In our example, the *MPC* was equal to 0.6, so the expenditure multiplier had the value $1/(1 - 0.6) = 1/0.4 = 2.5$. If the *MPC* had been 0.9 instead, the expenditure multiplier would have been equal to $1/(1 - 0.9) = 1/0.1 = 10$. The formula $1/(1 - MPC)$ can be used to find the multiplier for any value of the *MPC* between zero and one.

Using the general formula for the expenditure multiplier, we can restate what happens when investment spending increases:

$$\Delta GDP = \left[\frac{1}{(1 - MPC)} \right] \times \Delta I^p.$$

The multiplier effect is a rather surprising phenomenon. It tells us that an increase in investment spending ultimately affects GDP by *more* than the initial increase in investment. Further, it tells us that as long as annual investment spending remains $1,000 billion greater than it was previously, yearly GDP will remain higher than previously—$2,500 billion higher in our example. That is, a sustained increase in investment spending will cause a sustained increase in GDP.

By contrast, a one-time increase in investment—followed by a drop in investment back to its original level—will cause only a temporary change in GDP. That's because the multiplier process works in *both* directions, as you're about to see.

The Multiplier in Reverse

Suppose that, in Table 5, investment spending had *decreased* instead of increased. Then the initial change in spending would be −$1,000 billion ($\Delta I^p$ = −$1,000 billion). This would cause a $1,000 billion decrease in revenue for firms that produce investment goods, and they, in turn, would pay out $1,000 billion less in factor payments. In the next round, households, with $1,000 billion less in income, would spend $600 billion less on consumption goods, and so on. The final result would be a $2,500 billion *decrease* in equilibrium GDP.

Just as increases in investment spending cause equilibrium GDP to rise by a multiple of the change in spending, decreases in investment spending cause equilibrium GDP to fall by a multiple of the change in spending.

The multiplier formula we've already established will work whether the initial change in spending is positive or negative.

Other Spending Shocks

Shocks to the economy can come from other sources besides investment spending. In fact, when *any* sector's spending behavior changes, it will set off a chain of events similar to that in our investment example. Let's see how an increase in government spending could set off the same chain of events as an increase in investment spending.

Suppose that government agencies increased their purchases above previous levels. For example, the Department of Defense might raise its spending on new bombers, or state highway departments might hire more road-repair crews, or cities and towns might hire more teachers. If total government purchases rise by $1,000 billion, then, once again, household income will rise by $1,000 billion. As before, households will spend 60 percent of this increase, causing consumption, in the next round, to rise by $600 billion, and so on and so on. The chain of events is exactly like that of Table 5, with one exception: The first line in column 1 would read, "Initial Increase in Government Purchases" instead of "Initial Increase in Investment." Once again, output would increase by $2,500 billion.

Besides planned investment and government purchases, there are two other components of spending that can set off the same process. One is an increase in net exports (*NX*). Since *NX* = Exports − Imports, either an increase in the economy's exports or a *decrease* in imports will cause *net* exports to rise. For example, either an increase in exports of $1,000 billion, or a decrease in imports of $1,000 billion, would increase net exports by $1,000 billion and set off the same multiplier process described above.

Finally, a change in *autonomous consumption* can set off the process. For example, after a $1,000 billion increase in autonomous consumption spending we would see further increases in consumption spending of $600 billion, then $360 billion, and so on. This time, the first line in column 1 of Table 5 would read, "Initial Increase in Autonomous Consumption," but every entry in the table would be the same.

> *Changes in planned investment, government purchases, net exports, or autonomous consumption lead to a multiplier effect on GDP. The expenditure multiplier—1/(1 − MPC)—is what we multiply the initial change in spending by in order to get the change in equilibrium GDP.*

The following four equations summarize how we use the expenditure multiplier to determine the effects of different spending shocks in the short-run macro model. Keep in mind that these formulas work whether the initial change in spending is positive or negative.

$$\Delta GDP = \left[\frac{1}{(1 - MPC)} \right] \times \Delta I^p$$

$$\Delta GDP = \left[\frac{1}{(1 - MPC)} \right] \times \Delta G$$

$$\Delta GDP = \left[\frac{1}{(1 - MPC)} \right] \times \Delta NX$$

$$\Delta GDP = \left[\frac{1}{(1 - MPC)} \right] \times \Delta a$$

A Graphical View of the Multiplier

Figure 11 illustrates the multiplier using our aggregate expenditure diagram. The darker line is the aggregate expenditure line from Figure 7. The aggregate expenditure line intersects the 45° line at point *E*, giving us an equilibrium GDP of $6,000 billion.

Now, suppose that either autonomous consumption, investment spending, net exports, or government purchases rises by $1,000 billion. Regardless of which of these types of spending increases, the effect on our aggregate expenditure line is the same: It will *shift upward* by $1,000 billion, to the higher line in the figure. The new aggregate expenditure line intersects the 45° line at point *F*, showing that our new equilibrium GDP is equal to $8,500 billion.

What has happened? An initial spending increase of $1,000 billion has caused equilibrium GDP to increase from $6,000 billion to $8,500 billion, an increase of $2,500 billion. This is just what our multiplier of 2.5 tells us. In general,

$$\Delta GDP = \left[\frac{1}{(1 - MPC)} \right] \times \Delta \text{Spending}$$

and in this case,

$$\$2,500 \text{ billion} = 2.5 \times \$1,000 \text{ billion}.$$

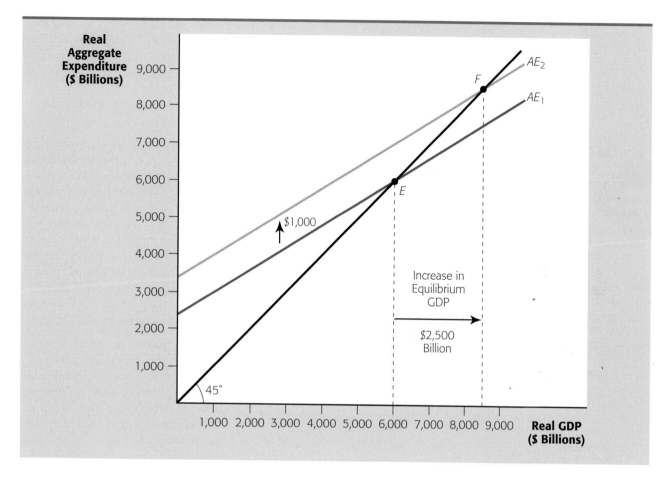

FIGURE 11
A Graphical View of the Multiplier

The economy starts off at point E with equilibrium real GDP of $6,000 billion. A $1,000 billion increase in spending shifts the aggregate expenditure line upward by $1,000 billion, triggering the multiplier process. Eventually, the economy will reach a new equilibrium at point F, where the new, higher aggregate expenditure line crosses the 45° line. At F, real GDP is $8,500, billion, an increase of $2,500 billion.

An increase in autonomous consumption spending, investment spending, government purchases, or net exports will shift the aggregate expenditure line upward by the initial increase in spending, causing equilibrium GDP to rise. The increase in GDP will equal the initial increase in spending times the expenditure multiplier.

Automatic Stabilizers and the Multiplier

In this chapter, we've presented a model to help us focus on the central relationship between spending and output. To keep the model as simple as possible, we've ignored many real-world factors that interfere with, and reduce the size of, the multiplier effect. These forces are called **automatic stabilizers** because, with a smaller multiplier, spending shocks will cause a much smaller change in GDP. As a result, economic fluctuations will be milder.

Automatic stabilizers reduce the size of the multiplier and therefore reduce the impact of spending shocks on the economy. With milder fluctuations, the economy is more stable.

Automatic stabilizers Forces that reduce the size of the expenditure multiplier and diminish the impact of spending shocks.

How do automatic stabilizers work? They shrink the additional spending that occurs in each round of the multiplier, and thereby reduce the final multiplier effect on equilibrium GDP. In Table 5, automatic stabilizers would reduce each of the numerical entries after the first $1,000 billion, and lead to a final change in GDP smaller than $2,500 billion.

Here are some of the real-world automatic stabilizers we've ignored in the simple, short-run macro model of this chapter:

DANGEROUS CURVES

The Two Kinds of Consumption Changes It's easy to become confused about the relationship between consumption spending and the expenditure multiplier. Does a change in consumption spending cause a multiplier effect? Or does the multiplier effect create an increase in consumption spending? Actually, the causation runs in both directions. The key is to recognize that there are two kinds of changes in consumption spending.

One kind is a change in autonomous consumption spending (the term "*a*" in the consumption function). This change will *shift* the aggregate expenditure line up or down, telling us that total spending will be greater or smaller at *any* level of income. It is the kind of change that *causes* a multiplier effect.

But consumption also changes when something other than autonomous consumption sets off a multiplier effect. This is because consumption depends on income, and income always increases during the successive rounds of the multiplier effect. Such a change in consumption is represented by a movement *along* the aggregate expenditure line, rather than a shift.

Whenever you discuss a change in consumption spending, make sure you know whether it is a change in autonomous consumption (a shift of the *AE* line) or a change in consumption caused by a change in income (a movement along the *AE* line).

Taxes. We've been assuming that taxes remain constant, so that a rise in income causes an equal rise in disposable income. But some taxes (like the personal income tax) rise with income. As a result, in each round of the multiplier, the increase in disposable income will be smaller than the increase in income. With a smaller rise in disposable income, there will be a smaller rise in consumption spending as well.

Transfer Payments. Some government transfer payments fall as income rises. For example, many laid-off workers receive unemployment benefits, which help support them for several months while they are unemployed. But when income and output rise, employment also rises, and newly hired workers must give up their unemployment benefits. As a result, a rise in income will cause a smaller rise in *disposable* income in each round, and a smaller rise in consumption.

Interest Rates. In a later chapter, you'll learn that an increase in output often leads to rising interest rates as well. This will crowd out some consumption and investment spending, making the increase in aggregate expenditure smaller than our simple story suggests.

Imports. Some additional spending is on goods and services imported from abroad. That is, instead of remaining constant as in our example, imports often rise as income rises, and net exports therefore fall as income rises. This helps to counteract any increase in spending caused by a rise in income.

Forward-looking Behavior. Consumers may be *forward-looking*. If they realize that the fluctuations in the economy are temporary, their consumption spending may be less sensitive to changes in their current income. Therefore, any change in income will cause a smaller change in consumption spending, and lead to a smaller multiplier effect.

Remember that each of these automatic stabilizers reduces the size of the multiplier, making it smaller than the simple formulas given in this chapter. For example, the simple formula for the expenditure multiplier is $1/(1 - MPC)$. With an *MPC* of about 0.9—which is in the ballpark for the United States and many other countries—we would expect the multiplier to be about 10 . . . *if the simple formula were accurate.* In that case, a $1,000 billion increase in government spending would cause output to rise by $10,000 billion—quite a large multiplier effect.

But after we take account of all of the automatic stabilizers, the multiplier is considerably smaller. How much smaller? Most of the forecasting models used by economists in business and government predict that the multiplier effect takes about nine months to a year to work its way through the economy. At the end of the process, the multiplier has a value of about 1.5. This means that a $1,000 billion increase in, say, government spending should cause GDP to increase by only about $1,500 billion in a year. This is much less than the $10,000 billion increase predicted by the simple formula $1/(1 - MPC)$ when the MPC is equal to 0.9.

> *In the real world, due to automatic stabilizers, spending shocks have much weaker impacts on the economy than our simple multiplier formulas would suggest.*

Finally, there is one more automatic stabilizer you should know about, perhaps the most important of all: the *passage of time.* Why is this an automatic stabilizer? Because, as you've learned, the impact of spending shocks on the economy is *temporary.* As time passes, the classical model—lurking in the background—stands ready to take over. And if we wait long enough—a few years or so—we will return to our potential output level. That is, after a shock pulls us away from full-employment GDP, the economy will eventually return to full-employment GDP, right where it started. We thus conclude that

> *in the long run, our multipliers have a value of zero: No matter what the change in spending or taxes, output will return to full employment, so the change in equilibrium GDP will be zero.*

Of course, the year or two we must wait can seem like an eternity to those who are jobless when the economy is operating below its potential. The short run is not to be overlooked. This is why, in the next several chapters, we will continue with our exploration of the short run, building on the macro model you've learned in this chapter. We'll be making the analysis more complete and more realistic by bringing in some of the real-world features that were not fully considered here.

COMPARING MODELS: LONG RUN AND SHORT RUN

Before leaving this chapter, it's important to note some startling differences between the long-run classical model you learned about a few chapters ago and the short-run macro model of this chapter. We've already discussed one of these differences: In the classical model, the economy operates *automatically* at potential GDP. In the short-run macro model, by contrast, the economy can operate above its potential or below its potential. The reason for the difference is that, in the short run, spending affects output: A negative spending shock can cause a recession that pushes output below potential GDP; a positive spending shock can cause a rapid expansion that pushes the economy above potential GDP, a boom.

There are two other important contrasts between the predictions of the two models. One concerns the role of saving in the economy, and the other concerns the effectiveness of fiscal policy. Let's explore each of these issues in turn.

The Role of Saving

In the long run, saving has positive effects on the economy. This was demonstrated two chapters ago, when—using the classical model—we discussed economic growth. Suppose, for example, that households decide to save more at any level of income. In the long run, the extra saving will flow into the loanable funds market, where it will be borrowed by business firms to purchase new plant and equipment. Thus, an increase in saving automatically leads to an increase in planned investment, faster growth in the capital stock, and a faster rise in living standards. Indeed, we can expect an increase in saving to have precisely these effects . . . in the long run.

But in the short run, the automatic mechanisms of the classical model do not keep the economy operating at its potential. On the contrary, *spending* influences output in the short run. If households decide to save more at each income level, they also, by definition, *spend less* at each income level. Or, putting it another way, an increase in saving is the same as a *decrease* in autonomous consumption spending, *a*. As you've learned in this chapter, a decrease in autonomous consumption spending causes a decrease in output through the multiplier process. If the economy is initially operating at full employment, the increase in saving will push output *below* its potential.

> *In the long run, an increase in the desire to save leads to faster economic growth and rising living standards. In the short run, however, it can cause a recession that pushes output below its potential.*

You can see that there are two sides to the "savings coin." The impact of increased saving is positive in the long run and potentially dangerous in the short run. Are you wondering how we get from the potentially harmful short-run effect of higher saving to the beneficial long-run effect? We'll address this question a few chapters later, when we examine how the economy adjusts from its short-run equilibrium to its long-run equilibrium.

The Effect of Fiscal Policy

In the classical model, you learned that fiscal policy—changes in government spending or taxes designed to change equilibrium GDP—is completely ineffective. More specifically, an increase in government purchases *crowds out* an equal amount of household and business spending: The rise in G is exactly matched by the decrease in C and I . . . in the long run.

But in the short run, once again, we cannot rely on the mechanisms of the classical model that are so effective in the long run. In the short run, *an increase in government purchases causes a multiplied increase in equilibrium GDP*. Therefore, in the short run, fiscal policy can actually change equilibrium GDP!

This important observation suggests that fiscal policy could, in principle, play a role in altering the path of the economy. If output begins to dip below potential, couldn't we use fiscal policy to pull us out of it or even prevent the recession entirely? For example, if investment spending decreases by $100 billion, setting off a negative multiplier effect, couldn't we just increase government purchases by $100 billion to set off an equal, positive multiplier effect? Why wait the many months or years it would take for the classical model to "kick in" and bring the economy back to full employment when we have such a powerful tool, fiscal policy, at our disposal?

Indeed, in the 1960s and early 1970s, this was the thinking of many economists. At that time, the popular view was that fiscal policy could effectively smooth out economic fluctuations, perhaps even eliminate them entirely. But very few economists believe this today. Why? In part, because of practical difficulties in executing the right fiscal policy at the right time. But more importantly, the rules of economic policy making have changed: The Federal Reserve now attempts to neutralize fiscal policy changes long before they can affect spending and output in the economy. In later chapters, we'll discuss the practical difficulties of executing fiscal policy and how the Federal Reserve has changed the "rules of the game."

USING THE THEORY
The Recession of 2001

Our most recent recession lasted from March 2001 to November 2001. Table 6 tells the story. Look first at the upper panel. The second column shows real GDP in 2000 dollars in each of several quarters. The figures are stated as *annual rates*. (For example, real GDP in the *second* quarter of 2001 was $9,906 billion. This means that *if* we had continued producing that quarter's GDP for an entire year, we *would* have produced a total of $9,906 billion worth of goods and services in the year 2001.) The other columns show investment spending (also at an annual rate) and the average level of employment for the quarter.

The lower panel, derived from the upper panel, gives a clearer picture of what happened during 2001. For each quarter, it shows the *change* in real GDP, investment spending, and average employment from the quarter before. As you can see, investment spending—which had been drifting downward—fell sharply during the second quarter of 2001 and continued to fall throughout the year. Employment mirrored this change, dropping in the second quarter and continuing to drop through the year. And real GDP—whose annual rate would normally have risen by $80 billion or so each quarter—fluctuated with almost no growth during the year.

What caused this recession? And can our short-run macro model help us understand it?

The decrease in investment spending is just the sort of spending shock that shifts the aggregate expenditure line downward. Over time, as the multiplier process takes place, a decrease in investment will bring down both GDP and employment, and that is just what began to happen in 2001.

But what caused these successive decreases in investment spending? In retrospect, we can see there were at least three causes.

First, during much of the late 1990s, there had been a boom in capital equipment spending as existing businesses rushed to incorporate the Internet into factories, offices, and their business practices in general. Firms like Avis, Wal-Mart, and Viacom needed servers and high-speed Internet connections, and the firms that supplied the new technology needed their own new offices, factories, and equipment. But as 2000 ended and 2001 began, firms had begun to catch up to the new technology. The rush ended and investment began to fall.

Another reason for the investment spending shock also had roots in the 1990s. During this period, the Internet and other new technologies made the public very optimistic about the future profits of American businesses, and hungry to own shares of stock in almost any company that had anything to do with the Internet. Share prices rose sky high. The optimism and high share prices encouraged entirely new businesses to start up—businesses that used the Internet to sell pet supplies, prescription drugs,

TABLE 6
The Recession of 2001

(a) Real GDP, Investment, and Employment

Quarter	Real GDP (Billions of 2000 Dollars)	Investment Spending (Billions of 2000 Dollars; excludes changes in inventories)	Average Employment (thousands)
4th quarter, 2000	9,888	1,689	137,341
Recession Quarters 1st quarter, 2001	9,876	1,678	137,719
2nd quarter, 2001	9,906	1,641	137,091
3rd quarter, 2001	9,871	1,622	136,729
4th quarter, 2001	9,910	1,577	136,222
1st quarter, 2002	9,994	1,560	136,096

(b) Change (from previous quarter) in Real GDP, Investment, and Employment

Quarter	Change in Real GDP (Billions of 2000 Dollars)	Change in Investment Spending (Billions of 2000 Dollars)	Change in Average Employment (thousands)
Recession Quarters 1st quarter, 2001	−12	−11	+378
2nd quarter, 2001	+30	−37	−628
3rd quarter, 2001	−35	−19	−362
4th quarter, 2001	+39	−45	−507
1st quarter, 2002	+84	−17	−126

Note: all figures based on most recent revisions of data (June, 2005) by the Bureau of Economic Analysis and Bureau of Labor Statistics.

and toys or to deliver videos, groceries, or even fresh hot pizzas. Of course, these new businesses needed their own capital equipment, warehouses, and office buildings, driving investment spending even further skyward in the late 1990s.

Unfortunately, in late 2000 and early 2001, reality set in. Competition was preventing many new firms from earning any profit, and many went bankrupt. Optimism shifted to pessimism. Share prices fell, and new business ventures—especially those having to do with the Internet—came to a halt. And so did the investment spending they had been undertaking. (We'll discuss the stock market in more detail in the "Using All the Theory" chapter at the end of this book.)

The final reason for the investment shock—more accurately, an exacerbation of the shock already occurring—was the infamous terrorist attacks on the World Trade Center and the Pentagon on September 11, 2001. The nation was traumatized by these events. What little optimism left in the future of the U.S. economy turned to uncertainty and fear. Millions of potential airline passengers no longer wanted to fly, forcing airlines to cancel flights and any orders for new aircraft. Hotel vacancy rates skyrocketed, and investment in new hotels and expansion of existing hotels came to a halt. Similar decisions were made in other industries, and investment spending fell sharply. (Although the table shows that investment declined only modestly in the third quarter, it is likely that most of the decrease occurred in September.)

One abnormal feature of the recession of 2001 was the behavior of consumption spending. Ordinarily, as income falls in a recession, consumption declines along with it. This is a movement leftward and downward along the consumption–income line (such as the line in Figure 3 of this chapter). Moreover, decreases in wealth from falling stock prices, and a sharp drop in consumer confidence after September 11, would ordinarily have caused a decrease in *autonomous* consumption spending (see Table 3), *shifting* the consumption–income line downward. Yet consumption spending (not shown) actually *rose* during every quarter of 2001. Since income fell during this time, the only way that consumption spending could rise was through an upward shift of the consumption–income line.

> **What Makes It a Recession?** Newspapers and television commentators often state that a recession occurs when real GDP declines for two consecutive quarters. But this is not correct.
>
> Actually, when a U.S recession begins and ends is determined by a committee within the National Bureau of Economic Research, an entirely private, nonprofit research organization headquartered in Boston.[2] The committee makes its decisions by looking at a variety of factors, including employment, industrial production, sales, and personal income, all of which are reported monthly. While it is true that each of these measures tends to move closely with real GDP, the latter is measured only quarterly, and plays only a supporting role in dating recessions.

DANGEROUS CURVES

Part of the reason for the upward shift was a 10-year tax cut that went into effect in June of 2001. But there were other reasons as well—which we'll look at two chapters from now. The increase in consumption spending was not enough to prevent the recession. The decline in investment spending—and the multiplier process it initiated—was too powerful.

The investment spending shock, and the recession it caused, are only half of the story of the recession of 2001. The other half, entirely ignored so far, is the response of government policy makers as they tried to prevent the economic storm from becoming a hurricane. Ultimately, their actions helped to make the recession relatively short and mild by historical standards. But to understand what these policy makers did, why they did it, and why it worked reasonably well, we must expand the short-run macro model. In the next chapter, we begin this process by learning about the banking system, the money supply, and the Federal Reserve.

---

[2] For the past few decades, the NBER's Business Cycle Dating Committee has been chaired by Robert E. Hall, a coauthor of this textbook.

Summary

In the short run, spending depends on income and income depends on spending. The short-run macro model was developed to explore this circular connection between spending and income.

Total spending is the sum of four aggregates: consumption spending by households, investment spending by firms, government purchases of goods and services, and net exports. Consumption spending (C) depends primarily on disposable income—what households have left over after paying taxes. The consumption function is a linear relationship between disposable income and consumption spending. The slope of the consumption function is the marginal propensity to con-

sume, a number between zero and one. It indicates the fraction of each additional dollar of disposable income that is consumed. The consumption–income line is the linear relationship between consumption and income. It has the same slope as the consumption function, but a different vertical intercept. For a given level of income, consumption spending can change as a result of changes in taxes, the interest rate, wealth, or expectations about the future. Each of these changes will shift the consumption–income line.

Investment spending (I^p), government purchases (G), and net exports (NX) are taken as given values, determined by forces outside our analysis. Aggregate expenditure (AE) is the sum $C + I^P + G + NX$; it varies with income because consumption spending varies with income.

Equilibrium GDP is the level of output at which aggregate expenditure is just equal to GDP (Y). If AE exceeds Y, then firms will experience unplanned decreases in inventories. They will respond by increasing production. If Y exceeds AE, firms will find their inventories increasing and will respond by reducing production. Only when $AE = Y$ will there be no unplanned inventory changes and no reason for firms to change production. Graphically, this occurs at the point where the aggregate expenditure line intersects the 45° line.

Spending shocks will change the economy's short-run equilibrium. An increase in investment spending, for example, shifts the aggregate expenditure line upward and triggers the multiplier process. The initial increase in investment spending causes income to increase. That, in turn, leads to an increase in consumption spending, a further increase in income, more consumption spending, and so on. The economy eventually reaches a new equilibrium with a change in GDP that is a multiple of the original increase in spending. Other spending shocks would have similar effects. The size of the *expenditure multiplier* is determined by the marginal propensity to consume.

There are several important differences between the short-run macro model and the long-run classical model. In the long run, the economy operates at potential output; in the short run, GDP can be above or below potential. In the long run, saving contributes to economic growth by making funds available for firms to invest in new capital. In the short run, increased saving means reduced spending and a lower level of output. Finally, fiscal policy is completely ineffective in the long run, but can have important effects on total demand and output in the short run.

Key Terms

Aggregate expenditure
Automatic stabilizers
Autonomous consumption spending

Consumption function
Consumption–income line
Equilibrium GDP

Expenditure multiplier
Marginal propensity to consume
Short-run macro model

Review Questions   *Answers to even-numbered Questions and Problems can be found on the text Web site at http://hall-lieb.swlearning.com.*

1. Briefly describe the four main categories of spending.

2. There are three different ways to interpret the marginal propensity to consume. What are they?

3. List, and briefly explain, the main determinants of consumption spending. Indicate whether a change in each determinant causes a movement along, or a shift of, the consumption–income line.

4. What are the main components of *planned investment* or *investment spending*? How does the definition of actual investment differ from planned investment?

5. What conditions must be satisfied in order for GDP to be at its equilibrium value? Is this equilibrium GDP the same as the economy's potential GDP? Why or why not?

6. Suppose that an increase in government purchases disturbs the economy's short-run equilibrium. Describe what happens as the economy adjusts to the change in spending.

7. What is the expenditure multiplier? How is it calculated, and how is it used?

8. What is an automatic stabilizer? List some automatic stabilizers for the U.S. economy. Which of these stabilizers do you think have gotten stronger, and which weaker, over the past several decades? Why?

9. Compare the macroeconomic role of saving in the short run and in the long run.

10. Does the short-run macro model reach the same conclusions about fiscal policy as the classical long-run model? Explain.

11. Refer to the relationship between real consumption spending and real disposable income shown in Figure 1. Based on this relationship, what should happen to real consumption spending during a recession? Did we see this behavior during the recession of 2001? Why or why not?

Problems and Exercises

1.

Y	C	I^P	G	NX
3,000	2,500	300	500	200
4,000	3,250	300	500	200
5,000	4,000	300	500	200
6,000	4,750	300	500	200
7,000	5,500	300	500	200
8,000	6,250	300	500	200

a. What is the marginal propensity to consume implicit in this data?

b. Plot a 45° line, and then use the data to draw an aggregate expenditure line.

c. What is the equilibrium level of real GDP? Illustrate it on your diagram.

d. Suppose that investment spending increased by 250 at each level of income. What would happen to equilibrium GDP?

2. a. Complete the following table when autonomous consumption is $30 billion, the marginal propensity to consume is 0.85, and net taxes are $0.

Real GDP ($ Billions)	Autonomous Consumption	MPC × Disposable Income	Consumption = Autonomous Consumption + (MPC × Disposable Income)
$0			
$100			
$200			
$300			
$400			
$500			
$600			

b. Given your answers in part (a), and given that planned investment is $40 billion, government spending is $20 billion, exports are $20 billion, and imports are $35 billion, complete the following table. (See table at bottom of page.)

c. Plot a 45° line, and then use your data to draw an aggregate expenditure line.

d. What is the equilibrium level of real GDP? Illustrate it on your diagram.

e. What will happen if the actual level of real GDP in this economy is $200 billion?

f. What will happen if the planned investment in this economy falls to $25 billion?

3.

Y	C	I^P	G	NX
7,000	6,100	400	1,000	500
8,000	6,900	400	1,000	500
9,000	7,700	400	1,000	500
10,000	8,500	400	1,000	500
11,000	9,300	400	1,000	500
12,000	10,100	400	1,000	500
13,000	10,900	400	1,000	500

a. What is the marginal propensity to consume implicit in these data?

b. What is the numerical value of the expenditure multiplier for this economy?

c. What is the equilibrium level of real GDP?

d. Suppose that government purchases (G) decreased from 1,000 to 400 at each level of income. What would happen to equilibrium real GDP?

4. Draw a graph showing a 45° line and an aggregate expenditures line.

a. Choose a point where real GDP is less than aggregate expenditures and label it GDP^A. Explain what will happen to inventories if the economy is operating at this point. What signal does this send to firms? Is GDP^A sustainable?

b. Choose a point where real GDP is greater than aggregate expenditures and label it GDP^B. Explain what will happen to inventories if the economy is operating at this point. What signal does this send to firms? Is GDP^B sustainable?

Real GDP ($ Billions)	Consumption Spending	Planned Investment	Government Spending	Net Exports	Aggregate Expenditure
$0					
$100					
$200					
$300					
$400					
$500					
$600					

5. Use an aggregate expenditure diagram to show the effect of each of the following changes:
   a. an increase in autonomous consumption spending due, say, to optimism on the part of consumers
   b. an increase in U.S. exports
   c. a decrease in taxes
   d. an increase in U.S. imports

   In each case, be sure to label the initial equilibrium and the new equilibrium.

6. What would be the effect on real GDP and total employment of each of the following changes?
   a. As a result of restrictions on imports into the United States, net exports (NX) increase.
   b. The federal government launches a new program to improve highways, bridges, and airports.
   c. Banks are offering such high interest rates that consumers decide to save a larger proportion of their incomes.
   d. The growth of Internet retailing leads business firms to purchase more computer hardware and software.

7. Using the data given in Problem 1, construct a table similar to Table 5 in this chapter.
   a. Show what would happen in the first five rounds following an increase in investment spending from 400 to 800.
   b. If investment spending stays at 800, what would be the ultimate effect on real GDP?
   c. How much would households spend on consumption goods in the new equilibrium?

8. Suppose that households become thriftier; that is, they now wish to save a larger proportion of their disposable income and spend a smaller proportion.
   a. In the table in Problem 1, which column of data would be affected?
   b. Draw an aggregate expenditure diagram and show how an increase in saving can be measured in that diagram.

   c. Use your aggregate expenditure diagram to show how an economy that is initially in short-run equilibrium will respond to an increase in thriftiness.

9. Calculate the change in real GDP that would result in each of the following cases:
   a. Planned investment spending rises by $100 billion, and the MPC is 0.9.
   b. Autonomous consumption spending decreases by $50 billion, and the MPC is 0.7.
   c. Government purchases rise by $40 billion, while at the same time, investment spending falls by $10 billion. The MPC is 0.6.

10. Calculate the changes in real GDP that would result in each of the following cases:
    a. Government purchases rise by $7,500, and the MPC is 0.95.
    b. Planned investment spending falls by $300,000 and the MPC is 0.65.
    c. Export spending rises by $60 billion at the same time that import spending rises by $65 billion, and the MPC is 0.75.

11. [Requires Appendix 2] Calculate the change in real GDP that would result in each of the following cases:
    a. Taxes fall by $30 billion, and the MPC is 0.8.
    b. Government spending and taxes *both* rise by $100 billion and the MPC is 0.9.

12. [Requires Appendix 2] Calculate the change in real GDP that would result in each of the following cases:
    a. Taxes rise by $400,000, and the MPC is 0.75.
    b. Taxes and government spending both fall by $500,000, and the MPC is 0.60.

13. Reread the last page of the "Using the Theory" section of this chapter. The consumption–income line shifted upward during the recession of 2001. But what happened to the aggregate expenditure line? How do we reconcile the shift in AE with the shift in the consumption–income line?

Challenge Questions

1. [Requires Appendix 1] Suppose that $a = 600$, $b = 0.75$, $T = 400$, $I^p = 600$, $G = 700$, and $NX = 200$. Calculate the equilibrium level of real GDP. Then check that the equilibrium value equals the sum $C + I^p + G + NX$.

2. [Requires Appendix 1] Suppose that $a = 1,000$, $b = 0.65$, $T = 700$, $I^p = 800$, $G = 600$, and $NX = -200$. Calculate the equilibrium level of real GDP. Then check that the equilibrium value equals aggregate expenditures.

3. The short-run equilibrium condition that $Y = C + I^p + G + NX$ can be reinterpreted as follows. First, subtract C from both sides to get $Y - C = I^p + G + NX$. Then note that all income not spent on consumption goods is either taxed or saved, so that $Y - C = S + T$. Now combine the two equations to obtain $S + T = I^p + G + NX$.

   Construct a diagram with real GDP measured on the horizontal axis. Draw two lines, one for $S + T$ and the other for $I^p + G + NX$. How would you interpret the point where the two lines cross? What would happen if investment spending increased?

4. Refer to your answer to Problem 12. Will your answer to part (b) change if the *MPC* is 0.8, rather than 0.60? Use

your finding to write a general statement about changes in government spending and taxes, and the resulting change in real GDP.

ECONOMIC Applications

These exercises require access to Hall/Lieberman Xtra! If Xtra! did not come with your book, visit http://www.bea.gov/bea/news-relarchive/2005/gdp105f.htm to purchase.

1. Use your Xtra! password at the Hall and Lieberman Web site (http://hallxtra.swlearning.com), select this chapter, and under Economic Applications, click on EconData. Choose *Macroeconomics: Employment, Unemployment, and Inflation,* and scroll down to find *Real GDP.* Read the definition and click on Updates and use the information to answer the following questions.

   a. Read the Bureau of Economic Analysis's new release http://www.bea.gov/bea/newsrelarchive/2005/gdp105f.htm and discuss the contributions of each component of the real GDP to growth in the period considered.

   b. Refer to the U.S. GDP and its Components data link http://www.economagic.com/fedstl.htm#GDP. Retrieve the data (in constant dollars), and the percent change of data for the four main components of aggregate expenditure: (1) Personal Consumption Expenditures, (2) Gross Private Domestic Investment, (3) Government Purchases, and (4) Net Exports.

   Which is the largest component? Which is the most volatile component?

   c. Refer to the U.S. GDP and its Components data link http://www.economagic.com/fedstl.htm#GDP. Retrieve the data (in constant dollars), for Personal Consumption and Disposable Income and chart Personal Consumption against Disposable Income. Draw a line to fit the trend and calculate its slope, which represents the marginal propensity to consume. Now calculate the simple multiplier. If spending increases by $1,000 billion, by how much will GDP increase?

   d. Refer to the U.S. GDP and its Components data link http://www.economagic.com/fedstl.htm#GDP. Click on the data series Change in Business Inventories, and then on GIF Chart. From this chart comment on the role of inventory adjustments in arriving at equilibrium, as discussed in this chapter.

APPENDIX 1

FINDING EQUILIBRIUM GDP ALGEBRAICALLY

The chapter showed how we can find equilibrium GDP using tables and graphs. This appendix demonstrates an algebraic way of finding the equilibrium GDP.

Our starting point is the relationship between consumption and disposable income given in the chapter. Letting Y_D represent disposable income:

$$C = a + bY_D$$

where a represents autonomous consumption spending and b represents the marginal propensity to consume. Remember that disposable income (Y_D) is the income that the household sector has left after net taxes. Letting T represent net taxes and Y represent total income or GDP, we have

$$Y_D = Y - T.$$

If we now substitute $Y_D = Y - T$ into $C = a + bY_D$, we get an equation showing consumption at each level of income:

$$C = a + b(Y - T).$$

We can rearrange this equation algebraically to read

$$C = (a - bT) + bY.$$

This is the general equation for the consumption–income line. When graphed, the term in parentheses $(a - bT)$ is the vertical intercept, and b is the slope. (Figure 3 shows a specific example of this line in which $a = $2,000$, $b = 0.6$, and $T = $2,000$.)

As you've learned, total spending or aggregate expenditure (AE) is the sum of consumption spending (C), investment spending (I^p), government spending (G), and net exports (NX):

$$AE = C + I^p + G + NX.$$

If we substitute for C the expression $C = (a - bT) + bY$, we get

$$AE = a - bT + bY + I^p + G + NX.$$

Now we can use this expression to find the equilibrium GDP. Equilibrium occurs when output (Y) and aggregate expenditure (AE) are the same. That is,

$$Y = AE$$

or, substituting the equation for AE,

$$Y = a - bT + bY + I^p + G + NX.$$

This last equation will hold true only when Y is at its equilibrium value. We can solve for equilibrium Y by first bringing all terms involving Y to the left-hand side:

$$Y - bY = a - bT + I^p + G + NX.$$

Next, factoring out Y, we get

$$Y(1 - b) = a - bT + I^p + G + NX.$$

Finally, dividing both sides of this equation by $(1 - b)$ yields

$$Y = \frac{a - bT + I^p + G + NX}{1 - b}.$$

This last equation shows how equilibrium GDP depends on a (autonomous consumption), b (the MPC), T (net taxes), I^p (investment spending), G (government purchases), and NX (net exports). These variables are all determined "outside our model." That is, they are given values that we use to determine equilibrium output, but they are not themselves affected by the level of output. If we use actual numbers for these given variables in the equation, we will find the same equilibrium GDP we would find using a table or a graph.

In the example we used throughout the chapter, the given values (found in Tables 1, 2, and 4) are, in billions of dollars, $a = 2,000$; $b = 0.6$; $T = 2,000$; $I^p = 700$; $G = 500$; and $NX = 400$. Plugging these values into the equation for equilibrium GDP, we get

$$Y = \frac{2,000 - (0.6 \times 2,000) + 700 + 500 + 400}{1 - 0.6}$$

$$= \frac{2,400}{0.4}$$

$$= 6,000.$$

This is the same value we found in Table 4 and Figure 7.

APPENDIX 2

THE SPECIAL CASE OF THE TAX MULTIPLIER

You learned in this chapter how changes in autonomous consumption, planned investment, and government purchases affect aggregate expenditure and equilibrium GDP. But there is another type of change that can influence equilibrium GDP: a change in taxes. For this type of change, the formula for the multiplier is slightly different from the one presented in the chapter.

Let's suppose that net taxes (T) *decrease* by $1,000 billion. Since disposable income is equal to total income − net taxes, the immediate impact of the tax cut is to *increase* disposable income by $1,000 billion. As a result, consumption spending will increase by $MPC \times$ $1,000 billion. Using the example in the chapter, with an MPC of 0.6, consumption spending would increase by $0.6 \times$ $1,000 billion = $600 billion. *This is the initial rise in spending caused by the tax cut.* Once consumption spending rises, the multiplier works as with any other change in spending: Consumption rises by another $0.6 \times$ $600 billion = $360 billion in the next round, and by another $0.6 \times$ $360 = $216 billion after that, and so on.

Now let's compare the full multiplier effect from a $1,000 billion cut in net taxes with the effect from a $1,000 billion increase in spending, such as planned investment spending. Look back at Table 5. There you can see that a $1,000 billion rise in investment spending causes a total increase in GDP of $1,000 billion + $600 billion + $360 billion + $216 billion + . . . = $2,500 billion. But when taxes are cut by $1,000 billion, the total increase in GDP is $600 billion + $360 billion + $216 billion + ... These two series of numbers are the same except that for the tax cut, the first $1,000 billion is missing. Therefore, the final rise in GDP from the tax cut must be $1,000 billion less than the final rise in GDP from the increase in investment spending. Since the $1,000 billion rise in investment spending raises GDP by $2,500 billion, a $1,000 billion cut in taxes must raise GDP by $2,500 billion − $1,000 billion = $1,500 billion.

Another way to say this is: For each dollar that taxes are cut, equilibrium GDP will increase by $1.50 rather than $2.50; the increase is one dollar less in the case of the tax cut. This observation tells us that the tax multiplier must have a numerical value *1.0 less than* the spending multiplier of the chapter.

Finally, there is one more difference between the spending multiplier of the chapter and the tax multiplier: While the spending multiplier is a positive number (because an increase in spending causes an increase in equilibrium GDP), the tax multiplier is a negative number, since a tax cut (a negative change in taxes) must be multiplied by a *negative* number to give us a *positive* change in GDP. Putting all this together, we conclude that

Thus, if the MPC is 0.6 (as in the chapter), so that the spending multiplier is 2.5, then the tax multiplier will have a value of $-(2.5 - 1) = -1.5$.

More generally, since the tax multiplier is 1.0 less than the spending multiplier and is also negative, we can write

Tax multiplier = −(spending multiplier − 1).

the tax multiplier is 1.0 less than the spending multiplier, and negative in sign.

Because the expenditure multiplier is $1/(1 - MPC)$, we can substitute to get

Tax multiplier $= -\left[\dfrac{1}{1 - MPC} - 1\right]$

$= -\left[\dfrac{1}{1 - MPC} - \dfrac{1 - MPC}{1 - MPC}\right]$

$= \dfrac{-MPC}{1 - MPC}.$

Hence,

the general formula for the tax multiplier is

$$\dfrac{-MPC}{(1 - MPC)}.$$

For any change in net taxes, we can use the formula to find the change in net equilibrium GDP as follows:

$$\Delta GDP = \dfrac{-MPC}{1 - MPC} \times \Delta T.$$

In our example, in which taxes were cut by \$1,000 billion, we have $\Delta T = -\$1{,}000$ billion and $MPC = 0.6$. Plugging these values into the formula, we obtain

$$\Delta GDP = \left[\dfrac{-0.6}{1 - 0.6}\right] \times -\$1{,}000 \text{ billion}$$

$$= \$1{,}500 \text{ billion}.$$

The Banking System and the Money Supply

CHAPTER OUTLINE

What Counts as Money

Measuring the Money Supply
Assets and Their Liquidity
M1 and M2

The Banking System
Financial Intermediaries
Commercial Banks
A Bank's Balance Sheet

The Federal Reserve System
The Structure of the Fed
The Functions of the Federal Reserve

The Fed and the Money Supply
How the Fed Increases the Money Supply
The Demand Deposit Multiplier
The Fed's Influence on the Banking System as a Whole
How the Fed Decreases the Money Supply
Some Important Provisos About the Demand Deposit Multiplier
Other Tools for Controlling the Money Supply

Using the Theory: Bank Failures and Banking Panics

Everyone knows that money doesn't grow on trees. But where does it actually come from? You might think that the answer is simple: The government just prints it. Right?

Sort of. It is true that much of our money supply is, indeed, paper currency, provided by our national monetary authority. But most of our money is *not* paper currency at all. Moreover, the monetary authority in the United States—the Federal Reserve System—is technically not a part of the executive, legislative, or judicial branch of government. Rather, it is a quasi-independent agency that operates *alongside* the government.

In future chapters, we'll make our short-run macro model more realistic by bringing in money and its effects on the economy. This will deepen your understanding of economic fluctuations, and help you understand our policy choices in dealing with them. But in this chapter, we focus on money itself, and the institutions that help create it. We will begin, in the next section, by taking a close look at what money is and how it is measured.

WHAT COUNTS AS MONEY

As discussed several chapters ago, money provides a nation with a *unit of account*, a standardized way of measuring the value of things that are traded. In this and the next chapter, we'll introduce money's function as a *store of value*, one of several ways in which households can hold their wealth. And most importantly, money is a *means of payment*: It can be used to buy things.

But now consider what *is* and what is *not* thought to be money in countries around the world. For example, paper currency, travelers checks, and funds held in checking accounts are all considered to be money in nations with well-established banking systems. That makes sense, because all of these can be used as means of payment. Yet credit cards are *not* considered money, even though you can use them to buy things. Why is this?

A more formal definition of money helps to answer questions like this.

Money An asset widely accepted as a means of payments.

> **Money** is an asset that is widely accepted as a means of payment in the economy.

Let's consider this definition more closely. First, only *assets*—things of value that people own—can be considered as money. Paper currency, travelers checks, and funds held in checking accounts are all examples of assets that people own, and these are all considered money in the United States. But *the right to borrow* is not an asset, so is not considered money. This is why the credit limit on your credit card, or your ability to go into a bank and borrow funds, is not considered *money* in the economy.

Second, only things that are *widely acceptable* as a means of payment are regarded as money. Coins and paper currency (usually called *cash*), travelers checks, and personal checks can all be used to buy things or pay bills. Other assets—such as stocks and bonds or even gold bars—can*not* generally be used for to pay for goods and services, and so they fail the acceptability test.

MEASURING THE MONEY SUPPLY

As you will learn in the next chapter, the amount of money in circulation can affect the macroeconomy. This is why governments around the world like to know how much money is available to their citizens—the total **money supply**.

Money supply The total amount of money held by the public.

In practice, measuring the money supply is not as straightforward as it might seem, and brings up some conceptual problems. For example, consider funds you might have in a savings account. While you can't use those funds to buy things directly, you can easily *move* the funds *into* your checking account, converting them to money. You might therefore regard your savings account as part of the means of payment that are easily available to you. Should they be included as part of the money supply?

Governments recognize this and other similar sticky questions, and have decided that the best way to deal with them is to have *different* measures of the money supply—in effect, alternative ways of defining what is and what is not money. Each measure includes a selection of *assets* that are *widely acceptable as a means of payment* and, as an additional criterion, *relatively liquid*.

Liquidity The property of being easily converted into cash.

> An asset is considered **liquid** if it can be converted to cash quickly and at little cost. An illiquid asset, by contrast, can be converted to cash only after a delay, or at considerable cost.

Checking account balances are highly liquid because you can convert them to cash at the ATM or by cashing a check. Travelers checks are also highly liquid. But stocks and bonds are *not* as liquid as checking accounts or travelers checks. Stock- and bondholders must go to some trouble and pay brokers' fees to convert these assets into cash.

But notice the phrase "*relatively* liquid." This does not sound like a hard-and-fast rule for measuring the money supply, and indeed it is not. This is why there are different measures of the money supply: Each interprets the phrase "relatively liquid" in a different way. To understand this better, let's look at the different kinds of liquid assets that people can hold.

Assets and Their Liquidity

Figure 1 lists a spectrum of assets, ranked according to their liquidity, along with the amounts of each asset in the U.S. public's hands on May 23, 2005. The most liquid asset of all is **cash in the hands of the public.** It takes no time and zero expense to convert this asset into cash, since it's *already* cash. In mid-2005, the public—including residents of other countries—held about $706 billion in U.S. cash.

Cash in the hands of the public Currency and coins held outside of banks.

Next in line are three asset categories of about equal liquidity. **Demand deposits** are the checking accounts held by households and business firms at commercial banks, including huge ones like the Bank of America or Citibank, and smaller ones like Simmons National Bank in Arkansas. These checking accounts are called "demand" deposits because when you write a check to someone, that person can go into a bank and, on demand, be paid in cash. This is one reason that demand deposits are considered very liquid: The person who has your check can convert it into cash quickly and easily. Another reason is that you can withdraw cash from your own checking account very easily—24 hours a day with an ATM card, or during banking hours if you want to speak to a teller. As you can see in the figure, the U.S. public held $332 billion in demand deposits in mid-2005.

Demand deposits Checking accounts that do not pay interest.

Other checkable deposits is a catchall category for several types of checking accounts that work very much like demand deposits. This includes *automatic transfers from savings accounts*, which are interest-paying savings accounts that automatically transfer funds into checking accounts when needed. On May 23, 2005, the U.S. public held $324 billion of these types of checkable deposits.

Travelers checks are specially printed checks that you can buy from banks or other private companies, like American Express. Travelers checks can be easily spent at almost any hotel or store. You can often cash them at a bank. You need only show an I.D. and countersign the check. In mid-2005, the public held about $8 billion in travelers checks.

Savings-type accounts at banks and other financial institutions (such as *savings and loan* institutions) amounted to $3,512 billion in mid-2005. These are less liquid than checking-type accounts, since they do not allow you to write checks. While it is easy to transfer funds from your savings account to your checking account, you must make the transfer yourself.

Next on the list are deposits in *retail money market mutual funds (MMMFs)*, which use customer deposits to buy a variety of financial assets. Depositors can withdraw their money by writing checks. In mid-2005, the general public held about $700 billion in such MMMFs.

Time deposits (sometimes called *certificates of deposit*, or *CDs*) require you to keep your money in the bank for a specified period of time (usually six months or

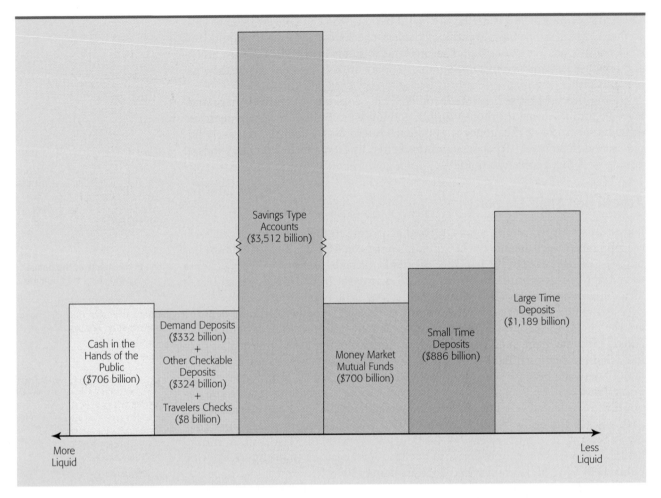

Source: http://www.federalreserve.gov,
Money Stock Measures, H.6, Tables 4
and 5.

FIGURE 1
Monetary Assets and Their Liquidity (May 23, 2005)

Assets vary according to their liquidity—the ease with which they can be converted into cash. Assets toward the left side of this figure are more liquid than those toward the right side.

M1 A standard measure of the money supply, including cash in the hands of the public, checking account deposits, and travelers checks.

longer), and impose an interest penalty if you withdraw early. In May 2005, the public held $886 billion in *small time deposits* (in amounts under $100,000) and $1,189 billion in *large time deposits* (in amounts over $100,000).

Now let's see how these assets have been used to define "money" in different ways.

M1 and M2

The standard measure of the money stock is called **M1.** It is the sum of the first four assets in our list: cash in the hands of the public, demand deposits, other checkable deposits, and travelers checks. These are also the four most liquid assets in our list.

M1 = cash in the hands of the public + demand deposits + other checking account deposits + travelers checks.

On May 23, 2005, this amounted to

M1 = $706 billion + $332 billion + $324 billion + $8 billion = $1,370 billion.

When economists or government officials speak about "the money supply," they usually mean M1.

But what about the assets left out of M1? While savings accounts are not as liquid as any of the components of M1, for most of us there is hardly a difference. All it takes is an ATM card and, presto, funds in your savings account become cash. Money market funds held by households and businesses are fairly liquid, even though there are sometimes restrictions or special risks involved in converting them into cash. And even time deposits—if they are not too large—can be cashed in early with only a small interest penalty. When you think of how much "means of payment" you have, you are very likely to include the amounts you have in these types of accounts. This is why another common measure of the money supply, **M2**, adds these and some other types of assets to M1:

M2 M1 plus savings account balances, retail money market mutual fund balances, and small time deposits.

$$M2 = M1 + \text{savings-type accounts} + \text{retail MMMF balances} + \text{small-denomination time deposits.}$$

Using the numbers for May 23, 2005 in the United States:

$$M2 = \$1{,}370 \text{ billion} + \$3{,}512 \text{ billion} + \$700 \text{ billion} + \$886 \text{ billion}$$

$$= \$6{,}468 \text{ billion.}$$

There are other official measures of the money supply besides M1 and M2 that add in assets that are less liquid than those in M2. But M1 and M2 have been the most popular, and most commonly watched, definitions.

It is important to understand that the M1 and M2 money stock measures exclude many things that people use regularly as a means of payment. Although M1 and M2 give us important information about the activities of the Fed and of banks, they do not measure all the different ways that people hold their wealth or pay for things. Credit cards, for example, are not included in any of the official measures of the money supply (they are not assets). But for most of us, unused credit *is* a means of payment, which we lump together with our cash and our checking accounts. As credit cards were issued to more and more Americans over the last several decades, the available means of payment increased considerably, much more than the increase in M1 and M2 suggests.

HTTP://

For information on electronic money systems around the world, see the "Survey of Electronic Money Developments" at http://www.bis.org/publ/cpss48.pdf.

Technological advances—now and in the future—will continue the trend toward new and more varied ways to make payments. For example, at the 1996 Olympics, people used electronic cash to make small transactions—smaller than would make sense with credit cards. You could buy a card worth $5, $10, or $20 and use it in place of cash or checks. In 1999, Citibank began testing similar electronic cash cards in the Upper West Side of Manhattan. In early 2002 electronic cash experiments were being conducted on several college campuses. But in spite of earlier optimistic forecasts, the idea has not yet caught on. Electronic cash is clearly a means of payment, even though it is not yet included in any measure of the money supply. If electronic cash were to become important in the economy, it would no doubt be included in M1.

Cash in Private Banks or the Fed In our definitions of money—whether M1, M2, or some other measure—we include cash (coin and paper currency) only if it is *in the hands of the public*. The italicized words are important. Some of the nation's cash is stored in bank vaults, and is released only when the public withdraws cash from their accounts. Other cash is in the hands of the Federal Reserve, which stores it for future release. But until this cash is released from bank vaults or the Fed, it is not part of the money supply. Only the cash possessed by households, businesses, or government agencies (other than the Fed) is considered part of the money supply.

DANGEROUS CURVES

Fortunately, the details and complexities of measuring money are not important for a basic understanding of the monetary system and monetary policy. For the rest of our discussion, we will make a simplifying assumption:

> *We will assume the money supply consists of just two components: cash in the hands of the public and demand deposits.*
>
> *Money supply = cash in the hands of public + demand deposits.*

As you will see later, our definition of the money supply corresponds closely to the liquid assets that our national monetary authority—the Federal Reserve—can control. While there is not much that the Federal Reserve can do directly about the amount of funds in savings accounts, MMMFs, or time deposits, or about the development of electronic cash or the ability to borrow on credit cards, it can tightly control the sum of cash in the hands of the public and demand deposits.[1]

We will spend the rest of this chapter analyzing how money is created and what makes the money supply change. Our first step is to introduce a key player in the creation of money: the banking system.

THE BANKING SYSTEM

Think about the last time you used the services of a bank. Perhaps you deposited a paycheck in the bank's ATM, or withdrew cash to take care of your shopping needs for the week. We make these kinds of transactions dozens of times every year without ever thinking about what a bank really is, or how our own actions at the bank—and the actions of millions of other bank customers—might contribute to a change in the money supply.

Financial Intermediaries

Financial intermediary A business firm that specializes in brokering between savers and borrowers.

Let's begin at the beginning: What are banks? They are important examples of **financial intermediaries**: business firms that specialize in assembling loanable funds from households and firms whose revenues exceed their expenditures, and channeling those funds to households and firms (and sometimes the government) whose expenditures exceed revenues. Financial intermediaries make the economy work much more efficiently than would be possible without them.

To understand this more clearly, imagine that Boeing, the U.S. aircraft maker, wants to borrow a billion dollars for three years. If there were no financial intermediaries, Boeing would have to make individual arrangements to borrow small amounts of money from thousands—perhaps millions—of households, each of which wants to lend money for, say, three months at a time. Every three months, Boeing would have to renegotiate the loans, and it would find borrowing money in this way to be quite cumbersome. Lenders, too, would find this arrangement troublesome. All of their funds would be lent to one firm. If that firm encountered difficulties, the funds might not be returned at the end of three months.

An intermediary helps to solve these problems by combining a large number of small savers' funds into custom-designed packages and then lending them to larger

---

[1] The Fed can also control some other types of checkable deposits. To keep our analysis as simple as possible, we consider only demand deposits.

borrowers. The intermediary can do this because it can predict—from experience—the pattern of inflows of funds. While some deposited funds may be withdrawn, the overall total available for lending tends to be quite stable. The intermediary can also reduce the risk to depositors by spreading its loans among a number of different borrowers. If one borrower fails to repay its loan, that will have only a small effect on the intermediary and its depositors.

Of course, intermediaries must earn a profit for providing brokering services. They do so by charging a higher interest rate on the funds they lend than the rate they pay to depositors. But they are so efficient at brokering that both lenders and borrowers benefit. Lenders earn higher interest rates, with lower risk and greater liquidity, than if they had to deal directly with the ultimate users of funds. And borrowers end up paying lower interest rates on loans that are specially designed for their specific purposes.

The United States boasts a wide variety of financial intermediaries, including commercial banks, savings and loan associations, mutual savings banks, credit unions, insurance companies, and some government agencies. Some of these intermediaries—called *depository institutions*—accept deposits from the general public and lend the deposits to borrowers. There are four types of depository institutions:

1. *Savings and loan associations (S&Ls)* obtain funds through their customers' time, savings, and checkable deposits and use them primarily to make mortgage loans.
2. *Mutual savings banks* accept deposits (called *shares*) and use them primarily to make mortgage loans. They differ from S&Ls because they are owned by their depositors rather than outside investors.
3. *Credit unions* specialize in working with particular groups of people, such as members of a labor union or employees in a specific field of business. They acquire funds through their members' deposits and make consumer and mortgage loans to other members.
4. *Commercial banks* are the largest group of depository institutions. They obtain funds mainly by accepting checkable deposits, savings deposits, and time deposits and use the funds to make business, mortgage, and consumer loans.

Since commercial banks will play a central role in the rest of this chapter, let's take a closer look at how they operate.

Commercial Banks

A commercial bank (or just "bank" for short) is a private corporation, owned by its stockholders, that provides services to the public. For our purposes, the most important service is to provide checking accounts, which enable the bank's customers to pay bills and make purchases without holding large amounts of cash that could be lost or stolen. Checks are one of the most important means of payment in the economy. Every year, U.S. households and businesses write trillions of dollars' worth of checks to pay their bills, and many wage and salary earners have their pay deposited directly into their checking accounts. And as you saw in Figure 1, the public holds about as much money in the form of demand deposits and other checking-type accounts as it holds in cash.

Banks provide checking account services in order to earn a profit. Where does a bank's profit come from? Mostly from lending out the funds that people deposit and charging interest on the loans, but also by charging for some services directly, such as check-printing fees or that annoying dollar or so sometimes charged for using an ATM.

TABLE 1
A Typical Commercial Bank's Balance Sheet

Assets		Liabilities and Net Worth	
Property and buildings	$ 5 million	Demand deposit liabilities	$100 million
Government and corporate bonds	$ 25 million	Net worth	$ 5 million
Loans	$ 65 million		
Cash in vault	$ 2 million		
In accounts with the Federal Reserve	$ 8 million		
Total Assets	$105 million	Total Liabilities plus Net Worth	$105 million

A Bank's Balance Sheet

Balance sheet A financial statement showing assets, liabilities, and net worth at a point in time.

We can understand more clearly how a bank works by looking at its *balance sheet,* a tool used by accountants. A **balance sheet** is a two-column list that provides information about the financial condition of a bank at a particular point in time. In one column, the bank's *assets* are listed—everything of value that it *owns.* On the other side, the bank's *liabilities* are listed—the amounts that the bank *owes.*

Table 1 shows a simplified version of a commercial bank's balance sheet.

Why does the bank have these assets and liabilities? Let's start with the assets side. The first item, $5 million, is the value of the bank's real estate—the buildings and the land underneath them. This is the easiest to explain, because a bank must have one or more branch offices in order to do business with the public.

Bond A promise to pay back borrowed funds, issued by a corporation or government agency.

Next, comes $25 million in *bonds,* and $65 million in *loans.* A **bond** is a promise to pay funds to the holder of the bond, issued by a corporation or a government agency when it borrows money.[2] A bond promises to pay back the loan either gradually (e.g., each month), or all at once at some future date. **Loans** are promises to pay back funds signed by households or noncorporate businesses. Examples are auto loans, student loans, small-business loans, and home mortgages (where the funds lent out are used to buy a home). Both bonds and loans generate interest income for the bank.

Loan An agreement to pay back borrowed funds, signed by a household or noncorporate business.

Next come two categories that might seem curious: $2 million in "vault cash," and $8 million in "accounts with the Federal Reserve." Vault cash, just like it sounds, is the coin and currency that the bank has stored in its vault. In addition, banks maintain their own accounts with the Federal Reserve, and they add and subtract to these accounts when they make transactions with other banks. Neither vault cash nor accounts with the Federal Reserve pay interest. Why, then, does the bank hold them? After all, a profit-seeking bank should want to hold as much of its assets as possible in interest-earning form: bonds and loans.

There are two explanations for vault cash and accounts with the Federal Reserve. First, on any given day, some of the bank's customers might want to

---

[2] We are using the term "bond" loosely to refer to *all* such promises issued by corporations and government agencies. Technically, a bond must be a long-term obligation to pay back money, 10 years or more from the time the money is first borrowed. Shorter-term obligations are called *notes* (between 1 and 10 years) or *bills* (1 year or less).

withdraw more cash than other customers are depositing. The bank must always be prepared to honor its obligations for withdrawals, so it must have some cash on hand to meet these requirements. This explains why it holds vault cash.

Second, banks are required by law to hold **reserves**, which are defined as *the sum of cash in the vault and accounts with the Federal Reserve.* The amount of reserves a bank must hold is called **required reserves.** The more funds its customers hold in their checking accounts, the greater the amount of required reserves. The **required reserve ratio,** set by the Federal Reserve, tells banks the fraction of their checking accounts that they must hold as required reserves.

For example, the bank in Table 1 has $100 million in demand deposits. If the required reserve ratio is 0.1, this bank's required reserves are 0.1 × $100 million = $10 million in reserves. The bank must hold *at least* this amount of its assets as reserves. Since our bank has $2 million in vault cash and $8 million in its reserve account with the Federal Reserve, it has a total of $10 million in reserves, the minimum required amount.

Now skip to the right side of the balance sheet. This bank's only liability is its demand deposits. Why are demand deposits a *liability*? Because the bank's customers have the right to withdraw funds from their checking accounts. Until they do, the bank *owes* them these funds.

Finally, the last entry. When we total up both sides of the bank's balance sheet, we find that it has $105 million in assets and only $100 million in liabilities. If the bank were to go out of business—selling all of its assets and using the proceeds to pay off all of its liabilities (its demand deposits)—it would have $5 million left over. Who would get this $5 million? The bank's owners: its stockholders. The $5 million is called the bank's **net worth.** More generally,

$$\text{Net worth} = \text{Total assets} - \text{Total liabilities.}$$

We include net worth on the liabilities side of the balance sheet because it is, in a sense, what the bank would owe to its owners if it went out of business. Notice that, because of the way net worth is defined, both sides of a balance sheet must always have the same total: *A balance sheet always balances.*

Private banks are just one of the players that help determine the money supply. Now we turn our attention to the other key player—the Federal Reserve System.

Reserves Vault cash plus balances held at the Fed.

Required reserves The minimum amount of reserves a bank must hold, depending on the amount of its deposit liabilities.

Required reserve ratio The minimum fraction of checking account balances that banks must hold as reserves.

Net worth The difference between assets and liabilities.

THE FEDERAL RESERVE SYSTEM

Every large nation controls its money supply with a **central bank**—the nation's principal monetary authority and the institution responsible for controlling its money supply. Most of the developed countries established their central banks long ago. For example, England's central bank—the Bank of England—was created in 1694. France was one of the latest in Europe, waiting until 1800 to establish the Banque de France. But the United States was even later. Although we experimented with central banks at various times in our history, we did not get serious about a central bank until 1913, when Congress established the *Federal Reserve System.*

Why did it take the United States so long to create a central bank? Part of the reason is the suspicion of central authority that has always been part of U.S. politics and culture. Another reason is the large size and extreme diversity of our country, and the fear that a powerful central bank might be dominated by the interests of one region to the detriment of others. These special American characteristics

Central bank A nation's principal monetary authority responsible for controlling the money supply.

FIGURE 2
The Geography of the Federal Reserve System

The United States is divided into 12 Federal Reserve districts, each with its own Federal Reserve Bank.

Source: Board of Governors of the Federal Reserve System (1994); *The Federal Reserve System, Purposes and Functions,* Eighth Edition, p. 8.

The Federal Open Market Committee meets in this room, inside the Fed's headquarters in Washington DC. The meetings are highly secretive. No one from the media, and no one representing Congress or the president, is permitted in the room during the meetings.

help explain why our own central bank is different in form from its European counterparts.

One major difference is indicated in the very name of the institution: the Federal Reserve System. It does not have the word *central* or *bank* anywhere in its title, making it less suggestive of centralized power.

Another difference is the way the system is organized. Instead of a single central bank, the United States is divided into 12 Federal Reserve districts, each one served by its own Federal Reserve Bank. The 12 districts and the Federal Reserve Banks that serve them are shown in Figure 2. For example, the Federal Reserve Bank of Dallas serves a district consisting of Texas and parts of New Mexico and Louisiana, while the Federal Reserve Bank of Chicago serves a district including Iowa and parts of Illinois, Indiana, Wisconsin, and Michigan.

Another interesting feature of the Federal Reserve System is its peculiar status within the government. Strictly speaking, it is not even a *part* of any branch of government. But the *Fed* (as the system is commonly called) was created by Congress, and could be eliminated by Congress if it so desired. Second, both the president and Congress exert some influence on the Fed through their appointments of key officials in the system.

The Structure of the Fed

Figure 3 shows the organizational structure of the Federal Reserve System. Near the top is the Board of Governors, consisting of seven members who are appointed by the president and confirmed by the Senate for a 14-year term. The most powerful person at the Fed is the *chairman* of the Board of Governors—one of the seven

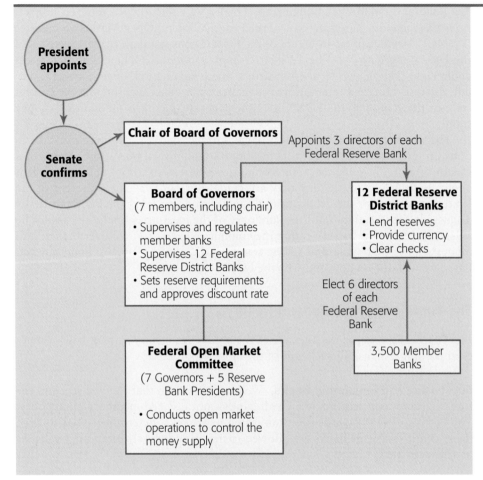

FIGURE 3
**The Structure of the
Federal Reserve System**

*Principal decision-making
power at the Fed is vested in the
Board of Governors, who are
appointed by the president and
confirmed by the Senate. Monetary policy is set by the Federal
Open Market Committee, which
consists of the seven governors
plus five of the presidents of
Federal Reserve Banks.*

governors who is appointed by the president, with Senate approval, to a four-year
term as chair. In order to keep any president or Congress from having too much influence over the Fed, the four-year term of the chair is *not* coterminous with the
four-year term of the president. As a result, every newly elected president inherits
the Fed chair appointed by his predecessor, and may have to wait several years before making an appointment of his own.

Each of the 12 Federal Reserve Banks is supervised by nine directors, three of
whom are appointed by the Board of Governors. The other six are elected by private commercial banks, the official stockholders of the system. The directors of
each Federal Reserve Bank choose a president of that bank, who manages its day-
to-day operations.

Notice that Figure 3 refers to "member banks." Only about a third of the
8,000 or so commercial banks in the United States are members of the Federal Reserve System. But they include all *national banks* (those chartered by the federal
government) and about a thousand *state banks* (chartered by their state governments). All of the largest banks in the United States (e.g., Citibank, Bank of America, and Fleet Bank) are nationally chartered banks and therefore member banks
as well.

Federal Open Market Committee (FOMC) A committee of Federal Reserve officials that establishes U.S. monetary policy.

The Federal Open Market Committee. Finally, we come to what most economists regard as the most important part of the Fed, the **Federal Open Market Committee** (**FOMC**). As you can see in Figure 3, the FOMC consists of all seven governors of the Fed, along with 5 of the 12 district bank presidents.[3] The committee meets about eight times a year to discuss current trends in inflation, unemployment, output, interest rates, and international exchange rates. After determining the current state of the economy, the FOMC sets the general course for the nation's money supply.

The word "open" in the FOMC's name is ironic, since the committee's deliberations are private. Summaries of its meetings are published only after a delay of a month or more. In some cases, the committee will release a brief public statement about its decisions on the day they are made. But not even the president of the United States knows the details behind the decisions, or what the FOMC actually discussed at its meeting, until the summary of the meeting is finally released. The reason for the word "open" is that the committee exerts control over the nation's money supply by buying and selling bonds in the public ("open") bond market. Later, we will discuss how and why the FOMC does this.

The Functions of the Federal Reserve

The Federal Reserve, as the overseer of the nation's monetary system, has a variety of important responsibilities. Some of the most important are:

Supervising and Regulating Banks. We've already seen that the Fed sets and enforces reserve requirements, which all banks—not just Fed members—must obey. The Fed also sets standards for establishing new banks, determines what sorts of loans and investments banks are allowed to make, and closely monitors banks' financial activities.

Acting as a "Bank for Banks." Commercial banks use the Fed in much the same way that ordinary citizens use commercial banks. For example, we've already seen that banks hold most of their reserves in reserve accounts with the Fed. In addition, banks can borrow from the Fed, just as we can borrow from our local bank. The Fed charges a special interest rate, called the **discount rate,** on loans that it makes to member banks. In times of financial crisis, the Fed is prepared to act as *lender of last resort,* to make sure that banks have enough reserves to meet their obligations to depositors.

Discount rate The interest rate the Fed charges on loans to banks.

Issuing Paper Currency. The Fed doesn't actually *print* currency; that is done by the government's Bureau of Engraving and Printing. But once printed, it is shipped to the Fed (under *very* heavy guard). The Fed, in turn, puts this currency into circulation. This is why every U.S. bill carries the label *Federal Reserve Note* on the top.

---

[3] Although all Reserve Bank presidents attend FOMC meetings, only 5 of the 12 presidents can vote on FOMC decisions. The president of the Federal Reserve Bank of New York has a permanent vote because New York is such an important financial center. But the remaining four votes rotate among the other district presidents.

Check Clearing. Suppose you write a check for $500 to pay your rent. Your building's owner will deposit the check into *his* checking account, which is probably at a different bank than yours. Somehow, your rent payment must be transferred from your bank account to your landlord's account at the other bank, a process called *check clearing*. In some cases, the services are provided by private clearinghouses. But in many other cases—especially for clearing out-of-town checks—the Federal Reserve system performs the service by transferring funds from one bank's reserve account to another's.

Controlling the Money Supply. The Fed, as the nation's monetary authority, is responsible for controlling the money supply. Since this function is so important in macroeconomics, we explore it in detail in the next section.

THE FED AND THE MONEY SUPPLY

Suppose the Fed wants to change the nation's money supply. (*Why* would the Fed want to do this? The answer will have to wait until the next chapter.) There are many ways this could be done. To increase the money supply, the Fed could print up currency and give it to Fed officials, letting them spend it as they wish. Or it could hold a lottery and give all of the newly printed money to the winner. To decrease the money supply, the Fed could require that all citizens turn over a portion of their cash to Fed officials who would then feed it into paper shredders.

These and other methods would certainly work, but they hardly seem fair or orderly. In practice, the Fed uses a more organized, less haphazard method to change the money supply: *open market operations.*

> *When the Fed wishes to increase or decrease the money supply, it buys or sells* government bonds *to bond dealers, banks, or other financial institutions. These actions are called* **open market operations***.*

Open market operations Purchases or sales of bonds by the Federal Reserve System.

We'll make two special assumptions to keep our analysis of open market operations simple for now:

1. Households and businesses are satisfied holding the amount of cash they are currently holding. Any additional funds they might acquire are deposited in their checking accounts. Any decrease in their funds comes from their checking accounts.
2. Banks never hold reserves in excess of those legally required by law.

Later, we'll discuss what happens when these simplifying assumptions do not hold. We'll also assume that the required reserve ratio is 0.1, so that each time deposits rise by $1,000 at a bank, its required reserves rise by $100.

How the Fed Increases the Money Supply

To increase the money supply, the Fed will *buy* government bonds. This is called an *open market purchase.* Suppose the Fed buys a government bond worth $1,000 from Lehman Brothers, a bond dealer that has a checking account at First

National Bank.[4] The Fed will pay Lehman Brothers with a $1,000 check, which the firm will deposit into its account at First National. First National, in turn, will send the check to the Fed, which will credit First National's reserve account by $1,000.

These actions will change First National's balance sheet as follows:

CHANGES IN FIRST NATIONAL BANK'S BALANCE SHEET

Action	Changes in Assets	Changes in Liabilities
Fed buys $1,000 bond from Lehman Brothers, which deposits $1,000 check from Fed into its checking account.	+$1,000 in reserves	+$1,000 in demand deposits

Notice that here we show only *changes* in First National's balance sheet. Other balance sheet items—such as property and buildings, loans, government bonds, or net worth—are not immediately affected by the open market purchase, so they are not listed here. As you can see, First National gains an asset—reserves—so we enter "+$1,000 in reserves" on the left side of the table. But there are also additional liabilities: the $1,000 that is now in Lehman Brothers' checking account and which First National owes to that firm. The additional liabilities are represented by the entry "+$1,000 in demand deposits" on the right side. Since First National's balance sheet was in balance before Lehman Brothers' deposit, and since assets and liabilities both grew by the same amount ($1,000), we know that the balance sheet is still in balance. Total assets are again equal to total liabilities plus net worth.

Before we go on, let's take note of two important things that have happened. First, the Fed, by conducting an open market purchase, has injected *reserves* into the banking system. So far, these reserves are being held by First National, in its reserve account with the Fed.

The second thing to notice is something that is easy to miss: *The money supply has increased.* How do we know? Because demand deposits are part of the money supply, and they have increased by $1,000. As you are about to see, even more demand deposits will be created before our story ends.

To see what will happen next, let's take the point of view of First National Bank's manager. He might reason as follows: "My demand deposits have just increased by $1,000. Since the required reserve ratio is 0.1, I must now hold $0.1 \times \$1,000 = \$100$ in additional reserves. But my *actual* reserves have gone up by more than $100; in fact, they have gone up by $1,000. Therefore, I have **excess reserves**—reserves above those I'm legally required to hold—equal to $1,000 − $100, or $900. Since these excess reserves are earning no interest, I should lend them out." Thus, we can expect First National, in its search for profit, to lend out $900 at the going rate of interest.

How will First National actually make the loan? It could lend out $900 in *cash* from its vault. It would be more typical, however, for the bank to issue a $900 *check* to the borrower. When the borrower deposits the $900 check into his own bank account (at some other bank), the Federal Reserve—which keeps track of these transactions for the banking system—will deduct $900 from First National's

Excess reserves Reserves in excess of required reserves.

---

[4] We'll limit our analysis to commercial banks, which hold demand deposits, although our story would be similar if other types of depository institutions were involved.

reserve account and transfer it to the other bank's reserve account. This will cause a further change in First National's balance sheet, as follows:

CHANGES IN FIRST NATIONAL BANK'S BALANCE SHEET

Action	Changes in Assets	Changes in Liabilities
Fed buys $1,000 bond from Lehman Brothers, which deposits $1,000 check from Fed into its checking account.	+$1,000 in reserves	+$1,000 in demand deposits
First National lends out $900 in excess reserves.	**−$900 in reserves** **+$900 in loans**	
The total effect on First National from beginning to end.	+$100 in reserves +$900 in loans	+$1,000 in demand deposits

Look at the boldface entries in the table. By making the loan, First National has given up an asset: $900 in reserves. This causes assets to change by −$900. But First National also gains an asset of equal value—the $900 loan. (Remember: While loans are liabilities to the borrower, they are assets to banks.) This causes assets to change by +$900. Both of these changes are seen on the assets side of the balance sheet.

Now look at the bottom row of the table. This tells us what has happened to First National from beginning to end. We see that, after making its loan, First National has $100 more in reserves than it started with, and $900 more in loans, for a total of $1,000 more in assets. But it also has $1,000 more in liabilities than it had before: the additional demand deposits that it owes to Lehman Brothers. Both assets and liabilities have gone up by the same amount. Notice, too, that First National is once again holding exactly the reserves it must legally hold. It now has $1,000 more in demand deposits than it had before, and it is holding $0.1 \times \$1,000 = \$100$ more in reserves than before. First National is finished ("loaned up") and cannot lend out any more reserves.

But there is still more to our story. Let's suppose that First National lends the $900 to the owner of a local business, Paula's Pizza, and that Paula deposits her loan check into *her* bank account at Second United Bank. Then, remembering that the Fed will transfer $900 in reserves from First National's reserve account to that of Second United, we'll see the following changes in Second United's balance sheet:

CHANGES IN SECOND UNITED'S BALANCE SHEET

Action	Changes in Assets	Changes in Liabilities
Paula deposits $900 loan check into her checking account.	**+$900 in reserves**	**+$900 in demand deposits**

Second United now has $900 more in assets—the increase in its reserve account with the Federal Reserve—and $900 in additional liabilities—the amount added to Paula's checking account.

Now consider Second United's situation from its manager's viewpoint. He reasons as follows: "My demand deposits have risen by $900, which means my required reserves have risen by $0.1 \times \$900 = \$90$. But my reserves have *actually* increased by $900. Thus, I have *excess reserves* of $\$900 − \$90 = \$810$, which I will lend out." After making the $810 loan, Second United's balance sheet will change once again (look at the boldface entries):

CHANGES IN SECOND UNITED'S BALANCE SHEET

Action	Changes in Assets	Changes in Liabilities
Paula deposits $900 loan check into her checking account.	+$900 in reserves	+$900 in demand deposits
Second United lends out $810 in excess reserves.	**−$810 in reserves** **+$810 in loans**	
The total effect on Second United from beginning to end.	+$ 90 in reserves +$810 in loans	+$900 in demand deposits

In the end, as you can see in the bottom row of the table, Second United has $90 more in reserves than it started with, and $810 more in loans. Its demand deposit liabilities have increased by $900. Notice, too, that the money supply has increased once again—this time, by $900.

Are you starting to see a pattern? Let's carry it through one more step. Whoever borrowed the $810 from Second United will put it into his or her checking account at, say, Third State Bank. This will give Third State excess reserves that it will lend out. As a result, its balance sheet will change as shown.

CHANGES IN THIRD STATE'S BALANCE SHEET

Action	Changes in Assets	Changes in Liabilities
Borrower from Second United deposits $810 loan check into checking account.	+$810 in reserves	+$810 in demand deposits
Third State lends out $729 in excess reserves.	**−$729 in reserves** **+$729 in loans**	
The total effect on Third State from beginning to end.	+$ 81 in reserves +$729 in loans	+$810 in demand deposits

As you can see, demand deposits increase each time a bank lends out excess reserves. In the end, they will increase by a *multiple* of the original $1,000 in reserves injected into the banking system by the open market purchase. Does this process sound familiar? It should. It is very similar to the explanation of the *expenditure multiplier* in the previous chapter, where in each round, an increase in spending led to an increase in income, which caused spending to increase again in the next round. Here, instead of spending, it is the *money supply*—or more specifically, *demand deposits*—that increase in each round.

The Demand Deposit Multiplier

By how much will demand deposits increase in total? If you look back at the balance sheet changes we've analyzed, you'll see that each bank creates less in demand deposits than the bank before. When Lehman Brothers deposited its $1,000 check from the Fed at First National, $1,000 in demand deposits was created. This led to an additional $900 in demand deposits created by Second United, another $810 created by Third State, and so on. In each round, a bank lent 90 percent of the deposit it received. Eventually the additional demand deposits will become so small that we can safely ignore them. When the process is complete, how much in additional demand deposits have been created?

Round	Additional Demand Deposits Created by Each Bank	Additional Demand Deposits Created by All Banks
First National Bank	$1,000	$ 1,000
Second United	$ 900	$ 1,900
Third State	$ 810	$ 2,710
Bank 4	$ 729	$ 3,439
Bank 5	$ 656	$ 4,095
Bank 6	$ 590	$ 4,685
. . .		
Bank 10	$ 387	$ 6,511
. . .		
Bank 20	$ 135	$ 8,784
. . .		
Bank 50	very close to zero	very close to $10,000

TABLE 2

Cumulative Increases in Demand Deposits After a $1,000 Cash Deposit

Table 2 provides the answer. Each row of the table shows the additional demand deposits created at each bank, as well as the running total. The last row shows that, in the end, $10,000 in new demand deposits has been created.

Let's go back and summarize what happened in our example. The Fed, through its open market purchase, injected $1,000 of reserves into the banking system. As a result, demand deposits rose by $10,000—10 times the injection in reserves. As you can verify, if the Fed had injected twice this amount of reserves ($2,000), demand deposits would have increased by 10 times *that* amount ($20,000). In fact, *whatever* the injection of reserves, demand deposits will increase by a factor of 10, so we can write

$$\Delta DD = 10 \times \text{reserve injection}$$

where "*DD*" stands for demand deposits. The injection of reserves must be *multiplied by* the number 10 in order to get the change in demand deposits that it causes. For this reason, 10 is called the *demand deposit multiplier* in this example.

> The *demand deposit multiplier* is the number by which we must multiply the injection of reserves to get the total change in demand deposits.

Demand deposit multiplier The number by which a change in reserves is multiplied to determine the resulting change in demand deposits.

The size of the demand deposit multiplier depends on the value of the required reserve ratio set by the Fed. If you look back at Table 2, you will see that each round of additional deposit creation would have been smaller if the required reserve ratio had been larger. For example, with a required reserve ratio of 0.2 instead of 0.1, Second United would have created only $800 in deposits, Third State would have created only $640, and so on. The result would have been a smaller cumulative change in deposits, and a smaller multiplier.

Now let's derive the formula we can use to determine the demand deposit multiplier for *any* required reserve ratio. We'll start with our example in which the required reserve ratio is 0.1. If $1,000 in reserves is injected into the system, the total change in deposits can be written as follows:

$$\Delta DD = \$1,000 + \$900 + \$810 + \$729 + \ldots$$

Factoring out $1,000, this becomes

$$\Delta DD = \$1,000 \times [1 + 0.9 + 0.9^2 + 0.9^3 + \ldots].$$

In this equation, $1,000 is the initial injection of reserves (Δreserves), and 0.9 is the fraction of reserves that each bank loans out, which is 1 minus the required reserve ratio ($1 - 0.1 = 0.9$). To find the change in deposits that applies to *any* change in reserves and *any* required reserve ratio (RRR), we can write

$$\Delta DD = \Delta\text{Reserves} \times [1 + (1 - RRR) + (1 - RRR)^2 + (1 - RRR)^3 + \ldots].$$

Now we can see that the term in brackets, the infinite sum $1 + (1 - RRR) + (1 - RRR)^2 + (1 - RRR)^3 + \ldots$, is our demand deposit multiplier. But what is its value?

Recall from the last chapter that an infinite sum

$$1 + H + H^2 + H^3 + \ldots$$

always has the value $1/(1 - H)$ as long as H is a fraction between zero and 1. In the last chapter, we replaced H with the MPC to get the expenditure multiplier. But here, we will replace H with $1 - RRR$ (which is always between zero and 1) to obtain a value for the deposit multiplier of $1/[1 - (1 - RRR)] = 1/RRR$.

For any value of the required reserve ratio (RRR), the formula for the demand deposit multiplier is 1/RRR.

In our example, the RRR was equal to 0.1, so the deposit multiplier had the value $1/0.1 = 10$. If the RRR had been 0.2 instead, the deposit multiplier would have been equal to $1/0.2 = 5$.

Using our general formula for the demand deposit multiplier, we can restate what happens when the Fed injects reserves into the banking system as follows:

$$\Delta DD = \left(\frac{1}{RRR}\right) \times \Delta\text{Reserves}.$$

Since we've been assuming that the amount of cash in the hands of the public (the other component of the money supply) does not change, we can also write

$$\Delta\text{Money Supply} = \left(\frac{1}{RRR}\right) \times \Delta\text{Reserves}.$$

The Fed's Influence on the Banking System as a Whole

We can also look at what happened to total demand deposits and the money supply from another perspective. When the Fed bought the $1,000 bond from Lehman Brothers, it injected $1,000 of reserves into the banking system. That was the only increase in reserves that occurred in our story. Where did the additional $1,000 in reserves end up? If you go back through the changes in balance sheets, you'll see that First National ended up with $100 in additional reserves, Second United ended up with $90, Third Savings with $81, and so on. Each of these banks is required to hold more reserves than initially, because its demand deposits have increased. In the end, *the additional $1,000 in reserves will be distributed among different banks in the system as required reserves.*

After an injection of reserves, the demand deposit multiplier stops working —and the money supply stops increasing—only when all the reserves injected are being held by banks as required *reserves.*

This observation helps us understand the demand deposit multiplier in another way. In our example, the deposit-creation process will continue until the entire injection of $1,000 in reserves becomes *required* reserves. But with an *RRR* of 0.1, each dollar of reserves entitles a bank to have $10 in demand deposits. Therefore, by injecting $1,000 of reserves into the system, the Fed has enabled banks, in total, to hold $10,000 in additional demand deposits. Only when $10,000 in deposits has been created will the process come to an end.

Just as we've looked at balance sheet changes for each bank, we can also look at the change in the balance sheet of the *entire banking system*. The Fed's open market purchase of $1,000 has caused the following changes:

"Creating Money" Doesn't Mean "Creating Wealth" Demand deposits are a means of payment, and banks create them. This is why we say that banks "create deposits" and "create money." But don't fall into the trap of thinking that banks create wealth. No one gains any additional wealth as a result of money creation.

DANGEROUS CURVES

To see why, think about what happened in our story when Lehman Brothers deposited the $1,000 check from the Fed into its account at First National. *Lehman Brothers* was no wealthier: It gave up a $1,000 check from the Fed and ended up with $1,000 more in its checking account, for a net gain of zero. Similarly, the *bank* gained no additional wealth: It had $1,000 more in cash, but it also *owed* Lehman Brothers $1,000—once again, a net gain of zero.

The same conclusion holds for any other step in the money-creation process. When Paula borrows $900 and deposits it into her checking account at Second United, she is no wealthier: She has $900 more in her account, but owes $900 to First National. And once again, the bank is no wealthier: It has $900 more in demand deposits, but owes this money to Paula.

Always remember that when banks "create money," they do not create wealth.

CHANGES IN THE BALANCE SHEET OF THE ENTIRE BANKING SYSTEM

Changes in Assets	Changes in Liabilities
+$1,000 in reserves	+$10,000 in demand deposits
+$9,000 in loans	

In the end, total reserves in the system have increased by $1,000—the amount of the open market purchase. Each dollar in reserves supports $10 in demand deposits, so we know that total deposits have increased by $10,000. Finally, we know that a balance sheet always balances. Since liabilities increased by $10,000, loans must have increased by $9,000 to increase total assets (loans and reserves) by $10,000.

How the Fed Decreases the Money Supply

Just as the Fed can increase the money supply by purchasing government bonds, it can also *decrease* the money supply by *selling* government bonds—an *open market sale.*

Where does the Fed get the government bonds to sell? It has trillions of dollars' worth of government bonds from open market *purchases* it has conducted in the past. Since, on average, the Fed tends to increase the money supply each year, it conducts more open market purchases than open market sales, and its bond holdings keep growing. So we needn't worry that the Fed will run out of bonds to sell.

Suppose the Fed sells a $1,000 government bond to a bond dealer, Merrill Lynch, which—like Lehman Brothers in our earlier example—has a checking account at First National Bank. Merrill Lynch pays the Fed for the bond with a $1,000 check drawn on its account at First National. When the Fed gets Merrill

Lynch's check, it will present the check to First National and deduct $1,000 from First National's reserve account. In turn, First National will deduct $1,000 from Merrill Lynch's checking account.

After all of this has taken place, First National's balance sheet will show the following changes:

CHANGES IN FIRST NATIONAL BANK'S BALANCE SHEET

Action	Changes in Assets	Changes in Liabilities
Fed sells $1,000 bond to Merrill Lynch, which pays with a $1,000 check drawn on First National.	−$1,000 in reserves	−$1,000 in demand deposits

Now First National has a problem. Since its demand deposits have decreased by $1,000, it can legally decrease its reserves by 10 percent of that, or $100. But its reserves have *actually* decreased by $1,000, which is $900 more than they are allowed to decrease. First National has *deficient reserves*—reserves smaller than those it is legally required to hold. How can it get the additional reserves it needs?

First National will have to *call in a loan* (ask for repayment) in the amount of $900.[5] A loan is usually repaid with a check drawn on some other bank. When First National gets this check, the Federal Reserve will add $900 to its reserve account, and deduct $900 from the reserve account at the other bank. This is how First National brings its reserves up to the legal requirement. After it calls in the $900 loan, First National's balance sheet will change as follows:

CHANGES IN FIRST NATIONAL BANK'S BALANCE SHEET

Action	Changes in Assets	Changes in Liabilities
Fed sells $1,000 bond to Merrill Lynch, which pays with a $1,000 check drawn on First National.	−$1,000 in reserves	−$1,000 in demand deposits
First National calls in loans worth $900.	**+$ 900 in reserves** **−$ 900 in loans**	
The total effect on First National from beginning to end.	−$ 100 in reserves −$ 900 in loans	−$1,000 in demand deposits

Look at the boldfaced terms. After First National calls in the loan, the composition of its assets will change: $900 more in reserves and $900 less in loans. The last row of the table shows the changes to First National's balance sheet from beginning to end. Compared to its initial situation, First National has $100 less in reserves (it lost $1,000 and then gained $900), $900 less in loans, and $1,000 less in demand deposits.

As you might guess, this is not the end of the story. Remember that whoever paid back the loan to First National did so by a check drawn on another bank. That

---

[5] In reality, bank loans are for specified time periods, and a bank cannot actually demand that a loan be repaid early. But most banks have a large volume of loans outstanding, with some being repaid each day. Typically, the funds will be lent out again the very same day they are repaid. But a bank that needs additional reserves will simply reduce its rate of new lending on that day, thereby reducing its total amount of loans outstanding. This has the same effect as "calling in a loan."

other bank, which we'll assume is Second United Bank, will lose $900 in reserves and experience the following changes in its balance sheet:

CHANGES IN SECOND UNITED BANK'S BALANCE SHEET

Action	Changes in Assets	Changes in Liabilities
Someone with an account at Second United Bank writes a $900 check to First National.	−$900 in reserves	−$900 in demand deposits

Now Second United Bank is in the same fix that First National was in. Its demand deposits have decreased by $900, so its reserves can legally fall by $90. However, its actual reserves have decreased by $900, which is $810 too much. Now it is Second United's turn to call in a loan. (On your own, fill in the rest of the changes in Second United Bank's balance sheet as it successfully brings its reserves up to the legal requirement.)

As you can see, the process of calling in loans will involve many banks. Each time a bank calls in a loan, demand deposits are destroyed—the same amount as were created in our earlier story, in which each bank *made* a new loan. The total decline in demand deposits will be a multiple of the initial withdrawal of reserves. Keeping in mind that a withdrawal of reserves is a *negative change in reserves*, we can still use our demand deposit multiplier—$1/(RRR)$—and our general formula:

$$\Delta DD = \left(\frac{1}{RRR}\right) \times \Delta \text{Reserves}.$$

Applying it to our example, we have

$$\Delta DD = \left[\frac{1}{0.1}\right] \times (-\$1,000) = -\$10,000.$$

In words, the Fed's $1,000 open market sale causes a $10,000 decrease in demand deposits. Since we assume that the public's cash holdings do not change, the money supply decreases by $10,000 as well.

To the banking system as à whole, the Fed's bond sale has done the following:

CHANGES IN BALANCE SHEET FOR THE ENTIRE BANKING SYSTEM

Changes in Assets	Changes in Liabilities
−$1,000 in reserves −$9,000 in loans	−$10,000 in demand deposits

Some Important Provisos About the Demand Deposit Multiplier

Although the process of money creation and destruction as we've described it illustrates the basic ideas, our formula for the demand deposit multiplier—$1/RRR$—is oversimplified. In reality, the multiplier is likely to be smaller than our formula suggests, for two reasons.

First, we've assumed that as the money supply changes, the public does *not* change its holdings of cash. But in reality, as the money supply increases, the public typically will want to hold part of the increase as demand deposits, and part of the increase as cash. As a result, in each round of the deposit-creation process, some

DANGEROUS CURVES

Selling Bonds: Fed Versus Treasury In this section, you learned how the Fed sells government bonds to decrease the money supply. It's easy to confuse this with another type of government bond sale, which is done by the U.S. Treasury.

The U.S. Treasury is the branch of government that collects tax revenue, disburses money for government purchases and transfer payments, and borrows money to finance any government budget deficit. The Treasury borrows funds by issuing *new* government bonds and *selling* them to the public—to banks, other financial institutions, and bond dealers. What the public pays for these bonds is what they are lending the government.

When the Fed conducts open market operations, however, it does not buy or sell *newly* issued bonds, but "secondhand bonds"—those already issued by the Treasury to finance past deficits. Thus, open market sales are *not* government borrowing; they are strictly an operation designed to change the money supply, and they have no direct effect on the government budget.

reserves will be *withdrawn* in the form of cash. This will lead to a smaller increase in demand deposits than in our story.

Second, we've assumed that banks will always lend out all of their excess reserves. In reality, banks often *want* to hold excess reserves, for a variety of reasons. For example, they may want some flexibility to increase their loans in case interest rates—their reward for lending—rise in the near future. Or they may prefer not to lend the maximum legal amount during a recession, because borrowers are more likely to declare bankruptcy and not repay their loans. If banks increase their holdings of excess reserves as the money supply expands, they will make smaller loans than in our story, and in each round, demand deposit creation will be smaller.

Other Tools for Controlling the Money Supply

Open market operations are the Fed's primary means of controlling the money supply. But there are two other tools that the Fed can use to increase or decrease the money supply.

- *Changes in the required reserve ratio.* In principle, the Fed can set off the process of deposit creation, similar to that described earlier, by lowering the required reserve ratio. Look back at Table 1, which showed the balance sheet of a bank facing a required reserve ratio of 0.1 and holding exactly the amount of reserves required by law—$10 million. Now suppose the Fed lowered the required reserve ratio to 0.05. Suddenly, the bank would find that its required reserves were only $5 million; the other $5 million in reserves it holds would become excess reserves. To earn the highest profit possible, the bank would increase its lending by $5 million. At the same time, all other banks in the country would find that some of their formerly required reserves were now excess reserves, and they would increase their lending. The money supply would increase.

  On the other hand, if the Fed *raised* the required reserve ratio, the process would work in reverse: All banks would suddenly have reserve deficiencies and be forced to call in loans. The money supply would decrease.

- *Changes in the discount rate.* The discount rate, mentioned earlier, is the rate the Fed charges banks when it lends them reserves. In principle, a lower discount rate, by enabling banks to borrow reserves from the Fed more cheaply, might encourage banks to borrow more. An increase in borrowed reserves works just like any other injection of reserves into the banking system: It increases the money supply.

  On the other side, a *rise* in the discount rate would make it more expensive for banks to borrow from the Fed, and decrease the amount of borrowed reserves in the system. This withdrawal of reserves from the banking system would lead to a decrease in the money supply.

Changes in either the required reserve ratio or the discount rate *could* set off the process of deposit creation or deposit destruction in much the same way outlined in this chapter. In reality, neither of these policy tools is used very often. The most recent change in the required reserve ratio was in April 1992, when the Fed lowered the required reserve ratio for most demand deposits from 12 percent to 10 percent. Changes in the discount rate are more frequent, but it is not unusual for the Fed to leave the discount rate unchanged for a year or more.

Why are these other tools used so seldom? Part of the reason is that they can have such unpredictable effects. When the required reserve ratio changes, all banks in the system are affected simultaneously. Even a tiny error in predicting how a typical bank will respond can translate into a huge difference for the money supply.

A change in the discount rate may have uncertain effects as well. In the past, many bank managers have preferred *not* to borrow reserves from the Fed, since it would put them under closer Fed scrutiny. And in the past, the Fed discouraged banks from borrowing reserves from it, unless the bank was in difficulty. Thus, a small change in the discount rate was unlikely to have much of an impact on bank borrowing of reserves, and therefore on the money supply.

In January 2003, however, the Fed changed its discount policy, and began to *encourage* banks to borrow. It established two different discount rates—one for banks in excellent financial condition and another, higher rate for banks considered more at risk. Banks in sound condition could borrow freely at the lower rate without Fed scrutiny. As a result, the discount rate may become a more effective, and more frequently used, policy tool in the future.

Still, open market operations will almost certainly remain the Fed's *principal* tool for controlling the money supply. One reason is that they can be so easily fine-tuned to any level desired. Another advantage is that they can be covert. No one knows exactly what the FOMC decided to do to the money supply at its last meeting for several weeks—unless the FOMC chooses to make an earlier announcement. And no one knows whether it is conducting more open market purchases or more open market sales on any given day (it always does a certain amount of both to keep bond traders guessing). By maintaining secrecy, the Fed can often change its policies without destabilizing financial markets, and also avoid the pressure that Congress or the president might bring to bear if its policies are not popular.

> *While other tools can affect the money supply, open market operations have two advantages over them: precision and secrecy. This is why open market operations remain the Fed's primary means of changing the money supply.*

The Fed's ability to conduct its policies in secret—and its independent status in general—is controversial. Some argue that secrecy and independence are needed so that the Fed can do what is best for the country—keeping the price level stable—without undue pressure from Congress or the president. Others argue that there is something fundamentally undemocratic about an independent Federal Reserve, whose governors are not elected and who can, to some extent, ignore the popular will. In recent years, because the Fed has been so successful in guiding the economy, the controversy has largely subsided.

© BETTMANN/CORBIS

USING THE THEORY
Bank Failures and Banking Panics

A bank failure occurs when a bank cannot meet its obligations to those who have claims on the bank. This includes those who have *lent* money to the bank, as well as those who deposited their money there. For example, if a bank has negative net worth—its total liabilities exceed its total assets—then even if the bank were to sell all of its assets, it could not repay what it borrowed *and* have sufficient assets to back up what it owes to its depositors. Some of the claims on the bank could not be honored.

Historically, many bank failures have occurred when depositors began to worry about a bank's financial health. For example, depositors may believe that their bank has made unsound loans that will not be repaid, so that it does not have enough assets to cover its demand deposit liabilities. In that case, everyone will want to be first in line to withdraw cash, since banks meet requests for withdrawals on a first-come, first-served basis. Those who wait may not be able to get any cash at all. This can lead to a **run on the bank,** with everyone trying to withdraw funds simultaneously.

Run on the bank An attempt by many of a bank's depositors to withdraw their funds.

Ironically, a bank can fail even when in good financial health, with more than enough assets to cover its liabilities, just because people *think* the bank is in trouble. Why should a false rumor be a problem for the bank? Because many of its assets are illiquid, such as long-term loans. A bank may be unable to sell these quickly enough to meet the unusual demands for withdrawal during a run on the bank.

For example, look back at Table 1, which shows a healthy bank with more assets than liabilities. But notice that the bank has only $2 million in vault cash. Under normal circumstances, that would be more than enough to cover a day of heavy withdrawals. But suppose that depositors hear a rumor that the bank has made many bad loans, and they want to withdraw $40 million. The bank would soon exhaust its $2 million in cash. It could then ask the Federal Reserve for more cash, using the $8 million in its reserve account, and the Fed would likely respond quickly, perhaps even delivering the cash the same day. The bank could also sell its $25 million in government bonds and obtain more cash within a few days. But altogether, this will give the bank only $35 million with which to honor requests for withdrawals. What then? Unless the bank is lucky enough to have many of its long-term loans coming due that week, it will be unable to meet its depositors' requests for cash. A false rumor could cause the bank to fail.

Banking panic A situation in which depositors attempt to withdraw funds from many banks simultaneously

A **banking panic** occurs when many banks fail simultaneously. In the past, a typical panic would begin with some unexpected event, such as the failure of a large bank. During recessions, for example, many businesses go bankrupt, so fewer bank loans are repaid. A bank that had an unusual number of "bad loans" would be in trouble, and if the public found out about this, there might be a run on that bank. The bank would fail, and many depositors would find that they had lost their deposits.

But that would not be the end of the story. Hearing that their neighbors' banks were short of cash might lead others to question the health of their own banks. Just to be sure, they might withdraw their own funds, preferring to ride out the storm and keep their cash at home. As we've seen, even healthy banks can fail under the pressure of a bank run. They, too, would have to close their doors, stoking the rumor mill even more, and so on.

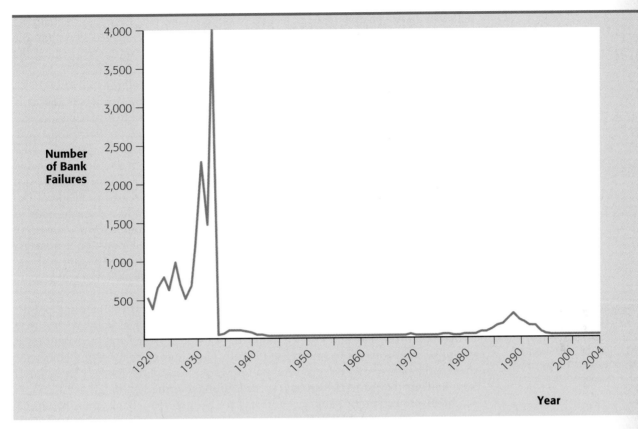

FIGURE 4
Bank Failures in the United States, 1921–2004

Bank failures continued after the Fed was created in 1913. During the Great Depression, a large number of banks failed. The creation of the Federal Deposit Insurance Corporation in 1933 strengthened faith in the stability of the banking system. Few banks have failed since that time.

Banking panics can cause serious problems for the nation. First, there is the hardship suffered by people who lose their accounts when their bank fails. Second, even when banks do not fail, the withdrawal of cash decreases the banking system's reserves. As we've seen, the withdrawal of reserves leads—through the demand deposit multiplier—to a larger decrease in the money supply. In the next chapter, you will learn that a decrease in the money supply can cause a recession. In a banking panic, the money supply can decrease suddenly and severely, causing a serious recession.

There were five major banking panics in the United States from 1863 to 1907. Indeed, it was the banking panic of 1907 that convinced Congress to establish the Federal Reserve System. From the beginning, one of the Fed's primary functions was to act as a lender of last resort, providing banks with enough cash to meet their obligations to depositors.

But the creation of the Fed did not, in itself, solve the problem. Figure 4 shows the number of bank failures each year since 1921. As you can see, banking panics continued to plague the financial system even after the Fed was created. The Fed did not always act forcefully enough or quickly enough to prevent the panic from spreading.

The Great Depression is a good example of this problem. In late 1929 and 1930, many banks began to fail because of bad loans. Then, from October 1930 until March 1933, more than one-third of all banks failed as frantic depositors stormed bank after bank, demanding to withdraw their funds—even from banks that were in reasonable financial health. Many economists believe that the banking panic of 1930–1933 turned what would have been just a serious recession into the Great Depression. Officials of the Federal Reserve System, not quite grasping the seriousness of the problem, stood by and let it happen.[6]

As you can see in Figure 4, banking panics were largely eliminated after 1933. Indeed, except for the moderate increase in failures during the late 1980s and early 1990s, the system has been almost failure free. In fact, for the five-year period ending in December 2004, a total of 29 banks failed, an average of about 6 per year. Why the dramatic improvement?

Largely for two reasons. First, the Federal Reserve learned an important lesson from the Great Depression, and it now stands ready to inject reserves into the system more quickly in a crisis. Moreover, in 1933 Congress created the Federal Deposit Insurance Corporation (FDIC) to reimburse those who lose their deposits. If your bank is insured by the FDIC (today, accounts are covered in 99 percent of all banks) and cannot honor its obligations for any reason—bad loans, poor management, or even theft—the FDIC will reimburse you up to the first $100,000 you lose in each of your bank accounts. (If you have more than $100,000 in a single bank account, you are not insured for the amount over $100,000.)

The FDIC has had a major impact on the psychology of the banking public. Imagine that you hear your bank is about to go under. As long as you have less than $100,000 in your account, you will not care. Why? Because even if the rumor turns out to be true, you will be reimbursed in full. The resulting calmness on your part, and on the part of other depositors, will prevent a run on the bank. This makes it very unlikely that bank failures will spread throughout the system.

FDIC protection for bank accounts has not been costless. Banks must pay insurance premiums to the FDIC, and they pass this cost on to their depositors and borrowers by charging higher interest rates on loans and higher fees for their services. And there is a more serious cost. If you are thoroughly protected in the event of a bank failure, your bank's managers have little incentive to develop a reputation for prudence in lending funds, since you will be happy to deposit your money there anyway. Without government regulations, banks could act irresponsibly, taking great risks with your money, and you would remain indifferent. Many more banks would fail, the FDIC would have to pay off more depositors, and banks—and their customers—would bear the burden of higher FDIC premiums.

This is the logic behind the Fed's continuing regulation of bank lending. Someone must watch over the banks to keep the failure rate low, and if the public has no incentive to pay attention, the Fed must do so. Most economists believe that if we want the freedom from banking panics provided by the FDIC, we must also accept the strict regulation and close monitoring of banks provided by the Fed and other agencies.

Look again at Figure 4 and notice the temporary rise in bank failures of the late 1980s and the early 1990s. Most of these failures occurred in state-chartered banks. These banks are less closely regulated by the Fed, and are often insured by state agencies instead of the FDIC. When a few banks went bankrupt because highly speculative loans turned sour, insurance funds in several states were drained. Citizens in those states began to fear that insufficient funds were left to insure their own deposits, and the psychology of banking panics took over. To many observers, the experience of the late 1980s and early 1990s was a reminder of the need for a sound insurance system and close monitoring of the banking system.

HTTP://

Fred Furlong and Simon Kwan, in "Rising Bank Risk?" (http://www.frbsf.org/econrsrch/wklyltr/wklyltr99/el99-32.html) explore recent developments in bank behavior.

---

[6] Milton Friedman and Anna Jacobson Schwartz, *A Monetary History of the United States, 1867–1960* (Princeton, NJ: Princeton University Press, 1963), especially p. 358.

Summary

In the United States, the standard measure of money—M1—includes currency, checking account balances, and travelers checks. Each of these assets is liquid and widely acceptable as a means of payment. Other, broader measures go beyond M1 to include funds in savings accounts and other deposits.

The amount of money circulating in the economy is controlled by the Federal Reserve, operating through the banking system. Banks and other financial intermediaries are profit-seeking firms that collect loanable funds from households and businesses, then repackage them to make loans to other households, businesses, and governmental agencies,

The Federal Reserve injects money into the economy by altering banks' balance sheets. In a balance sheet, assets always equal liabilities plus net worth. One important kind of asset is *reserves*—funds that banks are required to hold in proportion to their demand deposit liabilities. When the Fed wants to increase the money supply, it buys bonds in the open market and pays for them with a check. This is called an *open market purchase*. When the Fed's check is deposited in a bank, the bank's balance sheet changes. On the asset side, reserves increase; on the liabilities side, demand deposits (a form of money) also increase. The bank can lend some of the reserves, and the money loaned will end up in some other banks where it supports creation of still more demand deposits. Eventually, demand deposits, and the M1 money supply, increase by some multiple of the original injection of reserves by the Fed. The *demand deposit multiplier*, the inverse of the required reserve ratio, gives us that multiple.

The Fed can decrease the money supply by selling government bonds—an *open market sale*—causing demand deposits to shrink by a multiple of the initial reduction in reserves. The Fed can also change the money supply by changing either the required reserve ratio or the discount rate it charges when it lends reserves to banks.

Key Terms

Balance sheet	Excess reserves	Money
Banking panic	Federal Open Market Committee	Money supply
Bond	Financial intermediary	Open market operations
Cash in the hands of the public	Liquidity	Reserves
Central bank	Loan	Required reserves
Demand deposits	Net worth	Required reserve ratio
Demand deposit multiplier	M1	Run on the bank
Discount rate	M2	

Review Questions   *Answers to even-numbered Questions and Problems can be found on the text Web site at http://hall-lieb.swlearning.com.*

1. Describe the main characteristics of money. What purpose does money serve in present-day economies?

2. Which assets are included when measuring M1? . . . M2?

3. What is a depository institution? Give an example of each of the four types of depository institutions.

4. On a balance sheet, why is net worth listed on the liabilities side, rather than on the assets side?

5. What are reserves? What determines the amount of reserves that a bank holds? Explain the difference between required reserves and excess reserves.

6. What is the difference between the Federal Reserve Board (of Governors) and the Federal Open Market Committee?

7. What are the main functions of the Federal Reserve System?

8. Explain how the Federal Reserve can use open market operations to change the level of bank reserves. How does a change in reserves affect the money supply? (Give answers for both an increase and a decrease in the money supply.)

9. How does a "run on a bank" differ from a "banking panic"? What are their implications for the economy? What steps have been taken to reduce the likelihood of bank runs and bank panics?

10. Why do governments have more than one measure of the money supply?

11. "All U.S. cash is considered part of the U.S. money supply." True or false? Explain briefly.

12. Do banks create wealth when they create money? Explain.

13. Explain why the required reserve ratio and the discount rate have not been used very often, and why the discount rate may be a more frequently used tool in the future.

Problems and Exercises

1. Suppose the required reserve ratio is 0.2. If an extra $20 billion in reserves is injected into the banking system through an open market purchase of bonds, by how much can demand deposits increase? Would your answer be different if the required reserve ratio were 0.1?

2. If the Fed buys $50 million of government securities, by how much can the money supply increase if the required reserve ratio is 0.15? How will your answer be different if the required reserve ratio is 0.18?

3. Which of the following is considered part of the U.S. money supply? (Use the M1 measures.)
   a. A $10 bill you carry in your wallet
   b. A $100 travelers check you bought but did not use
   c. A $100 bill in a bank's vault
   d. The $325.43 balance in your checking account
   e. A share of General Motors stock worth $40

4. Given the following data (in billions of dollars), calculate the value of the M1 money supply and the value of the M2 money supply.

Bank reserves	50
Cash in the hands of the public	400
Demand deposits	400
Retail MMMF balances	880
Other checkable deposits	250
Savings-type account balances	1,300
Small time deposits	950
Travelers checks	10

5. Suppose bank reserves are $100 billion, the required reserve ratio is 0.2, and excess reserves are zero. Calculate how many dollars worth of demand deposits are being supported. Now suppose that the required reserve ratio is lowered to 0.1 and that banks once again become fully "loaned up" with no excess reserves. What is the new level of demand deposits?

6. Suppose bank reserves are $200 billion, the required reserve ratio is 0.2, and excess reserves are zero. Calculate how many dollars worth of demand deposits are being supported. If the Fed wants to decrease demand deposits by $50 billion by changing the required reserve ratio, what will the new required reserve ratio need to be set at?

7. Suppose that the money supply is $1 trillion. Decision makers at the Federal Reserve decide that they wish to reduce the money supply by $100 billion, or by 10 percent. If the required reserve ratio is 0.05, what does the Fed need to do to carry out the planned reduction?

8. Suppose that the money supply is $3.2 trillion. Decision makers at the Federal Reserve decide that they wish to increase the money supply by $500 billion. If the required reserve ratio is 0.10, what does the Fed need to do to carry out the planned increase? What if the required reserve ratio is 0.15?

9. For each of the following situations, determine whether the money supply will increase, decrease, or stay the same.
   a. Depositors become concerned about the safety of depository institutions.
   b. The Fed lowers the required reserve ratio.
   c. The economy enters a recession and banks have a hard time finding creditworthy borrowers.
   d. The Fed sells $100 million of bonds to First National Bank of Ames, Iowa.

10. Suppose that the Fed decides to increase the money supply. It purchases a government bond worth $1,000 from a private citizen. He deposits the check in his account at First National Bank, as in the chapter example. But now, suppose that the required reserve ratio is 0.2, rather than 0.1 as in the chapter.
    a. Trace the effect of this change through three banks—First National, Second United, and Third State. Show the changes to each bank's balance sheet as a result of the Fed's action.
    b. By how much does the money supply change in each of these first three rounds?
    c. What will be the ultimate change in demand deposits in the entire banking system?

11. Suppose accountants at the bank whose balance sheet is depicted in Table 1 discover that they've made an error: Cash in vault is only $1 million, not $2 million.
    a. Which other entries in the bank's balance sheet will change as a consequence of correcting this error?
    b. If the required reserve ratio is 0.10, does this bank now have excess reserves or deficient reserves? Of what value?

12. Assume that the Fed wants to keep the size of the money supply constant by adjusting the required reserve ratio only. How will it have to adjust the required reserve ratio to achieve this goal if
    a. people decide to hold more of their money as cash rather than as demand deposits?
    b. bankers decide to decrease their holdings of excess reserves?

Challenge Questions

1. Sometimes banks wish to hold reserves in excess of the legal minimum. Suppose the Fed makes an open market purchase of $100,000 in government bonds. The required reserve ratio is 0.1, but each bank decides to hold additional reserves equal to 5 percent of its deposits.
    a. Trace the effect of the open market purchase of bonds through the first three banks in the money expansion process. Show the changes to each bank's balance sheet.
    b. Derive the demand deposit multiplier in this case. Is it larger or smaller than when banks hold no excess reserves?
    c. What is the ultimate change in demand deposits in the entire banking system?

2. Suppose the Fed buys $100,000 in government bonds from Jonathan, and that the required reserve ratio is 0.1. Assume that Jonathan and each additional depositor always holds half of their money as cash.
    a. Trace the effect of this open market purchase through the first three banks in the money expansion process. Show the changes to each bank's balance sheet.
    b. Derive the demand deposit multiplier in this case. How does it compare with the demand deposit multiplier when depositors hold no cash?
    c. What is the ultimate change in demand deposits in the entire banking system?

 These exercises require access to Hall/Lieberman Xtra! If Xtra! did not come with your book, visit http://hallxtra.swlearning.com to purchase.

1. Use your Xtra! password at the Hall and Lieberman Web site (http://hallxtra.swlearning.com), select this chapter, and under Economic Applications, click on EconDebate. Choose *Macroeconomics: Money and the Financial System,* and scroll down to find the debate, "Should U.S. financial markets be deregulated?" Read the debate, and use the information to answer the following questions.
    a. Explain how the Federal Deposit Insurance Corporation (FDIC) increases the moral hazard problem.
    b. Do you expect the deregulation of U.S. financial markets to increase financial fragility and failures or not? Explain. Can you support your answer with an example from current events?

2. Use your Xtra! password at the Hall and Lieberman Web site (http://hallxtra.swlearning.com), select this chapter, and under Economic Applications, click on EconData. Choose *Macroeconomics: Money and the Financial System,* and scroll down to find *Stock Prices S&P 500*. Read the definition and click on Updates and use the information to answer the following questions.
    a. Click on the "review the latest S&P 500 Total Return data," and scroll down to see the percent change from last year for the year 2000 and onward. Describe the trend, and what might have contributed to it.
    b. Scroll down to the article "The Stock Market: Beyond Risk Lies Uncertainty." Read the article. In absence of regulations separating commercial from investment banking, how should the Federal Reserve System intervene to stabilize the financial system? Would Fed intervention exacerbate the moral hazard problem and lead to more instability or alternatively lead to long-term stability of financial markets? Explain.

The Money Market and the Interest Rate

CHAPTER OUTLINE

The Demand for Money
  An Individual's Demand for Money
  The Economy-Wide Demand for Money

The Supply of Money

Equilibrium in the Money Market
  How the Money Market Reaches Equilibrium

What Happens When Things Change?
  How the Fed Changes the Interest Rate
  How Do Interest Rate Changes Affect the Economy?
  Monetary Policy and the Economy
  Fiscal Policy (and Other Spending Changes) Revisited

Are There Two Theories of the Interest Rate?

Expectations and the Money Market

Using the Theory: The Fed and the Recession of 2001

Which of the following two newspaper headlines might you see in your daily paper?

1. "Motorists Fear Department of Energy Will Raise Gasoline Prices"
2. "Wall Street Expects Fed to Raise Interest Rates"

You probably know the answer: The first headline is entirely unrealistic. The Department of Energy, the government agency that makes energy policy, has no authority to set prices in any market. The Federal Reserve, by contrast, has full authority to influence the interest rate—the price of borrowing money. And it exercises this authority every day. This is why headlines such as the second one appear in newspapers so often.

In this chapter, you will learn how the Fed, through its control of the money supply, also controls the interest rate. We'll continue our focus on the short run, postponing any discussion about longer time horizons until the next chapter.

THE DEMAND FOR MONEY

Reread the title of this section. Does it appear strange to you? Don't people always want as much money as possible?

Indeed, they do. But when we speak about the *demand* for something, we don't mean the amount that people would desire if they could have all they wanted, without having to sacrifice anything for it. Instead, economic decision makers always face constraints: They must sacrifice one thing in order to have more of another. Thus, the *demand for money* does not mean how much money people would *like* to have in the best of all possible worlds. Rather, it means *how much money people would like to hold, given the constraints that they face.* Let's first consider the demand for money by an individual, and then turn our attention to the demand for money in the entire economy.

An Individual's Demand for Money

Money is one of the forms in which people hold their wealth. Unfortunately, at any given moment, the total amount of wealth we have is given; we can't just snap our fingers and have more of it. Therefore, if we want to hold more wealth in the form of money, we must hold less wealth in other forms: savings accounts, money market funds, time deposits, stocks, bonds, and so on. Indeed, people exchange one kind of wealth for another millions of times a day—in banks, stock markets, and bond markets. If you sell shares in the stock market, for example, you give up wealth in the form of corporate stock and acquire money. The buyer of your stock gives up money and acquires the stock.

These two facts—that wealth is given, and that you must give up one kind of wealth in order to acquire more of another—determine an individual's **wealth constraint.** Whenever we speak about the demand for money, the wealth constraint is always in the background, as in the following statement:

Wealth constraint At any point in time, total wealth is fixed.

> *An individual's* quantity of money demanded *is the amount of wealth that the individual chooses to hold as money, rather than as other assets.*

Why do people want to hold some of their wealth in the form of money? The most important reason is that money is a *means of payment;* you can buy things with it. Other forms of wealth, by contrast, are *not* used for purchases. (For example, we don't ordinarily pay for our groceries with shares of stock.) However, the other forms of wealth provide a financial return to their owners. For example, bonds, savings deposits, and time deposits pay interest, while stocks pay dividends and may also rise in value (which is called a *capital gain*). Money, by contrast, pays very little interest (some types of checking accounts) or none at all (cash and most checking accounts). Thus,

> *when you hold money, you bear an opportunity cost—the interest you could have earned by holding other assets instead.*

Each of us must continually decide how to divide our total wealth between money and other assets. The upside to money is that it can be used as a means of payment. The more of our wealth we hold as money, the easier it is to buy things at a moment's notice, and the less often we will have to pay the costs (in time, trouble, and commissions to brokers) to change our other assets into money. The downside to money is that it pays little or no interest.

To keep our analysis as simple as possible, *we'll use bonds as our representative nonmoney asset.* We'll also assume that all assets considered to be money pay no interest at all. In our discussion, therefore, people will choose between two assets that are mirror images of each other. Specifically,

> *individuals choose how to divide wealth between two assets: (1) money, which can be used as a means of payment but earns no interest; and (2) bonds, which earn interest, but cannot be used as a means of payment.*

This choice involves a clear trade-off: The more wealth we hold as money, the less often we will have to go through the inconvenience of changing our bonds into money . . . but the less interest we will earn on our wealth.

What determines how much money an individual will decide to hold? While tastes vary from person to person, three key variables have rather predictable impacts on most of us.

- *The price level.* The greater the number of dollars you spend in a typical week or month, the more money you will want to have on hand to make your purchases. A rise in the price level, which raises the dollar cost of your purchases, should therefore increase the amount of money you want to hold.
- *Real income.* Suppose the price level remains unchanged, but your income increases. Your purchasing power or *real* income will increase, and so will the number of dollars you spend in a typical week or month. Once again, since you are spending more dollars, you will choose to hold more of your wealth in the form of money.
- *The interest rate.* Interest payments are what you give up when you hold money—the *opportunity cost* of money. The greater the interest rate, the greater the opportunity cost of holding money. Thus, a rise in the interest rate *decreases* your quantity of money demanded.

The effect of the interest rate on the quantity of money demanded will play a key role in our analysis. But before we go any further, you may be wondering whether it is realistic to think that changes in the interest rate—which are usually rather small—would have any effect at all. Here, as in many aspects of economic life, you may not consciously think about the interest rate in deciding how to adjust your money-holding habits. Similarly, you may not rethink all your habits about using lights and computers every time the price of electricity changes. But in both cases, you may respond more casually. And when we add up everybody's behavior, we find a noticeable and stable tendency for people to hold less money when it is more expensive to hold it—that is, when the interest rate is higher.

The Demand for Money by Businesses. Our discussion of money demand has focused on the typical individual. But some money (not a lot in comparison to what individuals hold) is held by businesses. Stores keep some currency in their cash registers, and firms generally keep funds in business checking accounts. Businesses face the same types of constraints as individuals: They have only so much wealth, and they must decide how much of it to hold as money rather than other assets. The quantity of money demanded by businesses follows the same principles we have developed for individuals: They want to hold more money when real income or the price level is higher, and less money when the opportunity cost (the interest rate) is higher.

The Economy-Wide Demand for Money

When we use the term *quantity of money demanded* without the word *individual*, we mean the total demand for money by all wealth holders in the economy; businesses

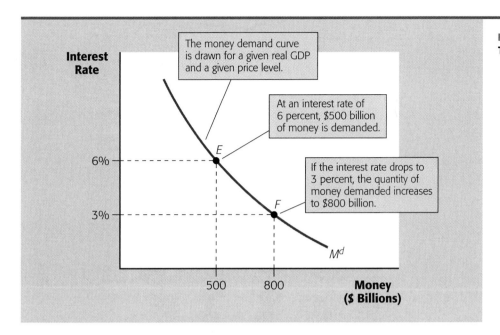

FIGURE 1
The Money Demand Curve

The money demand curve is drawn for a given real GDP and a given price level.

At an interest rate of 6 percent, $500 billion of money is demanded.

If the interest rate drops to 3 percent, the quantity of money demanded increases to $800 billion.

and individuals. And just as each person and each firm in the economy has only so much wealth, so, too, there is a given amount of wealth in the economy as a whole at any given time. In our analysis, this total wealth must be held in one of two forms: money or bonds.

The (economy-wide) quantity of money demanded is the amount of total wealth in the economy that all households and businesses, together, choose to hold as money rather than as bonds.

The demand for money in the economy depends on the same three variables that we discussed for individuals. In particular, (1) a rise in the price level will increase the demand for money; (2) a rise in real income (real GDP) will increase the demand for money; and (3) a rise in the interest rate will *decrease* the quantity of money demanded.

The Money Demand Curve. Figure 1 shows a **money demand curve**, which tells us *the total quantity of money demanded in the economy at each interest rate.* Notice that the curve is downward sloping. As long as the other influences on money demand don't change, a drop in the interest rate—which lowers the opportunity cost of holding money—will increase the quantity of money demanded.

Point *E*, for example, shows that when the interest rate is 6 percent, the quantity of money demanded is $500 billion. If the interest rate falls to 3 percent, we move to point *F*, where the quantity demanded is $800 billion. As we move along the money demand curve, the interest rate changes, but other determinants of money demand (such as the price level and real income) are assumed to remain unchanged.

Shifts in the Money Demand Curve. What happens when something *other* than the interest rate changes the quantity of money demanded? Then the curve shifts. For

Money demand curve A curve indicating how much money will be demanded at each interest rate.

FIGURE 2
**A Shift in the Money
Demand Curve**

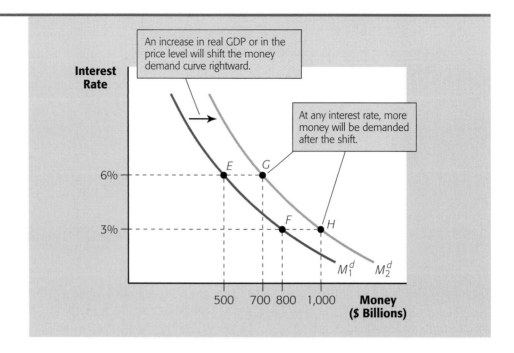

example, suppose that real income increases. Then, at each interest rate, individuals and businesses will want to hold *more* of their wealth in the form of money. The entire money demand curve will shift rightward. This is illustrated in Figure 2, where the money demand curve shifts rightward from M_1^d to M_2^d. At an interest rate of 6 percent, the quantity of money demanded rises from $500 billion to $700 billion; if the interest rate were 3 percent, the amount of money demanded would rise from $800 billion to $1,000 billion.

In general,

a change in the interest rate moves us along the money demand curve. A change in money demand caused by something other than the interest rate (such as real income or the price level) will cause the curve to shift.

Figure 3 summarizes how the key variables we've discussed so far affect the demand for money.

THE SUPPLY OF MONEY

Just as we did for money demand, we would like to draw a curve showing the quantity of money *supplied* at each interest rate. In the previous chapter, you learned how the Fed controls the money supply: It uses open market operations to inject or withdraw reserves from the banking system and then relies on the demand deposit multiplier to do the rest. Since the Fed decides what the money supply will be, we treat it as a fixed amount. That is, the interest rate can rise or fall, but the money supply will remain constant unless and until the Fed decides to change it.

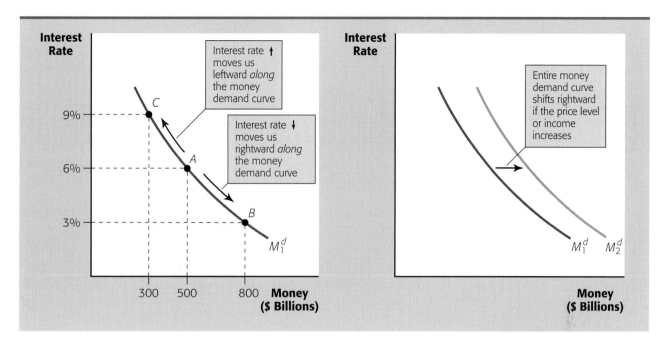

FIGURE 3
**Shifts and Movements
Along the Money Demand
Curve: A Summary**

Look at the vertical line labeled M_1^S in Figure 4. This is the economy's **money supply curve,** which shows the total amount of money supplied at each interest rate. The line is vertical because once the Fed sets the money supply, it remains constant until the Fed changes it. In the figure, the Fed has chosen to set the money supply at $500 billion. A rise in the interest rate from, say, 3 percent to 6 percent would move us from point J to point E along the money supply curve M_1^S, leaving the money supply unchanged.

Money supply curve A line showing the total quantity of money in the economy at each interest rate.

Now suppose the Fed, for whatever reason, were to *change* the money supply. Then there would be a *new* vertical line, showing a different quantity of money supplied at each interest rate. Recall from the previous chapter that the Fed raises the money supply by purchasing bonds in an open market operation. For example, if the demand deposit multiplier is 10, and the Fed purchases government bonds worth $20 billion, the money supply increases by 10 × $20 billion = $200 billion. In this case, the money supply curve shifts rightward, to the vertical line labeled M_2^S in the figure.

> *Open market purchases of bonds inject reserves into the banking system, and shift the money supply curve rightward by a multiple of the reserve injection. Open market sales have the opposite effect: They withdraw reserves from the system and shift the money supply curve leftward by a multiple of the reserve withdrawal.*

EQUILIBRIUM IN THE MONEY MARKET

Now let's combine money demand and money supply to find the equilibrium interest rate in the economy (step two in the three-step process). But before we do, a question may have occurred to you. Haven't we already discussed how the interest

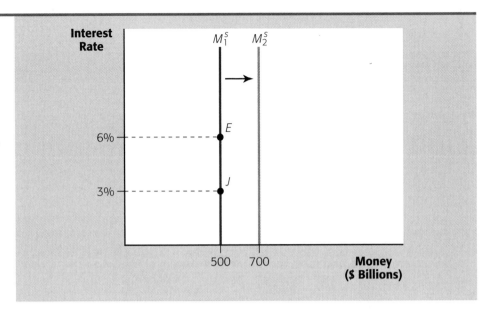

rate is determined? Indeed, we have. The classical model tells us that the interest rate is determined by equilibrium in the *loanable funds market,* where a flow of loanable funds is offered by lenders to borrowers. But remember: The classical model tells us how the economy operates in the *long run.* We can rely on its mechanisms to work only over long periods of time. Here, we are interested in how the interest rate is determined in the *short run,* so we must change our perspective. Toward the end of the chapter, we'll come back to the classical model and explain why its theory of the interest rate does not apply in the short run.

In the short run—our focus here—we look for the equilibrium interest rate in the *money market:* the interest rate at which the quantity of money demanded and the quantity of money supplied are equal. Figure 5 combines the money supply and demand curves. Equilibrium occurs at point *E*, where the two curves intersect. At this point, the quantity of money demanded and the quantity supplied are both equal to $500 billion, and the equilibrium interest rate is 6 percent.

It is important to understand what equilibrium in the money market actually means. First, remember that the money supply curve tells us the quantity of money, determined by the Fed, that *actually exists* in the economy. Every dollar of this money—either in cash or in checking account balances—is held by *someone.* Thus, the money supply curve, in addition to telling us the quantity of money supplied by the Fed, also tells us the quantity of money that people *are actually holding* at any given moment. The money demand curve, on the other hand, tells us how much money people *want* to hold at each interest rate. Thus, when the quantity of money supplied and the quantity demanded are equal, all of the money in the economy is being *willingly held.* That is, people are satisfied holding the money that they are *actually* holding.

> *Equilibrium in the money market occurs when the quantity of money people are* actually *holding (quantity supplied) is equal to the quantity of money they* want *to hold (quantity demanded).*

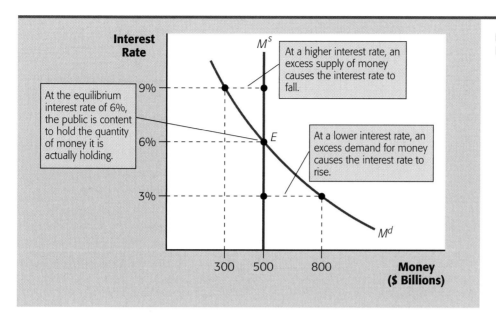

FIGURE 5
Money Market Equilibrium

In the figure:

Interest Rate (vertical axis)

At a higher interest rate, an excess supply of money causes the interest rate to fall.

At the equilibrium interest rate of 6%, the public is content to hold the quantity of money it is actually holding.

At a lower interest rate, an excess demand for money causes the interest rate to rise.

M^s

9%

6% — E

3%

M^d

300   500   800

Money ($ Billions)

Can we have faith that the interest rate will reach its equilibrium value in the money market, such as 6 percent in our figure? Indeed we can. In the next section, we explore the forces that drive the money market toward its equilibrium.

How the Money Market Reaches Equilibrium

To understand how the money market reaches its equilibrium, suppose that the interest rate, for some reason, were *not* at its equilibrium value of 6 percent in Figure 5. For example, suppose the interest rate were 9 percent. As the figure shows, at this interest rate the quantity of money demanded would be $300 billion, while the quantity supplied would be $500 billion. Or, put another way, people would *actually* be holding $500 billion of their wealth as money, but they would *want* to hold only $300 billion as money. There would be an **excess supply of money** (the quantity of money supplied would exceed the quantity demanded) equal to $500 billion − $300 billion = $200 billion.

Now comes an important point. Remember that in our analysis, money and bonds are the only two assets available. If people want to hold *less* money than they are currently holding, then, by definition, they must want to hold *more* in bonds than they are currently holding—an **excess demand for bonds**.

> *When there is an excess supply of money in the economy, there is also an excess demand for bonds.*

To understand this more clearly, imagine that instead of the money market, which can seem rather abstract, we were discussing something more concrete: the arrangement of books in a bookcase. Suppose that you have a certain number of books, and you have only two shelves on which to hold all of them: top and bottom. One day, you look at the shelves and decide that, the way you've arranged

Excess supply of money The amount of money supplied exceeds the amount demanded at a particular interest rate.

Excess demand for bonds The amount of bonds demanded exceeds the amount supplied at a particular interest rate.

things, the top shelf has *too many* books. Then, by definition, you must also feel that the bottom shelf has *too few* books. That is, an excess supply of books on the top shelf (it has more books than you want there) is the same as an excess demand for books on the bottom shelf (it has fewer books than you want there).

A similar conclusion applies to the money market. People allocate a given amount of wealth between two different assets: money and bonds. Too much in one asset implies too little in the other.

So far, we've established that if the interest rate were 9 percent, which is higher than its equilibrium value, there would be an excess supply of money, and an excess demand for bonds. What would happen? The public would demand more bonds. Just as there is a market for money, there is also a market for bonds. And as the public begins to demand more bonds, making them scarcer, *the price of bonds will rise*. We can illustrate the steps in our analysis so far as follows:

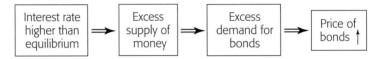

We conclude that, when the interest rate is higher than its equilibrium value, the price of bonds will rise. Why is this important? In order to take our story further, we must first take a detour for a few paragraphs.

An Important Detour: Bond Prices and Interest Rates. A bond, in the simplest terms, is a promise to pay back borrowed funds at a certain date or dates in the future. There are many types of bonds. Some promise to make payments each month or each year for a certain period and then pay back a large sum at the end. Others promise to make just one payment—perhaps 1, 5, 10, or more years from the date the bond is issued. When a large corporation or the government wants to borrow money, it issues a new bond and sells it in the marketplace; the amount borrowed is equal to the price of the bond.

Let's consider a very simple example: a bond that promises to pay to its holder $1,000 exactly one year from today. Suppose that you purchase this bond from the issuer—a firm or government agency—for $800. Then you are lending $800 to the issuer, and you will be paid back $1,000 one year later. What interest rate are you earning on your loan? Let's see: You will be getting back $200 more than you lent, so that is your *interest payment*. The annual interest *rate* is the interest payment over the year divided by the amount of the loan, or $200/$800 = 0.25 or 25 percent.

Now, what if instead of $800, you paid a price of $900 for this very same bond. The bond still promises to pay $1,000 one year from now, so your annual interest payment would now be $100, and your interest rate would be $100/$900 = 0.11 or 11 percent—a considerably lower interest rate. As you can see, the interest rate that you will earn on your bond depends entirely on the *price* of the bond. *The higher the price, the lower the interest rate*.

This general principle applies to virtually all types of bonds, not just the simple one-time-payment bond we've considered here. Bonds promise to pay various sums to their holders at different dates in the future. Therefore, the more you pay for any bond, the lower your overall rate of return, or interest rate, will be. Thus:

When the price of bonds rises, the interest rate falls; when the price of bonds falls, the interest rate rises.[1]

The relationship between bond prices and interest rates helps explain why the government, the press, and the public are so concerned about the *bond market,* where bonds issued in previous periods are bought and sold. This market is sometimes called the *secondary* market for bonds, to distinguish it from the *primary* market where newly issued bonds are bought and sold. When you hear that "the bond market rallied" on a particular day of trading, it means that prices rose in the secondary bond market. This is good news for bond holders. But it is also good news for any person or business that wants to borrow money. When prices rise in the secondary market, they immediately rise in the primary market as well, since newly issued bonds and previously issued bonds are almost perfect substitutes for each other. Therefore, a bond market rally not only means lower interest rates in the secondary market, it also means lower interest rates in the primary market, where firms borrow money by issuing new bonds. Sooner or later, it will also lead to a drop in the interest rate on mortgages, car loans, credit card balances, and even many student loans. This is good news for borrowers. But it is bad news for anyone wishing to lend money, for now they will earn less interest.

Now that you understand the relationship between bond prices and interest rates, let's return to our analysis of the money market.

Back to the Money Market. Look back at Figure 5, and let's recap what you've learned so far. If the interest rate were 9 percent, there would be an excess supply of money, and therefore an excess demand for bonds. The price of bonds would rise. Now we can complete the story. As you've just learned, a rise in the price of bonds means a *decrease* in the interest rate. The complete sequence of events is

Thus, if the interest is 9 percent in our figure, it will begin to fall. Therefore, 9 percent is *not* the equilibrium interest rate.

How far will the interest rate fall? As long as there continues to be an excess supply of money, and an excess demand for bonds, the public will still be trying to acquire bonds and the interest rate will continue to fall. But notice what happens in the figure as the interest rate falls: The quantity of money demanded *rises.* Finally, when the interest rate reaches 6 percent, the excess supply of money, and therefore the excess demand for bonds, is eliminated. At this point, there is no reason for the interest rate to fall further, so 6 percent is, indeed, our equilibrium interest rate.

---

[1] In our macroeconomic model of the economy, we refer to *the* interest rate. In the real world, there are many types of interest rates: a different one for each type of bond, and still other rates on savings accounts, time deposits, car loans, mortgages, and more. However, all of these interest rates usually move up and down together, even though some may lag behind a few days, weeks, or months. Thus, when bond prices rise, interest rates *generally* will fall, and vice versa.

We can also do the same analysis from the other direction. Suppose the interest rate were *lower* than 6 percent in the figure—say, 3 percent. Then, as you can see in Figure 5, there would be an *excess demand for money,* and an *excess supply of bonds.* In this case, the following would happen:

The interest rate would continue to rise until it reached its equilibrium value: 6 percent.

WHAT HAPPENS WHEN THINGS CHANGE?

Now that we have seen how the interest rate is determined in the money market, we turn our attention to *changes* in the interest rate. We'll focus on two questions: (1) What *causes* the equilibrium interest rate to change? and (2) What are the *consequences* of a change in the interest rate? As you are about to see, the Fed can change the interest rate as a matter of policy, or the interest rate can change on its own, as a by-product of other events in the economy. We'll begin with the Fed.

How the Fed Changes the Interest Rate

Changes in the interest rate from day to day, or week to week, are often caused by the Fed. Later in this chapter, you'll learn why the Fed often wants to manipulate the interest rate. For now, we'll focus on how the Fed does this.

Suppose the Fed wants to *lower* the interest rate. Fed officials cannot just declare that the interest rate should be lower. To change the interest rate, the Fed must change the *equilibrium* interest rate in the money market, and it does this by changing the money supply.

Look at Figure 6. Initially, with a money supply of $500 billion, the money market is in equilibrium at point *E*, with an interest rate of 6 percent. To lower the interest rate, the Fed *increases* the money supply through open market purchases of bonds. In the figure, the Fed raises the money supply to $800 billion, shifting the money supply curve rightward. (This is a much greater shift than the Fed would ever actually engineer in practice, but it makes the graph easier to read.) At the old interest rate of 6 percent, there would be an excess supply of money and an excess demand for bonds. This will drive the interest rate down until it reaches its new equilibrium value of 3 percent, at point *F*. The process works like this:

The Fed can *raise* the interest rate as well, through open market *sales* of bonds. In this case, the money supply curve in Figure 6 would shift leftward (not shown), setting off the following sequence of events:

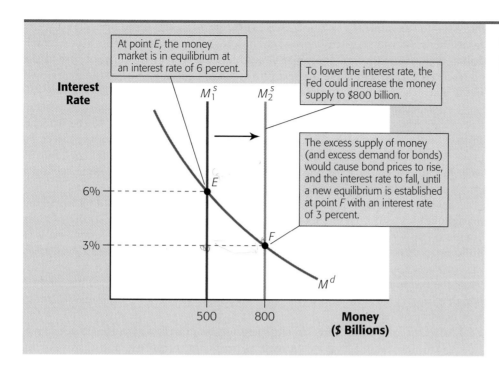

At point *E*, the money market is in equilibrium at an interest rate of 6 percent.

To lower the interest rate, the Fed could increase the money supply to $800 billion.

The excess supply of money (and excess demand for bonds) would cause bond prices to rise, and the interest rate to fall, until a new equilibrium is established at point *F* with an interest rate of 3 percent.

FIGURE 6
An Increase in the Money Supply

If the Fed increases the money supply by buying government bonds, the interest rate falls. If the Fed decreases the money supply by selling government bonds, the interest rate rises. By controlling the money supply through purchases and sales of bonds, the Fed can also control the interest rate.

HTTP://

You can find recent and historical data on the money supply and interest rates at the Fed's Web site: http://www.federalreserve.gov/rnd.htm.

How Do Interest Rate Changes Affect the Economy?

As you've just learned, if the Fed increases the money supply through open market purchases of bonds, the interest rate will fall. But what then? How is the macroeconomy affected? The answer is: *A drop in the interest rate will boost several different types of spending in the economy.*

How the Interest Rate Affects Spending. First, a lower interest rate stimulates business spending on plant and equipment. This idea came up a few chapters ago in the classical model, but we will go back over it here.

Remember that the interest rate is one of the key costs of any investment project. If a firm must borrow funds, it will have to pay for them at the going rate of interest—for example, by selling a bond at the going price. If the firm uses its *own* funds, so it doesn't have to borrow, the interest rate *still* represents a cost: Each dollar spent on plant and equipment *could* have been lent to someone else at the going interest rate. Thus, the interest rate is the *opportunity cost* of the firm's own funds when they are spent on plant and equipment.

A firm deciding whether to spend on plant and equipment compares the benefits of the project—the increase in future income—with the costs of the project. With a lower interest rate, the costs of funding investment projects are lower, so more projects will get the go-ahead. Other variables affect investment spending as well. But all else equal, a drop in the interest rate will cause an increase in spending on plant and equipment.

Interest rate changes also affect another kind of investment spending: spending on new houses and apartments that are built by developers or individuals. Most people borrow to buy houses or condominiums, and most developers borrow to build apartment buildings. The loan agreement for housing is called a *mortgage*, and mortgage interest rates tend to rise and fall with other interest rates. Thus, when the Fed lowers the interest rate, families find it more affordable to buy homes, and developers find it more profitable to build new apartments. Total investment in new housing increases.

Finally, in addition to investment spending, the interest rate affects consumption spending on big-ticket items such as new cars, furniture, and dishwashers. Economists call these *consumer durables* because they usually last several years. People often borrow to buy consumer durables, and the interest rate they are charged tends to rise and fall with other interest rates in the economy. Spending on new cars, the most expensive durable that most of us buy, is especially sensitive to interest rate changes. Since a lower interest rate causes higher consumption spending at *any* level of disposable income, it causes a *shift* of the consumption function, not a movement along it. Therefore, we consider this impact on consumption to be a rise in autonomous consumption spending, called *a* in our discussion of the consumption function.

We can summarize the impact of money supply changes as follows:

> *When the Fed increases the money supply, the interest rate falls, and spending on three categories of goods increases: plant and equipment, new housing, and consumer durables (especially automobiles). When the Fed decreases the money supply, the interest rate rises, and these categories of spending fall.*

Monetary Policy and the Economy

Two chapters ago ("The Short-Run Macro Model"), you learned that changes in aggregate expenditure cause changes in real GDP through the multiplier process. In this chapter, you've learned that the Federal Reserve, through its control of the money supply, can change the interest rate, and therefore influence aggregate expenditure. Thus, the Fed—through its control of the money supply—has the power to influence real GDP.

Monetary policy Control or manipulation of the money supply by the Federal Reserve designed to achieve a macroeconomic goal.

When the Fed controls or manipulates the money supply in order to achieve any macroeconomic goal—such as a change in the level of real GDP—it is engaging in **monetary policy.** Let's put all the pieces of our analysis together and see how monetary policy works.

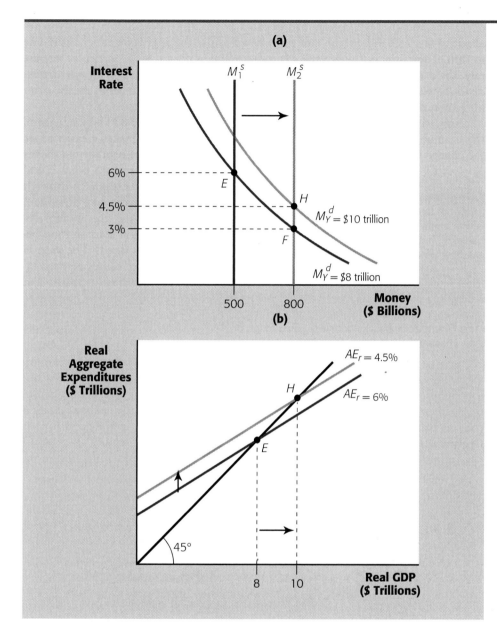

(a)

(b)

FIGURE 7
**Monetary Policy and
the Economy**

*Initially, the Fed has set the
money supply at $500 billion,
so the interest rate is 6 percent
(point E). Given that interest
rate, aggregate expenditure is
$AE_{r\,=\,6\%}$ in panel (b), and real
GDP is $8 trillion (point E).*

*If the Fed increases the
money supply to $800 billion,
money market equilibrium
moves temporarily to point F in
panel (a). The interest rate falls,
stimulating interest-sensitive
spending and driving aggregate
expenditures upward in panel
(b). Through the multiplier
process, real GDP increases. As
it does, the money demand curve
shifts rightward in panel (a). In
the new equilibrium, real GDP
is $10 trillion and the interest
rate is 4.5 percent (point H).*

In Figure 7, we revisit the short-run macro model, but we now include the
money market in our analysis. In panel (a), the Fed has initially set the money supply at $500 billion. Equilibrium is at point *E*, with an interest rate (*r*) of 6 percent.
Panel (b) shows the familiar short-run aggregate expenditure diagram, with equilibrium at point *E*, and equilibrium GDP equal to $8 trillion.

But notice the new labels in the figure. The letter *r* stands for the interest rate, and
Y stands for real GDP and real income. The aggregate expenditure line has the sub-
script "*r* = 6%," and the money demand curve has the subscript "*Y* = $8 trillion."
Why these additional labels?

Recall that the money demand curve will shift if there is a change in real income. Therefore, our particular money demand curve is drawn for a particular level

of real income, the level determined in panel (b), or \$8 trillion. Similarly, as you are about to see, a change in the interest rate will cause the aggregate expenditure line to shift. Therefore, our aggregate expenditure line is drawn for a particular interest rate, the one determined in the money market, or 6 percent. There is an *interdependence* between these two panels: The equilibrium in each one depends on the equilibrium in the other.

Now we suppose that the Fed increases the money supply to \$800 billion. (Again, this is an unrealistically large change in the money supply, but it makes it easier to see the change in the figure.) In the upper panel, the money market equilibrium moves from point E toward point F, and the interest rate begins to drop. (It won't drop all the way down to 3 percent, because the money demand curve will start shifting before we are finished.) The drop in the interest rate causes planned investment spending on plant and equipment and on new housing to rise. It also causes an increase in consumption spending—especially on consumer durables like automobiles—to rise at any level of income. This is an increase in au-

Shift Versus Movement Along the *AE* Line   When thinking about the effects of monetary policy, try not to confuse movements *along* the aggregate expenditure line with *shifts* of the line itself. We move *along* the line only when a change in *income* causes spending to change. The line shifts when something *other* than a change in income causes spending to change.

When the Fed changes the interest rate, both types of changes occur, but it's important to keep the order straight. *First,* the drop in the interest rate (something other than income) causes interest-sensitive spending to change, *shifting* the aggregate expenditure line. *Then,* increases in income in each round of the multiplier cause further increases in spending, moving us *along* the new aggregate expenditure line.

tonomous consumption spending (*a*). In the lower panel, the rise in spending causes the aggregate expenditure line to shift upward, setting off the multiplier effect and increasing equilibrium GDP. The rise in income causes the money demand curve to shift rightward, since the demand for money is greater when income is higher.

To find the final equilibrium in the economy, we would need quite a bit of information about how sensitive spending is to the drop in the interest rate, as well as how changes in income feed back into the money market to affect the interest rate. In Figure 7, we've illustrated just one possibility, in which the new equilibrium is at point H in both the money market and the aggregate expenditure diagrams. At this new equilibrium, the interest rate ends up at 4.5 percent, so the higher aggregate expenditure line is labeled "$r = 4.5\%$." Equilibrium GDP has risen to \$10 trillion, so the new higher money demand curve is labeled "$Y = \$10$ trillion." In the end, we see that the Fed, by increasing the money supply and lowering the interest rate, has increased the level of output.

We've covered a lot of ground to reach our conclusion, so let's review the highlights of how monetary policy works. This is what happens when the Fed conducts open market purchases of bonds:

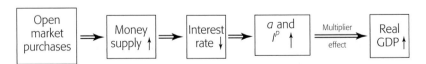

Open market *sales* by the Fed have exactly the opposite effects. In this case, the money supply curve in Figure 7 would shift leftward (not shown), driving the interest rate up. The rise in the interest rate would cause a decrease in interest-sensitive spending (*a* and I^p), shifting the aggregate expenditure line downward. Equilibrium GDP would fall by a multiple of the initial decrease in spending.

Fiscal Policy (and Other Spending Changes) Revisited

Two chapters ago, we discussed how fiscal policy affects the economy in the short run. For example, an increase in government purchases causes output to rise, and in successive rounds of the multiplier, spending and output rise still more. Now that we've added the money market to our analysis, it's time to revisit fiscal policy. As you'll see, its effects are now a bit more complicated.

Figure 8 shows the money market and the familiar short-run aggregate expenditure diagram. Initially, we have equilibrium in both panels. In panel (a), the money market equilibrium is point E, with the interest rate at 6 percent. In panel (b), the initial aggregate expenditure line, labeled "$r = 6\%$," is consistent with the interest rate we've found in the money market. As you can see, with this aggregate expenditure line, the equilibrium is at point E, with real GDP equal to $10 trillion, just as we assumed when we drew the money demand curve in panel (a).

An Increase in Government Purchases. Now let's see what happens when the government changes its fiscal policy, say, by increasing government purchases (G) by $2 trillion. Panel (b) shows the initial effect: The aggregate expenditure line shifts upward, by $2 trillion, to the topmost aggregate expenditure line. This new aggregate expenditure line is drawn for the same interest rate as the original line: $r = 6\%$. The shift illustrates what *would* happen if there were no change in the interest rate, as in our analysis of fiscal policy two chapters ago.

As you've learned, the increase in government purchases will set off the multiplier process, increasing GDP and income in each round. *If this were the end of the story,* the result would be a rise in real GDP equal to $[1/(1 - MPC)] \times \Delta G$. In our example, with an MPC of 0.6, the multiplier would be $1/(1 - 0.6) = 2.5$. The new equilibrium would be at point F, with GDP equal to $15 trillion—a rise of $5 trillion.

But point F is *not* the end of our story—not when we include effects in the money market. As income increases, the money demand curve in panel (a) will shift rightward, raising the interest rate. As a result, autonomous consumption (a) and investment spending (I) will decrease and shift the aggregate expenditure line downward. That is,

> *an increase in government purchases, which by itself shifts the aggregate expenditure line upward, also sets in motion forces that shift it downward.*

We can outline these forces as follows:

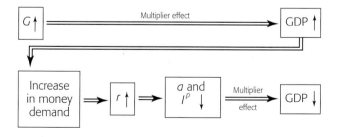

Net Effect: GDP↑, but by less due to effect of r ↑

FIGURE 8
Fiscal Policy and the
Money Market

The economy is initially in equilibrium with an interest rate of 6 percent in panel (a) and real GDP of $10 trillion in panel (b). An increase in government purchases shifts the aggregate expenditure line upward, triggering the multiplier process. If the interest rate did not change, equilibrium would be reestablished at point F in panel (b) with real GDP of $15 trillion. But the increase in GDP increases money demand in panel (a), driving the interest rate upward to 8 percent at point L. That reduces interest-sensitive spending, lowering aggregate expenditure to $AE_{r = 8\%}$ in panel (b) so that the real GDP at the new equilibrium is $13.5 trillion (point L).

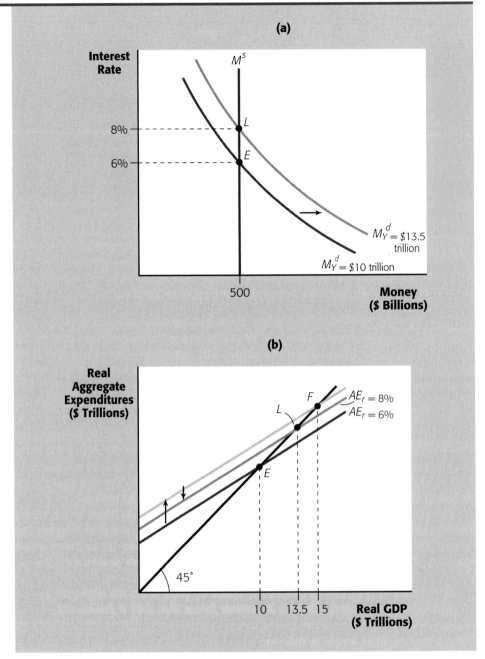

Thus, at the same time as the increase in government purchases has a *positive* multiplier effect on GDP, the decrease in *a* and *I* have *negative* multiplier effects. Which effect dominates? The positive multiplier effect. Why? Because the only force pulling GDP down—the higher interest rate—*depends upon* a rise in GDP. (It is the rise in GDP that shifts the money demand curve and drives up the interest rate.) If the negative effect on GDP were so strong that GDP actually decreased, then the money demand curve would shift leftward, not rightward. Therefore, the interest rate would be lower, not higher, and there would be no force pulling GDP down at all.

Thus, we know that an increase in government purchases causes GDP to rise. But the rise is smaller than the simple multiplier formula suggests. That's because the simple multiplier ignores the moderating effect of a rise in the interest rate on GDP.

> *In the short run, an increase in government purchases causes real GDP to rise, but not by as much as if the interest rate had not increased.*

Let's sum up the characteristics of the new equilibrium after an increase in government purchases:

- The aggregate expenditure line is higher, but by less than ΔG.
- Real GDP and real income are higher, but the rise is less than $[1/(1 - MPC)] \times \Delta G$.
- The money demand curve has shifted rightward, because real income is higher.
- The interest rate is higher, because money demand has increased.
- Autonomous consumption and investment spending are lower, because the interest rate is higher.

Figure 8 indicates one possible result that is consistent with all of these requirements. In the figure, the new equilibrium occurs at point L in both panels, with the new equilibrium GDP at \$13.5 trillion and the new equilibrium interest rate at 8 percent. Notice that real GDP has risen, but by only \$3.5 trillion—not the \$5 trillion suggested by the simple multiplier formula. Moreover, the two panels of the diagram are consistent with each other. The aggregate expenditure line (labeled "$r = 8\%$") corresponds to the equilibrium interest rate in the money market. The money demand curve (labeled "$Y = \$13.5$ trillion") corresponds to the equilibrium GDP in the aggregate expenditure diagram.

Crowding Out Once Again.   Our analysis illustrates an interesting by-product of fiscal policy. Comparing our initial equilibrium (point E in both panels) to the final equilibrium (point L), we see that government purchases increase. But because of the rise in the interest rate, *investment spending has decreased.*

What about consumption spending? It is influenced by two opposing forces. The rise in the interest rate causes *some* types of consumption spending (e.g., on automobiles) to decrease, but the rise in *income* makes other types of consumption spending *increase.* Thus, an increase in government purchases may increase or decrease consumption spending, depending on which effect is stronger.

Summing up:

> *When effects in the money market are included in the short-run macro model, an increase in government purchases raises the interest rate and crowds out some private investment spending. It may also crowd out consumption spending.*

This should sound familiar. In the classical, long-run model, an increase in government purchases also causes crowding out. But there is one important difference between crowding out in the classical model and the effects we are outlining here. In the classical model, there is *complete crowding out:* Investment spending and consumption spending fall by the same amount that government purchases rise. As a result, total spending does not change at all, and neither does real GDP. This is why, in the *long run,* we expect fiscal policy to have no effect on real GDP.

In the short run, however, our conclusion is somewhat different. While we expect *some* crowding out from an increase in government purchases, *it is not complete.* Investment spending falls, and consumption spending *may* fall, but together, they do not drop by as much as the rise in government purchases. In the short run, real GDP rises.

Other Spending Changes. So far, we've focused on the impact on the economy of a change in government purchases. But our analysis extends to *any* shock that shifts the aggregate expenditure line. Positive shocks would shift the aggregate expenditure line upward, just as in Figure 8. More specifically:

> *Increases in government purchases, planned investment, net exports, and autonomous consumption, as well as decreases in taxes, all shift the aggregate expenditure line upward. Real GDP rises, but so does the interest rate. The rise in equilibrium GDP is smaller than if the interest rate remained constant.*

For example, a $2 trillion increase in investment spending shifts the aggregate expenditure line upward by $2 trillion, as in Figure 8. If there were no rise in the interest rate, real GDP would rise according to the simple multiplier of $1/(1 - 0.6) = 2.5$. Applying this multiplier to a $2 trillion increase in investment tells us that real GDP would rise by a full $5 trillion. But once again, the rise in GDP does drive up the interest rate in the money market, which works to decrease investment and interest-sensitive consumption. And once again, GDP will rise, but not by as much as the simple multiplier suggests.

Negative shocks shift the aggregate expenditure line *downward.* More specifically:

> *Decreases in government purchases, investment, net exports, and autonomous consumption, as well as increases in taxes, all shift the aggregate expenditure line downward. Real GDP falls, but so does the interest rate. The decline in equilibrium GDP is smaller than if the interest rate remained constant.*

What About the Fed? In our analysis of spending shocks, we've made an implicit but important assumption. Look back at Figure 8. Notice that, from beginning to end, the money supply curve never shifted. This implies that the Fed just stands by, not interfering at all with the changes we've been describing. More specifically, we've been assuming that *the Fed does not change the money supply in response to shifts in the aggregate expenditure line.*

While this assumption has helped us focus on the impact of spending shocks, it is not the way the Fed has conducted policy during the past few decades. Instead, the Fed has usually responded to neutralize the impact of spending shocks. That is, it has used monetary policy to prevent spending shocks from changing GDP at all. You'll learn why, and how, the Fed does this when we revisit monetary policy in the chapter after next.

ARE THERE TWO THEORIES OF THE INTEREST RATE?

At the beginning of this chapter, you were reminded that you had already learned a different theory of how the interest rate is determined in the economy. In the classical model, the interest rate is determined in the *market for loanable funds.* In this chapter, you learned that the interest rate is determined in the *money market*, where people make decisions about holding their wealth as money and bonds. Which theory is correct?

The answer is: Both are correct. The classical model, you remember, tells us what happens in the economy in the *long run*. Therefore, when we ask what changes the interest rate over long periods of time—many years or even a decade—we should think about the market for loanable funds. But over shorter time periods—days, weeks, or months—we should use the money market model presented in this chapter.

Why don't we use the classical loanable funds model to determine the interest rate in the short run? Because, as you've seen, the economy behaves differently in the short run than it does in the long run. For example, in the classical model, output is automatically at full employment. But in the short run, output changes as the economy goes through booms and recessions. These changes in output affect the loanable funds market in ways that the classical model does not consider. For example, flip back to the chapter on the classical model and look at Figure 8 there. Recessions, which decrease household income, also decrease household saving at any given interest rate: With less income, households will spend less *and* save less. The supply of loanable funds curve would shift leftward in the diagram, and the interest rate would rise. The classical model—because it ignores recessions—ignores these short-run changes in the supply of loanable funds.

The classical model also ignores an important idea discussed in this chapter: that the public continuously chooses how to divide its wealth between money and bonds. In the short run, the public's preferences over money and bonds can change, and this, in turn, can change the interest rate. This idea does not appear in the classical model.

Of course, in the long run, the classical model gives us an accurate picture of how the economy and the interest rate behave. Recessions and booms don't last forever, so the economy returns to full employment. Thus, in the long run we needn't worry about recessions causing shifts in the supply of loanable funds curve. Also, changes in preferences for holding money and bonds are rather short-lived. We can ignore these changes when we take a long-run view.

> *In the long run, we view the interest rate as determined in the market for loanable funds, where household saving is lent to businesses and the government. In the short run, we view the interest rate as determined in the money market, where wealth holders adjust their wealth between money and bonds, and the Fed participates by controlling the money supply.*

EXPECTATIONS AND THE MONEY MARKET

One important insight of our money market analysis in this chapter is the inverse relationship between a bond's price and the interest rate it earns for its holder. When the interest rate falls, bond prices rise—and vice versa. Therefore, if people *expect* the interest rate to fall, they *expect* the price of bonds to rise. And this expectation, in turn, will affect the money market.

To see this more clearly, imagine (pleasantly) that you hold a bond promising to pay you $100,000 in exactly one year and that the going annual interest rate is 5 percent. The going price for your bond will be $95,238. Why? If someone bought your bond at that price, she would earn $100,000 − $95,238 = $4,762 in interest. Since the bond cost $95,238, the buyer's rate of return would be $4,762/$95,238 = 0.05, or

FIGURE 9
Interest Rate Expectations

If households and firms expect the interest rate to rise in the future, their demand for money will increase today. Starting from equilibrium at point E, an expected increase in the interest rate from 5 percent to 10 percent will increase money demand to M_2^d. The result is a self-fulfilling prophecy: The interest rate increases to 10 percent today.

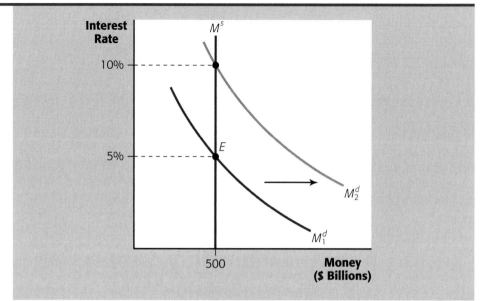

5 percent—the going rate of interest. If you tried to charge more than $95,238 for the bond, its rate of return would be less than 5 percent, so no one would buy it; they could always earn 5 percent by buying another bond that pays the going rate of interest.

Now suppose that you *expect* the interest rate to rise to 10 percent in the near future, say, next week. (This is an unrealistically large change in the interest rate in so short a time, but it makes the point dramatically.) Then you expect the going price for your bond to fall to about $90,909. At that price, a buyer would earn $100,000 − $90,909 = $9,091 in interest, so the buyer's rate of return would be $9,091/$90,909 = 0.10, or 10 percent. Thus, if you believe that the interest rate is about to rise from 5 to 10 percent, you also believe the price of your bond is about to fall from $95,238 to $90,909.

What would you do?

Logically, you would want to sell your bond *now*, before the price drops. If you still want to hold this type of bond later, you can always buy it back next week at the lower price and gain from the transaction. Thus, if you expect the interest rate to rise in the future, you will want to exchange your bonds for money *today*. Your demand for money will increase.

Of course, if *you* expect the interest rate to rise (and the price of bonds to drop), and your expectation is reasonable, others will probably feel the same way. They, too, will want to trade in their bonds for money. Thus, if the expectation is widespread, there will be an increase in the demand for money economy-wide.

> *A general expectation that interest rates will rise (bond prices will fall) in the future will cause the money demand curve to shift rightward in the present.*

Notice that when people expect the interest rate to rise, we *shift* the money demand curve, rather than move along it. People will want to hold more money at any *current* interest rate.

Figure 9 shows what will happen in the money market when people expect the interest rate to rise. Initially, with the money supply equal to $500 billion, the equilibrium is at point E and the interest rate is 5 percent. But the expected rise in the interest rate shifts the money demand curve rightward. After the shift, there is an excess demand for money and an excess supply of bonds at the original interest rate of 5 percent. The price of bonds will fall, which means the interest rate will rise.

How far will the interest rate rise? That depends. Imagine a simple case where *everyone* in the economy expected the interest rate to rise to 10 percent next week. Then no one would want to hold bonds at any *current* interest rate less than 10 percent. For example, if the interest rate rose to 9 percent, people would still expect it to rise further (and the price of bonds to fall further), so they would still want to sell their bonds. Therefore, to return the money market to equilibrium, the interest rate would rise to exactly the level that people expected. This is the case we've illustrated in Figure 9, where the money demand curve shifts rightward by just enough to raise the interest rate to 10 percent. More generally:

> *When the public as a whole expects the interest rate to rise in the future, they will drive up the interest rate in the present.*

When information comes along that makes people believe that interest rates will rise and bond prices fall in the near future, the result is an immediate rise in the interest rate and a fall in bond prices. This principle operates even if the information is false and there is ultimately no reason for the interest rate to rise. Thus, a general expectation that interest rates will rise can be a *self-fulfilling prophecy:* Because people believe it, it actually happens. Their expectation alone is enough to drive up the interest rate.

This immediate response to information about the future—and the possibility of a self-fulfilling prophecy—works in the opposite direction as well:

> *When the public expects the interest rate to drop in the future, they will drive down the interest rate in the present.*

In this case, the public expects bond prices to rise, so they try to shift their wealth from money to bonds. In Figure 9, the money demand curve would shift leftward (not shown). The price of bonds would rise, and the interest rate would fall, just as was originally expected.

USING THE THEORY
The Fed and the Recession of 2001

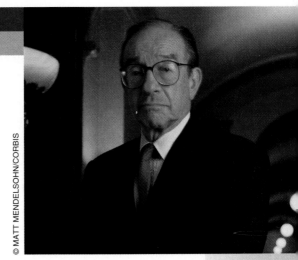

© MATT MENDELSOHN/CORBIS

Two chapters ago ("The Short-Run Macro Model"), we began an analysis of our most recent recession, which officially lasted from March to November of 2001. We saw that an investment spending shock caused a decrease in aggregate expenditure, which in turn caused equilibrium GDP and employment to drop. But we left two questions unanswered: (1) What did policy makers do to try to prevent the recession, and to deal with it once it started? and (2) Why did consumption spending behave abnormally, rising as income fell and preventing the recession from becoming a more serious downturn? Now that you've learned about monetary policy, we can begin to answer these questions.

Starting in January 2001—three months before the official start of the recession—the Fed began to worry. Although the economy was operating at its potential output (the unemployment rate the previous month was 3.9 percent), there was danger on the horizon: Investment spending had already decreased for two quarters in a row. The decrease in investment spending had started a negative multiplier effect, which was working its way through the economy and could ultimately cause a recession. Other factors made the Fed worry that investment spending could decrease further. And a sharp decrease in stock prices over the previous year—which had destroyed billions of dollars in household wealth—suggested that consumption spending might begin to fall as well.

The upper right panel (b) of Figure 10, which shows the aggregate expenditure diagram, illustrates the situation. Initially, the economy was at point *A*, with real GDP in January of 2001 (for this example, measured in 1996 dollars) equal to $9,242 billion.[2] The Fed feared that if it did nothing, the investment slowdown would shift the aggregate expenditure line downward, moving the equilibrium to a point like *B*, with GDP falling (in our diagram) to $9,000 billion.

The Fed decided to take action, indicated by the lower panels of Figure 10. The lower left panel (c) tracks the money supply measure M1 (monthly) from the period before and after January 2001. It shows that beginning in January, the Fed began increasing M1 rapidly. The lower right panel (d) shows changes in the *federal funds rate*—the interest rate that the Fed watches most closely when it conducts monetary policy. The **federal funds rate** is the interest rate that banks with excess reserves charge for lending reserves to other banks. Although it is just an interest rate for lending among banks, many other interest rates in the economy vary with it closely, so it gives us a good idea of how interest rates in general ("the interest rate" in our highly aggregated macro model) were changing during this period. As you can see, the federal funds rate fell continually and dramatically during the year, from 6.4 percent down to 1.75 percent. In September of 2001, during which real GDP probably hit bottom, the federal funds rate averaged about 3.1 percent.

Now look at the upper left panel (a), which shows the effect of the Fed policy in the money market. In January 2001, the money market was in equilibrium at point *A*, with the M1 measure of the money supply at $1,093 billion and the federal funds rate at 6.4 percent. As the money supply increased to an average of about $1,170 during the third quarter of 2001, the money supply curve shifted rightward and the interest rate fell. In panel (b), this had the effect of making the recession more mild: Instead of falling to point *B*, the economy ended up at point *C*, with real GDP hitting bottom at about $9,125 billion in September 2001. Notice that, in panel (a), the final money demand curve ($M^D{}_{Y = \$9,125 \text{ billion}}$) lies to the left of the initial money demand curve, because it is associated with a lower level of income. The new equilibrium for the money market— point *C*—is consistent with the new equilibrium in the aggregate expenditure diagram.

Although the Fed's policy did not completely prevent the recession, it no doubt saved the economy from a more severe and longer-lasting one. The lower interest rate was especially helpful in maintaining new-home construction, a category of investment spending that is especially sensitive to the interest rate.

The Fed's policy also helps us understand the other question we raised about the 2001 recession: the continued rise in consumption spending throughout the period. Lower interest rates, as you've now learned, stimulate consumption spending on consumer durables, especially automobiles. Indeed, helped by lower interest rates, auto sales rose in every quarter of 2001.

Federal funds rate The interest rate charged for loans of reserves among banks.

---

[2] This example makes use of monthly real GDP estimates in 1996 dollars provided by Macroeconomic Advisors, a private consulting firm, to the National Bureau of Economic Research (NBER) (available at *http://www.nber.org/cycles/hall.pdf*).

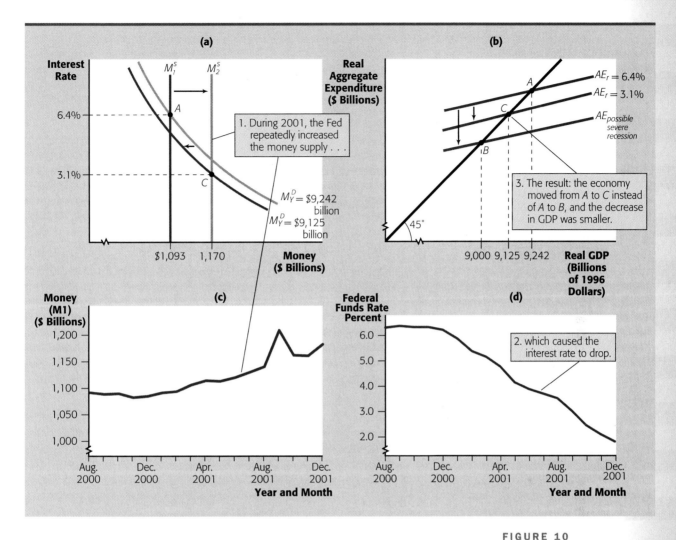

FIGURE 10
The Fed in Action: 2001

Moreover, when interest rates drop dramatically and rapidly—as they did in 2001—a frenzy of *home mortgage refinancing* can occur: Households rush to exchange their existing, higher-interest-rate mortgages for new mortgages at a lower interest rate. After a refinance, monthly mortgage payments are reduced, freeing up disposable income to be spent on goods and services. But many households go further, taking advantage of the refinancing to borrow even more than they owed on their original mortgage. This provides them with a one-time burst of cash to spend. Home refinancing and additional borrowing on homes seemed to play a major role in boosting consumption spending during the recession of 2001.

As you've read these pages, some questions may have formed in your mind. Why wasn't the Fed able to prevent the recession entirely? Couldn't the Fed have reduced the interest rate even more rapidly than it did?

There are, in general, good reasons for the Fed to be somewhat cautious in reducing interest rates. Over the next two chapters, you'll learn some of the reasons for the Fed's caution, and why most economists—despite the recession of 2001—give the Fed high marks for its actions during *that year*.

But you'll also learn that Fed policies during the year or so *before* 2001 may have actually contributed to the recession.

Summary

The interest rate is a key macroeconomic variable. This chapter explores how the supply and demand for money interact to determine the interest rate in the short run, and how the Federal Reserve can adjust the money supply to change the interest rate.

An individual's demand for money indicates the fraction of wealth that person wishes to hold in the form of money, at different interest rates. Money is useful as a means of payment, but holding money means sacrificing the interest that could be earned by holding bonds instead. The higher the interest rate, the larger the fraction of their wealth people will hold in the form of bonds, and the smaller the fraction they will hold as money.

The demand for money is sensitive to the interest rate, but it also depends on the price level, real income, and expectations. An increase in the price level, higher real income, or an increase in the expected future interest rate can each shift the money demand curve to the right.

The money supply is under the control of the Fed and is independent of the interest rate. Equilibrium in the money market occurs at the intersection of the downward-sloping money demand curve and the vertical money supply curve. The interest rate will adjust so that the quantity of money demanded by households and firms just equals the quantity of money supplied by the Fed and the banking system.

Conditions in the money market mirror conditions in the bond market. If the interest rate is above equilibrium in the money market, there will be an excess supply of money there.

People *want to* hold less money than they actually *do* hold, which means that they wish to hold more bonds than they do hold. (An excess supply of money means an excess demand for bonds.) The price of bonds will rise and the interest rate will fall. Thus, an excess supply of money will cause the interest rate to fall. Similarly, an excess demand for money will cause the interest rate to rise.

The Fed can increase the money supply through an open market purchase of bonds, and decrease it through an open market sale. An increase in the money supply creates an excess supply of money. Very quickly, the interest rate will fall so that the public is willing to hold the now-higher money supply. A decrease in the money supply will drive up the interest rate.

Changes in the interest rate affect interest-sensitive forms of spending—firms' spending on plant and equipment, new housing constructions, and households' purchases of "big-ticket" consumer durables. By lowering the interest rate, the Fed can stimulate aggregate expenditures and increase GDP through the multiplier process. Fiscal policy decisions to stimulate the economy, such as an increase in government purchases, raises the interest rate and causes a decrease in investment spending and (possibly) consumption spending. This partial crowding out of spending reduces the multiplier effect of fiscal policy. Finally, expectations of future interest rate changes can become self-fulfilling prophecies.

Key Terms

Excess demand for bonds   Monetary policy   Wealth constraint
Excess supply of money   Money demand curve
Federal funds rate   Money supply curve

Review Questions
Answers to even-numbered Questions and Problems can be found on the text Web site at http://hall-lieb.swlearning.com.

1. Why do individuals choose to hold some of their wealth in the form of money? Besides individual tastes, what factors help determine how much money an individual holds?

2. Why does the money demand curve slope downward? Which of the following result in a shift of the money demand curve and which result in a movement along the curve? If there is a shift, in which direction?
   a. The Fed lowers interest rates.
   b. The Fed raises interest rates.
   c. The price level falls.
   d. The price level rises.
   e. Income increases.
   f. Income decreases.

3. Why is the economy's money supply curve vertical? What causes the money supply curve to shift?

4. What sequence of events brings the money market to equilibrium if there is an excess supply of money? An excess demand for money?

5. The text mentions that starting in January 2001, the Fed began buying government bonds, and as a result, the interest rate fell. Explain how the Fed's purchase of bonds led to a lower interest rate.

6. Describe how an increase in the interest rate affects spending on the following:
   a. plant and equipment
   b. new housing
   c. consumer durables

7. Does a change in expectations about the interest rate result in a shift in the money demand curve or a movement

along it? Explain what happens in the money market when people expect the interest rate to fall.

8. Why do we have one theory for how the interest rate is determined in the long run (see the chapter on the classical model), and another theory of how the interest rate is determined in the short run (this chapter)? Briefly, what determines the interest rate in the short run? In the long run?

9. How do people reallocate their wealth holdings if they expect interest rates to fall? What effect do their actions have on the interest rate?

10. What is the *federal funds rate*?

Problems and Exercises

1. Assume the demand deposit multiplier is 10. For each of the following, state the impact on the money supply curve (the direction it will shift, and the amount of the shift).
   a. The Fed purchases bonds worth $10 billion.
   b. The Fed sells bonds worth $5 billion.

2. Assume the demand deposit multiplier is 7. For each of the following, state the impact on the money supply curve (the direction it will shift, and the amount of the shift).
   a. The Fed purchases bonds worth $28 million.
   b. The Fed sells bonds worth $17 million.

3. A bond promises to pay $500 one year from now. For the following prices, find the corresponding interest payments and interest rates that the bond offers.

Price	Amount Paid in One Year	Interest Payment	Interest Rate
$375	$500	____	____
$425	$500	____	____
$450	$500	____	____
$500	$500	____	____

As the price of the bond rises, what happens to the bond's interest rate?

4. A bond promises to pay $20,000 one year from now.
   a. Complete the following chart.

Price	Amount Paid in One Year	Interest Payment	Interest Rate	Quantity of Money Demanded
	$2000			$2300 billion
	$1500			$2600 billion
	$1000			$2900 billion
	$500			$3200 billion
	$0			$3500 billion

   b. Draw a graph of the money market, assuming that it is currently in equilibrium at an interest rate of 5.26 percent. What is the price of this bond? How large is the money supply?
   c. Find the new interest rate and the new bond price if the money supply increases by $300 billion. Show this on your graph.

5. "A general expectation that the interest rate will fall can be a self-fulfilling prophecy." Explain what this means.

6. Suppose that, in an attempt to prevent the economy from overheating, the Fed raises the interest rate. Illustrate graphically, using a diagram similar to Figure 7 in this chapter, the effect on the money supply, interest rate, and GDP.

7. For each of the following events, state (1) the impact on the money demand curve, and (2) whether the Fed should increase or decrease the money supply if it wants to keep the interest rate unchanged. (*Hint:* It will help to draw a diagram of the money market for each case.)
   a. People start making more of their purchases over the Internet, using credit cards.
   b. Greater fear of credit card fraud makes people stop buying goods over the Internet with credit cards, and discourages the use of credit cards in other types of purchases as well.
   c. A new type of electronic account is created in which your funds are held in bonds up to the second you make a purchase. Then—when you buy something—just the right amount of bonds are transferred to the ownership of the seller. (*Hint:* Would you want to increase or decrease the amount of your wealth in the form of money after this new type of account were available?)

8. A fellow student in your economics class stops you in the hallway and says: "An increase in the demand for money causes the interest rate to rise. But a rise in the interest rate causes people to demand *less* money. Therefore, increases in money demand largely cancel themselves out, and have very little effect on the interest rate." Is this correct? Why or why not? (*Hint:* Draw a graph.)

9. In a later chapter, you will learn that a drop in the interest rate has *another* channel of influence on real GDP: It causes a depreciation of the dollar (that is, it makes the dollar cheaper to foreigners), which, in turn, increases our net exports.

a. When we take account of the effect on net exports, does a given change in the money supply have *more* or *less* of an impact on real GDP?

b. Suppose that the Fed wants to stimulate the economy as during 2001. Should the Fed lower the interest rate by more or by less when it takes the impact on net exports into account (compared to the case of no impact on net exports)? Explain.

10. Figure 10 (c) shows a spike in money growth during September 2001. Using what you know about bonds versus money and the money demand curve, explain why this spike might have occurred.

Challenge Questions

1. Determine whether *fiscal policy* is *more* or *less* effective in changing GDP when autonomous consumption and investment spending are *very sensitive* to changes in the interest rate, and explain your reasoning.

2. In Problem 9, you were asked how the *net export* effect changes the potency of monetary policy. Answer the same question about fiscal policy (that is, does the net export effect make fiscal policy more or less potent in changing GDP?).

3. A fellow student in your economics class is confused again: "Economics makes no sense. On the one hand, we're told that if everyone expects the interest rate to rise, then everyone will sell bonds, and that will cause the price of bonds to fall (and the interest rate to rise). Fair enough. But in the real world, no one can sell a bond unless someone else buys it. And if everyone expects the price of bonds to fall, no one will buy them. Therefore,

no one can *sell* them either, and, therefore, there will be no change in the price of bonds or the interest rate." Can you resolve your friend's confusion?

4. Look back at Figure 10. Notice that from September to October 2001, the Fed actually *decreased* the money supply, and yet the interest rate continued to fall between those two months. Explain how that might be possible, and illustrate with a graph.

5. When the Fed intervenes in the economy it worries not only about how its decisions will affect the interest rate via changes in the money *supply,* but also about how its statements might affect the interest rate via changes in the money *demand.* Explain how statements by the Fed about its intentions can change the demand for money. How this can make the Fed's job in steering the economy more complex?

These exercises require access to Hall/Lieberman Xtra! If Xtra! did not come with your book, visit http://hallxtra.swlearning.com to purchase.

1. Use your Xtra! password at the Hall and Lieberman Web site (http://hallxtra.swlearning.com), select this chapter, and under Economic Applications, click on EconDebate. Choose *Macroeconomics: Money and the Financial System*, and scroll down to find the debate, "Does Dollarization Benefit Developing Economies?" Read the debate, and use the information to answer the following questions.

   a. What kind of policies result in high and unstable inflation rate for the developing economies. What is the cost of dollarization to these economies?

   b. Click on the following Web page: http://www.federalreserve.gov/releases/h15/data/m/fedfund.txt. What is the present intended federal funds rate? Can you explain the trend in this rate? Read the article titled "Open Market Operations in 1990s," *Federal Reserve Bulletin,* http://www.federalreserve.gov/pubs/buletin/1997/199711lead.pdf, and explain why the Fed relinquished M2 in setting interest rates.

Aggregate Demand and Aggregate Supply

CHAPTER OUTLINE

The Aggregate Demand Curve
Deriving the Aggregate Demand Curve
Understanding the *AD* Curve
Movements Along the *AD* Curve
Shifts of the *AD* Curve

The Aggregate Supply Curve
Costs and Prices
GDP, Costs, and the Price Level
Deriving the Aggregate Supply Curve
Movements Along the *AS* Curve
Shifts of the *AS* Curve

***AD* and *AS* Together: Short-Run Equilibrium**

What Happens When Things Change?
Demand Shocks in the Short Run
Demand Shocks: Adjusting to the Long Run
The Long-Run Aggregate Supply Curve
Supply Shocks

Some Important Provisos About the *AS* Curve

Using the Theory: The Story of Two Recessions and "Jobless" Expansions
The Recession of 1990–91
The Recession of 2001
Jobless Expansions

Economic fluctuations are facts of life. If you need a reminder, look back at Figure 1 in the chapter titled "Economic Fluctuations." There you can see that while potential GDP tends to move upward year after year, due to economic growth, *actual* GDP tends to rise above and fall below potential over shorter periods.

But the figure also reveals another important fact about the economy: Deviations from potential output don't last forever. When output dips below or rises above potential, the economy returns to potential output after a few quarters or years. True, in some of these episodes, government policy—either fiscal or monetary—helped the economy return to full employment more quickly. But even without corrective policies—such as during long parts of the Great Depression of the 1930s—the economy shows a remarkable tendency to begin moving back toward potential output. Why? And what, exactly, is the mechanism that brings us back to our potential when we have strayed from it? These are the questions we will address in this chapter. And we'll address them by studying the behavior of a variable that we've put aside for several chapters: the price level.

The chapter begins by exploring the relationship between the price level and output. This is a two-way relationship, as you can see in Figure 1 in *this* chapter. On the one hand, changes in the price level cause changes in real GDP. This causal relationship is illustrated by the *aggregate demand curve*, which we will discuss shortly. On

339

FIGURE 1
The Two-Way Relationship Between Output and the Price Level

the other hand, changes in real GDP cause changes in the price level. This relationship is summarized by the *aggregate supply curve,* to which we will turn later.

Once we've developed the aggregate demand and supply curves, we'll be able to use them to understand how changes in the price level—sometimes gently, other times more harshly—steer the economy back toward potential output.

THE AGGREGATE DEMAND CURVE

Our first step in understanding how the price level affects the economy is an important fact: When the price level rises, the money demand curve shifts rightward. Why? Remember that the money demand curve tells us how much of their wealth people want to hold as money (as opposed to bonds) at each interest rate. People hold bonds because of the interest they pay; people hold money because of its convenience. Each day, as we make purchases, we need cash or funds in our checking account to pay for them. If the price level rises, so that our purchases become more expensive, we'll need to hold more of our wealth as money just to achieve the same level of convenience. Thus, at any given interest rate, the demand for money increases, and the money demand curve shifts rightward.

The shift in money demand, and its impact on the economy, is illustrated in Figure 2. Panel (a) has our familiar money market diagram. We'll assume that, initially, the price level in the economy is equal to 100. With this price level, the money market is in equilibrium at point *E,* with an interest rate of 6 percent.

In panel (b), equilibrium GDP is at point *E,* with output equal to $10 trillion. The aggregate expenditure line is marked "*r* = 6%," which is the equilibrium interest rate we just found in the money market.

Now let's imagine a rather substantial rise in the price level, from 100 to 140. What will happen in the economy? The initial impact is in the money market. The money demand curve will start to shift rightward, and the interest rate will rise. Next, in panel (b), the higher interest rate decreases interest-sensitive spending—business investment, new housing, and consumer durables. The aggregate expenditure line shifts downward, and equilibrium real GDP decreases. All of these changes continue until we reach a new, consistent equilibrium in both panels. Compared with our initial position, this new equilibrium has the following characteristics:

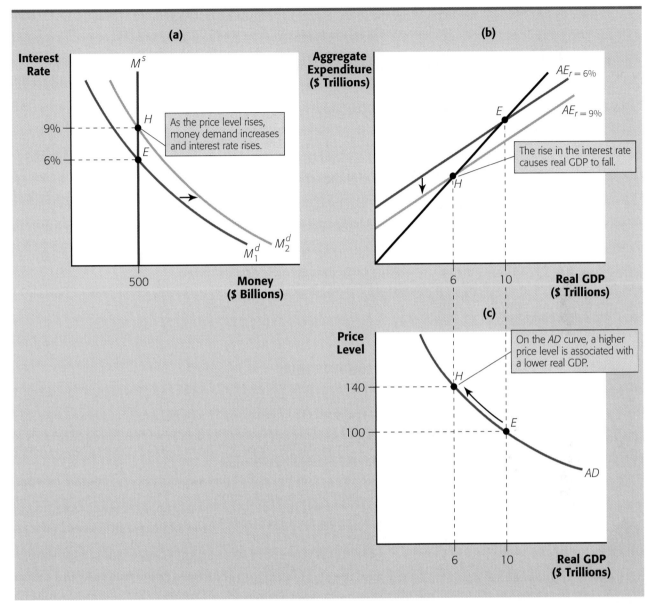

FIGURE 2
Deriving the Aggregate Demand Curve

- The money demand curve has shifted rightward.
- The interest rate is higher.
- The aggregate expenditure line has shifted downward.
- Equilibrium GDP is lower.

Remember that all of these changes are caused by a rise in the price level.

The points labeled H in panels (a) and (b) show one possible new equilibrium that meets these requirements. In panel (a), the money demand curve has shifted to M_2^d. The interest rate has risen to 9 percent. The aggregate expenditure line has shifted downward, to the one marked "$r = 9\%$." Finally, equilibrium output has fallen to $6 trillion.

Now recall the initial event that caused real GDP to fall: a rise in the price level. We've thus established an important principle:

A rise in the price level causes a decrease in equilibrium GDP.

Deriving the Aggregate Demand Curve

In panel (c), we introduce a new curve that directly shows the negative relationship between the price level and equilibrium GDP. In this panel, the price level is measured along the vertical axis, while real GDP is on the horizontal. Point *E* represents our initial equilibrium, with *P* = 100 and equilibrium GDP = $10 trillion. Point *H* represents the new equilibrium, with *P* = 140 and equilibrium GDP = $6 trillion. If we continued to change the price level to other values—raising it further to 150, lowering it to 85, and so on—we would find that each different price level results in a different equilibrium GDP. This is illustrated by the downward-sloping curve in the figure, which we call the *aggregate demand curve*.

Aggregate demand (*AD*) curve A curve indicating equilibrium GDP at each price level.

The aggregate demand (AD) *curve tells us the equilibrium real GDP at any price level.*

Understanding the *AD* Curve

The *AD* curve is unlike any other curve you've encountered in this text. In all other cases, our curves have represented simple behavioral relationships. For example, the demand curve for maple syrup shows us how a change in price affects the behavior of buyers in a market. Similarly, the aggregate expenditure line shows how a change in income affects total spending in the economy.

But the *AD* curve represents more than just a behavioral relationship between two variables. Each point on the curve represents a short-run *equilibrium* in the economy. For example, point *E* on the *AD* curve in Figure 2 tells us that when the price level is 100, *equilibrium* GDP is $10 trillion. Thus, point *E* doesn't just tell us that total spending is $10 trillion; rather, it tells us that when *P* = 100, spending and output are equal to each other only when they *both* are equal to $10 trillion.

Two Misconceptions About the *AD* Curve Watch out for two very common mistakes about the aggregate demand curve. The first is thinking that it is simply a "total demand" or "total spending" curve for the economy, telling us the total quantity of output that purchasers want to buy at each price level. This is an oversimplification. Rather, the *AD* curve tells us the *equilibrium* real GDP at each price level. Remember that equilibrium GDP is the level of output at which total spending *equals* total output. Thus, total spending is only part of the story behind the *AD* curve: The other part is the requirement that total spending and total output be equal.

A second, related mistake is thinking that the *AD* curve slopes downward for the same reason that a microeconomic demand curve slopes downward. This, too, is wrong: *Microeconomic* demand curves for individual products rely on an entirely different mechanism than the one we've described for the *AD* curve. In the market for maple syrup, for example, a rise in price causes quantity demanded to decrease, mostly because people switch to *other* goods that are now relatively cheaper. But along the *AD* curve, a rise in the price level generally causes the prices of *all* goods to increase *together*. In this case, there are no relatively cheaper goods to switch to!

The *AD* curve works in an entirely different way from microeconomic demand curves. Along the *AD* curve, an increase in the price level raises the interest rate in the money market, which decreases spending on interest-sensitive goods, causing a drop in equilibrium GDP.

As you can see, a better name for the *AD* curve would be the "equilibrium-output-at-each-price-level" curve—not a very catchy name. The *AD* curve gets its name because it *resembles* the demand curve for an individual product. It's a downward-sloping curve, with the price level (instead of the price of a single good) on the vertical axis and *equilibrium total output* (instead of the quantity of a single good demanded) on the horizontal axis. But there the similarity ends. The *AD* curve is not a demand curve at all, in spite of its name.

Movements Along the *AD* Curve

As you will see later in this chapter, a variety of events can cause the price level to change, and move us *along* the *AD* curve. It's important to understand what happens in the economy as we make such a move.

Look again at the *AD* curve in panel (c) of Figure 2. Suppose the price level rises, and we move from point *E* to point *H* along this curve. Then the following sequence of events occurs: The rise in the price level increases the demand for money, raises the interest rate, decreases autonomous consumption (*a*) and investment spending (I^p), and works through the multiplier to decrease equilibrium GDP. The process can be summarized as follows:

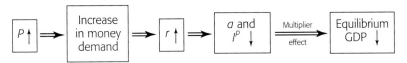

The opposite sequence of events will occur if the price level falls, moving us rightward along the *AD* curve:

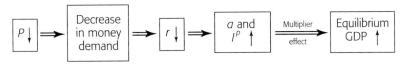

Shifts of the *AD* Curve

When we move along the *AD* curve in Figure 2, we assume that the price level changes but that other influences on equilibrium GDP are constant. When any of these other influences on GDP changes, the *AD* curve will shift. The distinction between movements along the *AD* curve and shifts of the curve itself is very important. Always keep the following rule in mind:

> *When a change in the price level causes equilibrium GDP to change, we move along the* AD *curve. Whenever anything other than the price level causes equilibrium GDP to change, the* AD *curve itself shifts.*

What are these other influences on GDP? They are the very same changes you learned about in previous chapters. Specifically, equilibrium GDP will change whenever there is a change in any of the following:

- government purchases
- taxes
- autonomous consumption spending
- investment spending
- net exports
- the money supply

Let's consider some examples and see how each causes the *AD* curve to shift.

FIGURE 3
A Spending Shock Shifts the
***AD* Curve**

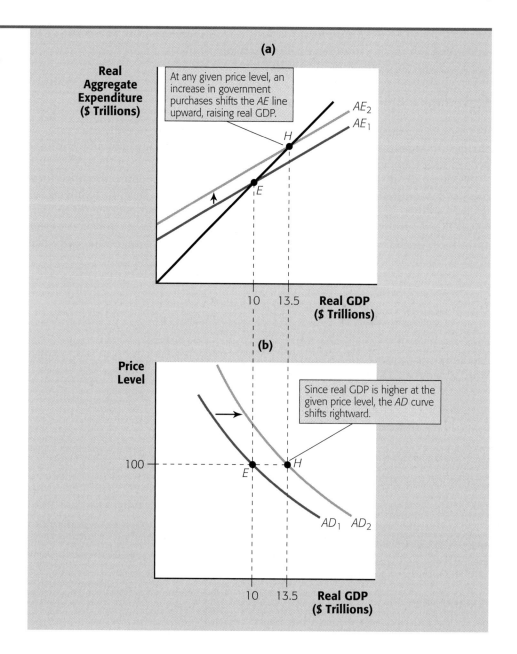

(a)

Real
Aggregate
Expenditure
($ Trillions)

At any given price level, an
increase in government
purchases shifts the *AE* line
upward, raising real GDP.

AE_2
AE_1

H

E

10 13.5 **Real GDP**
($ Trillions)

(b)

Price
Level

Since real GDP is higher at the
given price level, the *AD* curve
shifts rightward.

100

E *H*

AD_1 AD_2

10 13.5 **Real GDP**
($ Trillions)

An Increase in Government Purchases. In Figure 3, we assume that the economy
begins at a price level of 100. In the money market (not shown), the equilibrium interest rate is 6 percent and equilibrium output—given by point *E* in panel (a)—is $10
trillion. Panel (b) shows the same equilibrium as represented by point *E* on AD_1.

Now let's repeat an experiment from the previous chapter: We'll increase government purchases by $2 trillion and ask what happens if the price level remains at
100. If you flip back to Figure 8 in the previous chapter, you'll see that this rise in
government purchases caused the *AE* line to shift upward, but it also caused the
equilibrium interest rate to rise to 8 percent, causing the *AE* line to shift back downward a bit. The result was that equilibrium GDP rose to $13.5 trillion. This new

equilibrium is also shown in panel (a) of Figure 3. The aggregate expenditure line shifts upward to AE_2, and the equilibrium moves to point H. With the price level remaining at 100, equilibrium GDP increases.

Now look at panel (b) in Figure 3. There, the new equilibrium is represented by point H ($P = 100$, real GDP = \$13.5 trillion). This point lies to the right of our original curve AD_1. Point H, therefore, must lie on a *new AD* curve—a curve that tells us equilibrium GDP at any price level *after the increase in government spending*. The new AD curve is the one labeled AD_2, which goes through point H. What about the other points on AD_2? They tell us that, if we had started at any *other* price level, an increase in government spending would have increased equilibrium GDP at that price level, too. We conclude that *an increase in government purchases shifts the entire AD curve rightward.*

Any other factor that initially shifts the aggregate expenditure line upward will shift the AD curve rightward, just as in Figure 3. More specifically,

the AD curve shifts rightward when government purchases, investment spending, autonomous consumption spending, or net exports increase, or when net taxes decrease.

Our analysis also applies in the other direction. For example, at any given price level, a *decrease* in government spending shifts the aggregate expenditure line *downward*, decreasing equilibrium GDP. This in turn shifts the AD curve leftward.

The AD curve shifts leftward when government purchases, investment spending, autonomous consumption spending, or net exports decrease, or when net taxes increase.

Changes in the Money Supply. Changes in the money supply will also shift the aggregate demand curve. To see why, let's imagine that the Fed conducts open market operations to *increase* the money supply. As you learned in the previous chapter, this will cause the interest rate to decrease, increasing investment spending and autonomous consumption spending. Together, these spending changes will shift the aggregate expenditure line upward, just as in panel (a) of Figure 3, and increase equilibrium GDP. Since this change in equilibrium output is caused by something *other* than a change in the price level, the AD curve shifts. In this case, because the money supply *increased*, the AD curve shifts *rightward*, just as in panel (b) of Figure 3.

A decrease in the money supply would have the opposite effect: The interest rate would rise, the aggregate expenditure line would shift downward, and *equilibrium GDP at any price level would fall.* We conclude that

an increase in the money supply shifts the AD curve rightward. A decrease in the money supply shifts the AD curve leftward.

Shifts Versus Movements Along the *AD* Curve: A Summary. Figure 4 summarizes how some events in the economy cause a movement along the AD curve, and other events shift the AD curve. You can use the figure as an exercise, drawing diagrams similar to Figures 2 and 3 to illustrate why we move along or shift the AD curve in each case.

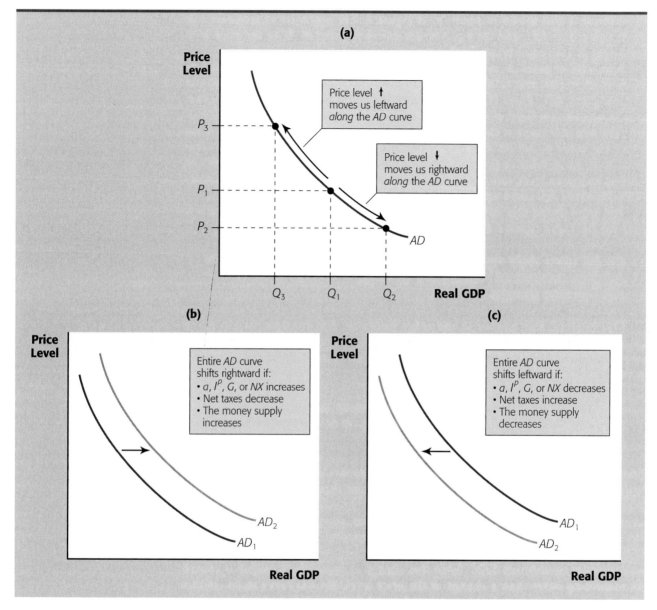

FIGURE 4
Effects of Key Changes on the Aggregate Demand Curve

Notice that panels (b) and (c) of Figure 4 tell us how a variety of events affect the *AD* curve, but *not* how they affect *real GDP*. The reason is that, even if we know which *AD* curve we are on, we could be at *any point* along that curve, depending on where the price level ends up.

But where will the price level end up? Our first step in answering that question is to understand the other side of the relationship between GDP and the price level.

THE AGGREGATE SUPPLY CURVE

Look back at Figure 1, which illustrates the *two-way* relationship between the price level and output. On the one hand, changes in the price level affect output. This is the relationship, summarized by the *AD* curve, that we've just explored in the previous section. On the other hand, changes in output affect the price level. This relationship—summarized by the *aggregate supply curve*—is the focus of this section.

The effect of changes in output on the price level is complex, involving a variety of forces. Current research is helping economists get a clearer picture of this relationship. Here, we will present a simple model of the aggregate supply curve that focuses on the link between prices and costs. Toward the end of the chapter, we'll discuss some additional ideas about the aggregate supply curve.

Costs and Prices

The price *level* in the economy results from the pricing behavior of millions of individual business firms. In any given year, some of these firms will raise their prices, and some will lower them. For example, during the 1990s, personal computers and long-distance telephone calls came down in price, while college tuition and the prices of movies rose. These types of price changes are subjects for *microeconomic* analysis, because they involve individual markets.

But often, all firms in the economy are affected by the same *macroeconomic* event, causing prices to rise or fall throughout the economy. This change in the price *level* is what interests us in macroeconomics.

To understand how macroeconomic events affect the price level, we begin with a very simple assumption:

> *A firm sets the price of its products as a markup over cost per unit.*

Fast-food restaurants, like other firms in the economy, charge a markup over cost per unit. The average markup in the economy is determined by competitive conditions, and tends to change slowly over time.

For example, if it costs Burger King $2.00, on average, to produce a Whopper (cost per unit is $2.00), and Burger King's percentage markup is 10 percent, then it will charge $2.00 + (0.10 \times $2.00) = $2.20 per Whopper.[1]

The percentage markup in any particular industry will depend on the degree of competition there. If there are many firms competing for customers in a market, all producing very similar products, then we can expect the markup to be relatively small. Thus, we expect a relatively low markup on fast-food burgers or personal computers. In industries where there is less competition—such as daily newspapers or jet aircraft—we would expect higher percentage markups.

In macroeconomics, we are not concerned with how the markup differs in different industries, but rather with the *average percentage markup* in the economy:

> *The average percentage markup in the economy is determined by competitive conditions in the economy. The competitive structure of the economy changes very slowly, so the average percentage markup should be somewhat stable from year to year.*

But a stable markup does not necessarily mean a stable price level, because unit costs can change. For example, if Burger King's markup remains at 10 percent, but the unit cost of a Whopper rises from $2.00 to $3.00, then the price of a Whopper will rise to $3.00 + (0.10 \times $3.00) = $3.30. Extending this example to all firms in the economy, we can say:

[1] In microeconomics, you learn more sophisticated theories of how firms' prices are determined. But our simple markup model captures a central conclusion of those theories: that an increase in costs will result in higher prices.

> *In the short run, the price level rises when there is an economy-wide increase in unit costs, and the price level falls when there is an economy-wide decrease in unit costs.*

GDP, Costs, and the Price Level

Our primary concern in this chapter is the impact of *total output or real GDP* on unit costs and, therefore, on the price level. Why should a change in output affect unit costs and the price level? We'll focus on three key reasons.

As total output increases:

Greater amounts of inputs may be needed to produce a unit of output. As output increases, firms hire new, untrained workers who may be less productive than existing workers. Firms also begin using capital and land that are less well suited to their industry. As a result, greater amounts of labor, capital, land, and raw materials are needed to produce each unit of output. Even if the prices of these inputs remain the same, unit costs will rise.

For example, imagine that Intel increases its output of computer chips. Then it will have to be less picky about the workers it employs, hiring some who are less well suited to chip production than those already working there. Thus, more labor hours will be needed to produce each chip. Intel may also have to begin using older, less-efficient production facilities, which require more silicon and other raw materials per chip. Even if the prices of all of these inputs remain unchanged, unit costs will rise.

The prices of nonlabor inputs rise. In addition to needing greater quantities of inputs, firms will also have to pay a higher price for them. This is especially true of inputs like land and natural resources, which may be available only in limited quantities in the short run. An increase in the output of final goods raises the demand for these inputs, causing their prices to rise. Firms that produce final goods experience an increase in unit costs, and raise their own prices accordingly.

The nominal wage rate rises. Greater output means higher employment, leaving fewer unemployed workers looking for jobs. As firms compete to hire increasingly scarce workers, they must offer higher nominal wage rates to attract them. Higher nominal wages increase unit costs, and therefore result in a higher price level. Notice that we use the nominal wage, rather than the real wage we've emphasized elsewhere in this book. That's because we are interested in explaining how firms' prices are determined. Since price is a nominal variable, it will be marked up over *nominal* costs.

A decrease in output affects unit costs through the same three forces, but with the opposite result. As output falls, firms can be more selective in hiring the best, most efficient workers and in choosing other inputs, decreasing their input requirements per unit of output. Decreases in demand for land and natural resources will cause their prices to drop. And as unemployment rises, wages will fall as workers compete for jobs. All of these contribute to a drop in unit costs, and a decrease in the price level.

The Short Run. All three of our reasons are important in explaining why a change in output affects the price level. However, they operate within different time frames.

When total output increases, new, less productive workers will be hired rather quickly. Similarly, the prices of certain key inputs—such as lumber, land, oil, and wheat—may rise within a few weeks or months.

But our third explanation—changes in the nominal wage rate—is a different story. While wages in some lines of work might respond very rapidly, we can expect wages in many industries to change very little or not at all for a year or more after a change in output.

> *For a year or so after a change in output, changes in the average nominal wage are less important than other forces that change unit costs.*

Here are some of the more important reasons why wages in many industries respond so slowly to changes in output:

- Many firms have union contracts that specify wages for up to three years. While wage increases are often built into these contracts, a rise in output will not affect the wage increase. When output rises or falls, these firms continue to abide by the contract.
- Wages in many large corporations are set by slow-moving bureaucracies.
- Wage changes in either direction can be costly to firms. Higher wages to attract new workers must be widely publicized in order to raise the number of job applicants at the firm. Lower wages can reduce the morale of workers—and their productivity. Thus, many firms are reluctant to change wages until they are reasonably sure that any change in their output will be long lasting.
- Firms may benefit from developing reputations for paying stable wages. A firm that raises wages when output is high and labor is scarce may have to lower wages when output is low and labor is plentiful. Such a firm would develop a reputation for paying unstable wages, and have difficulty attracting new workers.

In this section, we focus exclusively on the short run—a time horizon of a year or so after a change in output. Since the average nominal wage rate changes very little over the short run, we'll make the following simplifying assumption: *The nominal wage rate is fixed in the short run.* More specifically,

> *we assume that changes in output have no effect on the nominal wage rate in the short run.*

Keep in mind, though, that our assumption of a constant wage holds only in the *short run.* As you will see later, wage changes play a very important role in the economy's adjustment over the long run.

Since we assume a constant nominal wage in the short run, a change in output will affect unit costs through the other two factors we mentioned earlier. Specifically, in the short run, a rise in real GDP raises firms' unit costs because (1) input requirements per unit of output rise, and (2) the prices of nonlabor inputs rise. With a constant percentage markup, the rise in unit costs translates into a rise in the price level. Thus,

> *in the short run, a rise in real GDP, by causing unit costs to increase, will also cause a rise in the price level.*

FIGURE 5
The Aggregate Supply Curve

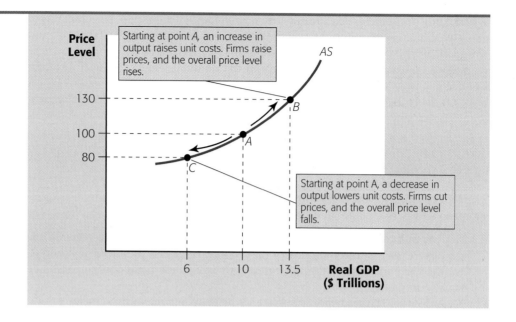

In the other direction, a *drop* in real GDP lowers unit costs because (1) input requirements per unit of output fall, and (2) the prices of nonlabor inputs fall. With a constant percentage markup, the drop in unit costs translates into a drop in the price level.

> *In the short run, a fall in real GDP, by causing unit costs to decrease, will also cause a decrease in the price level.*

Deriving the Aggregate Supply Curve

Figure 5 summarizes our discussion about the effect of output on the price level in the short run. Suppose the economy begins at point *A*, with output at $10 trillion and the price level at 100. Now suppose that output rises to $13.5 trillion. What will happen in the short run? Even though wages are assumed to remain constant, the price level will rise because of the other forces we've discussed. In the figure, the price level rises to 130, indicated by point *B*. If, instead, output *fell* to $6 trillion, the price level would fall—to 80 in the figure, indicated by point *C*.

As you can see, each time we change the level of output, there will be a new price level in the short run, giving us another point on the figure. If we connect all of these points, we obtain the economy's *aggregate supply curve:*

Aggregate supply (AS) curve A curve indicating the price level consistent with firms' unit costs and markups for any level of output over the short run.

> *The aggregate supply curve (or **AS** curve) tells us the price level consistent with firms' unit costs and their percentage markups at any level of output over the short run.*

A more accurate name for the *AS* curve would be the "short-run-price-level-at-each-output-level" curve, but that is more than a mouthful. The *AS* curve gets its name because it *resembles* a microeconomic market supply curve. Like the supply curve for maple syrup we discussed in Chapter 3, the *AS* curve is upward sloping, and it has a price variable (the price level) on the vertical axis and a quantity variable (total output) on the horizontal axis. But there, the similarity ends.

Movements Along the *AS* Curve

When a change in output causes the price level to change, we *move along* the economy's *AS* curve. But what happens in the economy as we make such a move?

Look again at the *AS* curve in Figure 5. Suppose we move from point *A* to point *B* along this curve in the short run. The increase in output raises the prices of raw materials and other (nonlabor) inputs and also raises input requirements per unit of output at many firms. Both of these changes increase costs per unit. As long as the markup remains somewhat stable, the rise in unit costs will lead firms to raise their prices, and the price level will increase. Thus, as we move upward along the *AS* curve, we can represent what happens as follows:

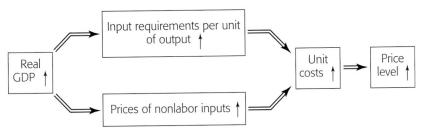

The opposite sequence of events occurs when real GDP falls, moving us downward along the *AS* curve:

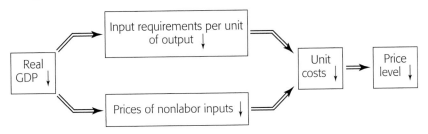

Shifts of the *AS* Curve

When we drew the *AS* curve in Figure 5, we assumed that a number of important variables remained unchanged. In particular, we assumed that the only changes in unit costs were those caused by a change in output. But in the real world, unit costs sometimes change for reasons *other* than a change in output. When this occurs, unit costs—*and* the price level—will change at *any* level of output, so the *AS* curve will shift.

In general, we distinguish between a movement along the *AS* curve, and a shift of the curve itself, as follows:

> *When a change in real GDP causes the price level to change, we move along the AS curve. When anything other than a change in real GDP causes the price level to change, the AS curve itself shifts.*

Figure 6 illustrates the logic of a shift in the *AS* curve. Suppose the economy's initial *AS* curve is AS_1. Now suppose that some economic event *other* than a change

FIGURE 6
Shifts of the Aggregate
Supply Curve

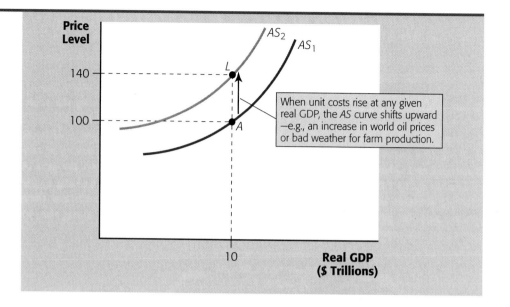

A Misconception About the *AS* Curve A common mistake about the *AS* curve is thinking that it describes the same kind of relationship between price and quantity as a microeconomic supply curve. There are two reasons why this is wrong.

First, the direction of causation between price and output is reversed for the *AS* curve. For example, when we draw the supply curve for maple syrup, we view changes in the price of maple syrup as causing a change in output supplied. But along the *AS* curve, it's the other way around: A change in *output* causes a change in the *price level*.

Second, the basic assumption behind the *AS* curve is very different from that behind a single market supply curve. When we draw the supply curve for an individual product, we assume that the prices of inputs used in producing the good remain fixed. This is a sensible thing to do, because an increase in production for a single good is unlikely to have much effect on input prices in the economy as a whole.

But when we draw the *AS* curve, we imagine an increase in *real GDP*, in which *all* firms are increasing their output. This will significantly raise the demand for inputs, so it is unrealistic to assume that input prices will remain fixed. Indeed, the rise in input prices is one of the important reasons for the *AS* curve's upward slope.

in output—for the moment, we'll leave the event unnamed—causes firms to raise their prices. Then the price level will be higher at *any* level of output we might imagine, so the *AS* curve must shift *upward*—for example, to AS_2 in the figure. At an output level of $10 trillion, the price level would rise from 100 to 140. At any other output level, the price level would also rise.

What can cause unit costs to change at any given level of output? The following are some important examples:

- *Changes in world oil prices.* Oil is traded on a world market, where prices can fluctuate even while output in the United States does not. And changes in world oil prices have caused major shifts in the *AS* curve. Three events over the past few decades—an oil embargo by Arab oil-producing nations in 1973–74, the Iranian revolution in 1978–79, and Iraq's invasion of Kuwait in 1990—all caused large jumps in the price of oil. Each time, costs per unit rose for firms across the country, and they responded by charging higher prices than before for *any* output level they might produce. As in Figure 6, the *AS* curve shifted upward. Conversely, oil prices fell sharply during 1997 and 1998. This caused unit costs to decrease at many firms, shifting the *AS* curve downward.

- *Changes in the weather.* Good crop-growing weather increases farmers' yields for any given amounts of land, labor, capital, and other inputs used. This decreases farms' unit costs, and the price of agricultural goods falls. Since many of these goods are final goods (such as fresh fruit and vegetables), the price drop will contribute directly to a drop in the price level and a downward shift of the *AS* curve. Additionally, agricultural products are important inputs in the production of many other goods. (For example, corn is an input in beef production.) Good weather thus leads to a drop in input prices for many other firms in the economy, causing their unit costs, and their prices, to decrease. For these reasons, we can expect good weather to shift the *AS* curve downward. Bad weather, which decreases crop yields, increases unit costs at any level of output and shifts the *AS* curve upward.

- *Technological change.* New technologies can enable firms to produce any given level of output at lower unit costs. In recent years, for example, we've seen revolutions in telecommunications, information processing, and medicine. The result has been steady downward shifts of the *AS* curve.

- *The Nominal Wage.* Remember that in our short-run analysis we're assuming the nominal wage rate does *not* change. As we move along the *AS* curve, we hold the nominal wage rate constant. But later in the chapter—when we extend our time horizon beyond a year or so—you'll see that changes in the nominal wage are an important part of the economy's long-run adjustment process. Here we just point out that, *if* the nominal wage were to increase for any reason, it would raise unit costs for firms at any level of output and therefore *shift* the *AS* curve *upward.* Similarly, *if* the nominal wage rate were to fall for any reason, it would *decrease* unit costs at any level of output and shift the *AS* curve downward. We'll come back to this important fact later.

Figure 7 summarizes how different events in the economy cause a movement along, or a shift in, the *AS* curve. But the *AS* curve tells only half of the economy's story: It shows us the price level *if* we know the level of output. The *AD* curve tells the other half of the story: It shows us the level of output *if* we know the economy's price level. In the next section, we finally put the two halves of the story together, allowing us to determine both the price level and output.

AD AND AS TOGETHER: SHORT-RUN EQUILIBRIUM

Where will the economy settle in the short run? That is, where is our **short-run macroeconomic equilibrium?** Figure 8 shows how to answer that question, using both the *AS* curve and the *AD* curve. If you suspect that the equilibrium is at point *E*, the intersection of these two curves, you are correct. At that point, the price level is 100 and output is $10 trillion. But it's worth thinking about *why* point *E*—and only point *E*—is our short-run equilibrium.

First, we know that in equilibrium, the economy must be at some point on the *AD* curve. For example, suppose the economy were at point *B*, which lies to the right of the *AD* curve. At this point, the price level is 140 and output is $14 trillion. But the *AD* curve tells us that with a price level of 140, *equilibrium* output is $6 trillion. Thus, at point *B*, real GDP would be greater than its equilibrium value. As you learned several chapters ago, this situation cannot persist for long, since inventories would pile up and firms would be forced to cut back on their production. Thus, point *B* cannot be our short-run equilibrium.

Second, short-run equilibrium requires that the economy be operating on its *AS* curve. Otherwise, firms would not be charging the prices dictated by their unit costs and the average percentage markup in the economy. For example, point *F* lies

Short-run macroeconomic equilibrium A combination of price level and GDP consistent with both the *AD* and *AS* curves.

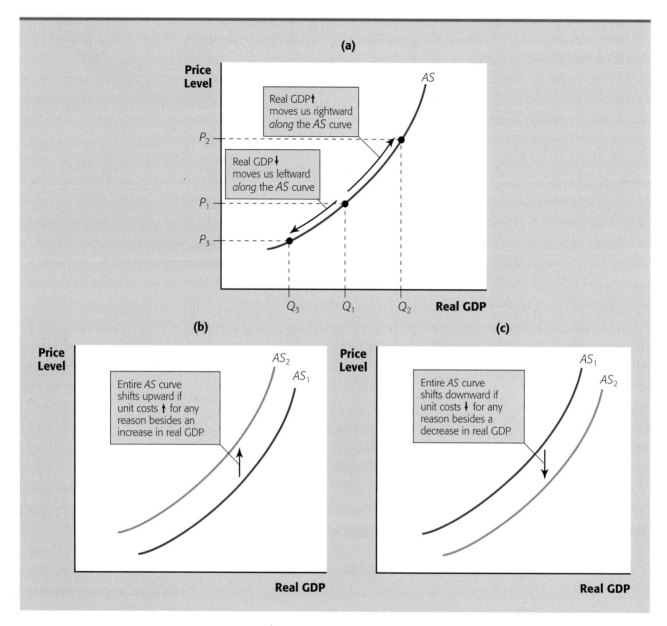

FIGURE 7
**Effects of Key Changes on the
Aggregate Supply Curve**

below the AS curve. But the AS curve tells us that if output is $14 trillion, based on the average percentage markup and unit costs, the price level should be 140 (point *B*), not something lower. That is, the price level at point *F* is *too low* for equilibrium. This situation will not last long either, since firms will want to raise prices, causing the overall price level to rise.

We could make a similar argument for any other point that is off the AS curve, off the AD curve, or off of both curves. Our conclusion is always the same: Unless the economy is on *both* the AS and the AD curves, the price level and the level of output will change. Only when the economy is at point *E*—on *both* curves—can we have a sustainable level of real GDP and the price level.

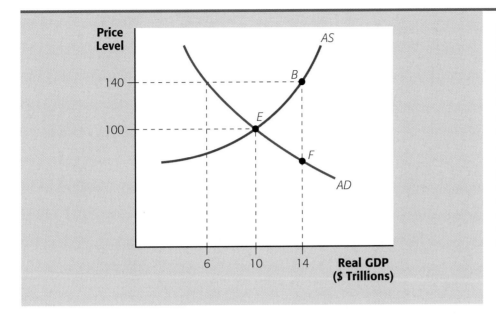

FIGURE 8
Short-Run Macroeconomic Equilibrium

Short-run equilibrium occurs where the AD and AS curves intersect. At point E, the price level of 100 is consistent with an output of $10 trillion along the AD curve. The output level of $10 trillion is consistent with a price level of 100 along the AS curve. At any other combination of price level and output, such as point F or point B, at least one condition for equilibrium will not be satisfied.

WHAT HAPPENS WHEN THINGS CHANGE?

Now that we know how the short-run equilibrium is determined, and armed with our knowledge of the *AD* and *AS* curves, we are ready to put the model through its paces. In this section, we'll explore how different types of events cause the short-run equilibrium to change.

Our short-run equilibrium will change when either the *AD* curve, the *AS* curve, or both, *shift*. Since the consequences for the economy are very different for shifts in the *AD* curve as opposed to shifts in the *AS* curve, economists have developed a shorthand language to distinguish between them:

*An event that causes the AD curve to shift is called a **demand shock**. An event that causes the AS curve to shift is called a **supply shock**.*

Demand shock Any event that causes the *AD* curve to shift.

Supply shock Any event that causes the *AS* curve to shift.

In earlier chapters, we've used the phrase *spending shock*: a change in spending by one or more sectors that ultimately affects the entire economy. As you're about to see, shifts in the aggregate demand curve or the aggregate supply curve both create changes in aggregate expenditure, although in different ways. So *demand shocks* and *supply shocks* are just two *different categories of spending shocks*.

In this section, we'll first explore the effects of demand shocks, both in the short run and during the adjustment process to the long run. Then, we'll take up the issue of supply shocks.

Demand Shocks in the Short Run

Figure 4, which lists the causes of a shift in the *AD* curve, also serves as a list of demand shocks to the economy. Let's consider some examples.

The Effect of a Demand Shock

Starting at point E, an increase in government purchases would shift the AD curve rightward to AD₂. Point J illustrates where the economy would move if the price level remained constant. But as output increases, the price level rises. Thus, the economy moves along the AS curve from point E to point H.

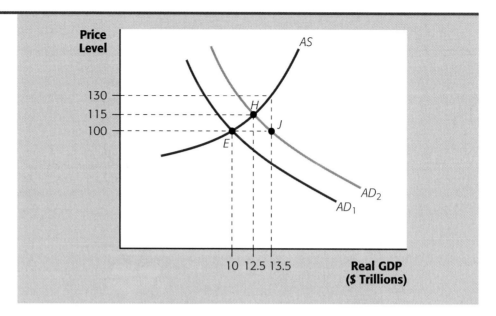

An Increase in Government Purchases. You've learned that an increase in government purchases shifts the *AD* curve rightward. Now we can see how it affects the economy in the short run. Figure 9 shows the initial equilibrium at point *E,* with the price level equal to 100 and output at $10 trillion. Now, suppose that government purchases rise by $2 trillion. Figure 4(b) tells us that the *AD* curve will shift rightward. What will happen to equilibrium GDP?

In our example in the previous chapter, a $2 trillion rise in government purchases increased output to $13.5 trillion, and also raised the interest rate in the money market to 8 percent. (Flip back to Figure 8 in that chapter to refresh your memory.)

But nowhere in our previous analysis did we consider any change in the price level. Thus, the rise in GDP to $13.5 trillion in the previous chapter makes sense *only if the price level does not change.* Here, in Figure 9, this *would* be a movement rightward, from point E to point J. However, *point J does not describe the economy's short-run equilibrium.* Why not? Because it ignores two facts that you've learned about in this chapter: The rise in output will change the price level, and the change in the price level will, in turn, affect equilibrium GDP.

To see this more clearly, let's first suppose that the price level did *not* rise when output increased, so that the economy actually *did* arrive at point J after the *AD* shift. Would we stay there? Absolutely not. Point J lies below the *AS* curve, telling us that when GDP is $13.5 trillion, the price level consistent with firms' unit costs, and average markup is 130, not 100. Firms would soon raise prices, and this would cause a movement leftward along *AD₂.* The price level would keep rising and output would keep falling, until we reached point *H.* At that point, with output at $12.5 trillion, we would be on both the *AS* and *AD* curves, so there would be no reason for a further rise in the price level and no reason for a further fall in output.

However, the process we've just described is not entirely realistic. It assumes that when government purchases rise, *first* output increases (the move to point J) and *then* the price level rises (the move to point H). In reality, output and the price level tend to rise *together.* Thus, the economy would likely *slide along* the *AS* curve from point *E* to point *H.* As we move along the *AS* curve, output rises, increasing unit costs and the price level. At the same time, the rise in the price level *reduces equilibrium GDP* (the level of output toward which the economy is heading on the *AD* curve) from point *J* to point *H.*

We can summarize the impact of a rise in government purchases this way:

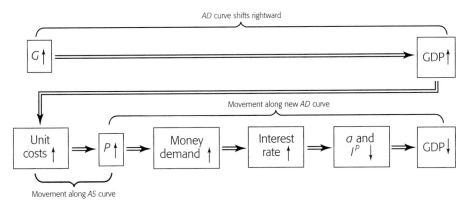

Net Effect: GDP↑, but by less due to effect of *P*↑

Let's step back a minute and get some perspective about this example of fiscal policy. This is the third time in this text that we've considered fiscal policy in the short run. Each time, the discussion became more realistic, and we've seen that the effect of fiscal policy becomes weaker. In our first analysis, we ignored any increase in the interest rate, and found that a rise in government purchases increased equilibrium GDP according to the simple multiplier formula $1/(1 - MPC)$. In our second analysis, in the chapter before this one, you learned that a rise in government purchases increases the interest rate, crowding out some interest-sensitive spending, thus making the rise in GDP smaller than it would otherwise be. The multiplier, therefore, was smaller than $1/(1 - MPC)$. Now you've learned that the rise in government purchases *also* increases the price level. This leads to a *further* rise in the interest rate, crowding out still *more* interest-sensitive spending, and making the rise in GDP *smaller still.* The size of the multiplier has been reduced yet again. (In our example, a $2 trillion increase in government purchases increases equilibrium GDP by $2.5 trillion, so the multiplier would be $2.5 trillion/$2 trillion = 1.25.) However, as you can see in Figure 9, the multiplier is still positive: A rise in government purchases—even when we take account of the rise in the price level—still raises GDP in the short run.

We can summarize the impact of price-level changes this way:

> *When government purchases increase, the horizontal shift of the* AD *curve measures how much real GDP would increase if the price level remained constant. But because the price level rises, real GDP rises by less than the horizontal shift in the* AD *curve.*

Now let's switch gears into reverse: How would we illustrate the effects of a *decrease* in government purchases? In this case, the *AD* curve would shift *leftward,* causing the following to happen:

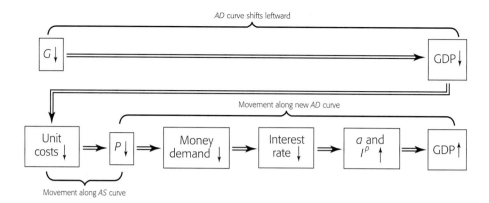

Net Effect: GDP↓, but by less due to effect of *P*↓

As you can see, the same sequence of events occurs in the same order, but each variable moves in the opposite direction. A decrease in government purchases decreases equilibrium GDP, but the multiplier effect is smaller because the price level falls.

An Increase in the Money Supply. Although monetary policy stimulates the economy through a different channel than fiscal policy, once we arrive at the *AD* and *AS* diagram, the two look very much alike. For example, an increase in the money supply, which reduces the interest rate, will stimulate interest-sensitive consumption and investment spending. Real GDP then increases, and the *AD* curve shifts rightward, just as in Figure 9. Once output begins to rise, we have the same sequence of events as in fiscal policy: The price level rises, so the increase in GDP will be smaller. We can represent the situation as follows:

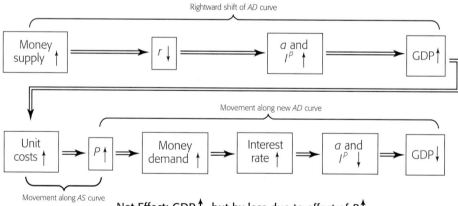

Net Effect: GDP↑, but by less due to effect of *P*↑

Other Demand Shocks. On your own, try going through examples of different demand shocks (see the list in Figures 4 (b) and (c)) and explain the sequence of events in each case that causes output and the price level to change. This will help you verify the following general conclusion about demand shocks:

> *A positive demand shock—one that shifts the* AD *curve rightward—increases both real GDP and the price level in the short run. A negative demand shock—one that shifts the* AD *curve leftward—decreases both real GDP and the price level in the short run.*

An Example: The Great Depression. As mentioned at the beginning of the chapter, the U.S. economy collapsed far more seriously during the period 1929 through 1933—the onset of the Great Depression—than it did at any other time in the country's history. Because the price level fell during this time, we know that the contraction was caused by an adverse demand shock. (An adverse supply shock would have caused the price level to *rise* as GDP fell.)

What do we know about the demand shocks that caused the depression? This question has been debated by economists almost continuously over the past 70 years. The candidates are numerous, and it appears that a combination of events was responsible. The 1920s were a period of optimism, with high levels of investment by businesses and spending by families on houses and cars. The stock market soared. In the fall of 1929, the bubble of optimism burst. The stock market crashed, and investment and consumption spending plummeted. Similar events occurred in other countries, and the demand for products exported by the United States fell. The Fed—then only 16 years old—reacted by cutting the money supply sharply, which added an adverse monetary shock to all of the cutbacks in spending. Each of these events contributed to a leftward shift of the *AD* curve, causing both output and the price level to fall.

Demand Shocks: Adjusting to the Long Run

In Figure 9, point *H* shows the new equilibrium after a positive demand shock *in the short run*—a year or so after the shock. But point *H* is not necessarily where the economy will end up in the long run. For example, suppose full-employment output is $10 trillion, and point *H*—representing an output of $12.5 trillion—is *above full-employment output*. Then, with employment unusually high and unemployment unusually low, business firms will have to compete to hire scarce workers, driving up the wage rate. It might take a year or more for the wage rate to rise significantly (recall our earlier list of reasons that wages adjust only slowly). But when we extend our horizon to several years or more, we must recognize that if output is above its potential, the wage rate will rise. Since the *AS* curve is drawn for a given wage, a rise in the wage rate will *shift* the curve upward, changing our equilibrium.

Alternatively, we could imagine a situation in which short-run equilibrium GDP was *below* its potential. In this case, with abnormally high unemployment, workers would compete to get scarce jobs, and eventually the wage rate would fall. Then the *AS* curve would shift downward, once again changing our equilibrium GDP.

> *In the short run, we treat the wage rate as given. But in the long run, the wage rate can change. When output is above full employment, the wage rate will rise, shifting the* AS *curve upward. When output is below full employment, the wage rate will fall, shifting the* AS *curve downward.*

Now we are ready to explore what happens over the long run in the aftermath of a demand shock. Figure 10 shows an economy in equilibrium at point *E*. We assume that the initial equilibrium is at full-employment output (Y_{FE}), since—as you are about to see—this is where the economy always ends up after the long-run adjustment process is complete. To make our results as general as possible, we'll use symbols, rather than numbers, to represent output and price levels.

Now suppose the *AD* curve shifts rightward due to, say, an increase in government purchases. In the short run, the equilibrium moves to point *H*, with a higher price level (P_2) and a higher level of output (Y_2). Point *H* tells us where the economy

FIGURE 10
The Long-Run Adjustment Process

Beginning at point E, *a positive demand shock would shift the aggregate demand curve to* AD$_2$, *raising both output and the price level. At point* H, *output is above the full-employment level,* Y$_{FE}$. *Firms will compete to hire scarce workers, thereby driving up the wage rate. The higher wage rate will shift the AS curve to* AS$_2$. *Only when the economy returns to full-employment output at point* K *will there be no further shifts in* AS.

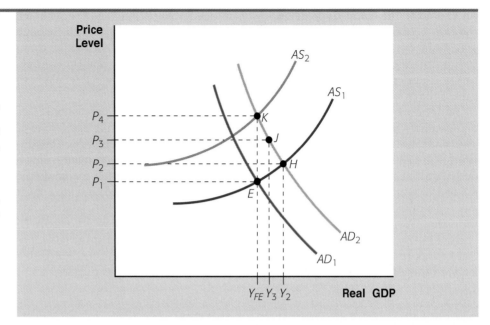

Self-correcting mechanism The adjustment process through which price and wage changes return the economy to full-employment output in the long run.

will be about a year after the increase in government purchases, before the wage rate has a chance to adjust. (Remember, along any given *AS* curve, the wage rate is assumed to be constant.)

But now let's extend our analysis beyond a year. Notice that Y_2 is greater than Y_{FE}. The wage will begin to rise, raising unit costs at any given output level and causing firms to raise prices. In the figure, the *AS* curve would begin shifting upward. Point *J* shows where the shifting aggregate supply curve might be two years after the shock, after the long-run adjustment process has begun. (You might want to pencil this intermediate *AS* curve into the figure, so that it intersects AD_2 at point *J*.) At this point, output would be at Y_3, and the rise in the price level has moved us along the new aggregate demand curve, AD_2.

Now, is point *J* our final, long-run equilibrium? No, it cannot be. At Y_3, output is *still* greater than Y_{FE}, so the wage rate will continue to rise and the *AS* curve will continue to shift upward. At point *J*, the long-run adjustment process is not yet complete. When will the process end? Only when the wage rate stops rising, that is, only when output has returned to Y_{FE}. This occurs when the *AS* curve has shifted all the way to AS_2, moving the economy to point *K*—our new, long-run equilibrium.

As you can see, the increase in government purchases has no effect on equilibrium GDP in the long run: The economy returns to full employment, which is just where it started. This is why the long-run adjustment process is often called the economy's **self-correcting mechanism.** And this mechanism applies to any demand shock, not just an increase in government purchases:

If a demand shock pulls the economy away from full employment, changes in the wage rate and the price level will eventually cause the economy to correct itself and return to full-employment output.

For a positive demand shock that shifts the *AD* curve rightward, the self-correcting mechanism works like this:

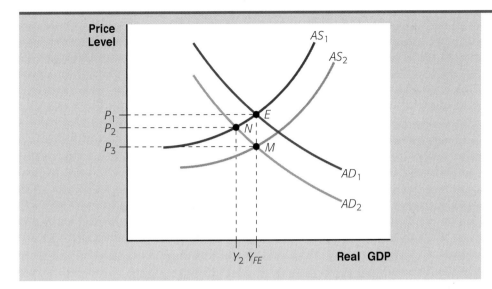

FIGURE 11
Long-Run Adjustment After a Negative Demand Shock

Starting from point E, a negative demand shock shifts the AD curve to AD$_2$, lowering GDP and the price level. At point N, output is below the full-employment level. With unemployed labor available, wages will fall, enabling firms to lower their prices. The AS curve shifts downward until full employment is regained at point M, with a lower price level.

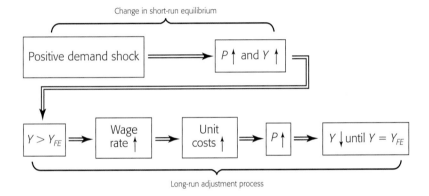

Figure 11 illustrates the case of a negative demand shock, in which the *AD* curve shifts leftward. Starting at point *E*, the short-run equilibrium moves to point *N* with real GDP below Y_{FE}. Over the long run, high unemployment drives the wage rate down, shifting the *AS* curve down as well. The price level decreases, causing equilibrium GDP to rise along the AD_2 curve. The process comes to a halt only when output returns to Y_{FE}. Thus, in the long run, the economy moves from point *E* to point *M*, and the negative demand shock causes no change in equilibrium GDP.

The complete sequence of events after a negative demand shock looks like this:

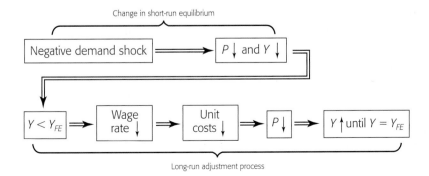

FIGURE 12
**The Long-Run
AS Curve**

This figure, like Figure 10, illustrates a positive demand shock, but focuses on the long-run effects. The initial equilibrium is at point E, with output at full employment (Y_{FE}) and price level P_1. After the positive demand shock and all the long-run adjustments to it, the economy ends up at point K with a higher price level (P_4), but the same full-employment output level (Y_{FE}). The long-run AS curve—a vertical line—shows all possible combinations of price level and output for the economy, skipping over the short-run changes. The vertical, long-run AS curve shows that in the long run, demand shocks can affect the price level but not output.

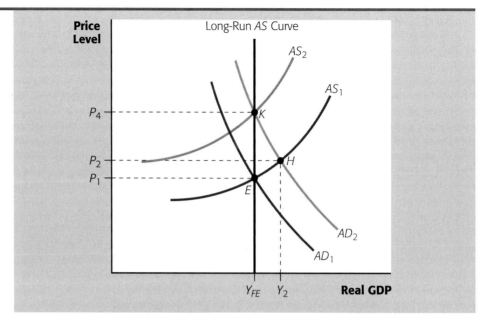

Pulling all of our observations together, we can summarize the economy's self-correcting mechanism as follows:

> *Whenever a demand shock pulls the economy away from full employment, the self-correcting mechanism will eventually bring it back. When output exceeds its full-employment level, wages will eventually rise, causing a rise in the price level and a drop in GDP until full employment is restored. When output is less than its full-employment level, wages will eventually fall, causing a drop in the price level and a rise in GDP until full employment is restored.*

The Long-Run Aggregate Supply Curve

The self-correcting mechanism provides an important link between the economy's long-run and short-run behaviors. It helps us understand why deviations from full employment don't last forever. Often, however, we are primarily interested in the long-run effects of a demand shock. In these cases, we may want to skip over the self-correcting mechanism and go straight to its end result. A new version of the *AS* curve helps us do this.

Now look at Figure 12, which illustrates the impact of a positive demand shock like the one in Figure 10. The economy begins at full employment at point *E*, then moves to point *H* in the short run (before the wage rate rises), and then goes to point *K* in the long run (after the rise in wages). If we skip over the short-run equilibrium, we find that the positive demand shock has moved the economy from *E* to *K*, which is vertically above *E*. That is, in the long run, the price level rises but output remains unchanged.

Now look at the vertical line in Figure 12, which shows another way of illustrating this long-run result. In the figure, the vertical line is the economy's **long-run aggregate supply curve**. It summarizes all possible output and price-level combinations at which the economy could end up in the long run. It is vertical because, in the long run, GDP will be the same—full-employment output—*regardless* of the position of

Long-run aggregate supply curve
A vertical line indicating all possible output and price-level combinations at which the economy could end up in the long run.

the *AD* curve. The price level, however, will depend on the position of the *AD* curve. In the long run, a positive demand shock shifts the *AD* curve rightward, moving the economy from *E* to *K*: a higher price level, but the same level of output. Similarly, in Figure 11, a negative demand shock—which shifts the *AD* curve leftward—moves the economy from *E* to *M* in the long run: a lower price level with the same level of output. (You may want to pencil in a vertical long-run aggregate supply curve in Figure 11 to help you see that it is the same curve as the one drawn in Figure 12.)

The long-run aggregate supply curve tells us something very important about the economy: In the long run, after the self-correcting mechanism has done its job, *the economy behaves as the classical model predicts.* In particular, the classical model tells us that demand shocks cannot change equilibrium GDP in the long run. Figure 12 brings us to the same conclusion: While demand shocks shift the *AD* curve, this only moves the economy up or down along a vertical long-run *AS* curve, leaving output unchanged.[2]

The long-run aggregate supply curve also illustrates another classical conclusion. In the classical model, an increase in government purchases causes *complete crowding out;* the rise in government purchases is precisely matched by a drop in consumption and investment spending, leaving total output and total spending unchanged. In Figure 12, the same result holds in the long run. How do we know? The figures tell us that, in the long run, the rise in government purchases causes no change in GDP. But if GDP is the same, and government purchases are higher, then the other components of GDP—consumption and investment—must decrease by the amount that government purchases increased.[3]

> *The self-correcting mechanism shows us that, in the long run, the economy will eventually behave as the classical model predicts.*

But notice the word *eventually* in the previous statement. It can take several years before the economy returns to full employment after a demand shock. This is why governments around the world are reluctant to rely on the self-correcting mechanism alone to keep the economy on track. Instead, they often use fiscal and monetary policies in an attempt to return the economy to full employment more quickly. We'll explore fiscal and monetary policies in more detail in the next two chapters.

Supply Shocks

In recent decades, supply shocks have been important sources of economic fluctuations. The most dramatic supply shocks have resulted from sudden changes in world oil prices. As you are about to see, supply shocks affect the economy differently from demand shocks.

Short-Run Effects of Supply Shocks. Figure 13 shows an example of a supply shock: an increase in world oil prices that shifts the aggregate supply curve upward, from AS_1 to AS_2. As rising oil prices increase unit costs, firms will begin raising prices and the price level will increase. The rise in the price level decreases equilibrium GDP

---

[2] Of course, full-employment output can increase from year to year, as you learned in the chapter on economic growth. When the economy is growing, the long-run *AS* curve will shift rightward. In that case, the level of output at which the economy will eventually settle increases from year to year.

[3] Net exports can be crowded out as well. In a later chapter, you'll learn that a higher interest rate causes a currency's value to increase relative to foreign currencies. This causes exports to fall and imports to rise.

FIGURE 13
The Effect of a Supply Shock

A negative supply shock would shift the AS curve upward from AS$_1$ to AS$_2$. In the short-run equilibrium at point R, the price level is higher and output is below Y$_{FE}$. Eventually, wages will fall, causing unit costs to fall, and the AS curve will shift back to its original position. A positive supply shock would have just the opposite effect.

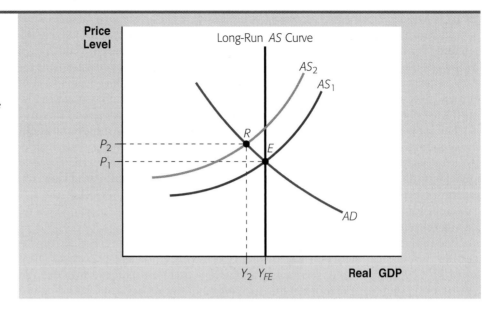

along the *AD* curve. In the short run, the price level will continue to rise, and the economy will continue to slide upward along its *AD* curve, until we reach the *AS$_2$* curve at point *R*. At this point, the price level is consistent with firms' unit costs and average markup (we are on the *AS* curve), and total output is equal to total spending (we are on the *AD* curve). As you can see, the short-run impact of higher oil prices is a rise in the price level and a fall in output. We call this a *negative* supply shock, because of the negative effect on output.

> *In the short run, a negative supply shock shifts the* AS *curve upward, decreasing output and increasing the price level.*

Notice the sharp contrast between the effects of negative supply shocks and negative demand shocks in the short run. After a negative demand shock (see, for example, Figure 11), both output and the price level fall. After a negative supply shock, output falls but the price level rises. Economists and journalists have coined the term **stagflation** to describe a *stag*nating economy experiencing in*flation*.

Stagflation The combination of falling output and rising prices.

> *A negative supply shock causes* stagflation *in the short run.*

Stagflation caused by increases in oil prices is not just a theoretical possibility. Three of our recessions in the last quarter century—in 1973–74, 1980, and 1990–91—followed increases in world oil prices. And each of these three recessions also saw jumps in the price level.

A *positive supply shock* would increase output by shifting the *AS* curve *downward*. (We call it positive, because of its effect on output.) As you can see if you draw such a shift on your own,

> *a positive supply shock shifts the* AS *curve downward, increasing output and decreasing the price level.*

Examples of positive supply shocks include unusually good weather, a drop in oil prices, and a technological change that lowers unit costs. In addition, a positive supply shock can sometimes be caused by government policy. A few chapters ago, we discussed how the government could use tax incentives and other policies to increase the rate of economic growth. These policies work by shifting the *AS* curve downward, thus increasing output while tending to decrease the price level.

Another type of policy tries to deal directly with negative supply shocks. For example, after the oil price shocks of the 1970s, the federal government built a strategic reserve of oil in huge underground storage areas. The idea was to release oil from the reserve if another oil price shock hit, in order to stabilize the price. The reserve has been used in this way, but not enough to make much difference in world oil prices.

Long-Run Effects of Supply Shocks. What about the effects of supply shocks in the long run? In some cases, we need not concern ourselves with this question, because some supply shocks are temporary. For example, except in unusual cases, periods of rising oil prices are followed by periods of falling oil prices. Similarly, supply shocks caused by unusually good or bad weather, or by natural disasters, are always short-lived. A temporary supply shock causes only a temporary shift in the *AS* curve; over the long run, the curve simply returns to its initial position, and the economy returns to full employment. In Figure 13, the *AS* curve would shift back from AS_2 to AS_1, the price level would fall, and the economy would move from point *R* back to point *E*.

In other cases, however, a supply shock can last for an extended period. One example was the rise in oil prices during the 1970s, which persisted for several years. In cases like this, is there a self-correcting mechanism that brings the economy back to full employment after a long-lasting supply shock? Indeed, there is, and it is the same mechanism that brings the economy back to full employment after a demand shock.

Look again at Figure 13. At point *R*, output is below full-employment output. In the long run, as workers compete for scarce jobs, the wage rate will decline. This will cause the *AS* curve to shift *downward*. The wage will continue to fall until the economy returns to full employment, that is, until we are back at point *E*.

> *In the long run, the economy self-corrects after a supply shock, just as it does after a demand shock. When output differs from its full-employment level, the wage rate changes and the* AS *curve shifts until full employment is restored.*

SOME IMPORTANT PROVISOS ABOUT THE *AS* CURVE

The upward-sloping aggregate supply curve we've presented in this chapter gives a realistic picture of how the economy behaves after a demand shock. In the short run, positive demand shocks that increase output also raise the price level. Negative demand shocks that decrease output generally put downward pressure on prices.

However, the story we have told about what happens as we move along the *AS* curve is somewhat incomplete.

First, we made the assumption that prices are completely flexible—that they can change freely over short periods of time. In fact, however, some prices take time to adjust, just as wages take time to adjust. Firms print catalogs containing prices that are good for, say, six months. The public utility commission in your state may set the prices of electricity, gas, water, and basic telephone service in advance for a year or more.

Second, we assumed that wages are completely *inflexible* in the short run. But in *some* industries, wages respond quickly. For example, in the construction industry, contractors hire workers for projects lasting a few months. When they can't find the workers they want, they immediately offer higher wages; they don't wait a year.

Third, there is more to the process of recovering from a shock than the adjustment of prices and wages. During a recession, many workers lose their jobs at the same time. It takes time for those workers to become reestablished in new jobs. As time passes, and job losers become job finders, the economy tends to recover. This process, in addition to the changes in wages and prices we've discussed, is part of the long-run adjustment process and helps to bring the economy back to full employment after a shock.

USING THE THEORY

The Story of Two Recessions and "Jobless" Expansions

The aggregate demand and aggregate supply curves are more than just abstract graphs; they're tools to help us understand important economic events. For example, they can help us understand why the economy suffered its two most recent recessions, and also how and why these recessions differed from one another.

The Recession of 1990–91

The story of the 1990–91 recession begins in mid-1990, when Iraq invaded Kuwait, a major oil producer. During this conflict, Kuwait's oil was taken off the world market, and so was Iraq's. The reduction in oil supplies resulted in a rapid and substantial increase in the price of oil, a key input to many industries. From the second to the fourth quarter of 1990, oil prices rose from $14 to $27 per barrel.

The left-hand panel of Figure 14 shows our *AS–AD* analysis of the shock. Initially, the economy was on both AD_{1990} and AS_{1990}. Equilibrium was at point *E*, and output was at the full-employment level. Then, the oil price shock shifted the *AS* curve upward, to AS_{1991}, while leaving the *AD* curve more or less unchanged. As the short-run equilibrium moved to point *R*, real GDP fell and the price level *rose*. Now look at the left side of the next figure (Figure 15). The upper panel shows the behavior of GDP during the period leading up to, and during, the recession. As you can see, consistent with our *AS–AD* analysis, real GDP fell—from a high of $7.13 trillion in the third quarter of 1990 to a low of $7.04 trillion in the first quarter of 1991 (a decrease of 1.3 percent). The lower panel shows the behavior of the Consumer Price Index (CPI). While the CPI was rising modestly before the recession began, it rose more rapidly during the second half of 1990, as the recession took hold. Once again, this is consistent with what our *AS–AD* analysis predicts for a negative supply shock, such as the rise in oil prices in 1990.

What about the recovery that followed this recession? Once you know what the Fed did, you have all the tools to answer this question yourself. Problem 8 at the end of this chapter takes you through the process.

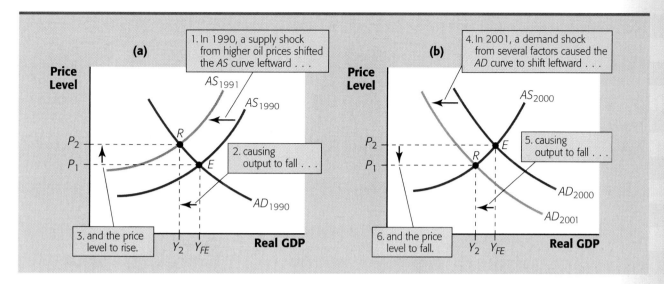

1. In 1990, a supply shock from higher oil prices shifted the *AS* curve leftward . . .

2. causing output to fall . . .

3. and the price level to rise.

4. In 2001, a demand shock from several factors caused the *AD* curve to shift leftward . . .

5. causing output to fall . . .

6. and the price level to fall.

FIGURE 14
An *AD* and *AS* Analysis of Two Recessions

The Recession of 2001

The story of the 2001 recession was quite different. This time, there was no spike in oil prices and no other significant supply shock to plague the economy. Rather, there was a demand shock, and a Federal Reserve policy during the year before the recession that might have made it a bit worse.

In earlier chapters, you learned that the major cause of the recession was a decrease in investment spending. To review: In the years leading up to 2001, businesses rushed to acquire and develop new equipment needed to exploit new technologies, such as the Internet and wireless communication. By 2001, many firms had sufficiently "caught up" and the flow of investment spending—while still positive and high—began to decrease relative to previous years. This decrease in investment spending was a demand shock to the economy: In 2001, the *AD* curve shifted leftward.

Now we can introduce another force that may have contributed to the recession of 2001: the policy of the Fed. During the late 1990s, the Fed had become concerned that the investment boom and consumer optimism were shifting the *AD* curve rightward too rapidly, creating a danger that we would overshoot potential GDP and set off higher inflation. The Fed responded by tightening up on the money supply and raising the interest rate. From mid-1999 to mid-2000, the Fed raised the federal funds rate six times—a total of almost two full percentage points in less than a year. The Fed then held the rate at a relatively high 6.50 percent for another six months until early 2001. In retrospect, the Fed may have continued raising and holding the rate high a bit too long, even after the *AD* curve stopped moving rightward. And the effects of this policy may have continued into early 2001, exacerbating the decrease in investment that was occurring for other reasons. In this way, the rate hikes themselves may have contributed to a further leftward shift of the *AD* curve.

The right-hand panel of Figure 14 shows our AS–AD analysis of this period. Initially, the economy was on both AD2000 and AS2000, with equilibrium at point E and output roughly at the full employment level. Then, the decrease in investment spending—helped along by the Fed—shifted the AD curve leftward, to AD2001, while leaving the AS curve more or less unchanged. As the short-run equilibrium moved to point R, real GDP fell. This is mirrored in Figure 15, where the upper

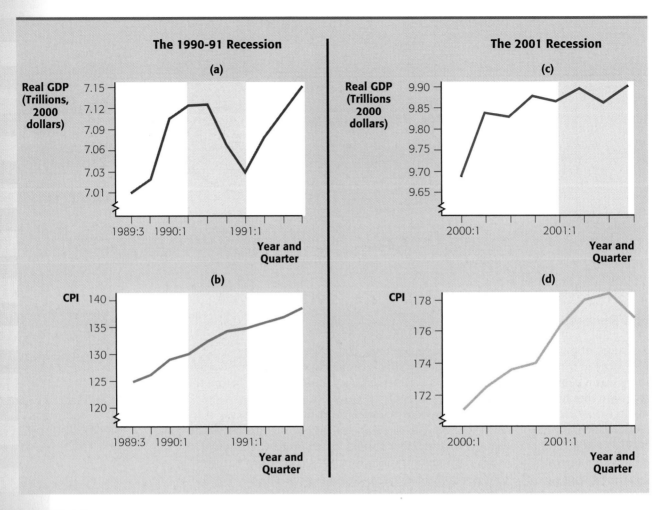

FIGURE 15
GDP and the Price Level
in Two Recessions

right-hand panel shows the behavior of GDP during the period leading up to, and during, the 2001 recession. As you can see, consistent with our AS–AD analysis, real GDP did fall in the first quarter of 2001, although it sputtered upward in the second quarter before falling again in the third.

But what about the price level? Here, we need to recognize that there is a slight difference between what our *AS–AD* analysis predicts and what actually happened. In the right panel of Figure 14, the price level falls. And indeed, in the lower right panel of Figure 15, you can see that the price level eventually fell—in the fourth quarter of 2001. But for much of the recession, instead of the price level falling we can see that it was rising, but more slowly as 2001 continued. In the next chapter, you will learn that inflation often has some momentum: When it's been rising at a certain rate for some time, then—left alone—it will continue to rise at that rate. The leftward shift in the *AD* curve meant that inflation was *not* left alone in early 2001, so while prices continued to rise, they rose more slowly due to the *AD* shift. And, as you can see, the *AD* shift's downward pressure on prices eventually overcame the inflationary momentum, causing a drop in the price level toward the end of 2001. This is just what we'd expect from our *AS–AD* analysis.

Months Before and After the Trough

FIGURE 16
The Average Expansion Versus Two Recent Jobless Expansions

Sources: "A Closer Look at Jobless Recoveries," *Economic Review,* Second Quarter 2003, Federal Reserve Bank of Kansas City, p. 48.

Jobless Expansions

After a recession, the economy enters the expansion phase of the business cycle. Typically, because real GDP is starting from such a low level, it grows rapidly in the first year or so of the expansion, as the economy catches back up to potential output. Employment usually grows rapidly during this period as well.

But in our two most recent recessions, the economy experienced abnormal, prolonged periods during which employment did not grow at all. These are *jobless expansions* (often called *jobless recoveries*).

Figure 16 illustrates the behavior of employment during our two most recent recessions, and the average of the six previous recessions. There is a lot going on in the figure, so let's go through it carefully.[4]

The horizontal axis measures the months before and after the *bottom* (or **trough**) of any given recession. For example, the month marked −2 is two months *before* the trough, when we were still in the *contraction* phase of the cycle. The month marked +6 is six months *after* the trough—six months into the expansion phase.

The vertical axis shows an employment index: employment *divided by* employment at the trough. For each recession, the employment index during any month will be higher or lower than 1.0, depending on whether employment is higher than or lower than it was at the trough. For example, an index number of 1.035 in some month would tell us that employment was 3.5 percent higher that month than during the trough of the recession, while an index number of .99 would tell us that employment was 1 percent lower.

Now, look at the blue line, which shows the average of the employment indices for the six business cycles *before* 1990–91. The blue line shows that employment falls during the contraction phase of the average cycle (the months up to 0), and

Trough The bottom point of a recession, when a contraction ends and an expansion begins.

[4] Analysis for this section is based on Stacey L. Schreft and Aarti Singh, "A Closer Look at Jobless Recoveries," *Economic Review,* Federal Reserve Bank of Kansas City, Second Quarter, 2003; Mark Schweitzer, "Another Jobless Recovery," *Economic Commentary,* Federal Reserve Bank of Cleveland, March 1, 2003; and "The NBER's Business Cycle Dating Procedure," July 17, 2003 (*http://www.nber.org/cycles/recessions.html*). Additional data on employment, hours, and real GDP from several tables at the Bureau of Economic Analysis (*www.bea.gov*) and the Bureau of Labor Statistics (*www.bls.gov*).

rises rapidly during the first year of the expansion phase (from months 0 to +12). But the red and pink lines show what happened in the first year of our two most recent expansions—during 1992 and 2002. In both cases, employment drifted slightly *downward,* telling us that the total number of jobs *decreased* during the year. These were jobless expansions. Why?

Explaining Jobless Expansions. Since the story is similar for both of the jobless expansions, we'll focus on the most recent case: the expansion after the recession of 2001. We can start by going back to the equation breaking down *potential* output into its different components, as we did several chapters ago ("Economic Growth and Rising Living Standards"):

$$\text{Total output} = \text{productivity} \times \text{average hours} \times \text{LFPR} \times \text{population}$$

where LFPR stands for the labor force participation rate—the fraction of the population that is either working or seeking work. Note that multiplying the last two terms (LFPR × population) gives us the total labor force, so we can write:

$$\text{Total output} = \text{productivity} \times \text{average hours} \times \text{labor force}$$

It makes sense to include the entire labor force in our calculations when studying economic growth, since—in the long run—the economy tends toward a fully employed labor force. But now we're interested in *deviations* in the economy *away* from full employment in the short run. Accordingly, we need to modify our equation so it explains our *actual* output, rather than our full employment output. The modification is very simple: we'll use *actual* employment (just those actually working) rather than the entire labor force in our equation:

$$\text{Real GDP} = \text{productivity} \times \text{average hours} \times \text{employment}$$

Next, we'll convert this equation into percentage changes (using the same method as in the earlier economic growth chapter):

$$\%\Delta \text{ Real GDP} \approx \%\Delta \text{ productivity} + \%\Delta \text{ average hours} + \%\Delta \text{ employment}$$

Finally, rearranging, we end up with:

$$\%\Delta \text{ employment} \approx \%\Delta \text{ real GDP} - \%\Delta \text{ productivity} - \%\Delta \text{ average hours}$$

$$(-0.5\%) \qquad (2.3\%) \qquad (3.5\%) \qquad (-0.7\%)$$

We'll get to the numbers in parenthesis in a moment. But notice what this equation tells us: in periods with no significant changes in average hours, the percentage change in total employment is equal to the rate of output growth minus the rate of productivity growth. If output grows faster than productivity, then %Δ employment will be positive: the number of jobs increases. If output grows slower than productivity, then %Δ employment will be negative: the total number of jobs decreases.

Now to the numbers in parenthesis under the last equation: these show the actual percentage changes in the first year of the expansion after the 2001 recession.[5] And they show us why that expansion was jobless: output grew much slower than productivity. Average hours actually *decreased* during the year, cushioning the drop in employment, but not preventing it. In the end, we have employment falling by $2.3\% - 3.5\% - (-0.7\%) = -0.5\%$.

But *why* didn't growth in real GDP keep up with productivity growth?

[5] Sources: Quarterly nonfarm business payroll employment, from EconStats (www.econstats.com/BLS); real GDP from Bureau of Economic Analysis (www.bea.gov); nonfarm business productivity and nonfarm business average hours from *Economic Report of the President,* 2005, Table B-49.

First, because growth in real GDP was unusually low. In the first year of an expansion, output typically grows about 6 percent, but during 2002 it grew by 2.3 percent—less than half its usual rate. Business investment spending gets most of the blame: It usually rises during the first year of an expansion, but in 2002 business investment *decreased*. The reasons for this may include continuing global uncertainty after September 11, 2001, which was followed by the war in Afghanistan and the buildup to war in Iraq. It may also be due to the high levels of investment in information technology and other capital equipment during the 1990s: Once firms caught up with the amount of capital they desired, they had no reason to maintain or return to those previously high rates of annual investment spending.

The second reason for the jobless recovery is productivity, which grew at about the *same* rate as in the average expansion, in spite of the low growth in output. Ordinarily, increases in the capital stock are a major source of productivity growth, but since business investment in new capital *decreased* during 2002, we might expect that productivity growth would slow down that year. But another factor was maintaining high productivity growth: firms' behavior in the labor market. Throughout the first year of the expansion, firms were reluctant to hire full-time, permanent workers, perhaps because the international instability discussed above created uncertainty about the strength and duration of the expansion. Instead, businesses expanded output by hiring part-time and temporary workers.

Why would this boost productivity? Because it enabled firms to adjust their workforce more easily to fluctuations in production. When firms hire regular, full-time employees, they tend to keep them employed at full-time hours even when production dips. But with temporary or part-time workers, firms can adjust employment or hours as production fluctuates. As a result, any given level of output can be produced, on average, with fewer total hours of employed labor. This increases productivity. Firms behaved similarly during the 1990s: Productivity growth exceeded output growth, largely because in 1992—as in 2002—firms relied more heavily on temporary and part-time workers than during a typical expansion.

It might seem odd to think of productivity growth as something harmful. After all, productivity growth is a good thing, the major reason that living standards grow . . . *in the long run.* But in the *short run,* as you've seen, if productivity grows faster than output, it threatens jobs. Keep in mind, though, that the phrase "jobless expansion" refers to just *part* of the expansion phase. Eventually, employment catches up, even to the higher levels of output made possible by productivity growth.

However, the problem can persist for some time. In the early 1990s, even after the expansion finally began to create new jobs after about a year, job creation was so slow that we remained significantly below full employment for another few years, into the mid-1990s. After the 2001 recession, when job growth finally resumed, employment grew so slowly that it did not reach its pre-recession level until late 2003 (according to the BLS household survey) or early 2005 (according to a different BLS survey of business employment).

It's too early to say if jobless expansions will become the norm in the first year of so after future recessions. Expansions are more likely to be jobless if the early phases of output growth are low—due to uncertainty, abnormally high investment in prior periods, or any other cause. And they are more likely if firms remain wary of hiring regular, full-time workers until the expansion is well under way. But jobless expansions are painful. They leave hundreds of thousands of additional workers without jobs even as the economy expands, and also raise the average *duration* of unemployment. Their mere possibility raises the stakes for the Fed and other government policy makers in trying to prevent future recessions.

Summary

The model of aggregate supply and demand explains how the price level and output are determined in the short run—a period of a year or so following a change in the economy—and how the economy adjusts over longer time periods as well.

The aggregate demand (AD) curve shows how changes in the price level affect equilibrium real GDP. A change in the price level shifts the money demand curve and alters the interest rate in the money market. The change in the interest rate, in turn, affects interest-sensitive forms of spending, shifts the aggregate expenditure curve, triggers the multiplier process, and leads to a new level of equilibrium real GDP. A lower price level means a higher equilibrium real GDP, and a higher price level means lower GDP. The downward-sloping AD curve is drawn for given values of government purchases, net taxes, autonomous consumption spending, and the money supply. Changes in any of those variables will cause the AD curve to shift.

The aggregate supply (AS) curve summarizes the way changes in output affect the price level. To draw the AS curve, we assume that firms set the price of individual products as a markup over their costs per unit, and that the economy's average markup is determined by competitive conditions. We also assume that the nominal wage rate is fixed in the short run. As we move upward along the AS curve, a rise in real GDP, by raising unit costs, causes the price level to increase.

When anything other than a change in real GDP causes the price level to change, the entire AS curve shifts.

AD and AS together determine real GDP and the price level. The economy must be on the AD curve, or real GDP would not be at its equilibrium level. It must be on the AS curve or firms would not be charging prices dictated by their unit costs and markups. Both conditions are satisfied at the intersection of the two curves.

The AD—AS equilibrium can be disturbed by a demand shock. An increase in government purchases, for example, shifts the AD curve rightward. As a result, the price level rises, and so does real GDP. In the long run, if GDP is above potential, wages will rise. This causes unit costs to rise and shifts the AS curve upward. Eventually, GDP will return to potential and the only long-run result of the demand shock is a higher price level. This implies that the economy's long-run aggregate supply curve is vertical at potential output.

The short-run AD—AS equilibrium can also be disturbed by a supply shock, such as an increase in world oil prices. With unit costs higher at each level of output, the AS curve shifts upward, decreasing real GDP and increasing the price level. Eventually, the shock will be self-correcting: With output below potential, the wage rate will fall, unit costs will decrease, and the AS curve will shift back downward until full employment is restored.

Key Terms

Aggregate demand (AD) curve
Aggregate supply (AS) curve
Demand shock

Long-run aggregate supply curve
Self-correcting mechanism
Short-run macroeconomic equilibrium

Stagflation
Supply shock
Trough

Review Questions   *Answers to even-numbered Questions and Problems can be found on the text Web site at http://hall-lieb.swlearning.com.*

1. What causal relationship does the aggregate demand curve describe? Why does the AD curve slope downward? What does each point on the AD curve represent?

2. "Only fiscal policy can shift the aggregate demand curve." True or false? Explain.

3. List three reasons why a change in output affects unit costs and subsequently the price level.

4. What causal relationship does the aggregate supply curve describe? Why does the AS curve slope upward?

5. Why does equilibrium occur only where the AD and AS curves intersect?

6. What is the economy's *self-correcting mechanism,* and how does it work?

7. What is the long-run aggregate supply curve? Why is it vertical?

8. Does the vertical shape of the long-run aggregate supply curve support the predictions of the classical model with regard to the effectiveness of fiscal policy and crowding out? Explain.

9. How does an economy recover from a permanent negative supply shock?

10. Explain why real GDP growth did not keep up with productivity in 2002.

Problems and Exercises

1. Redraw Figure 2, showing how a decrease in the price level will lead to an increase in equilibrium real GDP.

2. With a three-panel diagram—one panel showing the money market, one showing the aggregate expenditure diagram, and one showing the *AD* curve—show how a *decrease* in the money supply shifts the *AD* curve leftward.

3. Using a diagram showing the aggregate expenditure line, the money market, and the *AD* curve, describe how an increase in taxes affects the interest rate, real aggregate expenditure, and the aggregate demand curve. (Assume that the price level does not change.) What other changes would result in these same effects?

4. Suppose firms become pessimistic about the future and consequently investment spending falls. With an *AD* and *AS* graph, describe the short-run effects on real GDP and the price level. If the price level were constant, how would your answer change?

5. With an *AD* and *AS* diagram, explain the short-run effect of a decrease in the money supply on real GDP and the price level. What is the effect in the long run? Assume the economy begins at full employment.

6. Use an *AD* and *AS* graph to explain the short-run and long-run effects on real GDP and the price level of an increase in autonomous consumption spending. Assume the economy begins at full employment.

7. A new government policy successfully lowers firms' unit costs. What are the short-run and the long-run effects of such a policy? (Assume that full-employment output does not change.)

8. Make two copies of Figure 14(a) on a sheet of paper. Add curves to illustrate your answer to (a) on one copy and (b) on the other:
   a. What *would* have happened in the years after 1991 if the Fed had done nothing and the economy had relied solely on the self-correcting mechanism to return to full employment?
   b. What *did* happen as a result of the Fed bringing down the interest rate to end the recession?

   c. Is there a difference in the behavior of the price level during the recovery in these two cases? Explain.

9. Make two copies of Figure 14(b) on a sheet of paper. Add curves to illustrate the impacts of Fed policy for (a) on one copy and (b) on the other:
   a. What *would* have happened in the years following 2001 if the Fed had done nothing and the economy had relied solely on the self-correcting mechanism to return to full employment?
   b. What *did* happen as a result of the Fed's actual policy in 2001 (successive cuts in the interest rate throughout the year)?
   c. Is there a difference in the behavior of the price level during the recovery in these two cases? Explain.

10. Suppose that aggressive antitrust action by the U.S. Justice Department were to successfully increase the degree of competition in many U.S. industries. Use *AS* and *AD* curves to illustrate the short-run impact on the economy if, at the same time,
    a. The Fed does nothing.
    b. The Fed pursues a policy that successfully achieves the highest possible level of GDP with no rise in the price level.

11. (a) Use an *AD* and *AS* graph to show the effects of a decrease in net exports, assuming that the Fed intervenes to keep the economy at full employment. Assume the economy begins at full employment. (b) What would be the short-run and long-run effects if the Fed does not intervene?

12. a. Graphically show the effects of a temporary decrease in nonlabor input prices.
    b. How will your results change if this decrease lasts for an extended period?
    c. How would your results differ if the Fed intervened to keep the economy at full employment?

13. What will happen if real GDP grows by 4 percent while productivity grows by 4.6 percent?

Challenge Questions

1. Suppose that wages are slow to adjust downward but rapidly adjust upward. What would the *AS* curve look like? How would this affect the economy's adjustment to demand shocks (compared to the analysis given in the chapter)?

2. During the 1990s, because of technological change, the *AS* curve was shifting downward, but—except for a few months—the price level did not fall. Why not? (*Hint:* What was the Fed doing?)

ECONOMIC Applications

These exercises require access to Hall/Lieberman Xtra! If Xtra! did not come with your book, visit http://hallxtra.swlearning.com to purchase.

1. Use your Xtra! password at the Hall and Lieberman Web site (http://hallxtra.swlearning.com), select this chapter, and under Economic Applications, click on EconDebate. Choose *Monetary Policy*, and scroll down to find the debate, "Will the European Monetary Union Succeed?" Read the debate, and use the information to answer the following questions.

   a. This debate emphasizes the relationship between monetary and fiscal policy. Use the AD–AS framework to explain what would happen to the output and inflation rate of a country at full employment, if the European Central Bank engages in expansionary monetary policy and reduces interest rates.

   b. Use the AD–AS framework to explain what would happen to the output and inflation rate of a country

   in recession, if another (larger) country increases government borrowing to finance fiscal expenditures, and in the process raises the interest rates in all participating countries.

2. Use your Xtra! password at the Hall and Lieberman Web site (http://hallxtra.swlearning.com), select this chapter, and under Economic Applications, click on EconData. Choose *Monetary Policy*, and scroll down to find *Civilian Unemployment Rate*. Read the definition, then click on Diagrams/Data. The CPI Inflation Rate and the Unemployment Rate diagram illustrates the pattern of inflation and unemployment during the business cycle. Confirm that during recessions inflation rates fall while unemployment rates rise.

Inflation and Monetary Policy

CHAPTER OUTLINE

The Objectives of Monetary Policy
Low, Stable Inflation
Full Employment

The Fed's Performance

Federal Reserve Policy: Theory and Practice
Responding to Changes in Money Demand
Responding to Other Demand Shocks
Responding to Supply Shocks

Expectations and Ongoing Inflation
How Ongoing Inflation Arises
Ongoing Inflation and the Phillips Curve
Why the Fed Allows Ongoing Inflation

Using the Theory: Challenges for Monetary Policy
Information Problems
The Natural Rate of Unemployment
Rules Versus Discretion and the "Taylor Rule"
Deflation

In the late 1970s, the annual inflation rate in the United States reached 13 percent. At the time, polls showed that the public considered inflation the most serious economic problem facing the country. In the 13 years after 1991, however, the annual inflation rate never exceeded 3.5 percent in any year, and the problem receded as a matter of public concern. Bringing the inflation rate down, and keeping it low, was one of the solid victories of national economic policy.

But in late 2002 and early 2003, a new worry arose: that the inflation rate might be *too* low and the nation was in danger of experiencing *deflation*—an ongoing *decrease* in the price level.

Why was the inflation rate so high in the 1970s? How did the Fed bring the rate down? Why did the possibility of deflation keep some Fed officials awake at night? And finally, how should the Fed respond to future economic disturbances?

In this chapter, we'll be addressing these and other questions as we take a closer look at the Fed's conduct of monetary policy. Our earlier discussions of monetary policy were somewhat limited, because we lacked the tools—aggregate demand and aggregate supply—to explain changes in the price level. In this chapter, we'll explore monetary policy more fully, making extensive use of the *AD* and *AS* curves.

THE OBJECTIVES OF MONETARY POLICY

The Fed's objectives have changed over the years. When the Fed was first established in 1913, its chief responsibility was to ensure the stability of the banking system. By acting as a *lender of last resort*—injecting reserves into the banking system in times of crisis—the Fed was supposed to alleviate financial panics.

By the 1950s, the stability of the banking system was no longer a major concern, largely because the United States had not had a banking panic in decades. (Deposit insurance programs had effectively eliminated panics.) Accordingly, the Fed's objective in the 1950s and 1960s changed to keeping the interest rate low and stable. In the 1970s, the Fed's objectives shifted once again. As stated in the Federal Reserve Banking Act of 1978, which is still in force, the Fed is now responsible for achieving a low, stable rate of inflation, and full employment of the labor force. Let's consider each of these goals in turn.

Low, Stable Inflation

Why is a low rate of inflation important? Several chapters ago, we reviewed the social costs of inflation. When the inflation rate is high, society uses up resources coping with it—resources that could have been used to produce goods and services. Among these resources are the labor needed to update prices at stores and factories, as well as the additional time spent by households and businesses to manage their wealth and protect it from a loss of purchasing power.

In addition to keeping the inflation rate low, the Fed tries to keep it *stable* from year to year. For example, the Fed would prefer a steady yearly inflation rate of 3 percent to an inflation rate of 5 percent half the time, and 1 percent the other half, even though the average inflation rate would be 3 percent in both cases. The reason is that unstable inflation is difficult to predict accurately; it will often turn out higher or lower than people expected. As you learned several chapters ago, an inflation rate higher than expected redistributes real income from lenders to borrowers, while an inflation rate lower than expected has the opposite effect. Thus, unstable inflation adds to the risk of lending and borrowing, and interferes with long-run financial planning.

The Fed, as a public agency, chooses its policies with the costs of inflation in mind. And the Fed has another concern: Inflation is very unpopular with the public. Surveys show that most people associate high rates of inflation with a general breakdown of government and the economy.[1] A Fed chairman who delivers low rates of inflation is seen as popular and competent, while one who tolerates high inflation goes down in history as a failure.

Full Employment

"Full employment" means that unemployment is at normal levels. But what, exactly, is a *normal* amount of employment?

Recall that there are different types of unemployment. Some of the unemployed in any given month will find jobs after only a short time of searching. This *frictional* unemployment is part of the normal workings of the labor market and is not a

---

[1] Robert J. Shiller, "Public Resistance to Inflation: A Puzzle," *Brookings Papers on Economic Activity*, 1997.

serious social problem. Other job seekers will spend many months or years out of work because they lack the skills that employers require, or because they lack information about available jobs. While this *structural* unemployment is a serious social problem, it is best solved with *micro*economic policies, such as job-training programs or improved information flows.

Cyclical unemployment, by contrast, is a *macro*economic problem. It occurs during a recession, in which millions of workers lose their jobs and remain unemployed as they seek new ones. This is why macroeconomists use the term "full employment" to mean *the absence of cyclical employment*. When the economy achieves full employment according to this definition, macroeconomic policy has done all that it can do.

The Fed is concerned about cyclical unemployment for two reasons. First is its *opportunity cost*: the output that the unemployed could have produced if they were working. Part of this opportunity cost is paid by the unemployed themselves, in the form of lost earnings, and part is paid by people who remain employed but pay higher taxes to provide unemployment benefits to job losers. By maintaining full employment, the Fed can help society avoid this cost.

Second, cyclical unemployment represents a social failure. In a recession, people who have the right skills and who could be working actually *lose* their jobs. Excess unemployment lingers for several years after a recession strikes. Thus, cyclical unemployment caused by a recession is a partial breakdown of the system. The economy is not doing what it should do: provide a job for anyone who wants to work and who has the needed skills.

But why should the Fed try to eliminate only *cyclical* unemployment? Why not go further and push output above its full-employment level? After all, at higher levels of output, business firms would be more willing to hire *any* available workers. The frictionally unemployed would find jobs more easily, and some of the structurally unemployed would be hired as well. If unemployment is a bad thing, shouldn't the Fed aim for the lowest possible unemployment rate?

The answer is no. If the unemployment rate falls too low, GDP rises beyond its potential, full-employment level. As you learned in the last chapter, this causes the economy's self-correcting mechanism to kick in: The *AS* curve shifts upward, increasing the price level. Thus, unemployment that is too low compromises the Fed's other chief goal by creating inflation. And, as you will see later in the chapter, the Fed cannot keep the economy operating above full employment for more than a short time anyway. In the long run, its attempts to push the economy too hard would only create more inflation and would not succeed in lowering unemployment.

The unemployment rate at which GDP is at its full-employment level—that is, with no cyclical unemployment—is sometimes called the **natural rate of unemployment.**

Natural rate of unemployment
The unemployment rate when there is no cyclical unemployment.

> *When the unemployment rate is below the natural rate, GDP is greater than potential output. The economy's self-correcting mechanism will then create inflation. When the unemployment rate is above the natural rate, GDP is below potential output. The self-correcting mechanism will then put downward pressure on the price level.*

The word *natural* must be interpreted with care. The natural unemployment rate is not etched in stone, nor is it the outcome of purely natural forces that can't be influenced by public policy. But it is determined by rather slow-moving forces in the economy: how frequently workers move from job to job, how efficiently the unemployed can search for jobs and firms can search for new workers, and how well the skills of the unemployed match the skills needed by employers.

Still, the natural rate can change when any of these underlying conditions change. And it can also be influenced by government policies that provide incentives or disincentives for workers to find jobs quickly, or for employers to hire them. Indeed, economists generally believe that over the past decade, the natural rate has decreased in the United States—from 6 or 6.5 percent in the mid-1980s to perhaps as low as 4.5 percent today. Meanwhile, in many European countries, the natural rate of unemployment has increased over the last decade. In the late 1990s, the natural rate may have reached 10 percent in France and close to 20 percent in Spain. The causes of these changes in the natural rate, as well as the *extent* of the changes, are hotly debated by economists. But there is general agreement about the direction: down in the United States, up in continental Europe.

Why use the term *natural* for such a changeable feature of the economy? The term makes sense only from the perspective of *macroeconomic* policy. Simply put, there isn't much that macroeconomic policy can do about the natural rate. Stimulating the economy with fiscal or monetary policy may bring the *actual* unemployment rate down for a time, but it will not change the natural rate itself. And pushing unemployment below the natural rate would cause inflation. Thus, the natural rate of unemployment can be seen as a kind of goalpost for the Fed. The location of the goalpost may change over the years, but during any given year, it tells us where the Fed is aiming.

THE FED'S PERFORMANCE

How well has the Fed achieved its goals? Panel (a) of Figure 1 shows the annual inflation rate since 1950, as measured by the Consumer Price Index. You can see that monetary policy permitted extended periods of high inflation in the 1970s and early 1980s. You can also see, as noted at the beginning of the chapter, that the Fed has achieved great success in controlling inflation since then. Indeed, in the 20 years leading up to 2004, the annual inflation rate exceeded 4.6 percent only once—in 1990, during the supply shock caused by higher oil prices. And in recent years, inflation at 2.5 to 3.0 percent has become the norm.

Panel (b) shows the quarterly rate of unemployment since 1950. Over the last 20 years—a period during which the Fed has succeeded in keeping inflation in check—the Fed's performance on unemployment has been somewhat mixed. From 1984 through the end of 2004, the unemployment rate was 7 percent or greater—significantly above its natural rate—more than one-fourth of the time. But notice the remarkable improvement from mid-1992 and after, as the Fed slowly inched the unemployment rate down to 4 percent *without* heating up inflation. The Fed even managed to keep the unemployment rate hovering near 4 percent for more than two years until it began to rise during the recession of 2001.

As you can see, the Fed has mostly had a good—and improving—record in recent years. The inflation rate has been kept low and relatively stable, and—except for our most recent recession—unemployment has been near and even below most estimates of the natural rate. How has the Fed done it? Are there any general conclusions we can reach about how a central bank should operate to achieve the twin goals of full employment and a stable, low inflation rate? Indeed there are, as you'll see in the next section.

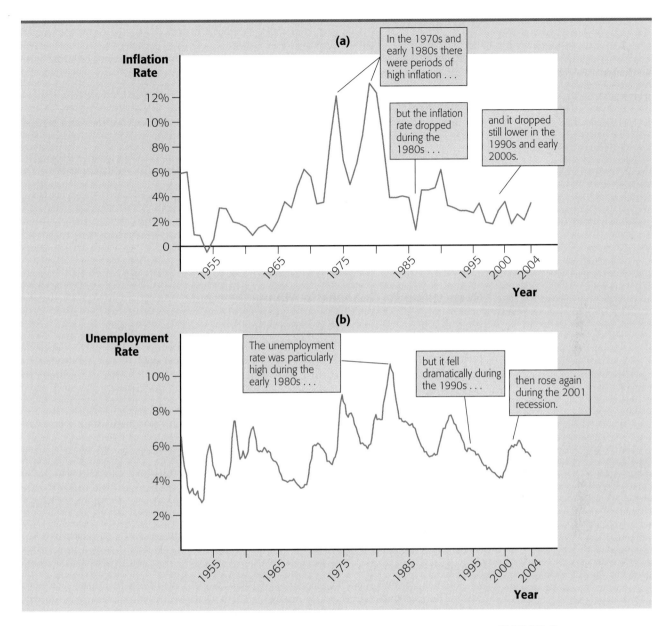

FIGURE 1
The Fed's Performance
Since 1950

FEDERAL RESERVE POLICY: THEORY AND PRACTICE

So far in this text, we've assumed that the Fed's response to demand shocks or supply shocks is a **passive monetary policy.** That is, in the face of these shocks, the Fed conducts neither open market purchases nor open market sales of bonds, and just keeps the money supply constant. While this was useful for understanding how different events can affect the economy, it is not a realistic description of the Fed's actions. In recent years, the Fed has tried to maintain a stable level of real GDP, rather than a stable money supply. Ideally, the Fed would like to keep the economy operating as close to its potential output as possible. If output falls

Passive monetary policy When the Fed keeps the money supply constant regardless of shocks to the economy.

below potential, there is painful and wasteful unemployment; if output rises above potential, there is a danger of inflation.

In order to keep real GDP as close as possible to its potential, the Fed must pursue an **active monetary policy,** in which it responds to events in the economy by *changing* the money supply. As you'll see, the required change in the money supply depends on what type of event the Fed is responding to.

In some cases, the proper response is easy to determine, because the same action that maintains full employment also helps maintain low inflation. But in other cases, the Fed must trade off one goal for another: Responses that maintain full employment will worsen inflation, and responses that alleviate inflation will create more unemployment.

We'll make a temporary simplifying assumption in this section: that the Fed's goal for the inflation rate is *zero.* In reality, the Fed's goal is *low,* but not zero, inflation. Later, we'll discuss why the Fed prefers a low inflation rate to a zero rate, and how this modifies our analysis.

Active monetary policy When the Fed changes the money supply in response to economic shocks.

Responding to Changes in Money Demand

Potential disturbances to the economy sometimes arise from a shift in the money demand curve. For example, two chapters ago, you learned about the effects of expectations on money demand. If people expect the interest rate to rise (the price of bonds to fall) in the near future, they will want to hold less wealth in the form of bonds and more in money, so the money demand curve will shift rightward. Larger and longer-lasting shifts in the money demand curve may occur for reasons that are not well understood, although leading suspects are the development of new types of financial assets and new methods of making payments.

How should the Fed respond to shifts in the money demand curve? Figure 2 shows the effect of a rightward shift of the money demand curve. Look first at panel (a). Initially, the money market is in equilibrium at point E, with the interest rate equal to r_1. When the money demand curve shifts rightward, to M_2^d, the equilibrium moves to point F, with the higher interest rate r_2. With a passive monetary policy—leaving the money supply unchanged—the rise in the interest rate would cause interest-sensitive spending to fall. This, in turn, would decrease equilibrium GDP at any given price level.

Panel (b) shows another way to view the effect of the change in money demand: The AD curve shifts leftward, from AD_1 to AD_2—a demand shock to the economy. With a passive monetary policy, the economy would slide down the AS curve from point E to point F, causing a recession. Since the economy began at full-employment output (Y_{FE}), the passive monetary policy would cause unemployment to rise above the natural rate and the price level would decrease.

If the Fed wants to maintain full employment with zero inflation (an unchanged price level) then a passive monetary policy is clearly the wrong response. Is there a better policy?

Indeed there is: an *active* monetary policy. By increasing the money stock—shifting the money supply curve rightward (indicated by the dashed arrow in panel (a))—the Fed can move the money market to a new equilibrium (directly to the right of point E), *preventing any rise in the interest rate.* If the Fed acts quickly enough, there will be no decrease in interest-sensitive spending and no shift in the AD curve.

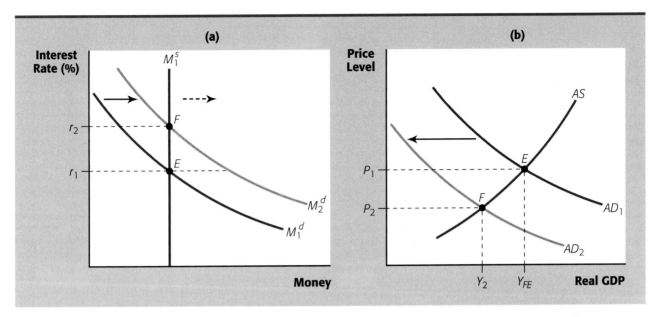

FIGURE 2
Responding to Shifts in Money Demand

Beginning at point E *in panel (a), an increase in money demand drives the interest rate up to* r_2 *(point* F*). Under a passive monetary policy, interest-sensitive spending would decrease, and the aggregate demand curve would shift leftward in panel (b). GDP falls from* Y_{FE} *to* Y_2. *The economy would suffer a recession. To maintain full employment, the Fed could increase the money supply (indicated by the dashed arrow), preventing any change in the interest rate and any shift in* AD.

Interest rate target The interest rate the Federal Reserve aims to achieve by adjusting the money supply.

In panel (b), the economy remains at point *E*, and the Fed maintains full employment with zero inflation.[2]

As you can see, shifts in the money demand curve present the Fed with a no-lose situation: By adjusting the money supply to prevent changes in the interest rate, the Fed can achieve both price stability and full employment. During most periods, when the economy is not affected by any shocks other than money demand shifts, the constant interest rate policy will keep the economy on an even keel. This is why, in its day-to-day operations, the Fed sets and maintains an **interest rate target** and then adjusts the money supply to achieve that target.

> *To deal with money demand shocks, the Fed sets an interest rate target and changes the money supply as needed to maintain the target. In this way, the Fed can achieve its goals of price stability and full employment simultaneously.*

How the Fed Keeps the Interest Rate on Target. A quick review of the day-to-day mechanics of Fed policy making shows how it sets and maintains its interest rate target in practice. Fed officials meet each morning to determine that day's monetary policy, based on information gathered the previous afternoon and earlier that morning. A key piece of information is what actually happened to the interest rate since the morning before. A rise in the interest rate means that the money demand curve has shifted rightward; a drop in the interest rate means the curve has shifted leftward.

Using this and other information about the banking system and the economy, the Fed decides what to do. At 11:30 A.M., if the interest rate is above target, the Fed buys government bonds. This increases the money supply and brings the interest rate back down to its target level, as in Figure 2. If, instead, the interest rate is

---

[2] Where will the money market end up in Figure 2 (a)? See Challenge Question #3 at the end of this chapter.

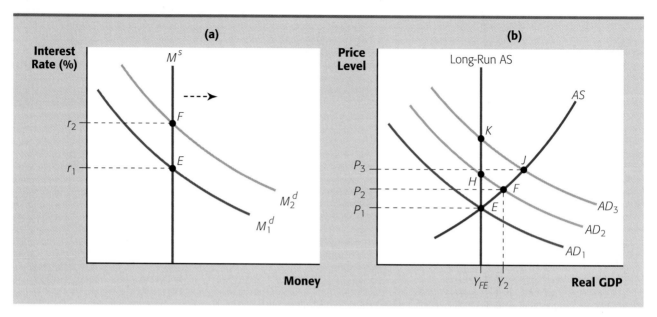

FIGURE 3

Responding to Demand Shocks that Originate with Aggregate Expenditure

A positive spending shock would shift the AD *curve rightward to* AD$_2$ *in panel (b), causing both the price level and output to rise. Under a passive monetary policy, that rise in income would cause the money demand curve to shift to* M$_2^d$ *in panel (a), driving the interest rate upward from* r$_1$ *to* r$_2$.

An active policy of maintaining the interest rate at r$_1$ *would make matters worse. To maintain the interest rate target, the Fed would have to increase the money supply (shown by the dashed arrow), causing an additional rightward shift of the* AD *curve to* AD$_3$ *and pushing the economy even further above full employment. The price level would increase to* P$_3$ *in the short run and even higher (at point* K*) in the long run.*

below target, the Fed sells government bonds, decreasing the money supply and raising the interest rate back up to its target level.[3]

Responding to Other Demand Shocks

You've just seen that changes in money demand shift the *AD* curve, so they are one kind of demand shock. But there are *other* demand shocks that originate with a shift in the aggregate expenditure line. The Fed has a more difficult time responding to this kind of demand shock than to shifts in money demand.

Figure 3 illustrates why. In panel (a) the money market is initially in equilibrium at point *E*, with the interest rate at its initial target level of *r*$_1$. In panel (b) the economy's short-run equilibrium is at point *E*, with output at full employment.

Now suppose that there is a positive demand shock that originates with an increase in aggregate expenditure. The shock might come from government policy—an increase in government purchases or a decrease in taxes—or in the private sector—an increase in investment or autonomous consumption or net exports. Whatever the source, the impact in panel (b) is the same: The *AD* curve will shift rightward—from *AD*$_1$ to *AD*$_2$—and output will rise. Back in panel (a), the rise in output will shift the money demand curve rightward to M$_2^d$, raising the interest rate. Now let's consider three possible responses by the Fed.

First, the Fed could follow a *passive* monetary policy, leaving the money supply unchanged. In this case, the interest rate would be allowed to rise above its target. In panel (b), the economy would slide upward along the *AS* curve, moving to point *F*. Both output and the price level would rise.

[3] In an earlier chapter, you learned that the interest rate targeted most directly by the Fed is the *federal funds rate*—the rate that banks charge when lending reserves to other banks. But the Fed knows that changes in the federal funds rate cause *other* interest rates to change—those that directly affect investment and consumption spending—and influencing these rates is the ultimate goal of the Fed.

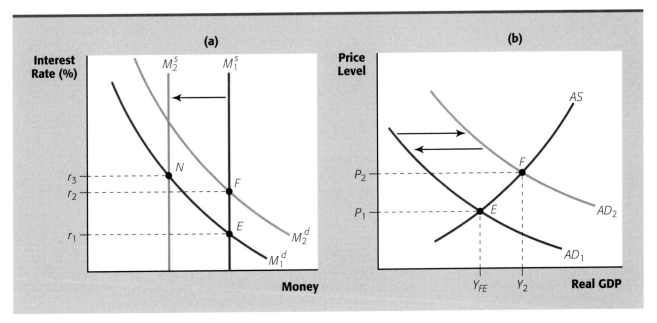

FIGURE 4
The Best Response to a Demand Shock Originating with Aggregate Expenditure

A demand shock that shifts the AD curve to AD$_2$ threatens to raise output beyond its full-employment level, and increase the price level as well. The Fed can neutralize that shift by raising its interest rate target to r$_3$ and decreasing the money supply to M$_2^s$ in order to achieve that target. The result is a decrease in interest-sensitive spending and a return of the AD curve to AD$_1$.

As you can see, the Fed would not want to respond to a demand shock with a passive monetary policy. Output would rise, bringing the unemployment rate below the natural rate. The price level would rise as well—to P_2. And in the long run, the price level would rise further as the self-correcting mechanism returned the economy to full employment at point H.

Would the active policy described earlier—maintaining an interest rate target—be an improvement? Actually, no; it would be even worse. To maintain the interest rate at r_1, the Fed would have to *increase* the money supply. But with no rise in the interest rate to crowd out some consumption and investment spending, the demand shock would shift the AD curve rightward even further—say, to AD_3. The new short-run equilibrium would then be at point J. As you can see, maintaining the interest rate target would push the economy even further beyond its potential output, and increase the price level even more, both in the short run (to P_3) and in the long run (to the higher price level at point K).

How, then, should the Fed respond to the demand shock? To maintain full employment and a stable price level, the Fed must pursue an active policy, but one that shifts the AD curve back to AD_1. And it can, indeed, do so. Look at Figure 4. Once again, the figure shows a demand shock that shifts the AD curve rightward to AD_2, increasing both output and the price level. In the money market, the higher price level and higher income shift the money demand curve rightward, raising the interest rate to r_2. But, as you saw in Figure 3, the rise to r_2 is not enough to choke off the increase in spending; it causes *some* crowding out of consumption and investment but not *complete* crowding out. In order to shift the AD curve back to AD_1, the Fed must raise the interest rate *further*, enough to cause *complete* crowding out. That is, it must raise the interest rate by just enough so that consumption and investment spending decline by an amount equal to the initial increase in aggregate expenditure. In the figure, we assume that an interest rate of r_3 will do the trick (point N). The Fed must decrease the money supply to M_2^s.

If the Fed acts quickly enough, it can prevent the demand shock from shifting the *AD* curve at all.[4]

> *To maintain full employment and price stability after a demand shock (other than a change in money demand), the Fed must change its interest rate target. A positive demand shock requires an increase in the target; a negative demand shock requires a decrease in the target.*

In recent years, the Fed has changed its interest rate target as frequently as needed to keep the economy on track. If the Fed observes that the economy is overheating—and that the unemployment rate has fallen below its natural rate—it will raise its target. The Fed, believing that the *AD* curve was shifting rightward too rapidly, reacted this way from June 2003 to June 2005, raising its interest rate target nine times in two years. When the Fed raises its target, it responds to forces that shift the *AD* curve rightward by creating an opposing force—a higher interest rate—to prevent the shift.

When the Fed observes that the economy is sluggish—and the unemployment rate has risen above its natural rate—the Fed will lower its target. The Fed did this aggressively throughout 2001, dropping its interest rate target 12 times that year. In this way, the Fed created a force opposing the leftward shift of the *AD* curve.

As you can see, demand shocks that originate with a shift of the aggregate expenditure line present the Fed with another no-lose situation: The same policy that helps to keep unemployment at its natural rate also helps to maintain a stable price level. However, these shocks present a challenge to the Fed that it doesn't face during other, less-eventful periods. To change the interest rate target by just the right amount, the Fed needs accurate information about how the economy operates. We'll return to this and other problems in conducting monetary policy in the "Using the Theory" section of this chapter.

The Interest Rate Target and the Financial Markets. The members of the Open Market Committee think very hard before they vote to change the interest rate target. In addition to its effects on the level of output and the price level, changes in the interest rate target can create turmoil in the stock and bond markets.

Why? Recall that the interest rate and the price of bonds are negatively related. Thus, when the Fed moves the interest rate to a higher target level, the price of bonds drops. Because the public holds trillions of dollars in government and corporate bonds, even a small rise in the interest rate—say, a quarter of a percentage point—causes the value of the public's bond holdings to drop by billions of dollars.

The stock market is often affected in a similar way. People hold stocks because they entitle the owner to a share of a firm's profits, and because stock prices are usually expected to rise as the economy grows and firms become more profitable. But stocks must remain competitive with bonds, or else no one would hold them. The lower the price of a stock, the more attractive the stock is to a potential buyer.

When the Fed raises the interest rate, the rate of return on bonds increases, so bonds become more attractive. As a result, stock prices must fall, so that stocks, too, will become more attractive. And that is typically what happens. Unless other changes are affecting the stock market, a rise in the interest rate causes people to try to sell their stocks in order to acquire the suddenly-more-attractive bonds. This

---

[4] Notice that the new money market equilibrium is along the original money demand curve M_1^d. Since this policy returns both the price level and income to their original values, the money demand curve returns to its original position.

causes stock prices to fall, until stocks are once again as attractive as bonds. Thus, a rise in the interest rate causes stock prices, as well as bond prices, to fall:

> *The stock and bond markets move in the opposite direction to the Fed's interest rate target: When the Fed raises its target, stock and bond prices fall; when it lowers its target, stock and bond prices rise.*

The destabilizing effect on stock and bond markets is one reason that, as a rule, the Fed prefers not to change its interest rate target very often. Frequent changes in the target would make financial markets less stable and the public more hesitant to supply funds to business firms by buying stocks and bonds.

Importantly, financial markets are also affected by *expected* changes in the interest rate target—whether or not they occur. If you expect the Fed to raise its target, you also expect stock and bond prices to fall. Therefore, you would want to dump these assets *now,* before their price drops. Similarly, an expectation of a drop in the interest rate target would make you want to buy stocks and bonds now, before their prices rise. Thus, *changes in expectations* about the Fed's future actions can be as destabilizing as the actions themselves.

This is why the financial press speculates constantly about the likelihood of changes in the interest rate target. Most of the time, the news is of the dog that didn't bark—the Federal Open Market Committee meets and decides to keep the target unchanged. Still, interest rates and stock prices often jump around in the days leading up to meetings of the Open Market Committee.

Once you understand the Fed's logic in changing its interest rate target, you can understand a phenomenon that—at first glance—appears mystifying: Stock and bond prices sometimes fall when good news about the economy is released, and rise when bad news is released. For example, if the Bureau of Labor Statistics announces that jobs are plentiful and the unemployment rate has dropped, or the Commerce Department announces that real GDP has grown rapidly in the previous quarter, the stock and bond markets may plummet. Why? Because owners of stocks and bonds believe that the Open Market Committee might interpret the good news as evidence that the economy is overheating. They would then expect the Committee to raise its interest rate target, so they try to sell their stocks and bonds before the committee even meets.

> *Good news about the economy sometimes leads to expectations that the Fed, fearing inflation, will raise its interest rate target. This is why good economic news sometimes causes stock and bond prices to fall. Similarly, bad news about the economy sometimes leads to expectations that the Fed, fearing recession, will lower its interest rate target. This is why bad economic news sometimes causes stock and bond prices to rise.[5]*

Responding to Supply Shocks

So far in this chapter, you've seen that demand shocks, in general, present the Fed with easy policy choices. By sticking to its interest rate target, it can neutralize any demand shocks that arise from shifts in money demand. And by changing its interest

HTTP://

Some income-distributional aspects of monetary policy are explored by Christina and David Romer in "Monetary Policy and the Well-Being of the Poor." It is available at **http://www.kc.frb.org/PUBLICAT/SYMPOS/1998/S98romer.pdf**.

---

[5] For a more complete discussion of the stock market, see the "Using All the Theory" chapter at the end of this book.

FIGURE 5
Responding to Supply Shocks

Starting at point E, a negative supply shock shifts the AS curve upward to AS₂. Under a passive monetary policy, a new short-run equilibrium would be established at point R, with a higher price level (P₂) and a lower level of output (Y₂). The Fed could prevent inflation by decreasing the money supply and shifting AD to AD$_{no\ inflation}$, but output would fall to Y₃. At the other extreme, it could increase the money supply and shift the AD curve to AD$_{no\ recession}$. This would keep output at the full-employment level, but at the cost of a higher price level, P₃.

For more information about supply shocks, download Bharat Trehan's "Supply Shocks and the Conduct of Monetary Policy," available at **http://www.frbsf.org/econrsrch/wklyltr/wklyltr99/el99-21.html**.

rate target from time to time, it can deal with demand shocks caused by changes that originate with aggregate expenditure. In each of these cases, the very policy that maintains a stable price level also helps to maintain full employment.

But adverse or negative *supply* shocks present the Fed with a true dilemma: If the Fed tries to preserve price stability, it will worsen unemployment; if it tries to maintain high employment, it will worsen inflation. And even though supply shocks are usually temporary, the shocks themselves—and the Fed's response—can affect the economy for several quarters or even years.

Figure 5 illustrates the Fed's dilemma when confronting an adverse supply shock. Initially, the economy is at point *E* (full employment). Then, a supply shock—say, a rise in world oil prices—shifts the *AS* curve up to *AS₂*. Under a passive monetary policy, the Fed would not change the money stock, keeping the *AD* curve at *AD₁*. The short-run equilibrium would then move from point *E* to point *R*, and the economy would experience *stagflation*—both inflation and a recession—with output falling to *Y₂* and the price level rising to *P₂*.

But the Fed can instead respond with an active monetary policy, changing the money supply in order to alter the short-run equilibrium. Which policy should it choose? The answer will depend on whether it is mostly concerned about rising prices or rising unemployment. Let's start by imagining two extreme positions.

First, the Fed could prevent inflation entirely by decreasing the money supply, shifting the *AD* curve leftward to the curve labeled *AD*$_{no\ inflation}$. This would move the short-run equilibrium to point *T*. Notice, though, that while the price level remains at *P₁*, output decreases to *Y₃*—even lower than under the passive policy.

At the other extreme, the Fed could prevent any fall in output. To accomplish this, the Fed would *increase* the money supply and shift the *AD* curve rightward, to *AD*$_{no\ recession}$. The equilibrium would then move to point *V*, keeping output at its full-employment level. But this policy causes more inflation, raising the price level all the way to *P₃*.

In practice, the Fed is unlikely to choose either of these two extremes to deal with a supply shock, preferring instead some intermediate policy. But the extreme positions help illustrate the Fed's dilemma:

> *A negative supply shock presents the Fed with a short-run trade-off: It can limit the recession, but only at the cost of more inflation; and it can limit inflation, but only at the cost of a deeper recession.*

The choice between the two policies is a hard one. After supply shocks, there are often debates within the Fed—and in the public arena—about how best to respond. Inflation *hawks* lean in the direction of price stability, and are willing to tolerate more unemployment in order to achieve it. In the face of an adverse supply shock, hawks would prefer a response that shifts the AD curve closer to $AD_{\text{no inflation}}$, even though it means higher unemployment. Inflation *doves* lean in the direction of a milder recession, and are more willing to tolerate the cost of higher inflation. They would prefer a response that brings the AD curve closer to $AD_{\text{no recession}}$.

Choosing Between Hawk and Dove Policies. When a supply shock hits, should the Fed use a hawk policy, should it employ a dove policy, or should it keep the AD curve unchanged? That depends. Over time, as the economy is hit by supply shocks, the hawk policy maintains more stability in the price level but less stability in output and employment. The dove policy gives the opposite result: more stability in output and less stability in the price level. The Fed should choose a hawkish policy if it cares more about price stability, and a dovish policy if it cares more about the stability of output and employment. Or it can pick an intermediate policy—one that balances price and employment stability more evenly.

The proper choice depends on how the Fed weights the harm caused by unemployment against the harm caused by inflation. And since the Fed is a public institution, its views should reflect the assessment of society as a whole. This is why supply shocks present such a challenge to the Fed: The public itself is divided between hawks and doves. Both inflation and unemployment cause harm, but of very different kinds. Inflation imposes a more general cost on society: the resources used up to cope with it. If the inflation is unexpected, it will also redistribute income between borrowers and lenders. The costs of unemployment are borne largely by the unemployed themselves—who suffer the harm of job loss—but partly by taxpayers, who provide funds for unemployment insurance. Balancing the gains and losses from hawk and dove policies is no easy task.

In recent years, some officials at the Fed have argued that having two objectives—stable prices *and* full employment—is unrealistic when there are supply shocks. The current chair of the Board of Governors, Alan Greenspan, has asked Congress to change the Fed's mandate to one of controlling inflation, period. But it would be difficult for the Fed to ignore the costs of higher unemployment, even if it were legally permitted to do so. Others have proposed that the Fed follow a predetermined rule, spelling out just how hawkish or dovish its response to supply shocks will be. We'll come back to this controversial idea in the "Using the Theory" section of this chapter.

Significant supply shocks—which have often been caused by higher oil prices—force the Fed to choose between a recession or a higher inflation rate.

© SUSAN VAN ETTEN

EXPECTATIONS AND ONGOING INFLATION

So far in this chapter, we've assumed that the Fed strives to maintain *zero* inflation, and that the price level remains constant when the economy reaches its long-run, full-employment equilibrium. But as we discussed earlier, this is not entirely realistic. Look again at panel (a) of Figure 1. There you can see that the U.S. economy has been characterized by *ongoing inflation.* Even in the 1990s and into early 2001—with unemployment at its natural rate—the annual inflation rate hovered around 2 to 3 percent. This means that, even though the economy was at full employment so the economy's self-correcting mechanism was not operating, prices were *continually rising.*

Even when the unemployment rate is *above* its natural rate—as in 2002 and 2003—prices keep rising. Why? And how does ongoing inflation change our analysis of the effects of monetary policy or the guidelines that the Fed should follow? We'll consider these questions next.

How Ongoing Inflation Arises

The best way to begin our analysis of ongoing inflation is to explore how it arises in an economy. We can do this by revisiting the 1960s, when the inflation rate rose steadily, and ongoing inflation first became a public concern.

What was special about the economy in the 1960s? First, it was a period of exuberance and optimism, for both businesses and households. Business spending on plant and equipment rose, and household spending on new homes and automobiles rose as well. At the same time, government spending rose—both military spending for the war in Vietnam and social spending on programs to help alleviate poverty. These increases in spending all contributed to rightward shifts of the *AD* curve; they were positive demand shocks. The unemployment rate fell below the natural rate—hovering around 3 percent in the late 1960s. And, as expected, the economy's self-correcting mechanism kicked in: Higher wages shifted the *AS* curve upward, causing the price level to rise.

As you've learned in this chapter, the Fed could have neutralized the positive demand shocks by raising its interest rate target (as in Figure 4), shifting the *AD* curve back to its original position. Alternatively, the Fed could have done nothing, allowing the self-correcting mechanism to bring the economy back to full employment with a higher—but stable—price level (as in the move from point *F* to point *H* in Figure 3). But in the late 1960s, the Fed made a different choice: It maintained its low interest rate target. This required the Fed to increase the money supply, thus adding its *own* positive demand shock to the spending shocks already hitting the economy. In Figure 3, this was the equivalent of moving the *AD* curve all the way out to *AD*$_3$, preventing any rise in interest rates but overheating the economy even more.

Why did the Fed act in this way? No one knows for sure, but one likely reason is that, in the 1960s, the Fed saw its job differently than it does today. The Fed's goal was to keep the interest rate stable and low, both to maintain high investment spending and to avoid instability in the financial markets. This is what it had been doing for years, with good effect: Americans had prospered in the previous decade, the 1950s, and financial markets were, indeed, stable.

But while this policy worked well in the 1950s, it did not serve the economy well during and after the demand shocks of the 1960s. That's because the Fed's policy—year after year—prevented the self-correcting mechanism from bringing the economy back to full employment. Instead, each time the price level began rising, and the economy began to self-correct, the Fed would increase the money supply *again*, causing output to remain *continually* above its potential output. And that, in turn, meant that the price level would continue to rise, year after year.

Now comes a crucial part of the story: As the price level continued to rise in the 1960s, the public began to *expect* it to rise at a similar rate in the future. This illustrates a more general principle:

When inflation continues for some time, the public develops expectations that the inflation rate in the future will be similar to the inflation rates of the recent past.

Why are expectations of inflation so important? Because when managers and workers expect inflation, it gets built into their decision-making process. Union contracts that set wages for the next three years will include automatic increases to compensate for the anticipated loss of purchasing power caused by future inflation. Nonunion wages will tend to rise each year as well, to match the wages in the unionized sector. And contracts for future delivery of inputs—like lumber, cement, and unfinished goods—will incorporate the higher prices everyone expects by the date of delivery.

A continuing, stable rate of inflation gets built into the economy. The built-in rate is usually the rate that has existed for the past few years.

Once there is built-in inflation, the economy continues to generate inflation even *after* the self-correcting mechanism has finally been allowed to do its job and bring us back to potential output. To see why, look at Figure 6. It shows what might happen over three years in an economy with built-in inflation. In the figure, output is at its full-employment level. Each year, the *AS* curve shifts upward and the *AD* curve shifts rightward, so the price level rises from P_1 to P_2 to P_3. Why does all this happen when there is built-in inflation?

Let's start with the reason for the upward shift of the *AS* curve. Unemployment is at its natural rate, so the self-correction mechanism is no longer contributing to any rise in wages or unit costs. But something else is causing unit costs to increase: inflationary expectations. Based on recent experience, the public expects the price level to rise as it has been rising in the past, so wages (and other input prices) will continue to increase, *even though output remains unchanged at full employment.* Thus,

in an economy with built-in inflation, the AS *curve will shift upward each year, even when output is at full employment and unemployment is at its natural rate. The upward shift of the* AS *curve will equal the built-in rate of inflation.*

For example, if the public expects inflation of 3 percent per year, then contracts will call for wages and input prices to rise by 3 percent per year. This means that unit costs will increase by 3 percent. Firms—marking up prices over unit costs—will raise their prices by 3 percent as well, and the *AS* curve will shift upward by 3 percent each year.

Explaining why the *AS* curve shifts upward is only half the story of the long-run equilibrium in Figure 6. We must also explain why the *AD* curve continues to shift rightward. The simple answer is: The *AD* curve shifts rightward because the Fed continues to increase the money supply. But *why* does the Fed shift the *AD* curve rightward, when it knows that doing so only prolongs inflation? One reason is that reducing inflation would be *costly* to the economy.

Imagine what would happen if, one year, the Fed decided *not* to shift the *AD* curve rightward as it had done in the past. During the year, the *AS* curve will shift upward anyway, by a percentage shift equal to the built-in rate of inflation. This will happen *no matter what the Fed does,* because the shift is based on expected inflation, which, in turn, is based on past experiences of inflation. There is nothing

FIGURE 6
**Long-Run Equilibrium
with Built-In Inflation**

*Each year, the aggregate supply
curve shifts upward by the built-
in rate of inflation. To keep the
economy at full employment,
the Fed shifts the AD curve
rightward each year by increasing the money supply.*

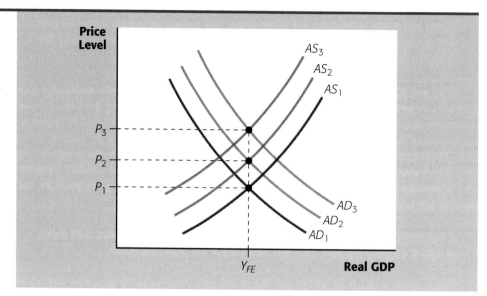

the Fed can do today to affect what has happened in the past, so each year, it must
accept the upward shift of the *AS* curve as a given.

But now suppose the Fed decides to reduce inflation by *not* shifting the *AD*
curve as it has in the past. Instead, it will just leave the *AD* curve where it was the
year before. For example, as the *AS* curve shifts from AS_2 to AS_3, the Fed might
keep the *AD* curve at AD_2. See if you can pinpoint the new, temporary equilibrium
that the Fed will achieve for the economy. (*Strong hint:* It's at the intersection of
AD_2 and AS_3.) If you've identified the point correctly, you'll see that the Fed would
achieve its goal of reducing the inflation rate that year. The price level would rise
from P_2 to something less than P_3, instead of all the way to P_3. But the reduction in
inflation is not without cost: The economy's output will decline—a recession.

> *In the short run, the Fed can bring down the rate of inflation by reducing the
> rightward shift of the* AD *curve, but only at the cost of creating a recession.*

Would the Fed ever purposely create a recession to reduce inflation? Indeed it
would, and it has—more than once. By far the most important episode occurred
during the early 1980s. As Figure 1 shows, annual inflation reached the extraordi-
nary level of 13.3 percent in 1979. Soon after, with some support from the newly
elected President Reagan, the Fed embarked on an aggressive campaign to bring
inflation down. The Fed stopped increasing the money supply, stopped shifting the
AD curve rightward, and a recession began in July of 1981. Unemployment
peaked, as shown earlier in in Figure 1, at 10.7 percent at the end of 1982. With
tremendous slack in the economy, the inflation rate fell rapidly, to below 4 percent
in 1982. The Fed deliberately created a serious recession, but it brought down the
rate of inflation.

Creating a recession is not a decision that the Fed takes lightly. Recessions are
costly to the economy and painful to those who lose their jobs. The desire to avoid
a recession is one reason that the Fed tolerated ongoing inflation for years and continued to play its role by shifting the *AD* curve rightward. We'll discuss other reasons for the Fed's tolerance of ongoing inflation a bit later.

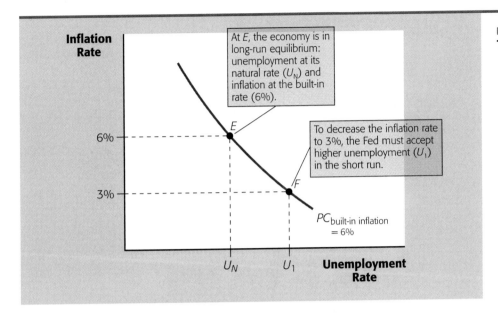

FIGURE 7
The Phillips Curve

The graph shows:
- **Inflation Rate** on the vertical axis
- **Unemployment Rate** on the horizontal axis
- At E, the economy is in long-run equilibrium: unemployment at its natural rate (U_N) and inflation at the built-in rate (6%).
- To decrease the inflation rate to 3%, the Fed must accept higher unemployment (U_1) in the short run.
- Point E at 6%, point F at 3%
- $PC_{\text{built-in inflation} = 6\%}$
- U_N, U_1

Ongoing Inflation and the Phillips Curve

Ongoing inflation changes our analysis of monetary policy. For one thing, it forces us to recognize a subtle, but important, change in the Fed's objectives: While the Fed still desires full employment, its other goal—price stability—is not zero inflation, but rather a *low and stable inflation rate.*

Another difference is in the graphs we use to illustrate the Fed's policy choices. Instead of continuing to analyze the economy with *AS* and *AD* graphs, when there is ongoing inflation, we usually use another powerful tool.

This tool is the *Phillips curve*—named after the late economist A. W. Phillips, who did early research on the relationship between inflation and unemployment. The **Phillips curve** illustrates the Fed's choices between inflation and unemployment in the short run, for a given built-in inflation rate.

Figure 7 shows a Phillips curve for the U.S. economy. The inflation rate is measured on the vertical axis, the unemployment rate on the horizontal. Point *E* shows the long-run equilibrium in the economy when the built-in inflation rate is 6 percent. At point *E*, unemployment is at its natural rate—U_N—and inflation remains constant from year to year at the built-in rate of 6 percent.

Notice that the Phillips curve is downward sloping. Why? Because it tells the same story we told earlier—with *AD* and *AS* curves—about the Fed's options in the short run. If the Fed wants to decrease the rate of inflation from 6 percent to 3 percent, it must slow the rightward shifts of the *AD* curve. This would cause a movement *along* the Phillips curve from point *E* to point *F*. As you can see, in moving to point *F*, the economy experiences a recession: Since output falls, unemployment rises above the natural rate.

> *In the short run, the Fed can move along the Phillips curve by adjusting the rate at which the* AD *curve shifts rightward. When the Fed moves the economy downward and rightward along the Phillips curve, the unemployment rate increases, and the inflation rate decreases.*

Phillips curve A curve indicating the Fed's choice between inflation and unemployment in the short run.

FIGURE 8
The Shifting Phillips Curve

Initially, the economy is at point E, with inflation equal to the built-in rate of 6%. If the Fed moves the economy to point F and keeps it there, the public will eventually come to expect 3% inflation in the future. At that point, the built-in inflation rate will fall and the curve will shift down to PC$_{built-in\ inflation\ =\ 3\%}$. The economy will move to point G in the long run, with unemployment at the natural rate and an actual inflation rate equal to the built-in rate of 3%.

Starting again at point E, suppose the Fed moved the economy to point H. The inflation rate would rise to 9 percent, and the unemployment rate would fall to U$_2$. If the Fed then held the economy at point H, the built-in inflation rate would rise to 9%, and the Phillips curve would shift up to PC$_{built-in\ inflation\ =\ 9\%}$. Eventually, the economy would move to point J. The vertical line connecting points E, G, and J is the long-run Phillips curve.

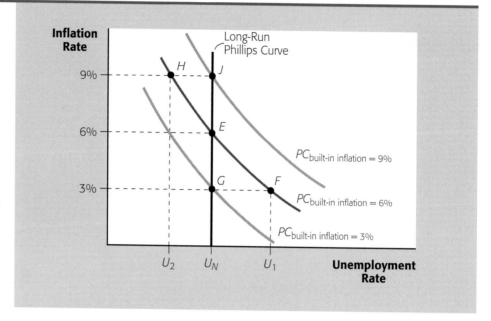

Now suppose the Fed keeps the economy at point *F*. In the long run, the public—observing a 3 percent inflation rate—will come to expect 3 percent inflation in the future. Thus, in the long run, 3 percent will become the economy's built-in rate of inflation. Figure 8 shows the effect on the Phillips curve (ignore the vertical line for now). When the economy's built-in inflation rate drops from 6 percent to 3 percent, the Phillips curve shifts downward, to the lower curve. At any unemployment rate, the inflation rate will be lower, now that the public expects inflation of only 3 percent rather than 6 percent.

> *In the long run, a decrease in the actual inflation rate leads to a lower built-in inflation rate, and the Phillips curve shifts downward.*

Once the Fed has reduced the built-in inflation rate, it can locate anywhere on the new Phillips curve by adjusting how rapidly it lets the money supply grow (and therefore, how rapidly the *AD* curve shifts rightward each year). Therefore, the Fed can choose to bring the economy back to full employment (point *G*), with a new, lower inflation rate of 3 percent rather than the previous 6 percent.

Riding Up the Phillips Curve. The process we've described—moving down the Phillips curve and thereby causing it to shift downward—also works in reverse: Moving *up* the Phillips curve will cause it to shift *upward*. Figure 8 also illustrates this case. Once again, assume the economy begins at point *E*, with a built-in inflation rate of 6 percent and unemployment at its natural rate. Now suppose the Fed begins to increase the money supply *more rapidly* than in the past, and begins shifting the *AD* curve further rightward than in Figure 6. In the short run, the economy would move *along* the Phillips curve from point *E* to point *H* in Figure 8. The inflation rate would rise to 9 percent, and the unemployment rate would fall below its natural rate—in the short run.

But suppose the Fed keeps the economy at point *H* for some time, continuing to shift the *AD* curve rightward at a faster rate than before. Then, in the long run, the public will begin to expect 9 percent inflation, and that will become the new built-in rate of inflation. The Phillips curve will then shift upward. At this point, if the Fed returns the economy to full employment, we end up at point J. The economy will be back in long-run equilibrium—but with a higher built-in inflation rate.

Long-Run Equilibrium. In Figure 8, you can see that the Fed's policy choices are different in the short run and in the long run. In the short run, the Fed can move along the Phillips curve, exploiting the trade-off between unemployment and inflation. But in the long run—once the public's expectations of inflation adjust to the new reality—the built-in inflation rate will change, and the Phillips curve will shift. Indeed, the Phillips curve will *keep* shifting whenever the unemployment rate is kept above or below the natural rate. (To see why, ask yourself what would happen in the future if the Fed tried to keep the unemployment rate *permanently* at a level like U_2—below the natural rate.) Thus, the economy cannot be in long-run equilibrium until the unemployment rate returns to its natural rate, and output is back to its potential level. In the long run, when we are at the natural rate of unemployment, the Fed can only choose *which* Phillips curve the economy will be on.

> *In the short run, there is a trade-off between inflation and unemployment: The Fed can choose lower unemployment at the cost of higher inflation, or lower inflation at the cost of higher unemployment. But in the long run, since unemployment always returns to its natural rate, there is no such trade-off.*

The Long-Run Phillips Curve. Let's reconsider what we've learned about the Fed's options in the long run. Figure 8 shows us that, when the Fed slows the rightward shifts of the *AD* curve, unemployment returns to the natural rate but the inflation rate is lower. The figure also shows us that, when the Fed allows the *AD* curve to shift rightward more rapidly than in the past, unemployment returns once again to the natural rate but the inflation rate is higher. As you can see,

> *in the long run, monetary policy can change the rate of inflation, but not the rate of unemployment.*

Now look at the vertical line in Figure 8. It tells us how monetary policy affects the economy in the long run, without the distractions of the short-run story. The vertical line is the economy's **long-run Phillips curve**, which tells us the combinations of unemployment and inflation that the Fed can choose in the long run. No matter what the Fed does, unemployment will always return to the natural rate, U_N, in the long run. However, the Fed can use monetary policy to select any rate of inflation it wants:

Long-run Phillips curve A vertical line indicating that in the long run, unemployment must equal its natural rate, regardless of the rate of inflation.

> *The long-run Phillips curve is a vertical line at the natural rate of unemployment. The Fed can select any point along this line in the long run, by using monetary policy to speed or slow the rate at which the* AD *curve shifts rightward.*

Why the Fed Allows Ongoing Inflation

Since the Fed can choose any rate of inflation it wants, and since inflation is costly to society, we might think that the Fed would aim for an inflation rate of zero. But a look back at panel (a) of Figure 1 shows that this is not what the Fed has chosen to do. In recent years, with unemployment very close to its natural rate, the Fed has maintained annual inflation at around 2 or 3 percent. Why doesn't the Fed eliminate inflation from the economy entirely?

One reason is a widespread belief that the Consumer Price Index (CPI) and other measures of inflation actually *overstate* the true rate of inflation in the economy. As you've learned, many economists believe that the CPI has overstated the true annual inflation rate by 1 to 2 percent—or more—in recent decades. Although the Bureau of Labor Statistics has been working hard to correct the problem, some significant upward bias remains. If the Fed forced the *measured* rate of inflation down to zero, the result would be an *actual* rate of inflation that was negative—*deflation*. In the "Using the Theory" section of this chapter, we'll discuss the special problems deflation would cause for the Fed and the economy.

Some economists have offered another explanation for the Fed's behavior: Low, stable inflation makes the labor market work more smoothly. The argument goes as follows: While no one wants a cut in their real wage rate, people seem to react differently, depending on *how* the real wage is decreased. For example, suppose there is an excess supply of workers in some industry, and a real wage cut of 3 percent would bring that labor market back to equilibrium. Workers would strongly resist a 3 percent cut in the nominal wage. But they would more easily tolerate a freeze in the nominal wage while the price level rises by 3 percent, even though in both scenarios, the real wage falls by 3 percent.

If this argument is correct, then a low or modest inflation rate would help wages adjust in different markets, helping to ensure that workers move to industries where they would be most productive as the structure of the economy changes over time. In some labor markets, real wages can be raised by increasing nominal wages faster than prices. In other labor markets, real wages can be cut by increasing nominal wages more slowly than prices, or not at all.

> The Fed has tolerated measured inflation at 2 to 3 percent per year because it knows that the true rate of inflation is lower, and because low rates of inflation may help labor markets adjust more easily.

USING THE THEORY
Challenges for Monetary Policy

So far in this chapter, we've described some clear-cut guidelines the Fed *can* and *does* follow in conducting monetary policy. We've seen that the proper policy for dealing with day-to-day changes in money demand is to set and *maintain* an interest rate target. The proper response to demand shocks that originate with aggregate expenditure is a *change* in the interest rate target. Dealing with a supply shock is more problematic, since it requires the Fed to balance its goal of low, stable inflation with its goal of full employment. But even here, once the Fed decides on the proper balance, its policy choice is straightforward: Shift the *AD* curve to achieve the desired combination of inflation and unemployment in the short run, and then guide the economy back to full employment in the long run.

© AFP/CORBIS

One might almost conclude from this chapter that monetary policy is akin to operating a giant machine—adjusting this or that knob, and making the occasional repair by consulting the manual. And policy making might appear rather uncontroversial, other than the occasional debate between those who favor hawkish and dovish policies toward inflation after a supply shock.

But the truth is very much the opposite. First, the Fed faces frequent criticism from members of Congress, the business community, the media and some academic economists—not just over its policy choices, but also the *way* it arrives at them. Second, the Fed, rather than operating a well-understood machine, must conduct monetary policy with highly imperfect information about the economy's course and precisely how its policies will alter it. Finally, in the early 2000s, the Fed found itself facing a new economic challenge—the possibility of deflation—requiring it to develop some new, untested tools for monetary policy . . . just in case. Let's consider each of these challenges facing the Fed.

Information Problems

The Federal Reserve has hundreds of economists carrying out research and gathering data to improve its understanding of how the economy works, and how monetary policy affects the economy. Research at the Fed is widely respected, and has made great progress. But because the economy is complex and constantly changing, serious gaps remain. Two of the most important gaps concern the time lag before monetary policy affects the economy, and knowledge of the natural rate of unemployment (or—equivalently—the economy's potential output).

Uncertain and Changing Time Lags. Suppose that we are in the midst of an expansion, and Fed officials begin to worry that the economy is about to overheat. They respond by raising their interest rate target. Eventually, the higher interest rate will dampen planned investment and consumption spending and cool the economy off. But when?

Monetary policy works with a time lag. Even after a rise in the interest rate, business firms will likely continue to build the new plants and new homes they've already started constructing. The most powerful effects on investment spending will be the cancellation of *new* projects currently being planned—projects that *would* have entered the pipeline of new spending many months later. The same applies in the other direction: When the Fed lowers the interest rate to stimulate additional spending, the full effects will be felt many months later, after new investment projects are planned and firms begin making the associated purchases.

The time lag in the effectiveness of monetary policy can have serious consequences. For example, by the time a higher interest rate target has its maximum effect, the economy may already be returning to full employment on its own, or it may be hit by a negative demand shock. In this case, the Fed—by raising its interest rate target—will be reining in the economy at just the wrong time, causing a recession.

Economists often use an analogy to describe this problem. Imagine that you are trying to drive a car with a special problem: When you step on the gas, the car will go forward . . . but not until five minutes later. Similarly, when you step on the brake, the car will slow, but also with a five-minute lag. It would be very difficult to maintain an even speed with this car: You'd step on the gas, and when nothing happened, you'd be tempted to step on it harder. By the time the car begins to move, you will have given too much gas and find yourself speeding down the road. So you try to slow down, but once again, hitting the brakes makes nothing happen. So you brake harder, and when the car finally responds, you come to a dead halt.

The Fed can make—and, in the past, has made—similar mistakes. When it tries to cool off an overheated economy, it may find that nothing is happening. Is it just a long time lag, or has the Fed not hit the brakes hard enough? If it hits the brakes harder, it runs the risk of braking the economy too much; if it doesn't, it runs the risk of continuing to allow the economy to overheat. Even worse, the time lag before monetary policy affects prices and output can change over the years: Just when the Fed may think it has mastered the rules of the game, the rules change.

The Natural Rate of Unemployment

In the Phillips curve diagram (Figure 8), we've assumed that the economy's natural rate of unemployment is known and remains constant, signified by the vertical long-run Phillips curve at some value U_N. In this case, once the economy achieved a long-run equilibrium, the Fed's job would be relatively straightforward: to shift the AD curve rightward by just the right amount each period to maintain the natural rate of unemployment with an acceptable rate of inflation.

But even though there is wide agreement that the natural rate rose in the 1970s and has fallen since the late 1980s, economists remain uncertain about its value during any given period. Many economists believe that today the natural rate is between 4.5 and 5 percent, but no one is really sure.

Why is this a problem? It's very much like the two mountain climbers who become lost. One of them pulls out a map. "Do you see that big mountain over there," he says, pointing off into the distance. "Yes," says the other. "Well," says the first, "according to the map, we're standing on top of it." In order to achieve its twin goals of full employment. And a stable, low rate of inflation, the Fed tries to maintain the unemployment rate as close to the natural rate as possible. If its estimate of the natural rate is wrong, it may believe it has succeeded when, in fact, it has not.

For example, suppose the Fed believes the natural rate of unemployment is 5 percent, but the rate is really 4.5 percent. Then—at least for a time—the Fed will be steering the economy toward an unemployment rate that is unnecessarily high and an output level that is unnecessarily low. We've already discussed the costs of cyclical unemployment. An overestimate of the natural rate makes society bear these costs needlessly. On the other hand, if the Fed believes the natural rate is 4.5 percent when it is really 5 percent, it will overheat the economy. This will raise the inflation rate—and a costly recession may be needed later in order to reduce it.

Trial and error can help the Fed determine the true natural rate. If the Fed raises unemployment above the true natural rate, the inflation rate will drop. If unemployment falls below the true natural rate, the inflation rate will rise. But (as we discussed earlier) trial and error works best when there is continual and rapid feedback. It can take some time for the inflation rate to change—six months, a year, or even longer. In the meantime, the Fed might believe it has been successful, even while causing avoidable unemployment, or planting the seeds for a future rise in the inflation rate.

Estimating the natural rate of unemployment is made even more difficult because the economy is constantly buffeted by shocks of one kind or another. If the Fed observes that the inflation rate is rising, does that mean that unemployment is below the natural rate? Or is the higher inflation being caused by a negative supply shock? Or by the Fed's response to an earlier, negative demand shock? This information is difficult to sort out, although the Fed has become increasingly sophisticated in its efforts to do so.

Rules Versus Discretion and the "Taylor Rule"

Over the last several decades, the Federal Reserve has formulated monetary policy using *discretion*: responding to demand and supply shocks in the way that Fed officials thought best at the time. In some cases, this seems to have helped the economy's performance, as when the Fed aggressively cut interest rates during 2001 and helped to make the recession of that year shorter and milder than it would otherwise have been. In other cases, discretion has worked less well. A notable example is during the late 1970s, when frequent changes in monetary policy contributed to wide fluctuations in output and a rapidly rising inflation rate that reached 13.3 percent in 1979. A more recent example is the Fed's policy in 2000: raising its interest rate target and, in retrospect, waiting too long before bringing it down again, missing an opportunity to begin an early fight against the recession of 2001.

Should the Federal Reserve have complete discretion to change its interest rate target in response to demand and supply shocks as it sees fit? Or should it stick to rules or guidelines in making monetary policy—rules that it announces in advance, with a justification required for any departure?

Some economists have suggested that the Fed's performance on average would be better with less discretion and more deference to predetermined rules. Currently, the most often-discussed rule is the **Taylor rule**, originally proposed in 1993 by economist John Taylor (currently Undersecretary of Treasury for International Affairs).

Taylor rule A proposed rule that would require the Fed to change the interest-rate by a specified amount whenever real GDP or inflation deviate from their pre-announced targets.

According to the Taylor rule, the Fed would announce a target for the inflation rate (say 2 percent per year) and another target for real GDP (equal to its estimate of potential GDP in that period). Then, the Fed would obligate itself to change its interest rate target by some predetermined amount for each percentage point that either output or inflation deviated from its respective target.

For example, suppose the economy began to overheat from a positive demand shock. Then either the inflation rate would begin to rise above its target rate, or real GDP would rise above potential, or both would occur. The Fed would then be obligated to raise its interest rate target by an amount that everyone knew in advance, depending on the changes observed in output and inflation. On the other side, if a negative demand shock started to threaten a recession, changes in inflation and/or output would commit the Fed to *lower* its interest rate target, and stimulate the economy back toward full employment.

What about a negative supply shock—such as a rise in oil prices—that causes the inflation rate to rise and output to fall? In this case, inflation would rise *higher* than its target, and output would fall *below* it. But the rule would identify in advance just how the Fed would respond. It would raise or lower the interest rate target depending on which variable—output or inflation—deviated the most, and depending on the response to each variable that the rule calls for. Thus, the hawk–dove debate that follows every supply shock would be settled—publically—in advance.

What would be the advantage of such a rule? First, if the Federal Reserve were committed to respond to the first signs of a boom, the public would know that the Fed would *not* allow the economy to continue overheating. This would discourage the formation of inflationary expectations. In effect, the Fed would be saying to the public, "Even though the inflation rate just rose, you know the rules. We have to bring the inflation rate back down, so don't get any ideas that we're going to let this continue." Similarly, if a negative demand shock sends the economy into a recession, and the Fed begins to stimulate the economy, the public needn't wonder whether the Fed will go too far and create ongoing, higher inflation. The rule says that the Fed will stimulate the economy only until we are back at potential output, and then maintain its original inflation rate target.

Second, the Taylor rule would give the Fed ammunition to fight inflation with a higher interest rate even when doing so might prove unpopular at the time. The Fed would only be following the rule that everyone understood in advance. This would help discourage the sort of discretion, and political pressure, that contributed to the high inflation rates of the late 1970s.

The Taylor rule is controversial. Opponents argue that it implies more advanced knowledge about the economy—and what an appropriate future response should be—than is realistically possible. And unless the rule were written into law—which only a few economists would advocate—the Fed would not be obligated to follow it. Since the public would know this, the existence of the rule might not be a strong deterrent to inflationary expectations.

Interestingly, the Fed's behavior under Alan Greenspan has followed reasonably close to the specific numerical rule that Taylor originally proposed. Whether the economy performed better or worse due to Greenspan's *deviations* from the rule remains controversial.

Deflation

During the first four years of the Great Depression, the price level fell an average of 10 percent per year—a very serious episode of deflation. Since then, episodes of deflation have been mild and short lived. In the early 2000s, however, deflation was back in the news. Not because the economy was experiencing it, but rather because of the fear that it would limit the Fed's ability to do its job. People pointed to Japan as an example. During the late 1990s and early 2000s, Japan's price level fell modestly, while the economy languished in recession. And Japan seemed unable to use monetary policy to stimulate its economy out of its recession.

Why does deflation create difficulties for monetary policy? To answer, we need to go back to the distinction between nominal and real interest rates you learned about several chapters ago. Recall that the nominal interest rate is the percentage rate in *dollars* that a borrower pays on a loan. The real interest rate, by contrast, is the percentage rate in *purchasing power* a borrower pays.

You also learned that the *real* rate that people expect to pay (or receive) over the life of a loan is what matters for decisions about borrowing and lending. Now we can extend this notion further: The expected *real* rate is what matters for decisions about consumption and investment spending. Businesses and households—in deciding whether to borrow for investment projects or consumer durables like automobiles—will base their decision on how much *purchasing power* they are giving up by taking out the loan.

The Federal Reserve, however, sets the *nominal* interest rate with its open market operations: the percentage paid in *dollars* when money is borrowed. The problem for the Fed—and for the central bank of Japan or any other country—is that the *nominal* interest rate cannot go below zero. After all, a nominal interest rate below zero would mean that borrowers would pay back fewer *dollars* than they borrowed. Under those circumstances, no one would ever lend money!

Now recall the relationship between the real and nominal interest rates:

$$\text{Real interest rate} = \text{Nominal interest rate} - \text{Rate of inflation.}$$

We can also write this in terms of the real interest rate that people *expect* to pay (or receive) on a loan:

Expected real interest rate = Nominal intererst rate − Expected rate of inflation.

This means that, when the expected inflation rate is positive, the expected real interest rate will be *less* than the nominal rate. For example, with annual inflation expected to be 4 percent, a nominal interest rate of 6 percent per year translates to an expected real interest rate of 2 percent. Under these circumstances, if the economy is in the midst of a recession, and the Fed lowers the nominal interest rate without creating expectations of higher inflation, the real interest rate will drop as well and spending will rise.

But suppose there is *deflation*—a *negative* rate of inflation—and suppose that people begin to expect continuing deflation. Then our equation tells us that the expected real interest rate will be *higher* than the nominal interest rate. For example, with expected deflation of 5 percent per year (expected inflation of −5 percent per year), a nominal interest rate of 4 percent translates to an expected real interest rate of 4 percent − (−5 percent) = 9 percent. And even if the nominal interest rate fell to 0 percent—the lowest it can go—the expected real interest rate would still be 5 percent—the negative of the rate of deflation. Thus,

ongoing, expected deflation puts a positive floor under the expected real interest rate. Once this floor is reached, the Fed cannot reduce the expected real interest rate—or stimulate aggregate expenditure—using the traditional tools of monetary policy.

In 2003—with the annual federal funds rate set at 1 percent and annual inflation running at about 2 percent—the *real* federal funds rate was −1 percent. This negative *real* interest rate was certainly helping to stimulate the economy, by encouraging borrowing for investment projects and consumer durables. But if the inflation rate dropped to zero—or turned negative—the real interest rate would rise. And if people expected deflation to continue, the *expected* real interest rate would rise. The Fed would then have only one percentage point left by which to cut the nominal interest rate. After that, any further deflation would automatically cause the real interest rate to *rise*, *decreasing* planned investment and consumption spending.

Deflation could then create a vicious cycle. The decreased spending—a negative demand shock—would further decrease the inflation rate (a greater *deflation* rate), which in turn would push the real interest rate even higher. And the Fed would be unable to fight the negative demand shock: With the nominal interest rate at zero, its normal tools—designed to lower the nominal interest rate—would be useless.

Fed officials have been aware of this problem, and in the early 2000s, they began to plan for the contingency of deflation. Part of their planning involved public announcements to reassure the public. First, they pointed out that while deflation of 5 or 10 percent a year would be a serious threat, a *modest* deflation rate was unlikely to create a downward spiral for the economy. (Japan's deflation rate, for example, had remained relatively stable for about a decade at 1 percent per year.) And a deflation perceived as temporary need not affect the economy significantly. What matters for spending is the real interest rate that people *expect* to pay over the life of a loan. As long as their expectations of future inflation remained positive and stable, an actual deflation needn't raise the expected real interest rate.

Second, the Fed announced that it was prepared to change the way it conducts monetary policy should the need arise. Instead of limiting its open market operations to injecting reserves into the federal funds market, it was prepared to start buying long-term government bonds.

Why would this help? The nominal interest rate on long-term bonds is generally higher than on short-term obligations, and higher than the very-short-term federal funds rate. This is mostly due to a greater risk that inflation will rise over a longer period, which would erode the *real* interest rate on the bond. In mid-2003, for example, the interest rate on longer-term government bonds was about 4 percent—substantially higher than the federal funds rate. By buying large quantities of long-term government bonds directly—thus adding to the demand for them and raising their price—the Fed could have lowered the interest rate on these bonds. Thus, even if the Fed could not reduce the federal funds rate any further once it hit zero, it could still have reduced *other* interest rates—not just on long-term government bonds, but also on long-term corporate bonds whose rates tend to move closely with their government counterparts.

Finally, the Fed has one other tool: its ability to influence expectations. By announcing that it would follow credible policies to raise the inflation rate to a modest, positive level, the Fed could create positive inflationary expectations *even in the midst of deflation*. Look again at the equation for the real interest rate. For a given nominal interest rate, every *rise* in the *expected* inflation rate causes a *decrease* in the real rate. Thus, even if all nominal interest rates in the economy hit zero, the Fed could try to convince the public that it would raise the inflation rate in the near future. If successful, it could continue to lower real interest rates merely by raising expected inflation. Most economists believed that the Fed would be able to convince the public, should the need arise.

Finally (although Fed officials did not stress this), even if *all* monetary policy tools were unable to stimulate spending, fiscal policy could be used: The government could increase purchases itself, or reduce taxes even further to raise disposable income. It might take time for the government to do this. But eventually, fiscal policy would work through the normal multiplier process to raise spending and output—a completely separate channel of influence over the economy from monetary policy. Indeed, modest increases in government purchases during the Great Depression helped to stop the economy's downward spiral. And what finally ended the last stages of the depression—very rapidly—was the huge increase in military purchases as the United States entered World War II.

As you can see, conducting monetary policy is not easy. The Fed has hundreds of economists carrying out research and gathering data to improve its information about the status of the economy and its understanding of how the economy works. And the effort seemed to have paid off during the decade leading up to 2001. But some economists believe that the Fed, in retrospect, could have done more to offset the forces that caused the recession that began in March 2001. They believe that the Fed raised the interest rate too high in 2000 and waited too long before starting to lower the interest rate in January 2001. This is an easy conclusion to come to with hindsight. But given the uncertainties faced by the Fed in conducting monetary policy, many economists continue to give the Fed high marks.

Will the Fed's success continue? If you are reading these words after January, 2006, Alan Greenspan has most likely left the Federal Reserve, and a new Chair has taken his place. What new shocks will the economy be facing? How much influence will the new Chair have within the FOMC? And how will the new Chair's approach differ from Greenspan's? Whether monetary policy remains successful hinges in large part on the answers to these questions.

Summary

As the nation's central bank, the Federal Reserve bears primary responsibility for maintaining a low, stable rate of inflation and for maintaining full employment of the labor force as the economy is buffeted by a variety of shocks. The money demand curve, for example, may shift, causing a change in the interest rate, a shift in the *AD* curve, and a change in output and employment. The Fed can neutralize such money demand shocks by setting an interest rate target. To maintain the target, it increases the money supply whenever money demand increases, and decreases the money supply when money demand decreases. This policy enables the Fed to stabilize both inflation and unemployment.

Demand shocks from spontaneous shifts in aggregate expenditure can also shift the *AD* curve, causing output to deviate from its full-employment level. The Fed can neutralize these shocks by adjusting its interest rate target—changing the money supply to shift the *AD* curve back to its original position.

The Fed's most difficult problem is responding to supply shocks. A negative supply shock—an upward shift of the *AS* curve—presents the Fed with a dilemma. In the short run, it must choose a point along that new *AS* curve. If it wishes to maintain price stability, it must shift the *AD* curve to the left and accept higher unemployment. If the Fed wishes to maintain full employment, it must shift the *AD* curve to the right and accept a higher rate of inflation. A "hawk" policy puts greater emphasis on price stability, while a "dove" policy emphasizes lower unemployment.

If Fed policy leads to ongoing inflation, then businesses and households come to expect the prevailing inflation rate to continue. As a result, the *AS* curve continues to shift upward at that built-in expected inflation rate. To maintain full employment, the Fed must shift the *AD* curve rightward, creating an inflation rate equal to the expected rate.

If the Fed wishes to change the built-in inflation rate, it must first change the expected inflation rate. For example, to lower the expected inflation rate, the Fed will slow down the rightward shifts of the *AD* curve. The actual inflation rate will fall, and expectations will eventually adjust downward. While they do so, however, the economy will experience a recession. The Fed's short-run choices between inflation and unemployment can be illustrated with the Phillips curve. In the short run, the Fed can move the economy along the downward-sloping Phillips curve by adjusting the rate at which the *AD* curve shifts. If the Fed moves the economy to a new point on the Phillips curve and holds it there, the built-in inflation rate will eventually adjust and the Phillips curve will shift. In the long run, the economy will return to the natural rate of unemployment with a different inflation rate. The long-run Phillips curve is a vertical line at the natural rate of unemployment.

In conducting monetary policy, the Fed faces several challenges. It has imperfect information about the time required for its policies to affect the economy, and also about the economy's potential GDP (or its natural rate of unemployment) during any given period. The Fed often faces criticism for using discretion rather than following rigid rules, especially when the economy does not perform well. And, in recent years, the Fed has had to worry about deflation and the need to develop new (and less tested) tools for conducting monetary policy.

Key Terms

Active monetary policy	Natural rate of unemployment	Taylor rule
Interest rate target	Passive monetary policy	
Long-run Phillips curve	Phillips curve	

Review Questions *Answers to even-numbered Questions and Problems can be found on the text Web site at http://hall-lieb.swlearning.com.*

1. "The Fed should aim for the lowest possible unemployment rate." True or false? Explain.

2. What effect does a change in the Fed's interest rate target have on financial markets? How do changes in expectations regarding the Fed's position on the interest rate target affect financial markets?

3. "The Fed should respond to any shift in the *AD* curve by maintaining its interest rate target." True or false? Explain.

4. Explain the trade-off that the Fed faces with regard to negative supply shocks. What do "hawks" and "doves" have to do with this trade-off?

5. Why do expectations of inflation have a significant impact on the economy? What is the impact?

6. What relationship does the Phillips curve illustrate? How does the Fed control movements along the Phillips curve? Why is the long-run Phillips curve vertical?

7. List and explain two reasons why the Fed tolerates some ongoing inflation.

8. What are the biggest information problems faced by the Fed?

9. Describe the Taylor rule. What are the advantages of following it? Why is it controversial?

10. How did the Fed plan for the contingency of deflation in the early 2000s?

Problems and Exercises

1. Suppose that a law required the Fed to do everything possible to keep the inflation rate equal to zero. Using *AD* and *AS* curves, illustrate and explain how the Fed would deal with (a) a rightward shift of the money demand curve, (b) a negative demand shock from a decrease in investment spending, and (c) an adverse aggregate supply shock. What would the costs and benefits of such a law be?

2. Suppose that, in a world with *no* ongoing inflation, the government raises taxes. Using *AD* and *AS* curves, describe the effects on the economy if the Fed decides to practice a passive monetary policy. Alternatively, how could the Fed use active policy to neutralize the demand shock?

3. Suppose that initially the price level is P_1 and GDP is Y_1, with no built-in inflation. The Fed reacts to a negative demand shock by shifting the aggregate demand curve in the appropriate direction. The next time the Fed receives data on GDP and the price level, it finds that the price level is above P_1 and GDP is above Y_1. Give a possible explanation for this finding.

4. Suppose the economy has been experiencing a low inflation rate. A new chair of the Federal Reserve is named, and he or she is known to be sympathetic to dove policies. Explain the possible effects on the Phillips curve.

5. "The idea of the Fed having to choose between hawk and dove policies in Figure 5 is silly. All the Fed has to do is shift the *AS* curve back to its original position, which would prevent *both* recession *and* inflation." Do you agree? Why or why not?

6. Using a graph similar to Figure 8, show what will happen in the future if the Fed tried to keep the unemployment rate permanently at a level like U_2—below the natural rate.

7. What would the Fed have to do to reduce the built-in inflation in our economy? Would it be likely to take this action if it was most concerned about achieving a lower unemployment rate, or if it was most concerned about preventing a loss of purchasing power?

8. One of your classmates stops you in the hall and says, "I was reading a statement from the Fed's Federal Open Market Committee (FOMC) meeting. It stated that the members were concerned that an already low rate of inflation might become lower. Why do they want to keep inflation rates high? I thought inflation was a bad thing." How should you explain to your classmate why the FOMC is worried about inflation becoming too low?

Challenge Questions

1. Suppose the economy is experiencing ongoing inflation. The Fed wants to reduce expected inflation, so it announces that in the future it will tolerate less inflation. How does the Fed's credibility affect the success of the reduction? How can the Fed build its credibility? Are there costs to building credibility? If so, what are they?

2. This chapter mentioned what would happen if the Fed over- or underestimated the natural rate of unemployment. Using the *AD–AS* model, suppose the economy is at the true natural rate of unemployment, so that GDP is at its potential level. Suppose, too, that the Fed wrongly believes that the natural rate of unemployment is higher (potential GDP is lower) and acts to bring the economy back to its supposed potential. What will the Fed do? What will happen in the short run? If the Fed continues to maintain output below potential, what will happen over the long run?

3. Look again at Figure 2. Suppose that the rightward money demand shift in the figure results from a permanent, one-time increase in tastes for holding money. Suppose, too, that the Fed wishes to pursue an active monetary policy to neutralize the impact of the shift. The Fed must increase the money supply by just enough to bring the interest rate back to r_1. However, as it does so, and as income increases in panel (b), the money demand curve will move rightward as well. (Why?) Identify the new, final equilibrium point in panel (a). (*Note*: This is not as easy as it seems. M_2^D is the money demand curve after the increase in tastes for holding money *and* the change in output to Y_2. You will have to draw in a *third* money demand curve that is consistent with the new tastes for holding money, but also consistent with output and income back at full employment.)

4. Given your answer to Problem 6, would you expect the short-run Phillips curve to shift by equal amounts in successive years?

5. The slope of the money demand curve helps to determine the effectiveness of Fed policy. Draw a graph to illustrate the concept that the steeper the money demand curve is, the more effective an increase in the money supply will be. Does this conclusion also hold for a decrease in the money supply?

ECONOMIC *Applications*   *These exercises require access to Hall/Lieberman Xtra! If Xtra! did not come with your book, visit http://hallxtra.swlearning.com to purchase.*

1. Use your Xtra! password at the Hall and Lieberman Web site (http://hallxtra.swlearning.com), select this chapter, and under Economic Applications, click on EconDebate. Choose *Monetary Policy*, and scroll down to find the debate, "Should the Fed Pursue a Fixed Policy Rule?" Read the debate, and use the information to answer the following questions.
   a. Why did Milton Friedman and other monetarists argue that the government should rely on fixed policy rules and avoid discretionary policies?
   b. What are the views of new-classical and new-Keynesian economists on discretionary monetary and fiscal policies?

2. Use your Xtra! password at the Hall and Lieberman Web site (http://hallxtra.swlearning.com), select this chapter, and under Economic Applications, click on EconData. Choose *Monetary Policy*, and scroll down to find *Money Supply (M2)*. Read the definition, click on Diagrams/Data, then use the information to answer the following questions.
   a. Considering the diagrams in this section, discuss the Fed's behavior with regard to monetary policy.
   b. Click on the Updates and read Governor Ben S. Bernanke's remarks titled: "Constrained Discretion" and Monetary Policy at http://www.federalreserve.gov/boarddocs/speeches/2003/20030203/default.htm. What are his views on monetary rules and discretion?

Fiscal Policy: Taxes, Spending, and the Federal Budget

CHAPTER OUTLINE

Thinking About Spending, Taxes, and the Budget

Spending, Taxes, and the Budget: Some Background
Government Outlays
Federal Tax Revenues
The Federal Budget and the National Debt

The Effects of Fiscal Changes in the Short Run
How Economic Fluctuations Affect the Federal Budget
How the Budget Affects Economic Fluctuations
Countercyclical Fiscal Policy

The Effects of Fiscal Changes in the Long Run
The National Debt

Using the Theory: The Bush Tax Cuts of 2001 and 2003
The Short Run: Countercyclical Fiscal Policy?
The Long Run: The Tax Cuts and the National Debt

Almost every year throughout the 1980s and early 1990s, a best-selling book would be published that predicted economic disaster for the United States and the world. In most of these books, the U.S. federal government played a central role. Arguments and statistics were offered to show that federal government spending—which was growing by leaps and bounds—was out of control, causing us to run budget deficits year after year. As a result, the United States was facing a growing debt burden that would soon swallow up all of our incomes, sink the United States economy, and bring about a worldwide depression.

During the late 1990s, as the federal budget picture improved, these disaster books quietly disappeared. Now, the federal government was running *surpluses*—raising more funds in tax revenues than it was spending. Moreover, the surpluses were projected to continue for at least a decade. News articles and public statements described a bright economic future in which our most pressing problem would be: What shall we do with our mounting budget surpluses?

Then, in 2002, another flip-flop: The government began running deficits again, with continued deficits projected through the end of the 2000s and beyond. Once again, concern over the budget and growing U.S. debt saturated the media, and the word *disaster* reappeared in the media.

What caused these flip-flops in the government's budget? And why should we care?

In this chapter, we'll take a close look at the government's role in the macroeconomy. You'll learn how to interpret trends in the government's budget, and how to identify the causes and effects of those trends. You'll also learn to distinguish between fiscal policy's long-run effects on the economy and its short-run effects.

THINKING ABOUT SPENDING, TAXES, AND THE BUDGET

Let's start with some simple numbers. In 1959, the federal government's total outlays for goods and services, transfer payments, and interest on its debt was $92 billion. By 2005, the total had grown to about $2,500 billion, an increase of more than 2,600 percent. Does this show that government spending is out of control?

Or consider the national debt—the total amount that the government owes to the general public from past borrowing in years in which it ran a budget deficit. In 1959, the national debt was $235 billion; by mid-2005, it had grown to $4,500 billion. Is this evidence that debt is crushing the economy?

Actually, these figures don't tell us much of anything. First, prices rose during that period, so *real* government outlays and the *real* national debt rose considerably less than these nominal figures suggest. In addition, from 1959 to 2005, the U.S. population grew, the labor force grew, and the average worker became more productive. As a result, real GDP and real income more than quadrupled during this period. Why is that important? Because *spending and debt should be viewed in relation to income.*

We automatically recognize this principle when we think about an individual family or business. Suppose you are told that a family is spending $50,000 each year on goods and services, and has a total debt—a combination of mortgage debt, car loans, student loans, and credit card balances—of $200,000. Is this family acting responsibly? Or is its spending and borrowing out of control? That depends. If the income of the household is less than its spending—say, $40,000—and is expected to remain so, then there is serious trouble. A family that spends more than it earns would see its debt grow every year until it could not handle the monthly interest payments.

But what if the family's income is $800,000 per year? Then our conclusion would change dramatically: We'd wonder why this family spends so *little*. And if it owed $200,000, we would not think it irresponsible at all. After all, the family could pay the interest on its debt—with a tiny fraction of its income.

What is true for an individual family is also true for the nation. Spending and debt are *relative* concepts. As a country's total income grows, it will want more of the things that government can provide—education, high environmental standards, domestic security, programs to help the needy, and more. Therefore, we expect government spending to rise as a nation becomes richer. Moreover, as its income grows, a country can *handle* higher interest payments on its debt. Government spending and the total national debt, considered in isolation, tell us nothing about how responsibly or irresponsibly the government is behaving.

> *Budget-related figures such as government outlays, tax revenues, or government debt should be considered relative to a nation's total income—as percentages of GDP.*

Viewing budget-related figures relative to GDP helps to put things in perspective. In 1959, the federal government's total outlays were 19 percent of GDP. In 2005, they were about 20 percent—reflecting a slight upward drift, but far from out of control. And relative to GDP, the national debt in the hands of the public was lower in mid-2005 than in 1959, shrinking from about 48 percent to 38 percent of GDP. This doesn't suggest that everything is fine with the federal budget, and we'll discuss some causes for concern in this chapter. But our concerns should be based on, and expressed with, the proper perspective.

In the rest of this chapter, as we explore recent trends in fiscal behavior and their effects on the economy, we'll do so with these lessons in mind. Accordingly, we'll look at fiscal variables as *percentages of GDP*.[1]

SPENDING, TAXES, AND THE BUDGET: SOME BACKGROUND

Our ultimate goal in this chapter is to understand how fiscal changes have affected, and continue to affect, the macroeconomy. But before we do this, some background will help. What has happened to the *composition* of government spending in recent decades? How does the U.S. tax system work, and what has happened to the government's tax revenues? Why has the national debt decreased in some years, risen slowly in other years, and risen very rapidly in still others? This section provides answers to these and other questions about the government's finances. Although state and local spending also play an important role in the macroeconomy, most of the significant macroeconomic changes in recent decades have involved the *federal* government. This is why we'll focus on spending, taxing, and borrowing at the federal level.

Government Outlays

The federal government's *outlays*—the total amount spent or disbursed by the federal government in all of its activities—can be divided into three categories:

- *government purchases*—the total value of the goods and services that the government buys (corresponding to "G" in GDP = C + I + G + NX)
- *transfer payments*—income supplements the government provides to people, such as Social Security benefits, unemployment compensation, and welfare payments
- *interest on the national debt*—the interest payments the government must make to those who hold government bonds

Government Purchases. Until the mid 1970s, government purchases of goods and services were the largest component of government spending. To understand how these purchases have changed over time, it's essential to divide them into two categories: military and nonmilitary. Figure 1 shows total federal purchases, as well as federal military and nonmilitary purchases, from 1959 to 2005.

One fact stands out from the figure: The federal government uses up only a tiny fraction of our national resources for nonmilitary purposes. These nonmilitary

---

[1] It makes no difference whether we divide *nominal* government outlays by *nominal* GDP, or *real* government outlays by *real* GDP; we get the same answer for government outlays as a percentage of GDP. When we measure a variable as a percentage of GDP, we adjust for inflation *and* for growth in real income at the same time.

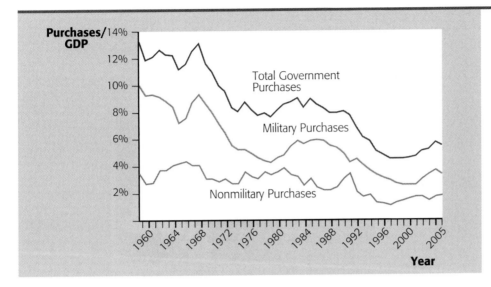

FIGURE 1
Federal Government Purchases as a Percentage of GDP

Over the last several decades, total government purchases have trended downward largely because nonmilitary purchases remained a stable, small percentage of GDP while military purchases have steadily decreased. Exceptions were the late 1960s (Vietnam War), 1980s (Reagan defense buildup) and the early 2000s (Bush defense buildup after September 11, 2001).

Source for this and most of the other figures in this chapter: Office of Management and Budget, *The Budget for Fiscal Year 2006, Historical Tables* (especially Tables 1.1, 1.3, 2.1, 2.3, 6.1, and 7.1). Data for 2005 are estimates.

purchases include the salaries paid to all government workers outside the Defense Department (for example, federal judges, legislators, and the people who run federal agencies), as well as purchases of buildings, equipment, and supplies. It also includes the spending of the new Homeland Security Department (established in 2003). Added together, all the different kinds of nonmilitary government purchases account for a stable, low fraction of GDP—about 2 percent.

This strongly contradicts a commonly held notion: that government spending is growing by leaps and bounds because of bloated federal bureaucracies. While it's true that government outlays have drifted upward over the last several decades, nonmilitary purchases have not been the cause.

As a percentage of GDP, nonmilitary government purchases have remained very low and stable. They have not contributed to growth in total government outlays.

What about military purchases? Here, we come to an even stronger conclusion:

As a percentage of GDP, military purchases declined dramatically over the past several decades. Like nonmilitary purchases, they have not contributed to the long-term upward drift in government outlays.

The decline in military purchases is shown by the middle line in Figure 1. They were around 10 percent of GDP in 1959, fell almost continuously to about 3 percent in the late 1990s, then rose again in the first half of the 2000s. In between, there were two large military buildups—one associated with the Vietnam War in the late 1960s and the other during the Reagan administration in the 1980s. But both of these buildups were temporary. From 1959 to 2001, the decline of military spending freed up resources amounting to 6½ to 7 percent of GDP (often called the "peace dividend" from the ending of the cold war). As you can see in Figure 1, the more recent rise in military purchases has taken back only a small part of the peace dividend.

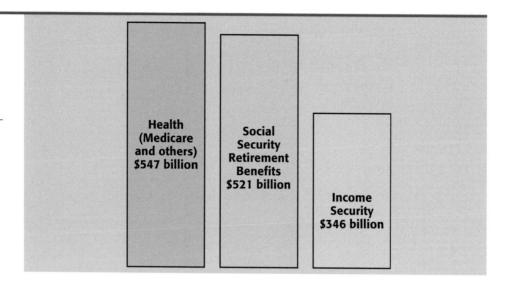

It is too early to say whether the current rise in military purchases will be temporary, or how large it will become. But given the current U.S. role in global politics, significant future cuts seem highly unlikely. The implications are tremendously important for thinking about the recent past and the future of the federal government's role in the economy:

*The decline in military spending in relation to GDP since the early 1960s
has made huge amounts of resources available for other purposes. Because
military spending has little room to fall further and is likely to rise over
the next decade, there will not be any similar freeing up of resources in
coming years.*

The resources released from military spending eased many otherwise tough decisions about resource allocation in the economy. In particular, they made it easy for the federal government to provide increases in resources to some parts of the population, through transfer payments. Now that this trend has ended, the government will be presented with difficult budget choices.

Social Security and Other Transfers. Transfer programs provide cash and in-kind benefits to people whom the federal government designates as needing or entitled to help. Figure 2 shows the three major categories of transfers.

The largest category of transfers—and the fastest-growing—occurs in health programs. The Social Security system provides health-related benefits to everyone aged 62 and over through Medicare. This is a health insurance plan for the elderly and some disabled people, which covers care at hospitals, nursing facilities, and outpatient physician services. Efforts have been made to control Medicare's rapidly rising costs, but they have continued to rise as a percentage of GDP. They are expected to rise even more rapidly over the next decade for two reasons: (1) the retirement of the baby boomers in the late 2000s, and (2) the addition of coverage for prescription drugs, to become fully effective in 2006. And in addition to funding Medicare, the federal government helps finance state-operated health plans for the poor, through a program called Medicaid. The costs of these programs have been rising rapidly as well.

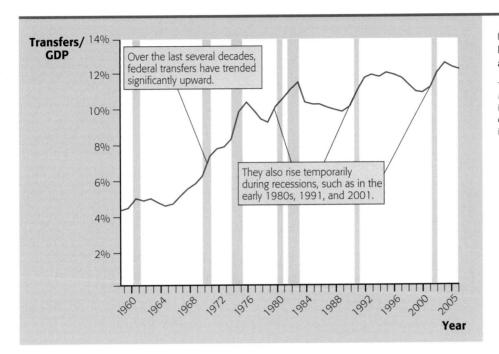

Transfers/ GDP

Over the last several decades, federal transfers have trended significantly upward.

They also rise temporarily during recessions, such as in the early 1980s, 1991, and 2001.

Year

FIGURE 3

Federal Transfer Payments as a Percentage of GDP

Note: Federal transfers in this chapter include grants to state and local governments that are used for health and income security assistance.

The second largest category is retirement benefits—the payments made by the Social Security system to retired people. Although the benefits are loosely related to past contributions to the Social Security system, workers whose earnings are low receive benefits that are worth far more than their contributions. And after age 72, even someone with no history of contributions receives the minimum benefit. Social Security outlays have grown rapidly over the last few decades, and are expected to rise even more rapidly as the baby-boom generation begins retiring and collecting benefits in the late 2000s.

Government "Outlays" Versus Government "Purchases" Don't confuse government outlays with government purchases, which are just one component of the government's outlays. The other components are transfer payments and interest on the debt.

DANGEROUS CURVES

The third and smallest of the three categories of transfers is *income security*—a catch-all for some federal retirement programs, as well as programs to help the poor and the unemployed. In recent years, the three largest components of spending in this category are (in order) retirement payments for federal government workers, unemployment insurance, and food stamps. Welfare payments to poor families are also in this category, but these payments are much smaller than outlays on food stamps.

Have transfer payments been growing as a fraction of GDP? Indeed, they have. All three categories of transfer programs have grown rapidly in recent decades. Figure 3 shows how *total* transfer payments as a percentage of GDP have trended upward.

In recent decades, transfers have been the fastest-growing part of federal government outlays and are currently equal to about 12.3 percent of GDP.

Growth in transfers relative to GDP was most rapid in the 1970s during the Nixon administration. During this period, government-financed retirement benefits

FIGURE 4
Federal Government Interest Payments as a Percentage of GDP

Federal interest payments relative to GDP rose rapidly during the 1980s as the national debt grew relative to GDP, then fell rapidly during the 1990s, as national debt fell relative to GDP. In spite of a rising debt-to-GDP ratio, interest payments relative to GDP have remained low in the 2000s, because interest rates have dropped.

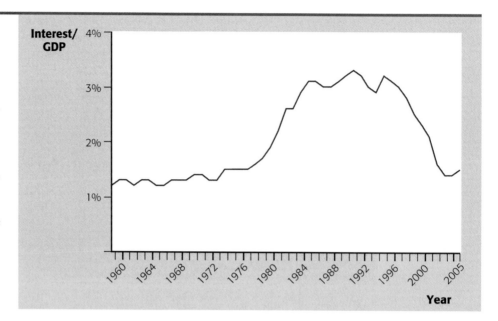

became much more generous, food stamps were introduced, and Medicare expanded. Since then, transfers have continued to rise modestly but are projected to soar as baby boomers retire and receive Social Security and Medicare benefits.

Notice, too, that transfers are sensitive to the ups and downs of the economy. Transfers as a fraction of GDP rise during recessions, as in 1974, 1981, 1991, and 2001. This is for two reasons. First, the number of needy recipients rises in a recession, so transfer payments—the numerator of the fraction—increase. Second, GDP—the denominator—falls in a recession. Similarly, transfers as a fraction of GDP tend to fall during expansions, such as the long expansion that ran from 1991 through early 2001. During expansions, the numerator of this fraction falls (why?), and the denominator rises. We will come back to these movements in transfers toward the end of the chapter.

Interest on the National Debt. Figure 4 shows the behavior of the third and smallest category of government spending: interest on the national debt. As you can see, interest as a percentage of GDP grew rapidly in the early 1980s, when the debt was growing and interest rates were rising. In the 1990s, interest as a fraction of GDP fell slowly at first, as growth in the debt slowed, and then fell dramatically as the national debt dropped from 1998 to 2001. Interest relative to GDP has remained low in the first half of the 2000s even though the national debt has been rising, because the Federal Reserve repeatedly lowered interest rates in 2001 and kept them very low through the first half of 2004.

Total Government Outlays. Figure 5 shows total outlays in relation to GDP over the past several decades. There are two important things to notice in the figure. The first is the *fluctuations* in government outlays over the period. There was a sharp increase in outlays in each recession (shaded) due to the jump in transfers that we saw in Figure 3. The recession of 1981–82 is a striking example. Also visible is the increase in military spending for the Vietnam War in the late 1960s.

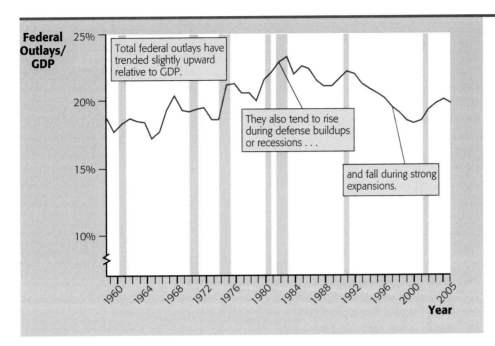

Federal Outlays/ GDP

Total federal outlays have trended slightly upward relative to GDP.

They also tend to rise during defense buildups or recessions . . .

and fall during strong expansions.

Year

FIGURE 5

Total Federal Outlays as a Percentage of GDP

The second thing to notice is the *upward trend* of federal outlays as a percentage of GDP:

> *For several decades up to the early 1990s, federal government outlays as a percentage of GDP drifted upward. The main causes were increases in transfer payments and increases in interest on the national debt that exceeded the decreases in military spending.*

Finally, notice the temporary *downward* movement in the mid- and late 1990s:

> *From 1992 to 2000, federal government outlays as a percentage of GDP fell. The main causes of the decline were sharp decreases in military spending (the "peace dividend"), and more modest decreases in transfer payments relative to GDP during a long expansion.*

However, Figure 5 also shows the appearance of a likely new trend:

> *In the first half of the 2000s, due to the ending of the "peace dividend" and continued increases in transfers, federal government outlays as a percentage of GDP began rising, and seem likely to continue rising through the decade.*

These trends in government outlays have important implications, but they are only half of the story. In order to understand their impact on the budget and the macroeconomy, we must look at the other side of the budget: tax revenue.

TABLE 1
Sources of Federal Revenue, 2003 (Estimated)

Source	Revenue (Billions of Dollars)	Percentage of Total Revenue
Personal income taxes	874	43%
Social Security taxes	794	39%
Corporate income taxes	230	11%
Excise taxes	73	4%
Other sources	65	3%
Total	2,036	

Source: Office of Management and Budget, *Budget of the United States Government, Fiscal Year 2006*, Historical Tables (Table 2.1).

Federal Tax Revenues

The federal government obtains most of its revenue from two sources: the personal income tax and the Social Security tax. Table 1 breaks down the revenue from these and other less-important sources.

The Personal Income Tax. The personal income tax is the most important source of revenue for the federal government and also the most conspicuous and painful. Almost every adult has to file Form 1040 or one of its shorter cousins. One of the signs of success as an American is seeing your federal tax return swell to the size of a magazine. Proposals to reduce both the amount of taxes people pay and the complexity of the tax forms are immensely popular.

Progressive tax A tax whose rate increases as income increases.

The personal income tax is designed to be **progressive**, to tax those at the higher end of the income scale at higher rates than those at the lower end of the scale, and to excuse the poorest families from paying any tax at all. Table 2 shows how the income tax works, in theory, by computing the amount of tax a family of four should have paid on its 2004 income if it took the standard deduction.[2] The table also shows the **average tax rate**—the fraction of total income a family pays in taxes—and the **marginal tax rate**—the tax rate paid on *each additional dollar* of income.

Average tax rate The fraction of a given income paid in taxes.

Marginal tax rate The fraction of an additional dollar of income paid in taxes.

We can see from Table 2 that the income tax is designed to be quite progressive. In principle, a family in the middle of the income distribution for married couples, earning $65,000 per year, should have paid about 9 percent of its income in taxes, while a family at the top should have paid almost 30 percent of its income in taxes. The table also shows that marginal tax rates on families with the highest income are in the range of 33 to 35 percent.

But the tax system shown in the table does not reflect the ways that people can avoid tax. Many people have deductions far above the standard deduction. Some people earn income that they never report to the government, thereby evading taxes entirely. And people can shelter income in their employer's retirement plan or in a

[2] The federal government allows households to deduct certain expenses (like medical care or the costs of moving to a new job) from their income before calculating the tax that they owe. Alternatively, they may deduct a standard amount (the *standard deduction*) from their income, regardless of their spending patterns.

Income	Tax	Average Tax Rate	Marginal Tax Rate
$ 10,000	$ 0	0%	0%
20,000	0	0	0
30,000	793	2.6	10
50,000	3,466	6.9	15
75,000	7,224	9.6	15
150,000	30,439	20.3	28
250,000	63,725	25.5	33
400,000	117,513	29.4	35

Source: Calculated from the 2004 Form 1040 tax table with the standard deduction of $9,700. First column shows income before standard deduction or deduction for dependents.

TABLE 2

The 2004 Personal Income Tax for a Married Couple with Two Children

plan of their own. Studies have shown that higher-income households avoid more taxes than poorer families and that the federal tax system—while still progressive—is much less progressive than suggested by Table 2.

Also, remember that we are looking at the *federal personal income* tax only. Households pay other taxes related to their income, some of which are **regressive**—taking a lower percentage in taxes as household income rises. For example, state and local sales taxes are regressive: Lower-income households *spend* a larger fraction of their incomes, so they pay a higher percentage of that income in sales taxes. Another example of a regressive tax is the federal payroll tax, earmarked to fund Social Security and Medicare, which we'll turn to now.

Regressive tax A tax that collects a lower percentage of income as income rises.

The Social Security Tax. The Social Security tax applies to wage and salary income only. It was put in place in 1936, to finance the Social Security system created in that year. Whereas the personal income tax is a nightmare of complex forms and rules, the Social Security tax is remarkably simple. The current tax rate (including the Medicare part of the tax) is a flat 15.3 percent,[3] except for one complication: Most of the tax is applied only on earnings below a certain amount ($90,000 in 2005, although the cap rises each year).

Because the payroll tax applies only to earnings below a certain level, it is regressive. For example, employees earning $90,000 or below in 2005 paid the full 15.3 percent of their income in taxes, while someone who earned twice that amount—$180,000—paid only 7.65 percent (since the tax applied to only half of their earnings). The Social Security tax is actually the largest tax paid by many Americans, especially those with lower incomes. These families pay little or no income tax, but pay the Social Security tax on all of their wage earnings. For example, a family with $30,000 of earnings in Table 2 would pay $793 in federal income tax, but Social Security taxes on those earnings would be $4,590.

HTTP://

The Congressional Budget Office maintains historical data on the U.S. federal budget. You can find it at http://www.cbo.gov/showdoc.cfm?index=1821&sequence=0&from=7#1.

[3] If you look at your own paycheck, it may seem that the Social Security tax (including Medicare) is only 7.65 percent instead of the 15.3 percent we've just mentioned. The reason is that your employer pays half the tax and you pay the other half. But the amount paid on your earnings is the sum, 15.3 percent.

Other Federal Taxes. Table 1 shows that the federal government also collects around $260 billion annually from other taxes aside from income and Social Security taxes. The most important of these is the *corporate profits tax*, which raised $230 billion in 2005 by taxing the profits earned by corporations at a rate of 35 percent.

The corporate profits tax is often criticized by economists because of two important problems. First, it applies only to corporations. Thus, a business owner can avoid it completely by setting up a sole proprietorship or partnership instead of a corporation. As a result, the tax causes many businesses to forego the benefits of being corporations because of the extra tax they would have to pay.

Second, the corporation tax results in *double taxation* on the portion of corporate profits that corporations pay to their owners. This portion of profits is taxed once when the corporation is taxed and again when the profits are included as part of the owners' personal income. The corporation tax is thus a prime target for tax reform. Almost all reform proposals put forward by economists involve integrating the taxation of corporations into the tax system in a way that avoids these two distortions.

The federal government also taxes the consumption of certain products, such as gasoline, alcohol, tobacco, and air travel. These are called *excise taxes*. Excise taxes raise additional revenue for the government, but they are usually put in place for other, nonrevenue reasons as well. The excise tax on gasoline is seen, in part, as a fee on drivers for the use of federal highways. The taxes on alcohol and tobacco are intended to discourage consumption of these harmful products.

Trends in Federal Tax Revenue. The top line in Figure 6 shows total federal government revenue, as a percentage of GDP, from all of the taxes we've discussed. Until recently, there was an upward trend. More specifically,

federal revenue trended upward from around 18 percent of GDP in the early 1960s to around 20 percent in the late 1990s.

But notice the sharp drop in the early 2000s. This was partly a short-run change (due to the very slow recovery from the 2001 recession) and partly the beginning of a new downward trend (due to significant long-term reductions in tax rates proposed by the Bush administration, and passed by Congress, in 2001 and 2003.)

In the early 2000s, federal tax revenues began a projected downward trend due to long-term reductions in tax rates.

We'll have much to say about these tax cuts in the "Using the Theory" section of this chapter.

Notice, also, that the *composition* of total federal revenue has changed dramatically. The lower two lines in Figure 6 show the part of federal revenue that comes from Social Security taxes and all other taxes. Notice the steady upward trend in Social Security tax revenue. Also notice that all other sources of revenue have trended slightly downward over the same period even before the sharp drop of the 2000s.

Why have Social Security taxes grown in importance? First, a little background. The Social Security system operates on a pay-as-you-go principle: It taxes people who are working now in order to pay benefits to those who worked earlier

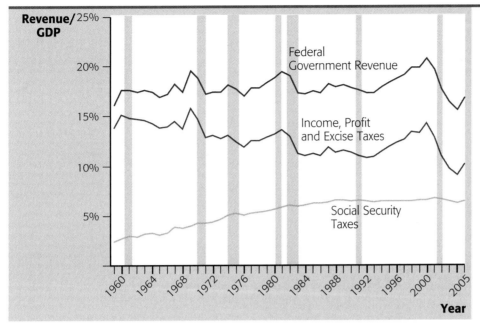

FIGURE 6

Federal Government Revenue as a Percentage of GDP

Until the 2000s, total federal revenue relative to GDP trended upward somewhat. But its composition has changed. All sources other than Social Security taxes have fallen relative to GDP while Social Security taxes have more than doubled relative to GDP.

and are now retired. For the first several decades after the system was established (in 1935), there were so few retirees that benefits could be funded with very low payroll tax rates on those currently working.

But now, demographic trends are working against the system. First, improved health is allowing people to spend a larger fraction of their lives in retirement. That is good from a human perspective, but from an accounting point of view, it means that the average retiree is drawing more benefits. At the same time, the baby boomers will begin retiring en masse in the late 2000s, which means greater *numbers* of people drawing benefits. Finally, these increased benefits will be funded by a smaller number of working taxpayers.

Anticipating these trends, the government had been raising Social Security tax rates for years, not just to keep the system solvent, but to go further—building up reserves in a separate government account (called the Social Security Trust Fund) for retiring baby boomers. This helped to create the rising Social Security tax line in Figure 6.

Note that keeping Social Security reserves in a separate trust fund makes little difference for policy. Its main importance has been psychological and political: making retirees and future retirees feel confident that the money was being held for them.

But the trust fund has imposed no constraints on Congress, legal or economic. In fact, the reserves built up in the trust fund have been (and continue to be) borrowed by the Treasury and spent on other government programs. Meanwhile, Congress has been (and continues to be) free to raise or lower social security benefits as it wishes, regardless of the balance in the trust fund.

Thus, the rising social security tax line in Figure 6—while it helped to fund past government outlays—did not "solve" the real social security problem. That problem is: Beginning in 2008, scheduled social security benefits as a percentage of GDP will begin rising (due to retiring baby boomers). Around the same time, payroll tax revenues as a percentage of GDP will begin falling (fewer baby boomers working and paying taxes). Similar but even larger changes will be occurring in Medicare, the government health program for retirees.

This combination—greater total benefits relative to GDP, and lower payroll taxes relative to GDP to pay for them—forces the country to choose among four unpleasant alternatives: (1) raise the payroll tax rate (or other tax rates) on current workers; (2) cut future retirement and/or health benefits as a fraction of GDP (say, by raising the retirement age, or cut projected growth of benefits for each retiree); (3) reduce *other* government outlays relative to GDP to pay the greater benefits; or (4) allow the overall annual buget deficit relative to GDP to rise.. (The last option occurs automatically if none of the others are chosen.) By mid-2005, it was still unclear which one (or combination) of these unpleasant options the country would ultimately choose.

HTTP://

Try your hand at managing the budget by using the National Budget Simulation at http://www.budgetsim.org/nbs.

The Federal Budget and the National Debt

Finally, we can bring together what we've learned about the government's tax revenue with what we've learned about the government's outlays (on purchases, transfers, and net interest). Look first at the upper panel in Figure 7. This shows total federal outlays (from Figure 5) and total federal revenue (from the top line in Figure 6). The difference between these two lines in any year is the federal budget deficit (when outlays exceed revenue) or surplus (when revenue exceeds outlays).

$$\text{Budget Surplus} = \text{Tax Revenue} - \text{Outlays}$$

$$\text{Budget Deficit} = \text{Outlays} - \text{Tax Revenue}[4]$$

The bottom panel shows the history of the budget in recent decades, with surpluses as positive values and deficits as negative values.[5] The lower panel looks much choppier because the scale of the diagram is different there. But you can see that there was a dramatic change in the behavior of the budget around 1975. Until that year, the government mostly ran deficits, but rarely more than 2 percent of GDP. But from 1975 until 1993, the deficit grew significantly. During that period, it was usually greater than 3 percent of GDP, and often more than 4 percent. Notice, for example, the especially large rise in the deficit that occurred in the early 1980s. This was the combined result of a severe recession, which caused

---

[4] Other than our current inclusion of interest payments as a category of government outlays, these are the same definitions given earlier in the text. To see this, just ignore interest payments in this chapter's definition of the deficit:

$$\begin{aligned}\text{Budget Deficit} &= \text{Outlays} - \text{Tax Revenue} \\ &= (\text{Government Purchases} + \text{Transfers}) - \text{Tax Revenue} \\ &= \text{Government Purchases} - (\text{Tax Revenue} - \text{Transfers}) \\ &= G - T\end{aligned}$$

The last line is the definition for the deficit given in the chapter on the classical model, where G is government purchases in GDP and T is net taxes.

[5] To measure the deficit or surplus, we have included all sources of federal revenue and all types of spending, whether part of the official federal budget or not. In particular, we've included Social Security taxes and Social Security payments even though they are officially considered "off budget" in U.S. government statistics.

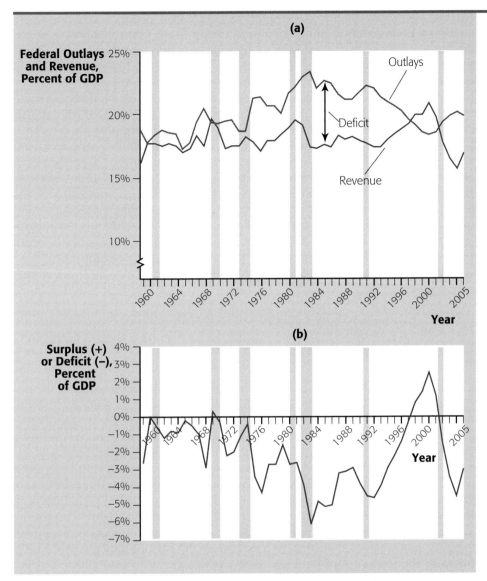

(a)

Federal Outlays and Revenue, Percent of GDP

Outlays

Deficit

Revenue

Year

(b)

Surplus (+) or Deficit (−), Percent of GDP

Year

FIGURE 7

The Federal Budget Deficit or Surplus as a Percentage of GDP

In any given year, the federal deficit (relative to GDP) is the difference between total federal revenue and total federal outlays relative to GDP. The deficit rises in recessions and after large tax cuts. Both occurred in the early 1980s and again in the early 2000s.

transfers to rise as shown in Figure 3, the buildup in military spending shown in Figure 1, and a large cut in income taxes during President Reagan's first term in office.

In the mid-1990s, the deficit began to come down, and finally, in the late 1990s, the federal government began running budget surpluses for a few years. But from 2002 to 2005, the budget was back into deficit, and the deficits were projected to continue through the end of the decade. Even though the world has changed much since the 1980s, the reasons for the deficits of the 2000s seem like a repeat of history: a recession, increased military spending, and a sizable, multi-year tax cut.

The National Debt. Before we consider the government's budget further, we need to address some common confusion among three related, but very different, terms: the federal *deficit,* the federal *surplus,* and the national *debt.* The federal deficit and surplus are *flow* variables: They measure the difference between government spending and tax revenue *over a given period,* usually a year. The national debt, by contrast, is a *stock* variable: It measures the total amount that the federal government owes *at a given point in time.* (See the chapter "Economic Growth and Rising Living Standards" if you need a refresher on stocks and flows.)

The relationship between these terms is this: Each year that the government runs a deficit, it must borrow funds to finance it, *adding to the national debt.* For example, in 1996, the federal government ran a deficit of $107 billion. During that year, it issued about $107 billion in new government bonds, adding that much to the national debt. On the other hand, if the government runs a surplus, it uses the surplus to *pay back* some of the national debt. For example, in 2000, the federal government ran a surplus of about $236 billion. That year, it purchased about that much in government bonds it had issued in the past, thus reducing the national debt.[6]

We can measure the national debt as the total value of government bonds held by the public. Thus,

> *deficits—which add to the public's holdings of government bonds—add to the national debt. Surpluses—which decrease the public's bond holdings—subtract from the national debt.*

Since the cumulative total of the government's deficits has been greater than its surpluses, the national debt has grown over the past several decades. For most of this period, it has also grown relative to GDP, as shown in Figure 8.

The rise and fall in the national debt also explains another trend we discussed earlier: the rise and fall in *interest payments* the government must make to those who hold government bonds. All else equal, the larger the national debt, the greater will be the government's yearly interest payments on the debt. As you saw in Figure 4, total interest payments rose rapidly during the 1980s—the same period in which the national debt zoomed upward. In the 1990s, as the national debt decreased relative to GDP, so did interest payments on the debt. If you compare Figure 4 with Figure 8, however, you'll see that, as a percentage of GDP, the national debt rose in the early 2000s while yearly interest payments fell. That's because all else was *not* equal during this period: As mentioned earlier, the Federal Reserve dramatically lowered interest rates in the early 2000s, which reduced the government's interest payments on each dollar of newly issued debt.

Now that we've outlined the recent history of federal government spending, taxes, and debt, we turn our attention to the relationship between fiscal changes and the economy.

THE EFFECTS OF FISCAL CHANGES IN THE SHORT RUN

In the short run, there is a two-way relationship between the government's budget and the macroeconomy. On the one hand, changes in the economy affect the gov-

---

[6] The increase or decrease in the national debt is never exactly the same as the annual deficit or surplus, because of accounting details.

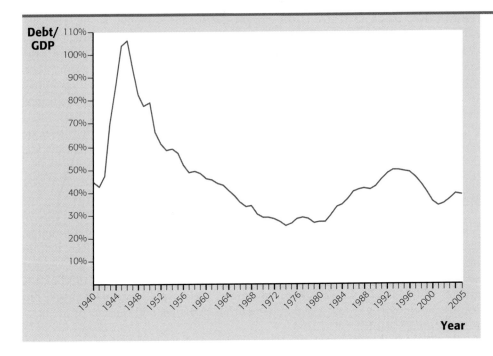

FIGURE 8

Federal Debt as a Percentage of GDP

Federal debt (the national debt) relative to GDP soared during World War II then fell steadily for several decades. It rose during the 1980s due to a combination of tax cuts and defense buildups during the Reagan administration, then fell during the shrinking deficits and expansion of the 1990s. In the early 2000s, a combination of recession and slow recovery, tax cuts and defense spending caused the debt-GDP ratio to begin rising.

Source: Office of Management and Budget. *Historical Tables, Budget of the United States Government, Fiscal Year 2003*, Table 7.1.

ernment's outlays and taxes; on the other hand, changes in outlays and taxes affect the economy. Let's begin by considering how economic fluctuations affect the government's budget.

How Economic Fluctuations Affect the Federal Budget

Economic fluctuations affect both transfer payments and tax revenues. In a recession, in which many people lose their jobs, the federal government contributes larger amounts to state-run unemployment insurance systems and pays more in transfers to the poor, since more families qualify for these types of assistance. Thus, a recession causes transfer payments to rise. Recessions also cause a drop in tax revenue, because household income and corporate profits—two important sources of tax revenue—decrease during recessions.

> *In a recession, because transfers rise and tax revenue falls, the federal budget deficit increases (or the surplus decreases).*

An expansion has the opposite effect on the federal budget: With lower unemployment and higher levels of output and income, federal transfers decrease and tax revenues increase. Thus,

> *in an expansion, because transfers decrease and tax revenue rises, the budget deficit decreases (or the surplus increases).*

Because the business cycle has systematic effects on spending and revenue, economists find it useful to divide the deficit into two components. The **cyclical deficit** is

Cyclical deficit The part of the federal budget deficit that varies with the business cycle.

the part that can be attributed to the current state of the economy. We have a cyclical deficit when output is below potential GDP, and a cyclical surplus when output is above potential. When the economy is operating just at full employment, the cyclical deficit is, by definition, zero.

Structural deficit The part of the federal budget deficit that is independent of the business cycle.

The **structural deficit** is the part of the deficit that is *not* caused by economic fluctuations. As the economy recovers from a recession, for example, the cyclical deficit goes away, but any structural deficit in the budget will remain.

Cyclical changes in the budget are not a cause for concern, because they average out to about zero, as output fluctuates above and below potential output. Thus, the cyclical deficit should not contribute to a long-run rise in the national debt.

How the Budget Affects Economic Fluctuations

Budget changes that occur automatically during expansions and recessions—that is, changes in the cyclical deficit or surplus—have an important impact: They help to make economic fluctuations milder than they would otherwise be. Recall that spending shocks have a multiplier effect on output. The larger the multiplier, the greater will be the fluctuations in output caused by any given spending shock. But changes in the cyclical deficit make the multiplier *smaller,* and thus act as an *automatic stabilizer.* How?

Let's use unemployment insurance as an example. In normal times, with the unemployment rate at around, say, 4.5 percent or lower, federal transfers for unemployment insurance are modest. But when a negative spending shock hits the economy, and output and income begin to fall, the unemployment rate rises. Federal transfers for unemployment insurance rise *automatically.* Without assistance from the government, many of the newly unemployed would have to cut back their consumption spending substantially. But unemployment insurance cushions the blow for many such families—at least for six months or sometimes longer—allowing them to make smaller cutbacks in consumption during that time. As a result, the total decline in consumption is smaller and GDP declines by less. Unemployment insurance thus reduces the multiplier.

Other transfer programs have a similar stabilizing effect on output. More people receive food stamps during recessions. Consequently, their consumption falls by less than it would if they did not have this help. And the tax system contributes to economic stability in a similar way. Income tax payments, for example, fall during a recession. With the government siphoning off a smaller amount of income from the household sector, the drop in consumption is smaller than it would be if tax revenues remained constant.

The same principle applies when a positive spending shock hits the economy. Transfer payments automatically decline, as the unemployed find jobs and fewer families qualify for government assistance. And tax revenues automatically rise, since income rises. As a result, the positive spending shock causes a smaller rise in GDP than would otherwise occur.

Many features of the federal tax and transfer systems act as automatic stabilizers. As the economy goes into a recession, these features help to reduce the decline in consumption spending, and they also cause the cyclical deficit to rise. As the economy goes into an expansion, these features help to reduce the rise in consumption spending, and they also cause the cyclical deficit to fall.

This immediately raises a question: If *automatic* changes in the budget help to stabilize the economy, can the government *purposely* change its spending or tax policy to make the economy even more stable?

Countercyclical Fiscal Policy

When the government uses fiscal policy to keep the economy closer to potential GDP in the short run, it is engaging in **countercyclical fiscal policy**. The government's tools in this effort are changes in government purchases, or changes in policy toward taxes or transfers. Notice the phrase "changes in policy"; the automatic changes in taxes or transfers that occur during the business cycle are not considered countercyclical fiscal policy because these occur without any government action.

Countercyclical fiscal policy
Changes in taxes or government spending designed to counteract economic fluctuations.

Figure 9 illustrates the idea behind countercyclical fiscal policy. It shows the aggregate expenditure line for an economy that is initially operating at point *A,* with full-employment output of $10 trillion. Now suppose that investment spending decreases. The aggregate expenditure line will start to shift downward, and the economy will begin heading toward point *B,* where—in the absence of government action—output would settle at $9 trillion. Note that, even if the government does nothing, automatic stabilizers will be at work: As output heads toward its new equilibrium of $9 trillion, tax revenue falls and transfers rise. In fact, without these stabilizers, output would decline further.[7]

But in theory, the government could try to *prevent* the recession with countercyclical fiscal policy. At the first signs of a contraction, it could increase government purchases (say, hiring more people to work with children in after-school programs). Alternatively, the government could increase transfers (further than they are rising automatically) with a change in policy—say, increasing the amount of unemployment insurance benefits paid to each unemployed worker. Or the government could decrease tax revenue (further than it is falling already) with a change in tax policy—say, an across-the-board decrease in everyone's income tax rate. Any of these actions would work to shift up the aggregate expenditure line. If taken early enough, the government could even stop the downward shift in its tracks and keep the economy close to full employment.

In the 1960s and 1970s, many economists and government officials believed that countercyclical fiscal policy could be an effective tool to counteract the business cycle. Today, however, economists tend to be more skeptical. Instead, they would put the Fed in charge of stabilizing the economy and reserve fiscal policy for addressing long-run issues of resource allocation. Why? Because countercyclical fiscal policy is plagued with several problems.

Timing Problems. It takes many months or even longer for most fiscal changes to be enacted. Consider, for example, a decision to decrease taxes in the United States. A tax bill originates in the House of Representatives and then goes to the Senate, where it is usually modified. Then a conference committee irons out the differences between the House and Senate versions, and the tax bill goes back to each chamber

---

[7] We've been drawing the aggregate expenditure line with a slope equal to the marginal propensity to consume. In more advanced treatments, automatic stabilizers are built into the slope of the aggregate expenditure line, making it flatter (a slope *less* than the MPC). With some experimentation, you can show that the flatter the line, the less any given decrease in investment spending will decrease equilibrium GDP.

FIGURE 9
Countercyclical Fiscal Policy

Initially, the economy's equilibrium is at full-employment output of $10,000 billion (point A). Then a decrease in investment spending shifts the aggregate expenditure line down to AE$_2$, and the economy starts heading toward point B—a recession. The government could shift the AE line back to its original position by increasing its own purchases, or by decreasing net taxes with a change in tax or transfer policies. If the change were enacted quickly enough, the government could prevent the recession.

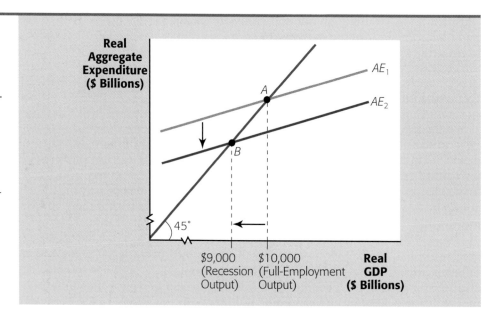

for a vote. Once the legislation has passed, the president must sign it. Even if all goes smoothly, this process can take many months.

But in most cases, it will *not* go smoothly. First, there is the thorny question of *distributing* the benefits of any total tax cut among different groups within the country—an issue about which Democrats and Republicans rarely agree. And some senators and representatives will see the bill as an opportunity to change the tax system in more fundamental ways, causing further political debate. All of these problems create the danger that the tax cut will take effect long after it is needed—stimulating the economy after it has recovered from recession and is beginning to overheat.

The same timing problem occurs in the opposite situation—when a tax hike is needed to counteract a boom—or when the fiscal policy is implemented through changes in government purchases or transfers. Because of delays, regular use of fiscal policy would be a *destabilizing* force in the economy—stepping on the gas when we should be hitting the brakes, or vice versa.

The Fed, by contrast, can increase or decrease the money supply *on the very day it decides that the change is necessary*. While there are time lags in the *effectiveness* of monetary policy (see the previous chapter), the ability to execute the policy in short order gives monetary policy an important advantage over fiscal policy for stabilizing the economy.

Irreversibility. To be effective, countercyclical fiscal policy must be reversible. In our example in Figure 9, a fiscal change is needed to counteract a decrease in investment spending. Therefore, once investment spending returns to normal levels, the fiscal stimulation should be reversed as well, so as not to overheat the economy. But reversing changes in government purchases or taxes is difficult. Spending programs that create new government departments or expand existing ones tend to become permanent, or at least difficult to terminate. Many temporary tax changes become permanent as well; the public is never happy to see a tax cut reversed, and the government is often reluctant to reverse a tax hike that has provided additional revenue for government programs.

Reversing monetary policy, while not painless, is easier to do. Fed governors are appointed to long terms and never have to stand for reelection. Thus, the Fed is at least somewhat insulated from the political process as it makes its decisions. Moreover, the public and Congress have largely accepted the Fed's role in stabilizing the economy, and expect that the interest rate will be adjusted as the condition of the economy changes.

The Fed's Reaction. Even if the government attempted to stabilize the economy with fiscal policy, it could usually not do so very effectively, because—to put it simply—the Fed would not allow it. The Fed views most changes in fiscal policy just as it views other changes in aggregate expenditure: as a change to be neutralized. In Figure 9, if the Fed had perceived that the aggregate expenditure line was beginning to shift downward, it would have *already* lowered its interest rate target, long before any fiscal change was enacted. The fiscal stimulus, when it finally took effect, would be counteracted with an offsetting rise in the interest rate target. As long as the Fed remains free to set its own course, and sees its goal as stabilizing the economy at full employment with low inflation, there is generally no opportunity—and no need—for countercyclical fiscal policy. (An exception discussed in the previous chapter is the very special circumstance in which the Fed has pushed the federal funds rate to zero, and exhausted all other tools to stimulate the economy out of a recession. In that case, fiscal policy would be an effective backup.)

THE EFFECTS OF FISCAL CHANGES IN THE LONG RUN

Fiscal changes have important effects on the economy over the long run. And, as you've learned, the classical model—which focuses on the determinants of potential output—provides a useful framework for analyzing these long-run effects.

Let's first list three important conclusions about fiscal policy in the classical model that you learned in earlier chapters:

- The government's tax and transfer policies can influence the rate of labor force participation. For example, higher tax rates on labor income (or household income, generally) or more generous transfers can reduce the labor force participation rate, and *decrease* the average standard of living. Lower tax rates or less generous transfers can raise the labor force participation rate and raise the standard of living.

- The government's tax policies can directly influence the rate of investment spending on new capital and R&D. Higher tax rates on the profits from investment projects will

Deficits and Growth: A Proviso This section has argued that rising deficits over the long run will come at the cost of lower investment spending and therefore reduce the rate of economic growth. But this is not *always* the case. It depends on what causes the deficit to increase. If the rise in the deficit results from a long-run rise in, say, transfer payments, the effects on growth will be negative. But suppose the deficit arises from an increase in government spending to improve the legal, financial, and physical infrastructure of the economy, or to improve education. All of these types of spending contribute to economic growth themselves. Thus, even if the deficits caused by this higher government spending crowd out private investment, their net effect on growth could be favorable.

DANGEROUS CURVES

lower investment spending and lead to slower growth in the average standard of living. Lower tax rates or other investment incentives will increase investment spending and lead to faster growth in living standards.

- The government's budget deficit can influence investment spending as well. An increase in the budget deficit causes the government to demand more loanable funds. This raises the interest rate, lowers investment spending, and slows the growth in living standards. Lower budget deficits reduce the government's demand for loanable funds, resulting in a lower interest rate, greater investment spending, and faster growth in living standards.

And, from this chapter, you've learned the following:

- Budget deficits add to the national debt.

But what are the *consequences* of adding to the national debt? Because there are so many widely held myths about this subject, it deserves a section of its own.

The National Debt

On a billboard in midtown Manhattan, a giant clocklike digital display tracks the U.S. national debt up to the second. In mid-2005, as the clock headed toward $8 trillion (rising by $761,000 per minute), the last four digits on the display changed so rapidly that they appeared as a blur.

The national debt clock was one of several public relations campaigns that spread fear among the American public.[8] How could we ever hope to repay all of this debt? Surely, we were speeding toward a debt disaster.

Economists do have concerns about the national debt. But they are very different from the concerns suggested by the national debt clock or other similar gimmicks.

Mythical Concerns About the National Debt. What bothers many people about a growing national debt is the belief that one day we will have to pay it all back. But although we might *choose* to repay the national debt, we do not have to. *Ever.* Moreover, there is nothing automatically wrong with a national debt that *grows* every year. That may sound surprising. How could a government keep borrowing funds without ever paying them back? Surely, no business could behave that way.

But actually, many successful businesses *do* behave that way. For example, the debt of many major corporations—like Pfizer and Verizon—continues to grow, year after year. While they continue to pay interest on their debt, they may have no plans to pay back the amount originally borrowed. As these companies' bonds become due, they simply *roll them over;* they issue new bonds to pay back the old ones.

Why don't these firms pay back their debt? Because they believe they have a better use for their funds: investing in new capital equipment and research and development to expand their businesses. This will lead to higher future profits.

---

[8] You can find similar debt clocks on the web (google "national debt clock"). But keep in mind that they all exaggerate the burden by using "total national debt," which includes amounts that one government agency owes to another. In mid-2005, when "total national debt" was approaching $8 trillion, the more relevant "publicly held debt" (what the government owed to everyone but itself) was $4.5 trillion.

Of course, this does not mean that *any* size debt would be prudent. Recall the important principle we discussed earlier in the chapter: *Debt and interest payments have meaning only in relation to income.* If a firm's income is growing by 5 percent each year, but its interest payments are growing by 10 percent per year, it would eventually find itself in trouble. Each year, its interest payments would take a larger and larger fraction of its income, and at some point interest payments would exceed total income. But even *before* this occurred, the firm would find itself in trouble. Lenders, anticipating the firm's eventual inability to pay interest, would cut the firm off. At that point, the firm would reach its *credit limit*—the maximum amount it can borrow based on lenders' willingness to lend. Since it could no longer roll over its existing debt with further borrowing, it would have to pay back any bonds coming due until its debt was comfortably below its credit limit.

All of these observations apply to the federal government as well. As long as the nation's total income is rising, the government can safely take on more debt. More specifically, if the nation's income is growing at least as fast as total interest payments, the debt can continue to grow indefinitely, without putting the government in danger.

The federal government *could* pay back the national debt—by running budget surpluses for many years. But the government could also choose to behave like most corporations and *not* pay back its debt. In fact, the government would better serve the public by not paying down the debt if it has better uses for its revenue than debt repayment.

But how rapidly could the government continue to accumulate debt? Or, equivalently, how large could annual deficits be without making the national debt a looming danger?

Let's see. As long as total national income grows at least as fast as interest payments on the debt, the ratio of interest payments to income will not grow. In that case, we could continue to pay interest without increasing the average tax rate on U.S. citizens. Let's use some round numbers to make this clearer. Suppose that the nominal GDP is $10 trillion and the national debt is $5 trillion. And suppose that annual interest payments average out to 7 percent of the national debt, or $350 billion. Then the ratio of interest payments to nominal GDP would be $350 billion/$10 trillion = 0.035 or 3.5 percent of GDP. Now suppose that, over some period of time, both nominal GDP and the national debt double, to $20 trillion and $10 trillion, respectively. Then interest payments would double as well, to $700 billion. But the ratio of interest payments to nominal GDP would remain constant, at $700 billion/$20 trillion = 0.035.

More generally,

> as long as the debt grows by the same percentage as nominal GDP, the ratios of debt to GDP and interest payments to GDP will remain constant. In this case, the government can continue to pay interest on its rising debt without increasing the average tax rate in the economy.

Genuine Concerns About the National Debt. When *should* we be concerned about a growing national debt? Our previous discussion has hinted at three scenarios that should cause concern.

A National Debt That Is Growing Too Rapidly. An important *minimal guideline* for responsible government is that the debt should grow no faster than nominal GDP. Whenever that guideline is violated, interest payments as a fraction of GDP rise, and the average tax burden on the public—taxes relative to GDP—grows. The violation cannot go on forever, because the tax burden has a mathematical upper limit of 100 percent of GDP. And even before that limit was reached, tax rates would become oppressive, harming growth and—if pushed too high—actually reducing living standards. However, if the violation of the guideline is temporary, and the debt begins growing at the same rate as nominal GDP again, tax payments as a fraction of GDP stop rising.

This has two important implications. First, to prevent a long-term disaster after too-rapid growth in the debt, we do not have to run budget surpluses. A surplus is only necessary if the goal is to reduce the *total* debt. But all that is required to put the economy on a *responsible path* is a reduction of the growth rate of the debt back to the growth rate of nominal GDP. After that, we can keep running deficits and the debt can keep rising indefinitely, as long as it rises no faster than nominal GDP.

But there is a second implication as well: Even a temporary violation of the guideline is costly. During the time that debt grows faster than nominal GDP, the tax burden rises. Then, after the debt starts growing at the same rate as nominal GDP again, the tax burden stops rising—but *the burden remains at its new, higher level.* Thus, while a temporary violation of the guideline does not mean a disaster, it *does* leave us with a permanently elevated tax burden . . . at least, until we do something about it.

How can the tax burden be brought back down after a temporary violation of the guideline? There are only two basic ways: (1) raise the growth rate of nominal GDP *above* the growth rate of the debt for some time; or (2) lower the growth rate of the debt below the growth rate of nominal GDP for some time. Either of these solutions could return the debt-to-GDP ratio back to its original level, so that interest payments relative to GDP and the tax burden could return to their original levels as well.

But these solutions are costly to society. Let's consider (1): raising the growth rate of nominal GDP. Since policy has only limited ability to influence the growth rate of *real* GDP over long periods, the only practical method to ensure a higher growth rate of *nominal* GDP is faster growth in the price level. This means allowing the inflation rate to rise for some time. But we've already seen that allowing the inflation rate to rise can be costly for society in numerous ways—including the buildup of inflationary expectations that would be difficult to reverse.

Now let's consider (2): slowing down the growth rate of the debt below the growth rate of nominal GDP. The only way to do this is to run *smaller deficits* as a fraction of GDP than we would otherwise be able to run. And the only way to reduce the deficit for some length of time is to raise tax rates or reduce government outlays during that period.

Thus,

> *a debt that rises too fast—faster than nominal GDP—for some period of time will impose an opportunity cost in the future. The cost will be either a permanently higher tax burden, a period of inflation, or a temporary period of reduced government outlays or higher taxes relative to GDP.*

This is not just theoretical, as the U.S. experience during the 1970s and 1980s demonstrates. During this time, nominal GDP was growing at about 9 percent per year—mostly due to increases in the price level. But the debt grew by an average of 11 percent per year, beyond the minimal guidelines for responsible government. The debt-to-GDP ratio therefore rose (see Figure 8) and so did interest payments relative to GDP (see Figure 4). This could not go on indefinitely, or interest payments on the debt would require an ever-larger share of GDP. How did we solve the problem? As we entered the 1990s, we gradually shrunk the budget deficit with higher tax rates and strict limits on the growth of government spending. Fortunately, the 1990s was a period of prolonged expansion and reduced military purchases, so lowering the deficit was not as painful as it might otherwise have been.

A Debt Approaching a National Credit Limit. If debt were to rise *too* rapidly relative to GDP, for *too* long, there is a theoretical danger of reaching the nation's credit limit—the amount of debt that would make lenders worry about the government's ability to continue paying interest. If this credit limit were approached, a nation would be truly flirting with disaster: a tiny increase in the ratio of debt to GDP would lead to a cutoff of further lending and require that the budget be balanced immediately. It could also cause a financial panic, with everyone trying to sell their government bonds at the same time, causing bond prices to fall and household wealth to plummet.

While this is *theoretically* possible, it's doubtful the U.S. will be anywhere near that type of limit in the next decade. Look at Figure 8. At the end of World War II, the debt reached 109 percent of GDP—almost triple its current percentage. Even then, no one doubted the U.S. government would continue to honor its obligations.

However, in the 2000s, economists have had a related concern. Roughly 45 percent of the "public" holding the U.S. national debt are foreigners. While they still have faith that the U.S. will honor its obligations, they may nevertheless have an upper limit on the proportion of total wealth they want to hold in dollar-denominated assets (say, to limit their risk in case the dollar falls in value against their own currency). If U.S. debt grows too rapidly, and foreigners find themselves with too much dollar-denominated wealth, they could suddenly, simultaneously, begin selling their U.S. bonds.

> *It is highly unlikely U.S. debt levels will approach an absolute credit limit based on loss of faith in the U.S. government. A more realistic concern is that rapidly rising debt causes foreign wealth portfolios to become too "dollar-heavy," leading to a destabilizing sell-off of U.S. bonds.*

We'll come back to this foreign-held debt in the chapter on exchange rates and macroeconomic policy.

Failing to Account for Future Obligations. Many students reading this book are getting financial help from parents to pay the costs of college. Planning for this obligation may have begun very early—perhaps even before you knew what college was. This makes sense: If a family wants to avoid a drastic decrease in its standard of living in the future, it should start accounting for future obligations early.

The federal government is in an analogous situation. It has effectively promised to provide Medicare and Social Security payments to millions of people at some time in the future. If we assume no changes in scheduled benefit policies, and if current cost trends continue, Social Security, Medicare, and Medicaid benefits are projected to rise significantly and continually over the next 75 years—from 8.5 percent of GDP in 2004 to 26.4 percent in 2050. If the federal government is to act like a responsible household, it should take these future obligations into account in its planning process. Otherwise, we may have to dramatically decrease *other* government outlays, dramatically increase taxes, or have an ever-rising debt-to-GDP ratio, leading to the dangers discussed earlier.

Of course, trying to project total federal revenues and outlays over the next 50 years is guesswork at best. Even official forecasts of *10-year* projections are typically widely off the mark. In 1989, for example, when the government made its fiscal projections for 1990–1999, no one could have predicted the development of the Internet and other technologies, and the rapid economic growth that would accompany them. And in 1999, when projections for 2000–2009 were completed, who could have predicted the events of September 11, 2001, and how it would change our spending on national defense and homeland security?

This uncertainty over future projections has led to divergent views about policy. Some argue that a responsible government should be exceedingly cautious, running budget surpluses now, paying down the national debt, and leaving us better prepared for any dramatic future rise in government outlays. Others argue that preparing for the worst would require huge sacrifices in the present—sacrifices that might be completely unnecessary in hindsight.

These divergent views formed part of the background for the controversy over the Bush tax cuts.

© WWW.OMB.GOV

USING THE THEORY
The Bush Tax Cuts of 2001 and 2003

In 2001, the Bush administration cut taxes over 10 years by $1.35 trillion, and in 2003, by another $350 billion. Marginal tax rates were reduced on all income brackets, as were tax rates on capital gains and dividends. There were additional reductions for taxpayers with children, and a reduction of the "marriage penalty" that taxed married couples at higher rates than if they were single. Also, the tax cuts in 2003 accelerated some of the 2001 reductions that had originally been postponed until 2006 and beyond.

Much of the debate over the tax reductions had to do with distribution: whether the cuts were apportioned fairly among different income groups. But they also raised two important macroeconomic issues that we've discussed in this chapter.

The Short Run: Countercyclical Fiscal Policy?

The tax cuts of 2001 and 2003 seem, at first glance, like perfect examples of well-timed countercyclical fiscal policy. After all, the first cuts were put in place in June 2001—in the middle of a recession that began just three months earlier. And the cuts in May 2003 took effect as the economy was still struggling with the weak expansion and joblessness of 2002 and 2003 (see the chapter "Aggregate Demand and Aggregate Supply") Does this show that countercyclical fiscal policy works?

Not really, because a closer look suggests that neither tax cut was really designed for that purpose. The tax cut of June 2001 had actually been proposed more than 18 months earlier by presidential candidate Bush as a long-run policy measure, to promote growth in potential output. At the time, the economy was in a boom, and the Federal Reserve was actively trying to slow it down. The fact that the tax cut was enacted during a recession was a stroke of luck, not an example of well-timed short-run fiscal policy.

Moreover, remember that countercyclical fiscal policy requires that changes in taxes be reversible when economic conditions change. But both of the Bush tax cuts were *long-term* policy changes: Some of their provisions applied through the end of the decade, and the others were expected to be extended at least that long, and probably beyond.

As so often happens in macroeconomic debates, however, politics took over. As the economy entered the recession of 2001, the debate over the 2001 tax cut quickly shifted to its short-run stimulus potential. And the 2003 cut—weighted heavily toward long-run reforms in the tax code—was both touted and opposed almost entirely on the basis of its ability to create jobs in the short run, during a slow recovery.

In between these two cuts, however, the Bush administration proposed a purely countercyclical, $60 billion tax cut. This was formulated and designed as an emergency measure, shortly after September 11, 2001, to prevent the economy from sliding further into recession. Timing was crucial, and the administration urged quick passage by Congress. If there was ever an opportunity to showcase the effectiveness of countercyclical fiscal policy, this was it. But the tax bill was debated for a full six months in the House and Senate, and was not signed by the president until March 2002. During these six months of debate, the Fed reduced its interest rate target four times, illustrating the greater flexibility of monetary policy as a countercyclical tool.

The Long Run: The Tax Cuts and the National Debt

Now let's consider the **long-run** macroeconomic controversies raised by the tax cuts. Table 3 shows two different projections of budget deficits and the national debt both issued less than two months after the 2003 tax cuts were signed into law. Let's start with the upper half of the table, which shows numbers released by the administration's Office of Management and Budget (OMB) as part of its midyear budget update in July 2003. The second column shows the projected deficit in each fiscal year, ending in September of the year indicated. The deficit is approximately equal to the rise in the debt from the end of the previous year to the end of the current year. For example, in 2005, the projected deficit was $304 billion, and the debt was expected to rise from $4,473 billion at the end of 2004 to $4,789 billion at the end of 2005, a rise of $4,789 − $4,473 = $316 billion. (The difference between the deficit and the annual rise in the debt is due to technical factors in measuring the official debt.)

Judging by the OMB's numbers, it appeared that the administration's fiscal policy was an example of a temporary violation of the guideline for responsible government: Debt would rise faster than GDP through 2006, and then stabilize and descend. (In 2003, the government issued only a 5-year projection, instead

TABLE 3
Projected Budget Deficits and the Rising National Debt

(a) Office of Management and Budget (White House) Projections

	Deficit: ($billion)	Debt (End of year) ($billion)	Nominal GDP ($billion)	Debt as Percentage of GDP
2002 (actual)	$158	$3,540	$10,446	33.8%
2003	$455	$4,036	$10,757	37.5%
2004	$475	$4,473	$11,303	39.6%
2005	$304	$4,789	$11,884	40.3%
2006	$238	$5,043	$12,483	40.4%
2007	$213	$5,272	$13,104	40.2%
2008	$226	$5,516	$13,752	40.1%

(b) House Budget Committee—Democratic Caucus Projections

	Deficit ($billion)	Debt (End of year) ($billion)	Nominal GDP ($billion)	Debt as Percentage of GDP
2002 (actual)	$158	$3,540	$10,446	33.8%
2003	$416	$3,956	$10,757	36.8%
2004	$489	$4,455	$11,303	39.4%
2005	$364	$4,809	$11,884	40.0%
2006	$345	$5,154	$12,483	41.3%
2007	$329	$5,483	$13,104	41.8%
2008	$343	$5,826	$13,752	42.4%
. . .				
2013	$2,090 (cumulative, 2009–2013)	$7,915	$17,505	45.2%

Sources: Office of Management and Budget, *Fiscal Year Budget, 2004,* Table 20, "Federal Government Financing and Debt," and House Budget Committee, Democratic Caucus, "Deficits Hit Record Levels," Press Release, July 16, 2003.

of the usual 10 years, citing uncertainties over the military occupation of Iraq and the war on terrorism.)

What did these numbers imply? Certainly not a debt disaster. But a fiscal policy with future costs. By raising the national debt as a percentage of GDP, interest payments relative to GDP and the tax burden would rise. Afterward, the debt-to-GDP ratio would come down a bit, but not enough to bring the tax burden back to where it was originally.

Where would this rise in the debt come from? Some of the early rise would come from *cyclical* deficits. Because of the economy's slow recovery after the recession in 2001, it was expected to remain below potential even into 2004, with lower tax revenues and higher transfers than would occur at full employment. But the continued deficits in 2006 and beyond—when the economy was assumed to have recovered—would be mostly *structural* deficits. According to the OMB's estimates, the two Bush tax cuts would account for about 25 percent of the total rise in the national debt over the projection period.

Now look at the lower table. It shows the numbers put out by the Democratic Caucus of the House Budget Committee in a press release, within days of the OMB document's release. It shows a more sharply rising deficit, and what looks like a *long-run* violation of the guideline for responsible government. The debt-to-GDP ratio was projected to rise continually, with no end in sight. Note that the Democratic Caucus projected 10 years forward instead of 5. But that accounted for only part of the dramatic difference in the fiscal story each side told. What accounted for the rest?

The answer is: the assumptions behind the numbers. The OMB deficit numbers left out estimates of government outlays for military operations in Iraq or Afghanistan beyond 2003. It also assumed that any provisions of the two tax cuts that were legally set to expire between 2004 and 2008 would, in fact, expire, thereby boosting tax revenues.

The Democrats made different assumptions. On the outlays side, they included the estimated cost of Iraq and Afghanistan from 2004 through 2006, and projected greater increases in other national defense spending. They also added the expenses of the proposed prescription drug benefit plan for Medicare, starting in 2006. (The plan did, in fact, go into effect in 2006.) On the revenue side, the Democrats not only assumed that expiring provisions of the tax cuts would be renewed, but that further changes in the tax code favored by the administration would also be enacted.

Using the Democratic numbers, virtually *all* of the rise in the debt during their 11-year projection period could be attributed to tax cuts of some form—either the original cuts in 2001 and 2003, or expected extensions and further expected reductions.

Note that, based on *either* set of numbers, we would be entering a period of rising debt that would entail the kinds of future costs we've discussed in the chapter. Under the Democrats' assumptions, the path would be unsustainable in the long run: Debt and interest payments would rise faster than GDP for 10 years and perhaps beyond. Under the Bush administration's assumptions, the path would be costly, but sustainable, with debt and interest payments topping out in 2006.

How did the first few years actually play out? From 2003 through 2005, GDP and federal tax revenues grew much faster than either side expected, but so did spending on the war in Iraq. Combining all three years, the total deficit was smaller, and the debt-to-GDP ratio ended up smaller than either side had predicted. (The preliminary estimate: debt was 38.1% of GDP at the end of fiscal 2005.) But by then, the battle had shifted forward to 2006–2010 projections, with the Democrats projecting deficits continually above $400 billion, and the administration projecting a steady drop to $207 billion.[9]

Ultimately, our conclusions about any economic policy must compare costs with *benefits*. And views about the benefits of the administration's fiscal plan diverge even more widely than views about its costs. Was the tax cut distributed in the right way? Should the United States have gone to war with Iraq? How much should younger workers sacrifice to care for retiring baby boomers? How one answers questions like these ultimately determines whether the costs of higher debt—whatever they turn out to be—are justified. But this is where economics leaves off and politics and ideology begins.

[9] House Budget Committee, Democratic Caucus, "The President's Budget," February 11, 2005, and Office of Management and Budget, Fiscal Year Budget, 2006, Historical Tables 1.1 and 7.1.

Summary

The U.S. federal government finances its spending through a combination of taxes and borrowing. When government outlays exceed tax revenue, the government runs a budget deficit. It finances that deficit by selling bonds, thereby adding to the national debt. When government outlays are less than tax revenue, the government runs a budget surplus. It uses that surplus to buy back bonds it has issued in the past, thus shrinking the national debt.

Federal government outlays consists of three broad categories: government purchases of goods and services, transfer payments, and interest on the national debt. Nonmilitary government purchases have traditionally accounted for a stable, low 2 percent of real GDP. Military purchases vary according to global politics; in recent years, they have declined dramatically relative to GDP, but seem likely to rise in 2002 and beyond. Transfer programs—such as Social Security, Medicare, and welfare—have been the fastest-growing part of government spending. They currently equal about 12.5 percent of GDP.

On the revenue side, the government relies on personal and corporate income taxes, Social Security taxes, and some smaller excise taxes and user fees. Federal revenue was trending mildly upward until the early 2000s.

From 1970 through the mid-1990s, federal spending exceeded federal revenues every year, so that the government ran budget deficits. Particularly large deficits occurred in the early 1980s. But in the 1990s, the deficit declined, and in 1998 the government began running yearly budget surpluses. In 2002, the budget picture flip-flopped again, as deficits were projected for several years.

In the short run, there is a two-way relationship between government outlays and taxes on the one hand and the level of output on the other. Changes in output affect government outlays and taxes. In recessions, for example, government tax revenues fall and transfer payments rise. In this way, the tax and transfer system acts as an automatic stabilizer, helping to smooth out fluctuations in output.

In principle, the government could use countercyclical fiscal policy—changing tax and transfer policies or government purchases in order to offset economic fluctuations. However, because of practical problems, most economists are skeptical about its effectiveness.

In the long run, fiscal changes have important effects. All else equal, we can expect larger budget deficits to slow growth in living standards, and smaller budget deficits or surpluses to speed the growth of living standards.

Over the 1970s and, especially, the 1980s, the average federal budget deficit was so large, and the national debt growing so rapidly, that interest payments were rising relative to GDP. While we were not on the brink of disaster, the deficits and the growing national debt did require a future sacrifice, which we paid in the 1990s by reducing the deficit through tight fiscal policy. The same scenario of high deficits and rising national debt relative to GDP is now projected for the coming decade. The rising debt-to-GDP ratio—even if temporary—will require future sacrifices.

Key Terms

Average tax rate
Countercyclical fiscal policy

Cyclical deficit
Marginal tax rate
Progressive tax

Regressive tax
Structural deficit

Review Questions

Answers to even-numbered Questions and Problems can be found on the text Web site at http://hall-lieb.swlearning.com.

1. Why is it misleading to compare the national debt of $235 billion in 1959 with the national debt of $3,878 billion in 2003?

2. List the three broad categories of federal government outlays. According to the most recent data in the chapter, which is the largest category? How have these types of spending changed relative to GDP over the past few years?

3. What is a *progressive* income tax?

4. List the main sources of federal revenue. How and why has the composition changed recently?

5. Explain the difference between the federal deficit and the national debt. Explain the relationship between the federal budget surplus and the national debt.

6. Define the cyclical deficit and the structural deficit. Why are changes in the cyclical deficit not a major long-run concern?

7. What is countercyclical fiscal policy? Is it an effective tool? Explain.

8. "A decrease in the national debt as a fraction of GDP requires the federal government to run budget surpluses." True or false? Explain.

9. While the national debt has been an important concern, most economists don't believe we were truly headed for disaster in the 1980s. Explain.

10. Judging from the Office of Management and Budget (OMB) numbers, explain whether or not the Bush administration is running a sustainable budget policy. Judge the same situation using the Democratic Caucus of the House Budget Committee's numbers. What accounts for the difference?

11. Explain why Medicare costs are expected to rise rapidly over the next two decades.

Problems and Exercises

1. Use the following statistics, in billions of units, to calculate the real national debt and the debt relative to GDP in 1990 and 2000 for this hypothetical country. Which figures would you use to compare the national debt in the two years?

National Debt in 1990:	1.2
National Debt in 2000:	13.8
Nominal GDP in 1990:	101.7
Nominal GDP in 2000:	552.2
Price Index in 1990:	35.2
Price Index in 2000:	113.3

2. You are running for president of the small nation of Utopia. You promise to cut tax rates, increase transfers and government purchases, reduce the government's budget deficit, and reduce the government's debt as a fraction of GDP. If elected, is it possible for you to keep all of your campaign promises in the short run? What about in the long run?

3. You are running for reelection as president of the nation of Utopia. Your opponents have criticized you for allowing the national debt to grow by almost 50 percent over the last four years. Use the following statistics, measured in millions of dollars, to defend yourself to Utopia's voters:

National debt in year 1 of your presidency:	$152
National debt in year 4 of your presidency:	$200
Nominal GDP in year 1 of your presidency:	$3042
Nominal GDP in year 4 of your presidency:	$4098
Price index in year 1 of your presidency:	45
Price index in year 4 of your presidency:	72

4. Suppose there is a country with 30 households divided into three categories (A, B, and C), with 10 households of each type. If a household earns 20,000 zips (the country's currency) or more in a year, it must pay 15 percent of its income in taxes. If the household earns less than 20,000 zips, it doesn't pay any tax. When the economy is operating at full employment, household income is 250,000 zips per year for each type A household, 50,000 zips for type B households, and 20,000 zips for type C households.

   a. If the economy is operating at full employment, how much revenue does the government collect in taxes for the year?

   b. Suppose a recession hits and household income falls for each type of household. Type A households now earn 150,000 zips, type B households earn 30,000 zips, and type C households earn 10,000 zips for the year. How much does the government collect in tax

revenue for the year? Assume the government spends all of the revenue it would have collected if the economy had been operating at full employment. Under this assumption, what is the effect of the recession on the government budget deficit (i.e., the effect on the cyclical deficit)?

   c. Suppose instead that the economy expanded and household incomes rose to 400,000 zips, 75,000 zips, and 30,000 zips, respectively, for the year. How much tax would the government collect for the year? What is the effect on the cyclical deficit (assume again that the government spends exactly the amount of revenue it collects when household income is at the values in part (a))? What does this problem tell you about the relationship between shocks to the economy and the budget deficit? structural deficit?

5. Suppose a nation's government purchases are equal to $2 trillion, regardless of the state of the economy. However, its taxes and transfers depend on economic conditions. When the economy is at potential output, net taxes (taxes minus transfers) equal $2.2 trillion. However, for each 1 percent GDP falls below potential output, net taxes fall by 5 percent.

   a. Suppose the economy was operating at potential output. What would be the structural deficit? The cyclical deficit?

   b. Suppose that real GDP was 5 percent below potential output. What would be the cyclical deficit? The structural deficit?

6. Are either of the following countries violating the minimal guidelines for responsible government as outlined in this text?

Country A
(Figures in Billions of $)

	Debt	GDP
1999	1	100
2000	2	110
2001	3	150

Country B
(Figures in Billions of $)

	Debt	GDP
1999	1236	1400
2000	1346	1550
2001	1406	1707

7. At the end of this chapter, you learned that in March 2002, a three-year fiscal stimulus package was put into effect. Suppose that when the stimulus began to have an impact, the economy had already returned to full employment.

   a. Show the likely effect of this policy on an AS–AD diagram, assuming that the Fed did nothing.

   b. What would be the Fed's normal response to such a fiscal stimulus? Why? Illustrate the effect of the Fed's policy on your AS–AD diagram.

   c. What can you conclude about the ultimate impact of an ill-timed fiscal stimulus on GDP and the price level when the Fed reacts as expected? Should the Fed be indifferent about such stimulus? Why or why not?

8. Assume that the unemployment rate in the small country of Economica is currently 6 percent, and that in this country government purchases = $10 million, tax revenue = $17 million, transfers and interest payments = $5 million, and the current unemployment rate is 6 percent.

   a. Find the size of the Economica's budget deficit.

   b. What can you tell about Economica's cyclical deficit and its structural deficit?

9. Complete this table for the small country of Microland. Assume that Microland started year one with no federal debt. What is the relationship between the deficit and the debt? How can the real national debt fall in the absence of a change in government outlays and tax revenue?

	Year						
	1	2	3	4	5	6	7
Price Index	100	103	105	110	118	133	140
Nominal GDP	$400	$500	$600	$700	$800	$900	$1000
Outlays	$100	$120	$125	$135	$133	$130	$ 130
Tax Revenue	$105	$126	$130	$132	$134	$138	$ 130
Deficit/Surplus							
Debt							
Real National Debt							
Debt to GDP							

Challenge Question

Suppose the United States were running a budget surplus and decided to eliminate it by either cutting taxes or increasing government spending.

   a. Compared to a policy of just accruing surpluses and paying down the national debt, what will this policy do to U.S. real GDP and interest rates in the *short run*? Illustrate your answer graphically. (*Hint*: Which macro model, and which graphs, should you use to illustrate effects on output and interest rates in the short run?)

   b. Compared to a policy of just accruing surpluses and paying down the national debt, what will this policy do to U.S. real GDP and interest rates in the *long run*? Illustrate your answer graphically.

   c. Going back to the short run, suppose the Fed responds by neutralizing the impact of the fiscal change in part (a) above. What will happen to real GDP and interest rates in the short run?

ECONOMIC *Applications*   *These exercises require access to Hall/Lieberman Xtra! If Xtra! did not come with your book, visit* http://hallxtra.swlearning.com *to purchase.*

1. Use your Xtra! password at the Hall and Lieberman Web site (http://hallxtra.swlearning.com), select this chapter, and under Economic Applications, click on EconDebate. Choose *Fiscal Policy*, and scroll down to find the debate, "How Should the U.S. Budget Surplus Be Used?" Read the debate, and use the information to answer the following questions.
    a. Explain the liberal and conservative views on budget deficit/surplus.
    b. Is the 2001 (and 2003) tax cut legislation, sponsored by the Bush administration, an example of counter-cyclical fiscal policy in light of recessions in these periods? Explain.

2. Use your Xtra! password at the Hall and Lieberman Web site (http://hallxtra.swlearning.com), select this chapter, and under Economic Applications, click on EconData. Choose *Taxes, Spending, and Deficits*, and scroll down to find *Real per-Capita Disposable Income*. Read the definition, click on Diagrams/Data.

    Disposable personal income is the portion of personal income that is available for consumption spending or saving after personal taxes are taken out. Confirm that in the short run, the increase in real per-capita disposable personal income is inversely related to personal tax rates, or directly related to personal consumption.

Exchange Rates and Macroeconomic Policy

CHAPTER OUTLINE

Foreign Exchange Markets and Exchange Rates
 Dollars per Pound or Pounds per Dollar?

The Demand for British Pounds
 The Demand for Pounds Curve
 Shifts in the Demand for Pounds Curve

The Supply of British Pounds
 The Supply of Pounds Curve
 Shifts in the Supply of Pounds Curve

The Equilibrium Exchange Rate

What Happens When Things Change?
 How Exchange Rates Change Over Time
 The Very Short Run: "Hot Money"
 The Short Run: Macroeconomic Fluctuations
 The Long Run: Purchasing Power Parity

Government Intervention in Foreign Exchange Markets
 Managed Float
 Fixed Exchange Rates
 Foreign Currency Crises, the IMF, and Moral Hazard
 The Euro

Exchange Rates and the Macroeconomy
 Exchange Rates and Demand Shocks
 Exchange Rates and Monetary Policy

Using the Theory: The Stubborn U.S. Trade Deficit
 From a Financial Inflow to a Trade Deficit
 The Growing Trade Deficit with China

If you've ever traveled to a foreign country, you were a direct participant in the **foreign exchange market**—a market in which one country's currency is traded for that of another. For example, if you traveled to Mexico, you might have stopped near the border to exchange some dollars for Mexican pesos.

 Even if you have never traveled abroad, you've been involved, at least indirectly, in all kinds of foreign exchange dealings. For example, suppose you buy some Mexican- grown tomatoes at a store in the United States, where you pay with dollars. Except for shipping and retailing services, the resources used to produce those tomatoes were Mexican. A Mexican farmer grew the tomatoes; Mexican truckers transported them to the distribution center in the nearest large city; and Mexican workers, machinery, and raw materials were used to package them. All of these people want to be paid in Mexican pesos, regardless of who buys the final product. After all, they live in Mexico, so they need pesos to buy things there. But you, as an American, want to pay for your tomatoes with dollars.

Foreign exchange market
The market in which one country's currency is traded for another country's.

Let's think about this for a moment. You want to pay for the tomatoes in dollars, but the Mexicans who produced them want to be paid in pesos. How can this happen?

The answer: *Someone,* here or abroad, must use the foreign exchange market to exchange dollars for pesos. For example, it might work like this: You pay dollars to your supermarket, which pays dollars to a U.S. importer, who pays dollars to the distributor in Mexico, who—finally—turns the dollars over to a Mexican bank in exchange for pesos. Finally, the Mexican distributor pays the Mexican farmer in pesos. In this case, the actual changing of dollars into pesos takes place in a Mexican bank. But why is the Mexican bank willing to trade pesos for dollars? Because the bank is a participant in the market for foreign exchange, and it also trades dollars for pesos.

In this chapter, we'll look at the markets in which dollars are exchanged for foreign currency. We'll also expand our macroeconomic analysis to consider the effects of changes in exchange rates. As you'll see, what happens in the foreign exchange market affects the economy, and changes in the economy affect the foreign exchange market. This has implications for the Fed as it tries to use monetary policy to steer the economy and keep it growing smoothly. Finally, in the "Using the Theory" section, you'll see how the tools of the chapter can help us understand why the United States has such a large and persistent trade deficit.

FOREIGN EXCHANGE MARKETS AND EXCHANGE RATES

Every day, all over the world, more than a hundred different national currencies are exchanged for one another in banks, hotels, stores, and kiosks in airports and train stations. Traders exchange dollars for Mexican pesos, Japanese yen, European euros, Indian rupees, Chinese yuan, and so on. In addition, traders exchange each of these foreign currencies for one another: pesos for euros, yen for yuan, euros for yen. . . . There are literally thousands of combinations. How can we hope to make sense of these markets—how they operate and how they affect us?

Our basic approach is to treat each pair of currencies as a separate market. That is, there is one market in which dollars are exchanged for euros, another in which Angolan kwanzas trade for yen, and so on. The physical locations where the trading takes place do not matter: Whether you exchange your dollars for yen in France, Germany, the United States, or even in Ecuador, you are a trader in the same dollar–yen market.

Exchange rate The amount of one country's currency that is traded for one unit of another country's currency.

In any foreign exchange market, the rate at which one currency is traded for another is called the **exchange rate** between those two currencies. For example, if you happened to trade dollars for British pounds on July 5, 2005, each British pound would have cost you about $1.76. On that day, the exchange rate was 1.7571 dollars per pound.

Dollars per Pound or Pounds per Dollar?

Table 1 lists exchange rates between the dollar and various foreign currencies on a particular day in 2005. But notice that we can think of any exchange rate in two ways: as so many units of foreign currency per dollar, or so many dollars per unit of

Country	Name of Currency	Symbol	Units of Foreign Currency per Dollar	Dollars per Unit of Foreign Currency
Brazil	real	R	2.3759	$0.4209
China	yuan	Y	8.2764	0.1208
European Monetary Union Countries	euro	€	0.8391	1.1917
Great Britain	pound	£	0.5691	1.7571
India	rupee	R	43.554	0.02296
Japan	yen	¥	111.59	0.008961
Mexico	peso	P	10.769	0.0929
Russia	ruble	R	28.827	0.03469

TABLE 1

Foreign Exchange Rates, July 5, 2005

foreign currency. For example, the table shows the exchange rate between the British pound and the dollar as 0.5691 pounds per dollar, or 1.7571 dollars per pound. We can always obtain one form of the exchange rate from the other by taking its reciprocal: 1/0.5691 = 1.7571, and 1/1.7571 = 0.5691.

In this chapter, we'll always define the exchange rate as "dollars per unit of foreign currency," as in the last column of the table. That way, from the American point of view, the exchange rate is just another *price*. The same way you pay a certain number of dollars for a gallon of gasoline (the price of gas), so, too, you pay a certain number of dollars for a British pound (the price of pounds).

The exchange rate is the price of foreign currency in dollars.

Table 1 raises some important questions: Why, in mid-2005, did a pound cost $1.76? Why not $1? Or $5? Why did one Japanese yen cost less than a penny? And a Russian ruble about three cents?

The answers to these questions certainly affect Americans who travel abroad. Suppose you are staying in a hotel in London that costs 100 pounds per night. If the price of the pound is $1, the hotel room will cost you $100, but if the price is $5, the room will cost you $500. And exchange rates affect Americans who stay at home, too. They influence the prices of many goods we buy in the United States, they help determine which of our industries will expand and which will contract, and they affect the wages and salaries that we earn from our jobs.

How are all these exchange rates determined? In most cases, they are determined by the familiar forces of supply and demand. As in other markets, each foreign exchange market reaches an equilibrium at which the quantity of foreign exchange demanded is equal to the quantity supplied.

In the next several sections, we'll build a model of supply and demand for a representative foreign exchange market: the one in which U.S. dollars are exchanged for British pounds. Taking the American point of view, we'll call this simply "the market for pounds." The other currency being traded—the dollar—will always be implicit.

THE DEMAND FOR BRITISH POUNDS

To analyze the demand for pounds, we start with a very basic question: *Who is demanding them?* The simple answer is, anyone who has dollars and wants to exchange them for pounds. But the most important buyers of pounds in the pound–dollar market will be American households and businesses. When Americans want to buy things from Britain, they will need to acquire pounds. To acquire them, they will need to offer U.S. dollars. To keep our analysis simple, we'll focus on just these American buyers. We'll also—for now—ignore any demand for pounds by the U.S. government.

> *In our model of the market for pounds, we assume that American households and businesses are the only buyers.*

Why do Americans want to buy pounds? There are two reasons:

* *To buy goods and services from British firms.* Americans buy sweaters knit in Edinburgh, airline tickets sold by Virgin Airways, and insurance services offered by Lloyd's. American tourists also stay in British hotels, use British taxis, and eat at British restaurants. To buy goods and services from British firms, Americans need to acquire pounds in order to pay for them.
* *To buy British assets.* Americans buy British stocks, British corporate or government bonds, and British real estate. In each case, the British seller will want to be paid in pounds, so the American buyer will have to acquire them.

The Demand for Pounds Curve

Demand curve for foreign currency A curve indicating the quantity of a specific foreign currency that Americans will want to buy, during a given period, at each different exchange rate.

Panel (a) of Figure 1 shows an example of a **demand curve for foreign currency,** in this case, the demand curve for pounds. The curve tells us *the quantity of pounds Americans will want to buy in any given period, at each different exchange rate.* Notice that the curve slopes downward: The lower the exchange rate, the greater the quantity of pounds demanded. For example, at an exchange rate of $2.25 per pound, Americans would want to purchase £200 million (point *A*). If the exchange rate fell to $1.50 per pound, Americans would want to buy £300 million (point *E*).

Why does a lower exchange rate—a lower price for the pound—make Americans want to buy more of them? Because the lower the price of the pound, the less expensive British goods are to American buyers. Remember that Americans think of prices in dollar terms. A British compact disc that sells for £8 will cost an American $18 at an exchange rate of $2.25 per pound, but only $12 if the exchange rate is $1.50 per pound.

Thus, as we move rightward *along* the demand for pounds curve, as in the move from point *A* to point *E*:

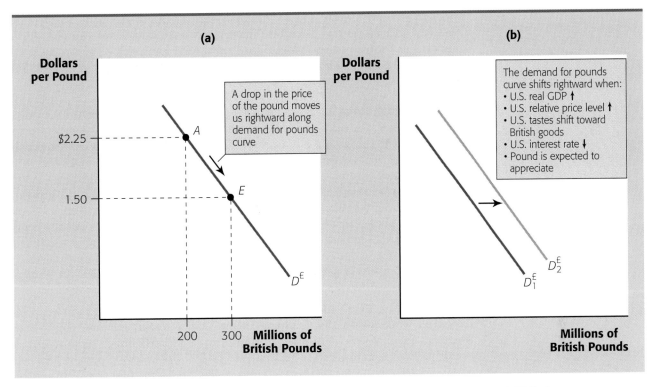

FIGURE 1
The Demand for British Pounds

Shifts in the Demand for Pounds Curve

In panel (a), you saw that a change in the exchange rate moves us *along* the demand for pounds curve. But other variables besides the exchange rate influence the demand for pounds. If any of these other variables changes, the entire curve will shift. As we consider each of these variables, keep in mind that we are assuming that only one of them changes at a time; we suppose the rest to remain constant.

U.S. Real GDP. Suppose real GDP and real income in the United States rise—say, because of continuing economic growth or a recovery from a recession. Then, Americans will buy more of everything, including goods and services from Britain. Thus, at any given exchange rate, Americans will demand more pounds. This is illustrated, in panel (b), as a rightward shift of the demand curve from $D_1^{£}$ to $D_2^{£}$.

Relative Price Levels. Suppose that the U.S. price level rises by 8 percent, while that in Britain rises by 5 percent. Then U.S. prices will rise *relative* to British prices. Americans will shift from buying their own goods toward buying the relatively cheaper British goods, so their demand for pounds will rise. That is, the demand for pounds curve will shift rightward.

Americans' Tastes for British Goods. All else being equal, would you prefer to drive a General Motors Aurora or a Jaguar? Do you prefer British-made films, like

Mansfield Park or *Hillary and Jackie,* or America's offerings, such as *American Beauty* or *Galaxy Quest*? These are matters of taste, and tastes can change. If Americans develop an increased taste for British cars, films, tea, or music, their demand for these goods will increase, and the demand for pounds curve will shift rightward.

Relative Interest Rates. Because financial assets must remain competitive in order to attract buyers, the rates of return on different financial assets—such as stocks and bonds—tend to rise and fall together. Thus, when one country's interest rate is high relative to that of another country, the first country's assets, *in general,* will have higher rates of return.

Now, suppose you're an American trying to decide whether to hold some of your wealth in British financial assets or in American financial assets. You will look very carefully at the rate of return you expect to earn in each country. All else being equal, a lower U.S. interest rate, relative to the British rate, will make British assets more attractive to you. Accordingly, as you and other Americans demand more British assets, you will need more pounds to buy them. The demand for pounds curve will shift rightward.

Expected Changes in the Exchange Rate. Once again, imagine you are an American deciding whether to buy an American or a British bond. Suppose British bonds pay 10 percent interest per year, while U.S. bonds pay 5 percent. All else equal, you would prefer the British bond, since it pays the higher rate of return. You would then exchange dollars for pounds at the going exchange rate and buy the bond.

But what if the price of the pound falls before the British bond becomes due? Then, when you cash in your British bond for pounds, and convert the pounds back into dollars, you'll be *selling your pounds at a lower price* than you bought them for. While you'd benefit from the higher interest rate on the British bond, you'd lose on the foreign currency transaction—buying pounds when their price is high and selling them when their price is low. If the foreign currency loss is great enough, you would be better off with U.S. bonds, even though they pay a lower interest rate.

As you can see, it is not just relative interest rates that matter to wealth holders; it is also *expected changes in the exchange rate.* An expectation that the price of the pound will fall will make British assets less appealing to Americans, since they will expect a foreign currency loss. In this case, the demand for pounds curve will shift leftward.

The opposite holds as well. If Americans expect the price of the pound to *rise,* they will expect a foreign currency *gain* from buying British assets. This will cause the *demand for pounds curve to shift rightward.*

THE SUPPLY OF BRITISH POUNDS

The demand for pounds is one side of the market for pounds. Now we turn our attention to the other side: the supply of pounds. And we'll begin with our basic question: *Who* is supplying them?

In the real world, pounds are supplied from many sources. Anyone who has pounds and wants to exchange them for dollars can come to the market and supply pounds. But the most important sellers of pounds are British households and businesses, who naturally have pounds and need dollars in order to make purchases from Americans. To keep our analysis simple, we'll focus on just these British sellers, and we'll ignore—for now—any pounds supplied by the British government:

> *In our model of the market for pounds, we assume that British households and firms are the only sellers.*

The British supply pounds in the dollar–pound market for only one reason: because they want dollars. Thus, to ask why the British supply pounds is to ask why they want dollars. We can identify two separate reasons:

- *To buy goods and services from American firms.* The British buy airline tickets on United Airlines, computers made by IBM and Apple, and the rights to show films made in Hollywood. British tourists stay in American hotels and eat at American restaurants. The British demand dollars—and supply pounds—for all of these purchases.
- *To buy American assets.* The British buy American stocks, American corporate or government bonds, and American real estate. In each case, the American seller will want to be paid in dollars, and the British buyer will acquire dollars by offering pounds.

The Supply of Pounds Curve

Panel (a) of Figure 2 shows an example of a **supply curve for foreign currency**—here, British pounds. The curve tells us *the quantity of pounds the British will want to sell in any given period, at each different exchange rate.* Notice that the curve slopes upward: The higher the exchange rate, the greater is the quantity of pounds supplied. For example, at an exchange rate of $1.50 per pound, the British would want to supply £300 million (point *E*). If the exchange rate rose to $2.25 per pound, they would supply £400 million (point *F*).

Why does a higher exchange rate—a higher price for the pound—make the British want to sell more of them? Because the higher the price for the pound, the more dollars someone gets for each pound sold. This makes U.S. goods and services less expensive to British buyers, who will want to buy more of them—and who will therefore need more dollars.[1]

To summarize, as we move rightward *along* the supply of pounds curve, such as the move from point *E* to point *F*:

Supply curve for foreign currency A curve indicating the quantity of a specific foreign currency that will be supplied, during a given period, at each different exchange rate.

---

[1] Actually, it is not a logical necessity for the supply of pounds curve to slope upward. Why not? When the price of the pound rises, it is true that the British will buy more U.S. goods and need more dollars to buy them. However, each dollar they buy costs *fewer pounds*. It might be that, even though the British obtain more dollars, they actually supply fewer pounds to get them at the higher exchange rate. In this case, the supply of pounds curve would slope downward. Economists believe, however, that a downward-sloping supply curve for foreign currency—while theoretically possible—is very rare.

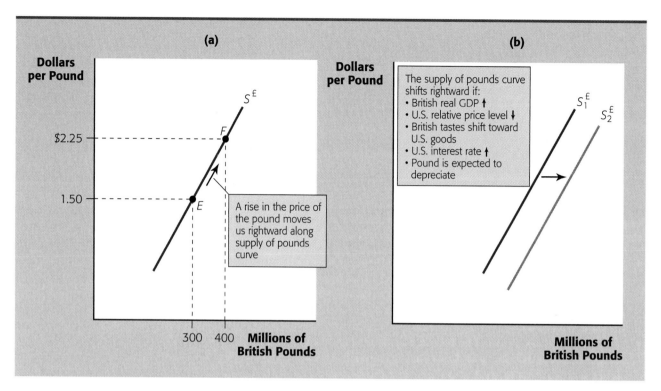

FIGURE 2
The Supply of British Pounds

Shifts in the Supply of Pounds Curve

When the exchange rate changes, we *move along* the supply curve for pounds, as in panel (a) of Figure 2. But other variables can affect the supply of pounds besides the exchange rate. When any of these variables change, the supply of pounds curve will shift, as shown in panel (b). What are these variables?

Real GDP in Britain. If real GDP and real income rise in Britain, British residents will buy more goods and services, including those produced in the United States. Since they will need more dollars to buy U.S. goods, they will supply more pounds. In panel (b) this causes a rightward shift of the supply curve, from $S_1^£$ to $S_2^£$.

Relative Price Levels. Earlier, you learned that a rise in the relative price level in the United States makes British goods more attractive to Americans. But it also makes *American* goods *less* attractive to the British. Since the British will want to buy fewer U.S. goods, they will want fewer dollars and will supply fewer pounds. Thus, a rise in the relative U.S. price level shifts the supply of pounds curve leftward.

British Tastes for U.S. Goods. Recall our earlier discussion about the effect of American tastes on the demand for pounds. The same reasoning applies to the effect of British tastes on the *supply* of pounds. The British could begin to crave things American—or recoil from them. A shift in British tastes toward American goods will shift the supply of pounds curve rightward. A shift in tastes *away* from American goods will shift the curve leftward.

Relative Interest Rates. You've already learned that a rise in the relative U.S. interest rate makes U.S. assets more attractive to Americans. It has exactly the same effect on the British. As the U.S. interest rate rises, and the British buy more U.S. assets, they will need more dollars and will supply more pounds. The supply of pounds curve will shift rightward.

Expected Change in the Exchange Rate. In deciding where to hold their assets, the British have the same concerns as Americans. They will look, in part, at rates of return; but they will *also* think about possible gains or losses on foreign currency transactions. Suppose the British *expect the price of the pound to fall.* Then, by holding U.S. assets, they can anticipate a foreign currency gain—selling pounds at a relatively high price and buying them back again when their price is relatively low. The prospect of foreign currency gain will make U.S. assets more attractive, and the British will buy more of them. *The supply of pounds curve will shift rightward.*

THE EQUILIBRIUM EXCHANGE RATE

Now we will make an important—and in most cases, realistic—assumption: that the exchange rate between the dollar and the pound *floats.* A **floating exchange rate** is one that is freely determined by the forces of supply and demand, without government intervention to change it or keep it from changing. Indeed, many of the world's leading currencies, including the Japanese yen, the British pound, the 11-nation euro, and the Mexican peso, do float freely against the dollar most of the time.

Floating exchange rate An exchange rate that is freely determined by the forces of supply and demand.

In some cases, however, governments do not allow the exchange rate to float freely, but instead manipulate its value by intervening in the market, or even *fix* it at a particular value. We'll discuss government intervention in foreign exchange markets later. In this section, we assume that both the British and U.S. governments leave the dollar–pound market alone.

When the exchange rate floats, the price will settle at the level where quantity supplied and quantity demanded are equal. Here, buyers and sellers are trading British pounds, and the price is the exchange rate—the *price of the pound.*

Look at panel (a) of Figure 3. The equilibrium in the market for pounds occurs at point *E,* where the supply and demand curves intersect. The equilibrium price is $1.50 per pound. As you can verify, if the exchange rate were higher, say, $2.25 per pound, there would be an *excess supply* of pounds, forcing the price of the pound back down to $1.50. If the exchange rate were *lower* than the equilibrium price of $1.50, there would be an *excess demand* for pounds, driving the price back up to $1.50.

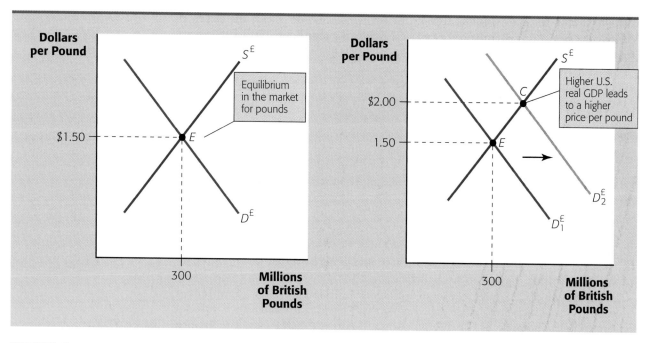

FIGURE 3
The Equilibrium Exchange Rate

When the exchange rate floats—that is, when the government does not intervene in the foreign currency market—the equilibrium exchange rate is determined at the intersection of the demand curve and the supply curve.

WHAT HAPPENS WHEN THINGS CHANGE?

What would cause the price of the pound to rise or fall? The simple answer to this question is, anything that shifts the demand for pounds curve, or the supply of pounds curve, or both curves together. Have another look at the right-hand panels of Figures 1 and 2. They summarize the major factors that can shift the demand and supply curves for pounds and therefore change the floating exchange rate.

Let's illustrate with a simple example. In panel (b) of Figure 3, the initial equilibrium in the market for pounds is at point *E*, with an exchange rate of $1.50 per pound. Now suppose that real GDP rises in the United States. As you've learned (see Figure 1), this rise in U.S. GDP will shift the demand for pounds curve rightward, from $D_1^{£}$ to $D_2^{£}$ in the figure. At the old exchange rate of $1.50 per pound, there would be an excess demand for pounds, which would drive the price of the pound higher. The new equilibrium—where the quantities of pounds supplied and demanded are equal—occurs at point *C*, and the new equilibrium exchange rate is $2.00 per pound.

To recap, the increase in American GDP causes the price of the pound to rise from $1.50 to $2.00. When the price of any floating foreign currency rises because

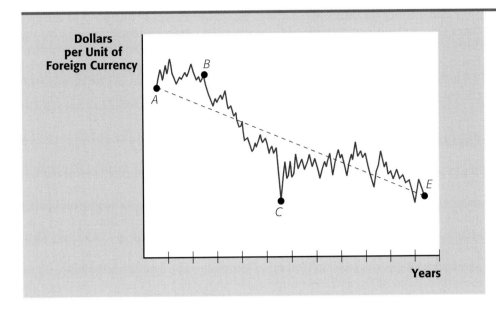

FIGURE 4

Hypothetical Exchange Rate Data Over Time

These hypothetical data show typical patterns of exchange rate fluctuations. Over the course of a few minutes, days, or weeks, the exchange rate can experience sharp up-and-down spikes. Over several months or a year or two, the exchange rate may rise or fall, as in the appreciation of the foreign currency from points A to B and the depreciation from B to C. Over the long run, there may be a general upward or downward trend, like the depreciation of the foreign currency illustrated by the dashed line connecting points A and E.

of a shift in the demand curve, the supply curve, or both, we call it an **appreciation** of the currency. In our example, the pound appreciates against the dollar. At the same time, there has been a **depreciation** of the dollar—a fall in its price in terms of pounds. (To see this, calculate the price of the dollar in terms of pounds before and after the shift in demand.)

Appreciation An increase in the price of a currency in a floating-rate system.

Depreciation A decrease in the price of a currency in a floating-rate system.

> *When a floating exchange rates changes, one country's currency will appreciate (rise in price) and the other country's currency will depreciate (fall in price).*

As you've learned, there are many other variables besides U.S. GDP that can change and affect the exchange rate. We could analyze each of these changes, using diagrams similar to panel (b) of Figure 3. However, we'll organize our discussion of exchange rate changes in a slightly different way.

How Exchange Rates Change Over Time

When we examine the actual behavior of exchange rates over time, we find three different kinds of movements. Look at Figure 4, which graphs hypothetical exchange rate data between the U.S. dollar and some other currency. We're using hypothetical data to make these three kinds of movements stand out more clearly than they usually do in practice.

Notice first the sharp up-and-down spikes. These fluctuations in exchange rates occur over the course of a few weeks, a few days, or even a few minutes—periods of time that we call the *very short run.*

Second, we see a gradual rise and fall of the exchange rate over the course of several months or a year or two. An example is the appreciation of the foreign currency from point *A* to *B* and its depreciation from point *B* to *C*. These are *short-run* movements in the exchange rate.

Finally, notice that while the price of the foreign currency fluctuates in the very short run and the short run, we can also discern a general *long-run* trend: This nation's currency seems to be depreciating in the figure. This long-run trend is illustrated by the dashed line connecting points A and E.

In this section, we'll explore the causes of movements in the exchange rate over all three periods: the very short run, the short run, and the long run.

The Very Short Run: "Hot Money"

Banks and other large financial institutions collectively have trillions of dollars worth of funds that they can move from one type of investment to another at very short notice. These funds are often called "hot money." If those who manage hot money perceive even a tiny advantage in moving funds to a different country's assets—say, because its interest rate is slightly higher—they will do so. Often, decisions to move billions of dollars are made in split seconds, by traders watching computer screens showing the latest data on exchange rates and interest rates around the world. Because these traders move such large volumes of funds, they have immediate effects on exchange rates.

Let's consider an example. Suppose that the relative interest rate in the United States suddenly rises. Then, as you've learned, U.S. assets will suddenly be more attractive to residents of both the United States and England, including managers of hot-money accounts in both countries. As these managers shift their funds from British to United States assets, they will be dumping billions of pounds on the foreign exchange market in order to acquire dollars to buy U.S. assets. This will cause a significant rightward shift of the supply of pounds curve.

In addition to affecting managers of hot-money accounts, the higher relative interest rate in the United States will affect ordinary investors. British investors will want to buy more American assets, helping to shift the supply of pounds curve further rightward. And American investors will want to buy fewer British assets than before, causing some decrease in the *demand* for pounds. Thus, in addition to the very large rightward shift in the supply of pounds, there will be a more moderate leftward shift in the demand for pounds.

Both of these shifts are illustrated in Figure 5: The supply of pounds curve shifts from $S_1^£$ to $S_2^£$, and the demand for pounds curve shifts from $D_1^£$ to $D_2^£$. The result is easy to see: The equilibrium in the market for pounds moves from point E to point G, and the price of the pound *falls* from $1.50 to $1.00. The pound depreciates and the dollar appreciates.

Expectations about future exchange rates can also trigger huge shifts of hot money, and Figure 5 also illustrates what would happen if American and British residents suddenly *expect* the pound to depreciate against the dollar. In this case, it would be the anticipation of foreign currency gains from holding U.S. assets, rather than a higher U.S. interest rate, that would cause the supply and demand curves to shift. As you can see in Figure 5, the expectation that the pound will depreciate actually *causes* the pound to depreciate—a self-fulfilling prophecy.

Sudden changes in relative interest rates, as well as sudden expectations of an appreciation or depreciation of a nation's currency, occur frequently in foreign exchange markets. They can cause massive shifts of hot money from the assets of one country to those of another in very short periods of time. For this reason,

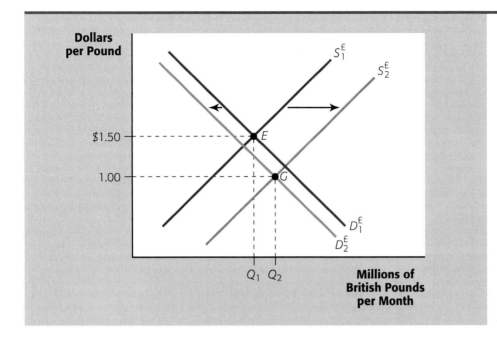

FIGURE 5
**Hot Money in the Very
Short Run**

The market for pounds is initially in equilibrium at point E, *with an exchange rate of $1.50 per pound. A rise in the U.S. interest rate relative to the British rate will make U.S. assets more attractive to both Americans and Britons. Hot-money managers in both countries will shift funds from British to U.S. assets, causing a rightward shift of the supply of pounds curve. American investors will want to buy fewer British assets, causing a decrease in the demand for pounds. The net effect is a lower exchange rate—$1.00 per pound at point* G.

relative interest rates and expectations of future exchange rates are the dominant forces moving exchange rates in the very short run.

The Short Run: Macroeconomic Fluctuations

Look again at Figure 4. What explains the movements in the *short-run* rate—the changes that occur over several months or a few years? In most cases, the causes are economic fluctuations taking place in one or more countries.

Suppose, for example, that both Britain and the United States are in a recession, and the U.S. economy begins to recover while the British slump continues. As real GDP rises in the United States, so does Americans' demand for foreign goods and services, including those from Britain. The demand for pounds curve will shift rightward, and—as shown in panel (a) of Figure 6—the pound will appreciate.

A year or so later, when Britain recovers from *its* recession, its real GDP will rise. British residents will begin to buy more U.S. goods and services, and supply more pounds so they can acquire more dollars. The supply of pounds curve will shift rightward, and—as shown in panel (b) of Figure 6—the pound will depreciate. Thus,

in the short run, movements in exchange rates are caused largely by economic fluctuations. All else equal, a country whose GDP rises relatively rapidly will experience a depreciation *of its currency. A country whose GDP falls more rapidly will experience an* appreciation *of its currency.*

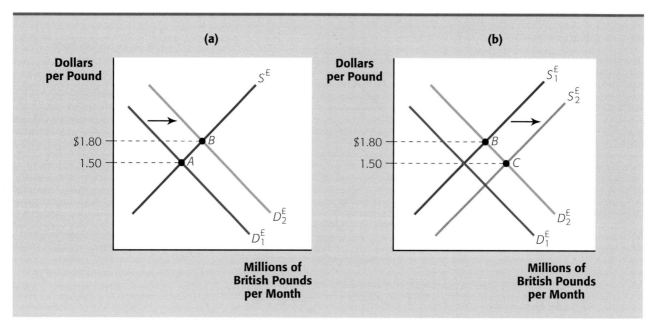

FIGURE 6
Exchange Rates in the Short Run

Panel (a) shows a situation in which the United States recovers from a recession first. U.S. demand for foreign goods and services increases, shifting the demand for pounds curve to the right. The result is an appreciation of the pound. Panel (b) shows Britain's subsequent recovery from its recession. As the British begin to buy more U.S. goods and services, the supply of pounds curve shifts rightward, causing the pound to depreciate.

This observation contradicts a commonly held myth: that a strong (appreciating) currency is a sign of economic health and a weak (depreciating) currency denotes a sick economy. The truth may easily be the opposite. Over the course of several quarters or a few years, the dollar could appreciate because the U.S. economy is *weakening*—entering a serious recession. This would cause Americans to cut back spending on domestic *and* foreign goods, and decrease the demand for foreign currency. Similarly, a *strengthening* U.S. economy—in which Americans are earning and spending more—would increase the U.S. demand for foreign currency and (all else equal) cause the dollar to depreciate.

Keep in mind, though, that other variables can change over the business cycle besides real GDP, including interest rates and price levels in the two countries. For example, a recession can be caused by a monetary contraction that raises the relative interest rate in a country. Or a monetary stimulus in the midst of a recession could result in a relatively low interest rate. These changes, too, will influence exchange rates over the business cycle.

The Long Run: Purchasing Power Parity

In mid-1992, you could buy about 100 Russian rubles for one dollar. In mid-1998, that same dollar would get you more than 6,000 rubles—so many that the Russian government that year created a new ruble that was worth 1,000 of the old rubles. (The ruble exchange rate in Table 1 is for the new ruble.) What caused the ruble to depreciate so much against the dollar during those six years?

This is a question about exchange rates over many years—the long run. Movements of hot money—which explain sudden, temporary movements of exchange rates—cannot explain this kind of long-run trend. Nor can business cycles, which are, by nature, temporary. What, then, causes exchange rates to change over the long run?

In general, long-run trends in exchange rates are determined by *relative price levels* in two countries. We can be even more specific:

> According to the **purchasing power parity (PPP) theory,** the exchange rate between two countries will adjust in the long run until the average price of goods is roughly the same in both countries.

Purchasing power parity (PPP) theory The idea that the exchange rate will adjust in the long run so that the average price of goods in two countries will be roughly the same.

To see why the PPP theory makes sense, imagine a basket of goods that costs $750 in the United States and £500 in Britain. If the prices of the goods themselves do not change, then, according to the PPP theory, the exchange rate will adjust to $750/£500 = $1.5 dollars per pound. Why? Because at this exchange rate, $750 can be exchanged for £500, so the price of the basket is the same to residents of either country—$750 for Americans and £500 for the British.

Now, suppose the exchange rate was *below* its PPP rate of $1.50 per pound— say, $1 per pound. Then a trader could take $500 to the bank, exchange it for £500, buy the basket of goods in Great Britain, and sell it in the United States for $750. She would earn a profit of $250 on each basket of goods traded. In the process, however, traders would be increasing the demand for pounds and raising the exchange rate. When the price of the pound reached $1.50, purchasing power parity would hold, and special trading opportunities would be gone. As you can see, trading activity will tend to drive the exchange rate toward the PPP rate. (An end-of-chapter review question asks you to explain the adjustment process when the exchange rate starts *higher* than the PPP rate.)

The PPP theory has an important implication:

> In the long run, the currency of a country with a higher inflation rate will depreciate against the currency of a country whose inflation rate is lower.

Why? Because in the country with the higher inflation rate, the relative price level will be rising. As that country's basket of goods becomes relatively more expensive, only a depreciation of its currency can restore purchasing power parity. And traders—taking advantage of opportunities like those just described—would cause the currency to depreciate.

Purchasing Power Parity: Some Important Caveats. While purchasing power parity is a good general guideline for predicting long-run trends in exchange rates, it does not work perfectly. For a variety of reasons, exchange rates can deviate from their PPP values for many years.

First, some goods—by their very nature—are difficult to trade. Suppose a haircut costs £5 in London and $30 in New York, and the exchange rate is $1.50 per pound. Then British haircuts are cheaper for residents of both countries. Could traders take advantage of this? Not really. They cannot take $30 to the bank in exchange for £20, buy four haircuts in London, ship them to New York, and sell them for a total of $120 there. Haircuts and most other personal services are nontradable.

Second, high transportation costs can reduce trading possibilities even for goods that *can* be traded. Our earlier numerical example would have quite a different ending if moving the basket of goods between Great Britain and the United States involved $500 of freight and insurance costs.

Third, artificial barriers to trade, such as special taxes or quotas on imports, can hamper traders' ability to move exchange rates toward purchasing power parity.

Still, the purchasing power parity theory is useful in many circumstances. Under floating exchange rates, a country whose relative price level is rising rapidly will almost always find that the price of its currency is falling rapidly. If not, all of its tradeable goods would soon be priced out of the world market.

Indeed, we often observe that countries with very high inflation rates have currencies depreciating against the dollar by roughly the amount needed to preserve purchasing power parity. For example, we've already mentioned the sharp depreciation of the Russian ruble from 1992 to 1998. During those six years, the number of rubles that exchanged for a dollar rose from around 100 to about 6,000. Over the same period, the annual inflation rate averaged about 200 percent in Russia, but only about 3 percent in the United States. As a result, the relative price level in Russia skyrocketed, leading to a dramatic depreciation of the ruble against the dollar. Another example is Turkey: From mid-1996 to mid-1997, its price level almost doubled, while the dollar price of its currency was cut in half.

GOVERNMENT INTERVENTION IN FOREIGN EXCHANGE MARKETS

As you've seen, when exchange rates float, they can rise and fall for a variety of reasons. But a government may not be content to let the forces of supply and demand change its exchange rate. If the exchange rate rises, the country's goods will become much more expensive to foreigners, causing harm to its export-oriented industries. If the exchange rate falls, goods purchased from other countries will rise in price. Since many imported goods are used as inputs by U.S. firms (such as oil from the Middle East and Mexico, or computer screens from Japan), a drop in the exchange rate will cause a rise in the U.S. price level. Finally, if the exchange rate is too volatile, it can make trading riskier or require traders to acquire special insurance against foreign currency losses, which costs them money, time, and trouble. For all of these reasons, governments sometime *intervene* in foreign exchange markets involving their currency.

Managed Float

Many governments let their exchange rate float *most of the time,* but will intervene on occasion when the floating exchange rate moves in an undesired direction or becomes too volatile. For example, look back at Figure 5, where the price of the British pound falls to $1 as hot money is shifted out of British assets. Suppose the British government does not want the pound to depreciate. Then its central bank—the Bank of England—could begin trading in the dollar–pound market itself. It would buy British pounds with dollars, thereby shifting the demand for pounds curve rightward. If it buys just the right amount of pounds, it can prevent the pound from depreciating at all. Alternatively, the U.S. government might not be happy with the *appreciation* of the dollar in Figure 5. In that case, the Federal Reserve can enter the market and buy British pounds with dollars, once again shifting the demand for pounds curve rightward.

The central banks of many countries—including the Federal Reserve—will sometimes intervene in this way in foreign exchange markets. When a government buys or sells its own currency or that of a trading partner to influence exchange rates, it is engaging in a "managed float" or a "dirty float."

> *Under a **managed float**, a country's central bank actively manages its exchange rate, buying its own currency to prevent depreciations, and selling its own currency to prevent appreciations.*

Managed float A policy of frequent central bank intervention to move the exchange rate.

Managed floats are used most often in the very short run, to prevent large, sudden changes in exchange rates. For example, during the week after the terror attacks of September 2001, the Bank of Japan (Japan's central bank) sold 2 trillion yen (about $17 billion worth) in order to stop a rapid *appreciation* of the yen against the dollar. On the other side—and on a smaller scale—Argentina's central bank purchased 15 million Argentinian pesos (about $9 million worth at the time) on January 15, 2002, in order to slow the *depreciation* of the peso against the dollar.

That last example raises a question. When a country—such as Argentina—wants to prevent or slow a depreciation against the dollar, it has to buy its own currency with dollars. Where does it get those dollars? Unfortunately for Argentina, it cannot print dollars; only the U.S. Federal Reserve can do that. Instead, Argentina must use its *reserves* of dollars—the dollars its central bank keeps on hand specifically to intervene in the dollar–peso market.

Almost every nation holds reserves of dollars—as well as euros, yen, and other key currencies—just so it can enter the foreign exchange market and sell them for its own currency when necessary. Under a managed float, periods of selling dollars are usually short-lived, and alternate with periods of buying dollars. Thus, countries rarely use up all of their dollar reserves when they engage in managed floats.

Managed floats are controversial. Some economists believe they help to avoid wide swings in exchange rates, and thus reduce the risks for international traders and investors. But others are critical of how managed floats often work out in practice. They point out that countries often intervene when the forces behind an appreciation or depreciation are strong. In these cases, the intervention only serves to delay inevitable changes in the exchange rate—sometimes, at great cost to a country's reserves of dollars and other key currencies.

Fixed Exchange Rates

A more extreme form of intervention is a **fixed exchange rate,** in which a government declares a particular value for its exchange rate with another currency. The government, through its central bank, then commits itself to intervene in the foreign exchange market any time the *equilibrium* exchange rate differs from the *fixed* rate.

Fixed exchange rate A government-declared exchange rate maintained by central bank intervention in the foreign exchange market.

For example, from 1987 to 1997, the government of Thailand fixed the value of its currency—the *baht*—at $0.04 per baht. The two panels of Figure 7 show the different types of intervention that might be necessary in the baht–dollar market to maintain this fixed exchange rate. Each panel shows a different set of supply and demand curves—and a different equilibrium exchange rate that might exist

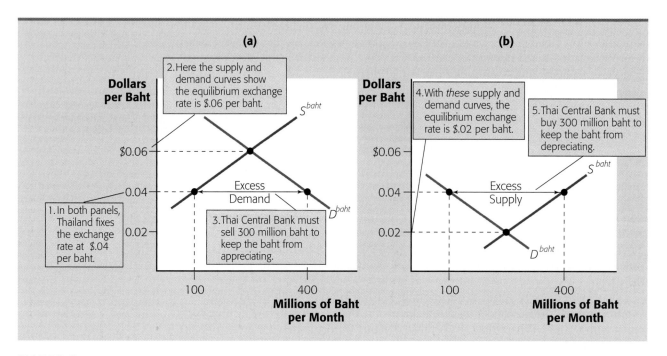

FIGURE 7
**A Fixed Exchange Rate
for the Baht**

for the baht. Look first at panel (a). Here, we assume that the equilibrium exchange rate is $0.06 per baht, so that the fixed rate is *lower* than the equilibrium rate. At the fixed rate of $0.04 per baht, 400 million baht would be demanded each month, but only 100 million would be supplied. There would be an *excess demand* of 300 million baht, which would ordinarily drive the exchange rate back up to its equilibrium value of $0.06. But the Thai government prevents this by entering the market and *selling* just enough baht to cover the excess demand. In panel (a), the Central Bank of Thailand would sell 300 million baht per month to maintain the fixed rate.

> *When a country fixes its exchange rate below the equilibrium value, the result is an excess demand for the country's currency. To maintain the fixed rate, the country's central bank must sell enough of its own currency to eliminate the excess demand.*

Panel (b) shows another possibility, where the equilibrium exchange rate is $0.02, so that the same fixed exchange rate of $0.04 per baht is now *above* the equilibrium rate. There is an excess *supply* of 300 million baht. In this case, to prevent the excess supply from driving the exchange rate down, the Central Bank of Thailand must *buy* the excess baht.

> *When a country fixes its exchange rate above the equilibrium value, the result is an excess supply of the country's currency. To maintain the fixed rate, the country's central bank must buy enough of its own currency to eliminate the excess supply.*

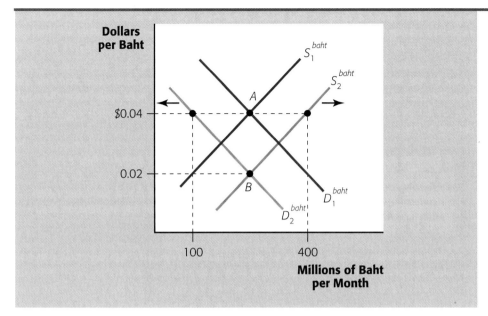

FIGURE 8
A Foreign Currency Crisis

Initially, the baht is fixed at the equilibrium rate of $0.04. When the supply and demand curves shift to D_2 and S_2, the equilibrium exchange rate falls to $0.02. If Thailand continues to fix the rate at $0.04, it will have to buy up the excess supply of 300 million baht per month, using dollars. As its dollar reserves dwindle, traders will anticipate a drop in the value of the baht, shifting the curves out further, as indicated by the arrows.

Fixed exchange rates present little problem for a country as long as the exchange rate is fixed at or very close to its equilibrium rate. But when the equilibrium exchange rate moves away from the fixed rate—as in the two panels of Figure 7—governments often try to maintain their fixed rate anyway, sometimes for long periods. This can create problems, especially when the exchange rate is fixed *above* the equilibrium rate.

Foreign Currency Crises, the IMF, and Moral Hazard

To see how a fixed exchange rate can be problematic, look at Figure 8. Initially, the supply and demand curves for baht are given by S_1 and D_1, respectively, so that the equilibrium exchange rate, $0.04, is equal to the fixed exchange rate. At this point, the central bank is neither selling nor buying baht. Now, suppose that, for some reason (we'll be more specific in a few paragraphs), the supply and demand curves shift to S_2 and D_2, respectively. The equilibrium rate falls, so the fixed rate of $0.04 is above the equilibrium rate of $0.02. The Central Bank of Thailand must now *buy* its own currency with dollars—at the rate of 300 million baht per month. Each baht costs the central bank 4 cents, so as the months go by, its dollar reserves are being depleted at the rate of 300 million × $0.04 = $12 million per month. Once those reserves are gone, Thailand will have only two choices: to let its currency float (which means an immediate depreciation to the lower, equilibrium rate) or to declare a new, lower fixed rate—a **devaluation** of its currency.

Of course, at a certain point, foreign exchange speculators and traders would see that Thailand doesn't have many dollars left. (Most countries' central banks regularly report their holdings of key currencies, and economists can estimate the holdings of countries that don't.) Looking ahead, these speculators and traders will

Devaluation A change in the exchange rate from a higher fixed rate to a lower fixed rate.

begin to *anticipate* a drop in the baht. And—as you've learned in this chapter—expected changes in the exchange rate *shift* supply and demand curves for foreign currency. In this case, an expected fall in the baht causes the supply curve for baht to shift further rightward and the demand curve to shift further leftward, as indicated by the heavy arrows in the diagram. In Figure 8, these shifts will *decrease* the equilibrium value of the baht, increase the *excess supply* of baht, and make the fixed rate of $0.04 even harder to maintain. The country is now experiencing a *foreign currency crisis*.

> A *foreign currency crisis* arises when people no longer believe that a country can maintain a fixed exchange rate above the equilibrium rate. As a consequence, the supply of the currency increases, demand for it decreases, and the country must use up its reserves of dollars and other key currencies even faster in order to maintain the fixed rate.

Once a foreign currency crisis arises, a country typically has no choice but to devalue its currency or let it float and watch it depreciate. And ironically, because the country waited for the crisis to develop, the exchange rate may for a time drop even lower than the original equilibrium rate. For example, in Figure 8, an early devaluation to $0.02 per dollar might prevent a crisis from occurring at all. But once the crisis begins, and the supply and demand curves shift out further than S_2 and D_2, the currency will have to drop *below* $0.02 to end the rapid depletion of dollar reserves.

Our analysis of a foreign currency crisis used the example of the Thai baht for good reason. In 1997 and 1998, Thailand was at the center of a financial crisis that rocked the world.

The crisis began when a lack of confidence in Thailand's financial system led to dramatic shifts in the supply and demand curves for baht—just as in Figure 8. While the *equilibrium* exchange rate fell, Thailand continued to fix the *actual* exchange rate at $0.04 per baht, above the equilibrium rate. As a result, Thailand's central bank was depleting its reserves of dollars and other foreign currencies. This, of course, led currency traders to anticipate a devaluation, shifting the supply and demand curves even further. Finally, in July 1997, the Thai central bank simply ran out of foreign currency reserves, and was forced to let its currency float. The baht immediately depreciated from $0.04 to $0.02.

But this was only the beginning of the story. Many of Thailand's banks—counting on the fixed exchange rate—had borrowed heavily in dollars, yen, and other foreign currencies, but then lent funds to Thai businesses in baht. Once the baht depreciated, these banks were obligated to make unchanged dollar and yen payments on their debts, while continuing to receive unchanged baht payments on the funds they had lent. The problem was that, after the depreciation, the baht coming in would no longer cover the dollars going out. Thailand's banks were in trouble.

And the trouble spread. Investors began to wonder if banks in *other* nearby countries were similarly vulnerable, and began to dump the foreign exchange of Indonesia, South Korea, Malaysia, and the Philippines. Before the crisis ended, it had even spread to several Latin American countries.

What ended the crisis? In large part, the crisis was resolved by the **International Monetary Fund (IMF)**, an international organization formed in 1945 in large part

---

Foreign currency crisis A loss of faith that a country can prevent a drop in its exchange rate, leading to a rapid depletion of its foreign currency (e.g., dollar) reserves.

HTTP://

Professor Nouriel Roubini of New York University maintains an excellent Web page devoted to global financial crises. You can find it at http://www.stern.nyu.edu/~nroubini/asia/AsiaHomepage.html.

International Monetary Fund (IMF) An international organization founded in 1945 to help stabilize the world monetary system.

to help nations avoid such foreign currency crises and help them recover when crises occur. In 1998, the IMF—in cooperation with the U.S. government—orchestrated a rescue package of more than $100 billion to cover the Asian economies' foreign debt.

The rescue was controversial, however. Why? Helping a troubled country leads other countries to expect that they, too, will get help if they pursue untenable policies and get themselves into trouble. This is an example of a more general problem which economists call *moral hazard*.

> ***Moral hazard*** *occurs when a decision maker (such as an individual, firm, or government) expects to be rescued in the event of an unfavorable outcome, and then changes its behavior so that the unfavorable outcome is more likely.*

Moral hazard When decision makers—expecting assistance in the event of an unfavorable outcome—change their behavior so that the unfavorable outcome is more likely.

Moral hazard plagues the insurance industry (are you as likely to lock your car if you're insured against theft?), efforts to care for the unemployed (will you look as hard for a new job after being laid off if you are collecting unemployment insurance?), and troubled business firms (will mega-corporations be careful not to take risks if they expect the government to rescue them in the event of a disaster?).

But here, our focus is on the international financial system. The problem of moral hazard helps explain the very different response of the IMF when, in late 2001 and early 2002, Argentina faced a somewhat similar foreign currency crisis. Like the Asian countries a few years earlier, Argentina needed billions of dollars of help to prevent it from devaluing its currency and defaulting on its foreign debt. This time, however, it was felt that Argentina's problems were unique, and so its foreign currency crisis—unlike the Asian crisis a few years earlier—was unlikely to spread to other countries. Accordingly, the Bush administration—concerned about the moral hazard problem—encouraged the IMF to take a tough stand. There was no rescue, and Argentina was forced into devaluation *and* default in January 2002.

The Euro

One answer to the problems that countries have encountered in managing their own currencies is to adopt another country's currency or an international currency. In 2001, both Ecuador and El Salvador scrapped their own national currencies and adopted the U.S. dollar as their official money. That same year, Guatemala passed legislation permitting the U.S. dollar and other foreign currency to circulate alongside the Guatemalan quetzal. And on January 1, 2002, 12 European countries—including Germany, France, Italy, and Spain—introduced their new common currency: the euro.

The European Central Bank has sole authority for changing the supply of euros. It determines a single monetary policy for all of Euroland, replacing the separate monetary policies of the different countries.

Why did these 12 European countries decide to do away with their national currencies?

There are several advantages. First, a single currency means that European firms—when they buy or sell across borders—no longer have to pay commissions

Euro coins and paper money became the official currency of 12 European countries in 2002.

© HOA QUI/INDEX STOCK IMAGERY

on the exchange of currency, or face the risk that exchange rates might change before accounts are settled. This will increase the volume of trade among the Euroland nations.

Second, the elimination of exchange rate risk makes it easier for European firms to sell stocks and bonds to residents anywhere in Euroland. This will help ensure that funds are channeled to the most profitable firms throughout the area. Third, adopting a single currency makes cross-country comparison shopping easier. This will help increase competition among firms, and help keep prices down to European consumers.

Finally, some of these countries—such as Italy—have had a history of loose monetary policy that has generated high rates of inflation and high expected inflation. By giving up the right to run an independent monetary policy, and leaving it to the (presumably stricter) European Central Bank, the high-inflation countries of Europe will benefit from lower inflation rates.

There are, however, downsides to the euro. In fact, some economists believe that—at least for a while—the euro will create significant problems for the Euroland countries. Why? With a single currency, there must be a single monetary policy, making it impossible to adjust the money supply and interest rates to the problems of individual nations. For example, suppose Spain goes into a recession. In the old days before the euro, its central bank would increase the Spanish money supply and lower interest rates. But now, what if while Spain is in recession, the rest of Europe has full employment or even a boom? Then, the European central bank will be tightening the money supply and raising interest rates, which will worsen conditions in Spain. Spain could always use fiscal policy. But, as you've learned, countercyclical fiscal policy is fraught with problems. Moreover, membership in Euroland requires countries to maintain strict fiscal discipline that might prevent them from using a fiscal stimulus when it is needed.

Optimum Currency Areas. The economists who worry about these problems question whether Europe is an **optimum currency area**—a region whose economies will perform better with a single currency rather than separate national currencies. To be an optimum currency area, the different nations in a region should face common, rather than national, shocks, so that they tend to go into booms and recessions together. In that case, a single monetary policy will be appropriate, because all nations will need stimulus or restraint at the same time. In Europe, unfortunately, the shocks are often national: Different countries are dominated by different industries, face different types of labor unions, and have different institutional frameworks and laws. They are therefore susceptible to national as well as regional shocks.

Another requirement for an optimum currency area is that labor is highly mobile from one country to another. That way, if one country is experiencing a negative shock and goes into a recession that can't be addressed with monetary or fiscal policy (for the reasons discussed earlier), at least its unemployed workers can find work in other countries whose economies are performing better. Indeed, this is what happens in the United States, where labor is highly mobile among states.

But at present, labor is much less mobile across European borders than across the American states. And if unemployed workers stay within a country, its government may feel pressure to abandon the euro so that it can use expansionary fiscal and monetary policy.

Optimum currency area A region whose economies perform better with a single currency than with separate national currencies.

In the very long run, the abolition of national currencies—and the creation of the euro—may work to increase labor mobility across Europe, especially if it changes the attitudes of European firms and workers toward cross-national employment. This would help make Europe more of an optimum currency area, and help make the euro a more workable common currency in the future.

EXCHANGE RATES AND THE MACROECONOMY

Exchange rates can have important effects on the macroeconomy—largely through their effect on net exports. And although we've included net exports in our short-run macro model, we haven't yet asked how exchange rates affect them. That's what we'll do now.

Exchange Rates and Demand Shocks

Suppose that the dollar depreciates against the foreign currencies of its major trading partners. (We'll discuss *why* that might happen in a later section.) Then U.S. goods would become cheaper to foreigners, and net exports would rise at each level of output. This increase in net exports is a positive demand shock to the economy—it increases aggregate expenditure and shifts the aggregate demand curve to the right. And, as you've learned, positive demand shocks increase GDP in the short run.

> *A depreciation of the dollar causes net exports to rise—a positive demand shock that increases real GDP in the short run. An appreciation of the dollar causes net exports to drop—a negative demand shock that decreases real GDP in the short run.*

The impact of net exports on equilibrium GDP—often caused by changes in the exchange rate—helps us understand one reason why governments are often concerned about their exchange rates. An unstable exchange rate can result in repeated shocks to the economy. At worst, this can cause fluctuations in GDP; at best, it makes the central bank's job more difficult as it tries to keep the economy on an even keel.

Exchange Rates and Monetary Policy

In several earlier chapters, we've explored how the Fed tries to keep the U.S. economy on an even keel with monetary policy. The central banks around the world are engaged in a similar struggle, and face many of the same challenges as the Fed. One challenge to central banks is that monetary policy causes changes in exchange rates, and thus has additional effects on real GDP that we have not yet considered.

To understand this, let's run through an example. Suppose the United States is in a recession, and the Fed decides to increase equilibrium GDP. As you've learned, the Fed—by increasing the money supply—brings down the interest rate.

Interest-sensitive spending rises, and so does aggregate expenditure. When we consider the foreign exchange market, however, there is an additional effect on aggregate expenditure.

By lowering the U.S. interest rate, the Fed makes *foreign* financial assets more attractive to Americans, which raises their demand for foreign currency. In the market for pounds, for example, this will shift the demand for pounds curve rightward. At the same time, U.S. financial assets become less attractive to foreigners, which decreases the supply of foreign exchange (in the market for pounds, a leftward shift in the supply of pounds curve). If you sketch out these shifts right now, you'll see that, as long as the exchange rate floats, the result is a *depreciation of the dollar* against the pound.

Now let's see how the depreciation of the dollar affects the economy. With dollars now cheaper to foreigners, they will buy more U.S. goods, raising U.S. exports. At the same time, with foreign goods and services more expensive to Americans, U.S. imports will decrease. Both the increase in exports and the decrease in imports contribute to a rise in net exports, *NX*. This, in turn, increases aggregate expenditure.

Thus, as you can see, the expansionary monetary policy causes aggregate expenditures to rise in two ways: first, by increasing interest-sensitive spending, and second, by increasing net exports. As a result, equilibrium GDP rises by more—and monetary policy is more effective—when the effects on exchange rates are included.

The channels through which monetary policy works are summarized in the following schematic:

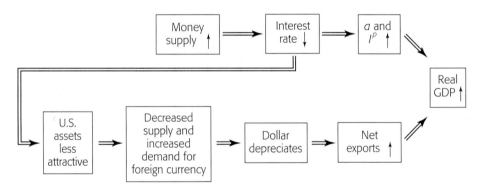

Net Effect: GDP ↑ by more when the exchange rate's effect on net exports is included

The top line shows the familiar effect on interest-sensitive spending: An increase in the money supply causes a drop in the interest rate, which increases autonomous consumption spending (*a*) and investment spending (I^p). The bottom line shows the *additional* effect on net exports through changes in the exchange rate—the effects we've been discussing.

The analysis of contractionary monetary policy is the same, but in reverse. A decrease in the money supply will not only decrease interest-sensitive spending, it will also cause the dollar to appreciate and net exports to drop. Thus, it will cause equilibrium GDP to fall by more than in earlier chapters, where we ignored the foreign exchange market.

The channel of monetary influence through exchange rates and the volume of trade is an important part of the full story of monetary policy in the United States. And in countries where exports are relatively large fractions of GDP—such as those of Europe—the trade channel is even more important. It is the main channel through which monetary policy affects the economy.

> *Monetary policy has a stronger effect when we include the impact on exchange rates and net exports, rather than just the impact on interest-sensitive consumption and investment spending.*

USING THE THEORY
The Stubborn U.S. Trade Deficit

The U.S. trade deficit is often in the news. But what, exactly, is it?

The trade deficit is the extent to which a country's imports exceed its exports:

$$\text{Trade deficit} = \text{imports} - \text{exports}.$$

On the other hand, when exports exceed imports, a nation has a trade surplus:

$$\text{Trade surplus} = \text{exports} - \text{imports}.$$

As you can see, the trade surplus is nothing more than a nation's net exports (NX). And when net exports are negative, we have a trade deficit.

The United States has had large trade deficits with the rest of the world since the early 1980s. In 2004, the trade deficit was $587 billion. Simply put, Americans bought $587 billion more goods and services from other countries than their residents bought from the United States.

Why does the United States have a trade deficit with the rest of the world? A variety of explanations have been offered in the media, including poor U.S. marketing savvy in selling to foreigners, and a greater degree of protectionism in foreign markets.

But economists believe that there is a much more important reason. In this section, we'll use what you've learned about exchange rates to show how the U.S. trade deficit arose and why it continues. To keep our analysis simple, we'll start by looking at the U.S. trade deficit with just one country—Japan—but our results will hold more generally to the trade deficit with other countries as well.

Before we analyze the causes of the trade deficit, we need to do a little math. Let's begin by breaking down the total quantity of yen demanded by Americans ($D^{¥}$) into two components: the yen demanded to purchase Japanese goods and

© DAN LAMONT/CORBIS

Trade deficit The excess of a nation's imports over its exports during a given period.

Trade surplus The excess of a nation's exports over its imports during a given period.

services (U.S. imports from Japan) and the yen demanded to buy Japanese assets:

$$D^{\yen} = \text{U.S. imports from Japan} + \text{U.S. purchases of Japanese assets.}$$

Similarly, we can divide the total quantity of yen supplied by the Japanese ($S^{\yen}$) into two components: the yen exchanged for dollars to purchase American goods (U.S. exports to Japan) and the yen exchanged for dollars to purchase American assets like stocks, bonds, or real estate:

$$S^{\yen} = \text{U.S. exports to Japan} + \text{Japanese purchases of U.S. assets.}$$

As long as the yen floats against the dollar without government intervention—which it does during most periods—we know that the exchange rate will adjust until the quantities of yen supplied and demanded are equal, or $D^{\yen} = S^{\yen}$. Substituting the foregoing breakdowns into this equation, we have

$$\left\{ \begin{array}{l} \text{U.S. imports from Japan} \\ + \text{ U.S. purchases of Japanese assets} \end{array} \right\} = \left\{ \begin{array}{l} \text{U.S. exports to Japan} \\ + \text{ Japanese purchases of U.S. assets.} \end{array} \right\}$$

Now let's rearrange this equation—subtracting U.S. exports from both sides—and subtracting American purchases of Japanese assets from both sides—to get

$$\left\{ \begin{array}{l} \text{U.S. imports from Japan} \\ - \text{ U.S exports to Japan} \end{array} \right\} = \left\{ \begin{array}{l} \text{Japanese purchases of U.S. assets} \\ - \text{ U.S. purchases of Japanese assets.} \end{array} \right\}$$

The term on the left should look familiar: It is the U.S. trade deficit with Japan. And since a similar equation must hold for every country, we can generalize it this way:

$$\left\{ \begin{array}{l} \text{U.S imports from other countries} \\ - \text{ U.S. exports to other countries} \end{array} \right\} = \left\{ \begin{array}{l} \text{foreign purchases of U.S. assets} \\ - \text{ U.S. purchases of foreign assets.} \end{array} \right\}$$

But what is the expression on the right? It tells us the extent to which foreigners are buying more of our assets than we are buying of theirs. It is often called the **net financial inflow** into the United States, because when the residents of other countries buy U.S. assets, funds flow into the U.S. financial market, where they are made available to U.S. firms and the U.S. government. Thus, the equation we've derived—which must hold true when exchange rates float—can also be expressed as

Net financial inflow An inflow of funds equal to a nation's trade deficit.

$$\text{U.S. trade deficit} = \text{U.S. net financial inflow.}$$

Why have we bothered to derive this equation? Because it tells us two very important things about the U.S. trade deficit. First, it tells us how the trade deficit is *financed*. Think about it: If the United States is running a trade deficit with, say, Japan, it means that the Japanese are providing more goods and services to Americans—more automobiles, VCRs, memory chips, and other goods—than Americans are providing to them. The Japanese are not doing this out of kindness. They must be getting *something* in return for the extra goods we are getting, and the equation tells us just what that is: U.S. assets. This is one reason why the trade deficit concerns U.S. policy makers: It results in a transfer of wealth from Americans to foreign residents.

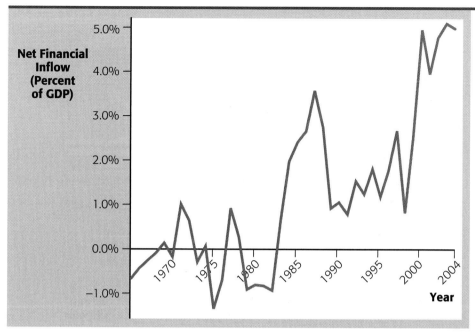

FIGURE 9
Net Financial Flows into the United States as a Percent of GDP

Beginning in the early 1980s, and continuing today, a massive financial inflow has led to a U.S. trade deficit.

The second important insight provided by the equation is that a trade deficit can arise *because* of forces that cause a financial inflow. That is, if forces in the global economy make the right side of the equation positive, then the left side must be positive as well, and we will have a trade deficit.

Indeed, economists believe this is just what has happened to the United States: that the U.S. trade deficit has been caused by the desire of foreigners to invest in the United States. The result was a massive financial inflow and trade deficit that arose in the early 1980s, as illustrated in Figure 9. This financial inflow was unprecedented in size and duration, and it reversed a long-standing pattern of ownership between the United States and other countries. For decades, American holdings of foreign assets far exceeded foreign holdings of U.S. assets. But the financial inflows of the 1980s changed that: By 1988, foreigners held about $500 billion more in U.S. assets than Americans held in foreign assets. By the end of 2004, the difference in asset holdings increased more than fivefold, and exceeded $2.5 trillion.

But how do the forces that create a financial inflow also *cause* a trade deficit?

From a Financial Inflow to a Trade Deficit

Figure 10 illustrates this process, using the yen–dollar market. We'll assume that initially, neither the Japanese nor the Americans are buying *assets* from the other country. Only goods and services are traded. Point *A* shows the initial equilibrium under this special assumption. Under these circumstances, the demand curve for yen would reflect U.S. *imports* of goods and services from Japan, and

FIGURE 10

How a U.S. Financial Inflow Creates a U.S. Trade Deficit

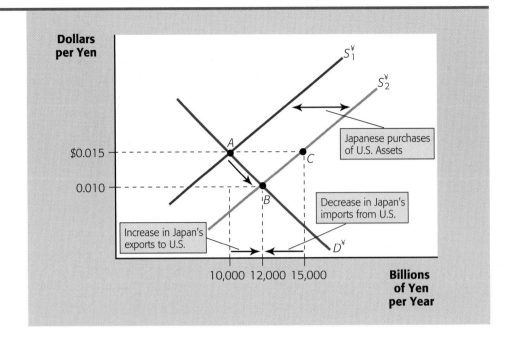

the supply curve would reflect U.S. *exports* of goods and services to Japan. The exchange rate would be $0.015 per yen (one-and-a-half cents per yen), and each year, 10,000 billion yen would be traded in exchange for 10,000 × .015 = 150 billion dollars. Since the quantity of yen demanded and supplied are equal in equilibrium, there is no trade deficit: The United States buys $150 billion in goods from Japan, and Japan buys $150 billion in goods from the United States.

Now suppose that the Japanese start to buy U.S. stocks, bonds, and real estate. Specifically, they want to purchase 5,000 billion yen worth of these assets from Americans each year. To do so, they need dollars, so they must supply additional yen to the foreign exchange market to get them. Accordingly, the supply of yen curve shifts rightward by 5,000 billion yen. The market equilibrium moves from point *A* to point *B*, and the new exchange rate is $.01 per yen. The yen depreciates against the dollar, and the dollar appreciates against the yen.

But something interesting happens in the market as the exchange rate changes. First, there is a *movement along the demand curve* for yen, from point *A* to point *B*. Why? The yen is now cheaper, so Americans—finding Japanese goods and services cheaper—buy more of them. Thus, the movement along the demand curve represents an *increase in Japan's exports to the U.S.* (valued in yen, the units on the horizontal axis). In the figure, Japan's exports—the quantity of yen demanded—rise by 2,000 billion yen as we move from *A* to *B*.

But there is a second movement as well. After the shift in the supply curve, *and at the old exchange rate of $0.015*, the Japanese want to supply 15,000 billion yen to the market (point *C*). But as the exchange rate falls, there is a movement from point *C* to point *B*—the quantity of yen supplied decreases. Why does this happen? Because as the yen depreciates (the dollar appreciates), U.S. goods and services become more expensive to the Japanese. Accordingly, they purchase fewer U.S. goods. Assuming that the Japanese still want to purchase the same 5,000 billion yen in U.S. *assets*, the entire decrease in the quantity of yen supplied as we move from *C* to *B* represents a *decrease in Japan's imports from the U.S.* (valued in yen). In the figure, Japan's imports decrease by 3,000 billion yen.

Let's recap: Because the Japanese wanted to purchase 5,000 billion yen in U.S. assets (a net financial inflow to the United States of 5,000 billion yen), the yen depreciated. This, in turn, made Japanese goods cheaper for Americans—increasing Japan's exports (U.S. imports) by 2,000 billion yen per year. It also made U.S. goods more expensive in Japan, decreasing Japan's imports (U.S. exports) by 3,000 billion yen per year. Since U.S. imports have risen by 2,000 billion ¥ and U.S. exports have fallen by 3,000 billion ¥, the United States—which initially had no trade deficit with Japan at point *A*—now has a trade deficit equal to 5,000 billion yen. This is exactly equal to the financial inflow—Japan's purchases of U.S. assets.

More generally,

an increase in the desire of foreigners to invest in the United States contributes to an appreciation of the dollar. As a result, U.S. exports—which become more expensive for foreigners—decline. Imports—which become cheaper to Americans—increase. The result is a rise in the U.S. trade deficit.

What explains the huge financial inflow that began in the 1980s, and has since grown larger? In the 1980s, an important part of the story was *a rise in U.S. interest rates relative to interest rates abroad*, which made U.S. assets more attractive to foreigners, and foreign assets less attractive to Americans. In the 1990s, however, U.S. interest rates were low relative to rates in other countries, yet the inflow continued. Why?

Even when U.S. interest rates are lower than abroad, it seems that foreign residents have a strong preference for holding American assets. In part, this is because of a favorable investment climate. The United States is a stable country with a long history of protecting individual property rights. People know that if they buy American stocks or bonds, unless they violate U.S. criminal law, the U.S. government is very unlikely to confiscate foreign-owned assets or suddenly impose punitive taxes when foreigners want to repatriate the funds to their home countries. This asymmetrical foreign preference for American assets helps explain why the U.S. net financial inflow has been *persistent*.

But why the recent *surge* in the inflow? One reason is that Americans have been saving less, and foreigners have been saving more. (In Europe and in Japan, aging populations have been saving heavily for retirement, while developing country governments have been reducing debt and building up financial reserves.) All of this new foreign wealth needs to be held in *some* country's assets, and—for reasons discussed earlier—the U.S. seems to be the favorite.[2]

Remember that, under floating exchange rates, the financial inflow equals the trade deficit. Thus, the story of the U.S. financial inflow of the 1980s, 1990s, and 2000s is also the story of the U.S. trade deficit:

[2] For a complete explanation of this argument, see the speech by Federal Reserve Governor Ben S. Bernanke, "The Global Saving Glut and the U.S. Current Account Deficit," April 14, 2005 (www.federalreserve.gov/boarddocs/speeches/2005)

FIGURE 11
The Growing U.S. Trade Deficit with China

Includes trade in goods only.
Source: Wayne M. Morrison, "China-U.S. Trade Issues," Congressional Research Service, Library of Congress, Updated May 16, 2003 and Economic Report of the President, 2005.

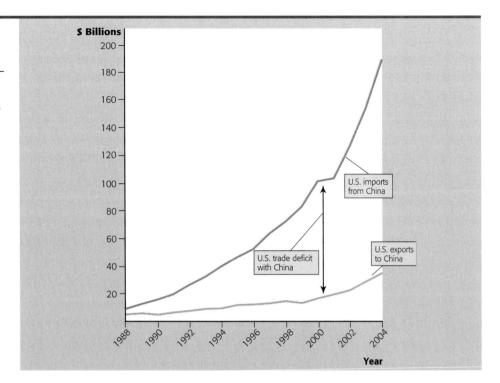

> *We can trace the rise in the trade deficit during recent decades to two important sources: first, relatively high interest rates in the 1980s, and second, a long-held preference for American assets that grew stronger in the 1990s. Each of these contributed to a large financial inflow, a higher value for the dollar, and a trade deficit.*

The Growing Trade Deficit with China

In addition to a strong desire to buy U.S. assets, a trade deficit can arise from another cause: a foreign currency fixed at an artificially low value. In the minds of many economists, this has contributed to the United States' growing trade deficit with China.

Figure 11 shows United States imports to, and exports from, China from 1988 to 2004. Trade in both directions expanded dramatically. But while United States exports to China increased seven-fold, United States *imports* from China increased almost 22-fold, from $8.5 billion in 1988 to $187 billion in 2004. During this period, China went from being a relatively unimportant trading partner of the United States to the fourth-largest trading partner. In the figure, the growing trade deficit is the increasing distance between the (higher) imports line and the (lower) exports line. In 2004, the United States had a larger trade deficit with China—$153 billion—than with any other country.

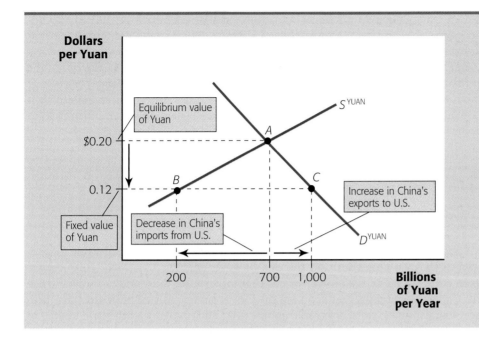

FIGURE 12
How an Undervalued Chinese Yuan Can Create a U.S. Trade Deficit

The U.S. trade deficit with China has been soaring for a variety of reasons, including special trade agreements during this period that gave China new access to U.S. markets, and Chinese trade policies that have encouraged exports and discouraged imports. But another factor, as mentioned above, is China's undervalued exchange rate. Since 1994, China has fixed the value of its currency (the yuan) against the dollar—first at 8.7 yuan per dollar, and since 1997, at a steady 8.27–8.28 yuan per dollar (about $.12 per yuan). This is widely believed to be lower than the equilibrium value of the yuan. (China's controls on trading the yuan make its equilibrium value difficult to determine.)

Figure 12 illustrates how an undervalued yuan can create a trade deficit for the United States. We'll assume that if the exchange rate were floating, the market equilibrium would be at point A, with an exchange rate of $0.20 per yuan. In this case, 700 billion yuan would be exchanged for 700 × .02 = 140 billion dollars each year.

Now we introduce the lower, fixed exchange rate of $.12 per yuan. Compared to the equilibrium exchange rate, the fixed exchange rate causes a movement along the *demand* for yuan curve, from point A to point C. The yuan is now cheaper, which makes Chinese goods and services cheaper to Americans, who buy more of them. Measured along the horizontal axis, *China's exports to the U.S. increase* by 300 billion yuan per year.

There is also a move from point A to point B along the *supply* curve; the quantity of yuan supplied decreases. A lower-valued yuan makes U.S. goods and services more expensive to Chinese households and businesses, so they purchase fewer of them. Along the horizontal axis, *China's imports from the U.S. decrease* by 500 billion yuan.

Since the fixed exchange rate has caused *China's imports from the U.S. to decrease* by 500 billion yuan, and *China's exports to the U.S. to increase* by 300 billion yuan, the U.S. trade deficit with China—valued in yuan—rises by 500 + 300 or 800 billion yuan per year. (If you convert the U.S. trade deficit to dollars, you'll see that our example comes close to the actual U.S. trade deficit with China.)

But wait . . . doesn't the rise in the U.S. trade deficit have to equal the rise in the net financial inflow? Indeed it does. Figure 11 shows an *excess demand for yuan* of $1,000 - 200 = 800$ billion at the fixed exchange rate. The Chinese government must supply these yuan, selling them for U.S. dollars. These dollars are then used to purchase U.S. assets, contributing to the U.S. net financial inflow.

> *When a U.S. trading partner fixes the dollar price of its currency below its equilibrium value, U.S exports—which become more expensive to foreigners—decline. U.S. imports—which become cheaper to Americans—increase. The result is a rise in the U.S. trade deficit.*

China's fixed exchange rate with the dollar is the source of considerable tension between the two countries. On the one hand, it enables Americans to purchase goods from China at even lower prices than otherwise. But rapidly growing trade with China also disrupts production in the U.S. economy, as U.S. businesses that produce sandals, shoes, suits, electronic goods, toys, and textiles find they are unable to compete with cheaper goods from China. The fixed exchange exacerbates their problem. By giving China an even *greater* cost advantage than it would otherwise have, U.S. firms and workers that compete in these markets must adjust more rapidly—and painfully—to the new pattern of international trade.

In July 2005, facing intense pressure from American officials to raise the value of its currency, China finally relented—a bit. First, it devalued the yuan (but by only 2.1%). More importantly, China ended its fixed exchange rate. Instead, it announced a managed float against a basket of currencies (not just the dollar). These changes might lead to further increases in the value of the yuan over time; if so, one of the forces driving the U.S. trade deficit with China would be weakened.

Summary

When residents of two countries trade with one another, one party ordinarily makes use of the foreign exchange market to trade one national currency for another. In this market, suppliers of a currency interact with demanders to determine an exchange rate—the price of one currency in terms of another.

In the market for U.S. dollars and British pounds, for example, demanders are mostly Americans who wish to obtain pounds in order to buy goods and services from British firms, or to buy British assets. A higher dollar price for the pound will lead Americans to demand fewer pounds—the demand curve slopes downward. Changes in U.S. real GDP, the U.S. price level relative to the British price level, Americans' tastes for British goods, interest rates in the United States relative to Britain, or expectations regarding the exchange rate can each cause the demand curve to shift.

Suppliers of pounds are mostly British residents who wish to buy American goods, services, or assets. A higher dollar price for the pound will lead Britons to supply more pounds—the supply curve slopes upward. The supply curve will shift in response to changes in British real GDP, prices in Britain relative to the United States, British tastes for U.S. goods, the British interest rate relative to the U.S. rate, and expectations regarding the exchange rate.

When the exchange rate floats, the equilibrium rate is determined where the supply and demand curves cross. If the equilibrium is disturbed by, say, a rightward shift of the demand curve, then the currency being demanded will appreciate—the exchange rate will rise. (The other country's currency will depreciate.) In a similar way, a rightward shift of the supply curve will cause the currency being supplied to depreciate.

Governments often intervene in foreign exchange markets. Many countries manage their float, buying and selling their own currency to alter the exchange rate. Some countries fix their exchange rate to the dollar or the currency of a major trading partner. And in Europe, 12 national governments have eliminated their national currencies and replaced them with the euro. Although these 12 nations may not yet be an optimum currency area, they are moving closer to one.

When a currency depreciates, its net exports rise—a positive demand shock. Monetary policy, in addition to its impact on interest-sensitive spending, also changes the exchange rate and net exports, adding to changes in output. This monetary policy is more effective in changing GDP when its effects on net exports are included.

The U.S. has had a persistent—and growing trade deficit—with the rest of the world. Much of this trade deficit can be explained by the growing U.S. financial inflow from the rest of the world. U.S. assets have been consistently more attractive to foreigners than foreign assets have been to Americans. The U.S. financial inflow causes the dollar to appreciate, which decreases U.S. exports and increases U.S. imports. In addition, an undervalued foreign currency can create a trade deficit. By making the U.S. dollar artificially more expensive to residents of the foreign country, it causes U.S. exports to decline and U.S. imports to rise.

Key Terms

Appreciation	Floating exchange rate	Net financial inflow
Demand curve for foreign currency	Foreign currency crisis	Optimum currency area
Depreciation	Foreign exchange market	Purchasing power parity (PPP) theory
Devaluation	International Monetary Fund	Supply curve for foreign currency
Exchange rate	Managed float	Trade deficit
Fixed exchange rate	Moral hazard	Trade surplus

Review Questions   *Answers to even-numbered Questions and Problems can be found on the text Web site at http://hall-lieb.swlearning.com.*

1. Why do Americans demand foreign currency? Why does the demand curve for foreign currency slope downward? What factors shift the demand curve for foreign currency to the right? What factors shift it to the left?

2. Why do foreigners supply foreign currency? Why does the supply of foreign currency curve slope upward? What factors shift the supply curve for foreign currency to the right? What factors shift it to the left?

3. Explain how an expected appreciation of a foreign currency can become a self-fulfilling prophecy.

4. What forces move exchange rates in the very short run? In the short run?

5. "A weak currency is a sign of a sick economy." True or false? Explain.

6. What is purchasing power parity? Why might exchange rates deviate from purchasing power parity?

7. Suppose the purchasing power parity exchange rate between the dollar and the pound is $1.50 per pound but the actual exchange rate is $2 per pound. Explain how a trader could profit by buying a basket of goods in one country (which country?) and selling it in the other. How would such actions by traders affect the exchange rate?

8. What is a managed float and why would a government use it?

9. How does an appreciation of the dollar affect U.S. real GDP?

10. According to economists, what caused the U.S. trade deficit in the 1980s? Why does the trade deficit persist?

11. Some nations might not be well suited to join together to use a common currency. What requirements are necessary for nations to be an optimum currency area?

12. Explain why managed floats are controversial.

Problems and Exercises

1. Do the following events cause the dollar to appreciate against the euro or to depreciate?
   a. Health experts discover that red wine, especially French and Italian red wine, lowers cholesterol.
   b. GDP in nations across Europe falls.
   c. The United States experiences a higher inflation rate than Europe does.
   d. The United States runs a large budget deficit.

2. Let the monthly demand for British pounds and the monthly supply of British pounds be described by the following equations:

$$\text{Demand for pounds} = 10 - 2e$$
$$\text{Supply of pounds} = 4 + 3e,$$

where the quantities are in millions of pounds and e is dollars per pound.

  a. Find the equilibrium exchange rate.

  b. Suppose the U.S. government intervenes in the foreign currency market and uses U.S. dollars to buy 2 million pounds each month. What happens to the exchange rate? Why might the U.S. government do this?

3. Let the demand and supply of Philippine pesos each month be described by the following equations:

$$\text{Demand for pesos} = 100 - 2,000e$$
$$\text{Supply of pesos} = 20 + 3,000e,$$

where the quantities are millions of pesos, and e is dollars per peso.

  a. Find the equilibrium exchange rate.

  b. Suppose the Philippine central bank wants to fix the exchange rate at 50 pesos per dollar and keep it there. Should the Philippine central bank buy or sell its own currency? How much per month?

4. Suppose the United States and Mexico are each other's sole trading partners. The Fed, afraid that the economy is about to overheat, decreases the U.S. money supply.

  a. Will the dollar appreciate or depreciate against the Mexican peso? Illustrate with a diagram of the dollar–peso foreign exchange market.

  b. What will happen to equilibrium GDP in the United States?

  c. How would your analyses in (a) and (b) change if, at the same time that the Fed was increasing the U.S. interest rate, the Mexican central bank increased the Mexican interest rate by an equivalent amount?

5. Jordan fixes its national currency—the dinar—against the dollar. In June, 2003, the fixed rate was 1.41 dinars per dollar.

  a. Draw a diagram illustrating the market in which Jordanian dinars are traded for U.S. dollars, assuming that the equilibrium exchange rate is 1.00 dinar per dollar. (In your diagram, put the number of dinars per month on the horizontal axis.)

  b. Under the assumption in (a) above, would Jordan's central bank be buying or selling Jordanian dinars in this market? Indicate the number of dinars per month that the central bank must buy or sell as a distance on your graph.

  c. Based on your diagram and your answers so far, could Jordan continue to fix its currency at 1.41 dinars per dollar forever? Why or why not?

  d. Suppose that foreign currency traders believe that Jordan will soon allow the dinar to float. How would this affect the current supply and demand curves for dinars? (Draw new curves to indicate the impact.)

  e. How would the events in (d) above affect the number of dinars that Jordan's central bank must buy or sell?

6. As in problem 5, note that Jordan fixes its national currency—the dinar—against the dollar at 1.41 dinars per dollar.

  a. Draw a diagram illustrating the market in which Jordanian dinars are traded for U.S. dollars, assuming that the equilibrium exchange rate is 2.00 dinars per dollar. (Put the number of dinars per month on the horizontal axis.)

  b. Under the assumption in (a) above, would Jordan's central bank be buying or selling Jordanian dinars in this market? Indicate the number of dinars per month that the central bank must buy or sell as a distance on your graph.

  c. Based on your diagram and your answers so far, could Jordan continue to fix its currency at 1.41 dinars per dollar forever? Why or why not?

  d. Suppose that foreign currency traders believe that Jordan will soon allow the dinar to float. How would this affect the current supply and demand curves for dinars? (Draw new curves to indicate the impact.)

  e. How would the events in (d) above affect the number of dinars that Jordan's central bank must buy or sell?

7. Some nations that fix their exchange rates make their currency more expensive for foreigners (an overvalued currency), while others make their currency artificially cheap to foreigners (an undervalued currency).

  a. Why would a country want an overvalued currency? How, specifically, would the country benefit? Would the policy cause harm to anyone in the country? Explain briefly.

  b. Why would a country want an undervalued currency? How, specifically, would the country benefit? Would the policy cause harm to anyone in the country? Explain briefly.

8. If the inflation rate in Country A is 4 percent and the inflation rate in Country B is 6 percent, explain what will happen to the relative value of each country's currency.

9. a. Use the information in the table below to find the exchange rate if the euro and the U.S. dollar are allowed to float freely.

Dollars per Euro	Quantity of Euros Demanded	Quantity of Euros Supplied
$1.20	500 million	2,600 million
$1.10	1,000 million	2,400 million
$1.00	1,500 million	2,200 million
$0.90	2,000 million	2,000 million
$0.80	2,500 million	1,800 million

b. What will happen to the exchange rate if the demand for euros rises by 700 million at each price if there is no intervention?

c. Assume that the European central bank currently owns 400 million dollars and the Fed currently owns 300 million euros. If the demand for Euros rises by 700 million at each price, what would the European central bank have to do to maintain a fixed exchange rate equal to the exchange rate you found in part (a)? Is this possible?

10. Use a diagram showing the market for British pounds, a money market diagram, and an AD–AS graph for the U.S. to show all the effects of an increase in the U.S. money supply on U.S. real GDP.

11. Refer to Figure 10 in the chapter. Remember that there was no trade deficit at point *A*. What is the U.S. trade deficit with Japan in *dollars* at point *B*?

Challenge Questions

1. It is often stated that the U.S. trade deficit with Japan results from Japanese trade barriers against U.S. goods.

   a. Suppose that Japan and the United States trade goods but not assets. Show—with a diagram of the dollar–yen market—that a U.S. trade deficit is impossible as long as the exchange rate floats. (*Hint:* With no trading in assets, the quantity of yen demanded at each exchange rate is equal in value to U.S. imports, and the quantity of yen supplied at each exchange rate is equal in value to U.S. exports.)

   b. In the diagram, illustrate the impact of a reduction in Japanese trade barriers. Would the dollar appreciate or depreciate against the yen? What would be the impact on U.S. net exports?

   c. Now suppose that the United States and Japan also trade assets, but that the Japanese buy more U.S. assets than we buy of theirs. Could the elimination of Japanese trade barriers wipe out the U.S. trade deficit with Japan? Why, or why not? (*Hint:* What is the relationship between the U.S. trade deficit and U.S. net financial inflow?)

2. Suppose that the U.S. government raises spending without increasing taxes. Will there be any effects on the foreign exchange market? (*Hint:* What does this policy do to U.S. interest rates?) When we add in the effects from the foreign exchange market and net exports, is fiscal policy more effective or less effective in changing equilibrium GDP in the short run?

 These exercises require access to Hall/Lieberman Xtra! If Xtra! did not come with your book, visit http://hallxtra.swlearning.com to purchase.

1. Use your Xtra! password at the Hall and Lieberman Web site (http://hallxtra.swlearning.com), select this chapter, and under Economic Applications, click on EconDebate. Choose *International Trade*, and scroll down to find the debate, "What Are the Pros and Cons of IMF Involvement with Global Economies?" Read the debate, and use the information to answer the following questions.

   a. What is the effect of volatility of exchange rates on international trade? Explain.

   b. Explain the debate over the austerity measures required for IMF loans in the case of the Asian crisis.

2. Use your Xtra! password at the Hall and Lieberman Web site (http://hallxtra.swlearning.com), select this chapter, and under Economic Applications, click on EconDebates Online. Choose *International Trade*, and scroll down to find the debate, "Does the U.S. Economy Benefit from the WTO?" Read the debate,

and use the information and explain the views of the proponents of the WTO. Which side of the debate do you find to have more plausible arguments? Explain why.

3. Use your Xtra! password at the Hall and Lieberman Web site (http://hallxtra.swlearning.com), select this chapter, and under Economic Applications, click on EconData. Choose *International Trade,* and scroll down to find *Current Account*. Read the definition and click on Diagrams/Data and use the information to answer the following questions.

   a. Consider the current account balance and the yen per dollar exchange rate diagram and explain what would happen to the current account balance if the dollar depreciates.

   b. Consider the current account balance and real personal income diagram and explain what happens to the current account balance during an economic recession.

Comparative Advantage and the Gains from International Trade

CHAPTER OUTLINE

The Logic of Free Trade

The Theory of Comparative Advantage
  Opportunity Cost and Comparative Advantage
  Specialization and World Production
  How Each Nation Gains from International Trade
  The Terms of Trade

How Potential Gains Turn into Actual Gains
  Some Important Provisos

The Sources of Comparative Advantage

Why Some People Object to Free Trade
  The Impact of Trade in the Exporting Country
  The Impact of Trade in the Importing Country
  Attitudes and Influence on Trade Policy

How Free Trade Is Restricted
  Tariffs
  Quotas

Protectionism
  Myths About International Trade
  Sophisticated Arguments for Protection
  Protectionism in the United States

Using the Theory: The U.S. Sugar Quota

Consumers love bargains. And the rest of the world offers U.S. consumers bargains galore: cars from Japan, computer memory chips from Korea, shoes and clothing from China, tomatoes from Mexico, lumber from Canada, and sugar from the Caribbean. But Americans' purchases of foreign-made goods have always been a controversial subject. Should we let these bargain goods into the country? Consumers certainly benefit when we do so. But don't cheap foreign goods threaten the jobs of American workers and the profits of American producers? How do we balance the interests of specific workers and producers on the one hand with the interests of consumers in general? These questions are important not just in the United States, but in every country of the world.

Over the post–World War II period, there has been a worldwide movement toward a policy of *free trade*—the unhindered movement of goods and services across national boundaries. An example of this movement was the creation—in 1995—of a new international body: the World Trade Organization (WTO). The WTO's goal is to help resolve trade disputes among its members, and to reduce obstacles to free trade around the world. And to some extent it has succeeded: Import taxes, import limitations, and all kinds of crafty regulations designed to keep out imports are gradually falling away. By mid-2005, 148 countries had joined the WTO, including the two most recent members, Cambodia and Nepal, which were admitted in 2004. And some 26 other countries, including Russia, Saudi Arabia, and Vietnam, were eager to join the free-trade group.

But while many barriers have come down, others are being put up. In 2005, the United States renewed its long-standing quota on sugar imports and took serious steps to limit imports of shrimp from Vietnam, Brazil, Thailand, and several other countries. The U.S. and Europe were using various methods to resist a surge of textile imports from China. The European Union continued to restrict the sale of U.S. beef, high-tech equipment, and entertainment programming. Japan and South Korea were resisting efforts to eliminate restrictions on the sale of U.S. automobiles and auto parts. And Mexico was actively trying to restrict imports of soft drinks.

Looking at the contradictory mix of trade policies that exist in the world, we are left to wonder: Is free international trade a good thing that makes us better off, or is it bad for us and something that should be kept in check? In this chapter, you'll learn to apply the tools of economics to issues surrounding international trade. Most important, you'll see how we can extend economic analysis to a global context, in which markets extend across international borders, and the decision makers are households, firms, and government agencies in different nations.

THE LOGIC OF FREE TRADE

Many of us like the idea of being self-reliant. A very few even prefer to live by themselves in a remote region of Alaska or the backcountry of Montana. But consider the defects of self-sufficiency: If you lived all by yourself, you would be poor. You could not *export* or sell to others any part of your own production, nor could you *import* or buy from others anything they have produced. You would be limited to consuming the goods and services that you produced. Undoubtedly, the food, clothing, and housing you would manage to produce by yourself would be small in quantity and poor in quality—nothing like the items you currently enjoy. And there would be many things you could not get at all—electricity, television, cars, airplane trips, or the penicillin that could save your life.

The defects of self-sufficiency explain why most people do not choose it. Rather, people prefer to specialize and trade with each other. In Chapter 2, you learned that specialization and exchange enable us to enjoy greater production and higher living standards than would otherwise be possible.

This principle applies not just to individuals, but also to *groups* of individuals, such as those living within the boundaries that define cities, counties, states, or nations. That is, just as we all benefit when *individuals* specialize and exchange with each other, so, too, we can benefit when *groups* of individuals specialize in producing different goods and services, and exchange them with other *groups*.

Imagine what would happen if the residents of your state switched from a policy of open trading with other states to one of self-sufficiency, refusing to import anything from "foreign states" or to export anything to them. Such an arrangement would be preferable to individual self-sufficiency; at least there would be specialization and trade *within* the state. But the elimination of trading between states would surely result in many sacrifices. Lacking the necessary inputs for their production, for instance, your state might have to do without bananas, cotton, or tires. And the goods that *were* made in your state would likely be produced inefficiently. For example, while residents of Vermont *could* drill for oil, and Texans *could* produce maple syrup, they could do so only at great cost of resources.

Thus, it would make no sense to insist on the economic self-sufficiency of each of the 50 states. And the founders of the United States knew this. They placed prohibitions against tariffs, quotas, and other barriers to interstate commerce right in the U.S. Constitution. The people of Vermont and Texas are vastly better off under free trade among the states than they would be if each state were self-sufficient.

What is true for states is also true for entire nations. The members of the WTO have carried the argument to its ultimate conclusion: National specialization and exchange can expand world living standards through free *international* trade. Such trade involves the movement of goods and services across national boundaries. Goods and services produced domestically, but sold abroad, are called **exports;** those produced abroad, but consumed domestically, are called **imports.** The long-term goal of the WTO is to remove all barriers to exports and imports in order to encourage among nations the specialization and trade that have been so successful within nations.

> **Exports** Goods and services produced domestically, but sold abroad.

> **Imports** Goods and services produced abroad, but consumed domestically.

THE THEORY OF COMPARATIVE ADVANTAGE

Economists who first considered the benefits of international trade focused on a country's *absolute advantage.*

> *A country has an **absolute advantage** in a good when it can produce it using fewer resources than another country.*

> **Absolute advantage** The ability to produce a good or service, using fewer resources than other producers use.

As the early economists saw it, the citizens of every nation could improve their economic welfare by specializing in the production of goods in which they had an absolute advantage and exporting them to other countries. In turn, they would import goods from countries that had an absolute advantage in those goods.

Way back in 1817, however, the British economist David Ricardo disagreed. Absolute advantage, he argued, was not a necessary ingredient for mutually beneficial international trade. The key was *comparative advantage:*

> *A nation has a **comparative advantage** in producing a good if it can produce it at a lower opportunity cost than some other country.*

> **Comparative advantage** The ability to produce a good or service at a lower opportunity cost than other producers.

Notice the difference between the definitions of absolute advantage and comparative advantage. While absolute advantage in a good is defined by the resources used to produce it, comparative advantage is based on the *opportunity cost* of producing it. And we measure the opportunity cost of producing a good not by the resources used to produce it, but rather by the *other goods* that these resources *could* have produced instead.

Labor Requirements per:	China	United States
Suit	125 hours	50 hours
Computer	625 hours	100 hours

TABLE 1
Labor Requirements per Unit

Ricardo argued that a potential trading partner could be absolutely inferior in the production of every single good—requiring more resources per unit of each good than any other country—and still have a comparative advantage in some good. The comparative advantage would arise because the country was *less* inferior at producing some goods than others. Likewise, a country that had an absolute advantage in producing everything could—contrary to common opinion—still benefit from trade. It would have a comparative advantage only in some, but not all, goods.

> *Mutually beneficial trade between any two countries is possible whenever one country is relatively better at producing a good than the other country is. Being relatively better means having the ability to produce a good at a lower opportunity cost—that is, at a lower sacrifice of other goods foregone.*

Opportunity Cost and Comparative Advantage

To illustrate Ricardo's insight, let's consider a hypothetical world of two countries, China and the United States. Both are producing only two goods, men's suits and computers. Could they better themselves by trading with one another? Ricardo would have us look at opportunity costs. But how do we determine the opportunity cost of a computer or a suit?

Let's start out as simply as possible. We'll imagine there is only one resource in each country—labor—and that it takes a constant number of hours to make one computer or one suit no matter how many units of these goods are produced. Table 1 lists the labor hours required. For example, the entry of 125 in the upper left corner tells us that it takes 125 hours of labor to make one suit in China, no matter how many suits are produced there. The upper right corner tells us that it takes 50 hours to make a suit in the United States.

This is all the information we'll need to find the opportunity cost of a computer or a suit in China or the United States.

First, suppose China were to produce one additional computer. Then it would have to divert 625 hours of labor from the suit industry. This, in turn, would require China to produce fewer suits. How many fewer? Since each suit uses up 125 hours of labor, then using 625 hours for one computer would require producing 625/125 = 5 fewer suits. Thus, the opportunity cost of a computer in China is *5 suits*. This opportunity cost is recorded in Table 2; check the table and make sure you can find this entry.

In the United States, producing an additional computer requires diverting 100 hours of labor from suit making. Since each suit requires 50 hours, this means a

Opportunity Costs per:	China	United States	TABLE 2
Suit	$\frac{1}{5}$ computer	$\frac{1}{2}$ computer	Opportunity Costs
Computer	5 suits	2 suits	

sacrifice of 2 suits. Thus, in the United States, the opportunity cost of one computer is 2 suits, which can also be found in Table 2.

Summing up, we see that in China, the opportunity cost of a computer is 5 suits; in the United States, it is 2 suits. Therefore, the United States—with the lower opportunity cost of producing computers—*has a comparative advantage in making computers*.

Notice that in Table 2, we do similar calculations for the opportunity cost of making a suit, measuring the opportunity cost in terms of *computers foregone*. These computations are summarized in the first row of the table. Make sure you can use these numbers to verify that China has a comparative advantage in producing suits.

Now we can use our conclusions about comparative advantage to show how both countries can gain from trade. The explanation comes in two steps. First, we show that if China could be persuaded to produce more suits and the United States more computers, the world's total production of goods will increase. Second, we show how each country can come out ahead by trading with the other.

Specialization and World Production

Using the numbers in Table 2, if China produced, say, 10 more suits, it would have to sacrifice the production of 2 computers as resources were shifted between the two industries. If the United States, simultaneously, produced 4 extra computers, it would have to sacrifice 8 suits—again because resources would have to be moved. But note: As a result of even this small change, the world's production of suits increases by 2, and its production of computers also rises by 2—despite the fact that no more labor is used than before. Table 3 summarizes the changes.

The additional production of suits and computers in this example represents the gain from specializing according to comparative advantage—a gain, as the next section will show, that the two trading partners will share. It is also the kind of gain that, multiplied a million times, lies behind the substantial benefits countries enjoy from free trade.

The particular example given here is not the only one that can be derived from our table of opportunity costs. For example, if China produced 20 more suits and, therefore, produced 4 fewer computers, while the United States changed as in Table 3, then world output of suits would increase by 12, while computer production would remain unchanged. And we could come up with other examples in which the world output of computers rises, but suits remain the same. (As an exercise, try to create such an example on your own.)

TABLE 3 A Small Change in Production		China	United States	World
Suit Production		+10	−8	+2
Computer Production		−2	+4	+2

In all cases, however, the key insight remains the same:

> *If countries specialize according to comparative advantage, a more efficient use of given resources occurs. That is, with the same resources, the world can produce more of at least one good, without decreasing production of any other good.*

How Each Nation Gains from International Trade

Now we proceed to the second step in Ricardo's case, showing that *both* countries can gain from trade. As you've seen (Table 3), when the two countries shift labor hours toward their comparative advantage good, they produce more of that good but less of the other. For example, China produces more suits but fewer computers. However, by *trading* some of its comparative advantage good for the other good, each country can consume more of *both* goods.

Table 4 shows just one example of trading that benefits both countries. The first row of numbers shows the changes in production in each country. These numbers have been taken from Table 3. For example, the first two entries in the first row tell us that when China produces 10 more suits (+10), it sacrifices 2 computers (−2).

The second row shows an example of China's trade with the United States. In this example, China—which has increased suit production by 10—trades 9 of those suits for 3 computers. The entry "−9" means China is giving up or *exporting* 9 suits, and the entry "+3" means it is getting or *importing* 3 computers in exchange for them. The result of these changes in production, as well as exports and imports, is shown in the third row. Since China increases suit production by 10, but exports 9, it is able to consume 1 more suit (+1) than it could before trade. At the same time, since China produces 2 fewer computers but imports 3, it is able to consume 1 more computer (+1) than before trade.

Continuing to the last two columns of the table, we see the numbers for the United States. Because we are dealing with only two countries, China's exports of suits must be the same as U.S. imports of suits, so in the second row, we show +9 for U.S. suit imports. And if China imports 3 computers from the United States, the United States must be exporting them to China, so the table shows −3 to represent U.S. computer exports. In the third row, we see that the United States—like China— gains from trade by being able to consume more of both goods. It produces 4 more computers, but exports only 3, so it gains 1 computer (+1). And it produces 8 fewer suits, but imports 9, so it gains 1 suit (+1).

Let's take a step back and consider what we've discovered. First, look back at Table 1. Note that based on the required labor hours, the United States has an *absolute advantage* in both goods: It can produce both suits and computers using

	China		United States		TABLE 4
	Suits	Computers	Suits	Computers	**The Gains from Specialization and Trade**
Change in Production	+10	−2	−8	+4	
Exports (−) or Imports (+)	−9	+3	+9	−3	
Net Gain	+1	+1	+1	+1	

fewer hours of labor than can China. But in Table 2, we saw that the United States has a *comparative advantage* in only *one* of these goods—computers—and China has a comparative advantage in the other—suits. This is because the *opportunity costs* of each good differ in the two countries. Then, in Table 3, we saw how world production of both goods increases when each country shifts its resources toward its comparative advantage good. Finally, in the last row of Table 4, we saw that *international trade* can enable *each* country to end up with more of *both* goods.

Of course, we've only been looking at a *small* change in production toward comparative advantage. But as long as such benefits continue, a country can gain even greater benefits by shifting more and more of its resources toward its comparative advantage good. In our example, China should *specialize* in suit production, and the United States should *specialize* in making computers.

> *As long as opportunity costs differ, specialization and trade can be beneficial to all involved. This remains true regardless of whether the parties are different nations, different states, different counties, or different individuals. It remains true even if one party has an all-round absolute advantage or disadvantage.*

The Terms of Trade

In our ongoing example, China exports 9 suits in exchange for 3 computers. This exchange ratio (9 suits for 3 computers, or 3 suits per computer) is known as the **terms of trade**—the quantity of one good that is exchanged for a unit of the other.

The terms of trade determine how the gains from international trade are *distributed* among countries. Our particular choice of 3 suits to 1 computer for the terms of trade happened to apportion the gains equally between the two countries: Both China and the United States each gain one suit and one computer every time they make the trade shown in Table 4. With *different* terms of trade, however, the benefits would have been distributed differently. For example, an end-of-chapter problem will ask you to calculate the gains for each country when the terms of trade (suits per computer) are 4 to 1 instead of 3 to 1. In that case, while both countries will still gain, the United States gains more than China.

But notice that the terms of trade were not even *used* in our example until we arrived at Table 4. The gains from trade for the *world as a whole* were demonstrated

Terms of trade The ratio at which a country can trade domestically produced products for foreign-produced products.

in Table 3, and were based entirely on the increase in world production when countries specialize according to comparative advantage.

> *For the world as a whole, the gains from international trade are due to increased production as nations specialize according to comparative advantage.* How *those world gains are distributed among specific countries depends on the terms of trade.*

We won't consider here precisely *how* the terms of trade are determined (it's a matter of supply and demand). But we *will* establish the limits within which the terms of trade must fall.

Look again at Table 2. China would never give up *more* than 5 suits to import 1 computer. Why not? Because it could always get 1 computer for 5 suits *domestically*, by shifting resources into computer production.

Similarly, the United States would never export a computer for *fewer than* 2 suits, since it can substitute 1 computer for 2 suits domestically (again, by switching resources between the industries). Therefore, the equilibrium terms of trade must lie *between* 5 suits for 1 computer and 2 suits for 1 computer. Outside of that range, one of the two countries would refuse to trade. Note that in our example, we assume terms of trade of 3 suits for 1 computer—well within the acceptable range.

HOW POTENTIAL GAINS TURN INTO ACTUAL GAINS

So far in this chapter, we have discussed the *potential* advantages of specialization and trade among nations, but one major question remains: How is that potential realized? Who or what causes a country to shift resources from some industries into others and then to trade in the world market?

Do foreign trade ministers at WTO meetings decide who should produce and trade each product? Does some group of omniscient and benevolent people in Washington and other world capitals make all the necessary arrangements? Not at all. Within the framework of the WTO, government officials are supposed to create the environment for free trade, but they do not decide who has a comparative advantage in what, or what should be produced in this or that country. In today's market economies around the world, it is individual consumers and firms who decide to buy things, at home or abroad. By their joint actions, they determine where things are produced and who trades with whom. That is, the promise of Ricardo's theory is achieved through markets. People only have to do what comes naturally: buy products at the lowest price. Without their knowing it, they are promoting Ricardo's vision.

In order to see how this works, we'll have to translate from the labor *hours* required to produce a good into labor *costs*. This is done in Table 5. Because Chinese firms keep books in Chinese yuan (CNY) and American firms in U.S. dollars, our cost data are expressed accordingly.

Going across the first row of the table, we see that one suit requires 125 hours of labor in China (just as it did before, in Table 1). The second column shows the

Countries gain when they shift production toward their comparative advantage goods (such as athletic shoes in China), and trade them for other goods from other countries.

© AFP/CORBIS

	China			United States			TABLE 5
	(1) Labor Hours per Unit	(2) Wage Rate	(3) Cost per Unit (1) × (2)	(4) Labor Hours per Unit	(5) Wage Rate	(6) Cost per Unit (4) × (5)	Costs of Production
Suits	125 hours	16 CNY per hour	**2,000 CNY**	50 hours	$10 per hour	**$500**	
Computers	625 hours	16 CNY per hour	**10,000 CNY**	100 hours	$10 per hour	**$1,000**	

wage rate in China (assumed to be 16 CNY per hour), so the total labor cost for one suit in China is 125 hours × 16 CNY per hour = 2,000 CNY. In the United States, a suit requires 50 hours of labor, which—at a wage rate of $10 per hour—implies a total labor cost of $500 per suit. The second row shows the same calculations for a computer, which has costs of 10,000 CNY in China, and $1,000 in the United States.

We can use the cost per unit of each good to determine *opportunity cost*. For example, suppose China wants to produce another computer. Then it will have to shift 10,000 CNY worth of resources (labor hours) out of suit production. This will require a sacrifice of 10,000 CNY / 2,000 CNY = 5 suits. So in China, the opportunity cost of one computer is 5 suits—just as it was earlier, in Table 2, before we translated from labor *hours* to labor *cost*. In fact, expressing resource requirements as *costs*, rather than hours, leads to the same opportunity cost numbers, and the same conclusions derived from them. That is, once again, China has a comparative advantage in suits, and the United States in computers.

Now, back to our question: What *makes* China shift resources into its comparative advantage good, suits, and away from computers? And what *makes* the United States shift resources in the other direction? The answer is: *prices*. In the absence of trade, the *price* of a good within a country will generally reflect the cost of the resources needed to produce another unit of that good. That is, if a suit requires 2,000 CNY worth of resources in China, then before trade, the price of a suit in China will be about 2,000 CNY. For the same reason, before trade, the price of a suit will be about $500 in the United States, because that's what it costs to make one there.

Now suppose we allow trade to open up between the two countries. Consider the decision of a U.S. consumer who can choose to purchase computers or suits in either country. To buy goods from Chinese producers (who want to be paid in their own currency) Americans must obtain yuan. Americans can get the needed yuan by going to the *foreign exchange market*, trading their dollars for yuan at the going **exchange rate**—the rate at which one currency can be exchanged for another. Using the exchange rate, we can calculate the *dollar* cost of a suit from China—what it would cost an American. Similarly, we can calculate the dollar

Exchange rate The amount of one currency that is traded for one unit of another currency.

	China		United States	
Per Suit	**2,000 CNY**	($250)	**$500**	(4,000 CNY)
Per Computer	**10,000 CNY**	($1,250)	**$1,000**	(8,000 CNY)

TABLE 6
Prices in China and the United States With an Exchange Rate of 8 CNY for $1

cost of a computer made in China, or the yuan cost of either good made in the United States.

This is done in Table 6. The bold numbers show the price of each good in each country in *local currency*. The numbers in parentheses show how these numbers translate to the *other country's currency* based on an exchange rate of 8 CNY per dollar.

It's not a big table, but there is a lot going on in it, so let's step carefully through it. Start with the entry in the upper left-hand corner. First, the entry tells us that the price of a suit in China is 2,000 CNY. If an American wants to buy this suit, he can do so—by exchanging dollars for yuan and then buying the suit. With an exchange rate of 8 CNY per dollar, it would take $250 to get 2,000 CNY, since $250 \times 8 = 2,000$. Thus, to the American, the dollar price of a Chinese suit is $250, which appears in parentheses next to the price in yuan. Similarly, the dollar price of a 10,000 CNY Chinese computer is $1,250—also in parentheses.

Looking at Table 6, you can see that, to an American, suits from China at $250 are cheaper than U.S. suits at $500, so *Americans will prefer to buy suits from China*. But when it comes to computers, we reach the opposite conclusion: A U.S. computer at $1,000 is cheaper than a Chinese computer at $1,250, so *Americans will prefer to buy computers in the United States*.

Now take the viewpoint of a Chinese consumer who can buy U.S. or Chinese goods. To buy U.S. goods, China's consumers will need dollars, which they can obtain at the going exchange rate: 8 CNY for $1. The last column of the table shows the prices of U.S. goods in yuan (in parentheses). To a Chinese buyer, Chinese suits at 2,000 CNY are cheaper than U.S. suits at 4,000 CNY, while U.S. computers at 8,000 CNY are cheaper than Chinese computers at 10,000 CNY. Thus, *a Chinese, just like an American, will prefer to buy computers from the United States and suits from China*.

Now suppose that trade in suits and computers had previously been prohibited, but is now opened up. Everyone would buy suits in China and computers in the United States, and the process of specialization according to comparative advantage would begin. Chinese suit makers would expand their production, while Chinese computer makers would suffer losses, lay off workers, and even exit the industry. Unemployed computer workers in China would find jobs in the suit industry. Analogous changes would occur in the United States, as production of computers expanded there. These changes in production patterns would continue until China specialized in suit production and the United States specialized in computer production—that is, until each country produced according to its comparative advantage.

Our example illustrates a general conclusion:

> *When consumers are free to buy at the lowest prices, they will naturally buy a good from the country that has a comparative advantage in producing it. That country's industries respond by producing more of that good and less of other goods. In this way, countries naturally move toward specializing in those goods in which they have a comparative advantage.*[1]

This conclusion applies even beyond the simple example we've been considering. It applies when there are many countries and many goods. And it applies when countries use a *variety* of resources to produce goods, rather than just labor. For example, the prices in Table 6 could come from the cost of *all* resources needed to make a unit of each good in each country—labor, capital equipment, entrepreneurship, and natural resources. The opportunity costs would still be as given in Table 2, and the entire story we've told about the gains from trade, and how they come about, would be the same.

Some Important Provisos

Look back at Tables 3 and 4. There you saw how a small change in production—with China shifting toward suits and the United States shifting toward computers—caused world production of both goods to rise. But if this can happen once, why not again? And again? And again? In fact, our simple example seems to suggest that countries should specialize *completely*, producing *only* the goods in which they have a comparative advantage. In our example, it seems that China should get out of computer production *entirely*, and the United States should get out of suit production *entirely*.

The real world, however, is more complicated than our simplified examples might suggest. Despite divergent opportunity costs, sometimes it does *not* make sense for two countries to trade with each other, or it might make sense to trade, but *not* completely specialize. Following are some real-world considerations that can lead to reduced trade or incomplete specialization.

Costs of Trading. If there are high transportation costs or high costs of making deals across national boundaries, trade may be reduced and even become prohibitively expensive. High transportation costs are especially important for perishable goods, such as ice cream, which must be shipped frozen, and most personal services, such as haircuts, eye exams, and restaurant meals. These goods are less subject to trade according to comparative advantage. (Imagine the travel cost for a U.S. resident to see an optometrist in China, where eye exams are less expensive.)

---

[1] Something may be bothering you about the way we reached this conclusion: We merely *asserted* that the exchange rate was 8 yuan per dollar. What if we had chosen another exchange rate? With a little work, you can verify that at any exchange rate between 4 yuan per dollar and 10 yuan per dollar, our conclusion will still hold: Countries will automatically produce according to their comparative advantage. Further, you can verify that if the exchange rate went *beyond* those bounds, the residents of both countries would want to buy both goods from just one country. This would change the demand for yuan or dollars, and force the exchange rate back between 8 yuan per dollar and 4 yuan per dollar.

The costs of making deals are generally higher for international trade than for trade within domestic borders. For one thing, different laws must be dealt with. In addition, there are different business and marketing customs to be mastered. High transportation costs and high costs of making deals help explain why nations continue to produce some goods in which they do not have a comparative advantage and why there is less than complete specialization in the world.

One final cost of international trade arises from the need to exchange domestic for foreign currency. In international trade, either importers or exporters typically take some risk that the exchange rate might change. For example, suppose a U.S. importer of suits from China agrees in advance to pay 100,000 CNY for a shipment of suits. At the time the agreement is made, the exchange rate is 8 CNY per dollar, so the importer figures the shipment will cost him $12,500. But suppose that, before he pays, the exchange rate changes to 5 CNY per dollar. Then the suit shipment—for which the importer must still pay 100,000 CNY— will cost him $20,000. The rise in costs could cause him to lose money on the shipment.

It is interesting to note that countries can work to reduce the cost of trading. Indeed, this was the primary reason behind the creation of a new, single currency— the *euro*—to be shared by 12 European countries, including France, Germany, Holland, and Italy. The euro was introduced into commerce in early 1999. In 2002, the French franc, the Italian lira, the German mark, and several other national currencies became relics of the past. The move to a single currency has eliminated the costs and risks of foreign exchange transactions from intra-European trade. This should enable these European countries to specialize more completely according to their comparative advantage, and increase the gains from trade even further.

Sizes of Countries. Our earlier example featured two large economies capable of fully satisfying each other's demands. But sometimes a very large country, such as the United States, trades with a very small one, such as the Pacific island nation of Tonga. If the smaller country specialized completely, its output would be insufficient to fully meet the demand of the larger one. While the smaller country would specialize *completely*, the large country would not. Instead, it would continue to produce both goods and would specialize only in the sense of producing *more* of its comparative advantage good after trade than it did before trade. This helps to explain why the United States continues to produce bananas, even though we do so at a much higher opportunity cost than many small Latin American nations.

Increasing Opportunity Cost. In all of our tables, we have assumed that opportunity cost remains constant as production changes. For example, in Table 2, the opportunity cost of a suit in China is ⅓ of a computer, regardless of how many suits or computers China makes. But more typically, the opportunity cost of a good rises as more of it is produced. (Why? You may want to review the law of increasing opportunity cost in Chapter 2.) In that case, each step on the road to specialization would change the opportunity cost. A point might be reached—before complete specialization—in which opportunity costs became *equal* in the two countries, and there would be no further mutual gains from trading. (Remember: Opportunity costs must *differ* between the two countries in order for trade to be mutually beneficial.) In the end, while trading will occur, there will not be complete specialization. Instead, each country will produce both goods, just as China and the United States each produce suits *and* computers in the real world.

Government Barriers to Trade. Governments can enact barriers to trading. In some cases, these barriers increase trading costs; in other cases, they make trade impossible. Since this is such an important topic, we'll consider government-imposed barriers to trade in a separate section, later in the chapter.

THE SOURCES OF COMPARATIVE ADVANTAGE

We've just seen how nations can benefit from specialization and trade when they have comparative advantages. But what determines comparative advantage in the first place?

In many cases, the answer is the *resources* a country has at its disposal.

> *A country that has relatively large amounts of a particular resource at its disposal will tend to have a comparative advantage in goods that make heavy use of that resource.*

This is most easy to see when the relevant resources are *gifts of nature*, such as a specific natural resource or a climate especially suited to a particular product.

The top part of Table 7 contains some examples. Saudi Arabia has a comparative advantage in the production of oil because it has oil fields with billions of barrels of oil that can be extracted at low cost. Canada is a major exporter of timber because its climate and geography make its land more suitable for growing trees than other crops. Canada is a good example of comparative advantage without absolute advantage: It grows a lot of timber, not because it can do so using fewer resources than other countries, but because its land is even more poorly suited to growing other things.

But now look at the bottom half of Table 7. It shows examples of international specialization that arise from some cause *other* than natural resources. Japan has a huge comparative advantage in making automobiles: it produces more of them than any other country. And the number would be even larger, except for laws that limit the import of Japanese cars into Europe. Yet none of the *natural* resources needed to make cars are available in Japan; the iron ore, coal, and oil needed to produce cars are all imported.

What explains the cases of comparative advantage in the bottom half of Table 7? In part, it is due to resources *other* than natural resources or climate. The United States is rich in both physical capital and human capital. As a result, the United States tends to have a comparative advantage in goods and services that make heavy use of computers, tractors, and satellite technology, as well as goods that require highly skilled labor. This, in part, explains the U.S. comparative advantage in the design and production of aircraft, a good that makes heavy use of physical capital (such as computer-based design systems) and human capital (highly trained engineers).

In less-developed countries, by contrast, capital and skilled labor are relatively scarce, but less-skilled labor is plentiful. Accordingly, these countries tend to have a

TABLE 7

Examples of National
Specialties in International
Trade

Country	Specialization Resulting from Natural Resources or Climate
Saudi Arabia	Oil
Canada	Timber
United States	Grain
Spain	Olive oil
Mexico	Tomatoes
Jamaica	Aluminum ore
Italy	Wine
Israel	Citrus fruit

Country	Specialization *Not* Based on Natural Resources or Climate
Japan	Cars, consumer electronics
United States	Software, movies, music, aircraft
Switzerland	Watches
Korea	Steel, ships
China	Textiles
Great Britain	Financial services
Pakistan	Textiles

comparative advantage in products that make heavy use of less-skilled labor, such as textiles and light manufacturing. Note, however, that as a country develops—and acquires more physical and human capital—its pattern of comparative advantage can change. Japan, Korea, and Singapore, after a few decades of very rapid development, acquired a comparative advantage in several goods that, at one time, were specialties of the United States and Europe—including automobiles, steel, and sophisticated consumer electronics.

But another aspect of the bottom half of Table 7 is harder to explain: Why do specific countries develop a *particular* specialty? For example, if you think you know why Japan dominates the world market for VCRs and other consumer electronics—say, some unique capacity to mass-produce precision products—be sure you can explain why Japan is a distant second in computer printers. The company that dominates the market for printers—Hewlett Packard—is a U.S. firm.

Similarly, we take the worldwide dominance of American movies for granted. But if you try to explain it based on the availability of resources like physical capital or highly skilled labor, or cultural traditions that encouraged artists, writers, or actors, then why not Britain or France? At the time the film industry developed in the United States, these two countries had similar endowments of physical and human capital, and much older and stronger theatrical traditions than the United States. Yet their film industries—in spite of massive government subsidies—are a very distant second and third compared to that of the United States.

In even the most remote corner of the world, the cars, cameras, and VCRs will be Japanese, the movies and music American, the clothing from Hong Kong or China, and the bankers from Britain. These specialties are certainly *consistent* with the capital and other resources each nation has at its disposal, but explaining why each *specific* case of comparative advantage arose in the first place is not easy.

We can, however, explain why a country retains its comparative advantage once it gets started. Japan today enjoys a huge comparative advantage in cars and consumer electronics in large part because it has accumulated a capital stock—both physical capital and human capital—well suited to producing those goods. The physical capital stock includes the many manufacturing plants and design facilities that the Japanese have built over the years. But Japan's human capital is no less important. Japanese managers know how to anticipate the features that tomorrow's buyers of cars and electronic products will want around the world. And Japanese workers have developed skills adapted for producing these products. The stocks of physical and human capital in Japan sustain its comparative advantage just as stocks of natural resources lead to comparative advantages in other countries. More likely than not, Japan will continue to have a comparative advantage in cars and electronics, just as the United States will continue to have a comparative advantage in making movies.

Countries often develop strong comparative advantages in the goods they have produced in the past, regardless of why they began producing those goods in the first place.

HTTP://

The International Trade Administration maintains a Web page that is full of information on U.S. international trade. Find it at http://www.ita.doc.gov/.

WHY SOME PEOPLE OBJECT TO FREE TRADE

Given the clear benefits that nations can derive by specializing and trading, why would anyone ever *object* to free international trade? Why do the same governments that join the WTO turn around and create roadblocks to unhindered trade? The answer is not too difficult to find: Despite the benefit to the nation as a whole, some groups within the country, in the short run, are likely to lose from free trade, even while others gain a great deal more. Unfortunately, instead of finding ways to compensate the losers—to make them better off as well—we often allow them to block free-trade policies. The simple model of supply and demand helps illustrate this story.

In our earlier example, after trade opens up, China exports suits and the United States imports them. Figure 1 illustrates the impact on the market for suits in the two countries. To keep things simple, we'll convert the price of suits in China into dollars, so that we can measure dollar prices on the vertical axis of both panels.

Before trade opens up, the Chinese suit market is in equilibrium at point *E*, with a price of $250 and quantity of 200,000 suits per month. The U.S. suit market is in equilibrium at point *F*, with price $500 and quantity 250,000. Notice that before trade opens up, the price is lower in China—the country with a comparative advantage in suits.

Now, when trade opens up, Americans will begin to buy Chinese suits, driving their price upward. As the price in China rises from $250 to $350, Chinese

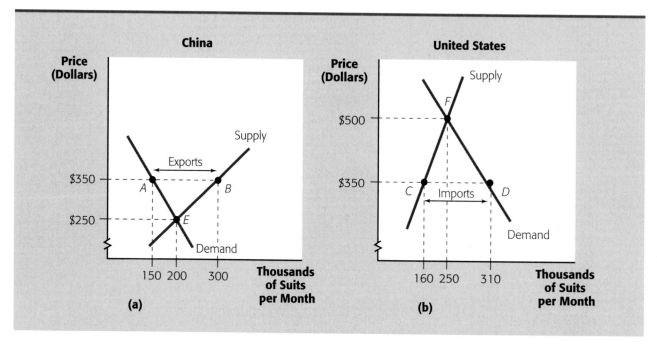

FIGURE 1
The Impact of Trade

Before trade, the Chinese suit market is in equilibrium at point E, and the U.S. market is in equilibrium at point F. When trade begins, Americans buy the cheaper Chinese suits, driving up their price. In response, Chinese manufacturers increase output, and Chinese consumers decrease their purchases. At the world equilibrium price, $350 per suit, Americans buy 150,000 Chinese suits each month (distance CD). China produces 300,000 suits, but Chinese consumers buy only 150,000, with the rest (distance AB) being exported to the United States.

producers increase their output to 300,000, moving from E to B along the supply curve, and Chinese consumers decrease their purchases to 150,000, moving from E to A along the demand curve. This seems to create an "excess supply" of suits in China, equal to distance AB or 300,000 − 150,000 = 150,000. But it is not *really* an excess supply, because that is precisely the number of suits that are exported to the United States. So, China's entire output of suits, 300,000, is purchased by either Chinese or Americans.

Now let's consider the effects in the United States. There, consumers are switching from suits made in the United States to suits made in China. With less demand for U.S. suits, their price will fall. With free trade, the United States must be able to buy Chinese suits at the same price as the Chinese (ignoring transportation costs), so the price of suits in the United States must fall to $350. As the price falls, U.S. suit producers will decrease their output to 160,000, moving from F to C along the supply curve, and U.S. consumers will increase their purchases to 310,000 moving from F to D along the demand curve. This seems to create a shortage of suits in the United States, equal to 310,000 − 160,000 = 150,000, but it is not a shortage: That is precisely the number of suits imported from China.

Now let's see how different groups are affected by the opening up of trade.

The Impact of Trade in the Exporting Country

When trade opens up in suits, China is the exporting country. How are different groups affected there?

- *Chinese suit producers and workers are better off.* Before international trade, producers sold 200,000 suits at $250 each, but with trade, they sell a larger quantity of 300,000 at a higher price of $350. The industry's workers are equally delighted because they undoubtedly share in the bonanza as the number of workers demanded rises along with the level of production. Both management and labor in the Chinese suit industry benefit from free trade.
- *Chinese suit buyers are worse off.* Why? Before trade, they bought 200,000 suits at price $250, and now they must pay the higher price, $350, and consume the smaller quantity 150,000.

> *When the opening of trade results in increased exports of a good, the producers of the good are made better off. Consumers of the good in the exporting country will be made worse off.*

The Impact of Trade in the Importing Country

Now let's consider the impact of free trade in suits on the United States, the importing country. Once again, it is easy to figure out who is happy and who is unhappy with the new arrangement.

- *U.S. suit producers and workers are worse off.* They formerly sold 250,000 at $500 each, but now they sell the lower quantity of 160,000 at the lower price, $350. The industry's workers suffer, too, because the number of workers demanded falls with the level of production.
- *U.S. suit buyers are better off.* They used to buy 250,000 at $500 each, but now they pay the lower price, $350, and consume the larger quantity, 310,000.

> *When the opening of trade results in increased imports of a product, the domestic producers of the product are made worse off. Consumers of the good in the importing country are better off.*

Attitudes and Influence on Trade Policy

In our examples, we've been discussing the impact of free trade in suits. We could tell the same story about free trade in computers. In this case, the United States has the role of exporter and China is the importer. But our conclusions about the impacts on different groups in exporting and importing countries would remain the same. These impacts are summarized in Table 8.

Each group in the table forms a natural constituency for government policies that encourage or discourage free trade. Notice, however, that one of the entries is italicized: producers of a good (and their employees) who would suffer from cheap imports. This group is emphasized because it typically has more influence on trade policy than the others in the table.

An example can help explain why. Imagine that a bill comes before Congress to permit completely free trade in apparel, allowing cheap clothing to enter the United States from China, Pakistan, and several other less-developed countries.

TABLE 8		In Export Sectors That Enjoy Comparative Advantage	In Import Sectors That Suffer from Comparative Disadvantage
The Impact of Free Trade			
	Gains from Trade	Owners of firms, workers	Consumers
	Harm from Trade	Consumers	*Owners of firms, workers*

The benefits to the United States as a whole would be huge, enjoyed mostly by American consumers of clothing—basically, the entire U.S. population. But because the benefits would be spread so widely, the gains for each *individual* consumer would be small. For example, if the benefits to *all* U.S. consumers amounted to $20 billion per year, the annual benefits to any single consumer would be less than $100. As a result, no single consumer has a strong incentive to lobby Congress, or to join a dues-paying organization that would act on his or her behalf.

By contrast, the harm that free trade would do to the owners and employees of domestic apparel firms would be highly concentrated on a much smaller group of people. An individual owner might lose millions of dollars competing with cheap imports, and a worker would face a substantially higher risk of being permanently laid off. These individuals have a powerful incentive to lobby against free trade. Not surprisingly, when it comes to trade policy, the voices raised *against imports* are loud and clear, while those *for imports* are often nonexistent. Since a country has the power to restrict imports from other countries, the lobbying can—and often does—lead to a restriction on free trade. The United States, for example, continues to keep out imports of cheap clothing from low-cost producers, largely due to powerful lobbying by the U.S. textile industry.

What about the export side? Here, as Table 8 suggests, it's the reverse: Individuals involved in the export sector who benefit from trade have the incentive to lobby, while individual consumers who would be harmed by higher prices have little incentive to act. Indeed, in the United States, farmers and cattle ranchers have been active advocates of free-trade policies so they can export corn, rye, soybeans, and beef. This suggests that the forces mounted for and against free trade might be evenly balanced. But notice in Table 8 that this group—firms and workers who benefit from exports—has not been emphasized. Why not?

The Antitrade Bias. While exporters have the incentive to lobby—and do—their effectiveness is limited. After all, it's not the U.S. government that is preventing them from exporting their products; it's some *foreign* government responding to pressure from its *own* producers who would be harmed by U.S. exports. The United States does not have the legal right to *force* another country to import American products. Indeed, European governments have for years used trade barriers to tightly restrict imports of American corn and American beef (officially attributed to environmental and health claims). Despite heavy lobbying from U.S. producers, the U.S. government has been unable to change European policy. Moreover, because the United States has so often given in to pressure from its own producers to restrict imports, it lacks the moral high ground.

> *The distribution of gains and losses creates a policy bias against free trade. Those who benefit from trade in a specific product either have little incentive to lobby for it (consumers of imports) or have limited power to influence policy (producers of exports). But one constituency harmed by trade—domestic producers threatened by imports—has both a powerful incentive to lobby and the ability to influence policy.*

There are, however, three antidotes to this policy bias.

Multilateral Agreements. In a bilateral or multilateral trade agreement, two or more countries agree to trade freely in many goods—or even *all* goods—simultaneously. Producers threatened by imports will lobby against such agreements in each country. But producers of potential exports will lobby just as strongly *for* the agreement. If the agreement is structured as an all-or-nothing proposition, a balance of influence is created that can enable governments to resist antitrade lobbying. An example was the North American Free Trade Agreement (NAFTA) between the United States, Canada, and Mexico, which went into effect in 1994, and has eliminated barriers on most products produced by the three nations. NAFTA was hotly opposed by many producers and some labor unions in all three countries who stood to lose from imports, but was just as hotly favored by producers and workers that stood to gain from exports. (The biggest gainers—consumers in the three countries—were hardly involved in the debate, for reasons we've discussed.) In mid-2005, a similar conflict arose over the proposed Central American Free Trade Agreement (CAFTA).

The World Trade Organization. Another antidote to anti-trade bias is the World Trade Organization (WTO). By setting standards for acceptable and unacceptable trade restrictions, and making rulings in specific cases, the WTO has some power to influence nations' trade policies. But its influence is limited because the WTO has no enforcement power. For example, the WTO has ruled several times against European trade barriers against U.S. beef, with little effect. Still, a negative WTO ruling puts public relations pressure on a country, and allows a nation harmed by restrictions on its exports to retaliate, in good conscience, with its own trade barriers.

Industries as Consumers. Whenever we use the word consumer, we naturally think of a household buying products for its own enjoyment. But the term can apply to any buyer of a product, including a firm that uses it as an input. If these firms are among the consumers in Table 8 who benefit from cheaper imports, and if the good is an important part of these firms' costs, they have an incentive to lobby for free trade in the good. Moreover, because the issue at stake—import restrictions—is under the control of the domestic government, lobbying by industrial consumers can influence policy. For example, in late 2004, the textile industry lobbied the Bush administration to slow the rise in clothing imports from China. But U.S. clothing retailers and importers—for whom clothing is an input—lobbied strongly *against* any trade barriers. While the retailers and importers ultimately lost the battle in May 2005, their opposition delayed the restrictions for months and influenced the final policy adopted.

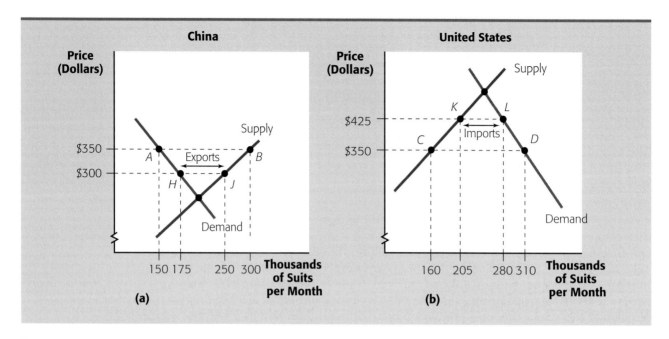

FIGURE 2
The Effects of a Tariff on Suits

A U.S. tariff of $125 on imported Chinese suits raises their price in the United States and reduces U.S. imports. It also lowers the price in China and reduces China's exports. In the new equilibrium, the price is $425 in the United States and $300 in China, the prices at which China's exports (distance HJ) are equal to U.S. imports (distance KL). The difference in the two prices—$125—is equal to the U.S. tariff on each imported suit.

Tariff A tax on imports.

HOW FREE TRADE IS RESTRICTED

So far in this chapter, you've learned that specialization and trade according to comparative advantage can dramatically improve the well-being of entire nations. This is why governments generally favor free trade. Yet international trade can, in the short run, hurt particular groups of people. These groups often lobby their government to restrict free trade.

When governments decide to accommodate the opponents of free trade, they are apt to use one of two devices to restrict trade: tariffs or quotas.

Tariffs

A **tariff** is a tax on imported goods. It can be a fixed dollar amount per physical unit, or it can be a percentage of the good's value. In either case, the effect in the tariff-imposing country is similar.

Figure 2 illustrates the effects of a U.S. government tariff on Chinese suits. Initially, before the tariff is imposed, the price of suits in both countries is $350, and China exports 150,000, given by the distance *AB*, while the United States imports the same number (represented by the distance *CD* in the U.S. market). Now, suppose the United States imposes a tariff of $125 on each suit imported from China. Since it is more costly for Chinese suit makers to sell suits in the United States than before, they will shift some of their output back to the home market in China. In the United States, at the old price of $350, this decrease in the supply of suits *would* create a shortage, but—as we know—shortages force the price up. In our diagram, the United States price rises to $425. As the price rises, the quantity of suits supplied domestically increases, and the quantity demanded domestically decreases. U.S. imports are accordingly cut back to *KL,* or 75,000 per month. In China, the sale of suits formerly exported drives the price there down to $300. Notice that—in the final equilibrium with U.S. price equal to $425 and the price in China equal to $300—U.S. imports (*KL*) and Chinese exports (*HJ*) are equal at 75,000. That is, every Chinese suit that is *not* bought by a Chinese consumer is bought by an American consumer. As you can see, American consumers are worse off: They pay a higher price for fewer suits. U.S. producers, on the other hand, are much better off: They sell more suits at a higher price. In China, the impact is the opposite: The price of suits falls, so Chinese producers lose and Chinese consumers gain.

But we also know this: Since the volume of trade has decreased, the gains from trade according to comparative advantage have been reduced as well. Both countries, as a whole, are worse off as a result of the tariff:

> *Tariffs reduce the volume of trade and raise the domestic prices of imported goods. In the country that imposes the tariff, producers gain and consumers lose. But the world as a whole loses, because tariffs decrease the volume of trade and therefore decrease the gains from trade.*

Quotas

A **quota** is a government decree that limits the imports of a good to a specified maximum physical quantity, such as 75,000 Chinese suits per month. Because the goal is to restrict imports, a quota is set below the level of imports that would occur under free trade. Its general effects are very similar to the effects of a tariff.

Figure 2, which we used to illustrate tariffs, can also be used to analyze the impact of a quota. In this case, we suppose that the U.S. government simply decrees that it will allow only 75,000 suits from China into the United States (the distance *KL*), and that it is able to enforce this quota. Once again, the U.S. market price in our example will rise to $425. (Why? Because at any price lower than $425, total imports of 75,000, plus the domestic quantity supplied of 205,000—given by the supply curve—would be smaller than quantity demanded. This would cause the price to rise.) And once again, the decrease in U.S. imports translates into a shrinkage in Chinese exports, down to 75,000, or the distance *HJ*. Both countries' suit markets end up in exactly the same place as if the United States had imposed a tariff that raised the U.S. price to $425.

The previous discussion seems to suggest that tariffs and quotas are pretty much the same. But even though prices in the two countries may end up at the same level with a tariff or a quota, there is one important difference between these two trade-restricting policies. A tariff, after all, is a *tax* on imported goods. Therefore, when a government imposes a tariff, it collects some revenue every time a good is imported. Even though the world loses from a tariff, the country that imposes it loses a bit less (compared to a quota) because at least it collects some revenue from the tariff. This revenue can be used to fund government programs or reduce other taxes, to the benefit of the country as a whole. When a government imposes a quota, however, it typically gains no revenue at all.

Quota A limit on the physical volume of imports.

> *Quotas have effects similar to tariffs: They reduce the quantity of imports and raise domestic prices. While both measures help domestic producers, they reduce the benefits of trade to the nation as a whole. However, a tariff has one saving grace: increased government revenue.*

Economists, who generally oppose measures such as quotas and tariffs to restrict trade, argue that, if one of these devices must be used, tariffs are the better choice. While both policies reduce the gains that countries can enjoy from specializing and trading with each other, the tariff provides some compensation in the form of additional government revenue.

PROTECTIONISM

This chapter has outlined the *gains* that arise from international trade, but it has also outlined some of the *pain* trade can cause to different groups within a country. While the country as a whole benefits, some citizens in both the exporting and importing countries are harmed. The groups who suffer from trade with other nations have developed a number of arguments against free trade. Together, these arguments form a position known as **protectionism**—the belief that a nation's industries should be *protected* from free trade with other nations.

Protectionism The belief that a nation's industries should be protected from foreign competition.

Myths About International Trade

Some protectionist arguments are rather sophisticated and require careful consideration. We'll consider some of these a bit later. But antitrade groups have also promulgated a number of myths to support their protectionist beliefs. Let's consider some of these myths.

Myth #1: "A HIGH-WAGE COUNTRY CANNOT AFFORD FREE TRADE WITH A LOW-WAGE COUNTRY. THE HIGH-WAGE COUNTRY WILL EITHER BE UNDERSOLD IN EVERYTHING AND LOSE ALL OF ITS INDUSTRIES, OR ELSE ITS WORKERS WILL HAVE TO ACCEPT EQUALLY LOW WAGES AND EQUALLY LOW LIVING STANDARDS."

It's true that some countries have much higher wages than others. Here are 2003 figures for average hourly wages of manufacturing workers, including benefits such as holiday pay and health insurance: Germany, $29.91; United States, $21.97; Japan, $20.09; Italy, $18.35; Korea, $10.28; Singapore, $7.41; Brazil, $2.67; Mexico, $2.48; and less than a dollar in China, India, and Bangladesh. This leads to the fear that the poorer countries will be able to charge lower prices for their goods, putting American workers out of jobs unless they, too, agree to work for low wages.

But this argument is incorrect, for two reasons. First, it is true that American workers are paid more than Chinese workers, but this is because the average American worker is more *productive* than his or her Chinese counterpart. After all, the American workforce is more highly educated, and American firms provide their workers with more sophisticated machinery than do Chinese firms. If an American could produce 25 times as much output as a Chinese worker in an hour, then even though wage rates in the United States may be about 20 times greater, cost *per unit* produced would still be lower in the United States. This is reflected in our example in Tables 5 and 6. If you look closely, you'll see that even though American workers are paid more than their Chinese counterparts, we've assumed that American workers can produce a computer with so much less labor input that labor costs per computer are actually lower in the United States.

But suppose the cost per unit *were* lower in China. Then there is still another, more basic argument against the fear of a general job loss or falling wages in the United States: comparative advantage. Let's take an extreme case. Suppose that labor productivity were the same in the United States and China, so that China—with lower wages—could produce *everything* more cheaply than the United States could. Both countries would still gain if China specialized in products in which its cost advantage was relatively large and the United States specialized in goods in which China's cost advantage was relatively small. That is, even though China would have an absolute advantage in everything, the United States would still have a comparative advantage in some things. The mutual gains from trade arise not from absolute advantage, but from comparative advantage.

Myth #2 "A LOW-PRODUCTIVITY COUNTRY CANNOT AFFORD FREE TRADE WITH A HIGH-PRODUCTIVITY COUNTRY. THE FORMER WILL BE CLOBBERED BY THE LATTER AND LOSE ALL OF ITS INDUSTRIES."

This argument is the flip side of the first myth. Here, it is the poorer, less-developed country that is supposedly harmed by trade with a richer country. But this myth, like the first one, confuses absolute advantage with comparative advantage. Suppose the high-productivity country (say, the United States) could produce *every* good with fewer resources than the low-productivity country (say, China). Once again, the low-productivity country would *still* have a comparative advantage in *some* goods. It would then gain by producing those goods and trading with the high-productivity country. This is the case in our hypothetical example depicted in Table 1 and Table 5. In that example, the United States has an absolute advantage in both goods, yet—as we've seen—trade still benefits both countries.

To make the point even clearer, let's bring it closer to home. Suppose there is a small, poor town in the United States where workers are relatively uneducated and work with little capital equipment, so their productivity is very low. Would the residents of this town be better off sealing their borders and not trading with the rest of the United States, which has higher productivity? Before you answer, think what this would mean: The residents of the poor town would have to produce everything on their own: grow their own food, make their own cars and television sets, and even provide their own entertainment. Clearly, they would be worse off in isolation. And what is true *within* a country is also true *between* different countries: Closing off trade will make a nation, as a whole, worse off, regardless of its level of wages or productivity. Even a low-productivity country is made better off by trading with other nations.

Myth #3: "IN RECENT TIMES, AMERICA'S UNSKILLED WORKERS HAVE SUFFERED BECAUSE OF EVER-EXPANDING TRADE BETWEEN THE UNITED STATES AND OTHER COUNTRIES."

True enough, unskilled workers lost ground in the 1980s and 1990s, for *some* reason. College graduates have enjoyed growing purchasing power from their earnings, while those with only a grade school education have lost purchasing power. Rising trade with low-wage countries has been blamed for this adverse trend.

But before we jump to conclusions, let's take a closer look. Our discussion earlier in this chapter tells us where to look for effects that come through trade. If the opening of trade has harmed low-skilled workers in the United States, it would have done so by lowering the prices of products that employ large numbers of those workers. A study taking this approach found almost no change in the relative prices of products in the United States that employ large numbers of unskilled workers. Studies that take other approaches have found only modest effects. In general, economists who have looked at the impact of trade on U.S. labor markets have concluded that foreign trade is a small contributor to the depressed earnings of low-wage workers. A much more important factor is technological change, and the greater skills needed to work with new technologies.[2]

Sophisticated Arguments for Protection

While most of the protectionist arguments we read in the media are based on a misunderstanding of comparative advantage, some more recent arguments for protecting domestic industries are based on a more sophisticated understanding of how markets work. These arguments have become collectively known as *strategic trade policy.* According to its proponents, a nation can gain in some circumstances by assisting certain *strategic industries* that benefit society as a whole, but that may not thrive in an environment of free trade.

Strategic trade policy is most effective in situations where a market is dominated by a few large firms. With few firms, the forces of competition—which ordinarily reduce profits in an industry to very low levels—will not operate. Therefore, each firm in the industry may earn high profits. These profits benefit not only the owners of the firm, but also the nation more generally, since the government will be able to capture some of the profit with the corporate profits tax. When a government helps an industry compete internationally, it increases the likelihood that high profits—and the resulting general benefits—will be shifted from a foreign country to its own country. Thus, interfering with free trade—through quotas, tariffs, or even a direct subsidy to domestic firms—might actually benefit the country.

Infant industry argument The argument that a new industry in which a country has a comparative advantage might need protection from foreign competition in order to flourish.

An argument related to strategic trade policy is the **infant industry argument.** This argument begins with a simple observation: In order to enjoy the full benefits of trade, markets must allocate resources toward those goods in which a nation has a comparative advantage. This includes not only markets for resources such as labor and land, but also *financial markets,* where firms obtain funds for new

---

[2] The studies include Robert Z. Lawrence and Matthew J. Slaughter, "Trade and U.S. Wages: Giant Sucking Sound or Small Hiccup?" Brookings Papers on Economic Activity: Microeconomics, 2:1993, pp. 161–210; Jeffrey D. Sachs and Howard J. Shatz, "Trade and Jobs in U.S. Manufacturing," Brookings Papers on Economic Activity, 1:1994, pp. 1–84; and Gary Burtless, Robert Lawrence, Robert Litan, and Robert Shapiro, Globaphobia: Confronting Fears About Free Trade (1998), The Brookings Institution Press (Washington, DC). See also the recent survey by Bernard Hoekman and L. Alan Winters, "Trade and Employment: Stylized Facts and Research Findings," mimeo, World Bank Development Research Group, March 2005.

products. But in some countries—especially developing countries—financial markets do not work very well. Poor legal systems or incomplete information about firms and products may prevent a new industry from obtaining financing, even though the country would have a comparative advantage in that industry once it was formed. In this case, protecting the infant industry from foreign competition may be warranted until the industry can stand on its own feet.

Strategic trade policy and support for infant industries are controversial. Opponents of these ideas stress three problems:

1. Once the principle of government assistance to an industry is accepted, special-interest groups of all kinds will lobby to get the assistance, whether it benefits the general public or not.
2. When one country provides assistance to an industry by keeping out foreign goods, other nations may respond in kind. If they respond with tariffs and quotas of their own, the result is a shrinking volume of world trade and falling living standards. If subsidies are used to support a strategic industry, and another country responds with its own subsidies, then both governments lose revenue, and neither gains the sought-after profits.
3. Strategic trade policy assumes that the government has the information to determine which industries, infant or otherwise, are truly strategic and which are not.

Still, the arguments related to strategic trade policy suggest that government protection or assistance *may* be warranted in some circumstances, even if putting this support into practice proves difficult. Moreover, the arguments help to remind us of the conditions under which free trade is most beneficial to a nation:

> *Production is most likely to reflect the principle of comparative advantage when firms can obtain funds for investment projects and when they can freely enter industries that are profitable. Thus, free trade, without government intervention, works best when markets are working well.*

This may explain, in part, why the United States, where markets function relatively well, has for decades been among the strongest supporters of the free trade ideal.

Protectionism in the United States

Americans can enjoy the benefits of importing many of the products listed in Table 7: olive oil from Spain, watches from Switzerland, tomatoes from Mexico, cars and VCRs from Japan. But on the other side of the ledger, U.S. consumers have suffered and U.S. producers have gained, from some persistent barriers to trade. Table 9 lists ten examples of American protectionism—through tariffs, quotas, or similar policies—that have continued for years.

As you can see, protection is costly. Quotas and tariffs on apparel and textiles, the most costly U.S. trade barrier, force American consumers to pay $33.6 billion more for clothes each year. And while protection saves an estimated 168,786

TABLE 9
**Some Examples of
U.S. Protectionism**[3]

Protected Industry	Annual Cost to Consumers	Number of Jobs Saved	Annual Cost per Job Saved
Apparel and Textiles	$33,629 million	168,786	$ 199,241
Maritime Services	$ 2,522 million	4,411	$ 571,668
Sugar	$ 1,868 million	2,261	$ 826,104
Dairy Products	$ 1,630 million	2,378	$ 685,323
Softwood Lumber	$ 632 million	605	$1,044,271
Women's Nonathletic Footwear	$ 518 million	3,702	$ 139,800
Glassware	$ 366 million	1,477	$ 247,889
Luggage	$ 290 million	226	$1,285,078
Peanuts	$ 74 million	397	$ 187,223

workers in this industry from having to make the painful adjustment of finding other work, it does so at an annual cost of $199,241 per worker. Both workers and consumers could be made better off if textile workers were paid any amount up to $199,241 *not* to work and consumers were allowed to buy inexpensive textiles from abroad.

In some cases, the cost per job saved is staggering. The table shows that trade barriers preventing Americans from buying inexpensive luggage save just a couple of hundred jobs, at a yearly cost of more than $1 million each. Trade barriers on sugar are almost as bad: While 2,261 jobs are saved, the annual cost per job is $826,104.

In addition to the dozens of industries in the United States permanently protected from foreign competition, dozens more each year are granted temporary protection when the U.S. government finds a foreign producer or industry guilty of *dumping*—selling their products in the United States at "unfairly" low prices that harm a U.S. industry. Most economists believe that these low prices are most often the result of comparative advantage, and that the United States as a whole would gain from importing the good. Vietnam, for example, has a clear comparative advantage in producing shrimp. But in 2005, based on a complaint by the Southern Shrimp Alliance, the U.S. government imposed tariffs of up to 26 percent on Vietnamese shrimp.

In the "Using the Theory" section that follows, we take a closer look at one of the longest-running examples of protectionism in the United States.

[3] *The Fruits of Free Trade*, Federal Reserve Bank of Dallas, Annual Report, 2002, Exhibit 11.

USING THE THEORY

The U.S. Sugar Quota[4]

The United States has protected U.S. sugar producers from foreign competition since the 1930s. Since the 1980s, the protection has been provided in the form of a price guarantee. Essentially, the government has promised U.S. sugar beet and sugar cane producers and processors that they can sell their sugar at a predetermined price—22 cents a pound—regardless of the world price of sugar. The promise is backed by a guarantee: If U.S. sugar prices fall *below* 22 cents, the government will buy the sugar at that price itself.

This may not sound like a high price for sugar. But in the rest of the world, people and businesses can buy sugar for a lot less. From 2000 to 2004, the world price of sugar has averaged about 8 cents a pound, while Americans have continued to pay 22 cents. Even in 1985, when the world price of sugar plunged to just 4 cents a pound—a bonanza for sugar buyers around the word—American buyers were not invited to the party: The United States price remained at 22 cents.

Because the world price of sugar is so consistently below the U.S. price, the government cannot keep its promise to support sugar prices while simultaneously allowing free trade in sugar. With free trade, the price of sugar in the United States would plummet and the government would have to spend billions of dollars each year making good on its guarantee to buy the sugar itself. The government's solution is a sugar quota. More accurately, the government decides how much foreign sugar it will allow into the United States each year, free of any tariff; all sugar beyond the allowed amount is hit with a heavy tariff of about 16 cents a pound. Since the tariff is so high, no country exports sugar to the United States beyond the allowed amount. So, in effect, the United States has a sugar quota.

The *primary* effects of the sugar quota are on sugar producers and sugar consumers. As you've learned, an import quota raises the domestic price of sugar (the quota's purpose). Sugar producers benefit. Sugar consumers are hurt.

And the harm is substantial. Table 9 shows that American consumers pay almost $2 billion more each year for sugar and products containing sugar due to the sugar quota. But spread widely over the U.S. population, this amounts to less than $15 per person per year. This probably explains why you haven't bothered to lobby for free trade in sugar.

[4] Information in this section is based on: Mark A. Groombridge "America's Bittersweet Sugar Policy," *Trade Briefing Paper No. 13*, Cato Institute, December 4, 2001; John C. Beghin, Barbara El Osta, Jar Y. Cherlow, and Samarendu Mohanty, "The Cost of the U.S. Sugar Program Revisited," *Working Paper 01-WP-273*, March 2001, Center for Agricultural and Rural Development, Iowa State University; Lance Gay, "Soured on Sugar Prices, Candy Makers Leave the U.S." *Scripps Howard News Service*, June 18, 2003; "Closing the 'Stuffed Molasses' Loophole," *White Paper*, United States Sugar Corporation (*http://www.ussugar.com/pressroom/white_papers/stuffed_molasses.html*).

But the costs of the sugar quota go beyond ordinary consumers. Industrial sugar users—such as the ice cream industry—are affected by the higher price too, not all of which can be passed on to consumers. So they try to avoid the quota's harm in other ways. One way is to waste resources buying sugar abroad disguised as other products. In the late 1990s and early 2000s, U.S. firms bought about 125,000 tons of sugar each year mixed with molasses, which was not restricted by the sugar quota. The sugar was then reseparated from the molasses. Even with these additional (and wasteful) processing costs, it was still a better deal to buy the disguised sugar abroad than to buy it through regular channels in the United States.

And sometimes a firm decides it's just not worth it anymore. In June 2003, Lifesavers was added to the list of other candy and baked-goods manufacturers who simply gave up trying to buy sugar in the United States, and moved their production facilities to Canada. In Canada, which doesn't have a quota, sugar can be purchased at the lower, world price.

Taxpayers, too, pay a cost for the sugar quota, because as part of its price support program, the U.S. government must occasionally buy excess sugar from producers. In 2005, the U.S. government was storing about 759,000 tons of sugar at a cost of more than $1 million per month. The government must also hire special agents to detect and prevent sugar from entering the country illegally.

But perhaps the most significant cost of the sugar quota is indicated by Figure 2 in this chapter. There we saw that a U.S. tariff or quota on Chinese suits raised their price in the United States, but lowered their price in China, the exporting country. The sugar quota has a similar effect: The price in the exporting "country" (in this case, the *rest of the world*) decreases. And since the United States is such a large potential importer of sugar, the quota—by keeping sugar out—causes greater quantities of sugar to be dumped onto the world market, depressing its price. This hurts the poorest countries in the world that rely on sugar as an important source of export revenue. The sugar quota's harm to these countries has been estimated at about $1.5 billion per year.

Why do we bear all of these costs? Because of lobbying by groups who enjoy highly concentrated benefits. There are about 13,000 sugar farms in the United States. When the $2 billion in additional spending by U.S. consumers is spread among this small number of farms, the additional revenue averages out to more than $150,000 per farm per year. Those benefits are sizable enough to mobilize sugar producers each time their protection is threatened.

But there is another group that receives concentrated benefits: producers of high-fructose corn syrup, the closest substitute for sugar. Because of the sugar quota, high-fructose corn syrup can be sold at a substantially higher price.

Not surprisingly, the largest producer of high-fructose corn syrup in the U.S. market—the Archer Daniels Midland (ADM) company—has funded organizations that lobby Congress and try to sway public opinion in the United States. Occasionally, you may see a full-page newspaper advertisement paid for by one of these groups, arguing that sugar in the United States is cheap. And it is . . . until you find out what the country next door is paying.

Summary

International specialization and trade enable people throughout the world to enjoy greater production and higher living standards than would otherwise be possible. The benefits of unrestrained international trade can be traced back to the idea of comparative advantage. Mutually beneficial trade is possible whenever one country can produce a good at a lower opportunity cost than its trading partner can. Whenever opportunity costs differ, countries can specialize according to their comparative advantage, trade with each other, and end up consuming more.

Despite the net benefits to each nation as a whole, some groups within each country lose, while others gain. When trade leads to increased exports, domestic producers gain and domestic consumers are harmed. When imports increase as a result of trade, domestic producers suffer and domestic consumers gain. The losers often encourage government to block or reduce trade through the use of tariffs (taxes on imported goods) and quotas (limits on the volume of imports).

A variety of arguments have been proposed in support of protectionism. Some are clearly invalid and fail to recognize the principle that both sides gain when countries trade according to their comparative advantage. More sophisticated arguments for restricting trade may have merit in certain circumstances. These include strategic trade policy—the notion that governments should assist certain strategic industries—and the idea of protecting "infant" industries when financial markets are imperfect.

Key Terms

Absolute advantage	Imports	Tariff
Comparative advantage	Infant industry argument	Terms of trade
Exchange rate	Protectionism	
Exports	Quota	

Review Questions

Answers to even-numbered Questions and Problems can be found on the text Web site at http://hall-lieb.swlearning.com.

1. Describe the theory of comparative advantage.

2. What is the difference between absolute advantage and comparative advantage?

3. What are the terms of trade and why are they important?

4. What are the sources of comparative advantage?

5. What makes a country shift resources into its comparative advantage good?

6. Briefly describe the antidotes to the antitrade bias.

7. What is a tariff? What are its main economic effects? How does a quota differ from a tariff?

8. What arguments have been made in support of protectionism? Which of them may be valid, and under what circumstances?

9. List the ways in which a quota on imported coffee would harm the nation that imposes it

Problems and Exercises

1. Suppose that the costs of production of winter hats and wheat in two countries are as follows:

	United States	Russia
Per Winter Hat	$10	5,000 rubles
Per Bushel of Wheat	$1	2,500 rubles

   a. What is the opportunity cost of producing one more winter hat in the United States? In Russia?

   b. What is the opportunity cost of producing one more bushel of wheat in the United States? In Russia?

   c. Which country has a comparative advantage in winter hats? In wheat?

   d. Construct a table similar to Table 3 that illustrates how a change in production in each country would increase world production.

e. If the exchange rate were 1,000 rubles per dollar, would mutually beneficial trade occur? If yes, explain what mechanism would induce producers to export according to their country's comparative advantage. If no, explain why not, and explain in which direction the exchange rate would change. (*Hint:* Construct a table similar to Table 6.)

f. Answer the same questions for an exchange rate of 100 rubles per dollar.

2. The following table gives information about the supply and demand for beef in Paraguay and Uruguay. (You may wish to draw the supply and demand curves for each country to help you visualize what is happening.)

	Paraguay			Uruguay	
Price	Quantity Supplied	Quantity Demanded	Price	Quantity Supplied	Quantity Demanded
0	0	1,200	0	0	1,800
5	200	1,000	5	0	1,600
10	400	800	10	0	1,400
15	600	600	15	0	1,200
20	800	400	20	200	1,000
25	1,000	200	25	400	800
30	1,200	0	30	600	600
35	1,400	0	35	800	400
40	1,600	0	40	1,000	200
45	1,800	0	45	1,200	0

a. In the absence of trade, what is the equilibrium price and quantity in Paraguay? In Uruguay?

b. If the two countries begin to trade, what will happen to the price of beef? How many sides of beef will be purchased in Paraguay and how many in Uruguay at that price?

c. How many sides of beef will be produced in Paraguay and how many in Uruguay? Why is there a difference between quantity purchased and quantity produced in each country?

d. Who benefits and who loses from the opening of trade between these two countries?

3. Use the data on supply and demand given in Question 2 to answer the following questions:

a. Suppose that Uruguay imposed a tariff that raised the price of beef imported from Paraguay to $25 per side. What would happen to beef consumption in Uruguay? To beef production there? How much beef would be imported from Paraguay?

b. How would the tariff affect Paraguay? Specifically, what would happen to the price of beef there after Uruguay imposed its tariff? How would Paraguay's production and consumption be affected?

4. Use the data on supply and demand given in Question 2 to answer the following questions:

a. Suppose that Uruguay imposed a quota on the import of beef from Paraguay—only 200 sides of beef can be imported each year. What would happen to the price of beef in Uruguay? What would happen to beef consumption in Uruguay? To beef production there?

b. How would the quota affect Paraguay? Specifically, what would happen to the price of beef there after Uruguay imposed its quota? How would Paraguay's production and consumption be affected?

5. Refer to Table 4 in the chapter. Calculate the gains for each country when the terms of trade (suits per computer) are 2 to 1, instead of 3 to 1. This time, assume that China increases suit production by 25 suits and exports 20, while the U.S. decreases suit production by 20. Which country gains more under these terms of trade?

6. Refer to Table 4 in the chapter. Calculate the gains for each country when the terms of trade (suits per computer) are 4 to 1, instead of 3 to 1. This time, assume that China increases suit production by 15 suits and exports 12, while the United States increases computer production by 4 computers. Which country gains more under these terms of trade?

7. The following table shows the hypothetical labor requirements per ton of wool and per hand-knotted rug, for New Zealand and for India.

Labor Requirements per Unit

	New Zealand	India
Per Ton of Wool	10 hours	20 hours
Per Hand-Knotted Rug	70 hours	100 hours

a. Use this information to calculate the opportunity cost in each country for each of the two products. Which country has a comparative advantage in each product?

b. Use this information to construct a table similar to Table 3 in the text, showing the overall gain in production if each country produces one unit less of the product for which it does not have a comparative advantage.

c. If India produces one more rug and exports it to New Zealand, what is the lowest price (measured in tons of wool) that it would accept? What is the highest price that New Zealand would pay? Where will the equilibrium terms of trade lie?

8. In Table 6 of this chapter, it was assumed that the exchange rate was 8 yuan per dollar. Recalculate the entries in parentheses in the table assuming that the exchange rate is 6 yuan per dollar. Will trade still take place? Explain briefly.

Challenge Questions

1. Suppose that the Marshall Islands does not trade with the outside world. It has a competitive domestic market for VCRs. The market supply and demand curves are reflected in this table:

Price ($/VCR)	Quantity Demanded	Quantity Supplied
500	0	500
400	100	400
300	200	300
200	300	200
100	400	100
0	500	0

a. Plot the supply and demand curves and determine the domestic equilibrium price and quantity.
b. Suddenly, the islanders discover the virtues of free exchange and begin trading with the outside world. The Marshall Islands is a very small country, and so its trading has no effect on the price established in the world market. It can import as many VCRs as it wishes at the world price of $100 per VCR. In this situation, how many VCRs will be purchased in the Marshall Islands? How many will be produced there? How many will be imported?
c. After protests from domestic producers, the government decides to impose a tariff of $100 per imported VCR. Now how many VCRs will be purchased in the Marshall Islands? How many will be produced there? How many will be imported?
d. What is the government's revenue from the tariff described in part (c)?

e. Compare the effect of the tariff described in part (c) with a quota that limits imports to 100 VCRs per year.

2. a. Use the information in the following table to plot supply and demand curves and determine the domestic equilibrium price and quantity for these two countries.

	Country A			Country B	
Price per Unit of Good X (measured in dollars)	Quantity Demanded of Good X	Quantity Supplied of Good X	Price per Unit of Good X (measured in dollars)	Quantity Demanded of Good X	Quantity Supplied of Good X
$10	1	25	$10	5	13
9	2	22	9	6	10
8	3	19	8	7	7
7	4	16	7	8	4
6	5	13	6	9	2
5	6	10	5	10	½
4	7	7	4	11	¼
3	8	4	3	12	⅛

b. Show graphically what will happen if these two countries begin to trade. What will happen to the price of Good X in each country? What will happen to consumption in each country? What will happen to production in each country? Which country has the competitive advantage in the production of Good X? Which country will export Good X? How many units will it export?

ECONOMIC *Applications*

These exercises require access to Hall/Lieberman Xtra! If Xtra! did not come with your book, visit http://hallxtra.swlearning.com to purchase.

1. Use your Xtra! password at the Hall and Lieberman Web site (http://hallxtra.swlearning.com), select this chapter, and under Economic Applications, click on EconDebate. Choose *World Economy: International Trade,* and scroll down to find the debate, "Does the United States economy benefit from the WTO?" Read the debate.

   a. What is the role of the WTO?

   b. Is free trade, as envisioned by the WTO, inconsistent with national sovereignty? That is, will WTO regulations require that nations give up some authority over their own environment, workplace rules, etc, in the name of free trade? Does that really matter? Explain your answer carefully.

2. Use your Xtra! password at the Hall and Lieberman Web site (http://hallxtra.swlearning.com), select this chapter, and under Economic Applications, click on EconDebate. Choose *World Economy: International Trade,* and scroll down to find the debate, "Does the anti-sweatshop movement help or harm workers in low-wage countries?" Read the debate, and write a short essay explaining how the anti-sweatshop movement works in concert with, or in opposition to, the theory of comparative advantage.

The Stock Market and the Macroeconomy

CHAPTER OUTLINE

Basic Background
Why Do People Hold Stock?
Tracking the Stock Market

Explaining Stock Prices
Step 1: Characterize the Market
Step 2: Find the Equilibrium
Step 3: What Happens When Things Change?

The Stock Market and the Macroeconomy
How the Stock Market Affects the Economy
How the Economy Affects the Stock Market

What Happens When Things Change?
A Shock to the Economy
A Shock to the Economy *and* the Stock Market: The High-Tech Boom of the 1990s
A Shock to the Economy *and* the Stock Market: The High-Tech Bust of 2000 and 2001
The Fed and the Stock Market

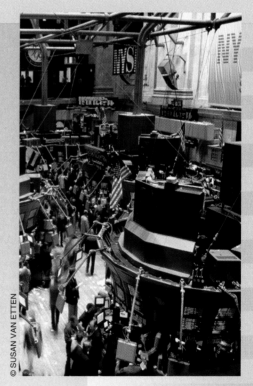

In December 1996, Alan Greenspan, the chair of the Federal Reserve Board, uttered two sentences that caught the world's attention. Speaking to a Washington research organization, he asked, "How do we know when irrational exuberance has unduly escalated asset values which then become the subject of unexpected and prolonged contractions . . . ? And how do we factor that assessment into monetary policy?"

Greenspan was referring to the rapid rise in stock prices that had occurred over the previous several years. By one broad measure, the average stock's price had doubled over this period—a very rapid rise by historical standards. But when the markets opened for trading at 9:30 A.M. on the morning after Greenspan's speech, stock prices dropped by about 2 percent almost immediately.

Everyone agreed that Greenspan's remarks had been designed to bring down stock prices and that he had succeeded somewhat. But this effort to "talk down the market" brought a wave of criticism in business and media circles. Who was Alan Greenspan to decide when stock prices are too high or too low? And what right did he have to try to bring stock prices down?

Flash forward to September 17, 2001. It was the first day of trading after the stock market had been closed for a week in the wake of the terrorist attacks of September 11. And it was not a good day. Stock prices fell on average more than 5 percent, with some airline and travel industry stocks plunging 40 to 50 percent. The next several days were little better, and by September 20, stocks had fallen more than 13 percent.

Alan Greenspan—still chair of the Federal Reserve—watched the market with deep concern that week. And when Congress called him to testify, they hoped he would have something encouraging to say. He did. In highly technical language, he reassured the nation that the Fed had responded appropriately and that, although the economy faced short-term uncertainty, there was no reason for long-run pessimism.

In the following days, the market began to rise—slowly at first, then more rapidly. And within a few weeks, stocks had regained all that they had lost after September 11. While there were many influences on the market during this time, no one doubted that Greenspan's reassuring words had helped to turn the tide and that he was once again trying to influence stock prices. Only this time, no one complained.

The events of 1996 and 2001 raise a number of important questions. *Why* does the stock market matter? What is its role in the economy? Why should public officials worry when stock prices are too high or too low? And why do stock prices sometimes fluctuate so widely? In this chapter—after providing some basic background about the stock market—we'll answer all these questions.

BASIC BACKGROUND

Let's start with the most basic question of all: What is a share of stock?

First, a share of stock is a private financial asset, like a corporate bond. In fact, stocks and corporate bonds are alike in two ways. Both are issued by corporations to raise funds for investment projects, and both offer future payments to their owners.

But there is also an important difference between these two types of assets. When a corporation issues a bond, it is *borrowing* funds; the bond is just a promise to pay back the loan. A share of stock, by contrast, is a share of *ownership* in a corporation. When a firm issues new shares of stock, those who pay for those shares provide the firm with new funds, and in return, the firm owes them—at some future date or dates—a share of the firm's profits.

When a firm issues new shares of stock—in what is called a *public offering*—the sale of stock generates funds for the firm. Once the newly issued shares are sold, however, the buyer is free to sell them to someone else. Indeed, virtually all of the shares traded in the stock market are previously issued shares, and this trading does not involve the firm that issued the stock.

But a firm is still *concerned* about the price of its previously issued shares for two reasons. First, the firm's owners—its stockholders—want high share prices because that is the price they can sell at. A management team that ignores the desires of stockholders for too long might find itself replaced by other managers who will pay more attention.

Moreover, the price of previously issued shares has an important impact on firms that are planning new public offerings. That's because previously issued shares are perfect substitutes for the firm's new shares, so the firm cannot expect to receive a higher price for its new shares than the going price on its old shares.

The higher the price for previously issued shares, the higher the price the firm will receive for *new* shares and the more funds it will obtain from any given public offering.

Why Do People Hold Stock?

Stock ownership in the United States is growing rapidly. In 1983, only 19 percent of Americans owned shares of stock either directly or through mutual funds—companies that invest in a variety of stocks for their clients. In 2003, almost half of all Americans owned stock in these two ways. If we included stocks in employer-managed retirement accounts, the percentage of Americans with a stake in the stock market would be much higher. And the stakes are significant.

Why do so many individuals choose to hold their wealth in stocks? You already know part of the answer: When you own a share of stock, you own part of the corporation. The fraction of the corporation that you own is equal to the fraction of the company's total stock that you own. For example, in July 2005, there were 302,074,000 shares outstanding in FedEx Corporation, which runs the overnight package delivery service Federal Express. If you owned 10,000 shares of FedEx stock, then you owned $10,000/302,074,000 = 0.000033$, or about three-thousandths of a percent of the company. That means that you are, in a sense, entitled to three-thousandths of a percent of the firm's after-tax profits.

In practice, however, most firms do not pay out *all* of their profit to shareholders. Instead, some is kept as *retained earnings*, for later use by the firm. The part of profit that is distributed to shareholders is called *dividends*. A firm's dividend payments benefit stockholders in much the same way that interest payments benefit bondholders, providing a source of steady income. Of course, as part owner of a firm, you are part owner of any retained earnings as well, even if you will not benefit from them until later.

Aside from dividends, a second—and usually more important—reason that people hold stocks is that they hope to enjoy *capital gains*. A capital gain is the return someone gets when they sell an asset at a higher price than they paid for it. For example, if you buy shares of FedEx at $60 per share, and later sell them at $65 per share, your capital gain is $5 per share. This is in addition to any dividends you earned while you owned the stock.

Some stocks pay no dividends at all, because the management believes that stockholders are best served by reinvesting all profits within the firm so that *future* profits will be even higher. The idea is to increase the value of the stock and create capital gains for the shareholders when the stock is finally sold. New or fast-growing companies—such as Yahoo! and Google—typically pay no dividends at all.

Over the past century, corporate stocks have generally been a good investment. Holding stocks was especially rewarding during the 1990s, as you'll see in the next section.

Tracking the Stock Market

In the United States, financial markets are so important that stock and bond prices are monitored on a continuous basis. If you wish to know the value of a

TABLE 1
The Performance of Three Stock Market Indexes

Index	Increase, 1 Year Ending June 30, 2005	Average Annual Increase, 3 Years Ending June 30, 2005	Average Annual Increase, 5 Years Ending June 30, 2005	Average Annual Increase, 10 Years Ending June 30, 2005
Dow Jones Industrial Average	−1.5%	3.6%	−0.3%	8.5%
Standard & Poor's 500	4.4%	6.4%	−3.9%	8.1%
NASDAQ	0.4%	12.0%	−12.3%	8.2%

Source: http://www.yahoo.com, and author's calculations.

stock, you can find out instantly by checking with a broker or logging onto a Web site (such as Yahoo.com, Morningstar.com, or thomsoninvest.com). In addition, stock prices and other information are reported daily in local newspapers and in specialized financial publications such as the *Wall Street Journal* and the *Financial Times*.

In addition to monitoring individual stocks, the media keep a close watch on many stock market indices or averages. These averages track movements in stock prices as a whole, or movements in particular types of stocks. The oldest and most popular average is the *Dow Jones Industrial Average (DJIA)*, which tracks the prices of 30 of the largest companies in the United States, including Microsoft, IBM, and Wal-Mart. Another popular average is the much broader *Standard & Poor's 500 (S&P 500)*, which tracks stock prices of 500 corporations chosen to represent all stocks in the market. Finally, the *NASDAQ* index tracks share prices of about 5,000 mostly newer companies whose shares are traded on the Nasdaq stock exchange, an association of stockbrokers who execute trades electronically. The companies in the NASDAQ include most of the new high-tech companies that are closely connected to the Internet sector.

Often, the three stock market averages will rise and fall at the same time, sometimes by the same percentage. That's because many of the shocks that hit the stock market affect most share prices *together*. But the indices can and do behave differently—sometimes very differently. For example, in 2000, Internet stocks fluctuated wildly from day to day, as new information changed public opinion about the future of the industry. There were many days on which the NASDAQ rose substantially while the Dow and the Standard & Poor's 500 fell, and vice versa.

Table 1 shows how the three averages performed over different lengths of time ending on June 30, 2005. The entries in the table tell us the average annual increase in each index over the period. For example, the entry 8.1 percent in the table (be sure you can find it) tells us that—over the period June 30, 1995, to June 30, 2005—the S&P 500 rose an average of 8.1 percent per year.

In spite of falling stock prices in 2000, 2001, and 2002, the last two decades have been good for stocks. Someone who invested $10,000 in a typical group of S&P 500 stocks on June 30, 1995, would have been able to sell them for $21,853 on June 30, 2005. A decade earlier (1985 to 1995—not shown), $10,000 invested in the S&P 500 would have grown to $28,534. However, you can also see that even a broad portfolio of stocks is risky in the short run. An investor who put $10,000 into S&P stocks in mid-2000 would have found them worth only $9,610 in mid-2005.

EXPLAINING STOCK PRICES

Why do stock prices change? And why do they change so often?

We can answer these questions—as we answer most questions about the economy—by using our three-step process.

Step 1: Characterize the Market

The price of a share of stock—like any other price—is determined in a market. But which market? Initially, we'll be focusing on price changes for shares of a particular stock, so the most useful way to organize our thinking is to look at the market for a single corporation's shares. That is, we'll view the "stock market" as a collection of *individual* markets, one for shares of stock in Time Warner, another for shares in FedEx, another for shares in Starbucks, and so on.

Further, we'll characterize the market for a company's shares as perfectly competitive. Indeed, markets for shares *do* satisfy the three requirements of perfect competition rather closely. There are many buyers and sellers (so many that no one of them can do much to change the market price of the stock).[1] There is a standardized product (it makes no difference to the buyer whether her FedEx shares are being sold to her by Smith or by Jones). And there is easy entry (virtually anyone with funds to invest can open up a brokerage account and buy or sell any publicly traded stock).

In sum,

> *we'll view the stock market as a collection of individual, perfectly competitive markets for particular corporations' shares.*

Step 2: Find the Equilibrium

Like all prices in competitive markets, stock prices are determined by supply and demand. However, in stock markets, our supply and demand curves require careful interpretations.

Figure 1 presents a supply and demand diagram for the shares of FedEx Corporation. Unlike most supply curves you've studied in this book—which show the quantity of something that suppliers want to *sell* over a given period of time—the supply curve in Figure 1 is somewhat different. It tells us the quantity of shares of FedEx stock *in existence* at any moment in time. This is the number of shares that people are *actually* holding.

---

[1] In some cases, a single buyer or seller holds such a large fraction of a company's shares that his or her decisions have a significant impact on market price. But these exceptions are rare for publicly traded shares.

The Market for Shares of FedEx Corporation

The supply curve shows the number of shares of FedEx stock people are holding. The curve is vertical at the number of shares outstanding—which was about 302 million in mid-2005. The demand curve tells us how many shares people want to hold. It slopes downward— the lower the price, the more shares people want to hold. At any price other than the equilibrium price of $90, there would be either an excess supply or an excess demand for shares.

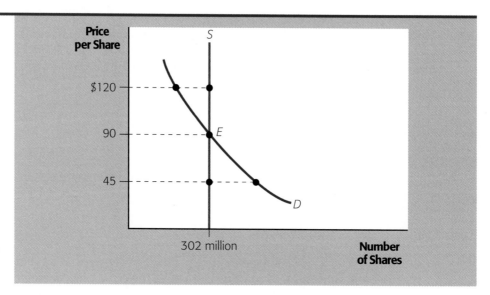

On any given day, the number of FedEx shares in existence is just the number that the firm has issued previously. By mid-2003, FedEx had issued about 302 million shares since the corporation began. Therefore, no matter what happens to the price of the stock on any particular day, the number of shares will remain unchanged, and so will the quantity supplied. This is why the supply curve in the figure is a vertical line at 302 million: We assume that over the time period we're analyzing, FedEx will not issue any new shares.

Now, just because 302 million shares of FedEx stock exist, that does not mean that this is the number of shares that people will *want* to hold. The desire to hold FedEx shares is given by the downward-sloping demand curve. As you can see, all else equal, the lower the price of the stock, the more shares of FedEx that people will want to hold. Why is this?

First, people have different expectations about the firm's future profits. Some may believe that FedEx will continue to grow as it has in the past. Others will think it is poised for a spurt of higher growth, while still others—more pessimistic—may believe that FedEx's best days are behind it. There will also be different opinions about the *risk* of those future profits. Thus, at any given moment, with an array of opinions about the company's future, each person will have a different price in mind that would make the stock an attractive buy. As the price per share falls, more and more people will find the stock to be a bargain, and want to hold it. This is what the downward-sloping demand curve tells us.

In the figure, you can see that at any price other than $90 per share, the number of shares people *are* holding (on the supply curve) will differ from the number they *want* to hold (on the demand curve). For example, at a price of $45 per share, people would want to hold more shares than they are currently holding. Many would try to buy the stock, bidding the price up. At $120 per share, the opposite occurs: People find themselves holding more shares than they want to hold, and they will try to get rid of the excess by selling them. The sudden sales would cause the price to drop. Only at the *equilibrium price* of $90—where the supply and demand curves intersect—are people satisfied holding the number of shares they are *actually* holding.

Stocks achieve their equilibrium prices almost instantly. There are so many stock traders—both individuals and professional fund managers—poised at their computers, ready to buy or sell a particular firm's shares at a moment's notice, that any excess supply or excess demand will cause the price to move within seconds. Thus, we can have confidence that the price of a share at any time is the equilibrium price.

But why do stock prices *change* so often? To answer that question, we need Step 3.

Step 3: What Happens When Things Change?

The *supply* curve for a corporation's shares, like the one in Figure 1, shifts rightward whenever there is a public offering. Can this explain changes in share prices? Not really. Public offerings occur only occasionally and with great fanfare. Moreover, most public offerings by existing companies are for a relatively small number of shares. They shift the supply curve only a little, and therefore have little impact on the market price of the stock. Thus, the changes in equilibrium prices we observe for most stocks are *not* caused by shifts of the supply curve.

That leaves only one explanation: shifts in *demand*.

> *The changes we observe in a stock's price—over a few minutes, a few days, or a few years—are virtually always caused by shifts in the demand curve.*

Panel (a) of Figure 2 shows how a rightward shift of the demand curve for shares of FedEx could cause the equilibrium price to rise to $75 per share. Indeed, on rare occasions, the demand curve for a firm's shares has shifted so far rightward in a single day that the share price doubled or even tripled.

But what causes these sudden changes in demand for a share of stock?

In almost all cases, it is one or more of the following three factors:

1. *Changes in expected future profits of the firm.* At any given time, people have an idea about the expected profits of every firm. But these ideas can change as new information becomes available. The new information can pertain to a scientific discovery, a corporate takeover or merger with another company, or a new government policy. Even information that suggests that one of these events *might* occur can change the attractiveness of stocks. After all, a stock in a company that has a 50 percent chance of making huge profits from a new invention is more attractive than a stock that has only a 20 percent chance of such profits.

   New information can be positive, shifting the demand curve rightward and increasing the price of the stock. But it can also be negative, shifting the demand curve leftward. A dramatic example was the plunge in passenger airline stocks when the market reopened on September 17, 2001. After the attacks of September 11, it was clear to everyone that fewer people would want to fly and that the cost of providing airline safety would soon rise. With fewer passengers and higher safety costs, profits were sure to fall; thus fewer people wanted to hold airline stocks at any given price.

FIGURE 2
Shifts in the Demand for Shares Curve

> *Any new information that* increases *expectations of firms' future profits—including announcements of new scientific discoveries, business developments, or changes in government policy—will shift the demand curves of the affected stocks rightward. New information that* decreases *expectations of future profits will shift the demand curves leftward.*

2. *Macroeconomic fluctuations.* When the economy is expanding, and real GDP is rising, firms *in general* tend to earn higher profits, and these profits are less risky. By contrast, in a recession, sales and profits decrease. For this reason,

> *any news that suggests the economy will enter an expansion, or that an expansion will continue, will shift the demand curves for most stocks rightward. Any news that suggests an economic slowdown or a coming recession shifts the demand curves for most stocks leftward.*

3. *Changes in the interest rate.* Stocks are not the only way that people can hold their wealth. They can also hold money and—more importantly—they can hold interest-earning assets like certificates of deposit or bonds. If the interest rate rises, these other assets become more attractive, and many people will want to shift their wealth *out* of stocks so they can buy them. Thus,

> *a rise in interest rates will shift the demand curves for most stocks to the left. Similarly, a drop in interest rates will shift the demand curves for most stocks to the right.*[2]

---

[2] If you've studied *microeconomics,* you've learned another way to view the impact of interest rate changes on stock prices: Higher interest rates reduce the *present value* of any given stream of future profits.

Even *expectations* of a future interest rate change can shift demand curves for stocks. This can create some rather convoluted—but logical—explanations for movements in stock prices. For example, suppose that a report comes out suggesting that real GDP is growing very rapidly. All else equal, this makes stocks more attractive. But . . . all else may *not* remain equal. In fact, you may surmise that the U.S. Federal Reserve and its influential chair—currently Alan Greenspan—will want to prevent inflation at almost any cost. You might then *anticipate* that the Fed—concerned about the economy overheating—will raise interest rates in the near future to slow down the growth in real GDP. You also know that—if the interest rate *does* rise—stock prices will fall, for the reasons we've just discussed. What should you do? *Dump your stocks now,* to avoid a capital loss later. Since you and many others will have access to the same information and feel the same way, the announcement of rapid economic growth could lead—almost immediately—to a *decrease* in stock prices.

Such an event occured on February 27, 2002, when Fed Chair Greenspan announced that it appeared the economy was recovering from its recession. Market participants felt that with this perception, the Fed was more likely to raise interest rates in the near future than lower them, and the Dow Jones Industrial Average dropped 200 points (about 2 percent).

Similarly, bad news about economic growth—if it leads to an expected decrease in interest rates—can cause stock prices to rise.

> *News that causes people to* anticipate *a rise in the interest rate will shift the demand curves for stocks leftward. Similarly, news that suggests a future drop in the interest rate will shift the demand curves for stocks rightward.*

Panels (a) and (b) of Figure 2 summarize the different forces that cause the demand curve for a stock to shift rightward or leftward.

THE STOCK MARKET AND THE MACROECONOMY

As you can see in Figure 3, there is a *two-way* relationship between the stock market and the economy. That is, the performance of the stock market affects the performance of the economy, and vice versa. In the next two sections of this chapter, we'll look at this two-way relationship. Let's start with the impact of the stock market on the economy, as illustrated by the upper arrow in the figure.

How the Stock Market Affects the Economy

On October 19, 1987, there was a dramatic drop in the stock market, one that made the decline on September 17, 2001 seem small by comparison. That day, the Dow Jones Industrial Average fell by 508 points—a drop of 23 percent—and about $500 billion in household wealth disappeared. That same evening, as President Reagan boarded his helicopter, a breathless Sam Donaldson of ABC News thrust a microphone in front of him and asked, "Mr. President, are you concerned about the drop in the Dow?" As Reagan entered his helicopter, he smiled calmly and replied, "Why, no, Sam. I don't own any stocks."

FIGURE 3
The Two-Way Relationship Between the Stock Market and the Economy

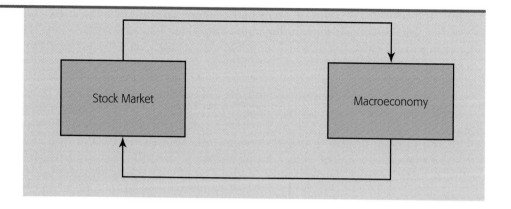

It was a curious exchange. Reagan was probably kidding—perhaps trying to calm a worried nation with his trademark humor. Or perhaps he was annoyed at a frantic reporter invading his personal space. Or he might have been caught off guard and said the first thing that popped into his head.

Whatever Reagan's intent, the statement was startling because, in fact, the stock market *does* matter to all Americans, whether they own stocks or not. As you are about to see, the ups and downs of stock prices—if they are big enough and sustained enough—can cause ups and downs in the overall economy.

The Wealth Effect. To understand how the market affects the economy, let's run through the following mental experiment: We'll suppose that, for *some* reason (we'll discuss specific reasons later), stock prices rise. As a result, those who own stock will feel wealthier. In fact, they *are* wealthier. After all, just as you measure the value of your house by the price at which you could sell it, the same is true of your financial assets, like stocks. When stock prices rise, so does household wealth.

What do households do when their wealth increases? Typically, they increase their spending. In our short-run macro model, we would classify this as an increase in *autonomous consumption*—an increase in consumption spending at *any* level of disposable income.

The link between stock prices and consumer spending is an important one, so economists have given it a name: the *wealth effect*. And the wealth effect works in both directions: Just as an increase in stock prices increases autonomous consumption, so will a drop in stock prices—which decreases household wealth—cause autonomous consumption spending to fall.

More generally,

> *the wealth effect tells us that autonomous consumption spending tends to move in the same direction as stock prices. When stock prices rise, autonomous consumption spending rises; when stock prices fall, autonomous consumption spending falls with it.*

The Wealth Effect and Equilibrium GDP. As you learned when you studied the short-run macroeconomic model, autonomous consumption is a component of to-

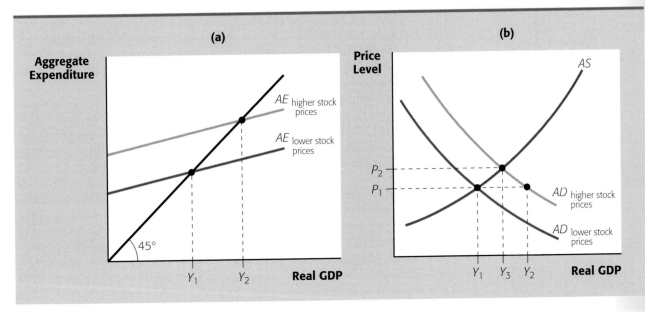

FIGURE 4
The Effect of Higher Stock Prices on the Economy

tal spending. And an increase in total spending tends to increase equilibrium real GDP, as shown in panel (a) of Figure 4. There, when stock prices rise, the increase in real wealth causes the aggregate expenditure line to shift upward, and increases the economy's equilibrium GDP from Y_1 to Y_2.

Panel (b) of Figure 4 shows a more complete way to view the impact of rising stock prices. In this panel, the increase in equilibrium GDP at any given price level is shown as a rightward shift in the economy's *AD* curve. And—in the absence of any change in government policy—this shift of the *AD* curve will increase both equilibrium GDP (to Y_3) and the price level (to P_2). (Why does equilibrium GDP increase by less in panel (b) than in panel (a)?)

We can summarize the logic of the wealth effect as follows:

Higher stock prices have a wealth effect on spending, increasing consumption spending at any level of real GDP. In panel (a), the wealth effect of higher stock prices shifts the aggregate expenditure line upward, raising equilibrium GDP from Y_1 to Y_2. Panel (b) shows a more complete way of illustrating the wealth effect: Higher stock prices shift the aggregate demand curve rightward, increasing both equilibrium real GDP and the price level.

In words:

Changes in stock prices—through the wealth effect—cause both equilibrium GDP and the price level to move in the same direction. That is, an increase in stock prices will raise equilibrium GDP and the price level, while a decrease in stock prices will decrease both equilibrium GDP and the price level.

How important is the wealth effect? Economic research shows that the *marginal propensity to consume out of wealth*—the change in consumption spending for each one-dollar rise in wealth—is between 0.03 and 0.05. In other words, when household wealth rises by a dollar, all else remaining the same, consumption spending tends to rise by between 3 and 5 cents. Moreover, recent research suggests that virtually *all* of the increase in consumption comes rather quickly—within one quarter (3 months) after the quarter in which stock prices rise.[3] Let's translate this into some practical numbers.

First, as a rule of thumb, a 100-point rise in the DJIA—which generally means a rise in stock prices in general—causes household wealth to rise by about $100 billion. This rise in household wealth, we've now learned, will increase autonomous consumption spending by between $3 billion and $5 billion—we'll say $4 billion. As you learned several chapters ago, the multiplier in the real world—after we take account of all the automatic stabilizers that reduce its value—is equal to about 1.5, with most of its impact in the first nine months to a year after a shock. Thus, a 100-point rise in the DJIA, which causes consumption spending to rise by about $4 billion, will cause real GDP to increase by about $4 billion × 1.5 = $6 billion. Extrapolating from these results, a 6,000- or so point rise in the Dow—as occurred in the second half of the 1990s—would generate about $240 billion in additional consumption spending and drive up real GDP by about $360 billion—an increase of about 4 percent. This is in addition to the normal rise in real GDP that would be occurring anyway, as income grows and spending grows with it. Thus,

> *rapid increases in stock prices can cause significant positive demand shocks to the economy, shocks that policy makers cannot ignore. Similarly, rapid decreases in stock prices can cause significant negative demand shocks to the economy, which would be a major concern for policy makers.*

How the Economy Affects the Stock Market

Now that we've explored how the stock market affects the economy, let's look at the other side of the two-way relationship: how the economy affects stock prices.

Actually, many different types of changes in the overall economy can affect the stock market. Some—like the revolution in telecommunications that took place in the 1990s—are rare, happening once or twice a century. Others—like the impact of macroeconomic fluctuations—happen much more frequently. In this section, we'll focus on the more frequent scenario: how the stock market responds as the economy goes through expansions and recessions in the short run.

Let's start by looking at the typical expansion, in which real GDP rises rapidly over several years. In the typical expansion, profits will rise along with GDP. Higher profits are themselves enough to make stocks look more attractive. But the process is further helped by another factor: an improvement in investor psychology. In an expansion, not only are corporate profits rising, but also the unemployment rate falls and household incomes rise. Memories of the last recession are dim, and it

---

[3] Sydney Ludvigson and Charles Steindel, "How Important Is the Stock Market Effect on Consumption?" New York Federal Reserve Bank *Policy Review*, July 1999. (Also available at *http://www.newyorkfed.org/research/staff_reports/research_papers/9821.html*) For a study that shows a somewhat larger effect of stockholder wealth on consumption, see Karen E. Dynan and Dean M. Maki, "Does Stock Market Wealth Matter for Consumption?" *Finance and Economics Discussion Series,* Board of Governors of the Federal Reserve System, May 2001.

looks as if the economy will continue to grow and grow, perhaps forever. This optimistic outlook raises estimates of future profits—sometimes dramatically. The demand curves for stocks will shift rightward and stock prices will rise.

We can summarize the impact of an *expansion* on the market as follows:

Of course, the process also works in reverse. When a *recession* strikes—such as the one from March through November 2001—corporate profits drop, unemployment rises, and the economy begins to look bleak. Stockholders turn pessimistic and expect lower profits in the future. The demand curves for stocks shift leftward, driving stock prices down:

In sum,

in the typical expansion, higher profits and stockholder optimism cause stock prices to rise. In the typical recession, lower profits and stockholder pessimism cause stock prices to fall.

WHAT HAPPENS WHEN THINGS CHANGE?

Now that you understand how stock prices affect the overall economy—and how the economy can affect stock prices—it's time to apply Step 3 one more time. But this time, we'll apply it very broadly: We'll observe how *both* the stock market and the macroeconomy are affected when *something* changes.

But . . . *what* changes?

Figure 5 illustrates three different types of changes we might explore. A change might have most of its initial impact on the overall economy rather than the stock market. For example, a change in government spending or taxes—with an unchanged interest rate target by the Fed—would initially affect real GDP rather than the stock market. Ultimately, stock prices would be affected, but primarily *through* the change in real GDP.

Alternatively, there might be a shock that initially affects the stock market. An example would be a change in the duration of patent protection for intellectual property, which would change the expected profits of firms and shift the demand curves for stocks. Direct shocks to the market—without simultaneously affecting the economy—are rare.

Finally, a shock could have powerful, initial impacts on *both* the stock market *and* the overall economy. Examples are the technological revolution of the late

FIGURE 5
Three Types of Shocks

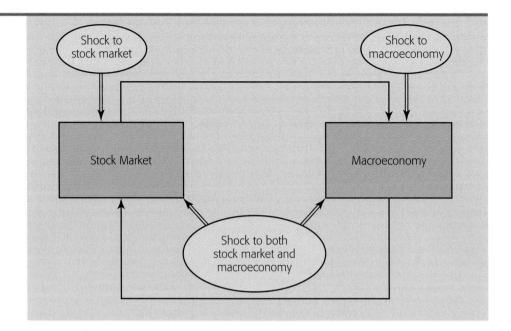

1990s and early 2000s and the collapse of dot-com shares in late 2000 and 2001. Each of these events rocked both the economy and the market simultaneously.

In the next section, we'll explore the consequences of an initial shock to the *economy*. Then, we'll turn our attention to shocks that simultaneously hit the market and the economy, as occurred during the 1990s and again in the early 2000s. Finally, in the end-of-chapter questions, you'll be asked to address the remaining case: a shock that initially hits just the stock market.

A Shock to the Economy

Imagine that new legislation greatly increases government purchases—say, to equip public schools with more sophisticated telecommunications equipment, or to increase the strength of our armed forces. This demand shock—and increase in government purchases—will have its primary initial impact on the overall economy, rather than the stock market. Let's suppose, too, that the Fed maintains its interest rate target, so there is no direct impact on the stock market from changes in the interest rate. What will happen?

As you've learned in your study of macroeconomics, the rise in government purchases will first increase real GDP through the expenditure multiplier:

In previous chapters, the multiplier process was a simple one: Increases in output and income cause increases in consumption, which cause further increases in output and income and then further increases in consumption, and so on. But now, there is a *new* contributor to the multiplier process: the stock market.

First, remember that increases in real GDP cause corporate profits to rise. This, in turn, leads to investor optimism about *future* profits, shifting the demand curves for stocks rightward and increasing the average price of stocks.

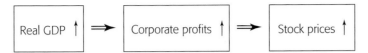

But the story doesn't end there. The increase in stock prices will—through the wealth effect—cause an increase in autonomous consumption spending. Note that this is *in addition* to the increase in consumption spending caused by the normal multiplier process. Indeed, the increase in autonomous consumption spending caused by the wealth effect sets off its *own* multiplier process, further increasing real GDP:

Now, look back at the three cause-and-effect chains just presented. You can see that an increase in government purchases will cause a *larger* rise in real GDP when we include the effects of the stock market. Another way of saying this is that,

> *when we include the effects of the stock market, the expenditure multiplier is larger. An increase in spending that increases real GDP will also cause stock prices to rise, causing still greater increases in real GDP. Similarly, a decrease in spending that causes real GDP to fall will also cause stock prices to fall, causing still greater decreases in real GDP.*

When you first learned about the multiplier, you learned about automatic stabilizers: features of the economy, such as the income tax or unemployment insurance payments, that make the expenditure multiplier smaller and thus help to stabilize real GDP. Now you can see that the normal behavior of the stock market—which makes the expenditure multiplier larger—works as an *automatic destabilizer*. This is one reason why stock prices are so carefully watched by policy makers, and matter for everyone—whether they own stocks themselves or not.

A Shock to the Economy *and* the Stock Market: The High-Tech Boom of the 1990s

The 1990s—especially the second half of the 1990s—saw a dramatic rise in stock prices. Both the Dow Jones Industrial Average and the Standard & Poor's 500 more than quadrupled over the period, and the NASDAQ increased almost ninefold.

The 1990s were also a period of rapid expansion, especially the period from 1995 to 2000, in which growth in real GDP averaged 4.2 percent per year—much faster than in previous decades.

In part, the economic expansion and the rise in stock prices were reinforcing: Each contributed to the other, as we've seen in this chapter. But the expansion and the climb in stocks were *initiated* by a common shock: a technological revolution, led by the Internet.

The Internet had a direct impact on the stock market through its effect on expected future profits of U.S. firms. In particular, stockholders (and potential stockholders) believed that the new technology would enable firms to produce goods and services at much lower costs than before, and that this reduction in costs would translate into an increase in profit. The increase in expected future profits translated into a rightward shift of the demand curve for stocks at virtually any firm that had the potential to exploit the new technology, or help other firms exploit it.

For example, during this period, AT&T positioned itself to be a major supplier of information and voice communication using the Internet and other new technologies. As a result, the demand curve for AT&T stock shifted rightward—enough to drive the price of AT&T stock from $28 per share in early 1997 to $60 in early 2000.

At the same time, the technological revolution was having a huge impact on the overall economy. Investment spending rose, as business firms—in order to take advantage of the new technology—invested in new plants and equipment. Autonomous consumption spending also rose: Consumers wanted new gadgets that would enable them to enjoy new types of services—new cellular phones, new computers, Palm Pilots, high-speed Internet connections, and more.

Faced with these demand shocks, the Federal Reserve would ordinarily have raised its interest rate target to prevent real GDP from exceeding potential output. But the technological revolution of the 1990s was having *another* effect on the economy: It *increased* potential output more rapidly than before. New computers, new software, and other forms of new capital equipment—along with the increased skills and training of the workforce—raised the typical worker's hourly output by about 22 percent over the decade.

The technological changes of the 1990s were an example of a shock to both the stock market *and* the economy. But remember that each of these also influences the other. As the expansion gained steam and real GDP was growing steadily and rapidly, profits and expected profits soared, pushing stock prices up further. And as stock prices rose, the wealth effect worked to propel consumer spending still higher. The result was a market and an economy that were feeding on each other, sending both to new performance heights. Was this a good thing?

Yes, and no. Higher stock prices certainly make stockholders happy. And a rapid expansion is good for workers, since it makes it easy to find jobs and forces firms to compete for workers by offering higher wages and better fringe benefits. Indeed, from a high of almost 8 percent in 1991, the unemployment rate dropped steadily during the 1990s, reaching 4 percent at the end of the decade.

But in spite of all this good news, there were dark clouds on the horizon. . . .

A Shock to the Economy *and* the Stock Market: The High-Tech Bust of 2000 and 2001

The market—especially high-tech NASDAQ stocks—began to decline in early 2000. By September 2001—even *before* September 11—the NASDAQ was down about 65 percent from its high. At the same time, a wave of pessimism was infecting the economy. The high-tech boom of the 1990s had become the high-tech bust of the early 2000s. What happened?

Both the economy and the market were being affected by several events discussed in earlier chapters of this book. Now let's bring these events together to understand what happened to the market and the economy.

First, during the 1990s, there had been an investment boom, as businesses rushed to incorporate the Internet into factories, offices, and their business practices in general. Firms across the country needed servers and high-speed Internet connections, and the high-tech firms that supplied these high-tech goods and services needed to expand, in order to meet the high demand of their clients. But as 2000 came to a close, firms had begun to catch up to the new technology. The rush had ended. Investment remained positive, but it was smaller than in previous periods. Of course, when investment is positive but smaller, this translates to a decrease in investment spending—a negative demand shock that set the stage for the recession that would begin a few months later.

The Fed may have played a role as well. Concerned about the economy overheating, the Fed raised interest rates throughout 2000. Some observers believe the Fed kept rates high for too long—into January 2001—and that this pulled investment spending down faster and further than it otherwise would have gone.

In any case, the decline in investment—and the recession it caused—can be regarded as a shock to the economy. As you've learned, though, shocks to the economy feed back to the market: Stock prices tend to fall during recessions. This was a part of the reason stock prices fell in 2001.

But in addition, there was a direct shock to the market: a change in expectations about the future. The late 1990s were a period of high optimimsm. The Internet and other new technologies seemed capable of increasing business profits to unprecedented heights. The public became hungry to own shares of stock in almost any company that had anything to do with the Internet, driving up share prices and encouraging the formation of many new businesses through public offerings.

Unfortunately, in late 2000 and early 2001, reality set in. Competition was preventing many new firms from earning any profit at all, and many went bankrupt. Optimism about future profits shifted rapidly to pessimism. Share prices fell. Ordinarily the drop in share prices would be expected to bring down consumption spending through the wealth effect. Surprisingly, though, consumption spending remained strong during the recession of 2001. Does this mean that there was no feedback effect from the market to the economy? Not really. A declining market *did* decrease real wealth, and this no doubt had some negative effect on consumption spending. But other forces (such as interest rate reductions by the Fed in 2001) helped to buoy consumption spending and keep it steady *in spite of* the negative wealth effect.

The Fed and the Stock Market

The experience of the late 1990s and early 2000s raised some important questions about the relationship between the Federal Reserve and the stock market—questions that have not been entirely resolved.

In 1995 and 1996, Greenspan began to worry that share prices might be rising out of proportion to the future profits corporations would be able to deliver to their owners. The Fed was worried that the market was experiencing a speculative *bubble*—a frenzy of buying that encouraged people to buy stocks and drive up their price because . . . well, just because their prices were rising.

In this view, the market in the late 1990s resembled the stock market in the 1920s, which is also often considered a bubble. While there were indeed reasons for optimism in the 1920s, there also seemed to be a speculative frenzy: Many investors borrowed money to buy stocks in companies they knew nothing about, just because of an anonymous tip or because they were watching the price of the stock go up. Indeed, the Dow Jones Industrial Average almost quadrupled from early 1920 to September 1929—just as it did during the 1990s. But when the bubble burst, it burst hard. From September 3, 1929, to July 8, 1932, the Dow fell from 381 to 41—about a 90 percent decline.[4] Many stocks of the most reliable and successful corporations (the so-called "blue chip" corporations) fell to only tiny fractions of their highs. General Electric stock, for example, fell from a high of $396\frac{1}{4}$ in 1929 to $8\frac{1}{2}$ in 1932; Bethlehem Steel from $140\frac{3}{8}$ to $7\frac{1}{4}$; and RCA from 101 to $2\frac{1}{2}$. Millions of people were financially wiped out—in itself, a human tragedy.

In 1996, when Alan Greenspan first made his "irrational exuberance" speech, he seemed to side with those who believed that the stock market was in the midst of a speculative bubble. His fear was that when the bubble burst—when people realized that there weren't sufficient buyers to keep propping up stock prices out of proportion to their future profits—then stock prices would come plummeting down to earth. And a burst bubble would be painful—millions of people would lose substantial amounts of wealth. Moreover, the Fed would be forced to intervene to prevent the wealth effect—this time in a negative direction—from creating a recession.

Could the Fed do so? Probably. We understand how the economy works much better today than we did in 1929, when—in retrospect—the Fed made several mistakes after the stock market crashed. But the Fed's knowledge isn't perfect and—as you've learned—Fed intervention is still fraught with uncertainty. There is always a chance the Fed will react too strongly, or not enough. From the Fed's point of view in the mid-1990s, the best economy would be one that hummed along without needing any policy intervention: That is, an economy with stock prices rising steadily and *slowly*, rather than a bubble that might burst and require a big policy shift.

In the mid-1990s, Greenspan seemed to be trying to "talk the market down" by letting stockholders know that he thought share prices were too high. The implied threat: If stocks rose any higher, the Fed would raise interest rates and bring them down. Indeed, according to many observers, merely hinting that the Fed *might* raise interest rates was designed to keep stock prices from rising too rapidly, and perhaps bring them down gently.

Only it didn't work. While Greenspan's irrational exuberance speech did bring the market down for a day or so, the relentless rise in stock prices continued. In October 1996, just before Greenpan's speech, the DJIA stood at about 6,500. By March 1999—less than three years later—it had reached 10,000.

---

[4] The Dow Jones Industrial Average measures *nominal* stock prices. Since the price level decreased over this period, the decline in *real* stock prices was less than 90 percent, but still a substantial loss.

Not only were Greenspan's efforts to "talk the market down" unsuccessful, they were also widely criticized. In the view of his critics, the value of stocks should be based on the decisions of those who buy and sell them. If people believe that a company is onto something good and that its future profits justify a doubling or tripling of its stock price within a short time, what business is it of the Fed to say they are wrong? After all, stock buying—and the funds it has made available to American corporations—is partly responsible for the remarkable rise in U.S. living standards over the past century. Moreover, the stock market has been especially effective in funneling funds to good ideas and away from bad ones because it relies on *decentralized* decision making. Those who put their money at risk decide for themselves what is and is not a good idea.

Greenspan himself seemed to change his tune as the 1990s continued. By 1998, he had stopped referring to exuberance—rational or irrational. Instead, he began to stress the remarkable changes in the economy, the rapid rise in productivity and potential output, and the fact that the American people—who buy and sell stocks—have a certain wisdom that should not be second-guessed by government officials. It was almost a complete reversal.

But as the 1990s came to a close, and the stock market continued to soar, the Fed faced a new problem: *the wealth effect*. Justified or not, share prices had continued to rise—and they rose a lot. In the two and a half years after Greenspan's famous irrational exuberance remarks in 1996, about $3 trillion in new wealth was created. Consumer spending was rising dramatically, and the Fed began to worry that the economy might be exceeding—or would soon exceed—its potential output.

Figure 6 shows one way we can view the Fed's problem: with aggregate demand and supply curves. In panel (a), the wealth effect of rising stock prices shifts the aggregate demand curve from AD_1 to AD_2, causing an increase in real GDP from Y_1 to Y_2 along with a rise in the price level. The question is: What happens next? That depends on where our potential output is relative to Y_2. If Y_2 is greater than potential output, the self-correcting mechanism will begin to work: The price level will rise further, bringing the economy back to potential output (assumed to be Y_1 in the figure). This is something the Fed has worked hard to avoid. As you've learned, inflation—once it begins—tends to be self-perpetuating. People begin to expect it. And once the inflation is embedded in the economy, eradicating it is painful: The Fed would have to raise interest rates and slow the economy by more than would have been necessary to prevent the inflation in the first place. Moreover, in the past, efforts to bring the inflation rate down have triggered deep recessions. From the Fed's point of view, preventing inflation in the first place is always the preferred alternative.

Figure 6 is useful, but it has a serious limitation: It doesn't take account of the rise in potential output. Each year, potential output increases because the population is growing, and because productivity—output per worker—is growing. In the 1990s and through early 2000, potential output was growing even more rapidly than in previous decades. We could illustrate this on an *AS–AD* diagram by shifting the *AS* curve rightward and downward over time. That is, due to changes in population and productivity, we could produce more output at any given price level, or have a lower price level at any given level of output. With a shifting *AS* curve, the Fed's goal is to shift the *AD* curve rightward each year by just enough to prevent inflation.

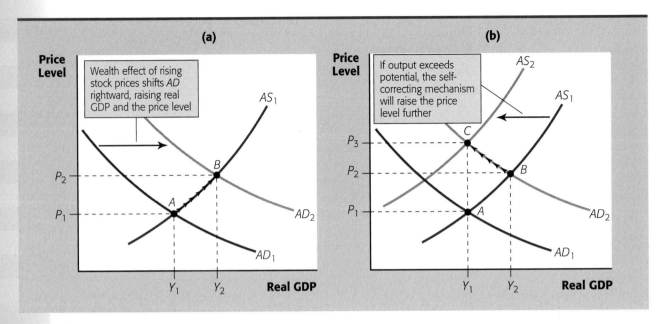

FIGURE 6
The Fed's Problem in 2000:
An *AS–AD* View

But the Phillips curve can illustrate the Fed's goal more easily. Look first at panel (a) of Figure 7, where the position of the economy in late 1999 and early 2000 is represented by point *A* on the Phillips curve PC_1: 4 percent unemployment and a 2.5 percent annual inflation rate. As you learned a few chapters ago ("Inflation and Monetary Policy"), the Fed can *keep* the economy at point *A* only if the actual unemployment rate, 4 percent, is also the *natural* rate of unemployment. In that case, the Fed—by keeping the economy at point *A*—would be allowing actual output to rise each year by just enough to keep it equal to potential output.

But what if the natural rate of unemployment is *greater* than 4 percent—say, 5 percent? Then, as you can see in panel (b), the economy would need to operate at point *B* to be at the natural rate. Point *A* now represents an overheated economy, with output greater than potential output. If we remain at point *A*, then over time the entire Phillips curve would shift upward, to the curve labeled PC_2, and point *A* would no longer be an option. If the Fed tried to maintain a 4 percent unemployment rate, the economy would then be at point *C*, with a rise in the inflation rate to 5 percent. To prevent any rise in inflation, the Fed would have to engineer a recession, bringing the economy to point *D* with unemployment above the natural rate.

To keep inflation low and stable without needing corrective recessions, the Fed strives to maintain unemployment at its natural rate. But no one—including the Fed—knows what the natural rate of unemployment *is* during any given year. We know that it is lower today than in the early 1990s—when it was believed to be about 5.5 or 6 percent. But no one knows how far it has fallen since then.

You might think that the Fed can estimate the natural rate by a process of trial and error, bringing the unemployment rate to a certain level (such as 4 percent) and seeing what happens to inflation. Then, if the inflation rate rises, the Fed would know that it had underestimated the natural rate. It could then slow the economy and bring unemployment back up to the natural rate.

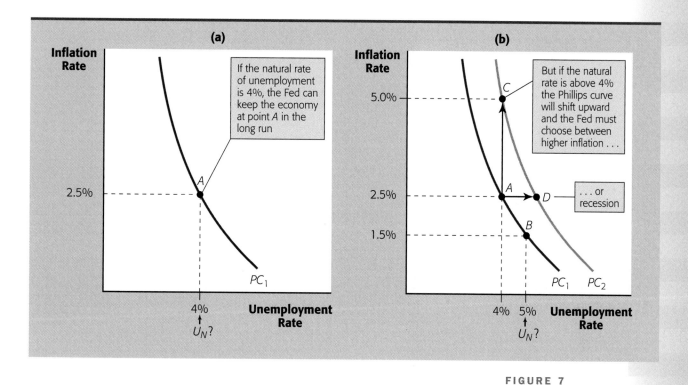

FIGURE 7
The Fed's Problem In 2000:
A Phillips Curve View

Unfortunately, things are not so simple. In the real world, when the economy overheats, the inflation rate begins to rise only after a lag of several quarters or longer. By the time the Fed notices a rise in the inflation rate, the economy may have been overheated for months, and the Fed may have to take even more drastic action to bring us back to potential output. For this reason, the Fed looks ahead and determines whether *current* economic conditions are likely to raise the inflation rate in the *future*.

And that is just what the Fed did beginning in mid-1999. With the unemployment rate near 4 percent, the economy growing at a rapid 3.8 percent clip for a year, and the stock market continuing to rise to record levels, Fed officials believed that the wealth effect would overheat the economy if nothing were done. So the Fed took action, even though inflation was still low and stable. From June 1999 through May 2000, the Fed raised its target for the federal funds rate six times: from 4.75 percent to 6.5 percent.

Of course, by raising interest rates to rein in the economy, the Fed *also* brought down stock prices—both by slowing economic growth and the growth in profits *and* through the direct effect of higher interest rates on stocks. Thus the Fed, in trying to steer the economy, was accused of trying to regulate stock prices. Indeed, the Fed itself continued to regard stock prices as one of its tools for steering the economy: Higher interest rates decrease (or slow the rise in) stock prices, and thus slow spending through the wealth effect.

By 2001, the high-tech bust, the recession of 2001, and the attacks of September 11 brought the criticism to an end. It was not that the Fed stopped paying attention to the stock market in making policy. Rather, now the Fed was concerned about a *falling* market and an economy slowing *too* much. The Fed's moves—dropping interest rates rapidly throughout 2001—were popular: They helped to prop up the economy and the market at the same time, with each feeding back to the other.

From 2003 to 2005, the story flipped again. As in the late 1990s, the Fed was concerned that a wealth effect would overheat the economy unless something was done. But this time, the wealth effect came not from the stock market (which had remained stable) but from rapidly rising housing prices. As a result, from June 2003 to June 2005, the Fed had already raised interest rates nine times, and signaled that it might not be done. By the time you read this, people may have begun accusing the Fed of trying to regulate the price of housing.

Problems and Exercises   *Answers to even-numbered Questions and Problems can be found on the text Web site at* http://hall-lieb.swlearning.com.

1. Consider the following statement: "The decade from 1993 to 2003 was good for stocks. Someone who invested $10,000 in a typical group of S&P 500 stocks on June 30, 1993, would have been able to sell them for $22,196 on June 30, 2003." Using information in the table below, demonstrate that this statement is correct. [*Hint:* Don't forget to compound the annual percentage changes.]

Index	Increase, 1 Year Ending June 30, 2003	Average Annual Increase, 3 Years Ending June 30, 2003	Average Annual Increase, 5 Years Ending June 30, 2003	Average Annual Increase, 10 Years Ending June 30, 2003
Dow Jones Industrial Average	−3.2%	−5.2%	0.1%	10.0%
Standard & Poor's 500	−0.3%	−12.6%	−7.6%	8.3%
NASDAQ	14.8%	−25.5%	−2.6%	9.0%

2. Use the table above to determine how much a $10,000 investment on June 30, 2000 in a typical group of Standard and Poor's 500 stocks would be worth three years later.

3. Use the table above to determine how much a $5,000 investment on June 30, 1993, in a typical group of Dow Jones industrial stocks, would be worth 10 years later.

4. Use the table above to answer the following questions.
   a. What was the *cumulative* percentage change in NASDAQ stocks from June 30, 1998 to June 30, 2003?
   b. What was the *cumulative* percentage change in the Standard and Poor's 500 from June 30, 2000 to June 30, 2003?

5. Use the table above to answer the following questions.
   a. What was the *cumulative* percentage change in the Dow Jones Industrial Average from June 30, 1993 to June 30, 2003?
   b. What was the *cumulative* percentage change in NASDAQ stocks from June 30, 2000 to June 30, 2003?

6. Suppose the corporate profits tax rate is reduced, and other taxes in the economy are increased by just enough to leave total tax revenue unchanged. Thus, the economy's equilibrium real GDP is unaffected, at least initially.
   a. Would this event have any impact on the stock market? Illustrate, using supply and demand curves for the typical stock. What will happen to the price of the typical stock?
   b. Using cause-and-effect diagrams like the ones in this chapter, show how this change in tax policy would first affect the stock market, then affect the economy, and then create feedback effects in the stock market.
   c. When we include feedback effects from the macro-economy, is the ultimate effect on stock prices greater or smaller than the initial impact in (a) above? Explain.

7. Sometimes corporations will use their profits to buy back their own shares.
   a. Explain why this action—using funds that could have been given to shareholders as dividends— might actually benefit shareholders. (*Hint:* Draw a supply and demand diagram for the corporation's shares. Which curve is affected by a stock buy-back?)
   b. In the United States, the tax rate on long-term capital gains (capital gains on assets held longer than one year) is lower than the tax rate on ordinary income, including income from dividends. Does this help explain why corporations sometimes buy back their own shares? Explain.

se that, over time, people become more sophisti-
...d about changes in stock prices. Specifically, they
realize that while stock prices go down in a recession,
they tend to rise when the recession ends. Would this
change the way the economy affects stock prices?
Would it change our view of the stock market as an automatic destabilizer over the business cycle? Explain.

9. Classify each of the following events as a shock that initially affects (a) primarily the economy; (b) primarily the
stock market; (c) both the stock market and the economy.
Justify your answer in each case.

   a. Government spending increases, while the Fed leaves
   its interest rate target unchanged.

   b. The Fed—beginning to worry about inflation—increases its interest rate target.

10. In the section "A Shock to the Economy," we explored
the impact of an increase in government purchases with
an unchanged interest rate target by the Fed.

   a. In order to maintain an unchanged interest rate target, will the Fed have to increase or decrease the
   money supply? Illustrate with a diagram of the money
   market.

   b. Suppose the Fed instead decides to pursue a completely passive monetary policy—leaving the *money
   supply* unchanged. What will happen to the interest
   rate? (Illustrate with another diagram of the money
   market.)

   c. Under a passive monetary policy, does the change
   in government spending have more or less of an
   initial impact on the stock market (compared to
   the policy of maintaining an unchanged interest
   rate target)?

11. When population and productivity are increasing, potential output increases each year. One way to illustrate this
is to shift the economy's *AS* curve rightward (and downward) each year. Assume that there is no expected inflation embedded in the economy, so that the ongoing inflation rate is zero. Using *AS–AD* diagrams, illustrate each
of the following scenarios.

   a. Potential output is increasing, and the Fed allows
   actual output to rise just enough to keep up with
   potential.

   b. Potential output is increasing, and the Fed allows actual output to rise above potential.

   c. Potential output is increasing, and the Fed allows
   so little growth that output falls below potential.

12. Using a diagram similar to panel (b) of Figure 7, show
what happens over time if the Fed maintains an unemployment rate of 4 percent when the *natural* rate of unemployment is actually 3.5 percent.

13. Figure 6 illustrates how a rise in stock prices can affect
the economy in the short run (panel (a)) and the long
run (panel (b)). Draw a diagram to illustrate the effect
of a *drop* in stock prices (such as occured in 2000 and
2001) in the short run and the long run under two assumptions:

   a. The Fed stands by and does nothing.

   b. The Fed takes action (as it did in 2001) to fight the
   impact of the fall in stock prices.

Challenge Question

1. In addition to its short-run effects on the economy via the
wealth effect, the stock market affects the economy in another way: It is part of the loanable funds market in
which households make their saving available to firms.
Thus, the *existence* of a stock market should affect the
economy in the long run.

   a. Do stocks have any advantages for households over
   other forms of saving? If so, what are they? (Think of
   yourself or your family. Why might you want to hold
   some of your wealth in the form of stocks, rather
   than hold all of it in other forms such as bonds or
   cash?)

   b. Using a loanable funds diagram, and your answer in
   part (a), show what happens—in an economy that is
   initially without a stock market—when a viable

   stock market is introduced. In particular, which
   curve will shift?

   c. Using your graph from part (b), how does introducing a stock market into the economy affect the level
   of investment spending and the standard of living
   over the long run?

   d. Do stocks have any advantages for business firms
   over other ways of obtaining funds for investment
   projects? If so, what are they?

   e. On your loanable funds diagram, and using your answer from part (d), illustrate the impact of the stock
   market on the investment demand curve. Does this
   contribute to, or work against, the impact of the stock
   market on the economy that you found in part (c)?

These exercises require access to Hall/Lieberman Xtra! If Xtra! did not come with your book, visit http://hallxtra.swlearning.com to purchase.

1. Use your Xtra! password at the Hall and Lieberman
    Web site (http://hallxtra.swlearning.com), select "Using
    All the Theory": The Stock Market and the Macroecon-
    omy, and under Economic Applications, click on Econ-
    Data. Under *Hot Data,* scroll down to click on *Stock
    Prices: S&P 500.* Read the definition and click on
    Diagrams/Data, and use the information to answer
    the following questions.

    a. In the "Using *All* the Theory" section, changes in ex-
        pected future profits of the firm is listed as a determi-
        nant of demand for a share of stock. Consider the
        S&P 500 and after-tax corporate profit diagram and
        confirm this relationship in aggregate. Why are these
        two graphs out of phase, i.e., why do the changes in
        the S&P 500 tend to be a leading indicator of corpo-
        rate after-tax profits.

    b. In the "Using *All* the Theory" section, changes in the
        interest rate are listed as a determinant of demand for
        a share of stock. Consider the S&P 500 and the 10-
        year treasury bond yield diagram and explain the
        strong inverse relationship between interest rates—
        such as the yield on the prominent 10-year U.S. trea-
        sury bond, and stock prices, as indicated by the S&P
        500 index.

    c. Consider the S&P 500 and the index of leading eco-
        nomic indicators diagram. Given that the S&P 500 is
        an element of the index of leading economic indica-
        tors, and that they tend to move together, what could
        be some of the possible reasons behind the decline in
        the indicator prior to each of the U.S. recessions
        since 1980, and the decline of the S&P 500 during
        these recessions?

Glossary

A

Absolute advantage The ability to produce a good or service, using fewer resources than other producers use.

Absolute advantage The ability to produce a good or service, using fewer resources than other producers use.

Active monetary policy When the Fed changes the money supply in response to economic shocks.

Aggregate demand (*AD*) curve A curve indicating equilibrium GDP at each price level.

Aggregate expenditure (*AE*) The sum of spending by households, business firms, the government, and foreigners on final goods and services produced in the United States.

Aggregate production function The relationship showing how much total output can be produced with different quantities of labor, with quantities of all other resources held constant.

Aggregate supply (*AS*) curve A curve indicating the price level consistent with firms' unit costs and markups for any level of output over the short run.

Aggregation The process of combining different things into a single category.

Alternate goods Other goods that a firm could produce, using some of the same types of inputs as the good in question.

Appreciation An increase in the price of a currency in a floating-rate system.

Automatic stabilizers Forces that reduce the size of the expenditure multiplier and diminish the impact of spending shocks.

Autonomous consumption spending The part of consumption spending that is independent of income; also the vertical intercept of the consumption function.

Average standard of living Total output (real GDP) per person.

Average tax rate The fraction of a given income paid in taxes.

B

Balance sheet A financial statement showing assets, liabilities, and net worth at a point in time.

Banking panic A situation in which depositors attempt to withdraw funds from many banks simultaneously

Bond A promise to pay back borrowed funds, issued by a corporation or government agency.

Boom A period of time during which real GDP is above potential GDP.

Budget deficit The excess of government purchases over net taxes.

Budget surplus The excess of net taxes over government purchases.

Business cycles Fluctuations in real GDP around its long-term growth trend.

Business demand for funds curve Indicates the level of investment spending firms plan at various interest rates.

C

Capital Something produced that is long-lasting and used to produce other goods.

Capital gains tax A tax on profits earned when a financial asset is sold at more than its acquisition price.

Capital per worker The total capital stock divided by total employment.

Capital stock The total value of all goods that will provide useful services in future years.

Capitalism A type of economic system in which most resources are owned privately.

Cash in the hands of the public Currency and coins held outside of banks.

Central bank A nation's principal monetary authority responsible for controlling the money supply.

Change in demand A shift of a demand curve in response to a change in some variable other than price.

Change in quantity demanded A movement along a demand curve in response to a change in price.

Change in quantity supplied A movement along a supply curve in response to a change in price.

Change in supply A shift of a supply curve in response to some variable other than price.

Circular flow A diagram that shows how goods, resources, and dollar payments flow between households and firms.

Classical model A macroeconomic model that explains the long-run behavior of the economy.

Command or centrally planned economy An economic system in which resources are allocated according to explicit instructions from a central authority.

Communism A type of economic system in which most resources are owned in common.

Comparative advantage The ability to produce a good or service at a lower opportunity cost than other producers.

Complement A good that is used together with some other good.

Complete crowding out A dollar-for-dollar decline in one sector's spending caused by an increase in some other sector's spending.

Consumer Price Index An index of the cost, through time, of a fixed market basket of goods purchased by a typical household in some base period.

Consumption (C) The part of GDP purchased by households as final users.

Consumption function A positively sloped relationship between real consumption spending and real disposable income.

Consumption tax A tax on the part of their income that households spend.

Consumption-income line A line showing aggregrate consumption spending at each level of income or GDP.

Corporate profits tax A tax on the profits earned by corporations.

Critical assumption Any assumption that affects the conclusions of a model in an important way.

Crowding out A decline in one sector's spending caused by an increase in some other sector's spending.

Cyclical deficit The part of the federal budget deficit that varies with the business cycle.

Cyclical unemployment Joblessness arising from changes in production over the business cycle.

D

Deflation A decrease in the price level from one period to the next.

Demand curve for foreign currency A curve indicating the quantity of a specific foreign currency that Americans will want to buy, during a given period, at each different exchange rate.

Demand deposit multiplier The number by which a change in reserves is multiplied to determine the resulting change in demand deposits.

Demand deposits Checking accounts that do not pay interest.

Demand schedule A list showing the quantities of a good that consumers would choose to purchase at different prices, with all other variables held constant.

Demand shock Any event that causes the *AD* curve to shift.

Depreciation A decrease in the price of a currency in a floating-rate system.

Depression An unusually severe recession.

Devaluation A change in the exchange rate from a higher fixed rate to a lower fixed rate.

Discount rate The interest rate the Fed changes on loans to banks.

Discouraged workers Individuals who would like a job, but have given up searching for one.

Disposable income Household income minus net taxes, which is either spent or saved.

E

Economic growth The increase in our production of goods and services that occurs over long periods of time.

Economic system A system of resource allocation and resource ownership.

Economics The study of choice under conditions of scarcity.

Entrepreneurship The ability and willingness to combine the other resources—labor, capital, and natural resources—into a productive enterprise.

Equilibrium GDP In the short run, the level of output at which output and aggregate expenditure are equal.

Equilibrium price The market price that, once achieved, remains constant until either the demand curve or supply curve shifts.

Equilibrium quantity The market quantity bought and sold per period that, once achieved, remains constant until either the demand curve or supply curve shifts.

Excess demand At a given price, the excess of quantity demanded over quantity supplied.

Excess demand for bonds The amount of bonds demanded exceeds the amount supplied at a particular interest rate.

Excess reserves Reserves in excess of required reserves.

Excess supply of money The amount of money supplied exceeds the amount demanded at a particular interest rate.

Excess supply At a given price, the excess of quantity supplied over quantity demanded.

Exchange The act of trading with others to obtain what we desire.

Exchange rate The amount of one currency that is traded for one unit of another currency.

Expansion A period of increasing real GDP.

Expenditure approach Measuring GDP by adding the value of goods and services purchased by each type of final user.

Expenditure multiplier The amount by which equilibrium real GDP changes as a result of a one-dollar change in autonomous consumption, investment spending, government purchases, or net exports.

Explicit cost The dollars sacrificed-and actually paid out—for a choice.

Exports Goods and services produced domestically, but sold abroad.

F

Factor payments Payments to the owners of resources that are used in production

Factor payments approach Measuring GDP by summing the factor payments earned by all households in the economy.

Federal funds rate The interest rate charged for loans of reserves among banks.

Federal Open Market Committee A committee of Federal Reserve officials that established U.S. monetary policy.

Federal Reserve System The central bank and national monetary authority of the United States.

Fiat money Anything that serves as a means of payment by government declaration.

Final good A good sold to its final user.

Financial intermediary A business firm that specializes in brokening between savers and borrowers.

Firm's quantity supplied The specific amount a firm would choose to sell over some time period, given (1) a particular price for the good; (2) all other constraints on the firm.

Fiscal policy A change in government purchases or net taxes designed to change total spending and thereby change total output.

Fixed exchange rate A government-declared exchange rate maintained by central bank intervention in the foreign exchange market.

Floating exchange rate An exchange rate that is freely determined by the forces of supply and demand.

Flow variable a variable measuring a process over some period

Foreign currency crisis A loss of faith that a country can prevent a drop in its exchange rate, leading to a rapid depletion of its foreign currency (e.g., dollar) reserves.

Foreign exchange market The market in which one country's currency is traded for another country's.

Frictional unemployment Joblessness experienced by people who are between jobs or who are just entering or reentering the labor market.

Full employment A situation in which there is no cyclical unemployment.

G

GDP price index An index of the price level for all final goods and services included in GDP.

Government demand for funds curve Indicates the amount of government borrowing at various interest rates.

Government purchases (G) Spending by federal, state, and local governments on goods and services.

Gross domestic product (GDP) The total value of all final goods and services produced for the marketplace during a given year, within the nation's borders.

H

Household's quantity demanded The specific amount a household would choose to buy over some time period, given (1) a particular price, (2) all other constraints on the household.

(Household) saving The portion of after-tax income that households do not spend on consumption.

Human capital The skills and training of the labor force.

I

Imperfectly competitive market A market in which a single buyer or seller has the power to influence the price of the product.

Implicit cost The value of something sacrificed when no direct payment is made.

Imports Goods and services produced abroad, but consumed domestically.

Income The amount that a person or firm earns over a particular period.

Index A series of numbers used to track a variable's rise or fall over time.

Indexation Adjusting the value of some nominal payment in proportion to a price index, in order to keep the real payment unchanged.

Infant industry argument The argument that an industry in which a country has a comparative advantage might need protection from foreign competition in order to flourish.

Inferior good A good that people demand less of as their income rises.

Inflation rate The percent change in the price level from one period to the next.

Injections Spending from sources other than households.

Input Anything (including a resource) used to produce a good or service.

Interest rate target The interest rate the Federal Reserve aims to achieve by adjusting the money supply.

Intermediate goods Goods used up in producing final goods.

International Monetary Fund (IMF) An international organization founded in 1945 to help stabilize the world monetary system.

Investment tax credit A reduction in taxes for firms that invest in capital.

Involuntary part-time workers Individuals who would like a full-time job, but who are working only part time.

L

Labor The time human beings spend producing goods and services.

Labor demand curve Indicates how many workers firms will want to hire at various real wage rates.

Labor force Those people who have a job or who are looking for one.

Labor force participation rate (LFPR) The percentage of the population that wants to be working.

Labor productivity The output produced by the average worker in an hour.

Labor supply curve Indicates how many people will want to work at various real wage rates.

Law of demand As the price of a good increases, the quantity demanded decreases.

Law of increasing opportunity cost The more of something that is produced, the greater the opportunity cost of producing one more unit.

Law of supply As the price of a good increases, the quantity supplied increases.

Leakages Income earned, but not spent, by households during a given year.

Liquidity The property of being easily converted into cash.

Loan An agreement to pay back borrowed funds, signed by a household or noncorporate business.

Loanable funds market The market in which households make their saving available to borrowers.

Long-run aggregate supply curve A vertical line indicating all possible output and price-level combinations at which the economy could end up in the long run.

Long-run Phillips curve A vertical line indicating that in the long run, unemployment must eqal its natural rate, regardless of the rate of inflation.

M

M1 A standard measure of the money supply, including cash in the hands of the public, checking account deposits, and travelers checks.

M2 M1 plus savings account balances, noninstitutional money market mutual fund balances, and small time deposits.

Macroeconomics The study of the behavior of the overall economy.

Managed float A policy of frequent central bank intervention to move the exchange rate.

Marginal propensity to consume The amount by which consumption spending rises when disposable income rises by one dollar.

Marginal tax rate The fraction of an additional dollar of income paid in taxes.

Market A group of buyers and sellers with the potential to trade with each other.

Market clearing Adjustment of prices until quantities supplied and demanded are equal.

Market economy An economic system in which resources are allocated through individual decision making.

Market quantity demanded The specific amount of a good that all buyers in the market would choose to buy over some time period, given (1) a particular price, (2) all other constraints they face.

Market quantity supplied The specific amount of a good that all sellers in the market would choose to sell over some time period, given (1) a particular price for the good; (2) all other constraints on firms.

Means of payment Anything acceptable as payment for goods and services.

Microeconomics The study of the behavior of individual households, firms, and governments; the choices they make; and their interaction in specific markets.

Model An astract representation of reality.

Monetary policy Control or manipulation of the money supply by the Federal Reserve designed to achieve a macroeconomic goal.

Money An asset widely accepted as a means of payments.

Money demand curve A curve indicating how much money will be willingly held at each interest rate.

Money supply The total amount of money held by the public.

Money supply curve A line showing the total quantity of money in the economy at each interest rate.

Moral hazard When decision makers—expecting assistance in the event of an unfavorable outcome—change their behavior so that the unfavorable outcome is more likely.

N

Natural rate of unemployment The unemployment rate when there is no cyclical unemployment.

Natural resources Land as well as the naturally occurring materials that come with it.

Net exports (NX) Total exports minus total imports.

Net financial inflow An inflow of funds equal to a nation's trade deficit.

Net investment Investment minus depreciation.

Net taxes Government tax revenues minus transfer payments.

Net worth The difference between assets and liabilities.

Nominal interest rate The annual percent increase in a lender's dollars from making a loan.

Nominal variable A variable measured without adjustment for the dollar's changing value.

Nonmarket production Goods and services that are produced but not sold in a market.

Normal good A good that people demand more of as their income rises.

Normative economics The study of what should be; it is used to make value judgments, identify problems, and prescribe solutions.

O

Open market operations Purchases or sales of bonds by the Federal Reserve System.

Opportunity cost What is given up when taking an action or making a choice.

Optimum currency area A region whose economies perform better with a single currency than with separate national currencies.

P

Passive monetary policy When the Fed keeps the money supply constant regardless of shocks to the economy.

Patent protection A government grant of exclusive rights to use or sell a new technology.

Perfectly competitive market A market in which no buyer or seller has the power to influence the price.

Phillips curve A curve indicating the Fed's choice between inflation and unemployment in the short run.

Physical capital The part of the capital stock consisting of physical goods, such as machinery, equipment, and factories.

Planned investment spending Business purchases of plant and equipment.

Positive economics The study of how the economy works.

Potential output The level of output the economy could produce if operating at full employment.

Price The amount of money that must be paid to a seller to obtain a good or service.

Price level The average level of dollar prices in the economy.

Private investment (*I*) The sum of business plant, equipment, and software purchases, new-home construction, and inventory changes; often referred to as just investment.

Production possibilities frontier (PPF) A curve showing all combinations of two goods that can be produced with the resources and technology currently available.

Productive inefficiency A situation in which more of at least one good can be produced without sacrificing the production of any other good.

Progressive tax A tax whose rate increases as income increases.

Protectionism The belief that a nation's industries should be protected from foreign competition.

Purchasing power parity (PPP) theory The idea that the exchange rate will adjust in the long run so that the average price of goods in two countries will be roughly the same.

Q

Quota A limit on the physical volume of imports.

R

Real interest rate The annual percent increase in a lender's purchasing power from making a loan.

Real variable A variable adjusted for changes in the dollar's value.

Recession A period of significant decline in real GDP.

Regressive tax A tax for which the percentage of income taxed falls as income rises.

Required reserve ratio The minimum fraction of checking account balances that banks must hold as reserves.

Required reserves The minimum amount of reserves a bank must hold, depending on the amount of its deposit liabilities.

Reserves Vault cash plus balances held at the Fed.

Resource allocation A method of determining which goods and services will be produced, how they will be produced, and who will get them.

Resources The labor, capital, land and natural resources, and entrepreneurship that are used to produce goods and services.

Run on the bank An attempt by many of a bank's depositors to withdraw their funds.

S

Say's law The idea that total spending will be sufficient to purchase the total output produced.

Scarcity A situation in which the amount of something available is insufficient to satisfy the desire for it.

Seasonal unemployment Joblessness related to changes in weather, tourist patterns, or other seasonal factors.

Self-correcting mechanism The adjustment process through which price and wage changes return the economy to full-employment output in the long run.

Short-run macro model A macroeconomic model that explains how changes in spending can affect real GDP in the short run.

Short-run macroeconomic equilibrium A combination of price level and GDP consistent with both the *AD* and *AS* curves.

Simplifying assumption Any assumption that makes a model simpler without affecting any of its important conclusions.

Socialism A type of economic system in which most resources are owned by the state.

Specialization A method of production in which each person concentrates on a limited number of activities.

Spending shock A change in spending that ultimately affects the entire economy.

Stagflation The combination of falling output and rising prices.

Stock variable a variable measuring a quantity at a moment in time.

Structural deficit The part of the federal budget deficit that is independent of the business cycle.

Structural unemployment Joblessness arising from mismatches between workers' skills and employers' requirements or between workers' locations and employers' locations.

Substitute A good that can be used in place of some other good and that fulfills more or less the same purpose.

Supply curve A graphical depiction of a supply schedule; a curve showing the quantity of a good or service supplied at various prices, with all other variables held constant.

Supply curve for foreign currency A curve indicating the quantity of a specific foreign currency that will be supplied, during a given period, at each different exchange rate.

Supply of funds curve Indicates the level of household saving at various interest rates.

Supply schedule A list showing the quantities of a good or service that firms would choose to produce and sell at different prices, with all other variables held constant.

Supply shock Any event that causes the AS curve to shift.

T

Tariff A tax on imports.

Taylor rule A proposed rule that would require the Fed to change the interest-rate by a specified amount whenever real GDP or inflation deviate from their preannounced targets.

Technological change The invention or discovery of new inputs, new outputs, or new production methods.

Terms of trade The ratio at which a country can trade domestically produced products for foreign-produced products.

Total demand for funds curve Indicates the total amount of borrowing at various interest rates.

Trade deficit The excess of a nation's imports over its exports during a given period.

Trade surplus The excess of a nation's exports over its imports during a given period.

Traditional economy An economy in which resources are allocated according to long-lived practices from the past.

Transfer payment Any payment that is not compensation for supplying goods or services.

Trough The bottom point of a recession, when a contraction ends and an expansion begins.

U

Unemployment rate The fraction of the labor force that is without a job.

Unit of value A common unit for measuring how much something is worth.

V

Value added The revenue a firm receives minus the cost of the intermediate goods it buys.

Value-added approach Measuring GDP by summing the value added by all firms in the economy.

W

Wealth The total value of everything a person or firm owns, at a point in time, minus the total value of everything owed.

Wealth constraint At any point in time, wealth is fixed.

Index

A

Absolute advantage, 36–38, 475
Active monetary policy, 380, 383
Aggregate demand *(AD)*, 375
Aggregate demand curve, 339, 340–346
  defined, 342
  deriving, 342–343
  Federal Reserve and, 384, 389, 523–524
  misconceptions about, 342
  movements along, 343
  shifts of, 343
  shifts versus movements along, 345–346
Aggregate expenditure, 253–254
  gross domestic product versus, 254
  income and, 254
Aggregate production function, 170, 261
Aggregate supply—aggregate demand diagram, 523–524
Aggregate supply *(AS)*, 375
Aggregate supply curve, 346–353
  defined, 350
  deriving, 350–351
  Federal Reserve and, 389, 523–524
  long-run, 362–363
  misconception about, 352
  movements along, 351
  provisos about, 365–371
  shifts of, 351–353
Aggregation, 53
  defined, 97
  in macroeconomics, 97

Agreements, multilateral, 491
Algebraic solution
  for equilibrium, 88
  for equilibrium gross domestic product, 280–281
Alternate goods, 70
American Airlines, 30, 264
American Express, 285
American Telephone & Telegraph (AT&T), 214, 241, 508, 520
Antitrade bias, 490–491
Apple Computer, 443
Appreciation of currency, 447, 452
Archer Daniels Midland, 500
Assets, 284
  liquidity of, 285–286
Assumptions
  of classical model, 166
  critical, 10
  simplifying, 9–10
Automated teller machine (ATM), 285
Automatic destabilizer, 551
Automatic stabilizers, 269–271
  expenditure multiplier and, 269–271
Automatic transfers from savings accounts, 285
Autonomous consumption, 249, 275, 546
Autonomous consumption spending, 245, 247
Average standard of living, 194
Average tax rate, 412
Avis, 273

B

Balance sheet
  bank and, 290–291
  defined, 290
Banking panic, 306–308
Banking system, 288–291
  Federal Reserve's influence on, 300–301
  financial intermediaries in, 288–289
Bank of America, 285, 293
Bank of England, 291
Bank(s)
  automatic teller machines and, 285
  balance sheet of, 290–291
  central, 291, 453
  commercial, 289
  European Central, 457
  failure of, 306
  Federal Reserve, 292
  national, 293
  run on the, 306
  state, 293
  supervising and regulating, 294
Banque de France, 291
Barriers to trade, government, 485
Base period, 140
Bethlehem Steel, 522
Bias
  antitrade, 490–491
  sources of, in Consumer Price Index (CPI), 152–154
  substitution, 152–153, 162
Blue-chip corporations, 522
Bond market, 321

Bonds
  defined, 290, 506
  excess demand for, 319
  interest rates of, 320–321
  secondary market for, 321
  selling, 304
Booms, 228, 234, 235, 236
Britain
  real gross domestic product in, 444
  tastes for U.S. goods in, 445
British goods, Americans' tastes for, 441–442
British pounds
  demand for, 440–442
  supply of, 442–445
Brown, Aaron, 163–164
Budget
  effect of, on economic fluctuations, 420–421
  Federal, 404, 416–420
  shrinking government, 209–211
Budgetary costs, 217–218
Budget deficit, 178, 210–211, 405, 418
  cyclical, 419–420
  fiscal policy with, 186–188
  impact of reduction in, on economic growth, 212
  structural, 420
Budget surpluses, 178, 404
  fiscal policy with, 188–189
Bündchen, Gisele, 41
Bureau of Economic Analysis (BEA), 107, 111–112, 118, 119
Bureau of Labor Statistics (BLS), 103–104, 129, 141, 151, 161, 202, 385

Bush, George W., 211
    tax cuts by, 428–431
Business
    demand for funds curve, 180
    demand for money by, 314
    increasing the incentive to in-
        vest by, 206–207
    purchases of plant equipment
        and software, 109–110
    spending by, 242
Business cycles, 164, 229. *See
    also* Booms; Depression;
    Economic fluctuations;
    Expansions; Recession
    defined, 93
    employment and, 93–94
Business firms
    number of, 71
    quantity supplied, 65
Buyers, in market, 54–55
By-product, 46

C

Capital, 32
    defined, 3
    human, 3, 111, 212–213
    per worker, 205
    physical, 3, 212
Capital formation, 109, 112
Capital gains, 313, 507
    long-term, 209
    tax on, 208
Capital goods, 109
Capitalism, 44
    centrally planned, 45
    market, 44, 45
Capital stock, 3, 109, 110
    growth in, 204–206
    investment and, 206
    private investment and,
        111–112
Carlyle, Thomas, 193
Cash
    electronic, 287
    in hands of public, 285
    vault, 290–291
Caterpillar, 263
Census Bureau Household
    Survey, 126–127
Central banks, 291, 453
Centrally planned capitalism, 45
Centrally planned economics, 40
Centrally planned socialism, 44,
    45
Certificates of deposit, 285–286
Chain-type annual weights GDP
    price index, 145n
Chain-type consumer expendi-
    tures price index, 158n

Changes
    in demand, 62
    in exchange rates, 447–448
    in interest rate, 322–324
    in investment spending,
        263–265
    in money demand, 380–382
    in quantity demanded, 62
    rate of, 15
Checkable deposits, 285, 288n
Check clearing, 295
China, growing trade deficit
    with, 466–468
Choices
    individual, 2–3
    quantity demanded and, 58
    quantity supplied and, 66
    social, 3–4
Circular flow, 172
Circular flow diagram, 172–173
Citibank, 285, 287, 293
Classical economics, 98
Classical labor market, 167
Classical long-run model,
    163–189, 228
    assumptions of, 166
    comparison with short-run
        macro model, 271–273
    in explaining economic fluctu-
        ations, 230–233
    fiscal policy in, 185–189
    loanable funds market in,
        178–184
    output in, 167–171
    spending in, 171–178
CNN *Moneyline,* 163
Coca-Cola, 264
Colleges
    opportunity cost of, 22–24
    supply and demand for
        administrators at,
        82–84
Command economy, 40
Commerce, U.S. Department of,
    103
Commercial banks, 289
Commodity money, 139
Communal ownership, 43
Communism, 43
Comparative advantage, 35–38,
    479
    defined, 475
    opportunity cost and,
        476–477
    sources of, 485–487
    theory of, 475–480
Competition
    in markets, 55–56
    perfect, 57
Competitive markets, 56

Complement, 63
Complete crowding out,
    186–187, 383
    consumption spending and,
        329
    defined, 186
Constraints, wealth, 313
Consumer durables, 111, 324
Consumer Price Index (CPI),
    95n, 141, 394
    accuracy of, 151–154
    behavior of, 142
    calculating, 161–162
    purpose of, 157–158
    sources of bias in, 152–154
    use and misuse of imperfect,
        154–158
    uses of, 142–143
Consumer(s)
    industries as, 491
    spending of, 523
Consumption
    autonomous, 249, 275, 514
    costs of, 218–219
    defined, 108
    disposable income and,
        244–247
    government, 112
    income and, 247–248
    kinds of changes in, 270
Consumption function, 245
Consumption goods, 54, 97
Consumption-income line, 248
    shifts in, 248–250
Consumption spending,
    108–109
    autonomous, 245, 247
    disposable income and,
        242–243
    expectations and, 243–244
    interest rate and, 243
    wealth and, 243
Consumption tax, 209
Contraction phase, 94, 369
Corporate profits tax, 207,
    414
Corporation, blue-chip, 522
Cost of living, 156
Costs
    budgetary, 217–218
    consumption, 218–219
    explicit, 23, 25
    implicit, 23
    opportunity, 21–34, 124,
        219–220, 476–477,
        484–485
    resource, of inflation,
        150–151
    of trading, 483–484
    of unemployment, 123–126

Countercyclical fiscal policy
    Bush tax cuts and, 428–431
    Federal Reserve and, 423
    irreversibility and, 422–423
    timing problems and,
        421–422
CPI. *See* Consumer Price Index
    (CPI)
CPI market basket, 141, 161
Credit cards, 287
Credit unions, 289
Creeping inflation, 150–151
Critical assumption, 10
Crowding out, 329–330
    complete, 186–187, 383
    defined, 186
Currency. *See also* Dollar(s)
    appreciation of, 447, 452
    euro as, 457–459
    exchange rates for, 438–439,
        442
    foreign
        crisis in, 455–456
        demand curve for, 440
        supply curve for, 443
    paper
        acceptance of, 139–140
        issuing, 294
Curved lines, 16
Cyclical deficit, 419–420
Cyclical unemployment, 123, 377

D

Debt, national, 188, 405, 406,
    410, 416–418, 424–431
Decision makers, constraints
    faced by, 81
Deficit. *See* Budget deficit;
    Trade deficit
Deflation
    costs of, 150
    defined, 96, 142, 375
    Federal Reserve and, 394,
        398–400
    in Japan, 398
Dell Computer, 132, 263
Demand, 57–65, 76. *See also*
    Supply and demand
    aggregate, 375
    for British pounds, 440–442
    combining with supply,
        73–75
    effect of supply on, 65
    effect on supply, 71
    excess, 73
    law of, 58–59
    for money, 312–316
    rise in income and, 76
    shifts in, 511

Demand curves. *See also* Aggregate demand curve
  aggregate, 339, 340–346
  defined, 59
  factors that shift, 61–65
  for foreign currency, 440
  labor, 168
  microeconomic, 342
  money, 315–316
  shifts versus movements along, 59–61
Demand deposit multiplier, 298–300, 303–304
Demand deposits, 285, 298
Demand for funds curve, 180–181
Demand for pounds curve, shifts in, 441–442
Demand schedule, 59
Demand shocks, 358
  adjusting to long-run, 359–362
  exchange rates and, 459
  Federal Reserve's response to, 379
  negative, 358, 361–362
  positive, 358, 360–361, 388
  responding to, 382–385
  in short run, 355–359
Dependent variable, 14, 20, 88
Depository institutions, 289
Depreciation
  of capital stock, 206
  of dollar, 447, 459
Depression, 94. *See also* Great Depression
Devaluation, 455
Dimminishing marginal returns to labor, 170
Dirty float, 453
Discounting, 154
Discount rate, 294
  changes in, 304–305
Discouraged workers, 127–128
Discretion, 397
Disney, 235, 264
Disposable income, 176, 242–247
  consumption and, 244–247
Dividends, 178, 507
Dollar(s). *See also* Currency
  appreciation of, 452
  depreciation of, 447, 459
  history of, 138–139
  per pound or pounds per dollar, 438–439
Donaldson, Sam, 513
Double taxation, 414
Dow Jones Industrial Average (DJIA), 508, 513, 516, 519, 522

Dumping, 498
DuPont Corporation, 214
Durables, consumer, 111, 324

E

Economic downturn, 31
Economic fluctuations, 164, 165, 228–237, 339
  aggregate expenditure in, 253–254
  classical model in explaining, 230–233
  effect of budget on, 420–421
  effect on budget, 419–420
  macroeconomic, 449–450, 512
  triggers of, 234–237
Economic growth, 32–34
  causes of, 32, 196–199
  cost of, 215–224
  expansion versus, 94
  human capital and, 212–213
  importance of, 194–196
  labor force participation rate and, 199–204
  in less-developed countries, 220–224
  living standards and, 193–224
  as macroeconomic goal, 90–91
  in productivity, 204–213
  rapid, 220
  technological change and, 32, 213–215
Economic growth rates from graphs, 92
Economic models, 9, 52–53. *See also* Models
  art of building, 9
  critical assumptions in, 10
Economics. *See also* Macroeconomics; Microeconomics
  centrally planned, 40
  classical, 98
  defined, 1–2
  methods of, 8–11
  normative, 5–6, 98
  positive, 5–6, 98
  scarcity and, 4–5
  special vocabulary of, 11
  studying, 6–8, 11
Economic systems, 34–49
  defined, 44
  resource allocation in, 39–43
  specialization and exchange in, 34–39
  types of, 44–46
Economists
  disagreements between, 6, 163–164
  study of choices by, 2–3

use of mathematical concepts by, 10
Economy
  centrally planned, 40
  command, 40
  determining output of, 169–171
  effect of, on stock market, 516–517
  effect of interest rate changes on, 323–324
  effect of stock market on, 513–516
  market, 41
  monetary policy and, 324–326
  real-world, 235
  traditional, 40
  underground, 119
Economy-wide demand for money, 314–316
Efficiency, in life saving, 46–49
Electronic cash, 287
Employment. *See also* Unemployment
  business cycle and, 93–94
  equilibrium, 200
  equilibrium gross domestic product and, 261–263
  full, 123, 169, 189, 228, 376–378
  high, 92–94
  methods of increasing, 202–204
Employment Act (1946), 92–93
Entrepreneurship, 3, 114
Equations
  linear, 16–18
  solving, 20
Equilibrium
  finding, 81–82
  in loanable funds market, 181–182
  long-run, 393
  in money market, 317–322
  short-run, 356
  solving for, algebraically, 88
  stocks that push economy away from shocks, 236
Equilibrium employment, 200
Equilibrium exchange rate, 445–446
Equilibrium gross domestic product, 255–263, 343
  defined, 256
  employment and, 261–263
  finding, with graph, 257–261
  finding algebraically, 280–281
  inventories and, 256–257
  wealth effect and, 514–516
Equilibrium price
  for stocks, 510–511
  in supply and demand, 73–75, 88

Equilibrium quantity, 73–75, 88
Erroneous logic, endless loop of, 76
Euro, 457–459
European Central Bank, 457
Excess demand, 73
  for bonds, 319
Excess reserves, 296
Excess supply, 74
  of money, 319
Exchange rates. *See also* Foreign exchange markets
  changes over time, 447–448
  defined, 438
  demand shocks and, 459
  elimination of risk, 458
  equilibrium, 445–446
  expectations about future, 448
  expected changes in, 442, 445
  fixed, 453–455
  floating, 445–446
  foreign exchange market and, 438–439, 481
  macroeconomy and, 459–461
  monetary policy and, 459–461
Excise taxes, 414
Expansions, 94, 228, 230, 369
  economic growth versus, 94
Expectations, 243–244
  money market and, 331–333
  ongoing inflation and, 387–394
Expected price, 63
  effect of, on supply curve, 71
Expenditure, aggregate, 253–254
Expenditure approach to gross domestic product, 107–113
Expenditure multiplier, 265–267, 298
  automatic stabilizers and, 269–271
  effect of fiscal policy, 272–273
  graphical view of, 268–269
  macroeconomics and, 518–519
  in reverse, 267
  role of saving, 272
Explicit costs, 23, 25
Exporting country, impact of trade in, 488–489
Exports, 475
  net, 113, 252–253, 363*n*

F

Factor markets, 172
Factor payments, 114, 172
  approach to gross domestic product, 114–116
Failures, bank, 306

Federal budget, 404. *See also* Budget
  effect of economic fluctuations on, 419–420
  national debt and, 416–418
Federal Deposit Insurance Corporation (FDIC), 308
Federal Express (FedEx), 507, 509–510, 511
Federal funds rate, 334, 382n
Federal Open Market Committee (FOMC), 294, 305, 385
Federal personal income tax, 413
Federal Reserve Banking Act (1978), 376
Federal Reserve Bank(s), 292
  of New York, 294n
Federal Reserve System, 291–305
  change of interest rates by, 322–323
  defined, 139
  deflation and, 394, 398–400
  demand shocks and, 520
  Federal Open Market Committee (FOMC), 294, 305, 385
  fiscal policy and, 185–189, 231, 272–273, 327–330, 421–423, 428–429
  foreign exchange markets and, 453
  functions of, 294–295
  inflation and, 387–394
  influence on banking system, 300–301
  interest rates and, 381–382, 384–385, 398–399
  monetary policy and, 324–326, 376–387, 394–400, 423, 459–461
  money supply and, 295–305
  objectives of, 376
  open market operations of, 295, 305, 326
  performance of, 378
  policy of, under Greenspan, 373–474, 387, 398, 513, 521–523
  response to September 11 terrorist attacks, 505–506, 511
  short-run macro model and, 333–335
  stock market and, 521–526
  structure of, 292–293
Federal surplus, 418

Federal tax revenues, 412–416
  trends in, 414–416
Final goods, 105
Final users, 105
Financial intermediaries, 288–289
Financial markets
  interest rate target and, 384–385
Financial Times, 540
Fiscal changes, effects of
  in long run, 423–428
  in short run, 418–423
Fiscal policy, 231, 327–330
  with budget deficit, 186–188
  with budget surplus, 188–189
  in classical model, 185–189
  countercyclical, 421–423, 428–429
  crowding out and, 329–330
  defined, 185
  effect of, 272–273
  government purchases and, 327–329
Fixed exchange rates, 453–455
Flat money, 139
Fleet Bank, 293
Floating exchange rate, 445–446
Flow variable, 206
Ford Motor Company, 55
Foregone income, 23
Foreign assistance, 224
Foreign currency
  crisis in, 455–456
  demand curve for, 440
  supply curve for, 443
Foreigners, 242
Foreign exchange markets, 481
  See also Exchange rates
  exchange rates and, 438–439, 481
  government intervention in, 452–459
Foreign investment, 224
Free trade, 473
  logic of, 474–476
  objections to, 487–492
  restrictions on, 492–494
Frictional unemployment, 120, 234, 376–377
Friedman, Milton, 29
Full employment, 123, 169, 189, 228, 376–378
Full Employment and Balanced Growth Act (1978), 93
Full-employment output, 363n
Future exchange rates, expectations about, 448

G

Gains, turning potential into actual, 480–485
Gates, Bill, 41
GDP. *See* Gross domestic product (GDP)
General Electric, 554
General Motors, 235, 236
The General Theory of Employment Interest and Money (Keynes), 98, 165n
Goods, 112
  alternate, 70
  consumption, 54, 97
  final, 105
  inferior, 62
  intermediate, 105, 132
  investment, 97
  normal, 61–62
  related, 62–65
Government
  barriers to trade, 485
  demand for funds, 181
  shrinking budget of, 209–211
Government agencies, 242
Government consumption, 112
Government intervention, in foreign exchange markets, 452–459
Government investment, 111, 112
Government outlays, 406–412
Government purchases, 112, 252, 406–408
  increase in, 327–329, 344–345, 356–359
Graphs, 14
  finding equilibrium gross domestic product with, 257–261
  growth rates from, 92
  straight-line, 15
Great Depression, 31, 92, 94, 165, 230, 307–308, 339, 359
Greenspan, Alan, 387, 398, 505–506, 513, 521–523
Gross domestic product (GDP), 103, 104
  aggregate expenditure versus, 254
  defined, 104–107
  equilibrium, 255–263, 343
  expenditure approach to, 107–113, 242
  inflation and measurement of, 145

measuring, 116
potential, 131
problems with, 118–120
real, 90, 97, 166
  inflation and measurement of, 145
  after September 11, 2001, 129–132
  uses of, 117–118
  value-added approach to, 114
Gross domestic product (GDP) price index, 145
Growth policies, 215

H

Handheld PCs, 78–80
High employment, 92–94
Home mortgage refinancing, 335
Horizontal intercept, 33
Hot money, 448–449
Households, 54, 242
  increasing the incentive to save by, 207–209
  quantity demanded, 57
  savings by, 176
Human capital, 3, 111
  economic growth and, 212–213

I

IBM, 443, 508
Imperfectly competitive markets, 55
Implicit costs, 23
Importing country, impact of trade in, 489
Imports, 474, 475
Incentives
  to invest, 206–207
  to save, 207–209
Income
  aggregate expenditure and, 254
  consumption and, 247–248
  disposable, 176, 242–243, 247
  effect on demand curve, 61
  foregone, 23
  interdependence between production and, 235
  rise in, and demand, 76
  wealth and, 63
Income security, 409
Income tax, personal, 412–413
Independent variable, 14
Index, 140
Indexation, 142
Indexing, 154–155

Index numbers, 140–141
Individuals
  demand for money of, 313–314
  opportunity cost for, 22–26
  scarcity and choice, 2–3
Industries
  as consumers, 491
  infant, 496–497
  strategic, 496
Infant industry argument,
  496–497
Inferior goods, 62
Inflation
  costs of, 145–151
  creeping, 150–151
  as economic problem, 375
  economy and, 96
  expectations and ongoing,
    387–394
  Federal Reserve and, 523,
    524–525
  low, stable, as objective of
    monetary policy, 376
  measurement of real gross do-
    mestic product and, 145
  measuring, 140–145
  Phillips curve and, 391–393
  purchasing power and,
    147–148
  real variables and adjustment
    for, 143–144
  redistributive cost of, 147–149
  resource cost of, 150–151
  rising prices versus rising, 143
  unexpected, and purchasing
    power, 149
Inflation rate, 142
Information, problems with,
  395–396
Injections, 177
Input prices, effect on supply
  curve, 69–70
Inputs, 4
An Inquiry into the Nature and
  Causes of the Wealth of Nations (Smith), 35
Intellectual property. See Patents
Interest, 178
  on national debt, 406, 410
Interest rates, 243
  bond prices and, 320–321
  changes in, 512–513
    by the Fed, 322–323
  effect of
    on economy, 323–324
    on spending, 323–324
  nominal, 148
  real, 148
  relative, 442, 445
  theories of, 330–331

Interest rate target, 381
  financial markets and,
    384–385
Intermediate goods, 105, 132
International Monetary Fund
  (IMF), 224, 456–457
International trade. See Trade
Inventories
  changes in, 110–111
  equilibrium gross domestic
    product and, 256–257
Inverse relationship, 14
Investment
  capital stock and, 206
  economics versus ordinary
    English, 112
  government, 111, 112
  methods of increasing,
    206–212
  net, 112
  private, 109
Investment goods, 97
Investment shock, 273–275
Investment spending, 251–252
  change in, 263–265
  planned, 174–175, 177, 186,
    206, 242
Investment tax credit, 207
Involuntary part-time workers,
  127–128

J

Japan
  Bank of, 453
  deflation, 398
  trade with U.S., 461–465
  Yen, 438–439, 456
Jobless expansions, 369–371
Jobless recoveries, 369

K

Kellogg, 55
Keynes, John Maynard, 98, 165,
  241
Keynesian model, 165
Kibbutzim, 43

L

Labor, 3, 97
Labor, U.S.Department of, 103
Labor demand, shifts in,
  231–232
Labor demand curve, 168
Labor force, 127
Labor force participation rate
  (LFPR), 197
  growth in, 199–204

Labor markets
  classical, 167
Labor productivity, 196
Labor supply, shifts in, 232–233
Labor supply curve, 167
Laissez-faire approach, 204
Law of demand, 58–59
Law of increasing opportunity
  cost, 28
Law of supply, 66–67
Leakages, 177
Lehman Brothers, 295–296,
  298, 301
Less-developed countries
  comparative advantage in,
    485–486
  economic growth in,
    220–224
Lifesaving resources, efficient al-
  location of, 48–49
Linear equations, 16–18
Lines
  curved, 16
  shifts versus movements
    along, 18–20
  slope of, 15
  tangent, 16
Liquidity, 284
  of assets, 285–286
Lives, saving efficiently, 46–49
Living standards, 91
  average, 194
  economic growth and,
    193–224
Loanable funds market,
  178–184
  equilibrium in, 181–182
  Say's Law and, 182–184
Loans, 290
Long-run, 361–362. See also
  classical long-run model
  distinction between short run
    and, 164
  effects of fiscal changes in,
    423–428
  impact of September 11 in,
    131–132
Long-run aggregate supply
  curve, 362–363
Long-run average total cost
  (LRATC) curve, mergers
  and, 20
Long-run effects of supply
  shocks, 365
Long-run equilibrium, 393
Long-run Phillips curve, 393
Long-term capital gains, 209
Low unemployment, 92–94
Lunch, search for free,
  29–34

M

M1, 286–287
M2, 287
Macro, 97
Macroeconomics, 96–100, 165
  aggregation in, 97
  controversies in, 98–99
  defined, 5
  exchange rates and, 459–461
  fluctuations in, 449–450, 512
  goals in, 89–96
    economic growth, 90–91
    high employment, 92–94
    low unemployment, 92–94
    stable prices, 95–96
  goods and services in, 54
  government transfer payments
    in, 175
  models in, 54, 164–166, 321n
  policy in, 378
  stock market and, 505–526
  studying, 31, 99–100
  three-step process in, 82
  total output and, 164
Malthus, Thomas, 193, 220
Managed float, 452–453
Marginal propensity to consume
  (MPC), 246–247, 264
Marginal tax rate, 412
Market capitalism, 44, 45
Market clearing, 166, 184
Market demand curves, 59
Market economy, 41
Market quantity demanded, 58
Market quantity supplied, 66
Market(s), 53–57
  bond, 321
  buyers in, 54–55
  characterizing, 81
  classical labor, 167
  competition in, 55–56
  competitive, 56. 247–257
  defined, 41, 53–54
  factor, 172
  financial, 384–385
  foreign exchange, 437,
    438–439, 452–459, 481
  imperfectly competitive, 55
  labor, 167
  for loanable funds, 178–184,
    330
  nature of, 41
  perfectly competitive, 56
  secondary, 321
  sellers in, 54–55
  supply and demand model in,
    56–57
  understanding, 46
Market socialism, 45

Marx, Karl, 43
McDonald's, 264
Means of payment, 138
    acceptance of paper currency
        as, 139–140
Medicaid, 409
Medicare, 409
Micro, 97
Microeconomics, 97
    aggregation in, 97
    defined, 5
    defining goals and constraints
        in, 81
    demand curves in, 342
    markets in, 54
    study of, 30, 56
    three-step process in, 82
Microeconomic unemployment,
    122
Military purchases, 407–408
Military spending, decline in, 408
Models, 8. See also Economic
    models
    classical long-run, 163–189,
        228
    Keynesian, 165
    macroeconomic, 54, 164–166
    short-run macro, 237,
        240–275, 333–335
Monetary policy
    active, 380, 383
    challenges for, 394–400
    defined, 324
    economy and, 324–326
    exchange rates and, 459–461
    objectives of, 376–378
    passive, 379, 382–383
    reversing, 423
    time lag and, 395–396
Monetary system, 137–158,
    138–140
    acceptance of paper currency,
        139–140
    functions of, 138
    history of the dollar, 138–139
    measuring price level and in-
        flation, 140–145
Money
    commodity, 139
    creating, 301
    defined, 283–284
    flat, 139
    hot, 448–449
Money demand, 312–316
    responding to changes in,
        380–382
Money demand curve, 315
    shifts in, 315–316
Money market
    equilibrium in, 317–322
    expectations and, 331–333

Money market mutual funds
    (MMMFs), 285, 288
Money supply, 316–317, 319
    changes in, 345
    controlling, 295
    defined, 284
    excess, 319
    Federal Reserve System and,
        295–305
    increase in, 358
    measuring, 284–288
    tools for controlling,
        304–305
Money supply curve, 317
Moral hazard, 457
Morrison, Toni, 41
Morningstar.com, 508
Multilateral agreements, 491
Multiplier
    demand deposit, 298–300,
        303–304
    expenditure, 265–267, 298
    tax, 281–282
Mutual funds, 507
    money market, 285, 288
    Mutual savings banks, 289

N

National Association of Security
    Dealers Automated Quota-
    tion (NASDAQ) Index,
    508, 519
National banks, 293
National Bureau of Economic
    Research (NBER), 334n
National debt, 188, 405
    federal budget and, 416–418
    genuine concerns about,
        425–428
    interest on, 406, 410
    mythical concerns about,
        424–425
    tax cuts and, 429–431
Natural events, effect of changes
    in, on supply curve, 71–73
Natural rate of unemployment,
    377–378, 396, 524
Natural resources, 3
Negative demand shock, 358,
    361–362
Negative net exports, 253
Negative relationship, 14
Negative spending shock, 420
Negative supply shock, 364
Net domestic product, 130
Net exports, 113, 252–253,
    363n
    negative, 253
Net financial inflow, 462
Net investment, 112

Net tax revenue, 175–176
Net worth, 291
New-home construction, 110
Nominal gross domestic prod-
    uct, 406n
    real gross domestic product
        versus, 116–117
Nominal interest rate, 148
Nominal variables, 116, 143
Nominal wage, 143, 348, 353
Nonlabor inputs, prices of, 348
Nonmarket production,
    119–120
Nonmilitary government
    purchases, 407
Normal goods, 61–62
Normative economics, 5–6, 98
North American Free Trade
    Agreement (NAFTA), 491,
    531

O

Oil prices
    changes in world, 352
    supply and demand in,
        82–84
Open market operations, 295,
    305
    purchases, 295
    sales, 295
Opportunity cost, 21–34
    of college, 22–24
    comparative advantage and,
        476–477
    defined, 21
    of health care, 26–27
    increasing, 28–29, 484–485
    for individuals, 22–26
    society and, 26
    unemployment and, 124
    of workers' time, 219–220
Optimum currency areas,
    458–459
Outputs, 97
    in classical long-run model,
        167–171
    determining, 169–171
    full-employment, 363n
    growth of potential, 164
    potential, 124

P

Paper currency
    acceptance of, 139–140
    issuing, 294
Part-time workers, involuntary,
    127–128
Passive monetary policy, 379,
    382–383

Patents, 214
Pay-as-you-go principle, 415
Perfect competition
    supply and demand in, 57
Perfectly competitive markets,
    56
Personal income tax, 412–413
Phillips, A. W., 391
Phillips curve, 391–393, 396
    long-run, 393
Physical capital, 3, 212
Planned investment, 251
Planned investment spending,
    174–175, 177, 186, 206, 242
Population, 63
Positive demand shock, 358,
    360–361
Positive economics, 5–6, 98
Positive relationship, 14
Positive spending shock, 420
Positive supply shock, 364–365
Potential gross domestic product,
    131
Potential output, 124
Price, equilibrium, 73–75,
    510–511
Price level, 140
    measuring, 140–145
    relative, 441, 444
Priceline.com, 30
Price(s)
    defined, 41
    equilibrium, 73–75, 88, 516,
        510–511
    expected, 63, 71
    importance of, 41–42
    input, 69–70
    quantity demanded and, 58
    of related goods, 62–63, 70
    rising, versus rising inflation,
        143
    stable, 95–96
Private goods, 529
Private investment, 109
    capital stock and, 111–112
Production
    interdependence between in-
        come and, 235
    nonmarket, 119–120
Production function, 170–171
    aggregate, 170
Production possibilities frontiers
    (PPF), 26–29
    defined, 27
    economic growth and, 218, 222
    operating inside, 29, 46
    shifts in, 512
Productive inefficiency, 29–30, 46
    defined, 30
Productivity, 196
    growth in, 204–213

Product(s). *See also* Gross domestic product (GDP)
net domestic, 130
potential gross domestic, 131
Profit(s), defined, 114
Progressive tax, 412
Protection, arguments for, 496–497
Protectionism, 494–498
in United States, 497–498
Public goods, government involvement and, 529–531
Public offering, 506, 511
Purchases, government, 252
Purchasing power, 166, 398
inflation and, 147–148, 149
Purchasing power parity (PPP) theory, 450–452

Q

Quality changes, 118–119
Quantity, equilibrium, 73–75
Quantity demanded, 57–58, 88
Quantity of money demanded, 314–315
Quantity supplied, 66, 76, 88
Quotas, 493–494, 497
U.S. sugar, 499–500

R

Rate of change, 15
Reagan, Ronald, 390, 417, 513–514
Real gross domestic product, 90, 97, 166, 406n
in Britain, 444
inflation and measurement of, 145
nominal gross domestic product versus, 116–117
per capita, 198
in United States, 441
Real interest rate, 148
Real saving, 166
Real variables, 116, 143
adjustment for inflation and, 143–144
Real wage, 143, 166, 167
Real-world economy, 235
Recession, 30–31, 234, 235
defined, 96
distinguishing, 275
explanation of, 232
Federal Reserve and, 333–335, 390
length of, 94, 230, 236
in 1981–82, 411
in 1990–91, 230, 366–367
output in, 228

severity of, 94, 96
tax revenue and, 419
in 2001, 230, 273–275, 333–335, 367–369, 517
unemployment and, 229, 230, 377
Regressive tax, 413
Related goods
effect of supply curve, 70
prices of, 62–63, 70
Relative interest rates, 442, 445
sudden changes in, 448
Relative price levels, 441, 444
Required reserve ratio (RRR), 291
changes in, 304
Required reserve ratio (RRR), 300
Required reserves, 291
Research and development (R&D), 33, 214–215
Resource allocation, 39–43
defined, 39
efficient, 46–49
markets and, 41
methods of, 40–41
prices and, 41–42
in United States, 42–43
Resource ownership, 43–44
Resource(s), 3–5, 32, 46
lifesaving, 48–49
natural, 3
Retained earnings, 507
Retirement benefits, 408
Ricardo, David, 475–476, 478, 480
Risks, elimination of exchange rate, 458
Run on the bank, 306

S

Saving(s)
household, 176
real, 166
role of, 272
Savings accounts, 285
automatic transfers to, 285
Savings and loan institutions, 285
Savings and loans associations (S&Ls), 289
Say, Jean Baptiste, 173
Say's Law, 173–174
defined, 173
loanable funds market and, 182–184
total spending and, 231, 237
Scarcity, 43
defined, 2

economics and, 4–5
individual choice and, 2–3
social choice and, 3–4
Seasonally adjusted, 107n
Seasonal unemployment, 121
Secondary market
for bonds, 321
Self-correcting mechanism, 360
Self-fulfilling prophecy, 333
Self-sufficiency, 474–475
Sellers, in market, 54–55
September 11, 2001
gross domestic product after, 129–132
terrorist attacks on, 505–506, 511
Services, 112
Share of stock, 506
Shaw, George Bernard, 98
Shocks
demand, 355–362, 379, 382–385, 459
negative, 358, 361–362
positive, 358, 360–361
investment, 273–275
spending, 267–268
negative, 420
positive, 420
supply, 355, 363–365, 397
that push economy away from equilibrium, 236
Short run
demand shocks in, 355–359
distinction between long run and, 164
effects of fiscal changes in, 418–423
impact of September 11 in, 131
Short-run effects of supply shocks, 363–365
Short-run equilibrium, 356
Short-run macroeconomic equilibrium, 353–354
Short-run macro model, 237, 240–275
change in investment spending in, 263–265
comparison with classical long-run model, 271–273
consumption spending in, 242–250
defined, 241
equilibrium gross domestic product in, 255–263
Federal Reserve System and, 333–335
total spending in, 251–255

Simmons National Bank, 285
Simplifying assumption, 9–10
Slope of line, 15
Smith, Adam, 35
Social choice, scarcity and, 3–4
Social goals, sacrifice of other, 220
Socialism, 44
centrally planned, 44, 45
market, 45
Social Security benefits, 406, 409
Social Security outlays, 408
Social Security payments, 242
Social Security tax, 413–414
Social Security Trust Fund, 415
Society, opportunity cost and, 26
Specialization, 477–478
Speculative bubble, 522
Spending, 241–242
consumption, 108–109, 242–250
effect of interest rate on, 323–324
investment, 251–252
planned, 174–175, 177, 186, 206, 242
private sector, for domestic security, 510
role of, in classical long-run model, 171–178
total, 172–178, 251–255
Spending shocks, 236, 267–268, 355
negative, 420
positive, 420
Stable prices, 95–96
Stagflation, 364, 386
Standard deduction, 412n
Standard & Poor's (S&P) 500 Index, 508, 519
Starbucks, 509
State banks, 293
Stockholders, 506
Stock market
effect of economy on, 516–517
effect on economy, 513–516
Federal Reserve System and, 521–526
high-tech boom of the 1920s, 519
high-tech bust of 2000 and 2001, 520–521
macroeconomy and, 505–526
tracking, 507–509
Stock(s)
capital, 3, 109, 110–112, 204–206
growth in, 204–206

investment and, 206
   private investment and,
      111–112
explaining prices, 509–513
reasons for holding, 507
share of, 506
Stock variable, 206
Store of value, 284
Straight-line graphs, 15
Strategic industries, 496
Structural deficit, 420
Structural unemployment, 121–123
Substitutes, 62–63
Substitution bias, 152–153, 162
Supply, 65–73. *See also* Supply
   and demand
   aggregate, 375
   of British pounds, 442–445
   combining with demand, 73–75
   effect of ice storm on, 77–78
   effect on, 65
   excess, 74
   law of, 66–67
Supply and demand, 52–53,
   73–75. *See also* Demand;
   Supply
   using, 56–57
Supply and demand model,
   52–53, 80
   in markets, 56–57
   steps in building, 80–82
Supply curve, 67–68, 543. *See
   also* Aggregate supply curve
   aggregate, 346–353, 365–371
      long-run, 362–363
   factors that shift, 69–73
   for foreign currency, 443
   labor, 167
   money, 317
   shifts versus movements
      along, 68–69
Supply of funds curve, 179–180
Supply of money, 316–317
Supply of pounds curve, shifts
   in, 444–445
Supply schedule, 67
Supply shocks, 355, 363–365
   adverse or negative, 386
   Federal Reserve's response to,
      379
   long-run effects of, 365
   negative, 364, 397
   positive, 364–365
   responding, 385–387
   short-run effects of, 363–365

T

Tables, 14
Tangent line, 16

Tariffs, 492–493, 497
Tastes, 63–65
Tax credits, investment, 207
Tax cuts, 163–164, 211
   Bush, 428–431
   national debt and, 429–431
Tax(es)
   capital gains, 208
   consumption, 209
   corporate profits, 207,
      414
   excise, 414
   income, 412–413
   progressive, 412
   regressive, 413
   Social Security, 413–414
Tax multiplier, 281–282
Tax revenue, net, 175–176
Taylor, John, 397
Taylor rule, 397–398
Technological advances, effect
   of supply curve on,
   70–71
Technological change, 353
   brand-new, as source of up-
      ward bias in Consumer
      Price Index, 153
   economic growth and, 32,
      213–215
Terms of trade, 479–480
Terrorist attacks of September
   11, 2001, 129–132,
   505–506, 511
Thomsoninvest.com, 508
Time as money, 24–26
Time deposits, 285–286
Time lags, uncertain and changing, 395–396
Time Warner, 507, 509
Total demand for funds, 181
Total government outlays,
   410–412
Total spending, 172–178,
   251–255
   changes in, 231
Trade
   absolute advantage and,
      36–38, 475
   antitrade bias and, 490–491
   attitudes and influence on pol-
      icy, 489–492
   comparative advantage and,
      35–38, 475–487
   costs of, 483–484
   exports in, 252–253, 363*n*,
      475–561
   free, 473
      logic of, 474–476
      objections to, 487–492
      restrictions on, 492–494

government barriers to,
   485
impact of
   in exporting country,
      488–489
   in importing country, 489
imports in, 474, 475
myths about, 494–496
national gains from,
   478–479
opportunity costs and,
   484–485
protectionism and,
   494–498
quotas and, 493–494, 497,
   499–500
tariffs and, 492–493, 497
terms of, 479–480
turning potential gains into
   actual gains, 480–485
Trade deficit
   growing, with China,
      466–468
   U.S., 461–468
Trade surplus, 461
Traditional economy, 40
Transfer payments, 175, 242,
   406
   defined, 112–113, 406
   disposable income and, 242
   in the macroeconomy, 175
Transfer programs, 408–410
   effect on output, 420
Travelers checks, 285
Trough, 369

U

Underground economy, 119
Unemployment, 30–31. *See also*
   Employment
   costs of, 123–126
   cyclical, 123, 377
   excess, 377
   frictional, 120, 234,
      376–377
   low, 92–94
   macroeconomic, 123
   measurement of, 126–127
      problems in, 127–129
   microeconomic, 122
   natural rate of, 377–378, 396,
      524
   seasonal, 121
   structural, 121–123
   types of, 120–123
Unemployment compensation,
   406
Unemployment insurance, 242,
   420

Unemployment rate, 92, 93,
   103, 104, 127, 230, 234
United Airlines, 443
U.S. goods, British tastes for,
   445
U.S. real gross domestic product,
   441
United States sugar quota,
   499–500
U.S. trade deficit, 461–468
Unit of account, 283
Unit of value, 138

V

Value-added approach to gross
   domestic product, 114
Variables
   dependent, 14, 20, 88
   flow, 206
   independent, 14
   nominal, 116, 143
   real, 116, 143–144
   stock, 206
Vault cash, 290–291
Vertical intercept, 17, 18*n*,
   33
Viacom, 273

W

Wage(s)
   nominal, 143, 348, 353
   real, 143, 166, 167
Wall Street Journal, 508
Wal-Mart, 273, 508
Wealth, 243
   effect on demand curve, 62
   income and, 63
Wealth constraint, 313
Wealth effect, 514, 520, 523
   equilibrium gross domestic
      product, 514–516
Weather
   changes in, 352–353
   effect of changes in, on supply
      curve, 71–73
Welfare payments, 406
Westinghouse, 263
World Bank, 224
World production, 477–478
World Trade Organization
   (WTO), 473–474, 475,
   480, 491

Y

Yahoo!, 539, 540